THE LONGMAN STANDARD HISTORY OF NINETEENTH CENTURY PHILOSOPHY

DANIEL KOLAK

William Paterson University of New Jersey

GARRETT THOMSON

College of Wooster

PEARSON

Longman

New York San Francisco Boston
London Toronto Sydney Tokyo Singapore Madrid
Mexico City Munich Paris Cape Town Hong Kong Montreal

Editor-in-Chief: Eric Stano
Executive Marketing Manager: Ann Stypuloski
Production Manager: Denise Phillip
Project Coordination, Text Design, and Electronic Page Makeup: West Words, Inc.
Senior Cover Design Manager/Cover Designer: Nancy Danahy
Cover Image: Tower Bridge, London, England (digitally enhanced). © Stone/Getty
    Images, Inc.
Senior Manufacturing Buyer: Dennis J. Para
Printer and Binder: Courier Corporation
Cover Printer: Courier Corporation

For permission to use copyrighted material, grateful acknowledgment is made to the copyright holders below.

Library of Congress Cataloging-in-Publication Data
Kolak, Daniel.
  The Longman standard history of philosophy / Daniel Kolak, Garrett Thomson.
      p. cm.
  Includes bibliographical references and index.
   ISBN 0-321-23511-8 (volume 6 (comprehensive) : alk. paper)—ISBN 0-321-23513-4
(volume 1 (ancient) : alk. paper)—ISBN 0-321-23512-6 (volume 3 (modern) : alk. paper)—ISBN 0-321-
23510-X (volume 5 (20th century) : alk. paper)
   1. Philosophy—History. I. Title: Standard history of philosophy. II. Thomson, Garrett. III. Title.
   B72.K635 2006
   190—dc22

                                                                            2002010370

Please visit us at http://www.ablongman.com

ISBN-13:   978-0-321-23515-2
ISBN-10:   0-321-23515-0

1 2 3 4 5 6 7 8 9 10—CRS—10 09 08 07

"Critique of Kantian Philosophy" by Arthur Schopenhauer, Appendix to *The World as Will and Presentation* translated, edited, annotated by Richard E. Aquila. Reprinted by permission.

"Independence and Dependence of Self-Consciousness: Relations of Master and Servant" translated by J.L.H. Thomas *from Hegel Selections: The Great Philosophers Series 1st Edition*, pp. 73–80, edited by M.J. Inwood, © 1989. Reprinted by permission of Pearson Education, Inc., Upper Saddle River, NJ.

From *Kierkegaard's Writings: Volume III* by Soren Kierkagaard, translated by David F. Swenson and Lillian Marvin Swenson. © 1987 Princeton University Press. Reprinted by permission of Princeton University Press.

From *Concluding Unscientific Postscript* by Soren Kierkagaard, translated by David F. Swenson and Walter Lowrie. © 1941 Princeton University Press, 1969 renewed. Reprinted by permission of Princeton University Press.

"Alienation" from *Economic and Philosophic Manuscripts of 1844* by Karl Marx, translated by Martin Milligan. Reprinted by permission of International Publishers.

"The Power of Money" from *Economic and Philosophic Manuscripts of 1844* by Karl Marx, translated by Martin Milligan. Reprinted by permission of International Publishers.

◆ CONTENTS ◆

◆ PREFACE ◆

Philosophy may not be the oldest profession, but it is the oldest discipline, the source of our views about reality, knowledge, and morality. To understand the revolutionary nature of the evolutionary history of philosophy is to understand ourselves and our world anew. Without the blinders of our answers and inspired by the intellectual intimacy that philosophy affords, the mind is broadened and refreshed. In that sense philosophy is always anything but old—awash with new possibilities for inquiry and understanding, the illuminating questions of philosophy liberate us from the blinding obviousness of present answers, the blinders of our individual and collective biases.

Philosophy progresses, evolves, and rarely stands still. Philosophers continually revise and often overthrow the views of their predecessors—sometimes even those of their own teachers. One of the most famous examples is the sequence of Socrates to Plato to Aristotle. And yet the evolution of thought that philosophy heralds remains much the same. It is the call to wonder, to dispute, to question, to liberate, to ponder, to inquire, to understand everything one can about the whole of our being—reality, knowledge, and morality—without allowing ourselves to become closed off. To behold the whole without being conquered by its vision is the sum and substance of the western intellectual tradition made possible by philosophy—a delicate balance that is anything but delicate when attained.

To see new wisdom in the old and old wisdom in the new is to be not just learned but wise. And to not merely tolerate such expansive openness but to *love* it is what it means to *be* a philosopher.

This book provides you with everything you need to understand the amazing world of nineteenth-century philosophy. With over 25 of the greatest works by 14 of the most important western philosophers of the nineteenth-century, this volume assembles into one book some of the most profound and edifying ideas from an astounding era of human thought. Suitable for a one-semester course on nineteenth-century philosophy, history of philosophy, history of ideas, or intellectual history, this book is a covert assembly with a covert purpose, to bring the profound philosophy of the nineteenth century to you, but even more importantly to bring you to a profound level of understanding of the ground-breaking ideas of this, one of the most fruitful eras of philosophical thought.

We have divided the book into six standard divisions: Part I, The Legacy of Kant: Avatar of Nineteenth Century Philosophy. Part II, The German Idealists, Part III, The Existentialists, Part IV, The Social Philosophers, Part V, The American Pragmatists and Idealists. Each part opens with a General Introduction that provides an overview of the standard major themes and historical developments of the era. A Prologue opens each chapter, and lets you in on what has come before, so you don't enter the conversation in the middle. Individual Biographical Histories give pertinent details about the life and times of each philosopher, such as Husserl. The purpose is to show you that philosophers are neither divine demigods nor depersonalized thinking machines, but individual human beings with a penchant for grappling with the perennial Big Questions, come what may. Often this has been perceived as radical because it is. The purpose of the Philosophical Overviews to each philosopher is two-fold: first, to show how that philosopher's thinking about reality, knowledge, and morality integrates into a coherent view; second, to integrate each particular philosopher's ideas into a broader philosophical context. Each reading selection comes with its own concise introduction designed to quicken your entry into the issues and prepare you for what is to come. The selections themselves have been chosen for their profundity and edited to highlight the central importance, while leaving in the all-important methods, processes, and development of the views expressed therein. Where translations are involved, we have in each case selected the most lucid. The Study Questions at the end of each reading provide comprehension questions as well as wider discussion questions; these are for you to test yourself to see how well you understand what you have read. The Philosophical Bridges, such as Marx's Influence, show how what has come before makes possible what comes after, and that philosophy's perennial questions lead to ever-more evolving views.

Special thanks to each of the following reviewers, whose comments about one or more of the volumes in the "Longman Standard History of Philosophy" series helped to enhance each book. Michael L. Anderson, University of Maryland; Marina P. Banchetti-Robino, Florida Atlantic University; David Boersema, Pacific University; Stephen Braude, University of Maryland Baltimore County; Cynthia K. Brown, Catholic University of America; Richard J. Burke, Oakland University; Marina Bykova, North Carolina State University; Jeffrey Carr, Christopher Newport University; James P. Cooney, Montgomery County Community College; Elmer H. Duncan, Baylor University; Christian Early, Eastern Mennonite University; Emma L. Easteppe, Boise State University; James E. Falcouner, Brigham Young University; Chris L. Firestone, Trinity International University; Merigala Gabriel, Georgia Southern University; Bruce Hauptli, Florida International University; Larry Hauser, Alma College; David J. Hilditch, Webster University; Mary Beth Ingham, Loyola Marymount University; Betty Kiehl, Palomar College; John H. Kulten, Jr., University of Missouri; Nelson P. Lande, University of Massachusetts; Dorothea Lotter, Wake Forest University; Charles S. MacKenzie, Reformed Theological Seminary; Thomas J. Martin, University of North Carolina Charlotte; D. A. Masolo, University of Louisville; Leemon B. McHenry, California State University, Northridge; John T. Meadors, Mississippi College; Glenn Melancon, Southeastern Oklahoma State University; Mark Michael, Austin Peay State University; Thomas Osborne, University of Nevada, Las Vegas; Walter Ott, East Tennessee State University; Anna Christina Ribeiro, University of Maryland; Stefanie Rocknak, Hartwick College; George Rudebusch, Northern Arizona University; Ari Santas, Valdosta State University; Candice Shelby, University of Colorado-Denver; Daniel Silber, Florida Southern College; Allan Silverman, Ohio State University; James K. Swindler, Illinois State University; David B. Twetten, Marquette University; Thomas Upton, Gannon University; Barry F. Vaughan, Mesa Community College; Daniel R. White, Florida Atlantic University; David M. Wisdo, Columbus State University; Evelyn Wortsman Deluty, Nassau Community College

We would like to thank the following people for their help. Brandon West of the College of Wooster for his sterling work as a student research assistant. Amy Erickson and Patrice Reeder of the College of Wooster for their unfailing secretarial help. Professors Martin Gunderson, Ron Hustwit, Henry Kreuzman, Adrian Moore, Elizabeth Schiltz, and Philip Turetzsky for their useful comments. Everyone at Longman Publishers for their very professional work, especially Priscilla McGeehon and Eric Stano, who have supported the project with tireless energy and enthusiasm. Our wives, Wendy and Helena, for their help and understanding. Finally, we would like to dedicate this volume to our children: Julia, Sophia, Dylan, and Andre Kolak; and to Andrew, Frances, Verena, Susana, and Robert Thomson.

GENERAL INTRODUCTION

The history of philosophy is sometimes presented as a genealogy with three main roots: the ancient Greek period, the modern, and the twentieth century/contemporary period. To make the extraordinary developments, upheavals, and innovations of nineteenth century wisdom a mere offshoot is no less a mistake than to ignore the medieval era, for two reasons. First, to simply leap from modern to contemporary thought makes what is going on today in philosophy so unmotivated as to be virtually incomprehensible to students and novices. This is no less true in science and mathematics, since neither quantum mechanics nor, for example, intuitionistic mathematics can appear as anything but bizarre without a thorough understanding of advances in idealism and idealist-inspired thought of the nineteenth century. More specifically, the role of mind and consciousness in contemporary thought owes far less to Berkeley's subjective idealism than the objective idealism of Fichte, Hegel, and Schelling, which in the twentieth century crossed over into physics via Niels Bohr, while in England, T. H. Green and F. H. Bradley and B. Bosanquet in France developed similar, absolute idealist, views of reality.

Second, to view philosophical works and the systems based on them merely as stepping stones in some great evolutionary scheme is no less grave an error than viewing artworks of a particular era as stepping stones to what happened in subsequent eras. It misses the intrinsic value of philosophy. Baroque art, no less so than Renaissance or nineteenth century art and music is not made irrelevant by Picasso or Pollock. On the contrary, they are and should be appreciated for their own value. This is no less true in philosophy.

The Origins of Nineteenth Century Thought:
The Kantian Legacy

This having been said, it must be pointed out that philosophy in the nineteenth Century revolved one way or the other around the groundbreaking developments resulting from the work of the great German enlightenment philosopher Immanuel Kant. His rejection of the assumptions underlying both rationalist and empiricist traditions opened up entire new lines of philosophical inquiry. No less important are his powerful demonstrations that sensation (i.e., sensible intuition) and the understanding (i.e., concepts) are both necessary for the having of experience as we know it. In this way Kant managed to accommodate in his vast system a complex but profound synthesis of all previous systems. Part of his success lay in his extraordinary ability to resolve the apparent contradictions between those earlier, modern, opposing systems of thought. His metaphysics is a bridge between idealism and realism, his epistemology a bridge between empiricism and rationalism, and his moral theory a secular rendition of a rule-based (deontological) universalism.

1

Kant's vast influence extended well beyond philosophy and science. All of Europe waxed metaphysical after Kant. Writers and composers like Schiller, Goethe, and Beethoven studied and quoted him in their own works. Ficthe, Schelling, Hegel, and Schopenhauer were inspired by his works to develop their own vast subsequent philosophies. Kant's criticism of the limits of rationality and his integration of feeling and emotion, especially with regard to the primacy of the will, inspired Schopenhauer and Nietzsche's voluntarism, Bergson's intuitionism, and even the pragmatism of William James owes more to Kant than to any other philosopher.

Kant's transcendental idealism inspired all subsequent idealists, starting with the Germans, most notably Fichte, Schelling, and Hegel. While all of these philosophers agreed with Kant's view of *phenomena*, broadly construed as appearances, perceptions, ideas, and representations as presented to consciousness, that is, "things in the mind," they disagreed with or in some cases rejected entirely his notion of *noumena*, broadly construed as what exists independently of consciousness, "things-in-themselves." The problem, as they saw it, is that there is a deep inconsistency in Kant's equivocation about whether anything can be said, known, or intuited about the noumenal world and the noumenal self, especially with regard to the will. Their notion of the Absolute as constituting by thought for the ideal objects in space and time resolves the inconsistency without falling into the solipsistic personal idealism of Berkeley. Schopenhauer, defending Kant, builds an elaborate scaffolding for the noumenal as constituted in and by the will, thereby altogether avoiding Hegel's notion of the Absolute.

The Influence of Hegel

In spite of Schopenhauer's brilliant efforts, Hegel's philosophy captured the thought of Britain and the United States. Ironically, however, the subsequent study of Hegel helped propel Kant's ideas forward, especially with regard to the idea that here was a way to save realism in philosophy without having to disregard phenomenalism or representationalism.

Especially after the French Revolution, some philosophers took a great interest in history: does history show a pattern of progress? Hegel proposed an idealist reading of history on a grand scale. He builds with Kantian thoroughness an idealist metaphysical system in which the mind does not merely structure and regulate reality but wholly generates and constitutes it, up to and including itself. What he calls "the Absolute," the world as it exists in itself, is mind or spirit, such that everything that is, was or will be is an evolving form within the world-mind, where the forces of evolution are driven not by events in the past or present, but by the still uncreated future.

Partly in reaction to the Enlightenment emphasis on reason, some nineteenth century thinkers stressed the importance of the non-rational side of human nature, such as feelings and the will. In the first half of the century, this took the form of Romanticism, which stressed the importance of the emotions. Later, it took the form of an emphasis on the will, especially in the works of Schopenhauer and Friedrich Nietzsche.

Mind and World: the Quest for Reality

Of no less importance was philosophy's influence on the thinking of the educated common man of the time. There are two commonly accepted philosophical views, shared by most ordinary individuals:

1. *There exists a mind-independent real world and*
2. *This mind-independent real world is directly experienced.*

These two beliefs tended to persist among the general public in spite of the various challenges posed to such "naïve realism" by those who called themselves the "new scientists" (Kepler, Galileo, Descartes) and the advent of modern philosophy and Kant, who even explained (with his notion of the transcendental illusion) why this should be so. But in the nineteenth century the wider public began to be affected by the various views in profound new ways, first mostly among the educated classes though this would soon filter down to ordinary citizens through the impact of a new breed of socially minded philosophers with an eye for revolution.

While many philosophers took different stands, pro and con, with regard to (1), hardly any philosopher accepted (2) at face value. Thus for instance subjective idealists, most notably Berkeley, denied wholeheartedly the existence of any such mind-independent world; whereas representationalists, most notably Kant, do not deny (1) but (2), arguing that there is a real world, in part created by mind—the phenomenal world—and created in part by things in themselves as they exist independently of the mind—the noumenal world. What all these views have in common is that any two-way relation between things in themselves and the mind must be explained in terms of individual minds affecting one and the same public reality. In other words, the underlying presupposition is that there exists one world, and that we all exist as different individuals in that one common world. The one real world is thus, ultimately, *objective*. Several extraordinary philosophers of the nineteenth century challenged this presupposition in a number of different ways, starting with Hegel and Schopenhauer, and followed by Kierkegaard and Nietzsche. By arguing that the thing-in-itself is the will, that the body itself is an expression of the will, Schopenhauer will make the case that subjectivity itself can be transcended in the social arena. Reality is an agreement among minds.

The Social Philosophers

But more than that. Following Kant, these philosophers went on to inspire Marx, Mill, and others to argue that the ego can create reality first by convincing other minds to think as you do and, even more importantly, by creating the right sort of social institutions. The process of building a new sort of individual not just through new and improved epistemologies and metaphysics but through the design of social institutions, became the sort of rallying cry heard around the world, as for instance Marx insisted: "The philosophers have only *interpreted* the world in various ways: the point however is to *change* it." Thus the shift: in Marx's view it is not individual consciousness that makes reality but, rather, social reality that makes individual consciousness.

The impact of these philosophical systems thus helped herald the new industrial revolution. The traditional end goal of philosophy up until this time was thought, ideas, or the attainment of certain special sorts of cognitive or emotive states. The nineteenth century shift into the social arena was thus brought about in part by a philosophical sea change concerning the question of what reality itself is. Instead of manipulating thoughts, propositions, opinions, and so on, the task of philosophy becomes constructing the lived reality. Thus Marx's dialectical materialism "turns Hegel upside down." Philosophy becomes less the realm of introspective analysis and more the realm of social, political, and economic activity.

American Pragmatism and Idealism

At the same time, in the United States philosophy had begun to take new shapes in the literary works of Emerson, Thoreau, Whitman, and took root in the profound new philosophical works of the first American philosophers, Peirce, James, Royce, and Dewey, the originators of two closely related movements: American pragmatism and American idealism. Before Kant, Hegel, and Nietzche, the common view among philosophers was that words are inert, ineffectual instruments employed by us to make meaning. Peirce, inspired by Kant, Hegel, and Nietzche, turns this relationship the other way around; the world, according to Peirce and his fellow pragmatists and idealists, is made, as are we ourselves, by signs, which are to words what numbers are to numerals, namely, logical functions. As such, they do not need to be created to exist. This is a notion inspired by Fichte's *act* (Section II).

It makes little sense, however, to delve further even in this most general introductory essay into any of these philosophies without first laying the groundwork for understanding the key concepts and ideas that either originated or came to a head in the work of Immanuel Kant. For this reason we begin, with Section I, with one of the best overviews of Kantian philosophy ever written, by his nineteenth century champion, Arthur Schopenhauer.

SECTION I

◆ THE LEGACY OF KANT: ◆ AVATAR OF NINETEENTH-CENTURY PHILOSOPHY

CRITIQUE OF KANTIAN PHILOSOPHY

Appendix to *The World as Will and Presentation*[1]

Arthur Schopenhauer

In this, one of the best introductions to the philosophy of Immanuel Kant ever written, Schopenhauer explains Kant's extraordinarily innovative and original, albeit extremely difficult, ideas. His goal is to uncover the true greatness of Kant's genius obscured by the glosses of his contemporaries, many of whom you will meet in the first section. He lays out Kant's essential doctrines and shows why they will forever alter the way philosophy is, can, and should be done. The most important of these doctrines, what he calls Kant's greatest achievement, is the distinction between phenomena and things-in-themselves.

He is careful, however, to avoid the superficial ways in which the distinction can easily be mired, and thereby dismissed, by a cursory understanding of what Kant means and why the problem cannot be avoided. Moreover, Schopenhauer tries to put Kantianism in a broader, global perspective by making bold, dramatic explanatory comparisons between Kant's system and the Hindu philosophy of the Vedas and Puranas.

However, Schopenhauer is not content merely to elevate Kant to what he feels is Kant's rightful position as one of the greatest philosophers of all time. Schopenhauer is critical of what he perceives as varying degrees of mistakes that, had Kant not made them, would have made him less prone to the attacks of his contemporaries. For instance, he argues that Kant did not do proper justice to the great modern British empiricist George Berkeley's insight, "no object without a subject," the cornerstone of subjective idealism. Kant's "grave mistake" was his failure to distinguish properly between perceptual and abstract cognition. This provides the impetus to Schopenhauer's new and original Kant-inspired philosophical system, expressed in the selection in the Schopenhauer section (4, Section I), where you will also find his biographical history and a general philosophical overview of his work.

It is much easier to display the failings and errors in the work of a great spirit than to articulate its value in explicit and complete terms. For the failings are something individual and finite, which therefore allow a complete survey. By contrast, it is precisely the mark that genius impresses on its works that what is excellent in them is unfathomable and inexhaustible; thus they indeed become never-aging teachers for many succeeding centuries. The masterpiece consummated by a truly great spirit will always have so deep and pervasive an effect on the whole of the human race that one could not calculate the distance of the centuries and lands within the reach of its illuminating influence. This will always be so. For however cultivated and rich the times may have been in which the work itself arose, yet genius always rises like a palm tree over the ground in which it is rooted.

But a deeply penetrating and widespread effect of this sort cannot occur suddenly, on account of the wide distance between the genius and ordinary humanity. The insight that this one individual has drawn immediately from life and the world in *one* lifetime—won and set forth for others as won and readied for them—can despite that fact not become the possession of humanity all at once; for the latter simply has no faculty for receiving as great as that which the former has for giving. Rather, even after surviving battle with unworthy opponents who would contest the life of the immortal from birth, and choke off humanity's salvation in the germ (comparable to the snake in the cradle of Hercules), that insight must then first wander the byways of countless false inter-

pretations and distorted applications, must survive attempts to unite it with old errors, and so live in a state of battle until there arises a new, unprejudiced generation for it that, even from its youth, gradually receives the content from the source in fragments through a thousand derivative channels, assimilates it bit by bit, and so comes to share in the benefaction which, proceeding from that great spirit, was destined to flow to humanity. Thus slowly goes the education of the human race, of that weak and yet recalcitrant pupil of the genius.

So too, only in time will the entire force and importance of Kant's doctrine become obvious, once the spirit of the times itself, gradually reshaped by the influence of that doctrine, altered in its most crucial and innermost features, comes to bear living witness to the power of that colossal spirit. But I would in no way here, in rash anticipation, take on the thankless role of Calchas and Cassandra.[2] Let it be but granted me, following what has been stated, to regard Kant's works as still most young, while many nowadays view them as already antiquated, indeed have laid them aside as over and done with or, as they put it, left them behind, and others, made bold by that fact, altogether ignore them and, with an iron brow, go on philosophizing about God and the soul under the presuppositions of the old realistic dogmatism and its scholasticism—which is as if one would have the doctrines of the alchemists apply in modern chemistry. In any case, Kant's works have no need of faint praises from me, but will of themselves eternally praise their master and, even if perhaps not in its letter, but in its spirit, live forever on earth.

Schopenhauer, from *Die Welt als Wille und Vorstellung,* translated by Richard E. Aquila, (Mannheim: F. A. Bockhaus, 1988). Copyright ©; Richard E. Aquila, 2005. Written especially for this volume.

[1]Translation based on the third edition (1859) of Volume One of *Die Welt als Wille and Vorstellung* (first edition, 1819), according to the version of the text edited by Julius Frauenstädt, revised by Arthur Hübscher, and published as reviewed by Angelika Hubscher, as Volume Two of Schopenhauer's *Sämtliche Werke* (Mannheim: F. A. Brockhaus, 1988 [4th ed.]).

[2]Figures in Greek mythology possessed of prophetic gifts.

Of course, if we look back on the immediate upshot of his doctrines, thus on the efforts and doings in the domain of philosophy during the time since elapsed, we find confirmation of a most disheartening pronouncement of Goethe's: "Just as the water that is displaced by a ship immediately plunges back together behind it, so when preeminent spirits have pushed error aside and made way for themselves, it is by nature most rapidly recomposed behind them" (*Poetry and Truth*, Part III, p. 521).[1] However, this period of time has been only an episode that, to be counted as part of the abovementioned fate of every new and great insight, is now unmistakably near its end, with its so persistently driven bubble now finally bursting. One is coming generally to be aware that actual and serious philosophy is still standing where Kant left it. In any case, I do not recognize anything as having happened between him and me; therefore, I take him as my immediate point of departure. . . .

I am altogether unable to justify the disagreements with Kant that nevertheless exist, however, except by accusing him of error on the particular points and exposing mistakes that he has made. Therefore, I must proceed in an altogether polemical manner against Kant in this appendix, and indeed with seriousness and with total engagement; for only thus can the error that clings to Kant's doctrine get sloughed off and its truth shine all the more brightly and stand more surely . . . So as nonetheless to avert any semblance of ill intent in the eyes of others, I would first further display my deeply felt reverence and gratitude toward Kant by briefly enunciating his main achievement as it appears to my eyes, and in particular from such general points of view that I am not compelled to touch on the points on which I must later contradict him.

Kant's greatest achievement is his distinction between phenomenon[2] and thing-in-itself—on the basis of a demonstration that between things and ourselves there stands always the *intellect*,[3] on account of which they cannot be cognized with respect to what they may be in themselves. He was led upon this path by Locke (see *Prolegomena to any Metaphysics*, § 13, Note 2).[4] The latter had demonstrated that the secondary qualities of things, such as sound, odor, color, hardness, softness, smoothness, and the like, being grounded in affections of the senses, did not pertain to objective bodies, to things in themselves, to which he rather attributed only the primary qualities, that is, those which merely presuppose space and impenetrability, thus extension, figure, solidity, number, motility. But this easily discoverable Lockean distinction, which remains merely on the surface of things, was but a youthful prelude, as it were, to the Kantian. The latter, namely, proceeding from an incomparably higher standpoint, explains all of what Locke had allowed to count as *qualitates primariae*, that is, qualities of the thing-in-itself, as likewise pertaining only to its appearance in our faculty of apprehension, and indeed precisely for the reason that we are cognizant a *priori* of its conditions, space, time, and causality. Thus Locke had removed from the thing-in-itself the share that the sense organs have in their appearance. Kant, however, then additionally removed the share had by brain-functions (although

---

[1]Johann Wolfgang von Goethe, from *Aus meinem Leben. Dichtung and Wahrheit (From my Life. Poetry and Truth* [1811–1814]), Book 15.

[2]*Erscheinung.* Following my translation of Schopenhauer's main work, I depart from standard recent translations of Kant as taken on his own, and use both "appearance" and "phenomenon" for *Erscheinung.* I use the former, however, only where the "appearing" *of* perceptual phenomena is in question.

[3]*Intellekt.* Both Schopenhauer and Kant also use this term interchangeably with *Verstand* ("understanding"). But they do not agree as to what it involves. Schopenhauer is also for the moment ignoring the role of *Ansehaumg* in Kant (See below for this term.) Unlike Kant, be consistently regards the latter as a function of "intellect," and he sees it as one of Kant's main failings that he was not only unclear as to why this should not be the case, but also inconsistent on the question.

[4]*Prolegomena zu einer jeden kunftigen Metaphysk, die als Wissenschaft wird auftreten können (Prolegomena to any Future Metaphysics that will be able to come forth as Science* [1783]).

not under this name),[1] whereby the distinction between phenomenon and thing-in-itself now acquired an infinitely greater significance and a very much deeper sense. To this purpose, he had to take up the great distinction between our cognition that is a priori and that which is *a posteriori*,[2] which had not yet ever been done before him with fitting rigor and completeness, nor with distinct consciousness; this accordingly became the main subject of his profound investigations. . . .

If, in accordance with the above, the distinction between phenomenon and thing-in-itself, thus the doctrine of the utter diversity of the ideal and real, is the hallmark of the Kantian philosophy, the arrival soon thereafter of a declaration of the absolute identity of the two is a sad confirmation of the pronouncement by Goethe earlier mentioned: all the more so given that it rested on nothing but the windbaggery of [purely] intellectual perception,[3] and was accordingly only a return to the crudeness of the common viewpoint, masked under the imposing ways of elegant airs, bombast, and sheer nonsense. It became the point of departure worthy of the still grosser nonsense of the plodding and spiritless[4] *Hegel*.

As then Kant's distinction of the phenomenon from the thing-in-itself, understood in the manner set forth above, far surpassed everything that had ever gone before in the profundity and thoughtful awareness of its grounding, it was also infinitely consequential in its results. For entirely in its own terms, in an utterly new manner, in a new aspect, and found upon a new path, he depicted therein the same truth that Plato already tirelessly repeats and in his own terminology usually expresses thus: this world appearing to the senses has no true being but only a ceaseless becoming, it is and also is not, and apprehension of it is not so much a case of cognition as of delusion. . . .

The same truth, depicted again in an entirely different way, is also one of the main doctrines of the Vedas and Puranas,[5] the doctrine of Maya, by which nothing other was understood than precisely what Kant calls phenomenon as opposed to thing in itself. For the work of Maya is said to be precisely this visible world in which we exist, a conjured illusion, an insubstantial semblance inherently without essence, comparable to optical illusions and dreams, a veil that envelops human consciousness, a something of which it is equally false and equally true to say that it is as that it is not. . . .

All of this rests, however, on a fundamental distinction between dogmatic and *critical*, or *transcendental*, philosophy. Anyone who would form a distinct idea of this and render it present with an example can do it in all brevity by perusing, as a spec-

---

[1]Kant himself did not attribute the functions by which things are determined to "appear" to us as brain-functions. He would at most have conceded they might be grounded in some "thing (or things) in itself' that *appears* to us, *qua* "phenomenon," as brain-functions. And despite often putting it in stronger-sounding terms, Schopenhauer at most holds that the matter composing brain-states is the essential *medium* for the cognitive functions in question. In turn, the inner being of that medium—Schopenhauer's "thing-in-itself"—is what he titles "will," meaning: an underlying force or energy that we are only able to *describe* in the misleading terms of what we call "our own" will. But over and above that medium and its inner being, there is also what Schopenhauer calls, in the main body of his work, the "pure" element in cognition, that is, precisely that *by virtue* of which any brain-state is indeed a medium for any sort of cognition in the first place. Thus in the main body of the work (e.g., § 24 in Book Two), Schopenhauer is forceful in his rejection of materialistic reductions of cognition, even precisely when attention is granted to the role of underlying forces.

[2]That is, cognition whose grounds have a "prior" or a "posterior" (derivative) status with respect to the possible appearance of anything to one's senses. The distinction has different connotations in different contexts (e.g., regarding the origin of "ideas," the grounding of judgments and knowledge-claims, etc.), but should in any case not be taken to rest, in either Kant or Schopenhauer, on the notion that we are actually *cognizant* of anything prior to our engagement in sensory experience.

[3]*intellektualer Anschauung*. Again, *Anschauung* essentially involves intellect for Schopenhauer himself. The objection here, aimed mainly against Fichte, is to the idea of perception *wholly* generated by way of the intellect (as opposed to intellect responding to sensation). Throughout, bracketed material in the text is interpolated by the translator.

[4]A joke in the light of the central role of spirit (*Geist*) in Hegel's philosophy.

[5]Sanskrit writings that provided the basis for much of Hinduism. As opposed to the Puranas, containing various myths of gods and heroes, the Vedas (of which the well-known *Bhagvadgita* is a part), were permitted only to the higher, Biahmanic, orders.

imen of dogmatic philosophy, an essay by Leibniz that bears the title *De rerum originatione radicali"* ["On the Ultimate Origination of Things"] . . . Here in a quite proper realistic-dogmatic manner, utilizing the ontological and cosmological proofs [of the existence of God], the origin and excellent makeup of the world are demonstrated a priori on the basis of *veritates aeternae* [eternal truths]—It is simply confessed in passing that experience reveals the exact opposite of the excellence of the world here demonstrated, whereupon, however, it is pointed out to experience that she understands nothing about it and should keep her mouth shut when philosophy has spoken a priori.

As an opponent of this entire method, there has now appeared with *Kant* the *Critical Philosophy* which has as its concern precisely the *veritates aetemae* that underlie all such dogmatic construction, examines them as to their origin, and then finds it in the human head, where they grow, namely, out of the forms that characteristically pertain to the latter, which it carries internally for the sake of apprehension of an objective world. Thus here, in the brain, is the quarry that provides the material for those proud dogmatic constructions. By virtue, however, of the fact that, to attain to this result, the critical philosophy had to *go beyond* the *veritates aeternae* in which all preceding dogmatism was grounded, in order to make them the very object of its investigation, it became *Transcendental* Philosophy. From this it then further ensues that the objective world, as we are cognizant of it, does not pertain to the essence of the thing-in-itself, but is its mere *phenomenon*, conditioned precisely by those forms, which lie a priori in the human intellect (that is, brain); therefore, they can indeed contain nothing but phenomena. . . .

He derived the thing-in-itself not in the correct way, as I will soon show, but by means of an inconsistency for which he had to atone through frequent and incontrovertible attacks upon this main part of his doctrine. He did not recognize the thing in itself directly in Will. But he took a major, groundbreaking step toward this recognition by depicting the undeniable moral significance of human action as entirely distinct and independent from the laws of the phenomenon and never explicable in accordance

with them, but rather as something that immediately touches the thing-in-itself: this is the second main point of view with respect to his achievement.

We can view the utter overthrow of scholastic philosophy as the third. With this name I would here designate in general terms the whole of the period beginning with Father of the Church Augustine and concluding close upon Kant. . . .

Speculative theology and the rational psychology[1] that was interconnected with it received their death blow from him. Since then, they have vanished from German philosophy, and one must not be misled by the fact that here and there the word is retained after the substance has been abandoned, or that some impoverished philosophy professor has the fear of his lord before his eyes and is leaving the truth to itself. The magnitude of this achievement by Kant can only be appreciated by someone who has observed the detrimental influence of those concepts on natural science, as well as philosophy, in all, even in the best writers of the seventeenth and eighteenth centuries. In German writings in natural science, the alteration in tone and in the metaphysical background entering the scene since Kant is striking; before him, matters stood in this as they now stand in England.

This achievement by Kant is connected with the fact that unreflective adherence to the laws of the phenomenon, elevation of these to eternal truths and thereby of fleeting phenomena to the true essence of the world, in short, *realism* undisturbed in its delusion by any reflection, had been altogether dominant in all the preceding philosophy of ancient, medieval, and modern times. *Berkeley*, who like *Malebranche* before him had already indeed been cognizant of the onesidedness, indeed the falsity of the latter, was unable to overturn it, because his attack was limited to a *single* point. Thus it was reserved to Kant to help bring to dominance, at least in philosophy in Europe, that basic idealistic view which is even, and indeed in its essentials, that of religion in the whole of non-Islamicized Asia. . . .

This little bit, and in no way exhausting the subject, may suffice as witness to my recognition of Kant's great achievements, borne here to my own satisfaction and because justice demanded that those achievements be recalled to the memory of anyone

---

[1] A philosophical undertaking aimed at an a priori grounding of pronouncements about a "soul."

who would follow me in relentlessly exposing his mistakes, to which I now proceed. . . .

We would first make explicit for ourselves and examine the basic thought in which the aim of the entire *Critique of Pure Reason* lies—Kant placed himself in the standpoint of his predecessors, the dogmatic philosophers, and in accordance therewith proceeded with them from the following presuppositions. (1) Metaphysics is the science of that which lies beyond the possibility of all experience. (2) Such a thing can never be found in accordance with principles that are themselves first drawn from experience (*Prolegomena*, § 1); rather, only that which we know *before*, thus *independently* of all experience can reach further than possible experience. (3) Within our faculty of reason, some principles of this sort are actually to be found; one comprehends them under the name of "cognition through pure reason."

Kant goes this far with his predecessors, but here is where he departs from them. They say: "These principles, or instances of cognition through pure reason, are expressions of absolute possibility with regard to things, *aeternae veritates*, sources of ontology; they stand above the world order as Fate stood above the gods of the ancients." Kant says: they are mere forms belonging to our intellect, laws not of the existence of things but of their presentations to us,[1] therefore they apply merely to our apprehension of things and can accordingly not—as was the concern of the point (1)—extend beyond the possibility of experience. For precisely the apriority of these cognitive forms, since it can only rest on their subjective origin, cuts us off forever from cognizance of the essence in itself of things and limits us to a world of mere phenomena, so that we can not even be cognizant *a posteriori*, let alone a priori, of things as they may be in themselves. Accordingly, metaphysics is impossible, and into its place

steps critique of pure reason. As opposed to the old dogmatism, Kant is utterly victorious here; therefore, all dogmatic efforts appearing since then have had to strike paths entirely different from the earlier ones.

In accordance with the pronounced aim of the critique in question, I will now conduct us to the justification of my own path. Namely, upon more exact examination of the argumentation above, one will have to confess that its very first basic assumption is a *petitio principii* [begs the question]. It lies in this proposition (set forth with particular distinctness in *Prolegomena* § 1): "The source of metaphysics must not be at all empirical, its principles and basic concepts must never be taken from experience, whether inner or outer." For a grounding of this cardinal assertion, however, nothing at all is cited but etymological argument based on the word "metaphysics."[2] But in truth things stand as follows. The world and our own existence is necessarily displayed as a riddle to us. Now it is assumed without further ado that the solution of the riddle cannot proceed from a thorough understanding of the world itself, but must be sought in something entirely distinct from the world (for that is what is meant by "beyond the possibility of all experience"), and that everything must be excluded from that solution of which we can have any sort of *immediate* cognizance (for that is what is meant by possible experience, both inner and outer); it must rather to be sought only in that to which we can attain in a merely mediated way, namely, by means of inferences on the basis of general propositions a priori.

Having in this way excluded the main source of all cognition and barred oneself from the direct path to the truth, one cannot wonder that the dogmatic efforts failed and that Kant was able to demonstrate the necessity of the failure; for one had assumed in advance that metaphysics and cognition a priori are

---

[1] Literally, "of our *Vorstellungen* of them." I translate as above because, in Schopenhauer, *Vorstellung* primarily signifies the status of something as object in relation to (as "presented" to) a cognitive subject's awareness. Thus, at least in most cases, the apparently possessive "our" signifies no more literal possession than when one says that "our presentation in this week's seminar will be a lecture by Professor Smith" or that "our (the audience's) performance this evening will be Shakespeare's *Hamlet*"; correspondingly, when what is in question is "our presentation of *x*," the *x* generally indicates just the "presentation" itself—what *gets presented*—but with the qualification: *as* presented, not "in itself." (Sometimes, of course, Schopenhauer rather wants to call attention precisely to the presenting *of* the matter in question, and *Vorstellung* has then a corresponding sense.)

[2] Signifying "beyond physics" or "beyond the physical."

identical. In addition, one would have had to prove in advance that what it takes to solve the riddle of the world simply cannot be contained within it itself, but is to be sought only outside of the world, in something to which one can attain only according to the directing principle of those forms of which we are conscious a priori. So long, however, as this has not been proven, we have no ground, in this most important and most difficult of all tasks, to stop up that source of cognition which is the richest of all in content, inner and outer experience, in order to work only with contentless forms.

I therefore say that the solution of the riddle of the world must proceed from an understanding of the world itself; thus that the task of metaphysics is not to fly beyond the experience within which the world exists, but to understand it in its depths, insofar as experience, outer and inner, is indeed the main source of all cognition; therefore, that the solution of the riddle of the world is possible only through a proper and correctly implemented connection of outer with inner experience. . . .

After dealing with space and time in isolation [in the Transcendental Aesthetic, the first of the two parts of the *Critique's* Transcendental Doctrine of Elements (A19/B33ff.)[1]], then having done with the entire world of perception in which we live and exist, which fills space and time, with the empty words, "the empirical content of perception is *given to us*" [A50/B74/ff., at the beginning of the Transcendental Logic, the second part of the Doctrine of Elements], he attains at once, with a *single leap*, to the *logical foundation of his entire philosophy*, to the *Table of Judgments* [A70/B95]. From the latter he deduces a proper dozen Categories, symmetrically stuck under four rubrics [Quantity, Quality, Relation, Modality (A80/B106)], which later become the frightful Procrustean bed into which he forcibly compels all the things of the world and all that transpires in human beings, eschewing no violence and shamed by no sophisms, only everywhere to be able to repeat the symmetry of that table. The first thing that is symmetrically derived from it is the pure physiological[2] table of the general principles of natural science, namely, the Axioms of Intuition (*Anschauung*), Anticipations of Perception (*Wahrnehmung*),[3] Analogies of Experience, and Postulates of Empirical Thought in General [A161/B200ff., in a chapter in the part of the Transcendental Logic called the Analytic of Principles] . . . The mere Categories were what he calls *concepts*, but these principles of natural science are *judgments* . . . In the same way there arise by application of *inferences* to the Categories—which business is accomplished by *reason*, in accordance with its supposed principle of seeking the unconditioned— the *Ideas* of Reason [A305/B362ff., in the part of the Transcendental Logic called the Transcendental Dialectic]. This then proceeds thus: the three Categories of Relation yield three exclusively possible types of major premise for inferences, with the latter likewise divided into three types, each of which is to be viewed as an egg from which reason hatches an Idea, namely, from the categorical mode of inference the Idea of *soul*, from the hypothetical the Idea of a *world*, and from the disjunctive the Idea of *God*.[4] In the middle case, that of the Idea of a world, the

---

[1]I follow the standard practice of referring to the first- and second-edition pagination as "A" and "B."

[2]That is, "physiological" in the sense of pertaining to the possibility of the physical sciences.

[3]For reasons not without ground, but to my mind insufficient, *Anschauung* is generally translated "intuition" in Kant, even though what Kant has in mind is nothing like what that term normally means in English. In a suitably broad sense, both *Anschauung* and *Wahrnehmung* are, for both philosophers, what we could comfortably call at least some kind of "perception." (The main broadening concerns the notion, accepted by both philosophers, of a pure, a priori "perception" of space and time as such, as opposed to the phenomena filling them as their contents.) I therefore generally use "perception" for both terms, and "intuition" and "intuitive" only where Kant uses *Intuition* and *intuitiv*. (Where they occur together, as above, one may simply translate *Anschauung* as "perception" and *Wahrnehmung* as, for example, "perceptual apprehension." I proceed otherwise above only to accommodate what may be most familiar to readers of Kant.)

[4]Respectively, the Paralogisms of Pure Reason (A341/B399ff.): major premise in the "categorical" or subject-predicate form; the Antinomy of Pure Reason (A408/B435ff.): major premise in the "hypothetical" or "if . . . then" form; the Ideal of Pure Reason (A567/B595ff.): major premise in the "disjunctive" or "either . . . or" form.

symmetry of the Table of Categories is then once again repeated, insofar as its four rubrics bring forth four Theses, each of which has its Antithesis as a symmetrical counterpart. . . .

I have put forth above, as Kant's main achievement, that he distinguishes the phenomenon from the thing-in-itself, explains this entire visible world as phenomenon, and therefore denies its laws any validity extending beyond the phenomenon. It is of course striking that he did not derive that merely relative existence of the phenomenon from the simple, so readily available, undeniable truth *"No object without a subject,"* in order to depict the object, because it altogether always exists only in relation to a subject, as in its very root dependent on the latter, conditioned by it, and therefore as a mere phenomenon that does not exist in itself, does not exist absolutely. Berkeley—to whose achievement Kant does not do justice—had already made that important principle the bedrock of his philosophy and thereby established the immortality of his memory . . . But when I later read Kant's main work in the first edition, already become rare, I saw to my great pleasure that all those contradictions vanished and, even if he does not employ the formula "no object without a subject," found that Kant, with just as much decisiveness as Berkeley and I, does explain the external world lying before us in space in time as a mere presentation to the subject cognizing it. Thus, for example, he says there at A383[1] without reservation: "If I take away the thinking subject, the entire corporeal word must fell away, as it is nothing but a phenomenon within our subject's sensibility and a species of its presentations." But the entire passage from A348–392, in which Kant sets forth his decided idealism in an exceedingly fine and distinct manner, was suppressed by him in the second edition and to the contrary a multitude of expressions inserted that are in conflict with it. . . .

In undeniable contradiction with the decidedly idealistic basic view so distinctly pronounced in the first edition of the *Critique of Pure Reason*, however, stands the way in which Kant introduces the *thing in itself*, and this is without doubt the main reason why in the second edition he suppressed the main idealistic passage in question and declared himself in straightforward opposition to Berkeleyan idealism;[2] thereby, however, he only brought inconsistencies into his work, without being able to rid it of its main infirmity . . . Kant grounds the presupposition of the thing in itself, although under the cover of all sorts of circumlocution, on an inference in accordance with the law of causality, namely, that empirical perception—more accurately, the *sensation* in our sense organs from which the latter proceeds—must have an external cause. But according to his own and accurate discovery, the law of causality is known to us a priori, is consequently a function of our intellect, thus of *subjective* origin; further, sensation itself, to which we are here applying the law of causality, is undeniably *subjective;* and finally, even the space into which, by means of this application, we set the cause of sensation as an object is something given a priori, consequently a *subjective* form belonging to our intellect. Hence empirical perception as a whole remains altogether on *subjective* ground and soil, as a mere process within us, and nothing entirely distinct from it, independent of it, can be brought into it as a *thing-in-itself* or demonstrated as its necessary presupposition. In actual fact, empirical perception remains mere presentation to us. It is the world as presentation. We can then attain to the essence in itself of the latter only upon the entirely different path that I have struck, by way of bringing in self-consciousness, which makes Will known to us as the in-itself of the phenomenon that we are. . . .

I now return to Kant's great mistake on which I have already touched above, that he did not properly distinguish between perceptual and abstract cognition . . . His "object of experience," of which he is constantly speaking, the real object of the Categories, is not a perceptual presentation, but it is not an abstract concept either, but rather distinct from both and yet at the same both, and an utter absurdity . . . and from this there comes the unfortunate confusion that I must now draw into the light. To this

---

[1] I "update" Schopenhauer's references to the *Critique* to what is currently standard, using "A" for the first edition and "B" for the second when Schopenhauer in fact refers to each.

[2] B70–71 and, in the "Refutation of Idealism" added in the edition of the *Critique*, B274.

purpose, I have to go in general terms through the entire Doctrine of Elements.[1]

The *Transcendental Aesthetic* is a work so altogether full of merit that it alone could suffice to render Kant's name eternal. It proves to have so full a power to convince that I count its theorems among the world's incontrovertible truths, just as without doubt they also belong among its most consequential, hence are to be regarded as the rarest thing in the world, namely, as an actual major discovery in metaphysics. The fact, rigorously proven by him, that a part of our cognition is known to us a priori, allows of no other explanation than that this comprises the forms belonging to our intellect.[2] . . .

After the detailed discussion of the general *forms* belonging to all perception given in the Transcendental Aesthetic, one must surely expect to gain some enlightenment regarding its *content*, regarding the way in which *empirical* perception enters our consciousness, how cognizance of this entire world, so real and so important for us, arises within us. But on this, Kant's entire doctrine really contains nothing further than the often repeated, empty expression: "The empirical element in perception is *given* from outside."

In this way here too, then, from the *pure forms belonging to perception*, Kant arrives with a leap at *thought*, at the *Transcendental Logic* . . . "Our cogni-tion," he says, "has two sources, namely, receptivity of impressions and spontaneity of concepts: the first is the capacity for receiving presentations, the second that for cognizance of an object through these presentations; through the first an *object* is given to us, through the second it is thought."[3]—That is wrong. For according to that the *impression,* for which alone we have mere receptivity, which thus comes from outside and is alone really "given," would already be a *presentation,* indeed already an *object.* But it is nothing further than a mere *sensation* in the sense organ, and only through application of the *understanding* (that is, of the law of causality) and of space and time as perceptual forms does our *intellect* transform this mere *sensation* into a *presentation* that now stands as an *object* in space and time and can be distinguished from the latter (from the object) only to the extent that one is asking about the thing-in-itself, but is otherwise identical with it.[4] I have set forth this process in detail in *The Fourfold Root of the Principle of Sufficient Ground,*[5] § 21. But with that, the business of the understanding and perceptual cognition is completed, and there is no need in it for any concepts or any thought; therefore even animals have these presentations.

With the addition of concepts, with the addition of thought—to which spontaneity can of course be

---

[1]The *Critique* is divided into a Transcendental Doctrine of Elements and a Transcendental Doctrine of Method, the former comprising eighty percent of the whole. The former is in turn divided into the Transcendental Aesthetic, focusing on sensibility, and a Transcendental Logic focusing on understanding (intellect) and reason; the Logic comprises ninety-five percent of the Doctrine of Elements.

[2]The "forms" in question are the space in time in which we are capable of apprehending phenomena: the pure, a priori forms belonging to human *Anschauung.* But again, it should be noted that Schopenhauer's use of the term 'intellect' is broader than Kant's, since the latter refers to a cognitive faculty essentially involving abstract concepts. For Schopenhauer, *reason* is the faculty for concepts; by contrast, in its proper relation to "sensibility," *understanding,* or *intellect,* is the faculty for "perception" (*Anschauung*) on an altogether pre-conceptual level. However, a major part of Schophenhauer's objection to Kant is precisely that he was confused as to whether *Anschauung* "presents" us with anything at all apart from concepts.

[3]A50/B74. Schopenhauer is not strictly quoting. Perhaps the only departure worth noting: Kant's emphasis in the passage is not on an *object* given, as opposed to thought, but on an object *given,* as opposed to being thought.

[4]Presumably, Schopenhauer is not proposing that something literally in our sense organs gets "transformed" into an object in space and time standing in a real relation to those very organs. What he more likely means is that any such object is, from the "transcendental" perspective, simply an empirically perceptible *portion* of the only space and time of which we can conceive; that the *space and time* in question are projected a priori as a kind of frame(s) for any such perception in the first place; and that the relevant portion of that space and time is apprehended as clothed in its particular sensory *quality* precisely because its apprehension is effected through the *medium* of particular sensations in one's sense organs (or more exactly: through the medium of particular sensations in what are "presented" to us as sense organs, insofar as they are in their own turn apprehended as objects).

[5]Or: . . . *Sufficient Reason;* the noun is *Grund.*

attributed—*perceptual* cognition is entirely abandoned, and an utterly different class of presentations, namely, of non–perceptual, abstract concepts enters into consciousness: this is the activity *of reason*, but it gets its entire content for our thought only from perception antecedent to it and their comparison with other perceptions and concepts. Thus Kant already brings thought into perception and lays the ground for that hopeless confusion of intuitive (*intuitiven*) and abstract cognition which it is my concern to criticize here. He lets perception taken by itself, without any understanding, be purely sensory, thus entirely passive, and an *object* be apprehended only through thought (Categories of the understanding); thus he brings *thought into perception*. But then on the other hand the object of *thought* is an individual, real object.[1] Thereby, thought forfeits its essential character of generality and abstraction and instead of general concepts gets individual things for its object, whereby, in turn, he brings *perception into thought*. From this there originates the hopeless confusion in question, and the consequences of this first false step extend over his entire theory of cognition. Through the entirety of the latter runs the complete confusion of perceptual and abstract presentation, to the point of something intermediate between the two, which he depicts as the object of cognition. . . .

It is not at all the *perceived object*, but it is conceptually added to perception in thought, as something corresponding to it, and thenceforth perception is experience (*Erfahrung*) and has value and truth, which it consequently obtains only through its relation to a concept (in diametrical opposition to our account, according to which concepts obtain their value and truth only from perception). The addition to perception in thought of this object with no possibility of direct presentation is then the real function of the Categories. "Only through perception is the object given, which is subsequently thought in accordance with the Category" (A399). This becomes particularly explicit from a passage at B125: "The question then arises whether concepts do not also precede a priori, as conditions under which alone something, even if not *perceived*, is nonetheless *thought* as an object in general," which he affirms. . . .

Kant ascribes objects themselves to *thought*, in order to make experience and the objective world thereby dependent on the *understanding*, but yet without having the latter be a faculty for *perception*. In this respect he of course distinguishes perception from thought, but makes individual things in part an object of perception, in part of thought. But they are actually only the former: our empirical perception is immediately *objective*, precisely because it proceeds from the causal nexus. Its object is immediately things, not presentations distinct from them. Individual things are perceived as such in the understanding and through the senses; in the process, the *one-sided* impression on the latter is supplemented by the imagination. As soon as we pass over to *thought*, by contrast, we abandon individual things and have only to do with general concepts without perceptibility, even if we subsequently apply the results of our thought to individual things. . . .

The unjustified interpolation of the hermaphrodite "object of presentation" is the source of Kant's errors. But with its removal, the doctrine of the Categories as a priori concepts also falls away, since they contribute nothing to perception and are not supposed to apply to the thing-in-itself, but by their means we only think that "object of presentations" and thereby transform presentation into experience. For every empirical perception is already experience, while every perception is empirical that proceeds from sensation through the senses: the understanding refers this sensation, by means of its single function (cognizance a priori of the law of causality) to its cause, which is precisely thereby displayed as an object of experience in space and time (forms belonging to pure perception), as a material object persisting in space through all time, but which nonetheless also remains as such always a presentation, just like space and time themselves. If we would go beyond this presentation, we are occupied with the question of the thing-in-itself, the answer to which is the theme of my entire work, as of all metaphysics in general. . . .

[A discussion follows of the "logical functions," or "logical forms"—supposed to belong a priori to the understanding as a capacity for judgment, and organ-

---

[1]That is, it is *supposed* to be an individual object, on Kant's view; for Schopenhauer, the objects of *thought* are mere abstractions, concepts.

ized into the Table of Judgments—and Kant's correlation of these functions with concepts supposed to be involved a priori in cognition relating one to "objects." These are the twelve Categories. Schopenhauer's conclusion: "I accordingly demand that we throw eleven of the Categories out the window and retain only that of causality." He then proceeds to the Analytic of Principles, where Kant attempts to provide a priori grounding for a number of judgments about objects in which those concepts are employed. The Analytic of Principles, also called the Transcendental Doctrine of Judgment, is the second part of the Transcendental Analytic; its first part is the Analytic of Concepts. A portion of this discussion follows:]

The principle of the *persistence of substance*[1] is derived from the Category of subsistence and inherence. But we know the latter only from the form of categorical judgments, that is, from the combination of two concepts as subject and predicate. How forcibly, therefore, that great metaphysical principle is made to depend on this simple, purely logical form! But it is only in fact done *pro forma* and for the sake of symmetry. The proof that is here given for this principle entirely sets aside its supposed origin from the understanding and from the Category, and is drawn from the pure perception of time. But this proof too is completely wrong. . . .

But of course our cognizance of the persistence of substance, that is, of matter, has to rest on an a priori insight, for it is elevated above all doubt, and therefore cannot be drawn from experience. I derive it from the fact that the principle of all becoming and passing, the law of causality of which we are a priori conscious, bears in its very essence only on *alterations*, that is, on the successive states of matter, thus is limited to the *form* but leaves the matter untouched, which therefore stands in our consciousness as the foundation of all things, subject to no becoming or passing, hence always having been and always remaining. A deeper grounding of the persistence of substance, drawn from analysis of the empirical world's perceptual presentation to us in general, can be found in our first Book,[2] § 4, where it was shown

that the essence of *matter* consists in completely *uniting space and time*, the uniting of which is possible only by means of the presentation of causality, consequently only with respect to the understanding, which is nothing but the subjective correlate of causality; therefore too, shown that there is never cognizance of matter otherwise than as operating, that is, as through and through causality, that being and operating are one in it, which is already indicated by the word *actuality*.[3] The intimate uniting of space and time, causality, matter, actuality are thus one thing, and the subjective correlate of this one thing is the understanding. . . .

Thus it is on the basis of the part played by *space* in matter, that is, in all the phenomena of actual reality—insofar as it is the contrary and opposite of time and therefore, in itself and outside of union with the latter, knows no change at all—that the principle of the persistence of substance, which everyone recognizes as a priori certain, has to be derived and explicated, but not on the basis of mere time, to which for this purpose Kant in all absurdity imputes a *lasting* character. . . .

[In what follows, Schopenhauer turns to the Transcendental Dialectic, which, along with the Analytic, makes up the Transcendental Logic] Kant opens it with an explanation of *reason*, which faculty is to play the main role in it, since so far only sensibility and understanding had been on the stage . . . Kant's exposition of this principle of reason is still rendered dim by indistinctness, indefiniteness, and fragmentation (A307/B364 and A322/B379). Distinctly pronounced, however, it is the following: "If the conditioned is given, so must also be given the totality of its conditions, hence also the *unconditioned* by which alone that totality is made complete." A most vivid sense of the seeming truth of this proposition will be gotten if the conditions and the conditioned are pictured as links of a hanging chain, the upper end of which is, however, not visible, and therefore might go on *ad infinitum*, but since the chain does not fall but is hanging, *one* link above must be the first and somehow fixed. Or more succinctly:

---

[1]The first of Kant's three Analogies of Experience (A182/B224*ff*.). The second and third concern causality and "reciprocity" in causal action. Schopenhauer rejects the very notion of reciprocity as unintelligible from the start.

[2]Book One of *The World as Will and Presentation*.

[3]*Wirken*="operate"; *Wirkung*="effect" (of some cause); *Wirklichkeit*="actuality," "reality," or "actual reality."

reason would like a point of attachment for infinitely retroverting causal chains; that would be a comfort to it. But we would examine the proposition not in pictures but in itself. . . .

Here it is in fact false that the conditions of something conditioned must as such constitute a *series*. Rather, the totality of conditions for anything conditioned must be contained in its *proximate* ground, from which it immediately proceeds and which is a *sufficient* ground only by that fact: thus, for example, the various determinations of the state that is its cause, which must all come together before the effect occurs. But the series, for example, the chain of causes, arises only by virtue of the fact that we consider in turn as something conditioned what was just now the condition, in which case the entire operation starts over again and the Principle of Sufficient Ground appears anew with its demand. But there can never be a truly successive *series* of conditions for something conditioned, which would exist merely as such and for the sake of the eventual final thing conditioned, but it is always an alternating series of conditions and things conditioned. With every link that we pass, however, the chain is interrupted and the demand of the Principle of Sufficient Ground is paid in full; it arises anew when the condition is made into something conditioned. Thus the Principle of *Sufficient* Ground always demands only completeness of the *proximate condition,* never completeness of a *series* . . . If instead of confronting the matter itself, on the other hand, one dwells within abstract concepts, those distinctions vanish: then a chain of alternating causes and effects, or of alternating logical grounds and consequences, is given out to be a chain of mere causes or grounds for the final effect, and the *completeness of conditions* by which alone a ground is made *sufficient* appears as completeness of that assumed *series* of mere grounds, which exist for the sake of the final consequence. The abstract principle of reason then steps most boldly forth with its demand for the unconditioned. But to recognize its invalidity, there is no need for a critique of reason by means of Antinomies and their resolu-

tion,[1] but only of a critique of reason understood in my sense, namely, an examination of the relation between abstract and immediately intuitive cognition by means of a descent from the indeterminate generality of the former to the solid determinateness of the latter. From such a critique it then results in this case that the essence of reason in no way consists in the demand for something unconditioned; for as soon as it proceeds with fully thoughtful awareness, it has to find of itself that something unconditioned is precisely a non-thing. As a cognitive faculty, reason can only deal with objects; but all objects for a subject are necessarily and irrevocably subordinated and subject to the Principle of Sufficient Ground, both *a parte ante* and *a parte post* [both with respect to what precedes and with respect to what follows]. . . .

In fact all of that talk about the Absolute, this almost exclusive theme of philosophies attempted since Kant, is nothing other than the cosmological proof [of the existence of God] *incognito*. The latter, namely, with the loss of all rights and declared an outlaw in consequence of the trial conducted against it by Kant, can no longer show itself in its true shape, therefore appears in all sorts of disguises, sometimes in elegant ones, cloaked in intellectual perception, or pure thought, sometimes as a suspicious vagabond who makes his demands—half begging, half defiant— in more modest philosophical theses. If those gentlemen would absolutely have an Absolute, then I would provide them with one that much better satisfies the demands on such a thing than the shadowy figures conveyed by their babbling: it is matter. It has not arisen and is imperishable, thus actually independent and *quod per se est et per se concipitur*.[2] From its womb everything proceeds, and everything returns to it; what more can one demand of an absolute? . . .

Now Kant himself, to be sure, denies all objective validity to this supposed principle of reason, but yet gives it out as a necessary subjective presupposition and thus introduces an irresolvable split into our cognition, which he soon lets come more distinctly to the fore. To this purpose, he further articulates that

---

[1] The Antinomy of Pure Reason—divided into four distinct antinomies, or sets of apparently counterbalancing.

[2] Theses and Antitheses with respect to four distinct issues—begins at A405/B432 in the Transcendental Dialectic. "that which exists through itself and is conceived through itself": with slight variation, Spinoza's definition of "substance."

principle of reason (A322/B379) in accordance with his favored method of architectonic symmetry. From the three Categories of Relation there spring three kinds of inferences, each of which provides the directing principle for the search for a special unconditioned, of which there are therefore three: soul, world (as object in itself and a closed totality), God. With this, one must immediately comment on a major contradiction of which Kant, however, takes no notice, because it would be very dangerous for the symmetry: two of these unconditioned beings are in fact themselves conditioned by the third, namely, soul and world by God, who is their productive cause; the former thus do not at all have the predicate of being unconditioned in common with the latter, but only that of being inferred in accordance with principles of experience beyond the possibility of experience.

This aside, we recognize in the three unconditioned beings at which, according to Kant, all reason following its essential laws must arrive, the three main objects around which the whole of Christianity-influenced philosophy has turned, from the scholastics on, down to Christian Wolff.[1] However accessible and current those concepts have now become for mere reason through all those philosophers, it is yet in no way thereby settled that they were bound to proceed, even without revelation, from the development of everybody's reason, as a product peculiar to the very essence of the latter. To settle this, we would have to bring in the aid of historical investigation, and thus to inquire whether ancient and non-European peoples, especially the Hindustani, and a number of the most ancient Greek philosophers had actually also arrived at those concepts, or whether, too good-naturedly, we merely ascribe these to them, just as the Greeks recognized their gods everywhere, insofar as we quite wrongly translate the Brahma of the Hindus and the Tien of the Chinese as "God"; or whether it is not rather that real theism is to be found only in the Jewish religion and the two that have proceeded from it, whose adherents have precisely for that reason grouped the followers of all other religions on earth under the name of heathens—a most simplistic and crude expression, incidentally, which should at least be banned from the writings of the learned, because it equates Brahmanists, Buddhists, Egyptians, Greeks, Romans, Germans, Gauls, Iroquois, Patagonians, Caribbeans, Tahitians, Australians, et. al., and sticks them in one bag. Such an expression is fitting for priests, but in the world of the learned it should be shown the door at once; it can travel to England and settle in Oxford. . . .

Such a historical investigation would have saved Kant from a dire strait into which he now gets, insofar as he has those three concepts necessarily originating from the nature of reason, and yet demonstrates that they are untenable and cannot be grounded by reason, and therefore turns reason itself into a sophist, saying (A339/B397): "They are sophistries not of people but of reason itself, from which even the wisest cannot free himself and perhaps, to be sure, wards off the error after much effort, but can never be free of the illusion, which incessantly torments and mocks him." According to that, these Kantian "Ideas of Reason" would be comparable to the focus in which, some inches in front of its surface, the rays reflected from a concave mirror converge, in consequence of which, through an unavoidable process of the understanding, an object is displayed to us there which is a thing with no reality.

The term *Idea (Idee)* for those three supposedly necessary productions of pure theoretical reason has been very unfortunately chosen and snatched from Plato, however, who with it designated the imperishable forms that, multiplied by way of space and time, are made partially visible in countless individual perishable things.[2] Plato's Ideas are consequently altogether perceptible, as indeed the word that he chose so definitely signifies, which one could only fittingly translate as "perceptibles" or "visibles." And Kant appropriated it in order to designate what lies so far from all possibility of perception that even abstract thought can only halfway attain to it. . . .

The refutation of *rational psychology*[3] is very much more detailed and thorough in the first edition

---

[1]Christian Wolff (1679–1754) wrote a number of works conveying Leibnizian ideas.

[2]Schopenhauer employs the term for his own purposes, making it the focus of Book Three.

[3]The Paralogisms of Pure Reason: A341/B399*ff.*

of the *Critique of Pure Reason* than in the second and following editions; one must therefore in this case make exclusive use of the former. This refutation has very great merit on the whole and much that is true in it. I am altogether of the opinion, however, that it is merely for the sake of his symmetry that, from that Paralogisms chapter, Kant derives the concept of the soul as necessary by means of an application of the demand for the unconditioned to the concept of *substance*, which is the first Category of Relation, and accordingly asserts that the concept of a soul arises in this manner in every speculating reason. If it really had its origin in the presupposition of an ultimate subject of all the predicates of a thing, then one would not only have assumed a soul in human beings, but also just as necessarily in every lifeless thing, since such a thing also demands an ultimate subject of all its predicates. But in general, Kant makes use of an entirely inadmissible expression when he speaks of a something that can exist only as subject and not as predicate (e.g., A323, B412; *Prolegomena*, §§ 46 and 47), although a precedent for it can be found in Aristotle's *Metaphysics* IV, ch. 8.[1] Things do not exist as subject and predicate at all; for these expressions pertain exclusively to logic and designate relations among abstract concepts. Now in the perceptual world, their correlate or representative is supposed to be substance and accident. But then we need look no further for something that exists only as subject and never as accident, but have it immediately with matter. It is the substance for all the properties of things, which are its accidents. It actually is, if one would retain the expression of Kant's just criticized, the ultimate subject of all the predicates of every empirically given thing, namely, that which remains after removal of all its predicates of every sort; and this applies to human beings as much as to animals, plants, or stones, and is so evident that not to see it requires a determined will not to see it. . . .

The contrast that has given occasion to the assumption of two fundamentally different substances, body and soul, is in truth that of the objective and subjective. If a person apprehends himself in outer perception, he finds a spatially extended and quite altogether corporeal being; if he apprehends himself by contrast in mere self-consciousness, thus purely subjectively, he finds something merely engaged in willing and presentation, free from all the forms belonging to perception, thus also without any of the properties belonging to bodies. Now he forms the concept of the soul, as he does of all the transcendent concepts that Kant called Ideas, by applying the Principle of Sufficient Ground, the form for all objects, to that which is not an object, in particular, in this case, to the subject of cognizing and willing. Namely, he considers cognizing, thinking, and willing as effects for which he is seeking a cause and cannot accept the body as such a thing, and thus posits a cause for them entirely distinct from the body. The first and the last dogmatist prove the existence of the soul in this manner, namely, of course Plato in the *Phaedrus* and also Wolff as well, namely, from thinking and willing as effects that direct us to that cause. Only after the concept of an immaterial, simple, indestructible being had arisen in this manner, through hypostasizing a cause corresponding to the effect, did the school develop and demonstrate the latter in terms of the concept *of substance*. But they had before that formed the latter itself quite particularly for the purpose. . . .

The Idea of soul was compelled to find its origin in the categorical form of inference. Now it is the turn for dogmatic ideas regarding the world-whole, conceived as an object in itself in its standing with respect to two limits, that of the smallest (an atom) and that of the greatest (the bounds of the world in time and space).[2] These have to proceed, then, from the hypothetical form of inference. In itself there is no special compulsion in this. For the hypothetical judgment gets its form from the Principle of Sufficient Ground, and in fact all of the so-called Ideas arise from unreflective, unconditioned application of this Principle . . . Thus, since the cognitive form from which only the cosmological Ideas are here derived, namely, the Principle of Sufficient Ground, is the origin of all of the ratiocinated hypostases, there is in this case no need for any sophisms; but they are all the more needed for classifying those Ideas in accor-

---

[1] See rather *Metaphysics* V, ch. 8.

[2] Section 1 of The Antinomy of Pure Reason, the "System of Cosmological Ideas" (A408/B435*ff.*).

dance with the four rubrics for the Categories [A415/B443].

1. The cosmological Ideas with respect to time and space,[1] thus the Ideas of the limits of the world in both respects, are boldly viewed as determined by the Category of *Quantity*,[2] with which they obviously have nothing in common but the chance fact of logic's designating the extension of the subject concept in a judgment with the word *quantity*, a figurative expression in place of which another could just as well have been chosen. But this is enough for Kant's love of symmetry to utilize the happy chance of the denomination and to attach transcendent dogmas regarding the extension of the world.

2. Even more boldly, Kant attaches transcendent Ideas about matter[3] to *Quality*, that is, affirmation or negation in a judgment, where not even a chance verbal similarity lies behind it; for it is precisely to the quantity and not the *quality* of matter that its mechanical (not chemical) divisibility refers. But even more, this whole idea of divisibility does not belong at all among inferences in accordance with the Principle of Sufficient Ground, from which, as the content of the hypothetical form, all cosmological Ideas are supposed to flow. For the assertion on which Kant rests in this, that the relation of parts to the whole is that of condition to conditioned, thus is a relation according to the Principle of Sufficient Ground, is to be sure a fine assertion but still a groundless sophism. That relation rather rests on the principle of contradiction. For the whole does not exist by way of the parts, nor these by way of that, but both necessarily exist together because they are one

thing, and their separation is only an arbitrary act. This latter supports the fact, in accordance with the principle of contradiction, that if the parts are thought away the whole is also thought away, and conversely; but it in no way supports the fact that the parts as *ground* condition the whole as *consequence* and that we would therefore, in accordance with the Principle of Sufficient Ground, be necessarily driven to seek ultimate parts in order to understand the whole on their basis, as its ground—Here, love of symmetry overcomes such great difficulties.

3. Under the rubric of *Relation*[4] would then quite properly come the Idea of the first cause of the world. But Kant has to save this for the fourth rubric, that of *Modality*[5] for which nothing would otherwise remain and under which he then forces that Idea by saying that the contingent (i.e., according to his explanation—which is diametrically contrary to the truth—any consequence following from its ground) is made necessary by the first cause. As a third Idea there thus appears, for the sake of symmetry, the concept of *freedom*. But by this is yet really meant the Idea of the cause of the world, the only one that after all really fits in here, as the Note on the Thesis of the Third Conflict distinctly states [A448/B476ff.]. The third and fourth conflicts are therefore basically tautologically the same.

Beyond all this, however, I find and assert that the entire Antinomy is a mere game of mirrors, a phony battle. Only the assertions of the *Antitheses* actually rest on forms belonging to our cognitive faculty, that is, if one puts it in objective terms, on necessary, a priori certain, universally general natural

---

[1]First Antinomy (A426/B454ff.). Thesis: "The world has a beginning in time, and is also enclosed within bounds in space"; Antithesis: "The world has no beginning and no bounds in space, but is rather, with respect to both time and space, infinite."

[2]Strictly, Quality is not the Category, but rather the rubric for the Categories unity, plurality, and totality.

[3]Second Antinomy (A434/B462ff.). Thesis: "Every composite substance in the world consists of simple parts, and there everywhere exists nothing but that which is simple or is composed of the simple"; Antithesis: "No composite thing in the world consists of simple parts, and there exists nothing simple anywhere in it."

[4]Third Antinomy (A444/B472ff.). Thesis: "Causation in accordance with laws of nature is not the only causality by which all of the world's phenomena can be derived. It is also necessary to assume a causality through freedom for their explanation"; Antithesis: "There *is* no freedom, but everything in the world happens only in accordance with laws of nature."

[5]Fourth Antinomy (A452/B480ff.). Thesis: "Something belongs to the world, either as a part of it or as its cause, that is an absolutely necessary being"; Antithesis: "There nowhere exists an absolutely necessary being, neither in the world nor beyond the world, as its cause." The Categories of Modality are the concepts of possibility, actuality, and necessity.

laws. Their proofs alone are therefore set out on the basis of objective grounds. By contrast, the assertions and proofs of the *Theses* have none other than a subjective ground, rest quite solely on the weakness of the ratiocinating individual, whose imagination tires in the face of an infinite regress and therefore puts an end to it with arbitrary presuppositions that it does its best to cover up, and whose judgment on this point is additionally paralyzed by early and firmly instilled prejudices. For this reason, the proof for the Thesis in all four conflicts is in every case only a sophism, while that for the Antithesis is an unavoidable inference by reason from laws of the world as presentation that are known to us a priori. Even Kant was only able to sustain the Theses with much effort and art, and have them make seeming onslaughts against opponents who are gifted with original force. . . .

[After brief discussion of the four Theses, Schopenhauer turns to Kant's resolution of apparent paradox that cogent arguments can be given in each case to both the Thesis and Antithesis.] Kant's ensuing "Critical Decision of the Cosmological Dispute" [A497/B525*ff*.] is, if one examines its real sense, not what it gives itself out as being, namely, resolution of the dispute by way of the disclosure that the two sides, proceeding from false presuppositions, are both wrong in the first and second conflict, but both right in the third and fourth; rather, it is in fact confirmation of the Antitheses through an elucidation of their pronouncements.

Kant first asserts in this resolution, obviously wrongly, that both sides proceeded from the presupposition, as a major premise, that with the conditioned the complete (thus closed) *series* of its conditions is also given. Only the *Thesis* grounded its assertions on this proposition, Kant's pure principle of reason; by contrast, the Antithesis everywhere expressly denied it and asserted the opposite. In addition, Kant burdens both sides with the presupposition that the world exists in itself, that is, independently of its being cognized and of the forms belonging to the latter, but yet again, this presupposition is only made by the Thesis; by contrast, the assertions of the Antithesis are so little grounded in it that it is even altogether incompatible with them. For it straightforwardly contradicts the concept of an infinite series that it be given in its entirety; it is therefore essential to it that it always exists only in passage through it,

but never independently thereof. By contrast, in the presupposition of determinate limits, there also lies that of a whole that exists in a self-subsistent manner and independently of taking its measure. Thus only the Thesis makes the false presupposition of a world-whole that is self-subsistent, that is, given in advance of all cognition, to which cognition would merely be added on. The Antithesis is altogether originally in dispute with this presupposition. For the infinitude of the series that it merely asserted under the direction of the Principle of Sufficient Ground can only exist to the extent that the regress is carried out, not independently of the latter. Just as, namely, any object at all presupposes the subject, so too the object determined as an *endless* chain of conditions necessarily presupposes the corresponding mode of cognition, namely, *constant pursuit* of the links of the chain, in the subject. But this is precisely what Kant provides as a resolution of the dispute and so often repeats: "The infinitude of the world's magnitude exists only *through* the regress, not *before* it" [A518/B546*ff*.]. This resolution of the conflict is thus really only a decision in favor of the Antithesis, in the assertion of which that truth already lies, just as it is entirely incompatible with the assertions of the Thesis. Had the Antithesis asserted that the world consists of infinite series of grounds and consequences, and yet at the same time exists independently of presentation and its regressive series, thus in itself, and therefore constitutes a given whole, then it would not only have contradicted the Thesis, but also itself; for something infinite can never be given as a *whole*, nor an *endless* series exist except insofar as it is endlessly traversed, nor something without limits constitute a whole. Thus only to the Thesis belongs that presupposition of which Kant asserts that it has led both sides astray. . . .

If indeed, proceeding in the opposite direction, one takes one's point of departure from what Kant provides as the conflict's resolution, assertion of the Antithesis follows directly just from that. Namely, if the world is not an unconditioned whole and does not exist in itself, but only in presentation, and if its series of grounds and consequences do not exist *before* the regress of presentations of them, but only *through* this regress, then the world cannot contain determinate and finite series, because their determination and limitation would have to be independent of the presentation that is only subsequently added on; rather, all of its series must be endless, that is, inexhaustible by any presentation.

At A506/B534, Kant would prove the transcendental ideality of phenomena from the fact that both sides are wrong, and begins: "If the world is a whole existing in itself, then it is either finite or infinite."— But this is false: a whole existing in itself cannot be at all infinite. Rather, the ideality in question can be inferred in the following way from the infinitude of series in the world: if the series of grounds and consequences in the world are altogether without end, then the world cannot be a whole given independently of presentation; for such a thing always presupposes determinate limits, just as, by contrast, an infinite series presupposes an infinite regress. Therefore, the presupposed infinitude of a series must be determined by the form of ground and consequence, and the latter by the subject's manner of cognition, thus the world as it is cognized must exist only in presentation to the subject.

Whether Kant himself knew or not that his critical decision of the dispute was really a pronouncement in favor of the Antithesis, I am unable to decide. For it depends on whether what Schelling somewhere most strikingly called Kant's "system of accommodations" extends that far, or whether Kant's spirit is here in fact caught up in an unconscious accommodation to the influence of his time and surroundings.

Resolution of the Third Antinomy, whose object was the Idea of freedom, deserves particular consideration, insofar as it is most noteworthy for us that, precisely here with the Idea of freedom, Kant is compelled to speak more extensively of the *thing-in-itself*, which was previously seen only in the background. This is very easily explicable for us after having recognized the thing-in-itself as *Will*. Here in general lies the point where Kant's philosophy leads to mine, or where the latter proceeds from it as from its stem. . . .

Kant never made the thing-in-itself the subject of a separate discussion or explicit derivation. Rather, whenever he needs it, he pulls it in at once with the inference that phenomena, thus the visible world, must surely have a ground, an intelligible cause, that would not be a phenomenon and would therefore belong to no possible experience. This he does after having incessantly emphasized that the Categories, thus also that of causality, have an employment altogether limited only to possible experience, are mere forms belonging to the understanding that serve to spell out the phenomena of the sensory world, beyond which they cannot, by contrast, have any meaning at all, etc., therefore most strictly banning their application to things beyond experience, and, in terms of its violation of this law, rightly explaining and at the same time overturning all earlier dogmatism.[1] The unbelievable inconsistency that Kant committed in this was soon noted by his first opponents and utilized for attacks against which his philosophy could offer no resistance. For of course we apply the law of causality in an indeed utterly a priori way, and prior to all experience, to alterations sensed in our sense organs; but precisely for this reason, it has just as subjective an origin as these sensations themselves, thus does not lead to the thing in itself. . . .

It has gone precisely the same for Kant with establishment of the thing-in-itself as with that of the apriority of the law of causality: both doctrines are correct, but their proof is wrong; thus they belong among correct conclusions from false premises. I have retained them both, but given them an entirely different and secure grounding.

I have not smuggled in the thing-in-itself nor inferred it in accordance with laws that exclude it insofar as they pertain rather to its phenomenon; nor have I attained to it by circuitous paths of any sort. Rather, I have immediately established it in the place where it immediately lies, in the Will that is revealed immediately to everyone as the in-itself of his own phenomenon.

And it is also this immediate cognizance of one's own will from which the concept of *freedom* proceeds in human consciousness. For of course Will as world-creating, as thing-in-itself, is free from the Principle of Sufficient Ground and thereby from all necessity, thus completely independent, free, indeed omnipotent. But this only applies, in truth, to Will in itself,

---

[1] This is in fact a disputed issue as regards to Kant, turning on the question of the extent to which the purely "logical" significance that would remain after abstraction from phenomenal conditions would at least make it possible to *think*, if not to make fully grounded knowledge claims, about a reality beyond phenomena: cf. Bxxxvi–xxxvii, A253–4/B309.

not to its phenomena, to individuals, which are indeed precisely through it, as its phenomena in time, unalterably determined. In common consciousness unpurified by philosophy, however, Will is at once confused with its phenomenon, and what belongs to it alone is attributed to the latter; thereby arises the illusion of the individual's unconditioned freedom. Spinoza says rightly, just for that reason, that even the stone that one throws, if it had consciousness, would believe it flew of its own free will.[1] For of course the in-itself of the stone is also the one and only free Will, but, as in all of its phenomena, here too where it makes its appearance as a stone, in fact utterly determined. . . .

Further, the proposed purpose, resolution of the Third Antinomy with the decision that both sides, each in its own sense, are right, is not achieved at all. For both Thesis and Antithesis in no way speak of the thing-in-itself, but altogether rather of the phenomenon, the objective world, the world as presentation. It is of this and altogether nothing else that, with the sophism that has been displayed, the Thesis would demonstrate that it contains unconditioned causes, and it is also this of which the Antithesis rightly denies the same thing. . . .

When speaking of cause and effect, the relation of the Will to its phenomenon (or of the intelligible character to the empirical)[2] must never be brought in, as is done here; for it is altogether distinct from the causal relation. In any case, it is also said in accord with the truth here, in this resolution of the Antinomy, that a human being's empirical character, like that of every other cause in nature, is unalterably determined, and actions thus necessarily proceed from it according to external effects on it; and therefore also, despite all transcendental freedom (that is, independence of the Will in itself from the laws for the interconnection of its phenomenon), no human being has a capacity for beginning a series of actions of himself, which latter is, to the contrary, asserted by the Thesis. Thus not even freedom has causality. For the only thing free is the Will that lies outside of nature or the phenomenon, which is precisely only its objectification but does not stand in a relation of

causality to it. This relation is met with only within the phenomenon, thus already presupposes it, cannot incorporate it and connect it with that which is expressly not a phenomenon. The world itself is only explicable on the basis of Will (since it is precisely the latter insofar as it makes its appearance), and not by causality. But *within the world* causality is the single principle of explanation, and everything happens only in accordance with laws of nature. Thus right lies entirely on the side of the Antithesis, which keeps to the subject under discussion and employs the principle of explanation that is applicable to it, and therefore is in need of no apology. By contrast, the Thesis is supposed to be pulled out of its difficulty with an apology that, first of all, makes a leap to something entirely different from what was in question, and then adopts a principle of explanation that is not applicable there. . . .

[After a brief comment dismissing the Fourth Antinomy, with its Idea of a necessary being, Schopenhauer comments on the Transcendental Ideal, dealt with in the third and last chapter of the Transcendental Dialectic, "The Ideal of Pure Reason." The issue concerns the logical form of disjunctive judgment as a supposedly a priori ground for the formation of the Idea of an *ens realissimum*, or "most real being." Then Schopenhauer turns to Kant's criticisms, in the same chapter, of attempts to prove the existence of God: the ontological proof, the cosmological proof, and the physico-theological proof]

Regarding the detailed refutation of speculative theology that now follows, I have only briefly to note that it is, like the entire critique of the three so-called Ideas of reason generally, thus the entire Dialectic of Pure Reason, to a certain extent the goal and purpose of the entire work. But this polemical part nonetheless does not really have, like the preceding doctrinal part, that is, the Aesthetic and Analytic, a quite general, lasting, and purely philosophical interest, but more of a temporal and local interest, insofar as it stands in a particular relation to the main features of philosophy holding sway in Europe up to Kant, although its utter overthrow through this polemic gained Kant immortal merit. He eliminated theism

---

[1] Letter to G. H. Schuller of October, 1674 (numbered, according to edition, as either Letter 62 or 58).

[2] A532/B560ff. Schopenhauer particularly employs these notions in §§ 20 and 28 in Book Two of the main body of *The World as Will and Presentation*.

from philosophy, since as a science, and not a doctrine of faith, only that which is either empirically given or established by tenable proofs can find a place in it. Here is meant, naturally, only actual philosophy, understood seriously, directed toward truth and nothing else, and in no way the joke that is university philosophy (die Spassphilosophie der Universitäteri), in which, as before, speculative theology plays the main role, just as indeed, as before, the soul appears without ceremony as a familiar character in it. For that is the philosophy which, lavished with stipends and honoraria, indeed even with courtly titles, takes no notice at all of folk such as I, looking proudly down from its heights for forty years, and which would gladly be rid of the old Kant with his critiques, so that deeply heartfelt toasts may be raised to Leibniz. . . .

In his critique of these proofs, as stated, Kant was merely concerned with speculative theology and limited himself to academics. If he had also, by contrast, had life and popular theology in mind, he would have been bound to add to the three proofs yet a fourth one, which for the vast mob is the really effective one and would most fittingly well be called, in Kant's technical terminology, the ceraunological[1] proof. It is that which is grounded in man's feeling of helplessness, impotence, and dependency in the face of infinitely superior, unfathomable, and largely menacing natural forces, paired with his natural tendency to personify everything, to which there is finally added the hope to accomplish something with pleading, and flattering, and of course, with gifts. In every human undertaking, namely, there is something that is not in our power and that does not enter into our calculations; the desire to win this over is the origin of the gods. . . .

But the ones whom Kant set into lasting embarrassment with his critique of speculative theology are the philosophy professors: salaried by Christian regimes, they could not leave the main article of their

faith in the lurch.[2] So how do the gentlemen help themselves?—They just say the existence of God is self-evident—So! after the ancient world, at the cost of its conscience, worked wonders to prove it, and the modern world, at the cost of its understanding, fielded ontological, cosmological, and physico-theological proofs—it is self-evident to these gentlemen. And on the basis of this self-evident God, they then explain the world: that is their philosophy. . . .

It is certainly not the least of the accomplishments of Frederick the Great that Kant was able to develop under his regime and permitted to publish the Critique of Pure Reason. A salaried professor would hardly have dared such a thing under any other regime. Kant already had to promise the successor of the great king that he would write no more. . . .

[Schopenhauer then turns to the distinction between theoretical and "practical" reason and Kant's attempt to ground ethics in the latter. Kant's main works in ethics are his Foundation for the Metaphysics of Morals (1785), Critique of Practical Reason (1788), Religion Within the Bounds of Mere Reason (1793), and The Metaphysics of Morals (1797).]

I have explained reason as the faculty for concepts. It is this wholly unique class of general, nonperceptual presentations, symbolized and fixed only by words, that distinguishes man from animals and gives him rule on earth. If animals are slave to the present, know no other than immediately sensory motives, and therefore, when they offer themselves to him, are as necessarily drawn to or repelled by them as iron in the case of a magnet, in man, to the contrary, by the gift of reason, thoughtful awareness (Besonnenheit) has dawned. This allows him, looking forward and back, to survey his life and the course of the world as a whole with ease, makes him independent of the present, lets him go to work with reflective consideration, with planning, and with circumspection, for evil

[1]From the Greek meaning to "strike with thunderbolts."

[2][Schopenhauer's footnote:] Kant said: "It is a most absurd thing to expect enlightenment from reason and yet prescribe to it in advance on what side it must necessarily fall" (A747/B775). By contrast, the following bit of naivete is the pronouncement of a philosophy professor of our time: "If a philosophy denies the reality of the basic ideas of Christianity, it is either false or, even if true, yet of no use"—scilicet [namely] for philosophy professors. It was the deceased Professor Bachmann who, in the Jena Literary Times of July 1840, pg. 126, so indiscreetly blurted out the maxim of all his colleagues. In any case, it is noteworthy here for a characterization of university philosophy how, if the truth will not adapt itself and fit in, it is shown the door in no uncertain terms, with a: "March, truth! we cannot make use of you. Do we owe you anything? Do you pay us?—So, march!"

as well as for good. But what he does, he does with complete self-consciousness. He knows exactly how his will decides, what he chooses in each case, and what other choice was factually possible, and from this self-conscious willing he comes to know himself and is reflected in his deeds.[1] In all these relations to human action reason is to be called *practical:* it is theoretical only so far as the objects with which it is occupied have no relation to the thinker's action, but have a merely theoretical interest; very few people are capable of this. . . .

Virtue and vice are really not in question with such rationality in one's ways, but this practical employment of reason validates the real advantage that human beings have over animals, and it is only in this respect that it makes sense and is permissible to speak of the dignity of man.

In all of the depicted cases and all that one might excogitate, the difference between rational and non-rational action reduces to the question whether the motives are abstract concepts or perceptual presentations. Precisely by that fact, the explanation that I have given of reason exactly agrees with the linguistic usage of all times and peoples, which one will surely not regard as something accidental or arbitrary, but rather see that it has proceeded precisely from the difference, of which everyone is conscious, between distinct mental faculties; one speaks in accord with this consciousness, but of course does not elevate it to the distinctness of an abstract definition. Our ancestors did not create the words without attributing a determinate sense to them, so that they would perhaps lie ready for philosophers who might come centuries later and determine what is to be thought thereby; rather, they designated entirely determinate concepts with them. The words are thus no longer without a master, and to attribute an entirely different sense to them than what they had up to now means to misuse them, means to introduce a license by which every word could be employed in an arbitrary sense; thereby, endless confusion is bound to arise. Locke has already demonstrated in detail that most disagreements in philosophy come from the mistaken use of words. Just take a look, for the sake of elucidation, at the shameful misuse that thought-impaired pseudo-philosophers nowadays make of the words substance, consciousness, truth, etc. . . .

One might have expected that Kant, in his critiques of theoretical and practical reason, would have taken his point of departure from an account of the essence of reason in general, and after having thus determined the *genus,* proceeded to explanation of the two *species,* demonstrating how one and the same reason expresses itself in two such diverse manners and yet, by retaining its main character, makes itself known as the same. But nothing of the sort is found. The unsatisfactory, vacillating, and conflicting character of the explanations he casually here and there gives of the faculty criticized in the *Critique of Pure Reason,* I have already demonstrated. *Practical* reason in fact turns up unannounced in the *Critique of Practical Reason,* and subsequently stands, in the *Critique* dedicated uniquely to it, as a settled affair, without a further accounting and without allowing the trampled linguistic usage of all times and peoples, or the conceptual determinations of the greatest earlier philosophers, to raise their voices. Overall, one can derive from individual passages that Kant's opinion goes something like this, cognition from a priori principles is an essential character of reason; since, then, cognizance of the ethical significance of action is not of empirical origin, it too must be an a *priori principium* and accordingly stems from reason, which is then to that extent *practical.*

Regarding the incorrectness of this explanation of reason, I have already sufficiently spoken. But even apart from that, how superficial and unfounded it is to utilize the single attribute of independence from experience here, to unite the most heterogeneous things while ignoring the rest of the fundamentally essential, immense distance between them. For even supposing, although not granting, that cognizance of the ethical significance of action originates from an imperative lying within us, from an unconditioned *Ought,* how fundamentally different such a thing would yet be from the general *forms*

---

[1]Schopenhauer does not mean to suggest that this is an easy matter. It involves the acquisition of "character" in a sense that Schopenhauer distinguishes from both the "empirical" and "intelligible" character mentioned above; on the other hand, it is also to be distinguished from what Schopenhauer means by "the real significance of the ethical content of actions" further below. For this notion of "acquired character," see § 55 in Book Four of the main body of the work.

belonging to cognition, the a priori consciousness of which Kant demonstrates in the *Critique of Pure Reason,* by virtue of which consciousness we are able to pronounce an unconditioned *Must* in advance, valid for all experience possible for us. The difference between this *Must,* this necessary form for all objects already determined in the subject, and that *Ought* of morality is so huge and so evident that one may well make a case, as a witty comparison, for their conjunction in the attribute "non-empirical mode of cognition," but not as a philosophical justification for equating their origins.

In any case, the birthplace of this child of practical reason, of this *absolute Ought* or categorical imperative, is not in the *Critique of Practical Reason,* but already in the *Critique of Pure Reason* (A802/B830). It is a forced birth and succeeds only by means of the forceps of a *Therefore,* which, boldly and brashly and one might even say shamelessly, intervenes between two propositions that are wildly foreign to one another and without any interconnection, in order to connect them as ground and consequence. Namely, the proposition from which Kant proceeds, expressing it as follows, is that not merely perceptual but also abstract motives determine us: "Not merely what stimulates, that is, immediately affects the senses, determines human choice, but through presentations of that which is itself more remotely useful or harmful, we have a faculty for overcoming impressions on our faculty of sensory desire. These reflections on that which is desirable with respect to our entire state, that is, good and useful, rest on reason." (Perfectly correct: would that he only always spoke so rationally of reason!) "This *therefore* (!) also yields laws that are imperatives, that is, objective laws of freedom, and that say what *ought* to happen, even if it perhaps never happens"[1]—!

Thus without any further accreditation, the categorical imperative leaps into the world, there to rule with its *unconditioned Ought*—A scepter of wooden iron. For in the concept of *Ought* there lies everywhere and essentially a consideration of threatened punishment, or promised reward, as a necessary condition, and it cannot be removed without nullifying the concept and depriving it of all meaning; therefore, an *unconditioned Ought* is a *contradictio in adjecto* [contradiction in terms]. This mistake had to be criticized, as closely as it is otherwise related to Kant's great achievement in ethics, which consists precisely in the fact that he freed ethics from all principles belonging to the world of experience, namely, from any doctrine of direct or indirect happiness, and quite truly showed that the realm of virtue is not of this world. . . .

Now the content of the absolute Ought, the basic law of practical reason, is the famous: "Act in such a way that the maxim of your will could always at the same time count as a principle for a general legislation."[2] This principle sets the task, for whomever demands regulation for his own will, of finding one for the will of quite everybody—Then the question comes up how such a thing is to be found. Obviously, to find the rule for my own behavior, I am not supposed to consider myself alone, but the totality of all individuals. Then, instead of my own well–being, the well–being of all, without distinction, becomes my purpose. But the latter is still in any case well–being. I find, then, that all can feel equally well off only if everyone sets the egoism of others as a limit to his own. From this it of course follows that I should harm nobody, because, this principle being accepted generally, *I* will not be harmed either; this, however, is the only ground I have, not yet possessing a moral law but still seeking one, for desiring to have this made a general law. But obviously, in this manner, desire for well–being, that is, egoism, remains the source of this ethical principle. As a basis for political theory that would be superb, as a basis for ethics it is worthless. For to meet that moral principle's task of establishing a rule for the will of all, anyone who is seeking it necessarily needs a rule for himself in turn; otherwise everything would be indifferent to him. But this rule can only be one's own egoism, since it is only upon this that the behavior of others has an influence, and

---

[1]The passage is somewhat altered by Schopenhauer, but apart from the emphases, and the exclamation mark, only in minor ways; I have added the parentheses around Schopenhauer's exclamation mark.]

[2]In the *Critique of Practical Reason* (but with "can" rather than "could"), p. 30 in Volume 5 of the Gentian "Academy edition" of Kant's worts; this pagination is regularly included in other editions. In *Foundation for the Metaphysics of Morals,* see secs. I–II.

therefore only by means of that egoism and in regard to it can someone seeking that rule have a will that bears on the actions of others, and can that action not be indifferent to him. . . .

But we have already spoken in detail at the end of our fourth Book of the possibility of a complete change of a person's disposition (rebirth), not by means of abstract cognition (ethics), but by means of intuitive cognition (effective grace); the content of this Book relieves me of any need to dwell on it longer here.

That Kant did not in any way penetrate into the real significance of the ethical content of actions, he shows us finally with his doctrine of the highest good as the necessary union of virtue and happiness, in par-

ticular with his doctrine that the former is worthiness for the latter.[1] In fact the logical objection applies to him here that the concept of worthiness that provides the standard in this case already presupposes an ethics as its standard, and so one cannot take it as a point of departure. It resulted in our fourth Book that all genuine virtue, having achieved its highest degree, leads one in the end to a state of utter renunciation in which all willing comes to an end; by contrast, happiness is satisfied willing, the two are thus fundamentally incompatible. For someone who has seen the evidence of my account, there is no need for further discussion of the total perverseness of this Kantian view of the highest good. And independently of my positive account, I have none further of the negative to give.[2]

STUDY QUESTIONS: SCHOPENHAUER, *CRITIQUE OF KANTIAN PHILOSOPHY*

1. Why does Schopenhauer think it will take some time before the true impact of Kant's philosophy will be fully appreciated?
2. What is Kant's greatest achievement, according to Schopenhauer?
3. How did Locke influence Kant?
4. What is Kant's distinction between phenomena and noumena? Why is it so important?
5. What is the difference between dogmatic and critical philosophy?
6. Did Kant derive the thing in itself in the proper way? Why? What is the main flaw, as Schopenhauer sees it?
7. What is metaphysics the science of?
8. What is the "riddle of the world?" What is its solution?
9. How is (post–Kantian) talk of the Absolute a regression to the cosmological proof for God?
10. What is the significance of what Schelling called Kant's "system of accommodations?"
11. What are the two main doctrines of Kant that Schopenhauer says are correct but whose proof is wrong?
12. What is the proper understanding of the role of the Will in relation to its phenomenon?
13. What is Schopenhauer's view of Leibniz?
14. What is reason the faculty for?
15. Did Kant do justice to the ethical content of actions? Why?

---

[1] A804/B832ff., in the *Critique of Practical Reason*, secs. V–IX of the Dialectic of Pure Practical Reason (pp. 124–148 in Academy vol. 5).

[2] Schopenhauer concludes with brief commentary on Kant's *Doctrine of Right*, Part One of *The Metaphysics of Morals* (Part Two is the *Doctrine of Virtue*), and the *Critique of Judgment*. The latter treats, in its first part, judgments of beauty and the sublime and related issues involving art and, as Kant argues, morality; in its second part it deals with judgments regarding purposiveness in natural objects. Schopenhauer's own positive account of virtue and vice is to be found in Book Four of *The World as Will and Presentation*.

SECTION II

THE GERMAN IDEALISTS

PROLOGUE

The remarkable blooming of philosophy in Germany at the turn of the nineteenth century—especially the four decades from 1780 to 1820—has been rightly compared to the golden age of philosophy in Greece, from Socrates to Aristotle. This happened in tandem with new and profound developments in literature and art nurtured by geniuses among which Kant, Fichte, Schelling, Schopenhauer, Goethe, Schiller, and Beethoven, were among the most illustrious.

The advent of Kantian philosophy rooted in the previous century provided much of the impetus, even and especially those who reacted against it. Indeed, it was the sudden departure from one central tenet of Kant's system that characterized the first aspect of the sudden new revolution in thought and led to a resurgence of grand new systems of idealism. This was the abandonment of the concept of the thing-in-itself that began with Johann Fichte (1762–1814). Kant immediately recognized Fichte as a great new thinker and helped launch his career. Fichte's fruitful advance from the Kantian philosophy paved the way for three important subsequent developments: absolute idealism, phenomenology, and existentialism. What enabled him to do this was his brilliant analysis of the real and primary function of the ego as a self-affirming primitive act of consciousness that constructs the objective world, not in accordance with, or based as a reaction to things-in-themselves, but purely from its own appearances. In this way Fichte paved the way for Schelling and Hegel. Friedrich Schelling (1775–1854) formed on the basis of such thinking his system of objective idealism, which so influenced his colleague and younger friend Hegel, and the Romanticism that inspired so much of subsequent thought, especially in development of literature and the arts. His *System of Transcendental Idealism* lays out his "philosophy of identity," in which the objective and subjective are unified under one systematic philosophy of nature, epistemology, and ethics.

Fichte (1762–1814)

Biographical History

The son of a farmer and linen-maker, Johann Gottlieb Fichte was born in the village of Rammenau in Upper (Saxon) Lusatia. After completing his studies in philosophy at the Universities of Jena and Leipzig he got a job tutoring students in Zurich. He published his first book at the age of 28, called *Aphorisms on Religion and God* (1790); it was inspired in part by Spinoza and even more so by Kant, who read it and invited him to Konigsberg. Fichte showed Kant the manuscript for his next work, *Essay Toward a Critique of All Revelation*. This work so impressed Kant that he sent it to his publisher on Fichte's behalf along with a Preface authored by Kant himself. The book came out two years later, in 1792, but because of a printer's error Fichte's name did not appear in the book and with the Preface by Kant everyone assumed that Kant was the author. By then it had already attracted much attention. Kant published a correction, stating clearly that the book was not by him but by Fichte and, moreover, that it happens to solve a major problem with Kant's own system that Kant himself had found impossible to solve! Overnight, Fichte became a legendary figure.

By the end of his life Fichte was generally acknowledged as one of the three leading successors to the great Immanuel Kant, along with Hegel and Schelling (see the sections following). At the University of Jena, where he had a full professorship, he commanded a huge following among the students and the public who attended his dynamic, standing-room-only lectures. However, jealousies from among his less popular colleagues led to a fight with the administration over academic freedom; against the students and the public's protest, Fichte was dismissed from his position for his "highly dangerous" views. In addition, he was ordered not to publish! Fichte steadfastly refused, stating that a philosopher's moral duty was to express his thoughts to all who would listen, including and especially his views about (and against) religion. After being dismissed from his post Fichte continued to give public lectures that were even more highly attended than before, and he continued to publish his works. In 1807, shortly after the French occupation, Fichte gave a famous speech, *Addresses to the German Nation*. Inspired by his call to moral regeneration through national unity and political reform, he commanded a wide political following that helped him to achieve, four years later, one of his ambitions: the founding of the new University of Berlin. There he remained for the rest of his life, teaching and writing.

Philosophical Overview

Kant's problem with his own philosophy, as he saw it, was this: His famous *Critique of Pure Reason*, arguably one of the greatest works of philosophy ever, calls all speculative theology into question and puts religion in a negative light. His *Critique of Practical Reason*, however, puts the central idea of Kant's philosophy, the moral law, at the center of any religion. This Kant saw as an inconsistency in his own position and a defect of his work. The problem, in a nutshell, is that this inconsistency in Kant's thought leaves open the question of under what conditions, if any, authentic religious belief is possible. Fichte answers this question. His *Critique of All Revelation* bridges the gap between Kant's two monumental works. In it, Fichte argues that the absolute requirements of the moral law themselves supply the necessary conditions that make revealed religion possible, a Kantian argument that even the great Kant could not see how to make.

In his other works Fichte departs from Kant and the Kantian approach to philosophy in specific ways that opened the door to subsequent improvements and developments, indeed, paved the way for the subsequent movements known as absolute idealism, phenomenology, and existentialism. Moreover, Fichte's astute analysis of the ego as the self-affirming primitive act of consciousness that constructs not only the objects of perception but the entire objective world, departs from Kant in the following dynamic way. Instead of constructing its objects in tandem with noumena, "things-in-themselves" (*ding-an-sich*), the ego constructs objects solely out of its own appearances.

THE SCIENCE OF KNOWLEDGE
Fichte

The work begins with an antinomy-like conflict between the inner sense of free will and the external sense that the world is completely determined. As he puts it, "In immediate consciousness, I appear to myself as free; by reflection on the whole of Nature, I discover that freedom is absolutely impossible." Add then to this dynamic equation the notion the only *immediate* knowledge of which we are capable is that of our own mind: "In all perception you perceive your own state." What you get is the sum and substance of Fichte's conclusions and the beginning of the departure, in the nineteenth century, from Kant, namely, the notion that the idea of things in themselves, the noumena, the *ding-an-sich*, are *themselves* but projections of the mind and, therefore, *not* something to which the consciousness mind is bound. Though it appears to be! This insight also opens the door to subsequent developments in philosophy that would come to be known as *existentialism*, predicated on the notion that the boundary by which we ordinarily distinguish self from other on the basis of what we can control apparently by a conscious act of will and what we cannot, is even if necessary for the having of experience, as Kant thought, an *inauthentic* way for the mind to relate to itself and the world.

What, then, is reality according to Fichte? What it means for something, anything, to be real—take, for instance, the chair on which you sit—is that it consists of *all possible experiences* that the object as such can generate within the mind of a potential observer. Take the chair apart, look at it from every angle, hit it, use it in various ways, the fact is that the reason you can perform any such acts with the chair is that the chair is a *containing space of all possibilities* of the object in relation to the perceiving subject. The universe itself according to Fichte is an Absolute Idea, animated by an *act* of consciousness which then unfolds one state into the next.

1.

Attend to yourself; turn your glance away from all that surrounds you and upon your own innermost self. Such is the first demand which philosophy makes of its disciples. We speak of nothing that is without you, but wholly of yourself.

In the most fleeting self-observation every one must perceive a marked difference between the various immediate determinations of his consciousness, which we may also call representations. Some of them appear entirely dependent upon our freedom, and it is impossible for us to believe that there is anything without us corresponding to them. Our imagination, our will, appears to us as free. Others, however, we refer to a truth, as their model, which is held to be established, independent of us; and in the

Fichte, from *Erste Einleisung in die Wissenschaftslehre*, translated by Benjamin Rand (Berlin: Sämmtlichte Werke, 1845).

attempt to determine such representations, we find ourselves conditioned by the necessity of their harmony with this truth. In the knowledge of their contents we do not consider ourselves free. In brief, we can say, some of our representations are accompanied by the feeling of freedom, others by the feeling of necessity.

The question cannot reasonably arise: why are the representations, which are directly dependent upon our freedom, determined in precisely this manner and not otherwise? For when it is affirmed that they are dependent upon our freedom, all application of the conception of a ground is dismissed; they are thus, because I have so determined them, and if I had determined them otherwise, then they would be different. But it is certainly a question worthy of reflection: what is the ground of the system of those representations which are accompanied by the feelings of necessity and of that feeling of necessity itself? To answer this question is the task of philosophy; and, in my opinion, nothing is philosophy but the science which solves this problem. The system of those representations which are accompanied by the feeling of necessity is also called *experience:* internal as well as external experience. Philosophy has therefore—to express the same thing in other words—to discover the ground of all experience.

Only three distinct objections can be raised against what has here been stated. Someone might deny that representations, accompanied by the feeling of necessity, and referred to a truth determined without our aid, are ever present in our consciousness. Such a person would either make the denial against better knowledge or be differently constituted from other men. In the latter case there would also be nothing for him that he denied, and hence no denial. We could therefore dismiss his protest without further ceremony. Or someone might say: the question raised is entirely unanswerable, we are and must remain in insuperable ignorance concerning it. To enter upon an argument with such a person is wholly superfluous. He is best refuted by an actual answer to the question; then all he can do is to test our attempt and to state where and why it appears to him insufficient. Finally, some one might dispute about the designation, and assert: philosophy is something else, or at least something more, than what you have above stated. It might easily be proved to such a one, that scholars

have at all times regarded exactly what has here been stated, to be philosophy, and that whatever else he might set up for it has already another name; that if this word is to signify anything at all, it must mean precisely this particular science.

Since, however, we are unwilling to enter upon any unfruitful controversy about words, we have on our part already abandoned the name of philosophy, and have called the science which has, properly speaking, the solution of the problem here indicated for its object, the *Science of Knowledge.*

2.

Only when speaking of something regarded as accidental, that is, which we suppose might also have been otherwise, though it was not determined by freedom, can we inquire concerning a ground. And precisely because of this asking concerning its ground does it become accidental to the inquirer. The problem involved in seeking the ground of anything means to find something else, from the special nature of which it can be seen why the accidental, among the manifold determinations which might have come to it, assumed precisely the one it did. The ground lies, by virtue of the mere thought of a ground, outside of that which is grounded; and both are, in so far as they are the ground and the grounded, opposed to each other, related to each other, and thus the latter is explained from the former.

Now philosophy seeks to discover the ground of all experience; hence its object lies necessarily *beyond all experience.* This proposition applies to all philosophy, and has also actually been so applied, down to the period of the Kantians and their facts of consciousness, that is, of inner experience.

No objection can be raised against the proposition here set forth; for the premise to our conclusion is a mere analysis of the above-stated conception of philosophy and from it the conclusion is drawn. If someone possibly should remind us that the conception of a ground must be differently explained, we certainly could not prevent him from forming another conception of it if he chooses; but we affirm with equal right, that in the above description of philosophy we wish nothing else to be understood by that word but what has been stated. Hence, if this meaning is not permitted, the possibility of philosophy, as we have described it, must be altogether denied; and to such a denial we have already made reply in our first section.

3.

The finite intelligence has nothing outside of experience. This it is that yields the entire material of its thinking. The philosopher is subject necessarily to similar conditions, and hence it appears inconceivable how he can raise himself above experience.

But he can abstract; that is to say, he can separate by the freedom of thinking what is united in experience. In experience, *the thing*, or, that which is to be determined independently of our freedom and in accordance with which our knowledge is to shape itself, and *the intelligence*, or that which is to acquire a knowledge of it, are inseparably united. The philosopher may abstract from both, and if he does, he has abstracted from experience and lifted himself above it. If he abstracts from the first, he retains an intelligence *in itself*, that is, abstracted from its relation to experience; if he abstracts from the latter, he retains the thing *in itself*, that is, abstracted from the fact that it occurs in experience. He thus retains either the intelligence in itself, or the thing-in-itself, as the ground of explanation of experience. The former mode of procedure is called *idealism*, the latter *dogmatism*.

Only these two philosophical systems (and of that these remarks should convince everybody) are possible. According to the first system, the representations which are accompanied by the feeling of necessity are products of the intelligence, which must be presupposed in their explanation; according to the latter system they are products of a thing in itself, which must be presupposed to explain them. If anyone desired to dispute this position, he would have to prove either that there is still another way to transcend experience than by means of abstraction, or that there exist in the consciousness of experience more than the two components just mentioned. Now, in regard to the first, it will appear below that what we have here called intelligence is actually present under another name in consciousness, and therefore is not something entirely produced by abstraction; but it will at the same time be shown that the consciousness of it is conditioned by an abstraction, which is wholly natural to mankind.

It will not be denied that it is possible to frame an entire system from fragments of these dissimilar systems, and that this illogical labor has actually very often been undertaken; but it is denied that more than these two systems are possible in any logical mode of procedure.

4.

Between the object (we shall call the explanatory ground of experience affirmed by a philosophy the *object of that philosophy*, since it appears to be only through and for such philosophy) of *idealism* and that of *dogmatism* there is a remarkable distinction in reference to their relation to consciousness. Everything of which I am conscious is called object of consciousness. There are three ways in which the object can be related to consciousness. Either the object appears to have been produced by the representation, or as existing without its aid; and in the latter case, either also as determined in regard to its structure, or as present merely with respect to its existence, but determinable in regard to its structure by the free intelligence.

The first relation applies merely to an imaginary object, whether with or without purpose; the second applies to an object of experience; and the third applies only to an object, which we shall forthwith describe.

I can determine myself by freedom to think this or that; for example, the thing-in-itself of the dogmatist. Now if I abstract from the thought and look simply upon myself, then I myself become the object of a particular representation. That I appear to myself as determined in precisely this manner and not otherwise, for example, as thinking, and among all possible thoughts as thinking just the thing-in-itself, is in my opinion to depend upon my freedom of self-determination: I have made myself such an object of my own free will. I have not, however, made myself, but I am compelled to presuppose myself as determinable through this self-determination. I am therefore myself my own object, the determinate character of which depends under certain conditions altogether upon intelligence, but the existence of which must always be presupposed.

Now this very I in itself is the object of idealism. The object of this system does not occur actually as something real in consciousness, as a *thing in itself*— for then idealism would cease to be what it is, and would be transformed into dogmatism—but it does appear as *I in itself*. It occurs not as object of experience—for it is not determined, but is solely determinable through me, and without this determination it would be nothing at all—but it appears as something raised above all experience.

The object of dogmatism, on the contrary, belongs to the objects of the first class, which are produced wholly by free thinking. The thing-in-itself is a mere invention, and has no reality at all. It does not occur in experience, for the system of experience is nothing else than thinking accompanied by the feeling of necessity; it cannot even be pretended to be anything else by the dogmatist, who, like every philosopher, has to give an explanation of it. The dogmatist, indeed, desires to assure reality to it, through the necessity of thinking it as the ground of all experience; and he would succeed, if he could prove that experience thereby can be, and can thereby only be explained. But this is the very question in dispute, and he cannot presuppose what must first be proved.

The object of idealism thus has the advantage over that of dogmatism, inasmuch as it is not to be deduced as the ground of explanation of experience—which would be a contradiction and would transform this system itself into a part of experience—but is nevertheless to be referred to as a part of consciousness. Whereas, the object of dogmatism can assume to be nothing but a mere invention, which attains realization only through the success of the system. This is cited merely to promote a clearer insight into the distinction between the two systems; but not to draw therefrom an argument against the *latter* system. That the object of every philosophy, as the explanatory ground of experience, must be beyond experience, is demanded by the very nature of philosophy, and is far from being derogatory to a system. But we have as yet discovered no reason why that object should be present also in a particular manner in consciousness.

If anybody should remain unconvinced of the truth of what has just been said, it still would not be impossible to convince him of the truth of the whole system, since the foregoing has only been incidental. Nevertheless, in conformity with our plan, we will also here take into consideration possible objections. Some one might deny the immediate self-consciousness affirmed to be in every free act of the mind. Such a one we have only again to remind of the conditions

of it above specified. This self-consciousness neither obtrudes itself, nor comes of its own accord; one must really have a free act, and then abstract from the object and attend entirely to one's self. No one can be compelled to do this, and also if he professes to have done it, one cannot know whether he has proceeded correctly. In a word, this consciousness cannot be proved to any one; but every one must produce it with freedom in himself. Against the second affirmation, that the thing-in-itself is a mere invention, an objection could only be made, because one misunderstood it. Such a one we would refer back to the preceding description of the origin of this conception.

5.

Neither of these two systems can directly refute the other; for their controversy is one about the first underivable principle. Each refutes the other, if only you admit its own first principle as established. Each denies everything to the opposite; and they have no point in common whereby they can attain a mutual understanding and reconciliation. Though they appear to agree on the words of a proposition, yet each one takes them in a different sense.

First of all, idealism cannot refute dogmatism. The former system, indeed, has, as we have seen, the advantage over the latter of being able to establish its explanatory ground of experience—the free acting intelligence—as a fact of consciousness. This fact the dogmatist must also concede to him, for otherwise he would render himself incapable of any further dealing with his opponent; but he transformed, however, the ground of explanation by a correct inference from his principle into an appearance and illusion, and thus disqualifies it for becoming an explanatory ground of anything else, since it cannot maintain its own existence in its own philosophy. According to the dogmatist everything that presents itself to our consciousness is a product of a thing-in-itself—even our pretended determinations by means of freedom, and the belief that we are free. This belief is produced in us by the effect upon ourselves of the thing and the determinations which we deduced from our freedom are similarly caused by it. Only, we are not aware of it in these instances, and hence ascribe it to no cause, that is, to our freedom. Every consistent dogmatist is necessarily a fatalist; he does not deny the fact of consciousness, that we regard ourselves as free, for this would be against all reason; but he proves from his principle the falsity of this view. He denies the independence of the ego upon which the idealist builds, and makes it merely a product of the thing, an *accident* of the world; hence the consistent dogmatist is necessarily also a materialist. He can only be refuted by the postulate of the freedom and independence of the ego; but this is directly what he denies.

Even as little can the dogmatist refute the idealist.

The principle of the former, the thing-in-itself, is nothing, and, as the defenders of it must admit, has no reality beyond that which it receives from the fact that experience can only be explained by it. But the idealist destroys this proof by explaining experience in another way, hence by denying precisely what the dogmatist assumes. The thing-in-itself is a complete chimera. There is no further reason why it should be assumed; and with its disappearance the entire structure of dogmatism falls.

From what has just been stated there follows likewise the absolute irreconcilability of the two systems; since the results of the one destroy those of the other. Wherever their union has been attempted the members would not fit into one another, and somewhere an enormous gap has appeared. Anyone who would deny the truth of this position must prove the possibility of such a union, that is, of a union which consists in a perpetual transition from matter to spirit, or, what is entirely the same, from necessity to freedom.

Since so far as we can perceive at present both systems appear to have the same speculative value, and since both cannot stand together, nor yet either of the two convince the other, it becomes a very interesting question what induces persons who comprehend this—and it is easily understood—to prefer the one to the other; and why it happens that skepticism, as the total renunciation of a reply to this problem, does not become universal.

The dispute between the idealist and the dogmatist is precisely the question whether the independence of the ego is to be sacrificed to that of the thing, or vice versa. What, then, is it which compels a reasonable man to decide in favor of the one or the other?

The philosopher discovers from the foregoing point of view—which is one where he must necessarily place himself if he is to be regarded as a philosopher, and which every man, in the progress of thinking, must necessarily sooner or later occupy—nothing further *than that he must represent to himself* both that he is free, and that there are determined things outside of him. It is, however, impossible for him to stop at this thought; the thought of the mere representation is only a half thought, a broken fragment of a thought. Something must be thought in addition as corresponding to the representation independent of it. In other words, the representation cannot exist by itself—it is something only in connection with something else, and in itself it is nothing. It is this necessity of thought which forces one from that point of view to the question, What is the ground of the representations? or, which is entirely the same, What is that which corresponds to them?

Now the representation of the independence of the ego and that of the thing can exist certainly together; but not the independence itself of both. Only one can be the first, the beginning, the independent; the second, by the very fact of being second, is necessarily dependent upon the first, with which it is to be connected.

Now which of the two is to be made the first? Reason affords no ground for a decision; for the question does not relate to the connecting of one link with another, where alone the grounds of reason extend; but to the beginning of the entire succession, which as an absolute first act is wholly dependent upon the freedom of thinking. The decision is therefore entirely arbitrary; and since the arbitrariness must have a cause, the decision is dependent upon *inclination* and *interest*. The last ground of the distinction between the dogmatist and the idealist is consequently the difference of their interest.

The highest interest, and hence the ground of all other interest, is that *for ourselves*. Thus with the philosopher. Not to lose his Self in his reasoning, but to retain and to assert it, this is the interest which unconsciously guides all his thinking. Now, there exist two grades of mankind; and in the progress of our race, before the last grade has been universally attained, two chief classes of men. The one class consist of those who have not raised themselves to the full feeling of their freedom and of absolute independence, but who are merely conscious of themselves in the representations of outward things. These have only a desultory self-consciousness, bound up with outward objects, and collected from their manifoldness. The image of their Self is reflected to them only from the things, as from a mirror. If the latter be taken from them, then they lose the Self at the same time. For their own sake, they cannot give up the belief in the independence of things, since they exist only together with these things. Whatever they are they have actually become through the external world. Whosoever is only a product of the things will never view himself in any other manner, and he is entirely correct, so long as he speaks merely of himself and of those like him. The principle of the dogmatist is: belief in the things for their own sake; hence, a mediated belief in his own desultory Self, as merely the result of the things.

But whosoever becomes conscious of his self-existence and independence from all outward things—and this one can only become by making something of one's self, by means of one's own self, independently of all external things—needs no longer the things in support of his Self, and cannot use them, because they destroy his self-existence and transform it into an empty appearance. The ego, which he possesses, and which interests him, destroys that belief in the things; he believes in his independence from inclination, and lays hold of it with affection. His belief in himself is immediate.

From this interest can be explained the various passions which commonly mingle with the defence of these philosophical systems. The dogmatist is actually in peril of losing his Self when his system is attacked; and yet he is not armed against this attack, because there is something in his inmost self which takes the side of the assailant; hence he defends himself with heat and bitterness. The idealist, on the contrary, cannot well refrain from looking down with disesteem upon the dogmatist, who can tell him nothing which he first has not long since known and thrown aside as useless, inasmuch as one arrives at idealism, if not through dogmatism itself, yet at least by the disposition thereto. The dogmatist gets angry, misconstrues, and would persecute, if he had the power; the idealist is cold, and inclined to ridicule the dogmatist.

What kind of a philosophy one chooses depends consequently upon what kind of a man one is; for a philosophical system is not a piece of dead household furniture, which one can use or lay aside at pleasure, but is animated by the soul of the man who has it. A person of a naturally indolent character, or who has become weak-minded and perverted through intellectual slavery, scholarly luxury, and vanity, will never elevate himself to idealism.

You can reveal to the dogmatist the inadequacy and inconsequence of his system; you can confuse and terrify him from all sides; but you cannot convince him, because he is unable quietly and coolly to hear and to examine what he cannot tolerate. If idealism should prove to be the only true philosophy, it will also appear that a man must be born a philosopher, be educated to be one, and educate himself to be one; but that by no human art can one be made a philosopher. Hence this science of knowledge expects few proselytes among men whose mental habits have already been moulded; but its hopes are centered in the rising generation, whose native vigor has not yet been impaired by the intellectual laxness of the present age.

STUDY QUESTIONS: FICHTE, *THE SCIENCE OF KNOWLEDGE*

1. What is the first demand that philosophy makes of its disciples?
2. Can you speak of anything that exists "without you?" Why?
3. What are representations?
4. What is so special about the feeling of necessity?
5. How are idealism and dogmatism related to consciousness?
6. What does Fichte mean by *I in itself*?
7. What is the ego?
8. What is the Self?
9. What is the importance of choosing a philosophy?

Philosophical Bridges: Fichte's Influence

The notion that you cannot speak of anything that is without you, as expressed in the beginning of the selection from Fichte's *Science of Knowledge*, has more than a little in common with the great twentieth century philosopher Wittgenstein's notion, expressed in his *Tractatus*. The ideas started by Fichte through Schelling and Hegel eventually found their way, by the end of the nineteenth century, to Schopenhauer, who was one of Wittgenstein's primary inspirations. But perhaps even more importantly, Fichte's notion of reality has been instrumental in getting some twentieth-century physicists to rethink the relationship between mind and reality, most notably, John Archibald Wheeler, who was inspired both by Fichte and Schelling (see subsequent section). In other words, Fichte's philosophy helped launch not just nineteenth century philosophical neo-Kantian idealisms but paved the way for twentieth century quantum mechanics. In quantum mechanics, what it means for something, anything—a particle, an event—to be *real*, at the *physical* level, is that the equation describing the thing allows the observer to list all possible solutions that it can generate. Beyond the range of those possibilities there simply is no mind-independent reality. Although Albert Einstein rejected the absolute idealisms in favor of explicitly Kantian transcendental idealism (Einstein himself having been inspired by Kant's *Prolegomena to Any Future Metaphysics*), others such as Niels Bohr and Werner Heisenberg were much more sympathetic to a Fichtean subjective idealist conception of reality.

Ficthe's philosophy also lay the metaphysical foundations for functionalist theories of mind developed in twentieth century computer and cognitive science, wherein reality itself can be viewed as a sort of program running on the abstract program (think "Absolute Idea") of a universal algorithm actualized by a Fichtean *act* of consciousness.

Schelling (1775–1854)

Biographical History

Friedrich Wilhelm Von Schelling was born in Leonburg, a small town of Würtenberg, Germany, and educated at the cloister school where his father was both chaplain and professory. He went on to study Spinoza, Kant, and especially Fichte at the theological seminary in Tübingen, where he befriended fellow student Georg Friedrich Handel. Together the two wunderkinds formed and edited a philosophy journal. After graduating in 1798 at the age of 23 Schelling became the youngest philosophy professor at the extraordinary University of Jena under the charge of its formidable rector, Duke Charles Augustus. When Hegel joined the department three years later, it became one of the greatest philosophy departments of all time, consisting of an illustrious faculty any one of which would have sufficed to make the department legendary: Fichte, Hegel, Schelling, Schlegel, Schiller, and Schopenhauer.

At Jena, Schelling became a leading champion of the Romantic movement (more on that below). He befriended other geniuses, such as Goethe, with whom he was quite close, and his colleagues in the department, most notably August von Schlegel and his wife Caroline, of whom he was deeply enamored. After a probable affair Schlegel divorced Caroline and she and Schelling married. This led to further alienation from other members in the department, and Schelling broke off his collaborative inquiries with both Fichte and Hegel; in search of a fresh start, he and Caroline moved to the new University of Würzburg. There he tangled with government officials over academic and political freedoms and in a few years moved (in 1806) to Munich, where he remained for 35 years, until 1841. He was elected to the academy of science, secretary of the academy of arts, eventually becoming secretary of the academy of sciences, a significant political appointment. He continued to lecture throughout this period at various universities, including Stuttgart.

Philosophical Overview

Schelling's most important and original contributions were to the development of Romanticism, the late eighteenth and early nineteenth-century philosophical movement that, inspired by Kant, evolved in opposition both to rationalism and empiricism. His elaborate philosophical system, which he did not fully develop until late in life, centers on the self, transcendentalism, and the transformational power of art and imagination, especially in literature and even more so music. His philosophy of nature, epistemology, and ethics taken together are an elaborate attempt to unify objective and subjective thought. What has since come to be known as his philosophy of identity is a system in which subject and object resolve into unity at the Absolute level, producing a mystical state of consciousness that can be attained not by religious ritual but intellectual intuition.

For Kant and Fichte, the ultimate goal of philosophy is morality. By contrast, for Schelling, the main goal is the creative act of the artist in which the identity between the subjective self and the objective world is expressed through works of art. As with Fichte, the only immediate object of knowledge is consciousness itself. The difference is that Schelling presents the objective world as a limiting condition of the dynamic evolutionary process from consciousness to self-consciousness, such that the mind becomes fully aware of itself through art. Thus the ultimate goal of philosophy in general and philosophical reflection in particular is to serve the imagination of the artist in the act of creating great and profound artworks.

Inspired by Spinoza's *Ethics*, Schelling distinguishes two very different sorts of knowledge. There is, on the one hand, *philosophical knowledge* of the rational faculties and, on the other, *confused knowledge* of the imagination. Each of these gives rise to a different form of existence. The infinite undivided existence of the absolute is the result of philosophical knowledge and the finite divided existence of individual things is the result of confused knowledge. Thus confused knowledge is not to be shunned or avoided but, as in Kant (and to a lesser extent Leibniz), is an essential and necessary ingredient to existence and experience as we know them. Objects in the phenomenal world are self-evolving, arising in thought alone; they possess no true reality, as in Leibniz: things appear particular to our dimmed representations of them. The philosopher, hower, can view objects *sub specie aeterni,* that is, from God's point of view, and apprehend them as ideas, in their totality. To understand and perceive objects as such the mind presents them to itself as they are in the totality of the world soul. Ultimately, all things are a whole, a Parmenidean One, existing as such at the Absolute. By "the Absolute" Schelling and the philosophers who followed him mean something like "the sum total of the whole of existence and everything in it considered as such."

System of Transcendental Idealism

In the following selection from his main work Schelling starts out with the Cartesian certainty of his own existence simultaneously denoted and expressed by the proposition *I Am.* He then shows how the *transcendental proposition* "there are things outside me" can also be known with the same absolute certainty. For Descartes, this process is guaranteed by a good God who would not deceive us (at least not with regard to our clear and distinct ideas). For Kant, this transcendental process does reach beyond the phenomena, that is, beyond the world of appearance, but *not* to the noumenal world of things in themselves. Rather, in Kant's view, what the mind reaches is its own cognitive faculties. In Schelling's view, by contrast, what the mind reaches through this process is the objective, absolute world itself.

The finitude of individual things in the world is broken up into a plurality of self-evolving individual entities. Among these are you and I. But even though we are particular individuals, the essential unity of the whole persists as such within us, in so far as we are each an expression of the absolute. Identity belongs to the absolute, and within us it thus exists in diminished form, diluted by differences. Ultimate reality is absolute and undivided; individual realities are relative. Nothing is purely objective or purely subjective, and there is identity both in individuality and in the totality. All existence and everything in it consists both of the objective and subjective. But from within any one perspective within the totality either the objective or the subjective will be more dominant. The phenomena of nature in Schelling's view are like the phenomena of the mind, not unity of matter and spirit but unity of real and ideal, objective and subjective.

Thus, in marked contrast to Berkely's idealism, according to which an "absolute other" (God) not identical to ourselves or the universe is responsible for sustaining the order and existence of everything, Schelling views reality as constructed internally from itself, a coherent universal system in which the absolute (think "God") is identical to the phenomenal. There are two major differences between what we might think of as Schelling's *absolute idealism* vs. Fichte's *subjective idealism*. According to Fichte, the subjective is primary and it is the subjective that posits the objective. Schelling has the opposite view: the objective posits the subjective. Now, for Fichte, as for Kant, a necessary condition for the having of experience as we know it is that what is experienced is interpreted to be other than mental phenomena. But whereas Schelling posits God as the first and the last, "the Alpha and the Omega; but as Alpha he is not what he is as Omega; and in so far as he is only the one—God 'in an immanent sense'—he cannot be the other God, in the same sense, or in strictness, be called God. For in that case, let it be expressly said, the unevolved god, *Deus implicitus*, would already be what, as Omega, the *Deus explicitus* is."

Schelling's vision of God is in marked contrast, also, with that of Spinoza's determinist God. God in Schelling's view makes freedom of choice possible within the real world by the presence of individual conscious beings such as ourselves, each one a direct manifestation of the actualizing, creative power of the Absolute (which is beyond space and time) acting in, and projecting itself, within space and time. It is not some "divine otherness" that creates the world; rather, it is we ourselves who are the true artists of reality. Schelling thus comes to the opposite conclusion from Plato with regard to the nature and significance of art; in Schelling's view art is the pinnacle of wisdom, neither separate from the world nor less important to its evolution than philosophy. Art is "the *univeral organum* of philosophy." (An *organum* is the polyphonic voice part that accompanies the *cantus firmus*, the plainsong Gregorian melody sung in unison, note for note, at a fourth, fifth or octave above or below.) In art and through art the mind becomes fully aware of itself, its presence and creative function in the world, its ultimate goal being the production of great and profound art through philosophical reflection.

SYSTEM OF TRANSCENDENTAL IDEALISM
Introduction to Idealism

SECTION I: IDEA OF TRANSCENDENTAL PHILOSOPHY

1.

All knowledge is based upon the agreement of an objective with a subjective. For we *know* only the true, and the truth is universally held to be the agreement of representations with their objects.

2.

The sum of all that is purely objective in our knowledge we may call Nature; whereas the sum of everything subjective may be termed the *ego,* or Intelligence. These two concepts are mutually opposed. Intelligence is originally conceived as that which solely represents, and nature as that which is merely capable of representation; the former as the conscious—the latter as the unconscious. But in all knowledge there is necessary a mutual agreement of the two—the conscious and the unconscious *per se.* The problem is to explain this agreement.

3.

In knowledge itself, in that I know, the objective and subjective are so united that one cannot say which of the two has priority. There is here no first and no second—the two are contemporaneous and one. In any attempt to explain this identity, I must already have resolved it. In order to explain it, inasmuch as there is nothing else given me as a principle of explanation except these two factors of knowledge, I must of necessity place the one before the other, that is to say, must set out from the one in order to arrive at the other. From which of the two I shall set out is not determined by the problem.

4.

There are, consequently, only two cases possible:

A. *Either the objective is made first, and the question arises how a subjective agreeing with it is superinduced.*

The idea of the subjective is not contained in the idea of the objective; on the contrary they mutually exclude each other. The subjective must therefore be *superinduced* upon the objective. It forms no part of the conception of Nature that there must be likewise an intelligence to represent it. Nature, to all appearance, would exist even if there were nothing to represent it. The problem may therefore likewise be expressed thus: How is the Intelligent superinduced upon Nature? Or, How does Nature come to be represented?

The problem assumes Nature, or the objective, as the first. It is, therefore, undoubtedly the task of natural science, which does the same. That natural science actually, and without knowing it, approximates, at least, to the solution of this problem can here be only briefly shown.

If all knowledge has, as it were, two poles, which mutually presuppose and demand each other, then they must seek each other in all sciences. There must, therefore, of necessity, exist two fundamental sciences; and it must be impossible to set out from one pole without being driven to the other. The necessary tendency of all natural science, therefore, is to proceed from Nature to the intelligent. This, and this alone, lies at the foundation of the effort to bring theory into natural phenomena. The final perfection of natural science would be the complete intellectualization of all the laws of Nature into laws of intuition and of thought. The phenomena, that is, the material, must completely vanish, and leave only the laws—that is, the formal. Hence it happens that the more the conformity to law is manifested in Nature, so much the more the wrapping disappears—the phenomena themselves become more intellectualized, and at length entirely cease. Optical phenomena are nothing more than a geometry whose lines are drawn by aid of the light; and even this light itself is already of doubtful materiality. In the phenomena of magnetism every trace of matter has already vanished: and of the phenomena of gravitation, which even the natural philosopher believed could be attributed only to direct spiritual influence, there remains nothing but

Translated from the German by Benjamin Rand, 1908, with emendation by Daniel Kolak their law, whose performance on a large scale is the mechanism of the heavenly motions. The complete theory of Nature would be that by virtue of which the whole of Nature should be resolved into an intelligence. The dead and unconscious products of Nature are only unsuccessful attempts of Nature to reflect itself, but the so-called dead Nature is merely an unripe Intelligence, hence in its phenomena the intelligent character appears, though still unconscious. Its highest aim, that is of becoming wholly self-objective, Nature does not attain, except in its highest and last reflection, which is none other than man, or more generally what we call reason. By its means Nature first turns completely back upon itself, and thereby it is manifest that Nature is originally identical with what in us is known as intelligent and conscious.

This may suffice to prove that natural science has a necessary tendency to render Nature intelligent. By this very tendency it becomes natural philosophy, which is one of the two necessary fundamental sciences of philosophy.

B. *Or the subjective is made first, and the problem is, how an objective is superinduced agreeing with it.*

If all knowledge is based upon the agreement of these two, then the problem to explain this agreement is undoubtedly the highest for all knowledge; and if, as is generally admitted, philosophy is the highest and loftiest of all sciences, it becomes certainly the chief task of philosophy.

But the problem demands only the explanation of that agreement generally, and leaves it entirely undetermined where the explanation shall begin, what it shall make its first, and what its second. Since also the two opposites are mutually necessary, the result of the operation is the same, from whichever point one sets out. To make the objective the first, and to derive the subjective from it, is, as has just been shown, the task of natural philosophy.

If, therefore, there is a transcendental philosophy, the only direction remaining for it is the opposite, that is: to proceed from the subjective as the first and the absolute, and to deduce the origin of the objective from it. Natural and transcendental philosophy have divided between themselves these two possible directions of philosophy. And if all philosophy must have for an aim to make either an Intelligence out of Nature or a Nature out of Intelligence,

then transcendental philosophy, to which this latter problem belongs, is the other necessary fundamental science of philosophy.

SECTION II: COROLLARIES

In the foregoing we have not only deduced the concept of transcendental philosophy, but have at the same time afforded the reader a glance into the whole system of philosophy. It is composed, as has been shown, of two fundamental sciences, which though opposed to one another in principle and direction, reciprocally demand and supplement each other. Not the entire system of philosophy, but only the one fundamental science of it, is here to be set up, and, in the first place, to be more strictly characterized in accordance with the idea of it already deduced.

1.

If, for transcendental philosophy, the subjective is the first and only ground of all reality, and the sole principle of explanation of everything else (§ 1), then it necessarily begins with universal doubt regarding the reality of the objective.

As the natural philosopher, wholly intent upon the objective, seeks nothing so much as to exclude every admixture of the subjective in his knowledge, so, on the other hand, the transcendental philosopher seeks nothing so much as the entire exclusion of the objective from the purely subjective principle of knowledge. The means of separation is absolute skepticism—not that partial scepticism which is directed merely against the common prejudices of men and never sees the foundation—but the radical scepticism which aims not at the individual prejudices, but against the fundamental prejudice, with which all others must stand or fall. For beyond the artificial and inculcated prejudices of man, there exist others of deeper origin which have been placed in him not by art or education, but by nature itself. These are regarded by all except the philosopher, as the principles of knowledge, and by the mere thinker of self, as the test of all truth.

The one fundamental prejudice, to which all others may be reduced, is this: that there exist things outside of us. This is an opinion, which, although it rests neither on proofs nor on conclusions (for there is not a single valid proof of it), yet as it cannot be uprooted by any opposite proof (*naturam furcâ expellas, tamen usque redibit*), lays claim to immediate certainty. But since it refers to something wholly distinct from us and, in fact, opposed to us, of which there is no evidence how it came into immediate consciousness, it must be regarded as nothing more than a prejudice—a natural and original one, to be sure, but nevertheless a prejudice.

The contradiction that a conclusion which in its nature cannot be immediately certain, is, nevertheless, blindly and without grounds, accepted as such, cannot be solved by transcendental philosophy, except on the assumption that this conclusion is implicitly, and without our being aware of it, not founded upon, but identical, and one and the same with an affirmation which is immediately certain. To demonstrate this identity will in reality be the task of transcendental philosophy.

2.

Now, even for the ordinary use of reason, there exists nothing immediately certain except the affirmation *I am*, which, since it loses all significance outside of immediate consciousness, is the most individual of all truths, and the absolute prejudice, which must be assumed, if anything else is to be made certain. The affirmation *There are things outside of us*, will therefore be certain for the transcendental philosopher, solely because of its identity with the affirmation *I am*; and its certainty will also only be equal to the certainty of the affirmation from which it derives its own.

According to this view transcendental knowledge would be distinguished from common knowledge in two particulars.

First. That for it the certainty of the existence of external things is a mere prejudice, which it transcends, in order to investigate the grounds of it. (It can never be the task for transcendental philosophy to prove the existence of things in themselves, but only to show that it is a natural and necessary prejudice to assume external objects as real.)

Second. That it separates the two affirmations, *I am* and *There are things outside of me*, which run together in the ordinary consciousness, and places the one before the other, in order to prove their identity and that immediate connection which in the other is only felt. By this act of separation, when it is completed, one transports one's self in the transcendental

act of contemplation, which is by no means a natural, but an artificial one.

3.

If the subjective alone has reality for the transcendental philosopher he will also make only the subjective directly his object. The objective will be for him only indirectly an object, and, whereas, in ordinary knowledge, knowledge itself—the act of knowing—disappears in the object, in transcendental knowledge, on the contrary, the object as such disappears in the act of knowing. Transcendental knowledge is therefore a knowledge of knowing, in so far as it is purely subjective.

Thus, for example, in intuition it is the objective only that reaches the ordinary consciousness; the act of intuition is itself lost in the object; whereas on the contrary the transcendental mode of observation gets only a glimpse of the object of intuition by the act of intuition. Thus the ordinary thinking is a mechanism, in which ideas prevail, without, however, being distinguished as ideas; whereas the transcendental act of thought interrupts this mechanism, and in becoming conscious of the idea as an act, rises to the idea of the idea. In ordinary action, the acting is itself forgotten in the object of the action; philosophizing is also an action, but not an action only. It is likewise a continued self-intuition in this action.

The nature of the transcendental mode of thought must consist, therefore, in general in this: that, in it, that which in all other thinking, knowing, or acting escapes the consciousness, and is absolutely non-objective, is brought into consciousness, and becomes objective. In brief, it consists in a continuous act of becoming an object to itself on the part of the subjective.

The transcendental art will therefore consist in the ability to maintain one's self constantly in this duplicity of acting and thinking.

SECTION III: PRELIMINARY DIVISION OF TRANSCENDENTAL PHILOSOPHY

This division is preliminary, because the principles of the division can be derived only from the science itself.

We return to the idea of science.

Transcendental philosophy has to explain how knowledge is possible at all, assuming that the subjective in it is accepted as the ruling or first element.

It is therefore, not a single part, nor a special object of knowledge, but knowledge itself, and knowledge in general, that it takes for its object.

Now all knowledge can be reduced to certain original convictions or original prejudices. These different convictions transcendental philosophy must trace to one original conviction. This ultimate conviction from which all others are derived, is expressed in the first principle of this philosophy, and the task of finding such is none other than to find the absolutely certain by which all other certainty is attained.

The division of transcendental philosophy is determined through those original convictions, whose validity it affirms. These convictions must, in the first place, be sought in the common understanding. If, therefore, we go back to the standpoint of the ordinary view, we find the following convictions deeply engraven in the human understanding:

A. That not only does there exist a world of things independent of us, but also that our representations agree with them in such a manner that there is nothing else in the things beyond what we represent by them. The necessity in our objective representations is explained by the belief that the things are unalterably determined, and that by this determination of things our representations appear to be mediately determined. By this first and most original conviction, the first problem of philosophy is determined, namely: to explain how representations can absolutely agree with objects which exist entirely independent of them. Since it is upon the assumption that things are exactly as we represent them, and that we therefore certainly know things as they are in themselves, that the possibility of all experience rests (for what would experience be, and where would physics, for example, stray to, without that presupposition of the absolute identity of being and seeming?), the solution of this problem is identical with theoretical philosophy, which has to investigate the possibility of experience.

B. The second equally original conviction is, that representations which originate in us freely and without necessity can pass over from the world of thought into the real world, and attain objective reality.

This conviction is opposed to the first. According to the first, it is assumed that objects are unalterably determined, and our representations by them; according to the other, that objects are changeable, and that, too, by the causality of representations in us. According to the first conviction, a transition takes place within us from the real world into the world of representations, or a determining of the representations by the objective, according to the second, a transition takes place from the world of representations into the world of reality, or a determining of the objective by a (freely conceived) representation in us.

By this second conviction, a second problem is determined, namely how, by something merely thought, an objective is changeable, so as entirely to correspond with that something thought.

Since the possibility of all free action rests upon that assumption, the solution of this problem is practical philosophy.

C. But with these two problems we find ourselves involved in a contradiction. According to B, the supremacy of thought (the ideal) over the world of sense is demanded. But how is such supremacy conceivable, if (according to A) the idea in its origin is already only the slave of the objective? On the other hand, if the real world is something wholly independent of us, and is something with which our ideas must conform as their pattern (by A), then it becomes inconceivable how, on the other hand, the real world can conform to the ideas in us (by B). In brief, in the theoretical certainty we lose the practical; in the practical we lose the theoretical. It is impossible that at the same time there should be truth in our knowledge and reality in our volition.

This contradiction must be solved, if there is to be a philosophy at all. The solution of this problem, or the answering of the question: How can ideas be conceived as conforming to objects, and at the same time objects as conforming to ideas? is not the first, but is the chief task of transcendental philosophy.

It is easy to see that this problem cannot be solved either in theoretical or practical philosophy, but in a higher one, which is the connecting link of both, and is neither theoretical nor practical, but both at the same time.

How at the same time the objective world conforms to representations in us, and representations in us conform to the objective world, cannot be conceived, unless there exists a preestablished harmony between the two worlds of the ideal and the real. But this preestablished harmony is itself not conceivable unless the activity by which the objective world is produced, is originally identical with that which displays itself in volition, and vice versa.

Now it is certainly a *productive* activity which manifests itself in volition. All free action is productive, but productive only with consciousness. If, then, since the two activities are only one in principle, we suppose that the same activity which is productive *with* consciousness in free action, is productive *without* consciousness in the production of the world, this preestablished harmony is a reality, and the contradiction is solved. If we suppose that all this is actually the case, then that original identity of the activity which is engaged in the production of the world, with that which exhibits itself in volition, must manifest itself in the productions of the former, and these must necessarily appear as the productions of an activity at once conscious and unconscious.

Nature, as a whole, no less than in its different productions, will of necessity appear as a work produced with consciousness and yet at the same time as the production of the blindest mechanism. It is the result of purpose without being explainable as such. The philosophy of the aims of Nature, or teleology, is therefore the required point of union of theoretical and practical philosophy.

D. Heretofore, we have posited only in general terms the identity of the unconscious activity which has produced Nature and the conscious activity which manifests itself in volition, without having decided where the principle of this activity lies, whether in Nature or in us.

But now the system of knowledge can be regarded as complete only when it reverts to its principle. Transcendental philosophy would therefore be completed only when it also could demonstrate that identity—the highest solution of its entire problem—in its principle (the *ego*).

It is therefore postulated, that activity, at once conscious and unconscious, can be shown in the subjective, that is in consciousness itself.

Such an activity can be no other than the *aesthetic*, and every work of art can only be conceived as the product of such. The ideal work of art and the real world of objects are therefore products of one and the same activity. The meeting of the two (of the conscious and the unconscious) gives *without* consciousness the real, *with* consciousness the aesthetic world.

The objective world is only the original still unconscious poetry of the soul. The universal organum of philosophy—the keystone of its entire arch—is the philosophy of art.

SECTION IV: ORGAN OF TRANSCENDENTAL PHILOSOPHY

1.

The only immediate object of transcendental consideration is the subjective (§ 2). The sole organ of this method of philosophizing is therefore the *inner sense*, and its object is of such a nature that, unlike that of mathematics, it can never become the object of external intuition. The object of mathematics, to be sure, exists as little outside of knowledge, as that of philosophy. The entire existence of mathematics depends upon the intuition. It exists, therefore, only in the intuition; but this intuition itself is an external one. In addition to this the mathematician has never to do immediately with the intuition—the construction itself—but only with the thing constructed, which can certainly be presented outwardly. The philosopher, however, regards only the act of construction itself, which is purely an internal one.

2.

Moreover, the objects of the transcendental philosopher have no existence, except in so far as they are freely produced. One cannot be compelled to this production any more than one can be compelled by the external drawing of a mathematical figure to regard it internally. Just as the existence of a mathematical figure depends upon external sense, so the entire reality of a philosophical concept depends upon the inner sense. The whole object of this philosophy is no other than the action of the intelligence according to fixed laws. This action can be conceived only through a peculiar, direct, inner intuition, and this again is possible only by production. But this is not enough. In philosophizing, one is not only the object, but is always at the same time the subject of the reflection. Two conditions are consequently demanded for the understanding of philosophy. First, the philosopher must be engaged in a continued inner activity, in a continuous production of those original actions of intelligence; second, he must be engaged in continuous reflection upon this productive action; in a word, he must at the same time always be the contemplated (producing) and the contemplating.

3.

By this continuous duplicity of production and of intuition, that must become an object which is otherwise reflected by nothing. It cannot be proved here, but will be proved later, that this becoming reflected on the part of the absolutely unconscious and non-objective, is possible only by an aesthetic act of the imagination. Nevertheless, it is certain from what has already been proved that all philosophy is productive. Philosophy, therefore, as well as art, rests upon the productive faculty, and the difference between the two consists merely in the different direction of the productive power. For whereas production in art is directed outward, in order to reflect the unconscious by products; philosophical production is directed immediately inward, in order to reflect it in intellectual intuition. The special sense by which this kind of philosophy must be grasped is therefore the aesthetic sense, and hence it is that the philosophy of art is the true organum of philosophy (§ 3).

From the vulgar reality there exist only two outlets: poetry, which transports us into the ideal world, and philosophy, which causes the real world wholly to vanish before us. It is not clear why the sense for philosophy should be more widely diffused than that for poetry, especially among the classes of men who have not wholly lost the aesthetic organ either by memory work (nothing destroys more directly the productive

power) or by dead speculation, which is ruinous to all imaginative power.

4.

It is unnecessary to occupy more time with the commonplaces about the sense of truth, or about entire disregard for results, although it might be asked, what other conviction can be sacred to one who questions the most certain of all—that there are things outside of us. We may rather take a glance at the so-called claims of the common understanding.

The common understanding in matters of philosophy has no claims whatsoever, except those which all objects of investigations have, namely, to be perfectly explained.

It is not, therefore, our business to prove that what is held for true, is true, but only to disclose the unavoidableness of its illusions. This implies that the objective world belongs only to the necessary limitations which render self-consciousness (the *I am*) possible; it is enough for the common understanding, if from this view the necessity of its own view is derived.

For this purpose it is necessary, not only that the inner machinery of our mental activity be disclosed, and the mechanism of necessary ideas revealed, but also that it should be shown by what peculiarity of our nature it is necessary that what has reality only in our intuition, is reflected to us as something existing outside of us.

As natural science produces idealism out of realism, when it intellectualizes the laws of nature into laws of intelligence, or superinduces the formal upon the material (§ 1), so transcendental philosophy produces realism out of idealism when it materializes the laws of intelligence into laws of nature, or introduces the material into the formal.

First Division: The Principle of Transcendental Idealism

EXPLANATIONS

A. If now we revert to the fundamental principle of identity A = A, we discover that we can derive our principle directly from it. In every identical proposition it was affirmed that the thought is compared with itself; this undoubtedly takes place by means of an act of thought. The proposition A = A therefore

presupposes a thought that becomes immediately an object to itself; but an act of thought which becomes its own object exists only in self-consciousness. It is certainly incomprehensible how one can seriously derive from a mere proposition of logic something real; but it is truly comprehensible how one can find in it by reflection upon the act of thought something real, for example the categories from the logical function of judgment, and similarly the act of self-consciousness from every identical proposition.

B. That the subject and object of thought are one in self-consciousness can become clear to every one solely by the act of self-consciousness itself. It is necessary for this purpose that one at the same time perform this act, and in so doing reflect again upon one's self. Self-consciousness is the act whereby the thinking itself immediately becomes the object, and conversely. This act and none other is self-consciousness. Such act is an absolutely free action, to which one can indeed be guided but cannot be compelled. The readiness to perceive one's self in this act, to discriminate one's self both as thought and as thinking, and again to recognize one's self as identical in such discrimination, is constantly presupposed in what follows.

C. Self-consciousness is an act, but by every act something is accomplished for us. Every thought is an act, and every definite thought is a definite act. By means of every such act there also arises in us a definite conception. The conception is nothing but the act of thinking itself, and abstracted from this act it is nothing. By the act of self-consciousness there must likewise originate a conception for us; and this is no other than the conception of the ego. While I regard myself as the object by means of self-consciousness there originates in me the conception of the ego; and conversely the conception of the ego is only the conception of self becoming its own object.

D. The conception of the ego is accomplished by the act of self-consciousness. Without the act, therefore, the ego is nothing; its entire reality depends solely upon this act. The ego can thus be conceived only as act, and it is otherwise nothing.

Whether the external object is nothing different from its conception, whether also here conception and object are one, is a question which is still to be decided. But that the conception of the ego, that is, the act whereby thought becomes its own object, and the ego itself (the object) are absolutely one, needs no proof, since the ego is clearly nothing apart from the act, and in general exists only in this act.

Here, therefore, is that original identity of thought and of object, of appearance and of being, which we sought, and which is nowhere else met with. The ego does not exist at all before that act whereby

the thought becomes its own object. It is therefore nothing other than the thought becoming itself the object, and consequently absolutely nothing apart from the thought. The reason why so many fail to see, in case of the ego, that its being conceived is identical with its being originated has its explanation solely in the fact, that they neither can perform the act of self-consciousness with freedom, nor are able to reflect upon what originates in this very act. As regards the first, it is to be remarked, that we make a clear distinction between self-consciousness as act, and mere empirical consciousness. What we commonly term consciousness is merely something which goes along with the representations of objects, something which maintains identity amid the change of representations. It is thus purely of an empirical character, for indeed I am thereby conscious of myself, but only as of one having representations. The act here spoken of is one, however, by which I am conscious of myself, not as having this or that determination, but originally, and this consciousness, in contrast with the other, is called pure consciousness, or self-consciousness.

The genesis of these two kinds of consciousness may be made clearer in the following way. Let one abandon himself wholly to the involuntary succession of representations, then, no matter how manifold or different these may be, they will nevertheless appear as belonging to one identical subject. But if I reflect upon this identity of the subject in the representations, there originates for me the proposition *I think*. It is this *I think* that accompanies all representations and maintains in them the continuity of consciousness. If however one frees one's self from every act of representation in order to become conscious of one's original self, there arises not the proposition *I think*, but the proposition *I am*, which is undoubtedly a higher one. In the proposition *I think* there exists already the expression of a determination or affection of the ego; the proposition *I am*, on the contrary, is an infinite proposition, because it is one which has no real predicate, but which, for that very reason, may have an infinity of possible predicates.

E. The ego is nothing distinct from the thought of it; the thought of the ego and the ego itself are absolutely one. The ego, therefore, is absolutely nothing apart from the thought; it is therefore also no thing, no affair, but endlessly the non-objective. This is to be understood in the following way. The ego is indeed object, but only for itself, and is thus not originally in the world of objects. It becomes an object only by the very fact that it makes itself its own object. It becomes the object not of something external, but always only of itself.

Everything that is not ego is originally object, and for this very reason is an object nor to itself, but to something perceiving outside of it. The original objective is always something known, never a knower. The ego is known only through its own self-knowledge. Matter is called self-less for the very reason that it has nothing innermost, and exists only as something perceived in a foreign perception.

F. If the ego is no thing, no affair, then one cannot ask concerning any predicate of the ego. It has none except this, that it is no thing. The character of the ego consists in having no other predicate except that of self-consciousness.

The same result can also be reached in other ways.

That which is the highest principle of knowledge cannot have its ground of knowledge in something higher. Its *principium essendi* and *cognoscendi*, must therefore be one, and coincide in one.

For this very reason the unconditioned can never be sought in any one thing; for what is object, is originally also object of knowledge; whereas what is a principle of all knowledge cannot become at all an object of knowledge, either originally or in itself, except only through a special act of freedom.

The unconditioned can therefore never be sought in the world of objects. (Therefore the purely objective, or matter, is for natural science nothing original, but is for it even as much appearance as it is for transcendental philosophy.)

Unconditioned is termed that which can by no means become a thing, or an affair. The first task of philosophy can therefore be thus expressed: to find something which absolutely cannot be thought as thing. But of this character is only the ego, and conversely, the ego is that which is in itself non-objective.

G. If now the ego is absolutely no object, no thing, it appears difficult to explain how in general a knowledge of it is possible, or what kind of knowledge we have of it.

The ego is pure act, pure doing, and, because it is the principle of all knowledge, must be absolutely non-objective in knowledge. If it is, therefore, to

become an act of knowledge, it can become known only in a way entirely different from common knowledge.

This knowledge must be:

1. Absolutely free, because all other knowledge is not free. It must, therefore, be a knowledge to which the way is not by proofs, conclusions, and the mediation of concepts. It is therefore in general an intuition.
2. It must also be a knowledge whose object is not independent of it, and is therefore a knowledge which is at the same time productive of its object. It is an intuition which is altogether freely productive, and in which the producing is one and the same with the produced.

Such an intuition is termed *intellectual intuition*, in contrast with the sensible intuition, which never appears as productive of its object, and in which therefore the perceiving-itself is distinct from the perceived.

Such an intuition is the ego, because through the knowledge the ego has of itself, the ego itself (the object) first originates. Since the ego (as object) is none other than this very knowledge of itself, the ego originates solely by the fact that it knows itself. The ego itself is, therefore, a knowledge which at the same time creates itself (as object).

The intellectual intuition is the organ of all transcendental thinking. For the whole aim of transcendental thought is freely to transform into its own object something which is otherwise no object. It presupposes a faculty to produce and at the same time to perceive certain functions of the soul, so that the producing of the object and the perceiving are absolutely one. This faculty, however, is precisely the faculty of intellectual intuition.

Transcendental philosophizing must therefore be constantly accompanied by intellectual intuition. All pretence that this philosophizing cannot be understood has its cause not in the unintelligibility of it, but in the defect of the organ whereby it must be comprehended. Apart from this intuition, philosophizing has itself no substratum that might cause and support thought. This very intuition supplies the place of the objective world in the transcendental thought, and, as it were, carries the flight of speculation. The ego itself is an object that exists by virtue of the fact that it has knowledge of itself, that is, it is a constant intellectual intuition. Since the sole object of transcendental philosophy is this self-producing activity, the intellectual intuition is for it precisely what space is for geometry. Just as without intuition of space, geometry would be absolutely incomprehensible, because all its constructions are only different methods and ways of qualifying that intuition, so without the intellectual intuition, all philosophy would be incomprehensible, because all its conceptions are only different qualifications of that production which has itself for an object, that is, of the intellectual intuition (cf. Fichte's "Einleitung in die Wissenschaftslehre" in the "Philosophisches Journal").

No reason need be given why people have perceived something mysterious in this intuition, some special sense feigned by a few, except that some persons are really without it. This, however, is no more strange than that they still entirely lack many another sense whose reality is as little involved in doubt.

H. The ego is nothing other than a producing which becomes its own object, that is it is an intellectual intuition. But this intellectual intuition is itself an absolutely free act. It can therefore not be demonstrated, but only demanded. The ego itself is solely this intuition; the ego therefore as principle of philosophy is itself only something that is postulated.

Since the time that Reinhold made the scientific founding of philosophy his aim, there has been much talk of a first fundamental proposition from which philosophy would have to proceed. By this one generally understood a theorem in which the entire philosophy should be involved. But it is easily perceived that transcendental philosophy can proceed from no theorem, because it proceeds from the subjective, that is, from that which can become objective only by a distinct act of freedom. A theorem is a proposition which depends upon being. Transcendental philosophy, however, proceeds from no being, but from a free act; and this can only be postulated. Every science that is not empirical must by its first principle already exclude all empiricism, that is, must presuppose its object as not already existing but must create it. In this way, for example, geometry proceeds, since it starts not from theorems but from postulates. It is because the most primal construction in it is postulated, and is left to the pupil to create, that he is at

the very outset sent back to self-construction. It is just the same with transcendental philosophy. Unless one bring to it the transcendental method of thought, one must find it incomprehensible. It is, therefore, necessary that one place one's self at the outset through freedom in that method of thought; and this takes place by means of the free act whereby the principle originates. If it be a fact that transcendental philosophy does not presuppose its objects, it certainly cannot presuppose its first object, the principle; it can postulate it only as one freely to be constructed. As the principle is of its own construction, so are also all its remaining concepts; and the entire science has to do with its own free constructions.

If the principle of philosophy is a postulate, then the object of this postulate must be the most primal construct for the inner sense, that is must be the ego, not in so far as it is determined in this or that particular way, but the ego in general, as production of itself. Through and in this primal construct, it is true, something definite is effected, just as always happens by every definite act of the soul. But the product is surely nothing without the construction; in fact it exists only in that it is constructed; abstracted from the construction it exists as little as the line of the geometer. The geometrical line also is nothing existing, for the line on the board is, as we know, not the line itself, but is recognized only as such because it is taken in connection with the original intuition of the line itself.

What the ego is, is for this reason just as little demonstrable as what the line is: one can only describe the action by which it originates. If the line could be demonstrated it would not need to be postulated. It is just the same with that transcendental line of the production which must be originally intuited in transcendental philosophy, and from which all other constructions of the science first proceed (cf. "Allgemeine Uebersicht der philosophischen Literatur" in New Philos. Journal, 10. Hft).

I. What comes to us by the original act of intellectual intuition can be expressed in a fundamental principle which one can term the first fundamental principle of philosophy. Now the ego originates through the intellectual intuition in so far as it is its own product, that is, is at the same time producing and produced. This identity between the ego in so far as it is the producing and the ego as produced is expressed in the proposition the I = I. This proposition, since it places opposites as equal, is by no means an identical, but a synthetic proposition.

By means of the proposition I = I, the proposition A = A is therefore transformed into a synthetical proposition, and we have found the point where the identical knowledge springs immediately from the synthetical, and the synthetical knowledge from the identical. But at this point also is found (Chap. 1) the principle of all knowledge. In the proposition I = I, therefore, the principle of all knowledge must be expressed, because this proposition is indeed the only possible one, that is at the same time identical and synthetical.

The mere reflection upon the proposition A = A could have led us to the same conclusion. The proposition A = A appears, to be sure, identical; it could, however, very well also have synthetical significance, that is, if the one A were opposed to the other. One would therefore have to substitute in the place of A, a conception which expresses the original duplicity of identity, and vice versa.

Such a conception is that of an object which is at the same time opposed to and on an equality with itself. But of such character is only an object which in itself is both cause and effect, producing and produced, subject and object. The conception of an original identity in duplicity, and conversely, is therefore solely the conception of a subject-object, and this occurs originally only in self-consciousness.

Natural science sets out from nature as at once arbitrarily the producing and the produced, in order to derive the individual from that conception. The unmediated object of knowledge is such an identity only in the unmediated self-consciousness, in the highest potency of becoming its own object, in which the transcendental philosopher at the outset places himself, not arbitrarily, but with freedom. The original duplicity in nature is itself ultimately explained only by assuming nature to be intelligible.

K. The proposition I = I meets at the same time the second demand which is made of the principle of knowledge, that it establish at once both the form and the content of knowledge. For the highest formal fundamental proposition A = A, is of course only possible by the act which is expressed by the proposition I = I, that is, by the act of thinking which becomes its own object, and is identical with itself.

The proposition I = I is therefore so far from being conditioned by the fundamental proposition of identity, that on the contrary this latter is conditioned by the former. For if I were not I, then A could also not be A, because the equality which is posited in that proposition expresses after all only an equality between the subject which judges and that in which A is posited as object, that is, an equality between the ego as subject and object.

GENERAL COMMENTS

1.

The contradiction which has been solved by the foregoing deduction is the following: the science of knowledge can proceed from nothing objective, since it begins precisely with the universal doubt in the reality of the objective. The unconditioned-certain, therefore, exists for it only in the absolute non-objective which also proves the non-objectivity of the identical propositions as the solely unconditioned-certain. But how the objective could arise from this original non-objective would not be conceivable, unless that non-objective were an ego, that is, a principle that becomes its own object. Only what is not originally object, can make itself the object, and thereby become an object. From this original duplicity in itself, every objective for the ego is evolved that comes into consciousness; and it is that original identity in duplicity which alone brings union and coherence into all synthetic knowledge.

2.

Some remarks may still be necessary on the use of language in this philosophy.

Kant in his anthropology finds it remarkable that a new world appears to spring up to the child as soon as it begins to speak of itself as I. This is in fact very natural: it is the intellectual world which reveals itself to him, since whatever can say I to itself lifts itself thereby above the objective world, and enters from a foreign intuition into its own. Philosophy must undoubtedly proceed from that conception in which the entire intellectuality is contained, and from which it is developed.

From this very fact one must see that in the conception of the ego there exists something higher than the mere expression of individuality. It is the very act of self-consciousness indeed, with which the consciousness of individuality makes its simultaneous appearance, but which itself contains nothing individual. Heretofore the discussion has been only of the ego as the mere act of self-consciousness; and from it all individuality must yet be derived.

Under the ego as principle, the individual I is thought of just as little as is the empirical I—the I which appears in empirical consciousness. The pure consciousness determined and restricted in a different way yields the empirical consciousness. The two, therefore, are separated merely by their restrictions. Remove the restrictions of the empirical and you have the absolute ego, which is here treated. The pure self-consciousness is an act which lies outside of all time and itself constitutes all time; the empirical consciousness is only one creating itself in time, and in the succession of representations.

The question whether the ego is a thing in itself, or a phenomenon, is of itself contradictory. It is in general no thing, neither thing in itself, nor phenomenon.

The dilemma which one may here bring forward in reply: Everything must either be something or nothing, etc., rests upon the ambiguity of the concept something. If the something in general is intended to designate something real in contrast with the merely imagined, then the ego must indeed be something real, since it is the principle of all reality. And just as clearly is it true that because the ego is principle of all reality, it cannot then be real in the same sense as that to which belongs merely derived reality. The reality which such objector regards as the true one, namely that of things, is merely derived, and is only the reflection of that higher reality. The dilemma strictly viewed is thus equivalent to saying: Everything is either a *thing* or nothing. This is manifestly false, since there certainly exists a higher conception than that of the thing, namely, that of the deed, or of the activity.

This conception must indeed be higher than that of the thing, since the things themselves are to be conceived only as modifications of an activity limited in different ways. The being of the thing does not indeed consist in mere rest or inactivity. For even all space-filling is only a degree of activity, and every thing is only a determined degree of activity with which space is filled.

Since none of the predicates which attach to things belong to the ego, the paradox is thereby explained, that one cannot say of the ego, that it is. One is unable to predicate being of the ego, just because the ego is being itself. The eternal act of self-consciousness conceived as in no time, which we term ego, is what gives existence to all things, and which therefore needs no other existence by which to be supported; but appears self-carrying and self-supporting, objectively as the eternal becoming, subjectively as the infinite producing.

3.

Before we proceed to the setting up of the system itself, it may be well to show how the principle can establish at the same time both theoretical and practical philosophy. That it does this is a necessary character of the principle, and is thus obvious.

That the principle should be at the same time the principle of theoretical and practical philosophy, is impossible, unless it be both theoretical and practical. Since now a theoretical principle is a theorem, but a practical principle is a command, something must be intermediate between the two. This is the postulate. It borders on the practical philosophy because it is a pure demand, and on the theoretical because it requires a purely theoretical construction. What the postulate derives its compulsory power from is explained by the fact that it is allied to the practical demands. The intellectual intuition is something that one can demand and expect. Whoever has not such faculty at least ought to have it.

4.

What every one who has attentively followed us thus far perceives for himself is that the beginning and the end of this philosophy is freedom, the absolutely indemonstrable, that which proves itself by itself. What in all other systems threatens the destruction of freedom is in this system derived from itself. Being, in this system, is only suspended freedom. In a system which makes being the first and highest, not only must knowledge be a mere copy of an original being, but all freedom must also be only a necessary deception, because one is ignorant of the principle whose movements constitute the apparent manifestations of freedom.

STUDY QUESTIONS: SCHELLING, *SYSTEM OF TRANSCENDENTAL IDEALISM*

1. On what is all knowledge based?
2. What is Nature?
3. Which is first, the objective or subjective?
4. What is intelligence?
5. What is the one fundamental prejudice?
6. What does Schelling mean by the "transcendental art?"
7. What is the universal organum of philosophy?
8. How are consciousness and the *I am* related?
9. What important principle can be derived from the fundamental principle of identity, A = A.
10. In what sense is self-consciousness an *act*?
11. How does Schelling establish the truth of the proposition I = I?
12. Why is freedom the beginning and end of Schelling's philosophy?

Philosophical Bridges: Schelling's Influence

As one the leading romantic philosophers of the nineteenth century, Schelling inspired the great English Romantic poets, such as Wordsworth and Shelley, and the writer Samuel Coleridge (1772–1834). In his own lifetime Schelling was a major source and influence on his fellow German idealists, especially Hegel and later his illustrious fellow colleagues at Jena. His distinction between the external, objective world of "nature" and the internal, subjective world of mind and spirit gave voice to the notion of a third, higher reality, the Absolute, which figured predominantly throughout the philosophy of the nineteenth century. The Absolute as conceived by Schelling and those who came after him is neither conscious nor unconscious and, like Kant's Noumenal Self, the Absolute in Schelling's view transcends the categories of thought. Yet it is personal and immanent; the Absolute desires to become conscious, it seeks individual existence in space and time, which it does by positing the existence of a material, inanimate, nonconscious world of matter on the basis of which it then by distinguishing itself from this unconscious notion of itself becomes a conscious mind. Schelling's idea that the Absolute, in opposition to its own concept of itself, becomes the relative, phenomenal world, without loss of identity, thus became one of the staples of idealist thought ever since, inspiring not only the German idealists but others in England (Frances Bradley, John McTaggart) and the United States, most notably Josiah Royce.

HEGEL (1770–1831)

Biographical History

Georg Wilhelm Friedrich Hegel was born and raised in Stuttgart, Germany. After graduating from the University of Tübingen he joined one of the most illustrious philosophy departments of all time, at the University of Jena, which included, besides Fichte and Schelling, the great writer, philosopher and critic Friedrich Von Schlegel (1772–1829), who helped originate the German Romantic movement, and one of the leading playwrights of the time, idealist philosopher Friedrich Schiller (1759–1805). During the French occupation by Napoleon, he was removed from his position as professor and moved to Bamberg, where he worked as a newspaper editor and then a school principal in Nuremberg. Eventually, in 1816, he returned to being a professor of philosophy, in Heidelberg; two years later he transferred to the university in Berlin and remained there for the rest of his life.

Philosophical Overview

The denial of Kant's distinction between phenomena, the known world of appearances, and the noumenal, the unknowable, noumenal world of things-in-themselves, was the starting point of Hegel's thought. Since in Kant's view the phenomenal world is not an illusion, but empirically real, and the noumenal world is in what ultimate reality consists, there are therefore necessarily two real worlds. In Hegel's view, as in his fellow idealists Fichte's and Schelling's, there is but one real world. Objects according to Hegel are created *completely* by the mind, just as in idealism. But where as Berkeley's denial of matter and any mind-independent realm matter makes room for (indeed, requires) God, according to Hegel the mind's own faculties are self-created, through its own historical evolution, itself resulting from an eternal opposition of itself against itself. Thus, in Hegel's metaphysical system, the mind generates, structures, and regulates the whole of reality, up to and including, most especially, itself.

By *the Absolute*, Hegel minds reality as it exists in itself; but it is not noumenal. The absolute is, itself, mind or, what the German word he uses explicitly implies, *spirit*. It should be kept in mind(!) that in German and Slavic languages there is no word for mind as such, and that the word Hegel and other German writers of the time use, *geist*, has as its root the meaning of ghost or spirit. Reality itself, all aspect of the world, is the result of a self-thinking thought. All existence in time is a teleological, goal-directed, evolutionary process in which being slowly becomes aware of itself, "the Absolute realizing itself," as Hegel calls it.

Unlike in Kant's transcendental idealism and Berkeley's subjective idealism, both of which are pluralistic, Hegel's notion of the Absolute is in the ancient and medieval monistic tradition according to which the whole existence is one substance. This one substance is spirit, or mind. What is new and different, albeit with an aspect of an Aristotelian nod to teleological forces, is that what drives evolution are not past or present events; rather, the still uncreated future draws us into itself as a way of the Absolute to come to realize itself. In that sense, the Kantian notion of a noumenal reality beyond the phenomenal world of appearances becomes in Hegel's view the real but as yet unpresent domain of future possibility, toward which everything must evolve as a manifest expression of the Absolute trying to realize itself. Philosophy itself, its history, its debates, its problems and resolutions, are all part of this grand cosmic evolution. Thus, as Hegel sees it, history is neither a succession of material objects rearranged into different geometrical positions, nor is it a succession of ideas that turns out to be false when there are new and better ideas to replace them. Philosophical developments through history are themselves changes in the Absolute, a gradual process in which the great cosmic mind comes to realize itself.

Hegel claims that Kant's notion of mind-independent reality, the "thing-in-itself," is ultimately unknowable and therefore immediately unintelligible. He starts with an analysis of Kant's notion of necessary truths that are not logically necessary, the synthetic a priori. This is the aspect of Kant's view that posits mind as existing not passively in relation to its objects but as an active force in object construction. It is a two-way process, according to

Kant: objects in the world, which are but representations of mind-independent things-in-themselves, contribute something to the mind as mind contributes something to them. The phenomenal world itself exists as a sort of superposition of the effects of objects as things-in-themselves and the effects of the faculties of the mind. Hegel then goes beyond Kant by putting an emphasis on necessary truths that are not necessary in the logical sense but come from within the mind itself. The laws of history as such express these necessities.

Because the laws of history according to Hegel follow a necessary process, they structure consciousness. For Hegel, as for Kant, necessary truths are mind-dependent and not logically necessary. The difference is that, for Hegel, these truths do not depend in any way on any sort of substance or reality beyond the reach of our minds. Truth is not a correspondence between some noumenal, mind-independent reality, and the phenomenal representations in the mind. Truth, as conceived by Hegel, is understood as *coherence within a complete system of thought*. "The true is the whole." What Hegel means by "complete system" is not something that in any way corresponds to some sort of objective, mind-independent reality but *is*, itself, objective reality. This Hegelian whole is not static. It evolves. Therefore, truth evolves. Nor is truth something beyond, or transcendental to, experience and the world. It is immanent. Like the world itself, truth is an evolutionary, developing *dialectic* process.

Hegel's theory of dialectic is an important and widely influential system of philosophizing in its own right. Dialectic begins with the *thesis*, some proposition that subsequent analysis will reveal to be false. This results in a contradictory proposition, the *antithesis*. This too will turn out to be false. This however does not end in paradox or skepticism but leads to a synthesis of the two initially contradictory propositions. This Hegel calls *sublation* (*Aufhebung*). The process then continues, leading to a new thesis, antithesis, and synthesis.

This process is never static. The dialectic leads to higher levels of discursive thought and enlightened consciousness, until distinctions derived from the false dichotomy between empiricist and rationalist systems of thought dissolve.

Consciousness itself is a culmination by-product of the dialectical process. The concept, *being*, as a thesis, gives rise to the opposite concept, the antithesis, *nonbeing*. Together in the mind, perplexed by thinking about these two concepts, is led its own logic to a new sublation of these two concepts, their synthesis, *becoming*. This is the creation, literally, of a new and higher realm of mind, namely, consciousness, the realm of becoming.

Phenomenology of Spirit: "Independence and Dependence of Self-Consciousness: Relations of Master and Servant"

In this essay Hegel begins with an explanation of what he calls the first phase in the dialectical evolution of consciousness. What he means by this is that, first, self-consciousness (I am, I exist, I am I) is from a logical point of view *impossible* unless at the same time there is the presence or interpretation of something that is not oneself, namely some "other." In other words, I am I to myself only to the degree that I am recognized as such by you. This is a deep and profound idea that will surface again, with great force, in subsequent existentialist thought. More to the point, according to Hegel, this fundamental realization, or actualization (albeit the result of a misinterpretation, since the whole of experience itself is but an aspect of the Absolute) creates a deep and fundamental feeling of anxiety, of threat, what some later thinkers (e.g. the existentialists) would no doubt call *dread*.

To avoid this awful, untenable state, the first stage of *alienation* or what the great American idealist philosopher Josiah Royce more simply and directly translates as "the unhappy consciousness," self-consciousness tries to establish itself as *free*. It asserts this freedom in a most unfriendly way, namely, by *dominating* the other and, perhaps equally importantly, to require that the other *acknowledges* it as master to which the other thus becomes *slave*. Struggle results—human, social, political, historical—and becomes thus the fundamental force of human evolution. The master dominates the servant who is then forced to produce material and other sorts of goods for the master's betterment, enjoyment, and subsequent further domination.

This evolutionary process, however, does not end happily for the master. Because the master is dependent upon the servant not only for the fundamental sustenance of life but also for recognition (without which the status of master and slave is moot), the master becomes insecure insofar as the master is vulnerable to the vagrancies of the slave. More-over, the master becomes more and more the consumer while the slave becomes more and more the creator (by making the products and services that the master needs). In this way the slave's self-consciousness evolves in relation to what the slave has created, further empowering the slave, while the master's consciousness may even devolve. In this way the dominator becomes dominated.

This dialectic process is one of the most pivotal and most influential ideas that Hegel has produced, which comes to full fruition in the explosive and revolutionary phi-losophy of his most famous pupil, Karl Marx.

PHENOMENOLOGY OF SPIRIT

INDEPENDENCE AND DEPENDENCE OF SELF-CONSCIOUSNESS: RELATIONS OF MASTER AND SERVANT

Self-consciousness is *in* and *for itself* in and through being in and for itself for another self-consciousness; that is, it is only as something acknowledged, or rec-ognized. The concept of this unity of self-consciousness in its duplication, of the infinitude realizing itself in self-consciousness, is a many-sided and many-sensed complex, so that the moments of this complex must both be held carefully apart, and at the same time taken and understood in this differentiation as not distinct, or always also in their opposed sense. The double-sensedness of what is distinguished lies in the essence of self-consciousness, of being infinite, or boundless, that is, immediately the contrary of the determination in which it is established. The laying-apart of the concept of this spiritual unity in its dupli-cation presents to us the movement of *acknowledging*.

There is for self-consciousness another self-consciousness; it has come *outside itself*. This has a twofold significance: *first*, self-consciousness has lost itself, for it finds itself as *another* being; *second*, it has thereby done away with the other, for it does not see the other either as the essential being, but *it itself* in the *other*.

Self-consciousness must do away with this *otherness it* has; this is the doing away with of the first double-sense, and hence itself a second double-sense: *first*, it must set out to do away with *the other* inde-pendent being in order thereby to become certain of *itself* as the essential being; *second*, in so doing it sets out to do away with *itself*, for this other being is itself.

This double-sensed doing away with its double-sensed otherness is equally a double-sensed return *into itself*; for, *first*, through doing away it gets itself back, for it becomes once more equal to itself through doing away with *its* otherness; *second*, however, it no

Hegel, from *Phenomenology of Spirit* (B, IV, A: "Independence and Dependence of Self-Consciousness: Relations of Master and Servant"), translated by J. L. H. Thomas. Reprinted from *Hegel: Selections*, edited by M. J. Inwood, *The Great Philoso-phers* series, Paul Edwards, general editor (New York: Macmillan, 1989).

less gives back the other self-consciousness to the latter again, for it had itself in the other, it does away with this being *it* has in the other, thus letting the other go free again.

This movement of self-consciousness in its relation to another self-consciousness has been presented in this way now, as *the doing of the one*; but this doing of the one has itself the two-fold significance of being as much *its doing* as *the doing of the other*; for the other is no less independent, shut up within itself, and there is nothing in it that is not owing to itself. The first self-consciousness does not have the object before it as the latter to begin with is merely for desire but an independent object existing for itself, over which therefore it has of itself no power, unless the object does with itself what self-consciousness does with it. The movement is thus in all respects the double movement of both self-consciousnesses. Each sees the *other one* do the same as it does; each does itself what it demands of the other, and so does what it does only inasmuch as the other does the same; a one-sided doing would be unavailing, because what it is intended should occur can come about only through both.

The doing is therefore double-sensed not only inasmuch as it is a doing as much *to itself as to the other*, but also inasmuch as it is undividedly as much the *doing of the one* as of the *other*.

In this movement we see the process repeat itself which presented itself as the play of forces, but in consciousness. What in the earlier process was for us, is here for the extremes themselves. The center is self-consciousness, which puts itself apart into the extremes; and each extreme is this exchanging of its determination and absolute going over into the opposed extreme. But though, as consciousness, it does indeed come *out of itself*, yet it is in its being-out-of-itself at the same time held back within itself, is *for itself*, and its "outside-itself" is *for it*. It is for consciousness that it immediately *is* and *is not* another consciousness; and, equally, that this other is only for itself in doing away with itself as something being for itself, and only in the being-for-itself of the other is for itself. Each is to the other the center through which each brings into relation and connects itself with itself, and each is to itself and to the other an immediate entity existing for itself, which at the same time is thus for itself only through this relating, or

mediation. They *acknowledge* one another as *mutually acknowledging one other*.

This pure concept of acknowledgment, the duplication of self-consciousness in its unity, will now be studied in the way in which its process appears for self-consciousness. This process will first present the facet of the *inequality* of the two, or the coming out of the center into the extremes, which, being extremes, are opposed to one another, the one acknowledged only, the other acknowledging only.

Self-consciousness is to begin with simple being-for-itself, equal-with-itself through the exclusion of everything *other from itself*; its essence and absolute object is to it "*I*"; and it is in this *immediacy*, or in this *being* of its being-for-itself, an *individual*. Whatever else there is for it, is as an inessential object, one marked with the character of the negative. But the other is also a self-consciousness: an individual comes on opposite an individual. Thus *immediately* coming on, they are for each other in the way of common objects: *independent* forms, consciousnesses immersed in the *existence of life*—for it is as life that the existent object has here determined itself—which have not yet carried out *for each other* the movement of absolute abstraction, of expunging all immediate existence and of being merely the purely negative existence of consciousness equal-with-itself, or which have not yet presented themselves to each other as pure *being-for-self*, that is, as *self*-consciousness. Each is indeed certain of itself, but not of the other, and consequently each's own certainty of itself has as yet no truth; for its truth could only be that its own being-for-itself had presented itself to it as an independent object or, what amounts to the same thing, that the object had presented itself as this pure certainty of itself. This, however, on the concept of acknowledgment is not possible, save that as the other does for the one, so the one does for the other, each with itself through its own activity, and again through the activity of the other, carrying out this pure abstraction of being-for-itself.

The *presentation* of oneself as the pure abstraction of self-consciousness, however, consists in showing oneself to be the pure negation of one's objective way of being, that is, in showing oneself not to be attached to a particular *concrete existence*, nor to the universal individuality of concrete existence in general, nor even to life. This presentation is a *double* doing: doing of the other, and doing through oneself. Inasmuch as it is the doing *of the other*, each then is set upon the death of the other. But in this there is present also the second doing, *the doing through oneself*; for the former contains within itself the staking of one's own life. The relation of the two self-consciousnesses is hence determined in such a way that through the combat for life and death they *prove* themselves and each other. They must enter this combat, for they must raise the certainty of themselves, *of being for themselves*, to truth in the other and in themselves. And it is solely through the staking of life that freedom arises, that it is confirmed to self-consciousness that it is not *being*, not the *immediate* way in which it comes on, not its being immersed in the expanse of life which is its essence—but that there is nothing present in it which is not for it a vanishing moment, that it is just pure *being-for-itself*. The individual that has not risked life can indeed be acknowledged as a *person*; but it has not attained the truth of this state of acknowledgment as that of an independent self-consciousness. Likewise, each must as much aim at the death of the other as it stakes its own life; for the other means no more to it than it itself does; the individual's essence presents itself to it as another, it is outside itself, it must do away with its being-outside-itself; the other is a consciousness engaged and existing in manifold ways; it must view its otherness as pure being-for-self, or as absolute negation.

This proving through death does away, however, with the truth that was to result from it, just as much as it thereby also does away with the certainty of oneself altogether; for just as life was the *natural* position of consciousness, independence without absolute negativity, so death is the *natural* negation of consciousness, negation without independence, which therefore remains without the required sense of acknowledgment. Through death the certainty has indeed arisen that both risked their life and despised it in themselves and in the other; though not for those who underwent this combat. They do away with their consciousness set in this alien essentiality that is natural concrete existence, or they do away with themselves, and are done away with as the *extremes* which would be for themselves. There thereby vanishes, however, from the play of exchange the essential moment of setting oneself apart into extremes of opposed determinations; and the center collapses into a dead unity, which is set apart into dead, merely existent, not opposed, extremes; and the two do not mutually give back and receive back themselves from each other through consciousness, but let each other free merely indifferently, as things. Their deed is abstract negation, not the negation of consciousness, which *does away* in such a manner that it *puts by* and *preserves* what is done away, and consequently survives its being-done-away.

In this experience self-consciousness comes to realize that life is as essential to it as pure self-consciousness is. In immediate self-consciousness the simple "I" is the absolute object, which however, for us or in itself, is absolute mediation and has existent independence as an essential moment. The dissolution of that simple unity is the result of the first experience; through it there is established a pure self-consciousness, and a consciousness which is not purely for itself, but is for another consciousness, that is, is as *existent*, or is consciousness in the form of *thinghood*. Both moments are essential; but as they are to begin with unequal and opposed, and their reflection into unity is not yet a reality, they are as two opposed forms of consciousness: one, the independent consciousness, to which being-for-self is the essence; the other, the dependent consciousness, to which life or being for another is the essence: the former is the *master*, the latter the *servant*.

The master is the consciousness existing *for itself*, though no longer merely the concept of the latter, but a consciousness existing for itself which is in mediate relation with itself through *another* consciousness, namely through one to whose essence it pertains to be synthesized with independent *being* or thinghood in general. The master relates himself to both these moments, to a *thing* as such, the object of desire, and to the consciousness to whom thinghood is what is essential; and since he (a), *qua* concept of self-consciousness, is immediate relation of *being-for-himself*, but (b) now is also as mediation, or as a being-for-self which is for itself only through another, so he relates himself (a) immediately to both and (b) mediately to each through the other. The master relates himself *to the servant mediately through independent being*; for it is precisely to this that the servant is kept; it is his chain, from which in the combat he could not abstract, and consequently showed himself to be dependent, to have his independence in thinghood. The master, however, is the power over the being in question, for he showed in the combat that it meant merely something negative to him; since he is the power over this being, while this being is the power over the other, the master thus has in this conjunction the other under himself. Likewise the master relates himself *mediately through the servant to the thing*, the servant relates himself, *qua* self-consciousness as such, to the thing negatively also, and does away with it; but the thing is at the same time independent for him, and hence he cannot through his negating dispose of it so far as to destroy it, or he *works* it merely. The master on the other hand *gains* through this mediation the *immediate* relation as the pure negation of the thing, or the *enjoyment*; where desire did not succeed, he succeeds, namely in disposing of the thing and in satisfying himself in the enjoyment of it. Desire did not succeed in this on account of the independence of the thing; the master, however, who has interposed the servant between the thing and himself, thereby connects himself only with the non-independence of the thing, and enjoys it in its purity; the facet of independence, on the other hand, he leaves to the servant, who works it.

In these two moments the master has his acknowledgment, or recognition, by another consciousness granted him; for the other consciousness establishes itself in these moments as something inessential, first, in the working of the thing, second, in the dependence upon a particular existence; in both it cannot achieve mastery over being and attain absolute negation. There is therefore present here the following moment of recognition, that the other consciousness does away with itself as being-for-it-self, and so itself does what the other does to it. Likewise the other moment is present, that this doing of the second consciousness is the first's own doing for what the servant does is really the doing of the master; to the latter, solely being-for-himself is the essence; he is the pure negative power to which the thing is nothing, and hence the pure essential doing in this situation; while the servant is not a pure doing, but an inessential one. But for true recognition there is lacking the moment that what the master does to the other he also does to himself, and what the servant does to himself he also does to the other. Thus there has arisen a one-sided and unequal recognizing.

The inessential consciousness is here for the master the object which constitutes the *truth* of the certainty of oneself. But it is evident that this object does not match its concept, and that there where the master has fulfilled himself, he has instead had something quite other than an independent consciousness come to be. It is not such a consciousness that is for him, but a dependent one rather; he is consequently not certain of *being-for-himself* as the truth, and his truth is rather the inessential consciousness, and the inessential doing of the latter.

The *truth* of independent consciousness is accordingly the servile or *subject consciousness*. The latter admittedly appears at first *outside* itself, and not as the truth of self-consciousness. But just as masterhood or dominion, showed that its essence is the converse of what it itself would be, so too, as we shall see, subjection will in its fulfillment turn rather into the contrary of what it is immediately; it will, *qua* consciousness *driven back* into itself, go into itself and turn about to true independence.

We have seen only what subjection is in the context of dominion. But the former is self-consciousness, and accordingly we shall now see what it is in and for itself. First of all, for subjection the master is the essence; hence the *independent consciousness existing for itself* is to subjection *the truth*, which however *for subjection* is not yet *in subjection*. But it has this truth of pure negativity and of *being-for-itself in the event in itself*; for subjection has *experienced* this essence within itself. This consciousness was, namely, not afraid for this or that, or for this instant or that, but for its whole being; for it has felt the fear of death, the absolute lord, or master. In this fear it has been internally broken up, it has been thoroughly shaken in itself, and everything fixed has trembled within it. This pure universal movement, the absolute becoming fluid of all that is permanent, is however the simple essence of self-consciousness, absolute negativity, *pure being-for-itself*, which is consequently *in* this consciousness. This moment of pure being-for-itself is also *for it*, for in the master it has it as its *object*. It is further not merely this universal dissolution *in general*, but in serving it *actually* brings it about; in serving it does away in all *particular* moments with its dependency on natural existence, and works that existence off.

But the feeling of absolute power, in general and in the particulars of service, is only the dissolution *in itself*, and although "the fear of the Lord is the beginning of wisdom," consciousness in this fear is *for its self*, not *being-for-itself*. Through work, however, it comes to itself. In the moment which corresponds to desire in the consciousness of the master, the facet of the inessential relation to the thing seemed to have fallen to the consciousness that serves, inasmuch as in this relation the thing retains its independence. Desire has reserved to itself the pure negating of the object and thereby the unmixed feeling-of-self. This satisfaction is on that account, however, itself just a vanishing, for it lacks the facet of the *object,* or *permanency*. Work by contrast is *contained* desire, *arrested* vanishing, or work *improves*. The negative relation to the object turns into the *form* of the object and into something *enduring,* precisely because to the worker the object has independence. This *negative* center, or the *activity* that forms, or fashions, is at the same time *the particularity*, or the pure being-for-self of consciousness, which now in work steps out of consciousness into the element of permanency; the consciousness that works therefore attains as a consequence a view of independent being *as itself*.

The fashioning has not only this positive significance, however, that in it the consciousness that serves has itself as pure *being-for-itself* become something *existent;* but also a negative significance as against its first moment, the fear. For, in the improving of the thing, the consciousness which serves has its own negativity, its being-for-itself, become object only by doing away with the opposed existent *form*. But this objective, *negative* thing is precisely the alien being before which it trembled. Now, however, it destroys this alien negative thing, sets *itself* as something negative into the element of permanency, and thereby comes to be *for itself,* something *existing-for-itself*. In the master it has being-for-self as *an other,* or as merely *for it;* in the fear being-for-self is *in the consciousness*

itself that serves; in the improving being-for-self comes to be for the consciousness that serves as *its own,* and the latter becomes conscious that it itself is in and for itself. Through being *set outside,* the form does not become to the consciousness that serves something other than the consciousness itself; for it is precisely the form that is its pure being-for-itself, which thereby to consciousness becomes the truth. Through this refinding of itself by itself, then, the consciousness that serves becomes a mind or *sense of its own,* and in the very work in which it seemed to be only *another's* sense. For this reflection both moments, that of fear and service in general, as well as that of improving, are necessary, and at the same time both in a general way. Without the discipline of service and obedience, fear remains at the formal stage, and does not spread itself upon the known reality of concrete existence. Without the improving, fear remains inward and silent, and consciousness does not become for itself. If consciousness fashions, or forms, without the initial absolute fear, it is merely a vain sense of self; for its form or negativity is not negativity *in itself,* and its fashioning cannot therefore give it the consciousness of itself as the essence. If it has not endured absolute fear, but only some anxiety, then it has the negative essence remain something external, its substance has not been infected through and through by the negative essence. Inasmuch as not all aspects of its natural consciousness have become insecure, it still *in itself* belongs to some particular existence; its self-sense is *self-will,* a freedom which as yet remains within subjection. No more than it can have the pure form become essence, no more is the form, regarded as something spread over individual things, a universal cultivating, an absolute concept, but is instead a dexterity which has power over merely some things, not over universal power and the whole objective realm of being.

STUDY QUESTIONS: HEGEL, *PHENOMENOLOGY OF SPIRIT*

1. Why is it important for me, according to Hegel, that you recognize me as being self-conscious?
2. How does self-consciousness come *outside itself?* What is the significance?
3. What is being-for-itself? How is it related to consciousness?
4. What is the role of *immediacy?*
5. What is the simple "I" an absolute object? What does Hegel mean by this?
6. What does he mean by "absolute negativity?"
7. When fear remains "inward and silent," what happens? Is this good or bad? Why?

Philosophy of Mind

Hegel begins by observing, as Kant did, that the notion that all is mind is not readily apparent to the mind. The idea that we are minds that exist within an objective material world consisting of mind-independent material objects is what Kant called the "transcendental illusion." This same illusion, which Hegel sees in a completely different light, he calls by a different name: "estrangement" or "alienation" (*Entfremdung*). What is the difference? For Hegel, the illusion is not an ontological boundary between the mental and non-mental world but is itself created by the mind within the mind. The mind draws a false boundary within itself, against itself, in opposition to itself. For Kant, for the mind to become aware of this illusion is the first necessary step to doing philosophy, which then continues as before, albeit arguably empowered by its wisdom. For Hegel, overcoming the illusion—realizing that what is before the mind is not mind-independent material objects but, itself, mind—is the first necessary step to overcoming the illusion. It is the first part of the thesis-antithesis-synthesis *philosophical revolution* culminating in the mind's return to itself.

Hegel's elaborate philosophy of mind is less a metaphysical theory of mind than it is a logical procedure for carrying out a systematic, revolutionary program into the faculties of human understanding. It can be viewed as an attempt to increase the logical space of the understanding. The aim of Hegel's philosophy of mind is not to transcend the phenomenal world outwardly, to things in themselves, nor inwardly, to the mental faculties of the understanding; the purpose, rather, is to break through the logical categories themselves.

PHILOSOPHY OF MIND: PART THREE OF THE ENCYCLOPAEDIA OF THE PHILOSOPHICAL SCIENCES

INTRODUCTION

377.

The knowledge of mind is the highest and hardest, just because it is the most 'concrete' of sciences. The significance of that 'absolute' commandment, *Know thyself*—whether we look at it in itself or under the historical circumstances of its first utterance—is not to promote mere self-knowledge in respect of the *particular* capacities, character, propensities, and foibles of the single self. The knowledge it commands means that of man's genuine reality—of what is essentially and ultimately true and real—of mind as the true and essential being. Equally little is it the purport of mental philosophy to teach what is called *knowledge of men*—the knowledge whose aim is to detect the *peculiarities*, passions, and foibles of other men, and lay bare what are called the recesses of the human heart. Information of this kind is, for one thing, meaningless, unless on the assumption that we know the *universal*—man as man, and, that always must be, as mind. And for another, being only engaged with casual, insignificant, and *untrue* aspects of mental life, it fails to reach the underlying essence of them all—the mind itself.

378.

Pneumatology, or, as it was also called, rational psychology, has been already alluded to in the Introduction to the Logic as an *abstract* and generalizing metaphysic of the subject. *Empirical* (or inductive) psychology, on the other hand, deals with the 'concrete' mind: and, after the revival of the sciences, when observation and experience had been made the distinctive methods for the study of concrete reality,

---

Hegel, from *the Encyclopedia of Philosophy* translated by William Wallace (Oxford, 1892).

such psychology was worked on the same lines as other sciences. In this way it came about that the metaphysical theory was kept outside the inductive science, and so prevented from getting any concrete embodiment or detail: whilst at the same time the inductive science clung to the conventional commonsense metaphysics with its analysis into forces, various activities, etc., and rejected any attempt at a 'speculative' treatment.

The books of Aristotle on the Soul, along with his discussions on its special aspects and states, are for this reason still by far the most admirable, perhaps even the sole, work of philosophical value on this topic. The main aim of a philosophy of mind can only be to reintroduce unity of idea and principle into the theory of mind, and so reinterpret the lesson of those Aristotelian books.

379.

Even our own sense of the mind's *living* unity naturally protests against any attempt to break it up into different faculties, forces, or, what comes to the same thing, activities, conceived as independent of each other. But the craving for a *comprehension* of the unity is still further stimulated, as we soon come across distinctions between mental freedom and mental determinism, antitheses between free *psychic* agency and the corporeity that lies external to it, whilst we equally note the intimate interdependence of the one upon the other. In modern times especially the phenomena of *animal magnetism* have given, even in experience, a lively and visible confirmation of the underlying unity of soul, and of the power of its 'ideality'. Before these facts, the rigid distinctions of practical common sense are struck with confusion; and the necessity of a 'speculative' examination with a view to the removal of difficulties is more directly forced upon the student.

380.

The 'concrete' nature of mind involves for the observer the peculiar difficulty that the several grades and special types which develop its intelligible unity in detail are not left standing as so many separate existences confronting its more advanced aspects. It is otherwise in external nature. There, matter and movement, for example, have a manifestation all their own—it is the solar system; and similarly the

differentiae of sense-perception have a sort of earlier existence in the properties of *bodies*, and still more independently in the four elements. The species and grades of mental evolution, on the contrary, lose their separate existence and become factors, states, and features in the higher grades of development. As a consequence of this, a lower and more abstract aspect of mind betrays the presence in it, even to experience, of a higher grade. Under the guise of sensation, for example, we may find the very highest mental life as its modification or its embodiment. And so sensation, which is but a mere form and vehicle, may to the superficial glance seem to be the proper seat and, as it were, the source of those moral and religious principles with which it is charged; and the moral and religious principles thus modified may seem to call for treatment as species of sensation. But at the same time, when lower grades of mental life are under examination, it becomes necessary, if we desire to point to actual cases of them in experience, to direct attention to more advanced grades for which they are mere forms. In this way subjects will be treated of by anticipation which properly belong to later stages of development (e.g. in dealing with natural awaking from sleep we speak by anticipation of consciousness, or in dealing with mental derangement we must speak of intellect).

What Mind (or Spirit) Is

381.

From our point of view mind has for its presupposition nature, of which it is the truth, and for that reason its *absolute prius*. In this its truth nature is vanished, and mind has resulted as the 'Idea' entered on possession of itself. Here the subject and object of the Idea are one—either is the intelligent unity, the notion. This identity is *absolute negativity*—for whereas in nature the intelligent unity has its objectivity perfect but externalized, this self-externalization has been nullified and the unity in that way been made one and the same with itself. Thus at the same time it *is* this identity only so far as it is a return out of nature.

382.

For this reason the essential, but formally essential, feature of mind is liberty: that is it is the notion's absolute negativity or self-identity. Considered as this formal aspect, it *may* withdraw itself from everything external and from its own externality, its very existence; it can thus submit to infinite *pain*, the negation of its individual immediacy: in other words, it can keep itself affirmative in this negativity and possess its own identity. All this is possible so long as it is considered in its abstract self-contained universality.

383.

This universality is also its determinate sphere of being. Having a being of its own, the universal is self-particularizing, while it still remains self-identical. Hence the special mode of mental being is 'manifestation'. The spirit is not some one mode or meaning which finds utterance or externality only in a form distinct from itself: it does not manifest or reveal *something*, but its very mode and meaning is this revelation. And thus in its mere possibility mind is at the same moment an infinite, 'absolute', *actuality*.

384.

Revelation, taken to mean the revelation of the *abstract* Idea, is an unmediated transition to nature which *comes* to be. As mind is free, its manifestation is to *set forth* nature as *its* world; but because it is reflection, it, in thus setting forth its world, at the same time *presupposes* the world as a nature independently existing. In the intellectual sphere to reveal is thus to create a world as its being—a being in which the mind procures the affirmation and *truth* of its freedom.

The absolute is mind (spirit)—this is the supreme definition of the absolute. To find this definition and to grasp its meaning and burden was, we may say, the ultimate purpose of all education and all philosophy: it was the point to which turned the impulse of all religion and science: and it is this impulse that must explain the history of the world. The word 'mind' (spirit)—and some glimpse of its meaning—was found at an early period: and the spirituality of God is the lesson of Christianity. It remains for philosophy in its own element of intelligible unity to get hold of what was thus given as a mental image, and what implicitly is the ultimate reality; and that problem is not genuinely, and by rational methods, solved so long as liberty and intelligible unity is not the theme and the soul of philosophy.

Subdivision

385.

The development of mind (spirit) is in three stages:

1. In the form of self-relation: within it it has the *ideal* totality of the idea—that is it has before it all that its notion contains: its being is to be self-contained and free. This is *Mind Subjective*.
2. In the form of *reality*: realized, that is in a *world* produced and to be produced by it: in this world freedom presents itself under the shape of necessity. This is *Mind Objective*.
3. In that unity of mind as objectivity and of mind as ideality and concept, which essentially and actually is and for ever produces itself, mind in its absolute truth. This is *Mind Absolute*.

386.

The two first parts of the doctrine of mind embrace the finite mind. Mind is the infinite idea, and finitude here means the disproportion between the concept and the reality—but with the qualification that it is a shadow cast by the mind's own light—a show or illusion which the mind implicitly imposes as a barrier to itself, in order, by its removal, actually to realize and become conscious of freedom as *its* very being, that is to be fully *manifested*. The several steps of this activity, on each of which, with their semblance of being, it is the function of the finite mind to linger, and through which it has to pass, are steps in its liberation. In the full truth of that liberation is given the identification of the three stages—finding a world presupposed before us, generating a world as our own creation, and gaining freedom from it and in it. To the infinite form of this truth the show purifies itself till it becomes a consciousness of it.

A rigid application of the category of finitude by the abstract logician is chiefly seen in dealing with mind and reason: it is held not a mere matter of strict logic, but treated also as a moral and religious concern, to adhere to the point of view of finitude, and the wish to go further is reckoned a mark of audacity, if not of insanity, of thought. Whereas in fact such a *modesty* of thought, as treats the finite as something altogether fixed and *absolute*, is the worst of virtues; and to stick to a post which has no sound ground in itself is the most unsound sort of theory. The category of finitude was at a much earlier period elucidated and explained at its place in the logic: an elucidation which, as in logic for the more specific though still simple thought-forms of finitude, so in the rest of philosophy for the concrete forms, has merely to show that the finite *is not*, that is is not the truth, but merely a transition and an emergence to something higher. This finitude of the spheres so far examined is the dialectic that makes a thing have its cessation by another and in another: but spirit, the intelligent unity and the *implicit* eternal, is itself just the consummation of that internal act by which nullity is nullified and vanity is made vain. And so, the modesty alluded to is a retention of this vanity—the finite—in opposition to the true: it is itself therefore vanity. In the course of the mind's development we shall see this vanity appear *as wickedness* at that turning-point at which mind has reached its extreme immersion in its subjectivity and its most central contradiction.

SECTION ONE—MIND SUBJECTIVE

387.

Mind, on the ideal stage of its development, is mind as *cognitive*. Cognition, however, being taken here not as a merely logical category of the idea (§ 223), but in the sense appropriate to the *concrete* mind.

Subjective mind is:

a. Immediate or implicit: a soul—the spirit in *nature*—the object treated by *anthropology*.
b. Mediate or explicit: still as identical reflection into itself and into other things: mind in correlation or particularization: consciousness—the object treated by the *Phenomenology of Mind*.
c. Mind defining itself in itself, as an independent subject—the object treated by *psychology*.

In the *soul* is the *awaking of consciousness*: Consciousness sets itself up as reason, awaking at one bound to the sense of its rationality: and this reason by its activity emancipates itself to objectivity and the consciousness of its intelligent unity.

For an intelligible unity or principle of comprehension each modification it presents is an advance of *development*: and so in mind every character under which it appears is a stage in a process of specification and development, a step forward towards its goal, in

order to make itself into, and to realize in itself, what it implicitly is. Each step, again, is itself such a process, and its product is that what the mind was implicitly at the beginning (and so for the observer) it is *for itself*—for the special form, namely which the mind has in that step. The ordinary method of psychology is to narrate what the mind or soul is, what happens to it, what it does. The soul is presupposed as a ready-made agent, which displays such features as its acts and utterances, from which we can learn what it is, what sort of faculties and powers it possesses—all without being aware that the act and utterance of what the soul is really invests it with that character in our conception and makes it reach a higher stage of being than it explicitly had before.

We must, however, distinguish and keep apart from the progress here to be studied what we call education and instruction. The sphere of education is the individuals only: and its aim is to bring the universal mind to exist in them. But in the philosophic theory of mind, mind is studied as self-instruction and self-education in very essence; and its acts and utterances are stages in the process which brings it forward to itself, links it in unity with itself, and so makes it actual mind.

A. Anthropology

The Soul

388.

Spirit (mind) *came into* being as the truth of nature. But not merely is it, as such a result, to be held the true and real first of what went before: this becoming or transition bears in the sphere of the notion the special meaning of '*free judgment*'. Mind, thus come into being, means therefore that nature in its own self realizes its untruth and sets itself aside: it means that mind presupposes itself no longer as the universality which in corporal individuality is always self-externalized, but as a universality which in its concretion and totality is one and simple. At such a stage it is not yet mind, but *soul*.

389.

The soul is no separate immaterial entity. Wherever there is nature, the soul is its universal immaterialism, its simple 'ideal' life. Soul is the *substance* or 'absolute' basis of all the particularizing and individualizing of mind: it is in the soul that mind finds the material on which its character is wrought, and the soul remains the pervading, identical ideality of it all. But as it is still conceived thus abstractly, the soul is only the *sleep* of mind—the passive of Aristotle, which is potentially all things.

The question of the immateriality of the soul has no interest, except where, on the one hand, matter is regarded as something true, and mind conceived as a *thing,* on the other. But in modern times even the physicists have found matters grow thinner in their hands: they have come upon *imponderable* matters, like heat, light, etc., to which they might perhaps add space and time. These 'imponderables', which have lost the property (peculiar to matter) of gravity and, in a sense, even the capacity of offering resistance, have still, however, a sensible existence and outness of part to part; whereas the 'vital' matter, which may also be found enumerated among them, not merely lacks gravity, but even every other aspect of existence which might lead us to treat it as material.

The fact is that in the idea of life the self-externalism of nature is *implicitly* at an end: subjectivity is the very substance and conception of life—with this proviso, however, that its existence or objectivity is still at the same time forfeited to the away of self-externalism. It is otherwise with mind. There, in the intelligible unity which exists as freedom, as absolute negativity, and not as the immediate or natural individual, the object or the reality of the intelligible unity is the unity itself; and so the self-externalism, which is the fundamental feature of matter, has been completely dissipated and transmuted into universality, or the subjective ideality of the conceptual unity. Mind is the existent truth of matter—the truth that matter itself has no truth.

A cognate question is that of the *community of soul and body.* This community (interdependence) was assumed as a *fact,* and the only problem was how to *comprehend* it. The usual answer, perhaps, was to call it an *incomprehensible* mystery; and, indeed, if we take them to be absolutely antithetical and absolutely independent, they are as impenetrable to each other as one piece of matter to another, each being supposed to be found only in the pores of the other, that is where the other is not—whence Epicurus, when

attributing to the gods a residence in the pores, was consistent in not imposing on them any connection with the world. A somewhat different answer has been given by all philosophers since this relation came to be expressly discussed. Descartes, Malebranche, Spinoza, and Leibniz have all indicated God as this *nexus.* They meant that the finitude of soul and matter were only ideal and unreal distinctions; and, so holding, there philosophers took God, not, as so often is done, merely as another word for the incomprehensible, but rather as the sole true identity of finite mind and matter. But either this identity, as in the case of Spinoza, is too abstract, or, as in the case of Leibniz, though his monad of monads brings things into being, it does so only by an act of judgment or choice. Hence, with Leibniz, the result is a distinction between soul and the corporeal (or material), and the identity is only like the *copula* of a judgment, and does not rise or develop into system, into the absolute syllogism.

390.

The Soul is at first

a. In its immediate natural mode—the natural soul, which only is.
b. Secondly, it is a soul which *feels,* as individualized, enters into correlation with its immediate being, and, in the modes of that being, retains an abstract independence.
c. Thirdly, its immediate being—or corporeity—is molded into it, and with that corporeity it exists as *actual* soul.

(a) The Physical Soul

391.

The soul universal, described, it may be, as an *anima mundi,* a world soul, must not be fixed on that account as a single subject; it is rather the universal *substance* which has its actual truth only in individuals and single subjects. Thus, when it presents itself as a single soul, it is a single soul which *is* merely: its only modes are modes of natural life. These have, so to speak, behind its ideality a free existence: that is they are natural objects for consciousness, but objects to which the soul as such does not behave as to something external. These features rather are *physical qualities* of which it finds itself possessed.

(a) Physical Qualities

392.

(1) While still a 'substance' (i.e. a physical soul) the mind takes part in the general planetary life, feels the difference of climates, the changes of the seasons, and the periods of the day, etc. This life of nature for the main shows itself only in occasional strain or disturbance of mental tone.

In recent times a good deal has been said of the cosmic, sidereal, and telluric life of man. In such a sympathy with nature the animals essentially live: their specific characters and their particular phases of growth depend, in many cases completely, and always more or less, upon it. In the case of man these points of dependence lose importance, just in proportion to his civilization, and the more his whole frame of soul is based upon a sub-structure of mental freedom. The history of the world is not bound up with revolutions in the solar system, any more than the destinies of individuals with the positions of the planets.

The difference of climate has a more solid and vigorous influence. But the response to the changes of the seasons and hours of the day is found only in faint changes of mood, which come expressly to the fore only in morbid states (including insanity) and at periods when the self-conscious life suffers depression.

In nations less intellectually emancipated, which therefore live more in harmony with nature, we find amid their superstitions and aberrations of imbecility *a few* real cases of such sympathy, and on that foundation what seems to be marvellous prophetic vision of coming conditions and of events arising therefrom. But as mental freedom gets a deeper hold, even these few and slight susceptibilities, based upon participation in the common life of nature, disappear. Animals and plants, on the contrary, remain forever subject to such influences.

393.

(2) According to the concrete differences of the terrestrial globe, the general planetary life of the nature-governed mind specializes itself and breaks up into the several nature-governed minds which, on the whole, give expression to the nature of the geographical continents and constitute the diversities of *race*.

The contrast between the earth's poles, the land towards the north pole being more aggregated and preponderant over sea, whereas in the southern hemisphere it runs out in sharp points, widely distant from each other, introduces into the differences of continents a further modification which Treviranus (*Biology*, Part II) has exhibited in the case of the flora and fauna.

394.

This diversity descends into specialities, that may be termed *local* minds—shown in the outward modes of life and occupation, bodily structure and disposition, but still more in the inner tendency and capacity of the intellectual and moral character of the several peoples.

Back to the very beginnings of national history we see the several nations each possessing a persistent type of its own.

395.

(3) The soul is further de-universalized into the individualized subject. But this subjectivity is here only considered as a differentiation and singling out of the modes which nature gives; we find it as the special temperament, talent, character, physiognomy, or other disposition and idiosyncrasy, of families or single individuals.

(b) Physical Alterations

396.

Taking the soul as an individual, we find its diversities, as alterations in it, the one permanent subject, and as stages in its development. As they are at once physical and mental diversities, a more concrete definition or description of them would require us to anticipate an acquaintance with the formed and matured mind.

(1) The first of these is the natural lapse of the ages in man's life. He begins with *Childhood*—mind wrapped up in itself. His next step is the fully developed antithesis, the strain and struggle of a universality which is still subjective (as seen in ideals, fancies, hopes, ambitions) against his immediate individuality. And that individuality marks both the world which, as it exists, fails to meet his ideal requirements, and the position of the individual himself, who is still short of independence and not fully

equipped for the part he has to play (*youth*). Thirdly, we see man in his true relation to his environment, recognizing the objective necessity and reasonableness of the world as he finds it—a world no longer incomplete, but able in the work which it collectively achieves to afford the individual a place and a security for his performance. By his share in this collective work he first is really *somebody*, gaining an effective existence and an objective value (*manhood*). Last of all comes the finishing touch to this unity with objectivity: a unity which, while on its realist side it passes into the *inertia* of deadening habit, on its idealist side gains freedom from the limited interests and entanglements of the outward present (*old age*).

397.

(2) Next we find the individual subject to a real antithesis, leading it to seek and find *itself* in *another* individual. This—the *sexual* relation—on a physical basis, shows, on its one side, subjectivity remaining in an instinctive and emotional harmony of moral life and love, and not pushing these tendencies to an extreme universal phase, in purposes political, scientific, or artistic; and on the other, shows an active half, where the individual is the vehicle of a struggle of universal and objective interests with the given conditions (both of his own existence and of that of the external world), carrying out these universal principles into a unity with the world which is his own work. The sexual tie acquires its moral and spiritual significance and function in the *family*.

398.

(3) When the individuality, or self-centralized being, distinguishes itself from its mere being, this immediate judgement is the *waking* of the soul, which confronts its self-absorbed natural life, in the first instance, as one natural quality and state confronts another state, namely *sleep*. The waking is not merely for the observer, or externally distinct from the sleep: it is itself the *judgment* (primary partition) of the individual soul—which is self-existing only as it relates its self-existence to its mere existence, distinguishing itself from its still undifferentiated universality. The waking state includes generally all self-conscious and rational activity in which the mind realizes its own distinct self. Sleep is an invigoration of this activity—

not as a merely negative rest from it, but as a return back from the world of specialization, from dispersion into phases where it has grown hard and stiff—a return into the general nature of subjectivity, which is the substance of those specialized energies and their absolute master.

The distinction between sleep and waking is one of those *posers*, as they may be called, which are often addressed to philosophy: Napoleon, for example, on a visit to the University of Pavia, put this question to the class of ideology. The characterization given in the section is abstract; it primarily treats waking merely as a natural fact, containing the mental element *implicate* but not yet as invested with a special being of its own. If we are to speak more concretely of this distinction (in fundamentals it remains the same), we must take the self-existence of the individual soul in its higher aspects as the ego of consciousness and as intelligent mind. The difficulty raised anent the distinction of the two states properly arises, only when we also take into account the dreams in sleep and describe these dreams, as well as the mental representations in the sober waking consciousness under one and the same title of mental representations. Thus superficially classified as states of mental representation the two coincide, because we have lost sight of the difference; and in the case of any assignable distinction of waking consciousness, we can always return to the trivial remark that all this is nothing more than mental idea. But the concrete theory of the waking soul in its realized being views it as *consciousness* and *intellect*: and the world of intelligent consciousness is something quite different from a picture of mere ideas and images. The latter are in the main only externally conjoined, in an unintelligent way, by the laws of the so-called *association of ideas*; though here and there of course logical principles may also be operative. But in the waking state man behaves essentially as a concrete ego, an intelligence: and because of this intelligence his sense-perception stands before him as a concrete totality of features in which each member, each point, takes up its place as at the same time determined through and with all the rest. Thus the facts embodied in his sensation are authenticated, not by his mere subjective representation and distinction of the facts as something external from the person, but by virtue of the concrete interconnection in which each part stands with all parts of this complex. The waking state is the concrete consciousness of this mutual corroboration of each single factor of its content by all the others in the picture as perceived. The consciousness of this interdependence need not be explicit and distinct. Still, this general setting to all sensations is implicitly present in the concrete feeling of self. In order to see the difference between dreaming and waking we need only keep in view the Kantian distinction between subjectivity and objectivity of mental representation (the latter depending upon determination through categories): remembering, as already noted, that what is actually present in mind need not be therefore explicitly realized in consciousness, just as little as the exaltation of the intellectual sense to God need stand before consciousness in the shape of proofs of God's existence, although, as before explained, these proofs only serve to express the net worth and content of that feeling. . . .

B. PHENOMENOLOGY OF MIND

Consciousness

413.

Consciousness constitutes the reflected or correlational grade of mind: the grade of mind as *appearance*. *Ego* is infinite self-relation of mind, but as subjective or as self-certainty. The immediate identity of the natural soul has been raised to this pure 'ideal' self-identity; and what the former *contained* is for this self-subsistent reflection set forth as an *object*. The pure abstract freedom of mind lets go from it its specific qualities—the soul's natural life—to an equal freedom as an independent *object*. It is of this latter, as external to it, that the *ego* is in the first instance aware (conscious), and as such it is consciousness. Ego, as this absolute negativity, is implicitly the identity in the otherness: the *ego* is itself that other and stretches over the object (as if that object were implicitly cancelled)—it is one side of the relationship and the whole relationship—the light, which manifests itself and something else too.

414.

The self-identity of the mind, thus first made explicit as the ego, is only its abstract formal ideality. As *soul* it was under the phase *of substantial* universality; now, as subjective reflection in itself, it is referred to this substantiality as to its negative, something dark and

beyond it. Hence consciousness, like reciprocal dependence in general, is the contradiction between the independence of the two sides and their identity in which they are merged into one. The mind as ego is *essence*; but since reality, in the sphere of essence, is represented as in immediate being and at the same time as 'ideal', it is as consciousness only the *appearance* (phenomenon) of mind.

415.

As the ego is by itself only a formal identity, the dialectical movement of its intelligible unity, that is the successive steps in further specification of consciousness, does not, to it, seem to be its own activity, but is implicit, and to the ego it seems an alteration of the object. Consciousness consequently appears differently modified according to the difference of the given object; and the gradual specification of consciousness appears as a variation in the characteristics of its objects. Ego, the subject of consciousness, is thinking: the logical process of modifying the object is what is identical in subject and object, their absolute interdependence, what makes the object the subject's own.

The Kantian philosophy may be most accurately described as having viewed the mind as consciousness, and as containing the propositions only of a *phenomenology* (not of a *philosophy*) of mind. The ego Kant regards as reference to something away and beyond (which in its abstract description is termed the thing-in-itself); and it is only from this finite point of view that he treats both intellect and will. Though in the notion of a power of *reflective* judgment he touches upon the *idea* of mind—a subject-objectivity, an *intuitive intellect*, etc., and even the idea of nature, still this Idea is again deposed to an appearance, that is to a subjective maxim (§ 58). Reinhold may therefore be said to have correctly appreciated Kantism when he treated it as a theory of consciousness (under the name of 'faculty of ideation'). Fichte kept to the same point of view: his non-ego is only something set over against the ego, only defined as in *consciousness*: it is made no more than an infinite 'shock', that is a thing-in-itself. Both systems therefore have clearly not reached the intelligible unity or the mind as it actually and essentially is, but only as it is in reference to something else.

As against Spinozism, again, it is to be noted that the mind in the judgement by which it 'constitutes' itself an ego (a free subject contrasted with its qualitative affection) has emerged from substance, and that the philosophy, which gives this judgement as the absolute characteristic of mind, has emerged from Spinozism.

416.

The aim of conscious mind is to make its appearance identical with its essence, to raise its *self-certainty to truth*. The *existence of* mind in the stage of consciousness is finite, because it is merely a nominal self-relation, or mere certainty. The object is only abstractly characterized as *its*; in other words, in the object it is only as an abstract ego that the mind is reflected into itself: hence its existence there has still a content, which is not as its own.

417.

The grades of this elevation of certainty to truth are three in number: first (a) consciousness in general, with an object set against it; (b) self-consciousness, for which *ego* is the object; (c) unity of consciousness and self-consciousness, where the mind sees itself embodied in the object and sees itself as implicitly and explicitly determinate, as reason, the *notion* of mind.

(a) Consciousness Proper

(a) Sensuous consciousness

418.

Consciousness is, first, *immediate* consciousness, and its reference to the object accordingly the simple, and underived certainty of it. The object similarly, being immediate, an existent, reflected in itself, is further characterized as immediately singular. This is sense-consciousness.

Consciousness—as a case of correlation—comprises only the categories belonging to the abstract ego or formal thinking; and these it treats as features of the object (§ 415). Sense-consciousness therefore is aware of the object as an existent, a something, an existing thing, a singular, and so on. It appears as wealthiest in matter, but as poorest in thought. That wealth of matter is made out of sensations: they are the *material* of consciousness (§ 414), the substantial

and qualitative, what the soul in its anthropological sphere is and finds *in itself*. This material the ego (the reflection of the soul in itself) separates from itself, and puts it first under the category of being. Spatial and temporal singularness, *here* and *now* (the terms by which in the *Phenomenology of the Mind*, I described the object of sense-consciousness) strictly belongs to *intuition*. At present the object is at first to be viewed only in its correlation to *consciousness*, that is a something *external* to it, and not yet as external on its own part, or as being beside and out of itself.

419.

The *sensible* as somewhat becomes an *other*: the reflection in itself of this *somewhat*, the *thing*, has *many* properties; and as a single (thing) in its immediacy has several *predicates*. The muchness of the sense-singular thus becomes a breadth—a variety of relations, reflectional attributes, and universalities. These are logical terms introduced by the thinking principle, that is in this case by the ego, to describe the sensible. But the ego as itself apparent sees in all this characterization a change in the object; and sensuous consciousness, so construing the object, is sense-perception.

(b) Sense-perception

420.

Consciousness, having passed beyond the sensible, wants to take the object in its truth, not as merely immediate, but as mediated, reflected in itself, and universal. Such an object is a combination of sense qualities with attributes of wider range by which thought defines concrete relations and connections. Hence the identity of consciousness with the object passes from the abstract identity of 'I am sure' to the definite identity of 'I know, and am aware'.

The particular grade of consciousness on which Kantism conceives the mind is perception: which is also the general point of view taken by ordinary consciousness, and more or less by the sciences. The sensuous certitudes of single apperceptions or observations form the starting-point: these are supposed to be elevated to truth, by being regarded in their bearings, reflected upon, and on the lines of definite categories turned at the same time into something necessary and universal, namely *experiences*.

421.

This conjunction of individual and universal is admixture—the individual remains at the bottom hard and unaffected by the universal, to which, however, it is related. It is therefore a tissue of contradictions—between the single things of sense apperception, which form the alleged ground of general experience, and the universality which has a higher claim to be the essence and ground—between the individuality of a thing which, taken in its concrete content, constitutes its independence and the various properties which, free from this negative link and from one another, are independent universal *matters*. This contradiction of the finite which runs through all forms of the logical spheres turns out most concrete, when the somewhat is defined as *object* (§§ 194 seqq.).

(c) The Intellect

422.

The proximate truth of perception is that it is the object which is an *appearance,* and that the object's reflection in self is on the contrary a self-subsistent inward and universal. The consciousness of such an object is *intellect*. This inward, as we called it, of the thing is, on one hand, the suppression of the multiplicity of the sensible, and, in that manner, an abstract identity: on the other hand, however, it also for that reason contains the multiplicity, but as an interior 'simple' difference, which remains self-identical in the vicissitudes of appearance. The simple difference is the realm of *the laws* of the phenomena—a copy of the phenomenon, but brought to rest and universality.

423.

The law, at first stating the mutual dependence of universal, permanent terms, has, in so far as its distinction is the inward one, its necessity on its own part; the one of the terms, as not externally different from the other, lies immediately in the other. But in this manner the interior distinction is, what it is in truth, the distinction on its own part, or the distinction which is none. With this new form-characteristic, on the whole, consciousness *implicitly* vanishes: for consciousness as such implies the reciprocal independence of subject and object. The ego in its judgment has an object which is not distinct from it—it has itself. Consciousness has passed into self-consciousness.

(b) Self-Consciousness

424.

Self-consciousness is the truth of consciousness: the latter is a consequence of the former, all consciousness of another object being as a matter of fact also self-consciousness. The object is my idea: I am aware of the object as mine; and thus in it I am aware of me. The formula of self-consciousness is I = I: abstract freedom, pure 'ideality'; and thus it lacks 'reality'. For as it is its own object, there is strictly speaking no object, because there is no distinction between it and the object.

425.

Abstract self-consciousness is the first negation of consciousness, and for that reason it is burdened with an external object, or, nominally, with the negation of it. Thus it is at the same time the antecedent stage, consciousness: it is the contradiction of itself as self-consciousness and as consciousness. But the latter aspect and the negation in general is in I = I potentially suppressed; and hence as this certitude of self against the object it is the *impulse* to realize its implicit nature, by giving its abstract self-awareness content and objectivity, and in the other direction to free itself from its sensuousness, to set aside the given objectivity and identify it with itself. The two processes are one and the same, the identification of its consciousness and self-consciousness.

(a) Appetite or Instinctive Desire

426.

Self-consciousness, in its immediacy, is a singular, and a desire (appetite)—the contradiction implied in its abstraction which should yet be objective—or in its immediacy which has the shape of an external object and should be subjective. The certitude of one's self, which issues from the suppression of mere consciousness, pronounces the *object* null: and the outlook of self-consciousness towards the object equally qualifies the abstract ideality of such self-consciousness as null.

427.

Self-consciousness, therefore, knows itself implicit in the object, which in this outlook is conformable to the appetite. In the negation of the two one-sided moments by the ego's own activity, this identity comes to be *for* the ego. To this activity the object, which implicitly and for self-consciousness is self-less, can make no resistance: the dialectic, implicit in it, towards self-suppression exists in this case as that activity of the ego. Thus while the given object is rendered subjective, the subjectivity divests itself of its one-sidedness and becomes objective to itself.

428.

The product of this process is the fast conjunction of the ego with itself, its satisfaction realized, and itself made actual. On the external side it continues, in this return upon itself, primarily describable as an individual, and maintains itself as such; because its bearing upon the self-less object is purely negative, the latter, therefore, being merely consumed. Thus appetite in its satisfaction is always destructive, and in its content selfish: and as the satisfaction has only happened in the individual (and that is transient) the appetite is again generated in the very act of satisfaction.

429.

But on the inner side, or implicitly, the sense of self which the ego gets in the satisfaction does not remain in abstract self-concentration or in mere individuality; on the contrary—as negation of *immediacy* and individuality the result involves a character of universality and of the identity of self-consciousness with its object. The judgment or direction of this self-consciousness is the consciousness of a *'free'* object, in which ego is aware of itself as an ego, which however is *also* still outside it.

(b) Self-consciousness Recognitive

430.

Here there is a self-consciousness for a self-consciousness, at first *immediately*, as one of two things for another. In that other as ego I behold myself, and yet also an immediately existing object, another ego absolutely independent of me and opposed to me. (The suppression of the singleness of self-consciousness was only a first step in the suppression, and it merely led to the characterization of it as *particular*.) This contradiction gives either self-consciousness the impulse to *show* itself as a free self, and to exist as such for the other: the process of *recognition*.

431.

The process is a battle. I cannot be aware of me as myself in another individual, so long as I see in that other an other and an immediate existence: and I am consequently bent upon the suppression of this immediacy of his. But in like measure I cannot be recognized as immediate, except so far as I overcome the mere immediacy on my own part, and thus give existence to my freedom. But this immediacy is at the same time the corporeity of self-consciousness, in which as in its sign and tool the latter has its own *sense of self,* and its being *for others*, and the means for entering into relation with them.

432.

The fight of recognition is a life and death struggle: either self-consciousness imperils the other's life, and incurs a like peril for its own—but only peril, for either is no less bent on maintaining his life, as the existence of his freedom. Thus the death of one, though by the abstract, therefore rude, negation of immediacy, it, from one point of view, solves the contradiction, is yet, from the essential point of view (i.e. the outward and visible recognition), a new contradiction (for that recognition is at the same time undone by the other's death) and a greater than the other.

433.

But because life is as requisite as liberty to the solution, the fight ends in the first instance as a one-sided negation with inequality. While the one combatant prefers life, retains his single self-consciousness, but surrenders his claim for recognition, the other holds fast to his self-assertion and is recognized by the former as his superior. Thus arises the status of *master and slave*.

In the battle for recognition and the subjugation under a master, we see, on their phenomenal side, the emergence of man's social life and the commencement of political union. *Force*, which is the basis of this phenomenon, is not on that account a basis of right, but only the necessary and legitimate factor in the passage from the state of self-consciousness sunk in appetite and selfish isolation into the state of universal self-consciousness. Force, then, is the external or phenomenal commencement of states, not their underlying and essential principle.

434.

This status, in the first place, implies *common* wants and common concern for their satisfaction—for the means of mastery, the slave, must likewise be kept in life. In place of the rude destruction of the immediate object there ensues acquisition, preservation, and formation of it, as the instrumentality in which the two extremes of independence and non-independence are welded together. The form of universality thus arising in satisfying the want, creates a *permanent* means and a provision which takes care for and secures the future.

435.

But secondly, when we look to the distinction of the two, the master beholds in the slave and his servitude the supremacy of his *single* self-hood resulting from the suppression of immediate self-hood, a suppression, however, which falls on another. This other, the slave, however, in the service of the master, works off his individualist self-will, overcomes the inner immediacy of appetite, and in this divestment of self and in 'the fear of his lord' makes 'the beginning of wisdom'—the passage to universal self-consciousness.

(c) Universal Self-consciousness

436.

Universal self-consciousness is the affirmative awareness of self in an other self: each self as a free individuality has his own 'absolute' independence, yet in virtue of the negation of its immediacy or appetite without distinguishing itself from that other. Each is thus universal self-consciousness and objective; each has 'real' universality in the shape of reciprocity, so far as each knows itself recognized in the other freeman, and is aware of this in so far as it recognizes the other and knows him to be free.

This universal reappearance of self-consciousness—the notion which is aware of itself in its objectivity as a subjectivity identical with itself and for that reason universal—is the form of consciousness which lies at the root of all true mental or spiritual life—in family, fatherland, state, and of all virtues, love, friendship, valor, honor, fame. But this appearance of the underlying essence may also be severed from that essence, and be maintained apart in worthless honor, idle fame, etc.

437.

This unity of consciousness and self-consciousness implies in the first instance the individuals mutually throwing light upon each other. But the difference between those who are thus identified is mere vague diversity—or rather it is a difference which is none. Hence its truth is the fully and really existent universality and objectivity of self-consciousness—which is *reason*.

Reason, as the *idea* as it here appears, is to be taken as meaning that the distinction between notion and reality which it unifies has the special aspect of a distinction between the self-concentrated notion or consciousness, and the object subsisting external and opposed to it.

(c) Reason

438.

The essential and actual truth which reason is, lies in the simple identity of the subjectivity of the notion with its objectivity and universality. The universality of reason, therefore, whilst it signifies that the object, which was only given in consciousness qua consciousness, is now itself universal, permeating and encompassing the ego, also signifies that the pure ego is the pure form which overlaps the object and encompasses it.

439.

Self-consciousness, thus certified that its determinations are no less objective, or determinations of the very being of things, than they are its own thoughts, is reason, which as such an identity is not only the absolute *substance*, but the truth that knows it. For truth here has, as its peculiar mode and immanent form, the self-centered pure notion, ego, the certitude of self as infinite universality. Truth, aware of what it is, is mind (spirit).

STUDY QUESTIONS: HEGEL, *PHILOSOPHY OF MIND*

1. What is the truth that consciousness learns from skepticism?
2. What does Hegel mean by self-ignorance? What is its cause?
3. What is the unhappy and broken consciousness?
4. What are our "two selves?" Why are they at war? Can we do anything about it?

5. What is the true self?
6. What is the changeless consciousness?
7. What is the divided consciousness?
8. What is Hegel's critique of the Stoic philosophers?
9. How can consciousness free itself?
10. What is the significance of "Know thyself?" Why is this the "absolute" commandment?
11. What is Rational Psychology?
12. Why does Hegel admire most about Aristotle's *On the Soul*?
13. What is the "concrete" nature of mind?
14. What is the mind, according to Hegel?
15. What does Hegel mean by *spirit*?
16. What are the three stages in the development of mind?
17. What does Hegel mean by "subjective" mind? With what is this contrasted? What is the significance of the distinction?
18. How did mind come into being?
19. What does Hegel mean by "free judgment," and what role does this play in his philosophy?
20. How is the soul related to what Aristotle, Aquinas, and Averroës called the passive intellect?
21. What does Hegel mean by *physical soul*?
22. What does Hegel mean by *substance*? What role does this concept play in relation to the mind?
23. Is the soul, according to Hegel, an individual? Why?
24. How is the soul "de-universalized" into the individualized subject?
25. What is the one permanent subject among the diversities of the soul?
26. How is the "sexual relation" stage of life related to Hegel's overall metaphysical conception?
27. What role does the Humean notion of the association of ideas play in his view of consciousness?
28. How does Hegel distinguish dreaming from waking states? Would Descartes agree or disagree? Why?
29. Why is the aim of conscious mind to make its appearance identical with its essence? How is this achieved?
30. What is the main weakness of Kant's *phenomenology* of mind, from Hegel's point of view?
31. Which aspects of Spinoza's conception of mind does Hegel accept, and which does he reject? Why?
32. How does Hegel distinguish self-consciousness from consciousness?
33. What is abstract self-consciousness? Why does Hegel define it as a negation?
34. What is universal self-consciousness? What role does freedom play?

LOGIC

Hegel uses Aristotle's logic to move into the realm of a higher logic in which contradictions are not errors but a revolutionary method of evolution. By "Logic" Hegel meant not formal logic but what he calls "the science of thought." In his view, since only thought exists, logic is neither psychological nor mathematical but metaphysical: "The Living Being is a syllogism whose very moments are syllogisms." Thinking itself is not merely an intellectual or psychological process in which a philosopher engages with other philosophers or with students; it is the very source and foundation of reality: "Being is thought."

1.

Philosophy misses an advantage enjoyed by the other sciences. It cannot like them rest the existence of its objects on the natural admissions of consciousness, nor can it assume that its method of cognition, either for starting or for continuing, is one already accepted. The objects of philosophy, it is true, are upon the whole the same as those of religion. In both the object is truth, in that supreme sense in which God and God only is the truth. Both in like manner go on to treat of the finite worlds of nature and the human mind, with their relation to each other and to their truth in God. Some *acquaintance* with its objects, therefore, philosophy may and even must presume, that and a certain interest in them to boot, were it for no other reason than this: that in point of time the mind makes general *images* of objects, long before it makes *notions* of them and that it is only through these mental images, and by recourse to them, that the thinking mind rises to know and comprehend *thinkingly.*

But with the rise of this thinking study of things, it soon becomes evident that thought will be satisfied with nothing short of showing the *necessity* of its facts, of demonstrating the existence of its objects, as well as their nature and qualities. Our original acquaintance with them is thus discovered to be inadequate. We can assume nothing, and assert nothing dogmatically: nor can we accept the assertions and assumptions of others. And yet we must make a beginning: and a beginning, as primary and underived, makes an assumption, or rather is an assumption. It seems as if it were impossible to make a beginning at all.

2.

This *thinking study of things* may serve, in a general way, as a description of philosophy. But the description is too wide. If it be correct to say, that thought makes the distinction between man and the lower animals, then everything human is human, for the sole and simple reason that it is due to the operation of thought. Philosophy, on the other hand, is a peculiar mode of thinking—a mode in which thinking becomes knowledge, and knowledge through notions.

However great therefore may be the identity and essential unity of the two modes of thought, the philosophic mode gets to be different from the more general thought which acts in all that is human, in all that gives humanity its distinctive character. And this difference connects itself with the fact that the strictly human and thought-induced phenomena of consciousness do not originally appear in the form of a thought, but as a feeling, a perception, or mental image—all of which aspects must be distinguished from the form of thought proper.

11.

The special conditions which call for the existence of philosophy may be thus described. The mind or spirit, when it is sentient or perceptive, finds its object in something sensuous; when it imagines, in a picture or image; when it wills, in an aim or end. But in contrast to, or it may be only in distinction from, these forms of its existence and of its objects, the mind has also to gratify the cravings of its highest and most inward life. That innermost self is thought. Thus the mind renders thought its object. In the best meaning of the phrase, it comes to itself; for thought is its principle, and its very unadulterated self. But while thus occupied, thought entangles itself in contradictions, that is loses itself in the hard-and-fast non-identity of its thoughts, and so, instead of reaching itself, is caught and held in its counterpart. This result, to which honest but narrow thinking leads the mere understanding, is resisted by the loftier craving of which we have spoken. That craving expresses the perseverance of thought, which continues true to itself, even in this conscious loss of its native rest and independence, "that it may overcome" and work out in itself the solution of its own contradictions.

To see that thought in its very nature is dialectical, and that, as understanding, it must fall into contradiction—the negative of itself, will form one of the main lessons of logic. When thought grows hopeless of ever achieving, by its own means, the solution of the contradiction which it has by its own action brought upon itself, it turns back to those solutions of

---

From *The Logic of Hegel*, 2d rev. ed., translated by William Wallace, (Oxford: Clarendon Press, 1892).

the question with which the mind had learned to pacify itself in some of its other modes and forms. Unfortunately, however, the retreat of thought has led it, as Plato noticed even in his time, to a very uncalled-for hatred of reason (misology); and it then takes up against its own endeavors that hostile attitude of which an example is seen in the doctrine that "immediate" knowledge, as it is called, is the exclusive form in which we become cognizant of truth.

12.

The rise of philosophy is due to these cravings of thought. Its point of departure is experience; including under that name both our immediate consciousness and the inductions from it. Awakened, as it were, by this stimulus, thought is vitally characterized by raising itself above the natural state of mind, above the senses and inferences from the senses into its own unadulterated element, and by assuming, accordingly, at first a stand-aloof and negative attitude towards the point from which it started. Through this state of antagonism to the phenomena of sense its first satisfaction is found in itself, in the idea of the universal essence of these phenomena: an idea (the Absolute, or God) which may be more or less abstract. Meanwhile, on the other hand, the sciences, based on experience, exert upon the mind a stimulus to overcome the form in which their varied contents are presented, and to elevate these contents to the rank of necessary truth. For the facts of science have the aspect of a vast conglomerate, one thing coming side by side with another, as if they were merely given and presented—as in short devoid of all essential or necessary connection. In consequence of this stimulus thought is dragged out of its unrealized universality and its fancied or merely possible satisfaction, and impelled onwards to a development from itself. On one hand this development only means that thought incorporates the contents of science, in all their specialty of detail as submitted. On the other it makes these contents imitate the action of the original creative thought, and present the aspect of a free evolution determined by the logic of the fact alone.

15.

Each of the parts of philosophy is a philosophical whole, a circle rounded and complete in itself. In each of these parts, however, the philosophical idea is found in a particular specificality or medium. The single circle, because it is a real totality, bursts through the limits imposed by its special medium, and gives rise to a wider circle. The whole of philosophy in this way resembles a circle of circles. The idea appears in each single circle, but, at the same time, the whole idea is constituted by the system of these peculiar phases, and each is a necessary member of the organisation.

17.

It may seem as if philosophy, in order to start on its course, had, like the rest of the sciences, to begin with a subjective presupposition. The sciences postulate their respective objects, such as space, number, or whatever it be; and it might be supposed that philosophy had also to postulate the existence of thought. But the two cases are not exactly parallel. It is by the free act of thought that it occupies a point of view, in which it is for its own self, and thus gives itself an object of its own production. Nor is this all. The very point of view, which originally is taken on its own evidence only, must in the course of the science be convened to a result—the ultimate result in which philosophy returns into itself and reaches the point with which it began. In this manner philosophy exhibits the appearance of a circle which closes with itself, and has no beginning in the same way as the other sciences have. To speak of a beginning of philosophy has a meaning only in relation to a person who proposes to commence the study, and not in relation to the science as science. The same thing may be thus expressed. The notion of science—the notion therefore with which we start—which, for the very reason that it is initial, implies a separation between the thought which is our object, and the subject philosophising which is, as it were, external to the former, must be grasped and comprehended by the science itself. This is in short the one single aim, action, and goal of philosophy—to arrive at the notion of its notion, and thus secure its return and its satisfaction.

18.

As the whole science, and only the whole, can exhibit what the idea or system of reason is, it is impossible to give in a preliminary way a general impression of a philosophy. Nor can a division of philosophy into its parts be intelligible, except in connection with the system. A preliminary division, like the limited conception from which it comes, can only be an anticipation. Here however it is premised that the idea turns out to be the thought which is completely identical with itself, and not identical simply in the abstract, but also in its action of setting itself over against itself, so as to gain a being of its own, and yet of being in full possession of itself while it is in this other. Thus philosophy is subdivided into three parts:

I. Logic: the science of the idea in and for itself.

II. The philosophy of nature: the science of the idea in its otherness.

III. The philosophy of mind: the science of the idea come back to itself out of that otherness.

As observed in § 15, the differences between the several philosophical sciences are only aspects or specializations of the one idea or system of reason, which and which alone is alike exhibited in these different media. In nature nothing else would have to be discerned, except the idea: but the idea has here divested itself of its proper being. In mind, again, the idea has asserted a being of its own, and is on the way to become absolute. Every such form in which the idea is expressed, is at the same time a passing or fleeting stage: and hence each of these subdivisions has not only to know its contents as an object which has being for the time, but also in the same act to expound how these contents pass into their higher circle. To represent the relation between them as a division, therefore, leads to misconception: for it coordinates the several parts or sciences one beside another, as if they had no innate development, but were, like so many species, really and radically distinct.

CHAPTER II

Preliminary Notion

19.

Logic is the science of the pure idea; pure, that is, because the idea is in the abstract medium of thought.

This definition, and the others which occur in these introductory outlines, are derived from a survey of the whole system, to which accordingly they are subsequent. The same remark applies to all prefatory notions whatever about philosophy.

Logic might have been defined as the science of thought, and of its laws and characteristic forms. But thought, as thought, constitutes only the general medium, or qualifying circumstance, which renders the idea distinctively logical. If we identify the idea with thought, thought must not be taken in the sense of a method or form, but in the sense of the self-developing totality of its laws and peculiar terms. These laws are the work of thought itself, and not a fact which it finds and must submit to.

From different points of view, logic is either the hardest or the easiest of the sciences. Logic is hard, because it has to deal not with perceptions, nor, like geometry, with abstract representations of the senses, but with pure abstractions; and because it demands a force and facility of withdrawing into pure thought, of keeping firm hold on it, and of moving in such an element. Logic is easy, because its facts are nothing but our own thought and its familiar forms or terms: and these are the acmé of simplicity, the a b c of everything else. They are also what we are best acquainted with: such as, "Is" and "Is not"; quality and magnitude; being potential and being actual; one, many, and so on. But such an acquaintance only adds to the difficulties of the study; for while, on the one hand, we naturally think it is not worth our trouble to occupy ourselves any longer with things so familiar, on the other hand, the problem is to become acquainted with them in a new way, quite opposite to that in which we know them already.

The utility of logic is a matter which concerns its bearings upon the student, and the training it may give for other purposes. This logical training consists in the exercise of thinking which the student has to go through (this science is the thinking of thinking): and in the fact that he stores his head with thoughts in their native unalloyed character. It is true that logic, being the absolute form of truth, and another name for the very truth itself, is something more than merely useful. Yet if what is noblest, most liberal and most independent is also most useful, logic has some claim to the latter character. Its utility must then be estimated at another rate than exercise in thought for the sake of the exercise.

◆ ◆ ◆

24.

With these explanations and qualifications, thoughts may be termed objective thoughts—among which are also to be included the forms which are more especially discussed in the common logic, where they are usually treated as forms of conscious thought only. *Logic therefore coincides with metaphysics, the science of things set and held in thoughts*—thoughts accredited able to express the essential reality of things.

(2) Logic is the study of thought pure and simple, or of the pure thought-forms. In the ordinary sense of the term, by thought we generally represent to ourselves something more than simple and unmixed thought; we mean some thought, the material of which is from experience. Whereas in logic a thought is understood to include nothing else but what depends on thinking and what thinking has brought into existence. It is in these circumstances that thoughts are *pure* thoughts. The mind is then in its own home-element and therefore free: for freedom means that the other thing with which you deal is a second self—so that you never leave your own ground but give the law to yourself. In the impulses or appetites the beginning is from something else, from something which we fed to be external. In this case then we speak of dependence. For freedom it is necessary that we should feel no presence of something else which is not ourselves. The natural man, whose motions follow the rule only of his appetites, is not his own master. Be he as self-willed as he may, the constituents of his will and opinion are not his own, and his freedom is merely formal. But when we *think,* we renounce our selfish and particular being, sink ourselves in the thing, allow thought to follow its own course—and, if we add anything of our own, we think ill.

If in pursuance of the foregoing remarks we consider logic to be the system of the pure types of thought, we find that the other philosophical sciences, the philosophy of nature and the philosophy of mind, take the place, as it were, of an applied logic, and that logic is the soul which animates them both. Their problem in that case is only to recognize the logical forms under the shapes they assume in nature and mind—shapes which are only a particular mode of expression for the forms of pure thought. If for instance we take the syllogism (not as it was understood in the old formal logic, but at its real value), we shall find it gives expression to the law that the particular is the middle term which fuses together the extremes of the universal and the singular. The syllogistic form is a universal form of all things. Everything that exists is a particular, which couples together the universal and the singular. But nature is weak and fails to exhibit the logical forms in their purity. Such a feeble exemplification of the syllogism may be seen in the magnet. In the middle or point of indifference of a magnet, its two poles, however they may be distinguished, are brought into one. Physics also teaches us to see the universal or essence in nature: and the only difference between it and the philosophy of nature is that the latter brings before our mind the adequate forms of the notion in the physical world.

It will now be understood that logic is the all-animating spirit of all the sciences, and its categories the spiritual hierarchy. They are the heart and center of things: and yet at the same time they are always on our lips, and, apparently at least, perfectly familiar objects. But things thus familiar are usually the greatest strangers. Being, for example, is a category of pure thought: but to make "is" an object of investigation never occurs to us. Common fancy puts the absolute far away in a world beyond. The absolute is rather directly before us, so present that so long as we think, we must, though without express consciousness of it, always carry it with us and always use it. Language is the main depository of these types of thought; and one use of the grammatical instruction which children receive is unconsciously to turn their attention to distinctions of thought.

◆ ◆ ◆

To ask if a category is true or not, must sound strange to the ordinary mind: for a category apparently becomes true only when it is applied to a given object, and apart from this application it would seem meaningless to inquire into its truth. But this is the very question on which everything turns. We must however in the first place understand clearly what we mean by truth. In common life truth means the agreement of an object with our conception of it. We thus pre-suppose an object to which our conception must conform. In the philosophical sense of the word, on the other hand, truth may be described, in general abstract terms, as the agreement of a thought-content with itself. This meaning is quite different from the one given above. At the same time the deeper and philosophical meaning of truth can be partially traced even in the ordinary usage of language. Thus we speak of a true friend; by which we mean a friend whose manner of conduct accords with the notion of friendship. In the same way we speak of a true work of art. Untrue in this sense means the same as bad, or self-discordant. In this sense a bad state is an untrue state; and evil and untruth may be said to consist in the contradiction subsisting between the function or notion and the existence of the object. Of such a bad object we may form a correct representation, but the import of such representation is inherently false. Of these correctnesses, which are at the same time untruths, we may have many in our heads. God alone is the thorough harmony of notion and reality. All finite things involve an untruth: they have a notion and an existence, but their existence does not meet the requirements of the notion. For this reason they must perish, and then the incompatibility between their notion and their existence becomes manifest. It is in the kind that the individual animal has its notion: and the kind liberates itself from this individuality by death.

The study of truth, or as it is here explained to mean, consistency, constitutes the proper problem of logic. In our everyday mind we are never troubled with questions about the truth of the forms of thought. We may also express the problem of logic by saying that it examines the forms of thought touching their capability to hold truth. And the question comes to this: What are the forms of the infinite, and what are the forms of the finite? Usually no suspicion attaches to the finite forms of thought; they are allowed to pass unquestioned. But it is from conforming to finite categories in thought and action that all deception originates.

◆　◆　◆

CHAPTER VI

Logic Further Defined and Divided

79.

In point of form logical doctrine has three sides: (α) the abstract side, or that of understanding; (β) the dialectical, or that of negative reason; (γ) the speculative, or that of positive reason.

These three sides do not make three *parts of logic*, but are stages or "moments" in every logical entity, that is, of every notion and truth whatever. They may all be put under the first stage, that of understanding, and so kept isolated from each other; but this would give an inadequate conception of them. The statement of the dividing lines and the characteristic aspects of logic is at this point no more than historical and anticipatory.

80.

(α) Thought, as *understanding*, sticks to fixity of characters and their distinctness from one another: every such limited abstract it treats as having a subsistence and being of its own.

In our ordinary usage of the term thought and even notion we often have before our eyes nothing more than the operation of understanding. And no doubt thought is primarily an exercise of understanding—only it goes further, and the notion is not a function of understanding merely. The action of understanding may be in general described as investing its subject matter with the form of universality. But this universal is an abstract universal: that is to say, its opposition to the particular is so rigorously maintained, that it is at the same time also reduced to the character of a particular again. In this separating and abstracting attitude towards its objects, understanding is the reverse of immediate perception and sensation, which, as such, keep completely to their native sphere of action in the concrete.

It is by referring to this opposition of understanding to sensation or feeling that we must explain the frequent attacks made upon thought for being hard and narrow, and for leading, if consistently developed, to ruinous and pernicious results. The answer to these charges, in so far as they are warranted by their facts, is, that they do not touch thinking in general, certainly not the thinking of reason, but only the exercise of understanding. It must be added however, that the merit and rights of the mere understanding should unhesitatingly be admitted. And that merit lies in the fact, that apart from understanding there is no fixity or accuracy in the region either of theory or of practice.

◆　◆　◆

81.

(β) In the dialectical stage these finite characterisations or formulae supersede themselves, and pass into their opposites.

(I) But when the dialectical principle is employed by the understanding separately and independently—especially as seen in its application to philosophical theories, dialectic becomes skepticism; in which the result that ensues from its action is presented as a mere negation.

(II) It is customary to treat dialectic as an advantageous art, which for very wantonness introduces confusion and a mere semblance of contradiction into definite notions. And in that light, the semblance is the nonentity, while the true reality is supposed to belong to the original dicta of understanding. Often, indeed, dialectic is nothing more than a subjective seesaw of arguments *pro* and *con*, where the absence of sterling thought is disguised by the subtlety which gives birth to such arguments. But in its true and proper character, dialectic is the very nature and essence of everything predicated by mere understanding—the law of things and of the finite as a whole. Dialectic is different from "reflection." In the first instance, reflection is that movement out beyond the isolated predicate of a thing which gives it some reference, and brings out its relativity, while still in other respects leaving it its isolated validity. But by dialectic is meant the in-dwelling tendency outwards by which the one-sidedness and limitation of the predicates of understanding is seen in its true light, and shown to be the negation of them. For anything to be finite is just to suppress itself and put itself aside. Thus understood the dialectical principle constitutes the life and soul of scientific progress, the dynamic which alone gives immanent connection and necessity to the body of science; and, in a word, is seen to constitute the real and true, as opposed to the external, exaltation above the finite.

✦ ✦ ✦

(1) . . . Dialectic, it may be added, is no novelty in philosophy. Among the ancients, Plato is termed the inventor of dialectic and his right to the name rests on the fact, that the Platonic philosophy first gave the free scientific, and thus at the same time the objective, form to dialectic. Socrates, as we should expect from the general character of his philosophising, has the dialectical element in a predominantly subjective shape, that of irony. He used to turn his dialectic, first against ordinary consciousness, and then especially against the Sophists. In his conversations he used to simulate the wish for some clearer knowledge about the subject under discussion, and after putting all sorts of questions with that intent, he drew on those with whom he conversed to the opposite of what their first impressions had pronounced correct. If, for instance, the Sophists claimed to be teachers, Socrates by a series of questions forced the Sophist Protagoras to confess that all learning is only recollection. In his more strictly scientific dialogues Plato employs the dialectical method to show the finitude of all hard and fast terms of understanding. Thus in the Parmenides he deduces the many from the one, and shows nevertheless that the many cannot but define itself as the one. In this grand style did Plato treat dialectic. In modern times it was, more than any other, Kant who resuscitated the name of dialectic, and restored it to its post of honor. He did it, as we have seen (§ 48), by working out the antinomies of the reason. The problem of these antinomies is no mere subjective piece of work oscillating between one set of grounds and another; it really serves to show that every abstract proposition of understanding, taken precisely as it is given, naturally veers round into its opposite.

✦ ✦ ✦

82.

(γ) The Speculative stage, or stage of positive reason, apprehends the unity of terms (propositions) in their opposition—the affirmative, which is involved in their disintegration and in their transition.

(1) The result of dialectic is positive, because it has a definite content, or because its result is not empty and abstract nothing, but the negation of certain specific propositions which are contained in the result—for the very reason that it is a resultant and not an immediate nothing. (2) It follows from this that the "reason" result, though it be only a thought and abstract, is still a concrete, being not a plain formal unity, but a unity of distinct propositions. Bare

abstractions or formal thoughts are, therefore, no business of philosophy, which has to deal only with concrete thoughts. (3) The logic of mere understanding is involved in speculative logic, and can at will be elicited from it, by the simple process of omitting the dialectical and "reasonable" element. When that is done, it becomes what the common logic is, a descriptive collection of sundry thought forms and rules which, finite though they are, are taken to be something infinite.

If we consider only what it contains, and not how it contains it, the true reason-world, so far from being the exclusive property of philosophy, is the right of every human being, on whatever grade of culture or mental growth he may stand; which would justify man's ancient title of rational being. The general mode by which experience first makes us aware of the reasonable order of things is by accepted and unreasoned belief; and the character of the rational, as already noted (§ 45), is to be unconditioned, and thus to be self-contained, self-determining. In this sense man above all things becomes aware of the reasonable order, when he knows of God, and knows him to be the completely self-determined. Similarly, the consciousness a citizen has of his country and its laws is a perception of the reason-world, so long as he looks up to them as unconditioned and likewise universal powers, to which he must subject his individual will. And in the same sense, the knowledge and will of the child is rational, when he knows his parents' will, and wills it.

Now, to turn these rational (of course positively-rational) realities into speculative principles, the only thing needed is that they be *thought*. The expression "speculation" in common life is often used with a very vague and at the same time secondary sense, as when we speak of a matrimonial or a commercial speculation. By this we only mean two things: first, that what is immediately at hand has to be passed and left behind; and secondly, that the subject matter of such speculations, though in the first place only subjective, must not remain so, but be realized or translated into objectivity.

83.

Logic is subdivided into three parts:

  I. The Doctrine of Being
 II. The Doctrine of Essence
III. The Doctrine of Notion and Idea

That is, into the Theory of Thought:

  I. In its immediacy: the notion implicit and in germ.
 II. In its reflection and mediation: the being-for-self and show of the notion.
III. In its return into itself, and its developed abiding by itself: the notion in and for itself.

The division of logic now given, as well as the whole of the previous discussion on the nature of thought, is anticipatory: and the justification, or proof of it, can only result from the detailed treatment of thought itself. For in philosophy, to prove means to show how the subject by and from itself makes itself what it is. The relation in which these three leading grades of thought, or of the logical idea, stand to each other must be conceived as follows. Truth comes only with the notion: or, more precisely, the notion is the truth of being and essence, both of which, when separately maintained in their isolation, cannot but be untrue, the former because it is exclusively immediate, and the latter because it is exclusively mediate. Why then, it may be asked, begin with the false and not at once with the true? To which we answer that truth, to deserve the name, must authenticate its own truth: which authentication, here within the sphere of logic, is given when the notion demonstrates itself to be what is mediated by and with itself, and thus at the same time to be truly immediate. This relation between the three stages of the logical idea appears in a real and concrete shape thus: God, who is the truth, is known by us in his truth, that is, as absolute spirit, only in so far as we at the same time recognize that the world which He created, nature and the finite spirit, are, in their difference from God, untrue.

CHAPTER VII

The Doctrine of Being

84.

Being is the notion implicit only: its special forms have the predicate "is"; when they are distinguished they are each of them an "other": and the shape which dialectic takes in them, that is their further specialization, is a passing over into another. This further determination, or specialization, is at once a forthputting and in that way a disengaging of the notion implicit in being; and at the same time the withdrawing of being inwards, its sinking deeper into itself. Thus the explication of the notion in the sphere of being does two things: it brings out the totality of being, and it abolishes the immediacy of being, or the form of being as such.

◆　◆　◆

A. Quality

(a) Being

86.

Pure Being makes the beginning: because it is on one hand pure thought, and on the other immediacy itself, simple and indeterminate; and the first beginning cannot be mediated by anything, or be further determined.

All doubts and admonitions, which might be brought against beginning the science with an abstract empty being, will disappear, if we only perceive what a beginning naturally implies. It is possible to define being "I = I," "absolute indifference" or identity, and so on. Where it is felt necessary to begin either with what is absolutely certain, that is the certainty of one's self, or with a definition or intuition of the absolute truth, these and other forms of the kind may be looked on as if they must be the first. But each of these forms contains a mediation, and hence cannot be the real first: for all mediation implies advance made from a first on to a second, and proceeding from something different. If I = I, or even the intellectual intuition, are really taken to mean no more than the first, they are in this mere immediacy identical with being: while conversely, pure being, if abstract no longer, but including in it mediation, is pure thought or intuition.

If we enunciate being as a predicate of the absolute, we get the first definition of the latter. The absolute is being. This is (in thought) the absolutely initial definition, the most abstract and stinted. It is the definition given by the Eleatics, but at the same time is also the well-known definition of God as the sum of all realities. It means, in short, that we are to set aside that limitation which is in every reality, so that God shall be only the real in all reality, the superlatively real.

◆　◆　◆

(2) . . . It is sufficient to mention here, that logic begins where the proper history of philosophy begins.

Philosophy began in the Eleatic school, especially with Parmenides. Parmenides, who conceives the absolute as being, says that "Being alone is and nothing is not." Such was the true starting-point of philosophy, which is always knowledge by thought: and here for the first time we find pure thought seized and made an object to itself.

Men indeed thought from the beginning (for thus only were they distinguished from the animals). But thousands of years had to elapse before they came to apprehend thought in its purity, and to see in it the truly objective. The Eleatics are celebrated as daring thinkers. But this nominal admiration is often accompanied by the remark that they went too far, when they made Being alone true, and denied the truth of every other object of consciousness. We must go further than mere being, it is true: and yet it is absurd to speak of the other contents of our consciousness as somewhat as it were outside and beside being, or to say that there are other things, as well as being. The true state of the case is rather as follows. Being, as being, is nothing fixed or ultimate: it yields to dialectic and sinks into its opposite, which, also taken immediately, is Nothing. After all, the point is, that Being is the first pure thought; whatever else you may begin with (the I = I, the absolute indifference, or God himself), you begin with a figure of materialized conception, not a product of thought; and that, so far as its thought content is concerned, such beginning is merely being.

87.

But this mere being, as it is mere abstraction, is therefore the absolutely negative: which, in a similarly immediate aspect, is just Nothing.

(1) Hence was derived the second definition of the absolute; the absolute is the nought. In fact this definition is implied in saying that the thing-in-itself is the indeterminate, utterly without form and so without content—or in saying that God is only the supreme being and nothing more; for this is really declaring him to be the same negativity as above. The nothing which the Buddhists make the universal principle, as well as the final aim and goal of everything, is the same abstraction.

◆　◆　◆

The distinction between being and nought is, in the first place, only implicit, and not yet actually made: they only *ought* to be distinguished. A distinction of course implies two things, and that one of them possesses an attribute which is not found in the other. Being however is an absolute absence of attributes, and so is nothing. Hence the distinction between the two is only meant to be; it is a quite nominal distinction, which is at the same time no distinction. In all other cases of difference there is some common point which comprehends both things. Suppose, for example, we speak of two different species: the genus forms a common ground for both. Both in the case of mere being and nothing, distinction is without a bottom to stand upon: hence there can be no distinction, both determinations being the same bottomlessness. If it be replied that being and nothing are both of them thoughts, so that thought may be reckoned common ground, the objector forgets that being is not a particular or definite thought, and hence, being quite indeterminate, is a thought not to be distinguished from nothing. It is natural too for us to represent being as absolute riches, and nothing as absolute poverty. But if when we view the whole world we can only say that everything *is*, and nothing more, we are neglecting all speciality and instead of absolute plenitude, we have absolute emptiness. The same stricture is applicable to those who define God to be mere being; a definition not a whit better than that of the Buddhists, who make God to be nothing, and who from that principle draw the further conclusion that self-annihilation is the means by which man becomes God.

88.

Nothing, if it be thus immediate and equal to itself, is also conversely the same as being is. The truth of being and of nothing is accordingly the unity of the two: and this unity is *becoming*.

◆ ◆ ◆

(3) It may perhaps be said that nobody can form a notion of the unity of being and nothing. As for that, the notion of the unity is stated in the sections preceding, and that is all: apprehend that, and you have comprehended this unity. What the objector really means by comprehension—by a notion—is more than his language properly implies: he wants a richer and more complex state of mind, a pictorial conception which will propound the notion as a concrete case and one more familiar to the ordinary operations

of thought. And so long as incomprehensibility means only the want of habituation for the effort needed to grasp and abstract thought, free from all sensuous admixture, and to seize a speculative truth, the reply to the criticism is, that philosophical knowledge is undoubtedly distinct in kind from the mode of knowledge best known in common life, as well as from that which reigns in the other sciences. But if to have no notion merely means that we cannot represent in imagination the oneness of being and nothing, the statement is far from being true; for every one has countless ways of envisaging this unity. To say that we have no such conception can only mean, that in none of these images do we recognise the notion in question, and that we are not aware that they exemplify it. The readiest example of it is becoming. Every one has a mental idea of becoming, and will even allow that it is *one* idea: he will further allow that, when it is analysed, it involves the attribute of being, and also what is the very reverse of being, namely nothing: and that these two attributes lie undivided in the one idea: so that becoming is the unity of being and nothing. Another tolerably plain example is a beginning. In its beginning, the thing is not yet, but it is more than merely nothing, for its being is already in the beginning. Beginning is itself a case of becoming; only the former term is employed with an eye to the further advance. If we were to adapt logic to the more usual method of the sciences, we might start with the representation of a beginning as abstractly thought, or with beginning as such, and then analyze this representation; and perhaps people would more readily admit, as a result of this analysis, that being and nothing present themselves as undivided in unity.

◆ ◆ ◆

As the first concrete thought term, becoming is the first adequate vehicle of truth. In the history of philosophy, this stage of the logical idea finds its analogue in the system of Heraclitus. When Heraclitus says, "all is flowing," he enunciates becoming as the fundamental feature of all existence, whereas the Eleatics, as already remarked, saw the only truth in Being, rigid processless being. Glancing at the principle of the Eleatics, Heraclitus then goes on to say: being no more is than not being: a statement expressing the negativity of abstract being, and its identity with not being, as made explicit in becoming: both abstractions being alike untenable. This may be looked at as an instance of the real refutation of one system by another. To refute a philosophy is to exhibit the dialectical movement in its principle, and thus reduce it to a constituent member of a higher concrete form of the idea. Even becoming however, taken at its best on its own ground, is an extremely poor term: it needs to grow in depth and weight of meaning. Such deepened force we find for example in life. Life is a becoming; but that is not enough to exhaust the notion of life. A still higher form is found in mind. Here too is becoming, but richer and more intensive than mere logical becoming. The elements, whose unity constitutes mind, are not the bare abstracts of being and of nothing, but the system of the logical idea and of nature.

B. QUANTITY

(a) Pure Quantity

99.

Quantity is pure being, where the mode or character is no longer taken as one with the being itself, but explicitly put as superseded or indifferent.

✦ ✦ ✦

Quantity, of course, is a stage of the idea: and as such it must have its due, first as a logical category, and then in the world of objects, natural as well as spiritual. Still even so, there soon emerges the different importance attaching to the category of quantity according as its objects belong to the natural or to the spiritual world. For in nature, where the form of the idea is to be other than, and at the same time outside, itself, greater importance is for that very reason attached to quantity than in the spiritual world, the world of free inwardness. No doubt we regard even spiritual facts under a quantitative point of view; but it is at once apparent that in speaking of God as a trinity, the number three has by no means the same prominence, as when we consider the three dimensions of space or the three sides of a triangle— the fundamental feature of which last is just to be a surface bounded by three lines. Even inside the realm of nature we find the same distinction of greater or less importance of quantitative features. In the inorganic world, quantity plays, so to say, a more promi-

nent part than in the organic. Even in organic nature when we distinguish mechanical functions from what are called chemical, and in the narrower sense, physical, there is the same difference. Mechanics is of all branches of science, confessedly, that in which the aid of mathematics can be least dispensed with— where indeed we cannot take one step without them. On that account mechanics is regarded next to mathematics as the science *par excellence;* which leads us to repeat the remark about the coincidence of the materialist with the exclusively mathematical point of view. After all that has been said, we cannot but hold it, in the interest of exact and thorough knowledge, one of the most hurtful prejudices, to seek all distinction and determinateness of objects merely in quantitative considerations. Mind to be sure is more than nature and the animal is more than the plant: but we know very little of these objects and the distinction between them, if a more and less is enough for us, and if we do not proceed to comprehend them in their peculiar, that is their qualitative character.

✦ ✦ ✦

(b) Quantum (How Much)

101.

Quantity, essentially invested with the exclusionist character which it involves, is quantum (or how much): that is limited quantity.

Quantum is, as it were, the determinate being of quantity: whereas mere quantity corresponds to abstract being, and the degree, which is next to be considered, corresponds to being-for-self. As for the details of the advance from mere quantity to quantum, it is founded on this: that while in mere quantity the distinction, as a distinction of continuity and discreteness, is at first only implicit, in a quantum the distinction is actually made, so that quantity in general now appears as distinguished or limited. But in this way the quantum breaks up at the same time into an indefinite multitude of quanta or definite magnitudes. Each of these definite magnitudes, as distinguished from the others, forms a unity, while on the other hand, viewed per se, it is a many. And, when that is done, the quantum is described as number.

✦ ✦ ✦

103.

The limit (in a quantum) is identical with the whole of the quantum itself. As *in itself* multiple, the limit is extensive magnitude; as in itself *simple* determinateness (qualitative simplicity), it is intensive magnitude or degree.

❖ ❖ ❖

104.

In degree the notion of quantum is explicitly put. It is magnitude as indifferent on its own account and simple: but in such a way that the character (or modal being) which makes it a quantum lies quite outside it in other magnitudes. In this contradiction, where the *independent* indifferent limit is absolute *externality*, the infinite quantitative progression is made explicit—an immediacy which immediately veers round into its counterpart, into mediation (the passing beyond and over the quantum just laid down), and vice versa.

Number is a thought, but thought in its complete self-externalisation. Because it is a thought, it does not belong to perception: but it is a thought which is characterised by the externality of perception. Not only therefore *may* the quantum be increased or diminished without end: the very notion of quantum is thus to push out and out beyond itself. The infinite quantitative progression is only the meaningless repetition of one and the same contradiction, which attaches to the quantum, both generally and, when explicitly invested with its special character, as degree. Touching the futility of enunciating this contradiction in the form of infinite progression, Zeno, as quoted by Aristotle, rightly says, "It is the same to say a thing once, and to say it for ever."

(1) If we follow the usual definition of the mathematicians, given in § 99, and say that magnitude is what can be increased or diminished, there may be nothing to urge against the correctness of the perception on which it is founded; but the question remains, how we come to assume such a capacity of increase or diminution. If we simply appeal for an answer to experience, we try an unsatisfactory course; because apart from the fact that we should merely have a material image of magnitude, and not the thought of it, magnitude would come out as a bare possibility (of increasing or diminishing) and we should have no key to the necessity for its exhibiting this behaviour. In the way of our logical evolution, on the contrary, quantity is

obviously a grade in the process of self-determining thought; and it has been shown that it lies in the very notion of quantity to shoot out beyond itself. In that way, the increase or diminution (of which we have heard) is not merely possible, but necessary.

(2) The quantitative infinite progression is what the reflective understanding usually relies upon when it is engaged with the general question of Infinity. The same thing however holds good of this progression, as was already remarked on the occasion of the qualitatively infinite progression. As was then said, it is not the expression of a true, but of a wrong infinity; it never gets further than a bare "ought," and thus really remains within the limits of finitude. The quantitative form of this infinite progression, which Spinoza rightly calls a mere imaginary infinity (*infinitum imaginationis*), is an image often employed by poets, such as Haller and Klopstock, to depict the infinity, not of Nature merely, but even of God himself. Thus we find Haller, in a famous description of God's infinity, saying:—

> I heap up monstrous numbers, mountains of millions; I pile time upon time, and world on top of world; and when from the awful height I cast a dizzy look towards Thee, all the power of number, multiplied a thousand times, is not yet one part of Thee.

Here then we meet, in the first place, that continual extrusion of quantity, and especially of number, beyond itself, which Kant describes as "eerie." The only really "eerie" thing about it is the wearisomeness of ever fixing, and anon unfixing a limit, without advancing a single step. The same poet, however, well adds to that description of false infinity the closing line:

> These I remove, and Thou liest all before me.

Which means, that the true infinite is more than a mere world beyond the finite, and that we, in order to become conscious of it, must renounce that *progressus in infinitum.*

❖ ❖ ❖

C. MEASURE

107.

Measure is the qualitative quantum, in the first place as immediate, a quantum, to which a determinate being or a quality is attached.

Measure, where quality and quantity are in one, is thus the completion of being. Being, as we first apprehend it, is something utterly abstract and characterless: but it is the very essence of being to characterize itself, and its complete characterization is reached in measure. Measure, like the other stages of being, may serve as a definition of the absolute: God, it has been said, is the measure of all things. It is this idea which forms the ground-note of many of the ancient Hebrew hymns, in which the glorification of God tends in the main to show that He has appointed to everything its bound: to the sea and the solid land, to the rivers and mountains; and also to the various kinds of plants and animals. To the religious sense of the Greeks the divinity of measure, especially in respect of social ethics, was represented by Nemesis. That conception implies a general theory that all human things, riches, honour, and power, as well as joy and pain, have their definite measure, the transgression of which brings ruin and destruction.

◆ ◆ ◆

CHAPTER VIII
The Doctrine of Essence

112.

The terms in essence are always mere pairs of correlatives, and not yet absolutely reflected in themselves: hence in essence the actual unity of the notion is not realized, but only postulated by reflection. Essence—which is being coming into mediation with itself through the negativity of itself—is self-relatedness, only in so far as it is relation to an other—this other however coming to view at first not as something which *is*, but as postulated and hypothesized. Being has not vanished; but, firstly, essence, as simple self-relation, is being, and secondly, as regards its one-sided characteristic of immediacy, being is deposed to a mere negative, to a seeming or reflected light—essence accordingly is Being thus reflecting light into itself.

The absolute is the essence. This is the same definition as the previous one that the absolute is being, in so far as being likewise is simple self-relation. But it is at the same time higher, because essence is being that has gone into itself: that is to say, the simple self-relation (in being) is expressly put as negation of the negative, as immanent self-mediation. Unfortunately when the absolute is defined to be the essence, the negativity which this implies is often taken only to mean the withdrawal of all determinate predicates. This negative action of withdrawal or abstraction thus falls outside of the essence—which is thus left as a mere result apart from its premises—the *caput mortuum* of abstraction. But as this negativity, instead of being external to being is its own dialectic, the truth of the latter, namely essence, will be being as retired within itself—immanent being. That reflection, or light thrown into itself, constitutes the distinction between essence and immediate being, and is the peculiar characteristic of essence itself.

Any mention of essence implies that we distinguish it from being: the latter is immediate, and, compared with the essence, we look upon it as mere seeming. But this seeming is not an utter nonentity and nothing at all, but being superseded and put by. The point of view given by the essence is in general the standpoint of "reflection." This word "reflection" is originally applied, when a ray of light in a straight line impinging upon the surface of a mirror is thrown back from it. In this phenomenon we have two things—first an immediate fact which is, and secondly the deputed, derivated, or transmitted phase of the same. Something of this sort takes place when we reflect, or think upon an object; for here we want to know the object, not in its immediacy, but as derivative or mediated. The problem or aim of philosophy is often represented as the ascertainment of the essence of things: a phrase which only means that things instead of being left in their immediacy, must be shown to be mediated by, or based upon, something else. The immediate being of things is thus conceived under the magic of a rind or curtain behind which the essence lies hidden.

◆ ◆ ◆

A. ESSENCE AS GROUND OF EXISTENCE

(a) The Pure Principles or Categories of Reflection

(α) IDENTITY

115.

The essence lights up *in itself* or is mere reflection: and therefore is only self-relation, not as immediate but as reflected. And that reflex relation is self-identity.

This identity becomes an identity in form only, or of the understanding, if it be held hard and fast, quite aloof from difference. Or, rather, abstraction is the imposition of this identity of form, the transformation of something inherently concrete into this form of elementary simplicity. And this may be done in two ways. Either we may neglect a part of the multiple features which are found in the concrete thing (by what is called analysis) and select only one of them; or, neglecting their variety, we may concentrate the multiple characters into one.

If we associate identity with the absolute, making the absolute the subject of a proposition, we get: The absolute is what is identical with itself. However true this proposition may be, it is doubtful whether it be meant in its truth: and therefore it is at least imperfect in the expression. For it is left undecided, whether it means the abstract Identity of understanding—abstract, that is, because contrasted with the other characteristics of essence, or the identity which is inherently concrete. In the latter case, as will be seen, true identity is first discoverable in the ground, and, with a higher truth, in the notion.

◆   ◆   ◆

Identity is, in the first place, the repetition of what we had earlier as being, but as *become*, through supersession of its character of immediateness. It is therefore being as ideality. It is important to come to a proper understanding on the true meaning of identity: and, for that purpose, we must especially guard against taking it as abstract identity, to the exclusion of all difference. That is the touchstone for distinguishing all bad philosophy from what alone deserves the name of philosophy. Identity in its truth, as an ideality of what immediately is, is a high category for our religious modes of mind as well as all other forms of thought and mental activity. The true knowledge of God, it may be said, begins when we know him as identity—as absolute identity. To know so much is to see that all the power and glory of the world sinks into nothing in God's presence, and subsists only as the reflection of His power and His glory. In the same way, identity, as self-consciousness, is what distinguishes man from nature, particularly from the brutes which never reach the point of comprehending themselves as "I," that is, pure self-contained unity. So again, in connection with thought, the main thing is not to confuse the true identity, which contains Being and its characteristics ideally transfigured in it, with an abstract identity,

identity of bare form. All the charges of narrowness, hardness, meaninglessness, which are so often directed against thought from the quarter of feeling and immediate perception, rest on the perverse assumption that thought acts only as a faculty of abstract identification. The formal logic itself confirms this assumption by laying down the supreme law of thought (so-called) which has been discussed above. If thinking were no more than an abstract identity, we could not but own it to be a most futile and tedious business, No doubt the notion, and the idea too, are identical with themselves; but identical only in so far as they at the same time involve distinction.

(β) DIFFERENCE

116.

Essence is mere identity and reflection in itself only as it is self-relating negativity, and in that way self-repulsion. It contains therefore essentially the characteristic of Difference.

Other-being is here no longer qualitative, taking the shape of the character or limit. It is now in essence, in self-relating essence, and therefore the negation is at the same time a relation—is, in short, distinction, relativity, mediation.

To ask, "How identity comes to difference," assumes that identity as mere abstract identity is something of itself, and difference also something else equally independent. This supposition renders an answer to the question impossible. If identity is viewed as diverse from difference, all that we have in this way is but difference; and hence we cannot demonstrate the advance to difference, because the person who asks for the how of the progress thereby implies that for him the starting point is nonexistent. The question then when put to the test has obviously no meaning, and its proposer may be met with the question what he means by identity; whereupon we should soon see that he attaches no idea to it at all, and that identity is for him an empty name. As we have seen, besides, Identity is undoubtedly a negative—not however an abstract empty nought, but the negation of being and its characteristics. Being so, identity is at the same time self-relation, and, what is more, negative self-relation; in other words, it draws a distinction between it and itself.

◆   ◆   ◆

(γ) THE GROUND

121.

The ground is the unity of identity and difference, the truth of what difference and identity have turned out to be—the reflection-into-self, which is equally a reflection-into-another, and vice versa. It is essence put explicitly as a totality.

The maxim of the ground runs thus: everything has its sufficient ground: that is, the true essentiality of any thing is not the predication of it as identical with itself, or as different (various), or merely positive, or merely negative, but as having its being in an other, which, being its self-same, is its essence. And to this extent the essence is not abstract reflection into self, but into an other. The ground is the essence in its own inwardness; the essence is intrinsically a ground; and it is a ground only when it is a ground of somewhat, of an other.

We must be careful, when we say that the ground is the unity of identity and difference, not to understand by this unity an abstract identity. Otherwise we only change the name, while we still think the identity (of understanding) already seen to be false. To avoid this misconception we may say that the ground, besides being the unity, is also the difference of identity and difference. In that case in the ground, which promised at first to supersede contradiction, a new contradiction seems to arise. It is however a contradiction which so far from persisting quietly in itself, is rather the expulsion of it from itself. The ground is a ground only to the extent that it affords ground: but the result which thus issued from the ground is only itself. In this lies its formalism. The ground and what is grounded are one and the same content: the difference between the two is the mere difference of form which separates simple self-relation, on the one hand, from mediation or derivativeness on the other. Inquiry into the grounds of things goes with the point of view which, as already noted (note to § 112), is adopted by reflection. We wish, as it were, to see the matter double, first in its immediacy, and secondly in its ground, where it is no longer immediate. This is the plain meaning of the law of sufficient ground, as it is called; it asserts that things should essentially be viewed as mediated. The manner in which formal logic establishes this law of thought, sets a bad example to other sciences. Formal logic asks these sciences not to accept their subject matter as it is immediately given; and yet herself lays down a law of thought without deducing it—in other words, without exhibiting its mediation. With the same justice as the logician maintains our faculty of thought to be so constituted that we must ask for the ground of everything, might the physicist, when asked why a man who falls into water is drowned, reply that man happens to be so organized that he cannot live under water; or the jurist, when asked why a criminal is punished, reply that civil society happens to be so constituted that crimes cannot be left unpunished.

Yet even if logic be excused the duty of giving a ground for the law of the sufficient ground, it might at least explain what is to be understood by a ground. The common explanation, which describes the ground as what has a consequence, seems at the first glance more lucid and intelligible than the preceding definition in logical terms. If you ask however what the consequence is, you are told that it is what has a ground; and it becomes obvious that the explanation is intelligible only because it assumes what in our case has been reached as the termination of an antecedent movement of thought. And this is the true business of logic: to show that those thoughts, which as usually employed merely float before consciousness neither understood nor demonstrated, are really grades in the self-determination of thought. It is by this means that they are understood and demonstrated.

B. APPEARANCE

131.

The essence must appear or shine forth. Its shining or reflection in it is the suspension and translation of it to immediacy, which, while as reflection-on-self it is matter or subsistence, is also form, reflection-on-something-else, a subsistence which sets itself aside. To show or shine is the characteristic by which essence is distinguished from being—by which it is essence; and it is this show which, when it is developed, shows itself, and is appearance. Essence accordingly is not something beyond or behind appearance, but just because it is the essence which exists—the existence is appearance (forth-shining).

Existence stated explicitly in its contradiction is appearance. But appearance (forth-shining) is not to be confused with a mere show (shining). Show is the proximate truth of being or immediacy. The immediate, instead of being, as we suppose, something independent, resting on its own self, is a mere show, and as such it is packed or summed up under the simplicity of the immanent essence. The essence is, in the first place, the sum total of the showing itself, shining in itself (inwardly); but, far from abiding in this inwardness, it comes as a ground forward into existence; and this existence being grounded not in itself, but on something else, is just appearance. In our imagination we ordinarily combine with the term appearance or phenomenon the conception of an indefinite congeries of things existing, the being of which is purely relative, and which consequently do not rest on a foundation of their own, but are esteemed only as passing stages. But in this conception it is no less implied that essence does not linger behind or beyond appearance. Rather it is, we may say, the infinite kindness which lets its own show freely issue into immediacy, and graciously allows it the joy of existence. The appearance which is thus created does not stand on its own feet, and has its being not in itself but in something else. God who is the essence, when He lends existence to the passing stages of his own show in himself, may be described as the goodness that creates a world: but He is also the power above it, and the righteousness, which manifests the merely phenomenal character of the content of this existing world, whenever it tries to exist in independence.

Appearance is in every way a very important grade of the logical idea. It may be said to be the distinction of philosophy from ordinary consciousness that it sees the merely phenomenal character of what the latter supposes to have a self-subsistent being. The significance of appearance however must be properly grasped, or mistakes will arise. To say that anything is a *mere* appearance may be misinterpreted to mean that, as compared with what is merely phenomenal, there is greater truth in the immediate, in that which *is*. Now in strict fact, the case is precisely the reverse. Appearance is higher than mere Being—a richer category because it holds in combination the two elements of reflection-into-self and reflection-into-another: whereas being (or immediacy) is still mere relationlessness, and apparently rests upon itself alone. Still, to say that anything is *only* an appearance suggests a real flaw, which consists in this, that

appearance is still divided against itself and without intrinsic stability. Beyond and above mere appearance comes in the first place actuality, the third grade of essence, of which we shall afterwards speak.

◆ ◆ ◆

C. ACTUALITY

142.

Actuality is the unity, become immediate, of essence with existence, or of inward with outward. The utterance of the actual is the actual itself: so that in this utterance it remains just as essential, and only is essential, in so far as it is in immediate external existence.

We have ere this met being and existence as forms of the immediate. Being is, in general, unreflected immediacy and transition into another. Existence is immediate unity of being and reflection; hence appearance: it comes from the ground, and falls to the ground. In actuality this unity is explicitly put, and the two sides of the relation identified. Hence the actual is exempted from transition, and its externality is its energizing. In that energizing it is reflected into itself: its existence is only the manifestation of itself, not of another.

Actuality and thought (or idea) are often absurdly opposed. How commonly we hear people saying that, though no objection can be urged against the truth and correctness of a certain thought, there is nothing of the kind to be seen in actuality, or it cannot be actually carried out! People who use such language only prove that they have not properly apprehended the nature either of thought or of actuality. Thought in such a case is, on one hand, the synonym for a subjective conception, plan, intention or the like, just as actuality, on the other, is made synonymous with external and sensible existence. This is all very well in common life, where great laxity is allowed in the categories and the names given to them: and it may of course happen that for example the plan, or so-called idea, say of a certain method of taxation, is good and advisable in the abstract, but that nothing of the sort is found in so-called actuality, or could possibly be carried out under the given conditions. But when the abstract understanding gets hold of these categories and exaggerates the distinction they imply into a hard and fast line of contrast, when it tells us that in this actual world we must knock ideas out of our heads, it is necessary energetically to protest against these doctrines, alike in the name of science and of sound reason. For on the one hand ideas are not confined to our heads merely, nor is the idea, upon the whole, so feeble as to leave the question of its actualization or non-actualization dependent on our will. The idea is rather the absolutely active as well as actual. And on the other hand actuality is not so bad and irrational, as purblind or wrong-headed and muddle-brained would-be reformers imagine. So far is actuality, as distinguished from mere appearance, and primarily presenting a unity of inward and outward, from being in contrariety with reason, that it is rather thoroughly reasonable, and everything which is not reasonable must on that very ground cease to be held actual. The same view may be traced in the usages of educated speech, which declines to give the name of real poet or real statesman to a poet or a statesman who can do nothing really meritorious or reasonable.

143.

(α) Viewed as an identity in general, actuality is first of all possibility—the reflection-into-self which, as in contrast with the concrete unity of the actual, is taken and made an abstract and unessential essentiality. Possibility is what is essential to reality, but in such a way that it is at the same time only a possibility.

✦ ✦ ✦

144.

(β) But the actual in its distinction from possibility (which is reflection-into-self) is itself only the outward concrete, the unessential immediate. In other words, to such extent as the actual is primarily (§ 142) the simple merely immediate unity of inward and outward, it is obviously made an unessential outward, and thus at the same time (§ 140) it is merely inward, the abstraction of reflection-into-self. Hence it is itself characterized as a merely possible. When thus valued at the rate of a mere possibility, the actual is a contingent or accidental, and, conversely, possibility is mere accident itself or chance.

145.

Possibility and contingency are the two factors of actuality—inward and outward, put as mere forms which constitute the externality of the actual. They have their reflection-into-self on the body of actual fact, or content, with its intrinsic definiteness which gives the essential ground of their characterization. The finitude of the contingent and the possible lies, therefore, as we now see, in the distinction of the form-determination from the content: and, therefore, it depends on the content alone whether anything is contingent and possible.

✦ ✦ ✦

147.

(γ) When this externality (of actuality) is thus developed into a circle of the two categories of possibility and immediate actuality, showing the intermediation of the one by the other, it is what is called real possibility. Being such a circle, further, it is the totality, and thus the content, the actual fact or affair in its all-round definiteness. While in like manner, if we look at the distinction between the two characteristics in this unity, it realises the concrete totality of the form, the immediate self-translation of inner into outer, and of outer into inner. This self-movement of the form is activity, carrying into effect the fact or affair as a *real* ground which is self-suspended to actuality, and carrying into effect the contingent actuality, the conditions; that is it is their reflection-in-self, and their self-suspension to another actuality, the actuality of the actual fact. If all the conditions are at hand, the fact (event) *must* be actual; and the fact itself is one of the conditions: for being in the first place only inner, it is at first itself only pre-supposed. Developed actuality, as the coincident alternation of inner and outer, the alternation of their opposite motions combined into a single motion, is necessity.

✦ ✦ ✦

The theory however which regards the world as determined through necessity and the belief in a divine providence are by no means mutually excluding points of view. The intellectual principle underlying the idea of divine providence will hereafter be shown to be the notion. But the notion is the truth of necessity, which it contains in suspension in itself; just as, conversely, necessity is the notion implicit. Necessity is blind only so long as it is not understood. There is nothing therefore more mistaken than the charge of blind fatalism made against the philosophy of history, when it takes for its problem to understand the necessity of every event. The philosophy of history rightly understood takes the rank of a Théodicée; and those, who fancy they honor divine providence by excluding necessity from it, are really degrading it by this exclusiveness to a blind and irrational caprice. In the simple language of the religious mind which speaks of God's eternal and immutable decrees, there is implied an express recognition that necessity forms part of the essence of God. In his difference from God, man, with his own private opinion and will, follows the call of caprice and arbitrary humor, and thus often finds his acts turn out something quite different from what he had meant and willed. But God knows what he wills, is determined in his eternal will neither by accident from within nor from without, and what he wills he also accomplishes, irresistibly.

159.

The passage from necessity to freedom, or from actuality into the notion, is the very hardest, because it proposes that independent actuality shall be thought as having all its substantiality in the passing over and identity with the other independent actuality. The notion, too, is extremely hard, because it is itself just this very identity. But the actual substance as such, the cause, which in its exclusiveness resists all invasion, is *ipso facto* subjected to necessity or the destiny of passing into dependency: and it is this subjection rather where the chief hardness lies. To think necessity, on the contrary, rather tends to melt that hardness. For thinking means that, in the other, one meets with one's self. It means a liberation, which is not the flight of abstraction, but consists in that which is actual having itself not as something else, but as its own being and creation, in the other actuality with which it is bound up by the force of necessity. As existing in an individual form, this liberation is called I: as developed to its totality, it is free spirit; as feeling, it is love; and as enjoyment, it is blessedness. The great vision of substance in Spinoza is only a potential liberation from finite exclusiveness and egoism: but the notion itself realizes for its own both the power of necessity and actual freedom.

When, as now, the notion is called the truth of Being and essence, we must expect to be asked, why we do not begin with the notion? The answer is that, where knowledge by thought is our aim, we cannot begin with the truth, because the truth, when it forms the beginning, must rest on mere assertion. The truth when it is thought must as such verify itself to thought. If the notion were put at the head of logic, and defined, quite correctly in point of content, as the unity of being and essence, the following question would come up: What are we to think under the terms "being" and "essence," and how do they come to be embraced in the unity of the notion? But if we answered these questions, then our beginning with the notion would be merely nominal. The real start would be made with being, as we have here done: with this difference, that the characteristics of being as well as those of essence would have to be accepted uncritically from figurate conception, whereas we have observed being and essence in their own dialectical development and learned how they lose themselves in the unity of the notion.

CHAPTER IX

The Doctrine of the Notion

160.

The notion is the principle of freedom, the power of substance self-realized. It is a systematic whole, in which each of its constituent functions is the very total which the notion is, and is put as indissolubly one with it. Thus in its self identity it has original and complete determinateness.

The position taken up by the notion is that of absolute idealism. Philosophy is a knowledge through notions because it sees that what on other grades of consciousness is taken to have being, and to be naturally or immediately independent, is but a constituent stage in the idea. In the logic of understanding, the notion is generally reckoned a mere form of thought, and treated as a general conception. It is to this inferior view of the notion that the assertion refers, so often urged on behalf of the heart and sentiment, that notions as such are something dead, empty, and abstract. The case is really quite the reverse. The notion is, on the contrary, the principle of all life, and thus possesses at the same time a character of thorough concreteness. That it is so follows from the whole logical movement up to this point, and need not be here proved. The contrast between form and content, which is thus used to criticize the notion when it is alleged to be merely formal, has, like all the other contrasts upheld by reflection, been already left behind and overcome dialectically or through itself. The notion, in short, is what contains all the earlier categories of thought merged in it. It certainly is a form, but an infinite and creative form, which includes, but at the same time releases from itself, the fulness of all content. And so too the notion may, if it be wished, be styled abstract, if the name concrete is restricted to the concrete facts of sense or of immediate perception. For the notion is not palpable to the touch, and when we are engaged with it, hearing and seeing must quite fail us. And yet, as it was before remarked, the notion is a true concrete; for the reason that it involves Being and essence, and the total wealth of these two spheres with them, merged in the unity of thought.

If, as was said at an earlier point, the different stages of the logical idea are to be treated as a series of definitions of the absolute, the definition which now results for us is that the absolute is the notion. That necessitates a higher estimate of the notion, however, than is found in formal conceptualist logic, where the notion is a mere form of our subjective thought, with no original content of its own. But if speculative logic thus attaches a meaning to the term notion so very different from that usually given, it may be asked why the same word should be employed in two contrary acceptations, and an occasion thus given for confusion and misconception. The answer is that, great as the interval is between the speculative notion and the notion of formal logic, a closer examination shows that the deeper meaning is not so foreign to the general usages of language as it seems at first sight. We speak of the deduction of a content from the notion, for example of the specific provisions of the law of property from the notion of property; and so again we speak of tracing back these material details to the notion. We thus recognize that the notion is no mere form without a content of its own: for if it were, there would be in the one case nothing to deduce from such a form, and in the other case to trace a given body of fact back to the empty form of the notion would only rob the fact of its specific character, without making it understood.

◆ ◆ ◆

162.
The doctrine of the notion is divided into three parts. (1) The first is the doctrine of the subjective or for-

mal notion. (2) The second is the doctrine of the notion invested with the character of immediacy, or of objectivity. (3) The third is the doctrine of the Idea, the subject-object, the unity of notion and objectivity, the absolute truth.

A. THE SUBJECTIVE NOTION

(a) The Notion as Notion

163.
The notion as notion contains the three following "moments" or functional parts. The first is universality—meaning that it is in free equality with itself in its specific character. The second is particularity—that is, the specific character, in which the universal continues serenely equal to itself. The third is individuality—meaning the reflection-into-self of the specific characters of universality and particularity—which negative self-unity has complete and original determinateness, without any loss to its self-identity or universality.

◆ ◆ ◆

164.
Universality, particularity, and individuality are, taken in the abstract, the same as identity, difference, and ground. But the universal is the self-identical, with the express qualification, that it simultaneously contains the particular and the individual. Again, the particular is the different or the specific character, but with the qualification that it is in itself universal and is as an individual. Similarly the individual must be understood to be a subject or substratum, which involves the genus and species in itself and possesses a substantial existence. Such is the explicit or realised inseparability of the functions of the notion in their difference (§ 160)—what may be called the clearness of the notion, in which each distinction causes no dimness or interruption, but is quite as much transparent.

No complaint is oftener made against the notion than that it is *abstract*. Of course it is abstract, if abstract means that the medium in which the notion exists is thought in general and not the sensible thing in its empirical concreteness. It is abstract also, because the notion falls short of the idea. To this extent the subjective notion is still formal. This however does not mean that it ought to have or receive another content than its own. It is itself the absolute form, and so is all specific character, but as that character is in its truth. Although it be abstract therefore, it is the concrete, concrete altogether, the subject as such. The absolutely concrete is the mind (see end of § 159)—the notion when it *exists* as notion distinguishing itself from its objectivity, which notwithstanding the distinction still continues to be its own. Everything else which is concrete, however rich it be, is not so intensely identical with itself and therefore not so concrete on its own part—least of all what is commonly supposed to be concrete, but is only a congeries held together by external influence. What are called notions, and in fact specific notions, such as man, house, animal, etc., are simply denotations and abstract representations. These abstractions retain out of all the functions of the notion only that of universality; they leave particularity and individuality out of account and have no development in these directions. By so doing they just miss the notion.

165.

It is the element of individuality which first explicitly differentiates the elements of the notion. Individuality is the negative reflection of the notion into itself, and it is in that way at first the free differentiating of it as the first negation, by which the specific character of the notion is realized, but under the form of particularity. That is to say, the different elements are in the first place only qualified as the several elements of the notion, and, secondly, their identity is no less explicitly stated, the one being said to be the other. This realized particularity of the notion is the judgment.

❖ ❖ ❖

(b) The Judgment

166.

The judgment is the notion in its particularity, as a connection which is also a distinguishing of its functions, which are put as independent and yet as identical with themselves, not with one another.

One's first impression about the judgment is the independence of the two extremes, the subject and the predicate. The former we take to be a thing or term per se, and the predicate a general term outside the said subject and somewhere in our heads. The next point is for us to bring the latter into combination with the former, and in this way frame a judgment. The copula "is" however enunciates the predicate *of* the subject, and so that external subjective subsumption is again put in abeyance, and the judgment taken as a determination of the object itself. The etymological meaning of the judgment (*Urtheil*) in German goes deeper, as it were declaring the unity of the notion to be primary, and its distinction to be the original partition. And that is what the judgment really is.

❖ ❖ ❖

B. THE OBJECT

194.

The object is immediate being, because insensible to difference, which in it has suspended itself. It is, further, a totality in itself, while at the same time (as this identity is only the *implicit* identity of its dynamic elements) it is equally indifferent to its immediate unity. It thus breaks up into distinct parts, each of which is itself the totality. Hence the object is the absolute contradiction between a complete independence of the multiplicity, and the equally complete nonindependence of the different pieces.

The definition, which states that the absolute is the object, is most definitely implied in the Leibnitzian monad. The monads are each an object, but an object implicitly "representative," indeed the total representation of the world. In the simple unity of the monad, all difference is merely ideal, not independent or real. Nothing from without comes into the monad, it is the whole notion in itself, only distinguished by its own greater or less development. None the less, this simple totality parts into the absolute multitude of differences, each becoming an independent monad. In the monad of monads, the preestablished harmony of their inward developments, these substances are in like manner again reduced to "ideality" and unsubstantiality. The philosophy of Leibnitz, therefore, represents contradiction in its complete development.

❖ ❖ ❖

(2) Objectivity contains the three forms of mechanism, chemism, and teleology. The object of mechanical type is the immediate and undifferentiated object. No doubt it contains difference, but the different pieces stand, as it were, without affinity to

each other, and their connection is only extraneous. In chemistry, on the contrary, the object exhibits an essential tendency to differentiation, in such a way that the objects are what they are only by their relation to each other: this tendency to difference constitutes their quality. The third type of objectivity, the teleological relation, is the unity of mechanism and chemism. Design, like the mechanical object, is a self-contained totality, enriched however by the principle of differentiation which came to the fore in chemism, and thus referring itself to the object that stands over against it. Finally, it is the realization of design which forms the transition to the idea.

✦ ✦ ✦

C. THE IDEA

213.

The idea is truth in itself and for itself—the absolute unity of the notion and objectivity. Its "ideal" content is nothing but the notion in its detailed terms: its "real" content is only the exhibition which the notion gives itself in the form of external existence, whilst yet, by enclosing this shape in its ideality, it keeps it in its power, and so keeps itself in it.

The definition, which declares the absolute to be the idea, is itself absolute. All former definitions come back to this. The idea is the truth: for truth is the correspondence of objectivity with the notion—not of course the correspondence of external things with my conceptions—for these are only *correct* conceptions held by *me*, the individual person. In the idea we have nothing to do with the individual, nor with figurate conceptions, nor with external things. And yet, again, everything actual, in so far as it is true, is the idea, and has its truth by and in virtue of the idea alone. Every individual being is some one aspect of the idea: for which, therefore, yet other actualities are needed, which in their turn appear to have a self-subsistence of their own. It is only in them altogether and in their relation that the notion is realized. The individual by itself does not correspond to its notion. It is this limitation of its existence which constitutes the finitude and the ruin of the individual.

When we hear the idea spoken of, we need not imagine something far away beyond this mortal sphere. The idea is rather what is completely present: and it is found, however confused and degenerated, in every consciousness. We conceive the world to ourselves as a great totality which is created by God, and so created that in it God has manifested himself to us. We regard the world also as ruled by divine providence: implying that the scattered and divided parts of the world are continually brought back, and made conformable, to the unity from which they have issued. The purpose of philosophy has always been the intellectual ascertainment of the idea; and everything deserving the name of philosophy has constantly been based on the consciousness of an absolute unity where the understanding sees and accepts only separation. It is too late now to ask for proof that the idea is the truth. The proof of that is contained in the whole deduction and development of thought up to this point. The idea is the result of this course of dialectic. Not that it is to be supposed that the idea is mediate only, that is mediated through something else than itself. It is rather its own result, and being so, is no less immediate than mediate. The stages hitherto considered, namely those of being and essence, as well as those of notion and of objectivity, are not, when so distinguished, something permanent, resting upon themselves. They have proved to be dialectical; and their only truth is that they are dynamic elements of the idea.

214.

The idea may be described in many ways. It may be called reason (and this is the proper philosophical signification of reason); subject-object; the unity of the ideal and the real, of the finite and the infinite, of soul and body; the possibility which has its actuality in its own self; that of which the nature can be thought only as existent, etc. All these descriptions apply, because the idea contains all the relations of understanding, but contains them in their infinite self-return and self-identity.

It is easy work for the understanding to show that everything said of the idea is self-contradictory. But that can quite as well be retaliated, or rather in the idea the retaliation is actually made. And this work, which is the work of reason, is certainly not so easy as that of the understanding. Understanding may demonstrate that the idea is self-contradictory: because the subjective is subjective only and is always confronted by the objective—because being is different from notion and therefore cannot be picked out of it—because the finite is finite only, the exact antithesis of the infinite, and therefore not identical with it; and so on with every term of the description. The reverse of all this however is the doctrine of logic. Logic shows that the subjective which is to be subjective only, the finite which would be finite only, the infinite which would be infinite only, and so on, have no truth, but contradict themselves, and pass over into their opposites. Hence this transition, and the unity in which the extremes are merged and become factors, each with a merely reflected existence, reveals itself as their truth.

The understanding, which addresses itself to deal with the idea, commits a double misunderstanding. It takes *first* the extremes of the idea (be they expressed as they will, so long as they are in their unity), not as they are understood when stamped with this concrete unity, but as if they remained abstractions outside of it. It no less mistakes the relation between them, even when it has been expressly stated. Thus, for example, it overlooks even the nature of the copula in the judgment, which affirms that the individual, or subject, is after all not individual, but universal. But, in the *second* place, the understanding believes *its* "reflection"—that the self-identical idea contains its own negative, or contains contradiction—to be an external reflection which does not lie within the idea itself. But the reflection is really no peculiar cleverness of the understanding. The idea itself is the dialectic which for ever divides and distinguishes the self-identical from the differentiated, the subjective from the objective, the finite from the infinite, soul from body. Only on these terms is it an eternal creation, eternal vitality, and eternal spirit. But while it thus passes or rather translates itself into the abstract understanding, it for ever remains reason. The idea is the dialectic which again makes this mass of understanding and diversity understand its finite nature and the pseudo-independence in its productions, and which brings the diversity back to unity. Since this double movement is not separate or distinct in time, nor indeed in any other way—otherwise it would be only a repetition of the abstract understanding—the idea is the eternal vision of itself in the other—notion which in its objectivity *has* carried out *itself*—object which is inward design, essential subjectivity.

The different modes of apprehending the idea as unity of ideal and real, of finite and infinite, of identity and difference, etc., are more or less formal. They designate some one stage of the *specific* notion. Only the notion itself, however, is free and the genuine universal: in the idea, therefore, the specific character of the notion is only the notion itself—an objectivity, namely, into which it, being the universal, continues itself, and in which it has only its own character, the total character. The idea is the infinite judgment, of which the terms are severally the independent totality; and in which, as each grows to the fulness of its own nature, it has thereby at the same time passed into the other. None of the other specific notions exhibits this totality complete on both its sides as the notion itself and objectivity.

215.

The idea is essentially a process, because its identity is the absolute and free identity of the notion, only in so far as it is absolute negativity and for that reason dialectical. It is the round of movement, in which the notion, in the capacity of universality which is individuality, gives itself the character of objectivity and of the antithesis thereto; and this externality which has the notion for its substance, finds its way back to subjectivity through its immanent dialectic.

As the idea is (*a*) a process, it follows that such an expression for the Absolute as *unity* of thought and being, of finite and infinite, etc., is false; for unity expresses an abstract and merely quiescent identity. As the idea is (*b*) subjectivity, it follows that the expression is equally false on another account. That unity of which it speaks expresses a merely virtual or underlying presence of the genuine unity. The infinite would thus seem to be merely *neutralised* by the finite, the subjective by the objective, thought by being. But in the negative unity of the idea, the infinite overlaps and includes the finite, thought overlaps being, subjectivity overlaps objectivity. The unity of the idea is thought, infinity, and subjectivity, and is in consequence to be essentially distinguished from the idea as *substance*, just as this overlapping subjectivity, thought, or infinity is to be distinguished from the one-sided subjectivity, one-sided thought, one-sided infinity to which it descends in judging and defining.

The idea as a process runs through three stages in its development. The first form of the idea is life: that is, the idea in the form of immediacy. The second form is that of mediation or differentiation; and this is the idea in the form of knowledge, which appears under the double aspect of the theoretical and practical idea. The process of knowledge eventuates in the restoration of the unity enriched by difference. This gives the third form of the idea, the absolute idea: which last stage of the logical idea evinces itself to be at the same time the true first, and to have a being due to itself alone.

◆ ◆ ◆

STUDY QUESTIONS: HEGEL, LOGIC

1. What advantage do the sciences have over philosophy?
2. What is the notion of the mind's *acquaintance* with objects?
3. What cravings of thought give rise to philosophy?
4. What is logic the science of?
5. How are pure ideas related to logic?
6. How are logic and metaphysics related?
7. Is the absolute beyond this world, or present in the world?
8. What are the "three sides" of logic, and how are they related?
9. How is dialectic different from reflection?
10. Did Kant improve on Plato's dialectic?
11. What is the "doctrine of being?"
12. What does Hegel mean by "pure being?"
13. Are *being* and *nothingness* related?
14. What is "becoming?"
15. How does Hegel define *quantum*?
16. How does Hegel make use of Zeno?
17. What is the "doctrine of essence?"
18. How does Hegel define *identity*?
19. What does the unity of identity and difference make?
20. How is appearance related to actuality?
21. What is the significance of the concept "reflection-into-self?"
22. Why is possibility essential to reality?
23. What is the importance of the notion of *necessity*? How is it related to freedom?
24. What does Hegel mean by the will?
25. What does Hegel mean by "the notion as notion"?
26. What is truth in itself and for itself?
27. How are *reason* and *idea* related?

THE PHENOMENOLOGY OF MIND

Kant already conceived the mind not in passive terms, where impressions and ideas are merely effects of the object, as in the views of the British empiricists, but in active terms: objects themselves are but representations consisting of phenomena and thus partly the effects of the activity of mind. What is different about Hegel's phenomenology is that he sees this entire Kantian process as *itself* being explained in strictly fixed terms, and, therefore, a mistake. The mind according to Kant works using its faculties, creating thereby the phenomenal world, and the noumenal world impacts the mind's faculties but the whole process is passive. Hegel sees this whole process as being one created by the mind's own activity. Kant's view is, according to Hegel, flawed because ultimately everything that is, is mind. But not mind as something separate, as in theistic systems that conceive of a God as something existing apart from, or beyond, the universe; nor mind conceived as transcendental terms, a mind behind the mind. Rather, the mind according to Hegel consists not only of phenomena but is, itself, the entire conceptual framework all the way down to the logic of thought. It is itself both relative and absolute.

Whereas in Kant's philosophy the mind actively creates the phenomenal world, this process is itself a passive fact about the way the world is. This phenomenal-noumenal totality of reality includes all aspects of the mind, including the ego and transcendental ego, in relation to which the noumenal world is Godlike, otherworldly, unknowable. Hegel goes beyond this aspect of Kant's metaphysics by drawing the boundary between the unknowable thing in itself and the knowable phenomena as itself existing *within* the real world, moving from past to future. The future exists in the not-yet realm of infinite possibility, as inaccessible from the present moment as Kant's noumenal reality is from phenomenal reality.

In skepticism consciousness learns in truth, that it is divided against itself. And from this experience there is born a new type of consciousness, wherein are linked the two thoughts which skepticism had kept asunder. The thoughtless self-ignorance of skepticism must pass away; for in fact the two attitudes of skepticism express one consciousness. This new type of consciousness is therefore explicitly aware of its own doubleness. It regards itself on the one hand as the deliverer, changeless and self-possessed; on the other hand it regards itself as the absolutely confounded and contrary; and it is the awareness of this its own contradiction. In stoicism the self owns itself in the simplicity of freedom. In skepticism it gives itself embodiment, makes naught of other embodied reality, but, in the very act of so doing, renders itself the rather twofold and is now parted in twain. Hereby the same duplication that was formerly shared between two individuals, the lord and the slave, has now entered into the nature of one individual. The differentiation of the self, which is essential to the notion of mind, is already present, but not as constituting an organic unity, and the un-happy consciousness is this awareness of the self as the divided nature, wherein is only conflict.

This unhappy and broken consciousness, just because the conflict of its nature is known as belonging to one person, must forever, in each of its two forms, have the other also present to it. Whenever, in either form, it seems to have come to victory and unity, it finds no rest there, but is forthwith driven over to the other. Its true homecoming, its true reconciliation with itself, will, however, display to us the nature of the mind, as he will appear when, having come to life, he has entered the world of his manifestation. For it already belongs to the unhappy consciousness to be one undivided soul in the midst of its doubleness. It is in fact the very gazing of one self into another; it is both these selves; it has no nature save insofar as it unites the two. But thus far it knows not yet this its own real essence; it has not entered into possession of this unity.

For the first then, the unhappy consciousness is but the unwon unity of the two selves. To its view the two are not one, but are at war together. And accordingly it regards one of them, namely, the simple, the changeless consciousness, as the true self. The other, the multiform and fickle, it regards as the false self. The unhappy consciousness finds these two as mutually estranged. For its own part, because it is the awareness of this contradiction, it takes sides with the changeless consciousness, and calls itself the false self. But since it is aware of the changeless, that is of the true self, its task must be one of self-deliverance, that

Hegel, from the translation by Josiah Royce in *Modern Classical Philosophers* (Boston: Houghton Mifflin, 1908).

is, the task of delivering itself from the unreality. For on the one hand it knows itself only as the fickle; and the changeless is far remote from it. And yet the unhappy consciousness is in its genuine selfhood one with the simple and changeless consciousness; for therein lies its own true self. But yet again it knows that it is not in possession of this true self. So long as the unhappy consciousness assigns to the two selves this position, they cannot remain indifferent to each other; or, in other words, the unhappy consciousness cannot itself be indifferent to the changeless. For the unhappy consciousness is, as a fact, of both kinds, and knows the relation of the changeless to the fickle as a relation of truth to falsehood. The falsehood must be turned to naught; but since the unhappy consciousness finds both the false and the true alike necessary to it, and contradictory, there remains to it only the contradictory movement, wherein neither of the opposed elements can find repose in going over to its opponent but must create itself anew in the opponent's very bosom.

To win, then, in this strife against the adversary, is rather to be vanquished. To attain one goal, is rather to lose it in its opposite. The whole life, whatever it be, whatever it do, is aware only of the pain of this being and doing. For this consciousness has no object besides its opposite, the true self, and its own nothingness. In aspiration it strives hence towards the changeless. But this aspiration is itself the unhappy consciousness, and contains forthwith the knowledge of the opposite, namely of its own individuality. The changeless, when it enters consciousness, is sicklied over with individuality, is present therewith; instead of being lost in the consciousness of the changeless, individuality arises ever afresh therein.

But one thing the unhappy consciousness thus learns, namely that individuality is made manifest in the changeless, and that the changeless is made manifest in individuality. It finds that in general individuality belongs to the changeless true self, and that in fact its own individuality also belongs thereto. For the outcome of this process is precisely the unity of this twofold consciousness. This unity, then, comes to light, but for the first only as an unity wherein the diversity of the two aspects plays the chief part. For the unhappy consciousness there thus result three ways in which individuality and the changeless are linked. First, it rediscovers itself as again banished into its opposition to the changeless self; and it is cast back to the beginning of the strife, which latter still remains the element of the entire relationship. In the second place, the unhappy consciousness learns that individuality belongs to the very essence of the changeless, is the incarnation of the changeless; and the latter hereupon assumes the burden of this whole range of phenomena. In the third place, the unhappy consciousness discovers itself to be the individual who dwells in the changeless. In the first stage the changeless appears to consciousness only as the remote self, that condemns individuality. In passing through the second stage, consciousness learns that the changeless is as much an incarnate individual as it is itself; and thus, in the third stage, consciousness reaches the grade of the mind, rejoices to find itself in the mind, and becomes aware that its individuality is reconciled with the universal.

What is here set forth as the character and relationship of the changeless has appeared as the experience that the divided consciousness obtains in its woe. This experience is to be sure not its own one-sided process; for it is itself the changeless consciousness, and the latter is also an individual consciousness; so that the process is all the while a process in the changeless consciousness, belonging to the latter quite as much as to the other. For the changeless consciousness passes through the three stages, being first the changeless as in general opposed to the individual, then becoming an individual over against another individual, and finally being united with the latter. But this observation, in so far as it is made from our own point of view as observers, is here premature; for thus far we have come to know the changeless only in so far as consciousness has defined it. Not, as yet, the true changeless, but the changeless as modified by the duality of consciousness, has come to our sight; and so we know not how the developed and self-possessed changeless will behave. What has resulted from the foregoing is only this, that the mentioned characteristics appear, to the consciousness now under consideration, as belonging to the changeless.

Consequently the changeless consciousness itself also preserves even in its incarnate form the character and principle of separation and isolation as against the individual consciousness. From the latter's point of view, the fact that the changeless takes on the form of individuality appears as something which somehow *comes to pass*. The opposition to the changeless is something, moreover, which the individual consciousness merely finds as a fact. The relation seems to it merely a result of its natural constitution. As for the final reconciliation, the individual consciousness looks upon this as in part its own deed, the result of its own individuality; but it also regards a part of the unity as due, both in origin and in existence, to the changeless. The element of opposition thus remains even in the unity. In fact, in taking on its incarnate form, the changeless has not only retained but actually confirmed its character of remoteness. For although, in assuming a developed and incarnate individuality, it seems on the one hand to have approached the individual, still, on the other hand, it now stands over against him as an opaque fact of sense, with all the stubbornness of the actual about it. The hope that the individual may become one with the changeless must remain but hope, empty and distant; for between hope and fruition stand now the fatal chance and the lifeless indifference which have resulted from that very incarnation wherein lies the foundation of the hope. Because the changeless has thus entered the world of facts, has taken on the garments of actuality, it follows necessarily that in the world of time it has vanished, that in space it is far away, and forever far remains.

If at the outset the mere notion of the divided consciousness demanded that it should undertake the destruction of its individuality, and the growth into the changeless, the present result defines the undertaking thus: that the individual should leave off its relation with the formless ideal, and should come only into relations with the changeless as incarnate. For it is now the fact of the unity of the individual and the changeless which has become the truth and the object for consciousness, as before, in the mere notion, only the abstract and disembodied changeless was the essential object; and consciousness now finds the total separation of the notion as the relation which is to be forgotten. The thing which has now to be reduced to unity is the still external relation to the embodied ideal, insofar as the latter is a foreign actuality.

The process whereby the unreal self seeks to reach this unity is once more threefold, since it will be found to have a threefold relation to its incarnate but remote ideal. In the first place it will appear as the devout consciousness; in the second place, as an indi-vidual, whose relation to the actuality will be one of aspiration and of service; in the third place it will reach the consciousness of self-possession. We must now follow these three states of being, to see how they are involved in the general relation, and are determined thereby.

Taking the first state, that of the devout consciousness, one finds indeed that the incarnate changeless, as it appears to this consciousness, seems to be present in all the completeness of its being. But as a fact the fashion of the completed being of the changeless has not yet been developed. Should this completed being be revealed to consciousness, the revelation would be, as it were, rather the deed of the Ideal than the work of the devour consciousness; and thus the revelation would come from one side alone, would be no full and genuine revelation, but would remain burdened with incompleteness and with duality.

Although the unhappy consciousness still lacks the presence of its ideal, it is nevertheless as we see beyond the stage of pure thought, whether such thought were the mere abstract thinking of Stoicism, which forgets all individuality, or the merely restless thinking of scepticism, which in fact embodies individuality in its ignorant contradictions and its ceaseless unrepose. Both of these stages the unhappy consciousness has transcended. It begins the synthesis of pure thought and of individuality and persists therein. But it has not yet risen to the thought which is aware of the reconciliation of the conscious individual with the demands of pure thought. The unhappy consciousness stands between the two extremes, at the place where pure thought and the individual consciousness meet. It is in fact itself this meeting place; it is the unity of pure thought and individuality. It even knows that pure thought, yes the changeless itself, is essentially individual. But what it does not know is that this its object, the changeless, which it regards as having necessarily assumed an incarnate individuality, is identical with its own self, with the very individual as he is in consciousness.

Its attitude, then, in this first form, in which it appears as the devout consciousness, is not one in which it explicitly thinks about its object. It is implicitly indeed the consciousness of a thinking individual, and its object also is a thinking individual. But the relation between these two is still one that defies pure thought. Consciousness accordingly as it were makes but a feint at thinking, and takes the form of adoration. Such thought as it has remains the mere formless tinkling of an altar bell, or the wreathing of warm incense smoke—a thinking in music, such as never reaches an organized notion, wherein alone an inner objectivity could be attained. This limitless and devout inner feeling finds indeed its object, but as something uncomprehended, and so as a stranger. Thus comes to pass the inward activity of the devout soul, which is indeed self-conscious, but only in so far as it possesses the mere feeling of its sorrowful disharmony. This activity is one of ceaseless longing. It possesses the assurance that its true self is just such a pure soul—pure thought in fact, taking on the form of individuality—and that this being, who is the object of the devotion, since he possesses the thought of his own individuality, recognizes and approves the worshipper. But at the same time this Being is the unapproachable and remote. As you seize hold upon him he escapes, or rather he has already gone away. He has already gone away; for he is the ideal giving himself in thought the form of an individual and therefore consciousness gets without hindrance its self-fulfilment in him—gets self-fulfilment, but only to learn that it is the very opposite of this ideal. Instead of seizing hold on the true self, its mere feeling is all. It sinks back into itself. Unable at the moment of union to escape finding itself as the very opposite of the ideal, it has actually seized hold upon its own untruthfulness, not upon the truth. In the true self it has sought to find its own fulfilment; but *its own* means only its isolated individual reality. For the same reason it cannot get hold upon the true self in so far as he is at once an individual and a reality. Where one seeks him, the true self is not to be found; for by definition he is the remote self, and so is to be found nowhere. To seek him in so far as he is an individual is not to look for his universal, his ideal individuality, nor for his presence as the law of life, but merely to seek him as an individual thing, as a fact amongst facts, as something that sense could touch unhindered. But as such an object the ideal exists only as a lost object. What consciousness finds is thus only the sepulchre of its true life. But this sepulchre is now the actuality, and, moreover, one that by its nature forbids any abiding possession; and the presence of this tomb means only the strife of a search

that must be fruitless. But consciousness thus learns that there is no real sepulchre which can contain its true lord, the changeless. As lord who has been taken away he is not the true lord. The changeless will no longer be looked for here below, or grasped after as the vanished one. For hereby consciousness learns to look for individuality as a genuine and universal ideal.

In the next place then, the return of the soul to itself is to be defined as its knowledge that in its own individuality it has genuine being. It is the pure heart, which potentially, or from our point of view, has discovered the secret of self-satisfaction. For although in feeling it is sundered from its ideal, still this feeling is in essence a feeling of self-possession. What has been felt is the ideal as expressed in terms of pure feeling; and this ideal is its own very self. It issues from the process then as the feeling of self-possession, and so as an actual and independent being. By this return to itself it has, from our point of view, passed to its second relationship, that of aspiration and service. And in this second stage consciousness confirms itself in the assurance of self-possession (an assurance which we now see it to have attained), by overcoming and feeding upon the true self, which, in so far as it was an independent thing, was estranged. From the point of view of the unhappy consciousness, however, all that yet appears is the aspiration and the service. It knows not yet that in finding these it has the assurance of self-possession as the basis of its existence, and that its feeling of the true self is a self-possessed feeling. Not knowing this, it has still ever within it the fragmentary assurance of itself. Therefore any confirmation which it should receive from toiling and from communion would still be a fragmentary confirmation. Yes, itself it must destroy even this confirmation also, finding therein indeed a confirmation of something, but only of its isolation and its separation.

The actual world wherein the aspiration and the service find their calling, seems to this consciousness no longer an essentially vain world, that is only to be destroyed and consumed, but rather, like the consciousness itself, a world broken in twain, which is only in one aspect vain, while in another aspect it is a sanctified world, wherein the changeless is incarnate. For the changeless has retained the nature of individuality, and being, as changeless, an universal, its individuality has in general the significance of all actuality.

If consciousness were now aware of its independent personality, and if it regarded the actual world as essentially vain, it would get the feeling of its independence in its service and in its communion, since it would be aware of itself as the victory that overcometh the world. But because the world is regarded by it as an embodiment of the ideal, it may not overcome by its own power. It does indeed attain to conquest over the world and to a feasting thereon, but to this end it is essential that the changeless should itself give its own body as the food. And in this respect consciousness appears as a mere matter of fact having no part in the deed; but it also appears inwardly broken in twain, and this doubleness, its division into a self that stands in a genuine relation to itself and to reality, and a self whose life is hidden and undeveloped, is now apparent in the contrast between its service and its communion. As in actual relation to the world, consciousness is a doer of works, and knows itself as such, and this side belongs to its individuality. But it has also its undeveloped reality. This is hidden in the true self, and consists in the talents and virtues of the individual. They are a foreign gift. The changeless grants them to consciousness that they may be used.

In doing its good works, consciousness is, for the first, parted into a relationship between two extremes. On one side stands the toiler in the world here below; on the other side stands the passive actuality in whose midst he toils. Both are related to each other; both however are also referred to the changeless as their source, and have their being hidden therein. From each side, then, there is but a shadowy image let free to enter into play with the other. That term of the relationship which is called the actuality is overcome by the other term, the doer of good works. But the former term, for its part, can only be overcome because its own changeless nature overcomes it, divides itself in twain, and gives over the divided part to be the material for deeds. The power that does the deeds appears as the might that overcometh the world. But for this very reason the present consciousness, which regards its true self as something foreign, must regard this might also, whereby it works, as a thing remote from itself. Instead of winning self-possession from its good works, and becoming thereby sure of itself, consciousness relates all this activity back again to the other member of the relationship, which thus proves itself to be the pure universal, the absolute might, whence flows every form of activity, and wherein lies the truth both of the mutually dissolving terms, as they first appeared, and of their interchanging of relationship.

The changeless consciousness sacrifices its body, and gives it over to be used. On the other hand the individual consciousness renders thanks for the gift, forbids itself the satisfaction of a sense of independence, and refers all its doings to the changeless. In these two aspects of the mutual sacrifice made by both the members of the relation, consciousness does indeed win the sense of its own oneness with the changeless. But at the same time this oneness is still beladen with the separation, and is divided in itself. The opposition between the individual and the universal comes afresh to sight. For consciousness only *seems* to resign selfish satisfaction. As a fact it gets selfish satisfaction. For it still remains longing, activity, and fulfilment. As consciousness it has longed, it has acted, it has been filled. In giving thanks, in acknowledging the other as the true self, in making naught of itself, it has still been doing its own deed. This deed has repaid the deed of the other, has rendered a price for the kindly sacrifice. If the other has offered its own image as a gift, consciousness, for its part, has made its return in thanks, and has herein done actually more than the other, since it has offered its all, namely, its good works, while the other has been parted with its mere image. The entire process returns then back to the side of the individual, and does so not merely in respect of the actual aspiration, service, and communion, but even in respect of the very act of giving thanks, an act that was to attain the opposite result. In giving thanks consciousness is aware of itself as this individual, and refuses to be deceived by its own seeming resignation. What has resulted is only the twofold reference of the process to its two terms; and the result is the renewed division into the conflicting consciousness of the changeless on the one hand, and, on the other hand, the consciousness of the opposed will, activity, and fulfilment, and even of the very resignation itself; for these constitute in general the separated individuality.

Herewith begins the third phase of the process of this consciousness, which follows from the second as a consciousness that in truth, by will and by deed, has proved its independence. In the first phase it was the mere notion of a live consciousness, an inner life that had not yet attained actuality by service and communion. The second phase was the attainment, as outer activity and communion. Returned from this outer activity, consciousness has now reached the stage where it has experienced its own actuality and power, where it knows in truth that it is fully self-possessed. But now the enemy comes to light in his most genuine form. In the struggle of the inner life the individual had existence only as an abstraction, as "passed in music out of sight." In service and in communion, as the realization of this unreal selfhood, it is able in its immediate experience to forget itself, and its consciousness of its own merit in this actual service is turned to humiliation through the act of thankful acknowledgment. But this humiliation is in truth a return of consciousness to itself, and to itself as the possessor of its own actuality.

This third relationship, wherein this genuine actuality is to be one term, is that relationship of the actuality to the universal, wherein the actuality is nevertheless to appear as an unreality; and the process of this relationship is still to be considered.

In the first place, as regards the conflicting relationship of consciousness, wherein its own reality appears to it as an obvious nothingness, the result is that its actual work seems to it a doing of naught, and its satisfaction is but a sense of its misery. Work and satisfaction thus lose all universal content and meaning; for if they had any, then they would involve a full self-possession. Both of them sink to the level of individuality; and consciousness, turning upon this individuality, devotes itself to making naught of it. Consciousness of an actual individual is a consciousness of the mere animal functions of the body. These latter are no longer naïvely carried out as something that is altogether of no moment, and that can have no weight or significance for the spirit; on the contrary, they become the object of earnest concern, and are of the very weightiest moment. The enemy arises anew in his defeat. Consciousness holds him in eye, yet frees itself not from him, but rather dwells upon the sight, and sees constantly its own uncleanness. And because, at the same time, this object of its striving, instead of being significant, is of the most contemptible, instead of being an universal is of the most individual, we therefore behold at this stage only a brooding, unhappy and miserable personality, limited solely to himself and his little deeds.

But all the while this person links both to the sense of his misery and to the worthlessness of his deeds, the consciousness that he is one with the ideal. For the attempted direct destruction of individuality is determined by the thought of the ideal, and takes place for the sake of the Ideal. This relation of dependence constitutes the essence of the negative onslaught upon individuality. But the dependence is as such potentially positive, and will bring consciousness to a sense of its own unity.

This determinate dependence is the rational tie, whereby the individual who at first holds fast by his opposition to the true self, is still linked to the other term, yet only by means of a third element. This mediating element reveals the true self to the false self, which in its turn knows that in the eyes of the true self it has existence only by virtue of the dependence. It is the dependence then which reveals the two terms of the relationship to one another, and which, as mediator, takes the part of each one of the terms in presence of the other. The mediator too is a conscious being, for its work is the production of this consciousness as such. What it brings to pass is that overcoming of individuality which consciousness is undertaking.

Through the mediator, then, consciousness frees itself from regarding its good works and its communion as due to its private merit. It rejects all claim to independence of will. It casts upon the mediator, the intercessor, the burden of its self-will, its freedom of choice, and its sins. The mediator, dwelling in the immediate presence of the ideal, gives counsel as to what is to be done. And what is done, being in submission to the will of another, is no longer one's own act. What is still left to the untrue self is the objective result of the deed, the fruit of the toil, the satisfaction. But this too it refuses to accept as its own, and resigns not only its self-will, but the actual outcome of its service and its satisfaction. It resigns this outcome, first, because the latter would involve an attainment of self-conscious truth and independence (and this consciousness lives in the thought and the speech of a strange and incomprehensible mystery). Secondly, moreover, it resigns the outcome in so far as the latter consists of worldly goods, and so it abandons, in a measure, whatever it has earned by its labor. Thirdly, it resigns all the satisfaction which has fallen to its lot, forbidding itself such satisfaction through fasting and through penance.

By these characteristics, by the surrender of self-will, of property, and of satisfaction, and by the further and positive characteristic of its undertaking of a mysterious task, consciousness does in truth free itself completely from any sense of inner or outer freedom, from any trust in the reality of its independence. It is sure that it has verily surrendered its ego, and has reduced its natural self-consciousness to a mere thing, to a fact amongst facts. Only by such a genuine self-surrender could consciousness prove its own resignation. For only thus does there vanish the deceit that lies in the inner offering of thanks with the heart, with the sentiments, with the lips. Such offering does indeed strip from the individual all independent might, and ascribes all the glory to the heavenly giver. But the individual even when thus stripped, retains his outer self-will, for he abandons not his possessions; and he retains his inner self-will, for he is aware that it is he who undertakes this self-sacrifice, and who has in himself the virtue involved in such an undertaking—a virtue which he has not exchanged for the mysterious grace that cometh from above.

But in the genuine resignation, when once it has come to pass, consciousness, in laying aside the burden of its own deeds, has also, in effect, laid aside the burden of its grief. Yet that this laying aside has already, in effect, taken place, is due to the deed of the other member of the tie, namely to the essential self. The sacrifice of the unreal self was made not by its own one-sided act, but involved the working of the other's grace. For the resignation of self-will is only in part negative, and on the other hand involves in its very notion, or in its beginning, the positive transformation of the will, and, in particular, its trans-formation from an individual into an universal will. Consciousness finds this positive meaning of the denial of self-will to consist in the will of the changeless, as this will is done, not by consciousness itself, but through the counsel of the mediator. Consciousness becomes aware, then, that its will is universal and essential, but it does not regard itself as identical with this essential nature. Self-resignation is not seen to be in its very notion identical with the positive work of the universal will. In the same way the abandonment of possession and of satisfaction has only the same negative significance, and the universal that thus comes in sight does not appear to consciousness as its own deed. The unity of truth and of self-possession implied in the notion of this activity, an unity which consciousness accordingly regards as its essence and its reality, is not recognized as implied in this very notion. Not is the unity recognized by consciousness as its own self-created and immediately possessed object. Rather does consciousness only hear, spoken by the mediator's voice, the still fragile assurance that its own grief is, in the yet hidden truth of the matter, the very reverse, namely the bliss of an activity which rejoices in its tasks, that its own miserable deeds are, in the same hidden truth, the perfect work. And the real meaning of this assurance is that only what is done by an individual is or can be a deed. But for consciousness both activity and its own actual deeds remain miserable. Its satisfaction is its sorrow, and the freedom from this sorrow, in a positive joy, it looks for in another world. But this other world, where its activity and its being are to become, even while they remain its own, real activity and being—what is this world but the image of Reason—of the assurance of consciousness that in its individuality it is and possesses all reality?

STUDY QUESTIONS: HEGEL, *PHENOMENOLOGY OF MIND*

1. What does consciousness learn from skepticism?
2. What is the "unhappy and broken" consciousness? How does it arise?
3. What is the "changeless" consciousness?
4. What is the "unreal self?"
5. How is the "return of the soul to itself defined?
6. What is the third phase of consciousness?
7. How can consciousness free itself from its good works?
8. What is the role of reason in relation to consciousness, individuality, and reality?

THE PHILOSOPHY OF HISTORY

In Hegel's view, the evolutionary changes in philosophy are not merely conceived as the abstract work of human philosophers trying to understand themselves and the world. Rather, philosophy, like history itself, is but the world (the absolute) trying to understand itself. Because this process cannot be understood without thorough knowledge of all these developing stages of thought as represented by the history of philosophy, trying to understand philosophy without understanding the history of philosophy is impossible. The history of philosophy has been an important facet of philosophy ever since. The idea that in reading the history of philosophy we are viewing not merely the struggles of individuals to understand themselves and the world, but are witnessing the evolution of the world's understanding of itself, can be thoroughly inspiring.

The only thought that philosophy brings with it to the contemplation of history, is the simple conception of reason; that reason is the sovereign of the world; that the history of the world, therefore, presents us with a rational process. This conviction and intuition is a hypothesis in the domain of history as such. In that of philosophy it is no hypothesis. It is there proved by speculative cognition, that reason—and this term may here suffice us, without investigating the relation sustained by the universe to the divine being—is substance, as well as infinite power, its own infinite material underlying all the natural and spiritual life which it originates, as also the infinite form—that which sets this material in motion. On the one hand, reason is the substance of the universe, namely that by which and in which all reality has its being and subsistence. On the other hand, it is the infinite energy of the universe; since reason is not so powerless as to be incapable of producing anything but a mere ideal, a mere intention—having its place outside reality, nobody knows where; something separate and abstract, in the heads of certain human beings. It is the infinite complex of things, their entire essence and truth. It is its own material which it commits to its own active energy to work up; not needing, as finite action does, the conditions of an external material of given means from which it may obtain its support and the objects of its activity. It supplies its own nourishment, and is the object of its own operations. While it is exclusively its own basis of existence, and absolute final aim, it is also the energizing power realizing this aim; developing it not only in the phenomena of the natural, but also of the mental, universe—the history of the world. That this "idea" or "reason" is the true, the eternal, the absolutely powerful essence, that it reveals itself in the world, and that in that world nothing else is revealed but this and its honor and glory—is the thesis which, as we have said, has been proved in philosophy, and is here regarded as demonstrated.

In those of my hearers who are not acquainted with philosophy, I may fairly presume, at least, the existence of a belief in reason, a desire, a thirst for acquaintance with it, in entering upon this course of lectures. It is, in fact, the wish for rational insight, not the ambition to amass a mere heap of acquirements, that should be presupposed in every case as possessing the mind of the learner in the study of science. If the clear idea of reason is not already developed in our minds, in beginning the study of universal history, we should at least have the firm, unconquerable faith that reason *does* exist there; and that the world of intelligence and conscious volition is not abandoned to chance, but must show itself in the light of the self-aware idea. Yet I am not obliged to make any such preliminary demand upon your faith. What I have said thus provisionally, and what I shall have further to say, is, even in reference to our branch of science, not to be regarded as hypothetical, but as a summary view of the whole; the result of the investigation we

Hegel, from *Philosophy of History*, translated by J. Sibree (London: Ciradel Press, 1900).

are about to pursue; a result which happens to be known to *me*, because I have traversed the entire field. It is only an inference from the history of the world that its development has been a rational process; that the history in question has constituted the rational necessary course of the world-mind— that mind whose nature is always one and the same, but which unfolds this one nature in the phenomena of the world's existence. This must, as before stated, present itself as the ultimate result of history. But we have to take the latter as it is. We must proceed historically—empirically. Among other precautions we must take care not to be misled by professed historians who . . . are chargeable with the very procedure of which they accuse the philosopher—introducing a priori inventions of their own into the records of the past. It is, for example, a widely current fiction that there was an original primeval people, taught immediately by God, endowed with perfect insight and wisdom, possessing a thorough knowledge of all natural laws and spiritual truth; that there have been such or such sacerdotal peoples; or, to mention a more specific assertion, that there was a Roman Epos, from which the Roman historians derived the early annals of their city, etc. A priorities of this kind we leave to those talented historians by profession, among whom . . . their use is not uncommon. We might then announce it as the first condition to be observed, that we should faithfully adopt all that is historical. But in such general expressions as "faithfully" and "adopt" lies the ambiguity. Even the ordinary, the "impartial" historian, who believes and professes that he maintains a simply receptive attitude, surrendering himself only to the data supplied him, is by no means passive as regards the exercise of his thinking powers. He brings his categories with him, and sees the phenomena presented to his mental vision exclusively through these media. And, especially in all that pretends to the name of science, it is indispensable that reason should not sleep, that reflection should be in full play. To him who looks upon the world rationally, the world in its turn, presents a rational aspect. The relation is mutual. But the various exercises of reflection—the different points of view—the modes of deciding the simple question of the relative importance of events (the first category that occupies the attention of the historian), do not belong to this place.

I will only mention two phases and points of view that concern the generally diffused conviction that reason has ruled, and is still ruling in the world, and consequently in the world's history, because they give us, at the same time, an opportunity for more closely investigating the question that presents the greatest difficulty, and for indicating a branch of the subject that will have to be enlarged on in the sequel.

(1) One of these points is the historical fact that the Greek Anaxagoras was the first to enunciate the doctrine that nous, understanding in general, or reason, governs the world. It is not intelligence as self-conscious reason, not a spirit as such, that is meant; and we must clearly distinguish these from each other. The movement of the solar system takes place according to unchangeable laws. These laws are reason, implicit in the phenomena in question. But neither the sun nor the planets that revolve around it according to these laws can be said to have any consciousness of them.

A thought of this kind—that nature is an embodiment of reason; that it is unchangeably subordinate to universal laws—appears nowise striking or strange to us. We are accustomed to such conceptions, and find nothing extraordinary in them. And I have mentioned this extraordinary occurrence partly to show how history teaches that ideas of this kind, which may seem trivial to us, have not always been in the world; that on the contrary, such a thought marks an epoch in the annals of human intelligence. Aristotle says of Anaxagoras, as the originator of the thought in question, that he appeared as a sober man among the drunken. Socrates adopted the doctrine from Anaxagoras, and it forthwith became the ruling idea in philosophy—except in the school of Epicurus, who ascribed all events to chance. "I was delighted with the sentiment," Plato makes Socrates say, "and hoped I had found a teacher who would show me nature in harmony with reason, who would demonstrate in each particular phenomenon its specific aim, and in the whole, the grand object of the universe. I would not have surrendered this hope for a great deal. But how very much was I disappointed, when, having zealously applied myself to the writings of Anaxagoras, I found that he adduces only external causes, such as air, ether, water, and the like." It is evident that the defect Socrates complains of respecting Anaxagoras' doctrine does not concern the principle itself but the shortcoming of the propounder in applying it to nature in the concrete. Nature is not deduced from that principle: the latter remains in fact a mere abstraction, inasmuch as the former is not comprehended and exhibited as a development of it—an organization produced by and from reason. I wish, at the very outset, to call your attention to the important difference between a conception, a principle, a truth limited to an *abstract* form and its determinate application and concrete development. This distinction affects the whole fabric of philosophy; and among other bearings of it there is one to which we shall have to revert at the close of our view of universal history, in investigating the aspect of political affairs in the most recent period.

(2) We have next to notice the rise of this idea— that reason directs the world—in connection with a further application of it, well known to us: in the form, namely of the religious truth that the world is not abandoned to chance and external contingent causes, but that a providence controls it. I stated above that I would not make a demand on your faith with regard to the principle announced. Yet I might appeal to your belief in it, in this religious aspect, if, as a general rule, the nature of philosophical science allowed it to attach authority to presuppositions. To put it in another form, this appeal is forbidden, because the science of which we have to treat proposes itself to furnish the proof (not indeed of the abstract truth of the doctrine, but) of its correctness as compared with facts. The truth, then, that a providence (that of God) presides over the events of the world, consorts with the proposition in question; for divine providence is wisdom endowed with an infinite power, which realizes its aim, viz. the absolute rational design of the world. Reason is thought conditioning itself with perfect freedom. But a difference—rather a contradiction—will manifest itself, between this belief and our principle, just as was the case in reference to the demand made by Socrates in the case of Anaxagoras' dictum. For that belief is similarly indefinite; it is what is called a belief in a general providence, and is not followed out into definite application, or displayed in its bearing on the grand total—the entire course of human history. But to *explain* history is to depict the passions of mankind,

the genius, the active powers, that play their part on the great stage; and the providentially determined process that these exhibit constitutes what is generally called the "plan" of providence. Yet it is this very plan which is supposed to be concealed from our view: which it is deemed presumption even to wish to recognize. The ignorance of Anaxagoras as to how intelligence reveals itself in actual existence was ingenuous. Neither in his consciousness nor in that of Greece at large had that thought been further expanded. He had not attained the power to apply his general principle to the concrete, so as to deduce the latter from the former. It was Socrates who took the first step in comprehending the union of the concrete with the universal. Anaxagoras, then, did not take up a hostile position towards such an application. The common belief in providence *does*; at least it opposes the use of the principle on the large scale, and denies the possibility of discerning the plan of providence. In isolated cases this plan is supposed to be manifest. Pious persons are encouraged to recognize in particular circumstances something more than mere chance, to acknowledge the guiding hand of God—for example when help has unexpectedly come to an individual in great perplexity and need. But these instances of providential design are of a limited kind, and concern the accomplishment of nothing more than the desires of the individual in question. But in the history of the world, the individuals we have to do with are peoples, totalities that are states. We cannot, therefore, be satisfied with what we may call this "peddling" view of providence, to which the belief alluded to limits itself. Equally unsatisfactory is the merely abstract, undefined belief in a providence, when that belief is not brought to bear upon the details of the process which it conducts. On the contrary our earnest endeavor must be directed to the recognition of the ways of providence, the means it uses, and the historical phenomena in which it manifests itself; and we must show their connection with the general principle above mentioned. . . .

The enquiry into the essential destiny of reason— as far as it is considered in reference to the world— is identical with the question, what is the ultimate design of the world? And the expression implies that that design is destined to be realized. Two points of consideration suggest themselves: first, the import of this design, its abstract definition, and second, its realization.

It must be observed at the outset that the phenomenon we investigate—universal history—belongs to the realm of mind. The term "world" includes both physical and psychical nature. Physical nature also plays its part in the world's history, and attention will have to be paid to the fundamental natural relations thus involved. But mind, and the course of its development, is our substantial object. Our task does not require us to contemplate nature as a rational system in itself—though in its own proper domain it proves itself such—but simply in its relation to mind. On the stage on which we are observing it—universal history—mind displays itself in its most concrete reality. Notwithstanding this (or rather for the very purpose of comprehending the general principles which this, its form of concrete reality, embodies) we must premise some abstract characteristics of the nature of spirit. Such an explanation, however, cannot be given here under any other form than that of bare assertion. The present is not the occasion for unfolding the idea of mind speculatively; for whatever has a place in an introduction must, as already observed, be taken as simply historical, something assumed as having been explained and proved elsewhere, or whose demonstration awaits the sequel of the science of history itself.

We have therefore to mention here:

1. The abstract characteristics of the nature of mind.
2. The means mind uses in order to realize its idea.
3. The form that the perfect embodiment of mind assumes: the state.

1. FREEDOM AS THE GOAL OF MIND

The nature of mind may be understood by a glance at its direct opposite—matter. As the essence of matter is gravity, so, on the other hand, we may affirm that the essence, the substance, of mind is freedom. All will readily assent to the doctrine that, among other properties, mind is also endowed with freedom; but philosophy teaches that all the qualities of mind exist only through freedom, that all are but means for attaining freedom, that all seek and produce this and this alone. It is a finding of speculative philosophy that freedom is the sole truth of mind. . . .

The destiny of the mental world, and—since this is the substantial world, while the physical remains subordinate to it, or, in the language of speculation, has no truth as against the mental—the final cause of the world at large, we allege to be the consciousness of its own freedom on the part of mind, and *ipso facto* the reality of that freedom. But that this term "freedom," without further qualification, is an indefinite and incalculably ambiguous term, and that, while what it represents is the *ne plus ultra* of attainment, it is liable to an infinity of misunderstandings, confusions and errors, and can become the occasion for all imaginable excesses—has never been more clearly known and felt than in modern times. Yet, for the present, we must content ourselves with the term itself without further definition. Attention was also directed to the importance of the infinite difference between a principle in the abstract and its realization in the concrete. In the process before us, the essential nature of freedom—which involves in it absolute necessity—is to be displayed as coming to a consciousness of itself (for it is in its very nature self-consciousness) and thereby realizing its existence. It is its own object of attainment, and the sole aim of mind. This is the result at which the process of the world's history has been continually aiming, and to which the sacrifices that have ever and anon been laid on the vast altar of the earth, through the long lapse of ages, have been offered. This is the only aim that sees itself realized and fulfilled, the only pole of repose amid the ceaseless change of events and conditions, and the sole efficient principle that pervades them. This final aim is God's purpose with the world; but God is the absolute perfect Being, and can, therefore, will nothing other than himself—his own will. The nature of His will—that is, His nature itself—is what we here call the idea of freedom, translating the language of religion into that of thought. The question, then, which we may next put, is: What means does this principle of freedom use for its realization? This is the second point we have to consider.

2. THE ROLE OF THE INDIVIDUAL

The question of the means by which freedom develops itself into a world conducts us to the phenomenon of history itself. Although freedom is, primarily, an inward idea, the means it uses are external and phenomenal, presenting themselves in history to our sensuous vision. The first glance at history convinces us that the actions of men proceed from their needs, their passions, their characters and talents, and impresses us with the belief that such needs, passions and interests are the sole springs of action—the efficient agents in this scene of activity. Among these may, perhaps, be found aims of a liberal or universal kind, benevolence it may be, or noble patriotism; but such virtues and general views are but insignificant as compared with the world and its doings. We may perhaps see the ideal of reason actualized in those who adopt such aims, and within the sphere of their influence; but they bear only a trifling proportion to the mass of the human race, and the extent of that influence is limited accordingly. Passions, private aims, and the satisfaction of selfish desires, are on the other hand most effective springs of action. Their power lies in the fact that they respect none of the limitations that justice and morality would impose on them, and that these natural impulses have a more direct influence over man than the artificial and tedious discipline that tends to order and self-restraint, law and morality. When we look at this display of passions and the consequences of their violence, the irrationality which is associated not only with them, but even (rather we might say especially) with good designs and righteous aims—when we see the evil, the vice, the ruin that has befallen the most flourishing kingdoms which the mind of man ever created, we can scarce avoid being filled with sorrow at this universal taint of corruption: and, since this decay is not the work of mere nature, but of the human will—a moral embitterment—a revolt of the good mind (if it have a place within us) may well be the result of our reflections. Without rhetorical exaggeration, a simply truthful account of the miseries that have overwhelmed the noblest of nations and polities, and the finest exemplars of private virtue, forms a picture of most fearful aspect, and excites emotions of the profoundest and most hopeless sadness, counter-balanced by no consolatory result. We endure in beholding it a mental torture, allowing no defense or escape but the consideration that what has happened could not be otherwise, that it is a fatality no intervention could alter. And at last

we draw back from the intolerable disgust with which these sorrowful reflections threaten us, into the more agreeable environment of our individual life—the present formed by our private aims and interests. In short we retreat into the selfishness that stands on the quiet shore, and thence enjoy in safety the distant spectacle of "wrecks confusedly hurled." But even regarding history as the slaughter-bench at which the happiness of peoples, the wisdom of states, and the virtue of individuals have been made victims, the question involuntarily arises: to what principle, to what final aim these enormous sacrifices have been offered. . . .

The first remark we have to make, one which—though already presented more than once—cannot be too often repeated when the occasion seems to call for it, is that what we call principle, aim, destiny, or the nature and idea of mind, is something merely general and abstract. Principle, plan of existence, law, is a hidden, undeveloped essence, which as such—however true in itself—is not completely real. Aims, principles, etc., have a place in our thoughts, in our subjective design only, but not yet in the sphere of reality. What exists only for itself is a possibility, a potentiality, but has not yet emerged into existence. A second element must be introduced in order to produce actuality—namely realization, activity whose motive power is the will, the activity of man in the widest sense. It is only by this activity that that idea, or abstract characteristics generally, can be realized, actualized; for of themselves they are powerless. The motive power that puts them in operation, and gives them determinate existence, is the need, instinct, inclination, and passion of man. . . .

We assert then that nothing has been accomplished without interest on the part of the actors; and—if interest be called passion, inasmuch as the whole individuality, to the neglect of all other actual or possible interests and claims, is devoted to an object with every fibre of volition, concentrating all its desires and powers upon it—we may affirm absolutely that nothing great in the world has been accomplished without passion. Two elements, therefore, enter into the object of our investigation: the first, the idea, the second, the complex of human passions; the one, the warp, the other, the woof, of the vast tapestry of universal history. The concrete mean and union of the two is liberty, under the conditions of morality in a state. . . .

From this comment on the second essential element in the historical embodiment of an aim, we infer—glancing at the institution of the state in passing—that a state is then well constituted and internally powerful when the private interest of its citizens is one with the common interest of the state, when the one finds its gratification and realization in the other—a proposition in itself very important. But in a state many institutions must be adopted, much political machinery invented, accompanied by appropriate political arrangements, necessitating long struggles of the understanding before what is really appropriate can be discovered—involving, moreover, contentions with private interest and passions, and a tedious discipline of these latter, in order to bring about the desired harmony. The epoch when a state attains this harmonious condition marks the period of its blossoming, its virtue, its vigor, and its prosperity. But the history of mankind does not begin with a conscious aim of any kind, as it is the case with the particular circles into which men form themselves of set purpose. The mere social instinct implies a conscious purpose of security for life and property, and when society has been constituted this purpose becomes more comprehensive. The history of the world begins with its general aim—the realization of the idea of mind—only in an *implicit* form that is, as nature, a hidden (most profoundly hidden) unconscious instinct; and the whole process of history (as already observed) is directed to rendering this unconscious impulse a conscious one. Thus appearing in the form of merely natural existence, natural will—which has been called the subjective side—physical craving, instinct, passion, private interest, as also opinion and subjective conception, spontaneously present themselves at the very start. This vast congeries of volitions, interests and activities, constitutes the instruments and means of the world-mind for attaining its object, bringing it to consciousness, and realizing it. And this aim is none other than finding itself—coming to itself—and contemplating itself in concrete actuality. But that those manifestations of vitality on the part of individuals and peoples, in which they seek and fulfil their own purposes, are, at the same time, the means and instruments of a higher and broader purpose of which they know nothing, which they

realize unconsciously, might be made a matter of question—indeed has been questioned, and in every variety of form denied, decried and condemned as mere dreaming and "philosophy." But on this point I announced my view at the very outset, and asserted our hypothesis—which, however, will appear finally in the form of a legitimate inference—and our belief that reason governs the world and has consequently governed its history. In relation to this independently universal and substantial existence, all else is subordinate, subservient to it, and the means for its development. . . .

He is happy who finds his condition suited to his special character, will, and fancy, and so enjoys himself in that condition. The history of the world is not the theatre of happiness. Periods of happiness are blank pages in it, for they are periods of harmony, periods when the antithesis is in abeyance. Reflection on self—the freedom above described—is abstractly defined as the formal element of the activity of the absolute idea. The realizing *activity* of which we have spoken is the middle term of the syllogism, one of whose extremes is the universal essence, the *idea*, which reposes in the hidden depths of mind, and the other, the complex of external things, objective matter. That activity is the medium by which the universal latent principle is translated into the domain of objectivity.

I will endeavor to make what has been said more vivid and clear by examples.

The building of a house is, in the first instance, a subjective aim and design. On the other hand we have, as means, the several substances required for the work—iron, wood, stones. The elements are made use of in working up this material: fire to melt the iron, wind to blow the fire, water to set wheels in motion, in order to cut the wood, etc. The result is that the wind, which has helped to build the house, is shut out by the house; so also are the violence of rains and floods, and the destructive powers of fire, so far as the house is made fire-proof. The stones and beams obey the law of gravity, press downwards, and so high walls are carried up. Thus the elements are made use of in accordance with their nature, and yet are made to cooperate for a product by which their operation is limited. Thus the passions of men are gratified; they develop themselves and their aims in accordance with their natural tendencies, and build up the edifice of human society, thus fortifying a position for right and order against themselves.

The connection of events above indicated, involves also the fact that in history an additional result is commonly produced by human actions beyond what they aim at and obtain, what they immediately recognize and desire. They gratify their own interest; but something further is thereby accomplished, latent in the actions in question, though not present to their consciousness and not included in their design. An analogous example is the case of a man who, from a feeling of revenge—perhaps not an unjust one, but produced by injury on the other's part—burns that other man's house. A connection is immediately established between the deed itself and a train of circumstances not directly included in it, considered in abstraction. In itself it consisted in merely presenting a small flame to a small portion of a beam. Events not involved in that simple act follow of themselves. The part of the beam that was set fire to is connected with its remote portions; the beam itself is united with the woodwork of the house generally, and this with other houses, so that a wide conflagration ensues, which destroys the goods and chattels of many others besides the man against whom the act of revenge was first directed—perhaps even costs not a few men their lives. This lay neither in the deed considered in itself, nor in the design of the man who committed it. But the action has a further general bearing. In the design of the doer it was only revenge executed against an individual in the destruction of his property, but it is moreover a crime, and that involves punishment also. This may not have been present to the mind of the perpetrator, still less in his intention; but his deed itself—the general principles it calls into play, its substantial content—entails it. By this example I wish only to impress on you the point that in a simple act something further may be implicated than lies in the intention and consciousness of the agent. The example before us involves, however, this additional consideration, that the substance of the act, consequently we may say the act itself, recoils upon the perpetrator—reacts upon him with destructive tendency. This union of the two extremes—the embodiment of a general idea in the form of direct reality, and the elevation of a particularity into connection with universal truth—is brought to pass, at first sight, under the conditions of an utter diversity of nature between the two, and an indifference of the one extreme towards the other. The aims that the agents set before themselves are limited and special; but it must be remarked that the agents themselves are intelligent thinking beings. The purport of their desires is interwoven with general, essential considerations of justice, good, duty, etc.; for mere desire—volition in its rough and savage forms—falls not within the scene and sphere of universal history. Those general considerations, which form at the same time a norm for directing aims and actions, have a determinate purport; for such an abstraction as "good for its own sake" has no place in living reality. If men are to act, they must not only intend the good, but must have decided for themselves whether this or that particular thing is a good. What special course of action, however, is good or not is determined, as regards the ordinary contingencies of private life, by the laws and customs of a state; and here no great difficulty is presented. Each individual has his position; he knows on the whole what a just, honorable course of conduct is. As to ordinary, private relations, the assertion that it is difficult to choose the right and good—regarding it as the mark of an exalted morality to find difficulties and raise scruples on that score—may be set down to an evil or perverse will that seeks to evade duties not in themselves of a perplexing nature, or, at any rate, to an idly reflective habit of mind, where a feeble will affords no sufficient exercise to the faculties, leaving them therefore to find occupation within themselves, and to expend themselves on moral self-adulation.

It is quite otherwise with the comprehensive relations that history has to do with. In this sphere are presented those momentous collisions between existing, acknowledged duties, laws, and rights, and those contingencies which are adverse to this fixed system, which assail and even destroy its foundations and existence, whose tenor may nevertheless seem good, on the whole advantageous—yes, even indispensable and necessary. These contingencies realize themselves in history: they involve a general principle of a different order from that on which depends the permanence of a people or a state. This principle is an essential phase in the development of the creating idea, of truth striving and urging towards itself. Historical men—world-historical individuals—are those in whose aims such a general principle lies.

Caesar—in danger of losing a position, not perhaps at that time of superiority, yet at least of equality with the others who were at the head of the state, and of succumbing to those who were just on the point of becoming his enemies—belongs essentially to this category. These enemies, who were at the same time pursuing *their* personal aims, had the form of the constitution, and the power conferred by an appearance of justice, on their side. Caesar was contending for the maintenance of his position, honor, and safety; and, since the power of his opponents included the sovereignty over the provinces of the Roman Empire, his victory secured for him the conquest of that entire Empire, and he thus became—though leaving the form of the constitution—the autocrat of the state. What secured for him the execution of a design, which in the first instance was of negative import—the autocracy of Rome—was, however, at the same time an independently necessary feature in the history of Rome and of the world. It was not, then, his private gain merely, but an unconscious impulse that occasioned the accomplishment of that for which the time was ripe. Such are all great historical men, whose own particular aims involve those large issues which are the will of the world-mind. They may be called heroes, inasmuch as they have derived their purposes and their vocation, not from the calm, regular course of things, sanctioned by the existing order, but from a concealed fount—one that has not attained to phenomenal, present existence—from that inner mind, still hidden beneath the surface, which, impinging on the outer world as on a shell, bursts it in pieces, because it is a different kernel from that which belongs to that shell. They are men, therefore, who appear to draw the impulse of their life from themselves, and whose deeds have produced a condition of things and a complex of historical relations that appear to be only their interest and their work.

Such individuals have no consciousness of the general idea they were unfolding, while prosecuting those aims of theirs; on the contrary, they were practical, political men. But at the same time they were thinking men, who had an insight into the requirements of the time—what was ripe for development. This was the very truth for their age, for their world, the genus next in order, so to speak, and which was already formed in the womb of time. It was theirs to know this nascent principle, the necessary, directly sequent step in progress that their world was to take, to make this their aim, and to expend their energy in promoting it. World-historical men—the heroes of an epoch—must, therefore, be recognized as its clear-sighted ones; their deeds, their words are the best of that time. Great men have formed purposes to satisfy themselves, not others. Whatever prudent designs and counsels they might have learned from others would be the more limited and inconsistent features in their career, for it was they who best understood affairs, from whom others learned, and whose policy was approved, or at least acquiesced in. For that mind which had taken this fresh step in history is the inmost soul of all individuals, but in a state of unconsciousness which the great men in question awoke. Their fellows therefore follow these soul leaders, for they feel the irresistible power of their own inner mind thus embodied. If we go on to cast a look at the fate of these world-historical persons whose vocation it was to be the agents of the world-mind, we shall find it to have been no happy one. They attained no calm enjoyment; their whole life was labor and trouble; their whole nature was nothing but their master passion. When their object is attained they fall off like empty hulls from the kernel. They die early, like Alexander; they are murdered, like Caesar; transported to St. Helena, like Napoleon. This fearful consolation—that historical men have not enjoyed what is called happiness, of which only private life (and this may be passed under very various external circumstances) is capable—this consolation those may draw from history who stand in need of it; and it is craved by envy, vexed at what is great and transcendent, striving, therefore, to belittle it and to find some flaw in it. Thus in modern times it has been demonstrated *ad nauseam* that princes are generally unhappy on their thrones; in consideration of which the possession of a throne is tolerated, and men acquiesce in the fact that not themselves but the personages in question are its occupants. The free man, we may observe, is not envious, but gladly recognizes what is great and exalted, and rejoices that it exists.

It is in the light of those common elements which constitute the interest and therefore the passions of individuals that these historical men are to be regarded. They are great men, because they willed and accomplished something great, not a mere fancy, a mere intention, but what met the case and fell in with the needs of the age. This mode of considering them also excludes the so-called "psychological" view, which—serving the purpose of envy most effectually—contrives to refer all actions to the heart, to bring them under a subjective aspect—so that they appear to have done everything under the impulse of some passion, mean, or grand—some morbid craving—and on account of these passions and cravings to have been not moral men. Alexander of Macedonia partly subdued Greece, and then Asia; therefore he was possessed by a morbid craving for conquest. He is alleged to have acted from greed of fame and conquest; and the proof that these were the impelling motives is that what he did resulted in fame. What pedagogue has not demonstrated of Alexander the Great, of Julius Caesar, that they were moved by such passions, and were consequently immoral men? By which it is implied that he, the pedagogue, is a better man than they, because he has not such passions; a proof of which lies in the fact that he does not conquer Asia, vanquish Darius and Porus, but while he enjoys life himself lets others enjoy it too. These psychologists are particularly fond of contemplating those peculiarities of great historical figures which appertain to them as private persons. Man must eat and drink; he sustains relations to friends and acquaintances; he has passing impulses and ebullitions of temper. "No man is a hero to his valet," is a well-known proverb; I have added—and Goethe repeated it two years later—"but not because the former is no hero, but because the latter is a valet." He takes off the hero's boots, assists him to bed, knows that he prefers champagne, etc. Historical personages waited upon in historical literature by such psychological valets do not make out well; they are brought down by their attendants to a level with—or rather a few degrees below the level of—the morality of such exquisite discerners of spirits. Homer's Thersites, who abuses the kings, is a standing figure for all times. Blows—that is beating with a solid cudgel—he does not get in every age, as in the Homeric one; but his envy, his egotism, is the thorn he has to carry in his flesh; and the undying worm that gnaws him is the tormenting consideration that his excellent views and vituperations remain absolutely without effect in the world. But our satisfaction at the fate of Thersitism also may have its sinister side.

A world-historical individual is not so unwise as to indulge a variety of wishes to divide his regards. He is devoted to the one aim, regardless of all else. It is even possible that such men may treat other great, even sacred, interests inconsiderately—conduct which is indeed obnoxious to moral reprehension. But so mighty a form must trample down many an innocent flower, crush to pieces many an object in its path.

The special interest of passion is thus inseparable from the active development of a general principle: for it is from the special and determinate, and from its negation, that the universal results. Particularity contends with its like, and some loss is involved in the issue. It is not the general idea that is implicated in opposition and combat and that is exposed to danger. It remains in the background, untouched and uninjured. This may be called the cunning of reason—that it sets the passions to work for itself, while what develops its existence through such impulsion pays the penalty, and suffers loss. For it is *phenomenal* being that is so treated, of which part is of no value, part is positive and real. The particular is for the most part of too trifling value as compared with the general: individuals are sacrificed and abandoned. The idea pays the penalty of determinate existence and of corruptibility, not from itself, but from the passions of individuals. . . .

3. THE ROLE OF THE STATE

The third point to be analyzed is, therefore: what object is to be realized by these means, that is what form it assumes in the realm of reality. We have spoken of means; but in the carrying out of a subjective, limited aim, we have also to take into consideration the material that either is already present or has to be procured. Thus the question would arise: What is the material in which the ideal of reason is wrought out? The primary answer would be: personality itself, human desires, subjectivity generally. In human knowledge and volition, as its material element, reason attains positive existence. We have considered subjective volition where it has an object that is the truth and essence of a reality, namely where it constitutes a great world-historical passion. As a subjective will, occupied with limited passions, it is dependent, and can gratify its desires only within the limits of this dependence. But the subjective will has also a substantial life, a reality, in which it moves in the region of essential being and has the essential itself as the object of its existence. This essential being is the union of the subjective with the rational will: it is the moral whole, the state, which is that form of reality in which the individual has and enjoys his freedom, but on the condition of his recognizing, believing in, and willing what is common to the whole. And this must not be understood as if the subjective will of the social unit attained its gratification and enjoyment through that common will, as if this were a means provided for its benefit, as if the individual, in his relations to other individuals, thus limited his freedom, in order that this universal limitation—the mutual constraint of all—might secure a small space of liberty for each. Rather, we affirm that law, morality, government, and they alone, are the positive reality and completion of freedom. Freedom of a low and limited order is mere caprice, which finds its exercise in the sphere of particular and limited desires.

Subjective volition, passion, is what sets men in activity, and effects "practical" realization. The idea is the inner spring of action; the state is the actually existing, realized moral life. For it is the unity of the universal essential will with that of the individual; and this is "morality." The individual living in this unity has a moral life, possesses a value that consists in this substantiality alone. Sophocles in his *Antigone,* says, "The divine commands are not of yesterday, nor of today; no, they have an infinite existence, and no one could say whence they came." The laws of morality are not accidental, but are the essentially rational. It is the very purpose of the state that what is essential in the practical activity of men, and in their dis-

positions, should be duly recognized, that it should have a manifest existence, and maintain its position. It is the absolute interest of reason that this moral whole should exist; and herein lies the justification and merit of heroes who have founded states, however rude these may have been. In the history of the world, only those peoples that form a state can come under our notice. For it must be understood that this latter is the realization of freedom, that is of the absolute final aim, and that it exists for its own sake. It must further be understood that all the worth the human being possesses, all spiritual reality, he possesses only through the state. For his spiritual reality consists in this, that his own essence—reason—is objectively present to him, that it possesses objective immediate existence for him. Thus only is he fully conscious; thus only is he a partaker of morality, of a just and moral social and political life. For truth is the unity of the universal and subjective will; and the universal is to be found in the state, in its laws, its universal and rational arrangements. The state is the divine idea as it exists on earth. We have in it, therefore, the object of history in a more definite shape than before—that in which freedom obtains objectivity, and lives in the enjoyment of this objectivity. For law is the objectivity of mind, volition in its true form. Only that will which obeys law is free, for it obeys itself—it is independent and so free. When the state, our country, constitutes a community of existence, when the subjective will of man submits to laws, the contradiction between liberty and necessity vanishes. The rational has necessary existence, as being the reality and substance of things, and we are free in recognizing it as law, and following it as the substance of our own being. The objective and the subjective will are then reconciled, and present one identical homogeneous whole.

STUDY QUESTIONS: HEGEL, *PHILOSOPHY OF HISTORY*

1. How are history and philosophy related?
2. What is a self-aware idea? What would be an example?
3. What is the important historical point that Anaxagoras first enunciated?
4. How is nature an embodiment of reason?
5. What is the essential destiny of reason?
6. What is one of the main goals of the mind? How is it attained?
7. What is the main role of the individual in relation to history?

8. What is the key to happiness, according to Hegel?
9. Why have the leading figures of history not been happy, in Hegel's view? What does this show?
10. What is a "world-historical individual?"
11. What is the chief role of the state?

Philosophical Bridges: Hegel's Influence

Hegel's influence on the nineteenth century and beyond was immense. Even philosophers who reacted strongly against his system developed their ideas directly in response to him. Among these, most notably, were Kierkegaard, Nietzsche, and Marx whose philosophies would have been inconceivable without Hegel. (Discussed in the sections following.)

Hegel's overall system and the subsequent philosophical movements to which it gave rise in the nineteenth century have been central to subsequent developments in philosophy, mathematics, physics, and computer science. The new logical analysis of the relationships between being and thought and language initiated by the ideas of Kant, Hegel, and the nineteenth-century German idealists, were developed to new heights by physicists like Einstein, Niels Bohr, and John Archibald Wheeler. Philosophically gifted mathematicians like Alan Turing and logicians like Kurt Gödel and Alonzo Church used the formal dissolution of the distinction between representation and reality to create a new level of logical rigor that could be encodeable into algorithmic processes and would ultimately become universal machines known as computers. What Hegel and the German idealists did in equating reality with the process of thought is remarkably analogous to what the computer scientist does in viewing the universe as equivalent to its simulation, conceived as a universal program.

The conception of human beings as sub-programs functioning as such within the general universal program owes much to Hegel's demise of the universe conceived as a Kantian noumenal thing-in-itself, which is excluded not just by the absolute idealists but also by the twentieth-century logical systems of the type invented by Kurt Gödel and Alonzo Church. Today, "*models*" of what a real computer program is and a "*real*" computer program are identical objects, in exactly the way that Hegel envisioned. The universe, regarded as an abstract program, can thus be conceived as a Hegelian absolute idea that has exactly the same nature as our individual human minds, the programs or subroutines running within it. The absolute idealists' conception of individual intellectual *acts*, none of which are substances or things in themselves but are abstract objects, can thus be seeen as analogous to the fundamental map, that is, the procedure, program, or algorithm, that takes the universal program, that is, being, from one state into the next. Reality can thus be viewed as a series of operations of an abstract universal machine. We, as individual parts of the whole, subsisting within the universal program, are but necessary elements for making the whole; in a Hegelian system the philosophers and philosophies themselves are part of the construction of reality writing itself into existence. Such Hegelian thinking, involving a bootstrap metaphysics where the future brings about the past, is exactly of the sort found in recent quantum models of the universe, such as that of John Archibald Wheeler. According to Wheeler, we live in a "participatory universe" in which our own acts of consciousness actualize reality retroactively, just as envisioned by Hegel and other German idealists. Thus Hegel's philosophy, a synthesis of Fichte's subjective idealism and Schelling's objective idealism, can be seen as an early avatar for subsequent developments of Kant's concept of a mind-independent, noumenal reality, applied by metaphysically inspired physicists such as Einstein in his development of relativity and quantum mechanics.

SCHOPENHAUER (1788–1860)

Biographical History

Arthur Schopenhauer was born to a prominent German family in the free city of Danzig, in a Baltic province (consisting of East Prussia and Pomerania, that after World War II became Gdansk in Poland). Schopenhauer was only 17 when his father, a wealthy traveling merchant, was found drowned in the river, probably a suicide. From early on he had a broad education; his mother, a writer in her own right, had a salon—a private meeting place popular among writers, artists and intellectuals during the nineteenth century—frequented by the likes of Goethe, Schubert, the Grimm brothers, and other prominent figures of the time. After studying history, mathematics, Greek and Latin at the Gymansium in Gotha, Schopenhauer went in 1809 to the University of Göttingen, where he studied physics, astronomy, meteorology, medicine, botany, law, and philosophy. For his graduate work he went to the University of Berlin to study with Fichte, and completed his doctorate at Jena.

Although Schopenhauer was only 30 years old when he published his most important work, *The World as Will and Idea,* he did not receive the attention he deserved until much later in life. It took nearly three decades before anyone took serious notice of his work. Like Hume, who had lamented that his own work had "fallen stillborn from the press," Schopenhauer was deeply hurt that his masterpiece was ignored. It did, however, help him to get a teaching position at the University of Berlin in the same department as Hegel, the most famous and talked about philosopher of the time, whom Schopenhauer both envied and despised.

How much of Schopenhauer's distaste of Hegel was the result merely of envy and jealousy, how much from his substantive criticisms of Hegel's views, is a matter of controversy. However, Schopenhauer did write that "the minds of the present generation of scholars are disorganized by Hegelian nonsense, incapable of thinking, coarse and stupefied, they become prey to the shallow materialism that has crept out of the basilisk's egg." Schopenhauer tried in vain to compete with his departmental colleague Hegel by scheduling his own lectures at the same time as Hegel's; as a result, hardly anyone attended Schopenhauer's classes, whereas Hegel's were packed, standing room only. Meanwhile, Hegel's philosophy grew ever more popular throughout Germany, dominating European thought. Schopenhauer was outraged: "Hegel, installed from above by the powers that be as the certified great philosopher, was a flat-headed, insipid, nauseating, illiterate charlatan, who reached the pinnacle of audacity in scribbling together and dishing up the craziest mystifying nonsense."

In 1844, at the age of 56, Schopenhauer published an expanded revision of *The World as Will and Idea.* Much to his surprise, this time it drew great attention. Already by then in his sixties, suddenly he found himself the center of a rapidly growing international following of devoted philosophers, psychologists, writers, and musicians who found him deeply inspirational and profound. His reputation quickly spread by word of mouth. Some of his most famous and devoted adherents included Friedrich Nietzsche, Richard Wagner, Leo Tolstoy, Joseph Conrad, Marcel Proust, Thomas Mann, and Sigmund Freud.

Philosophical Overview

The biggest influences on Schopenhauer were Plato and Kant, the latter whom he regarded as the greatest philosopher of all time. Following Kant, Schopenhauer developed his own unique brand of idealism in marked contrast to Hegel. Schopenhauer's unique blend of Kantian and Platonic metaphysics and epistemology, Indian mysticism, and Goethe's Romanticism, was tempered by a deep respect for Descartes, Locke and Hume. Hegel, as already mentioned, was widely influential throughout the nineteenth century and beyond in both a positive and negative sense. The most substantive similarity and difference, put most simply, is that although Hegel's and Schopenhauer's philosophies had much in common, having both developed from within a Kantian framework, Schopenhauer vehemently and openly opposed Hegel's emphasis on reason, which in Schopenhauer's view stemmed from a deeply profound neglect of the underlying concept of *will*, the basic force of our existence.

The sum and substance of Schopenhauer's philosophy is revealed in a nutshell by the very title of his book, *The World as Will and Idea*. What is the world? The world—the sum total of everything you know, experience, touch, feel—consists in, and is, at the most fundamental level, a dynamic system with a dual aspect: *idea* and *will*. The world is idea. Schopenhauer credits this discovery to Berkeley. Your world is your idea. The world and everything in it is a dream, *your* dream. But, more than that, the world is not *just* a dream; it is a dream guided by firm logical rules of engagement within and among ideas, empowered by will, itself ruled by the principle of sufficient reason. In his doctoral dissertation, *The Fourfold Root of the Principle of Sufficient Reason*, he gives four underlying aspects, or meanings—"roots"—of this fundamental principle:

1. No physical phenomena are possible without a prior cause
2. No logical truths are possible without a priori derivation
3. No mathematical theorem is possible without a geometrical proof
4. No human or animal action is possible without a motive.

These four roots of the principle of sufficient mean, basically, that just about anything and everything that is, was, or will be, can always ultimately be *explained*. Schopenhauer identifies this principle at the core of philosophers ranging from Plato, Aristotle, the Stoics, Descartes, and Spinoza, and attributes the discovery of the full import of this "main principle of all knowledge and science" to Leibniz.

THE WORLD AS WILL AND IDEA

Schopenhauer

In this, his greatest and most influential work, Schopenhauer explains how the world is a dream and then asks: if everything is your dream, why is your world not perfect? Why do you suffer? Why is your life not perfect bliss? Nor are you alone in the trials and tribulations of life. Why all the wars, suffering, and all manner of unhappiness? Schopenhauer's answer, revealed in the second aspect of his fundamental equation, is that the world is not just idea but also will. The will is anything but kind or sentimental. To understand why this is so, recall the Kantian distinction between the world of appearances—the phenomenal world—and the world of things in themselves—the noumenal world. In Kant's view, the noumenal world of things in themselves is forever beyond reach of our experience or our reason. The noumenal world is unknowable. In Schopenhauer's view, on the other hand, the noumenal world of things in themselves is, itself, involved in each and every aspect of our existence, because it is none other than *your will*. In other words, the noumenal is not some abstract realm; you experience the noumenal when you experience your own life, and yourself in it: your body, for instance, and all the physical phenomena in which your experience of tables, trees, and other people consists, is a direct apprehension of your will. Everything you see, touch, and in any way experience is the active construction of the will. Moreover, we are each to ourselves a phenomenal object, just as the physical phenomena in which tables and chairs consist. The difference is that our own self-consciousness reveals to each one of us that we are, also, more. Our bodies, as physical phenomena in space and time, do not just respond merely in reaction to other physical phenomena in which the environment and everything in it consists. Rather, our bodies themselves directly respond to the will, which guides all our actions. But wishing isn't willing. Wishing is psychological, merely mental phenomena without power to cause changes among physical phenomena; the will is manifest in physical phenomena.

Thus, as the missing link between phenomena and noumena, the will is not the sort of rational world-mind envisioned by Hegel, or the sort of benevolent God envisioned by western religion. It is a dark, nonrational, blind force that creates all and destroys all. It generates all the myriad creatures and fills them with insatiable cravings of sex, violence, greed, war, and domination—life and death, a perpetual metaphysical struggle.

In the end, Schopenhauer places a great emphasis on art, and the aesthetic experience, as a way of transcending the tyranny of the will. Because the will is not rational, yet controls everything, the world cannot be understood by rational means but only through aesthetic experience. In that sense art is the transcendental reality of existence without will. Because art is not subservient to science and rationality, it is the highest form of understanding, making possible the attainment, however brief, of freedom—not of the known, but from the known.

BOOK I: THE WORLD AS IDEA

1.

"The world is my idea"—this is a truth which holds good for everything that lives and knows, though man alone can bring it into reflective and abstract consciousness. If he really does this, he has attained to philosophical wisdom. It then becomes clear and certain to him that what he knows is not a sun and an earth, but only an eye that sees a sun, a hand that feels an earth; that the world which surrounds him is there only as idea, that is, only in relation to something else, the consciousness, which is himself. If any truth can be asserted a priori, it is this: for it is the expression of the most general form of all possible and thinkable experience: a form which is more general than time, or space, or causality, for they, all presuppose it; and each of these, which we have seen to be just so many modes of the principle of sufficient reason, is valid only for a particular class of ideas; whereas the antithesis of object and subject is the common form of all these classes, is that form under which alone any idea of whatever kind it may be, abstract or intuitive, pure or empirical, is possible and thinkable. No truth therefore is more certain, more independent of all others, and less in need of proof than this, that all that exists for knowledge, and therefore this whole world, is only object in relation to subject, perception of a perceiver, in a word, idea. This is obviously true of the past and the future, as well as of the present, of what is farthest off, as of what is near; for it is true of time and space themselves, in which alone these distinctions arise. All that in any way belongs or can belong to the world is inevitably thus conditioned through the subject, and exists only for the subject. The world is idea.

Schopenhauer, from *The World as Will and Idea,* translated by R. B. Haldane and J. Kemp (London: Trübner, 1883), vol. 1. with emendation by Daniel Kolak.

This truth is by no means new. It was implicitly involved in the skeptical reflections from which Descartes started. Berkeley, however, was the first who distinctly enunciated it, and by this he has rendered a permanent service to philosophy, even though the rest of his teaching should not endure. Kant's primary mistake was the neglect of this principle. . . . How early again this truth was recognized by the wise men of India, appearing indeed as the fundamental tenet of the Vedânta philosophy ascribed by Vyasa, is pointed out by Sir William Jones in the last of his essays: "On the Philosophy of the Asiatics" (*Asiatic Researches*, vol. iv, p. 164), where he says, "The fundamental tenet of the Vedanta school consisted not in denying the existence of matter, that is, of solidity, impenetrability, and extended figure (to deny which would be lunacy), but in correcting the popular notion of it, and in contending that it has no essence independent of mental perception; that existence and perceptibility are convertible terms." These words adequately express the compatibility of empirical reality and transcendental ideality.

In this first book, then, we consider the world only from this side, only so far as it is idea. The inward reluctance with which any one accepts the world as merely his idea, warns him that this view of it, however true it may be, is nevertheless one-sided, adopted in consequence of some arbitrary abstraction. And yet it is a conception from which he can never free himself. The defectiveness of this view will be corrected in the next book by means of a truth which is not so immediately certain as that from which we start here; a truth at which we can arrive only by deeper research and more severe abstraction, by the separation of what is different and the union of what is identical. This truth, which must be very serious and impressive if not awful to every one, is that a man can also say and must say, "The world is my will."

In this book, however, we must consider separately that aspect of the world from which we start; its aspect as knowable, and therefore, in the meantime, we must, without reserve, regard all presented objects, even our own bodies (as we shall presently show more fully), merely as ideas, and call them merely ideas. By so doing we always abstract from will (as we hope to make clear to every one further on), which by itself constitutes the other aspect of the world. For as the world is in one aspect entirely *idea,* so in another it is entirely *will.* A reality which is neither of these two, but an object in itself (into which the thing-in-itself has unfortunately dwindled in the hands of Kant), is the phantom of a dream, and its acceptance is an *ignis fatuus* in philosophy.

2.

That which knows all things and is known by none is the subject. Thus it is the supporter of the world, that condition of all phenomena, of all objects which is always presupposed throughout experience; for all that exists, exists only for the subject. Every one finds himself to be subject, yet only in so far as he knows, not in so far as he is an object of knowledge. But his body is object, and therefore from this point of view we call it idea. For the body is an object among objects and is conditioned by the laws of objects, although it is an immediate object. Like all objects of perception, it lies within the universal forms of knowledge, time and space, which are the conditions of multiplicity. The subject, on the contrary, which is always the knower, never the known, does not come under these forms, but is presupposed by them; it has therefore neither multiplicity nor its opposite unity. We never know it, but it is always the knower wherever there is knowledge.

So then the world as idea, the only aspect in which we consider it at present, has two fundamental, necessary, and inseparable halves. The one half is the object, the forms of which are space and time, and through these multiplicity. The other half is the subject, which is not in space and time, for it is present, entire and undivided, in every percipient being. So that any one percipient being, with the object, constitutes the whole world as idea just as fully as the existing millions could do; but if this one were to disappear, then the whole world as idea would cease to be. These halves are therefore inseparable even for thought, for each of the two has meaning and existence only through and for the other, each appears with the other and vanishes with it. They limit each other immediately; where the object begins the subject ends. The universality of this limitation is shown by the fact that the essential and hence universal forms of all objects, space, time, and causality, may, without knowledge of the object, be discovered and fully known from a consideration of the subject, that is in Kantian language, they lie a priori in our consciousness. That he discovered this is one of Kant's principal merits, and it is a great one. I however go beyond this, and maintain that the principle of sufficient reason is the general expression for all these forms of the object of which we are a priori conscious; and that therefore all that we know purely a priori, is merely the content of that principle and what follows from it; in it all our certain a priori knowledge is expressed. In my essay on the principle of sufficient reason I have shown in detail how every possible object comes under it; that is, stands in a necessary relation to other objects, on the one side as determined, on the other side as determining: this is of such wide application, that the whole existence of all objects, so far as they are objects, ideas and nothing more, may be entirely traced to this their necessary relation to each other, rests only in it, is in fact merely relative; but of this more presently. I have further shown, that the necessary relation which the principle of sufficient reason expresses generally, appears in other forms corresponding to the classes into which objects are divided, according to their possibility; and again that by these forms the proper division of the classes is tested. I take it for granted that what I said in this earlier essay is known and present to the reader, for if it had not been already said it would necessarily find its place here.

5.

It is needful to guard against the grave error of supposing that because perception arises through the knowledge of causality, the relation of subject and object is that of cause and effect. For this relation subsists only between the immediate object and objects known indirectly, thus always between objects alone. It is this false supposition that has given rise to the foolish controversy about the reality of the outer world; a controversy in which dogmatism and skepticism oppose each other, and the former appears, now as realism, now as idealism. Realism treats the object as cause, and the subject as its effect. The idealism of Fichte reduces the object to the effect of the subject. Since however, and this cannot be too much emphasized, there is absolutely no relation according to the principle of sufficient reason between subject and object, neither of these views could be proved, and therefore skepticism attacked them both with success. Now, just as the law of causality precedes perception

and experience as their condition, and therefore cannot (as Hume thought) be derived from them, so object and subject precede all knowledge, and hence the principle of sufficient reason in general, as its first condition; for this principle is merely the form of all objects, the whole nature and possibility of their existence as phenomena: but the object always presupposes the subject; and therefore between these two there can be no relation of reason and consequent. My essay on the principle of sufficient reason accomplishes just this: it explains the content of that principle as the essential form of every object—that is to say, as the universal nature of all objective existence, as something which pertains to the object as such; but the object as such always presupposes the subject as its necessary correlative; and therefore the subject remains always outside the province in which the principle of sufficient reason is valid. The controversy as to the reality of the outer world rests upon this false extension of the validity of the principle of sufficient reason to the subject also, and starting with this mistake it can never understand itself. On the one side realistic dogmatism, looking upon the idea as the effect of the object, desires to separate these two, idea and object, which are really one, and to assume a cause quite different from the idea, an object in itself, independent of the subject, a thing which is quite inconceivable; for even as object it presupposes subject, and so remains its ideas. Opposed to this doctrine is skepticism, which makes the same false presupposition that in the idea we have only the effect, never the cause, therefore never real being; that we always know merely the action of the object. But this object, it supposes, may perhaps have no resemblance whatever to its effect, may indeed have been quite erroneously received as the cause, for the law of causality is first to be gathered from experience, and the reality of experience is then made to rest upon it. Thus both of these views are open to the correction, firstly, that object and idea are the same; secondly, that the true being of the object of perception is its action, that the reality of the thing consists in this, and the demand for an existence of the object outside the idea of the subject, and also for an essence of the actual thing different from its action, has absolutely no meaning, and is contradiction: and that the knowledge of the nature of the effect of any perceived object, exhausts such an object itself, so far as it is object, that is idea, for beyond this there is nothing more to be known. So far then, the perceived world in space and time, which makes itself known as causation alone, is entirely real, and is throughout simply what it appears to be, and it appears wholly and without reserve as idea, bound together according to the law of causality. This is its empirical reality. On the other hand, all causality is in the understanding alone, and for the understanding. The whole actual, that is, active world is determined as such through the understanding, and apart from it is nothing. This, however, is not the only reason for altogether denying such a reality of the outer world as is taught by the dogmatist, who explains its reality as its independence of the subject. We also deny it, because no object apart from a subject can be conceived without contradiction. The whole world of objects is and remains idea, and therefore wholly and for ever determined by the subject; that is to say, it has transcendental ideality. But it is not therefore illusion or mere appearance; it presents itself as that which it is, idea, and indeed as a series of ideas of which the common bond is the principle of sufficient reason. It is according to its inmost meaning quite comprehensible to the healthy understanding, and speaks a language quite intelligible to it. To dispute about its reality can only occur to a mind perverted by over-subtlety, and such discussion always arises from a false application of the principle of sufficient reason, which binds all ideas together of whatever kind they may be, but by no means connects them with the subject, nor yet with a something which is neither subject nor object, but only the ground of the object; an absurdity, for only objects can be and always are the ground of objects. If we examine more closely the source of this question as to the reality of the outer world, we find that besides the false application of the principle of sufficient reason generally to what lies beyond its province, a special confusion of its forms is also involved; for that form which it has only in reference to concepts or abstract ideas, is applied to perceived ideas, real objects; and a ground of knowing is demanded of objects, whereas they can have nothing but a ground of being. Among the abstract ideas, the concepts united in the judgment, the principle of sufficient reason appears in such a way that each of these has its worth, its validity, and its whole existence, here called *truth*, simply and solely

through the relation of the judgment to something outside of it, its ground of knowledge, to which there must consequently always be a return. Among real objects, ideas of perception, on the other hand, the principle of sufficient reason appears not as the principle of the ground of *knowing*, but of *being*, as the law of causality: every real object has paid its debt to it, inasmuch as it has come to be, that is has appeared as the effect of a cause. The demand for a ground of knowing has therefore here no application and no meaning, but belongs to quite another class of things. Thus the world of perception raises in the observer no question or doubt so long as he remains in contact with it: there is here neither error nor truth, for these are confined to the province of the abstract—the province of reflection. But here the world lies open for sense and understanding; presents itself with naive truth as that which it really is—ideas of perception which develop themselves according to the law of causality.

So far as we have considered the question of the reality of the outer world, it arises from a confusion which amounts even to a misunderstanding of reason itself, and therefore thus far, the question could be answered only by explaining its meaning. After examination of the whole nature of the principle of sufficient reason, of the relation of subject and object, and the special conditions of sense perception, the question itself disappeared because it had no longer any meaning. There is, however, one other possible origin of this question, quite different from the purely speculative one which we have considered, a specially empirical origin, though the question is always raised from a speculative point of view, and in this form it has a much more comprehensible meaning than it had in the first. We have dreams; may not our whole life be a dream? Or more exactly: is there a sure criterion of the distinction between dreams and reality? Between phantasms and real objects? The assertion that, what is dreamed is less vivid and distinct than what we actually perceive is not to the point, because no one has ever been able to make a fair comparison of the two; for we can only compare the recollection of a dream with the present reality. Kant answers the question thus: "the connection of ideas among themselves, according to the law of causality, constitutes the difference between real life and dreams." But in dreams, as well as in real life, anything is connected individually at any rate, in accordance with the principle of sufficient reason in all its forms, and this connection is broken only between one dream and another. Kant's answer therefore could only run thus: the *long* dream (life) has throughout complete connection according to the principle of sufficient son; it has not this connection, however, with *short* dreams, although each of these has in itself the same connection: the bridge is therefore broken between the former and the latter and on this account we distinguish them.

But to institute an enquiry according to this criterion, as to whether something was dreamed or seen, would always be difficult and often impossible. For we are by no means in a position to trace link by link the causal connection between any experienced event and the present moment, but we do not on that account explain it as dreamed. Therefore in real life we do not commonly employ that method of distinguishing between dreams and reality. The only sure criterion by which to distinguish them is in fact the entirely empirical one of awaking, through which at any rate the causal connection between dreamed events and those of waking life, is distinctly and sensibly broken off. This is strongly supported by the remark of Hobbes in the second chapter of Leviathan, that we easily mistake dreams for reality if we have unintentionally fallen asleep without taking off our clothes, and much more so when it also happens that some undertaking or design fills all our thoughts, and occupies our dreams as well as our waking moments. We then observe the awaking just as little as the falling asleep, dream and reality run together and becomes confounded. In such a case there is nothing for it but the application of Kant's criterion; but if, as often happens, we fail to establish by means of this criterion, either the existence of causal connection with the present, or the absence of such connection, then it must for ever remain uncertain whether an event was dreamed or really happened. Here, in fact, the intimate relationship between life and dreams is brought out very clearly, and we need not be ashamed to confess it, as it has been recognised and spoken of by many great men. The Vedas and Puranas have no better simile than a dream for the whole knowledge of the actual world, which they call the web of Mâyâ, and they use none more frequently. Plato often says that men live only

in a dream; the philosopher alone strives to awake himself. . . . Beside which most worthily stands Shakespeare:

> We are such stuff
> As dreams are made on, and our little life
> Is rounded with a sleep. —*Tempest*, Act IV. Sc. i.

Lastly, Calderon was so deeply impressed with this view of life that he sought to embody it in a kind of metaphysical drama, "Life a Dream."

After these numerous quotations from the poets, perhaps I also may be allowed to express myself by a metaphor. Life and dreams are leaves of the same book. The systematic reading of this book is real life, but when the reading hours (that is, the day) are over, we often continue idly to turn over the leaves, and read a page here and there without method or connection: often one we have read before, sometimes one that is new to us, but always in the same book. Such an isolated page is indeed out of connection with the systematic study of the book, but it does not seem so very different when we remember that the whole continuous perusal begins and ends just as abruptly, and may therefore be regarded as merely a larger single page.

Thus although individual dreams are distinguished from real life by the fact that they do not fit into that continuity which runs through the whole of experience, and the act of awaking brings this into consciousness, yet that very continuity of experience belongs to real life as its form, and the dream on its part can point to a similar continuity in itself. If therefore, we consider the question from a point of view external to both, there is no distinct difference in their nature, and we are forced to concede to the poets that life is a long dream.

Let us turn back now from this quite independent empirical origin of the question of the reality of the outer world, to its speculative origin. We found that this consisted, first, in the false application of the principle of sufficient reason to the relation of subject and object; and secondly, in the confusion of its forms, inasmuch as the principle of sufficient reason of knowing was extended to a province in which the principle of sufficient reason of being is valid. But the question could hardly have occupied philosophers so constantly if it were entirely devoid of all real content, and if some true thought and meaning did not lie at its heart as its real source. Accordingly, we must assume that when the element of truth that lies at the bottom of the question first came into reflection and sought its expression, it became involved in these confused and meaningless forms and problems. This at least is my opinion, and I think that the true expression of that inmost meaning of the question, which it failed to find, is this: what is this world of perception besides being my idea? Is that of which I am conscious only as idea, exactly like my own body, of which I am doubly conscious, in one aspect as *idea,* in another aspect as *will?* The fuller explanation of this question and its answer in the affirmative, will form the content of the second book, and its consequences will occupy the remaining portion of this work.

6.

For the present, however, in this first book we consider every thing merely as idea, as object for the subject. And our own body, which is the starting point for each of us in our perception of the world, we consider, like all other real objects, from the side of its knowableness, and in this regard it is simply an idea. Now the consciousness of everyone is in general opposed to the explanation of objects as mere ideas, and more especially to the explanation of our bodies as such; for the thing in itself is known to each of us immediately in so far as it appears as our own body; but in so far as it objectifies itself in the other objects of perception, it is known only indirectly. But this abstraction, this one-sided treatment, this forcible separation of what is essentially and necessarily united, is only adopted to meet the demands of our argument; and therefore the disinclination to it must, in the meantime, be suppressed and silenced by the expectation that the subsequent treatment will correct the one-sidedness of the present one, and complete our knowledge of the nature of the world.

At present therefore the body is for us immediate object; that is to say, that idea which forms the starting point of the subject's knowledge; because the body, with its immediately known changes, precedes the application of the law of causality, and thus supplies it with its first data. The whole nature of matter consists, as we have seen, in its causal action. But

cause and effect exist only for the understanding, which is nothing but their subjective correlative. The understanding, however, could never come into operation if there were not something else from which it starts. This is simple sensation—the immediate consciousness of the changes of the body, by virtue of which it is immediate object. Thus the possibility of knowing the world of perception depends upon two conditions; the first, *objectively expressed,* is the power of material things to act upon each other, to produce changes in each other, without which common quality of all bodies no perception would be possible, even by means of the sensibility of the animal body. And if we wish to express this condition *subjectively* we say: The understanding first makes perception possible; for the law of causality, the possibility of effect and cause, springs only from the understanding, and is valid only for it, and therefore the world of perception exists only through and for it. The second condition is the sensibility of animal bodies, or the quality of being immediate objects of the subject which certain bodies possess. The mere modification which the organs of sense sustain from without through their specific affections, may here be called ideas, so far as these affections produce neither pain nor pleasure, that is, have no immediate significance for the will, and are yet perceived, exist therefore only for *knowledge.* Thus far, then, I say that the body is immediately *known,* is *immediate object.* But the conception of object is not to be taken here in its fullest sense, for through this immediate knowledge of the body, which precedes the operation of the understanding, and is mere sensation, our own body does not exist specifically as *object,* but first the material things which affect it: for all knowledge of an object proper, of an idea perceived in space, exists only through and for the understanding; therefore not before, but only subsequently to its operation. Therefore the body as object proper, that is, an idea perceived in space, is first known indirectly, like all other objects, through the application of the law of causality to the action of one of its parts upon another, as, for example, when the eye sees the body or the hand touches it. Consequently the form of our body does not become known to us through mere feeling, but only through knowledge, only in idea; that is to say, only in the brain does our own body first come to appear as extended, articulate, organic. A man born blind receives this idea only little by little from the data afforded by touch. A blind man without hands could never come to know his own form; or at the most could infer and construct it little by little from the effects of other bodies upon him. If, then, we call the body an immediate object, we are to be understood with these reservations. . . .

12.

Rational knowledge is then all abstract knowledge— that is, the knowledge which is peculiar to the reason as distinguished from the understanding. Now, as reason only reproduces, for knowledge, what has been received in another way, it does not actually extend our knowledge, but only gives it another form. It enables us to know in the abstract and generally, what first became known in sense-perception, in the concrete. But this is much more important than it appears at first sight when so expressed. For it depends entirely upon the fact that knowledge has become rational or abstract knowledge, that it can be safely preserved, that it is communicable and susceptible of certain and wide-reaching application to practice. Knowledge in the form of sense-perception is valid only of the particular case, extends only to what is nearest, and ends with it, for sensibility and understanding can only comprehend one object at a time. Every enduring, arranged, and planned activity must therefore proceed from principles (that is, from abstract knowledge) and it must be conducted in accordance with them. Thus, for example, the knowledge of the relation of cause and effect arrived at by the understanding, is in itself far completer, deeper and more exhaustive than anything that can be thought about it in the abstract; the understanding alone knows in perception directly and completely the nature of the effect of a lever, of a pulley, or a cog wheel, the stability of an arch, and so forth. But on account of the peculiarity of the knowledge of perception just referred to, that it only extends to what is immediately present, the mere understanding can never enable us to construct machines and buildings. Here reason must come in, it must substitute abstract concepts for ideas of perception, and take them as the guide of action; and if they are right, the anticipated result will happen. In the same way we have perfect knowledge in pure perception of the nature and constitution of the parabola, hyperbola, and spiral; but if we are to make trustworthy application of this knowledge to the real, it must first become abstract knowledge, and by this it certainly loses its character of intuition or perception, but on the other hand it gains the certainty and preciseness of abstract knowledge. The differential calculus does not really extend our knowledge of the curve, it contains nothing that was not already in the mere pure perception of the curve; but it alters the kind of knowledge, it changes the intuitive into an abstract knowledge, which is so valuable for application. . . .

The greatest value of rational or abstract knowledge is that it can be communicated and permanently retained. It is principally on this account that it is so inestimably important for practice. Anyone may have a direct perceptive knowledge through the understanding alone, of the causal connection, of the changes and motions of natural bodies, and he may find entire satisfaction in it; but he cannot communicate this knowledge to others until it has been made permanent for thought in concepts. Knowledge of the first kind is even sufficient for practice, if a man puts his knowledge into practice himself, in an action which can be accomplished while the perception is still vivid; but it is not sufficient if the help of others is required, or even if the action is his own but must be carried out at different times, and therefore requires a preconceived plan. Thus, for example, a practiced billiard player may have a perfect knowledge of the laws of the impact of elastic bodies upon each other, merely in the understanding, merely for direct perception; and for him it is quite sufficient; but on the other hand it is only the man who has studied the science of mechanics who has, properly speaking, a rational knowledge of these laws, that is, a knowledge of them in the abstract. . . . It is, however, remarkable that in the first kind of activity—in which we have supposed that one man alone, in an uninterrupted course of action, accomplishes something— abstract knowledge, the application of reason or reflection, may often be a hindrance to him; for example in the case of billiard playing, of fighting, of tuning an instrument, or in the case of singing. Here perceptive knowledge must directly guide action; its passage through reflection makes it uncertain, for it divides the attention and confuses the man.... In the same way it is of no use to me to know in the abstract the exact angle in degrees and minutes at which I must apply a razor if I do not know it intuitively, that is, if I have not got it in my touch. The knowledge of physiognomy, also, is interfered with by the application of reason. This knowledge must be gained directly through the understanding. We say that the expression, the meaning of the features, can only be *felt*, that is, it cannot be put into abstract concepts. Every man has his direct intuitive method of physiognomy and pathognomy, yet one man understands more clearly than another these *signatura rerum*. But an abstract science of physiognomy to be taught and learned is not possible; for the distinctions of difference are here so fine that concepts cannot reach them; therefore abstract knowledge is related to them as a mosaic is to a painting by a Van der Werft or a Denner. In mosaics, however fine they may be, the limits of the stones are always there, and therefore no continuous passage from one color to another is possible, and this is also the case with regard to concepts, with their rigidity and sharp delineation; however finely we may divide them by exact definition they are still incapable of reaching the finer modifications of the perceptible, and this is just what happens in the example we have taken, knowledge of physiognomy.

This quality of concepts by which they resemble the stones of a mosaic, and on account of which perception always remains their asymptote, is the reason why nothing good is produced in art by their means. If the singer or the virtuoso attempts to guide his execution by reflection he remains silent. And this is equally true of the composer, the painter, and the poet. The concept always remains unfruitful in art; it can only direct the technical part of it, its sphere is science....

Lastly, virtue and holiness do not proceed from reflection, but from the inner depths of the will, and its relation to knowledge. The exposition of this belongs to another part of our work; this, however, I may remark here, that the dogmas relating to ethics may be the same in the reason of whole nations, but the action of every individual different; and the converse also holds good; action, we say, is guided by *feelings*—that is, simply not by concepts, but as a mat-

ter of fact by the ethical character. Dogmas occupy the idle reason; but action in the end pursues its own course independently of them, generally not according to abstract rules, but according to unspoken maxims, the expression of which is the whole man himself. Therefore, however different the religious dogmas of nations may be, yet in the case of all of them, a good action is accompanied by unspeakable satisfaction, and a bad action by endless remorse. No mockery can shake the former; no priest's absolution can deliver from the latter. Notwithstanding this, we must allow that for the pursuit of a virtuous life, the application of reason is needful; only it is not its source, but has the subordinate function of preserving resolutions which have been made, of providing maxims to withstand the weakness of the moment, and give consistency to action. It plays the same part ultimately in art also, where it has just as little to do with the essential matter, but assists in carrying it out, for genius is not always at call, and yet the work must be completed in all its parts and rounded off to a whole.

As regards the *content* of the sciences generally, it is, in fact, always the relation of the phenomena of the world to each other, according to the principle of sufficient reason, under the guidance of the *why*, which has validity and meaning only through this principle. *Explanation* is the establishment of this relation. Therefore explanation can never go further than to show two ideas standing to each other in the relation peculiar to that form of the principle of sufficient reason which reigns in the class to which they belong. If this is done we cannot further be asked the question, *why*: for the relation proved is that one which absolutely cannot be imagined as other than it is, that is it is the form of all knowledge. Therefore we do not ask why $2 + 2 = 4$; or why the quality of the angles of a triangle determines the equality of the sides; or why its effect follows any given cause; or why the truth of the conclusion is evident from the truth of the premises. Every explanation which does not ultimately lead to a relation of which no "why" can further be demanded, stops at an accepted *qualitas occulta*; but this is the character of every original force of nature. Every explanation in natural science must ultimately end with such a *qualitas occulta*, and thus with complete obscurity. It must leave the inner nature of a stone just as much unexplained as that of a human being; it can give as little account of the weight, the cohesion, the chemical qualities, etc, of the former, as of the knowing and acting of the latter. . . . Philosophy is the most general rational knowledge, the first principles of which cannot therefore be derived from another principle still more general. The principle of contradiction establishes merely the agreement of concepts, but does not itself produce concepts. The principle of sufficient reason explains the connections of phenomena, but not the phenomena themselves; therefore philosophy cannot proceed upon these principles to seek a *causa efficiens* or a *causa finalis* of the whole world. My philosophy, at least, does not by any means seek to know *whence* or *wherefore* the world exists, but merely *what* the world is. But the *why* is here subordinated to the *what*, for it already belongs to the world, as it arises and has meaning and validity only through the form of its phenomena, the principle of sufficient reason. We might indeed say that every one knows what the world is without help, for he is himself that subject of knowledge of which the world is the idea; and so far this would be true. But that knowledge is empirical, is in the concrete; the task of philosophy is to reproduce this in the abstract, to raise to permanent rational knowledge the successive changing perceptions, and in general, all that is contained under the wide concept of feeling and merely negatively defined as not abstract, distinct, rational knowledge. It must therefore consist of a statement in the abstract, of the nature of the whole world, of the whole and of all the parts. . . .

BOOK II: THE WORLD AS WILL

First Aspect. The Objectification of the Will

17.

. . . What now impels us to inquiry is, that we are not satisfied with knowing that we have ideas, that they are such and such, and that they are connected according to certain laws, the general expression of which is the principle of sufficient reason. We wish to know the significance of these ideas; we ask whether this world is merely idea; in which case it would pass by us like an empty dream or a baseless vision, not worth our notice; or whether it is also something else, something more than idea, and if so, what. Thus much is certain, that this something we seek for must

be completely and in its whole nature different from the idea; that the forms and laws of the idea must therefore be completely foreign to it; further, that we cannot arrive at it from the idea under the guidance of the laws which merely combine objects, ideas, among themselves, and which are the forms of the principle of sufficient reason.

Thus we see already that we can never arrive at the real nature of things from without. However much we investigate, we can never reach anything but images and names. We are like a man who goes round a castle seeking in vain for an entrance, and sometimes sketching the facades. And yet this is the method that has been followed by all philosophers before me.

18.

In fact, the meaning for which we seek of that world which is present to us only as our idea, or the transition from the world as mere idea of the knowing subject to whatever it may be besides this, would never be found if the investigator himself were nothing more than the pure knowing subject (a winged cherub without a body). But he is himself rooted in that world; he finds himself in it as an *individual*, that is to say, his knowledge, which is the necessary supporter of the whole world as idea, is yet always given through the medium of a body, whose affections are, as we have shown, the starting-point for the understanding in the perception of that world. His body is, for the pure knowing subject, an idea like every other idea, an object among objects. Its movements and actions are so far known to him in precisely the same way as the changes of all other perceived objects, and would be just as strange and incomprehensible to him if their meaning were not explained for him in an entirely different way. Otherwise he would see his actions follow upon given motives with the constancy of a law of nature just as the changes of other objects follow upon causes, stimuli, or motives. But he would not understand the influence of the motives any more than the connection between every other effect which he sees and its cause. He would then call the inner nature of these manifestations and actions of his body which he did not understand a force, a quality, or a character, as he pleased, but he would have no further insight into it. But all this is not the case; indeed the answer to the riddle is given to the subject of knowledge who appears as an individual, and the answer is *will*. This and this alone gives him the key to his own existence, reveals to him the significance, shows him the inner mechanism of his being, of his action, of his movements. The body is given in two entirely different ways to the subject of knowledge, who becomes an individual only through his identity with it. It is given as an idea in intelligent perception, as an object among objects and subject to the laws of objects. And it is also given in quite a different way as that which is immediately known to every one, and is signified by the word *will*. Every true act of his will is also at once and without exception a movement of his body. The act of will and the movement of the body are not two different things objectively known, which the bond of causality unites; they do not stand in the relation of cause and effect; they are one and the same, but they are given in entirely different ways—immediately, and again in perception for the understanding. The action of the body is nothing but the act of the will objectified, that is passed into perception. It will appear later that this is true of every movement of the body, not merely those which follow upon motives, but also involuntary movements which follow upon mere stimuli, and, indeed, that the whole body is nothing but objectified will, that is will become idea. All this will be proved and made quite clear in the course of this work. In one respect, therefore, I shall call the body the *objectivity of will*; as in the previous book, and in this essay on the principle of sufficient reason, in accordance with the onesided point of view intentionally adopted there (that of the idea), I called it *the immediate object*. Thus in a certain sense we may also say that will is the knowledge a priori of the body, and the body is the knowledge *a posteriori* of the will. Resolutions of the will which relate to the future are merely deliberations of the reason about what we shall will at a particular time, not real acts of will. Only the carrying out of the resolve stamps it as will, for till then it is never more than an intention that may be changed, and that exists only in the reason *in abstracto*. It is only in reflection that to will and to act are different; in reality they are one. Every true, genuine, immediate act of will is also, at once and immediately, a visible act of the body. And, corresponding to this, every impression upon the body is also, on the other hand,

at once and immediately an impression upon the will. As such it is called pain when it is opposed to the will; gratification or pleasure when it is in accordance with it. The degrees of both are widely different. It is quite wrong, however, to call pain and pleasure ideas, for they are by no means ideas, but immediate affections of the will in its manifestation, the body; compulsory, instantaneous willing or not-willing of the impression which the body sustains. There are only a few impressions of the body which do not touch the will, and it is through these alone that the body is an immediate object of knowledge, for, as perceived by the understanding, it is already an indirect object like all others. These impressions are, therefore, to be treated directly as mere ideas, and excepted from what has been said. The impressions we refer to are the affections of the purely objective senses of sight, hearing, and touch, though only so far as these organs are affected in the way which is specially peculiar to their specific nature. This affection of them is so excessively weak an excitement of the heightened and specifically modified sensibility of these parts that it does not affect the will, but only furnishes the understanding with the data out of which the perception arises, undisturbed by any excitement of the will. But every stronger or different kind of affection of these organs of sense is painful, that is to say, against the will, and thus they also belong to its objectivity. Weakness of the nerves shows itself in this, that the impressions which have only such a degree of strength as would usually be sufficient to make them data for the understanding reach the higher degree at which they influence the will, that is to say, give pain or pleasure, though more often pain, which is, however, to some extent deadened and inarticulate, so that not only particular tones and strong light are painful to us, but there ensues a generally unhealthy and hypochondriacal disposition which is not distinctly understood. The identity of the body and the will shows itself further, among other ways, in the circumstance that every vehement and excessive movement of the will, that is every emotion, agitates the body and its inner constitution directly, and disturbs the course of its vital functions. . . .

Lastly, the knowledge which I have of my will, though it is immediate, cannot be separated from that which I have of my body. I know my will, not as a whole, not as a unity, not completely, according to its nature, but I know it only in its particular acts, and therefore in time, which is the form of the phenomenal aspect of my body, as of every object. Therefore the body is a condition of the knowledge of my will. Thus, I cannot really imagine this will apart from my body. In the essay on he principle of sufficient reason, the will, or rather the subject of willing, is treated as a special class of ideas or objects. But even there we saw this object become one with the subject; that is, we saw it cease to be an object. We there called this union the miracle, and the whole of the present work is to a certain extent an explanation of this. So far as I know my will specially as object, I know it as body. But then I am again at the first class of ideas laid down in that essay, that is real objects. As we proceed we shall see always more clearly that these ideas of the first class obtain their explanation and solution from those of the fourth class given in the essay, which could no longer be properly opposed to the subject as object, and that, therefore, we must learn to understand the inner nature of the law of causality which is valid in the first class, and of all that happens in accordance with it from the law of motivation which governs the fourth class.

The identity of the will and the body, of which we have now given a cursory explanation, can only be proved in the manner we have adopted here. We have proved this identity for the first time, and shall do so more and more fully in the course of this work. By "proved" we mean raised from the immediate consciousness, from knowledge in the concrete to abstract knowledge of the reason, or carried over into abstract knowledge. On the other hand, from its very nature it can never be demonstrated, that is, deduced as indirect knowledge from some other more direct knowledge, just because it is itself the most direct knowledge; and if we do not apprehend it and stick to it as such, we shall expect in vain to receive it again in some indirect way as derivative knowledge. It is knowledge of quite a special kind, whose truth cannot therefore properly be brought under any of the four rubrics under which I have classified all truth in the essay on the principle of sufficient reason, § 29, the logical, the empirical, the metaphysical, and the metalogical, for it is not, like all these, the relation of an abstract idea to another idea, or to the necessary form of perceptive or of abstract ideation, but it is the relation of a judgment to the connection which an idea of perception, the body, has to that which is not an idea at all, but something *toto genere* different, will. I should like therefore to distinguish this from all other truth, and call it *philosophical truth*. We can turn the expression of this truth in different ways and say: my body and my will are one—or, what as an idea of perception I call my body, I call my will, so far as I am conscious of it in an entirely different way which cannot be compared to any other—or, my body is the *objectivity* of my will—or, my body considered apart from the fact that it is my idea is still my will, and so forth.

19.

In the first book we were reluctantly driven to explain the human body as merely idea of the subject which knows it, like all the other objects of this world of perception. But it has now become clear that what enables us consciously to distinguish our own body from all other objects which in other respects are precisely the same, is that our body appears in consciousness in quite another way *toto genere* different from idea, and this we denote by the word *will*; and that it is just this double knowledge which we have our own body that affords us information about it, about its action and movement following on motives and also about what it experiences by means of external impressions; in a word, about what is it, not as idea, but as more than idea; that is to say, what it is *in itself*. None of this information have we got directly with regard to the nature, action, and experience of other real objects.

It is just because of this special relation to one body that the knowing subject is an individual. For regarded apart from this relation, his body is for him, only an idea like all other ideas. But the relation through which the knowing subject is an *individual,* is just on that account a relation which subsists only between him and one particular idea of all those which he has. Therefore he is conscious of this one idea, not merely as an idea, but in quite a different way as a will. If, however, he abstracts from that special relation, from that two-fold and completely heterogeneous knowledge of what is one and the same, then that *one*, the body, is an idea like all other ideas. Therefore, in order to understand the matter, the individual who knows must either assume that what distinguishes that one idea from others is merely the fact that his knowledge stands in this double relation to it alone; that insight in two ways at the same time is open to him only in the case of this one object of perception, and that this is to be explained not by the difference of this object from all others, but only by the difference between the relation of his knowledge to this one object, and its relation to all other objects. Or else he must assume that this object is essentially different from all others; that it alone of all objects is at once both will and idea, while the rest are only ideas, that is only phantoms. Thus he must assume that his body is the only real individual in the world, that is the only phenomenon of will and the only immediate object of the subject. That other objects, considered merely as *ideas*, are like his body, that is, like it, fill space (which itself can only be present as idea), and also, like it, are causally active in space, is indeed demonstrably certain from the law of causality which is a priori valid for ideas, and which admits of no effect without a cause; but apart from the fact that we can only reason from an effect to a cause generally, and not to a similar cause, we are still in the sphere of mere ideas, in which alone the law of causality is valid, and beyond which it can never take us. But whether the objects known to the individual only as ideas are yet, like his own body, manifestations of a will, is, as was said in Book I the proper meaning of the question as to the reality of the external world. To deny this is *theoretical egoism*, which on that account regards all phenomena that are outside its own will as phantoms, just as in a practical reference exactly the same thing is done by practical egoism. For in it a man regards and treats himself alone as a person, and all other persons as mere phantoms. Theoretical egoism can never be demonstrably refuted, yet in philosophy it has never been used otherwise than as a skeptical Sophism, that is a pretense. As a serious conviction, on the other hand, it could only be found in a madhouse, and as such it stands in need of a cure rather than a refutation. We do not therefore combat it any further in this regard, but treat it as merely the last stronghold of skepticism, which is always polemical. Thus our knowledge, which is always bound to individuality and is limited by this circumstance, brings with it the necessity that each of us can only *be*

one, while, on the other hand, each of us can *know all;* and it is this limitation that creates the need for philosophy. We therefore who, for this very reason, are striving to extend the limits of our knowledge through philosophy, will treat this skeptical argument of theoretical egoism which meets us, as an army would treat a small frontier fortress. The fortress cannot indeed be taken, but the garrison can never sally forth from it, and therefore we pass it by without danger, and are not afraid to have it in our rear.

The double knowledge which each of us has of the nature and activity of his own body, and which is given in two completely different ways, has now been clearly brought out. We shall accordingly make further use of it as a key to the nature of every phenomenon in nature, and shall judge of all objects which are not our own bodies, and are consequently not given to our consciousness in a double way but only as ideas; according to the analogy of our own bodies, and shall therefore assume that as in one respect they are idea, just like our bodies, and in this respect are analogous to them, so in another aspect, what remains of objects when we set aside their existence as idea of the subject, must in its inner nature be the same as that in us which we call *will.* For what other kind of existence or reality should we attribute to the rest of the material world? Whence should we take the elements out of which we construct such a world? Besides will and idea nothing is known to us or thinkable. If we wish to attribute the greatest known reality to the material world which exists immediately only in our idea, we give it the reality which our own body has for each of us; for that is the most real thing for every one. But if we now analyze the reality of this body and its actions, beyond the fact that it is idea, we find nothing in it except the will; with this its reality is exhausted. Therefore we can nowhere find another kind of reality which we can attribute to the material world. Thus if we hold that the material world is something more than merely our idea, we must say that besides being idea, that is, in itself and according to its inmost nature, it is that which we find immediately in ourselves as *will.* I say according to its inmost nature; but we must first come to know more accurately this real nature of the will, in order that we may be able to distinguish from it what does not belong to itself, but to its manifestation, which has many grades. . . .

20.

As we have said, the will proclaims itself primarily in the voluntary movements of our own body, as the inmost nature of this body, as that which it is besides being object of perception, idea. For these voluntary movements are nothing else but the visible aspect of the individual acts of will, with which they are directly coincident and identical, and only distinguished through the form of knowledge into which they have passed, and in which alone they can be known, the form of idea.

But these acts of will have always a ground or reason outside themselves in motives. Yet these motives never determine more than what I will at *this* time, in *this* place, and under *these* circumstances, not *that* I will in general, or *what* I will in general, that is, the maxims which characterize my volition generally. Therefore the inner nature of my volition cannot be explained from these motives; but they merely determine its manifestation at a given point of time: they are merely the occasion of my will showing itself; but the will itself lies outside the province of the law of motivation, which determines nothing but its appearance at each point of time. It is only under the presupposition of my empirical character that the motive is a sufficient ground of explanation of my action. But if I abstract from my character, and then ask why, in general, I will this and not that, no answer is possible, because it is only the manifestation of the will that is subject to the principle of sufficient reason, and not the will itself, which in this respect is to be called *groundless*. . . .

Thus, although every particular action, under the presupposition of the definite character, necessarily follows from the given motive, and although growth, the process of nourishment, and all the changes of the animal body take place according to necessarily acting causes (stimuli), yet the whole series of actions, and consequently every individual act, and also its condition, the whole body itself which accomplishes it, and therefore also the process through which and in which it exists, are nothing but the manifestation of the will, the becoming visible, *the objectification of the will*. Upon this rests the perfect suitableness of the human and animal body to the human and animal will in general, resembling, though far surpassing, the correspondence between an instrument made for a purpose and the will of the maker, and on this account appearing as design, that is, the teleological explanation of the body. The parts of the body must, therefore, completely correspond to the principal desires through which the will manifests itself; they must be the visible expression of these desires. Teeth, throat, and bowels are objectified hunger; the organs of generation are objectified sexual desire; the grasping hand, the hurrying feet, correspond to the more indirect desires of the will which they express. As the human form generally corresponds to the human will generally, so the individual bodily structure corresponds to the individually modified will, the character of the individual, and therefore it is throughout and in all parts characteristic and full of expression. . . .

21.

Whoever has now gained from all these expositions a knowledge *in abstracto*, and therefore clear and certain, of what every one knows directly *in concreto*, that is, as feeling, a knowledge that his will is the real inner nature of his phenomenal being, which manifests itself to him as idea, both in his actions and in their permanent substratum, his body, and that his will is that which is most immediate in his consciousness, though it has not as such completely passed into the form of idea in which object and subject stand over against each other, but makes itself known to him in a direct manner, in which he does not quite clearly distinguish subject and object, yet is not known as a whole to the individual himself, but only in its particular acts—whoever, I say, has with me gained this conviction will find that of itself it affords him the key to the knowledge of the inmost being of the whole of nature; for he now transfers it to all those phenomena which are not given to him, like his own phenomenal existence, both in direct and indirect knowledge, but only in the latter, thus merely onesidedly as *idea* alone. He will recognize this will of which we are speaking not only in those phenomenal existences which exactly resemble his own, in men and animals as their inmost nature, but the course of reflection will lead him to recognize the force which germinates and vegetates in the plant, and indeed the force through which the crystal is formed, that by which the magnet turns to the North Pole, the force whose shock he experiences from the contact of two different kinds of metals, the force which appears in the elective affinities of matter as repulsion and attraction, decomposition and combination, and, lastly, even gravitation, which acts so powerfully throughout matter, draws the stone to the earth and the earth to the sun—all these, I say, he will recognize as different only in their phenomenal existence, but in their inner nature as identical, as that which is directly known to him so intimately and so much better than anything else, and which in its most distinct manifestation is called *will*. It is this application of reflection alone that prevents us from remaining any longer at the phenomenon, and leads us to the *thing in itself*. Phenomenal existence is idea and nothing more. All idea, of whatever kind it may be, all *object*, is *phenomenal* existence, but the *will* alone is a *thing in itself*. As such, it is throughout not idea, but *toto genere* different from it; it is that of which all idea, all object, is the phenomenal appearance, the visibility, the objectification. It is the inmost nature, the kernel, of every particular thing, and also of the whole. It appears in every blind force of nature and also in the preconsidered action of man; and the great difference between these two is merely in the degree of the manifestation, not in the nature of what manifests itself.

25.

We know that *multiplicity* in general is necessarily conditioned by space and time, and is only thinkable in them. In this respect they are called the *principium individuationis*. But we have found that space and time are forms of the principle of sufficient reason. In this principle all our knowledge a priori is expressed but, as we showed above, this a priori knowledge, as such, only applies to the knowableness of things, not to the things themselves, that is it is only our form of knowledge, it is not a property of the thing-in-itself. The thing-in-itself is, as such, free from all forms of knowledge, even the most universal, that of being an object for the subject. In other words, the thing-in-itself is something altogether different from the idea. If, now, this thing-in-itself is *the will*, as I believe I have fully and convincingly proved it to be; then, regarded as such and apart from its manifestation, it lies outside time and space, and therefore knows no multiplicity, and is consequently *one*. Yet, as I have said, it is not one in the sense in which an individual or a concept is one, but as something to which the

condition of the possibility of multiplicity, the *principium individuationis*; is foreign. The multiplicity of things in space and time, which collectively constitute the objectification of will, does not affect the will itself, which remains indivisible notwithstanding it. It is not the case that, in some way or other, a smaller part of will is in the stone and a larger part in the man, for the relation of part and whole belongs exclusively to space, and has no longer any meaning when we go beyond this form of intuition or perception. The more and the less have application only to the phenomenon of will, that is, its visibility, its objectification. Of this there is a higher grade in the plant than in the stone; in the animal a higher grade than in the plant indeed, the passage of will into visibility, its objectification, has grades as innumerable as exist between the dimmest twilight and the brightest sunshine, the loudest sound and the faintest echo. We shall return later to the consideration of these grades of visibility which belong to the objectification of the will, to the reflection of its nature. But as the grades of its objectification do not directly concern the will itself, still less is it concerned by the multiplicity of the phenomena of these different grades, that is, the multitude of individuals of each form, or the particular manifestations of each force. For this multiplicity is directly conditioned by time and space, into which the will itself never enters. The will reveals itself as completely and as much in *one* oak as in millions. Their number and multiplication in space and time has no meaning with regard to it, but only with regard to the multiplicity of individuals who know in space and time, and who are themselves multiplied and dispersed in these. The multiplicity of these individuals itself belongs not to the will, but only to its manifestation. We may therefore say that if, *per impossibile*, a single real existence, even the most insignificant, were to be entirely annihilated, the whole world would necessarily perish with it. The great mystic Angelus Silesius feels this when he says:

> I know God cannot live an instant without me,
>   He must give up the ghost if I should cease to be.

Men have tried in various ways to bring the immeasurable greatness of the material universe nearer to the comprehension of us all, and then they have seized the opportunity to make edifying remarks.

They have referred perhaps to the relative smallness of the earth, and indeed of man; or, on the contrary, they have pointed out the greatness of the mind of this man who is so insignificant—the mind that can solve, comprehend, and even measure the greatness of the universe, and so forth. Now, all this is very well, but to me, when I consider the vastness of the world, the most important point is this, that the thing-in-itself, whose manifestation is the world—whatever else it may be—cannot have its true self spread out and dispersed after this fashion in boundless space, but that this endless extension belongs only to its manifestation. The thing-in-itself, on the contrary, is present entire and undivided in every object of nature and in every living being. Therefore we lose nothing by standing still beside any single individual thing, and true wisdom is not to be gained by measuring out the boundless world, or, what would be more to the purpose, by actually traversing endless space. It is rather to be attained by the thorough investigation of any individual thing, for thus we seek to arrive at a full knowledge and understanding of its true and peculiar nature.

The subject which will therefore be fully considered in the next book, and which has, doubtless, already presented itself to the mind of every student of Plato, is, that these different grades of the objectification of will which are manifested in innumerable individuals, and exist as their unattained types or as the eternal forms of things, not entering themselves into time and space, which are the medium of individual things, but remaining fixed, subject to no change, always being, never becoming, while the particular things arise and pass away, always become and never are—that these *grades of the objectification of will* are, I say, simply *Plato's Ideas*. I make this passing reference to the matter here in order that I may be able in future to use the word *Idea* in this sense. In my writings, therefore, the word is always to be understood in its true and original meaning given to it by Plato, and has absolutely no reference to those abstract productions of dogmatising scholastic reason, which Kant has inaptly and illegitimately used this word to denote, though Plato had already appropriated and used it most fitly. By Idea, then, I understand every definite and fixed grade of the objectification of will, so far as it is thing-in-itself, and therefore has no multiplicity. These grades are

related to individual things as their eternal forms or prototypes. . . .

26.

The lowest grades of the objectification of will are to be found in those most universal forces of nature which partly appear in all matter without exception, as gravity and impenetrability, and partly have shared the given matter among them, so that certain of them reign in one species of matter and others in another species, constituting its specific difference, as rigidity, fluidity, elasticity, electricity, magnetism, chemical properties, and qualities of every kind. They are in themselves immediate manifestations of will, just as much as human action; and as such they are groundless, like human character. Only their particular manifestations are subordinated to the principle of sufficient reason, like the particular actions of men. They themselves, on the other hand, can never be called either effect or cause, but are the prior and presupposed conditions of all causes and effects through which their real nature unfolds and reveals itself. It is therefore senseless to demand a cause of gravity or electricity, for they are original forces. . . . It is therefore a mistake to say "gravity is the cause of a stone falling," for the cause in this case is rather the nearness of the earth, because it attracts the stone. Take the earth away and the stone will not fall, although gravity remains. The force itself lies quite outside the chain of causes and effects, which presupposes time, because it only has meaning in relation to it; but the force lies outside time. . . .

In the higher grades of the objectivity of will we see individuality occupy a prominent position, especially in the case of man, where it appears as the great difference of individual characters, that is, as complete personality, outwardly expressed in strongly marked individual physiognomy, which influences the whole bodily form. None of the brutes have this individuality in anything like so high a degree, though the higher species of them have a trace of it; but the character of the species completely predominates over it, and therefore they have little individual physiognomy. . . .

Thus every universal, original force of nature is nothing but a low grade of the objectification of will, and we call every such grade an eternal *Idea* in Plato's sense. But a *Law of Nature* is the relation of the Idea to the form of its manifestation. This form is time, space, and causality, which are necessarily and inseparably connected and related to each other. Through time and space the Idea multiplies itself in innumerable phenomena, but the order according to which it enters these forms of multiplicity is definitely determined by the law of causality; this law is as it were the norm of the limit of these phenomena of different Ideas, in accordance with which time, space, and matter are assigned to them. This norm is therefore necessarily related to the identity of the aggregate of existing matter, which is the common substratum of all those different phenomena. If all these were not directed to that common matter in the possession of which they must be divided, there would be no need for such a law to decide their claims. They might all at once and together fill a boundless space throughout an endless time. Therefore, because all these phenomena of the eternal Ideas are directed to one and the same matter, must there be a rule for their appearance and disappearance; for if there were not, they would not make way for each other. Thus the law of causality is essentially bound up with that of the permanence of substance; they reciprocally derive significance from each other. Time and space, again, are related to them in the same way. For time is merely the possibility of conflicting states of the same matter, and space is merely the possibility of the permanence of the same matter under all sorts of conflicting states. . . .

27.

. . . It follows from all that has been said that it is certainly an error on the part of natural science to seek to refer the higher grades of the objectification of will to the lower; for the failure to recognize, or the denial of, original and self-existing forces of nature is just as wrong as the groundless assumption of special forces when what occurs is merely a peculiar kind of manifestation of what is already known. Thus Kant rightly says that it would be absurd to hope for a blade of grass from a Newton, that is, from one who reduced the blade of grass to the manifestations of physical and chemical forces, of which it was the chance product, and therefore a mere freak of nature, in which no special Idea appeared, that is, the will did not directly reveal itself in it in a higher and specific grade, but just as in the phenomena of unorganized nature and

by chance in this form. On the other hand, it is not to be overlooked that in all Ideas, that is, in all forces of unorganized, and all forms of organized nature, it is *one and the same* will that reveals itself, that is to say, which enters the form of the idea and passes into *objectivity*. Its unity must therefore be also recognizable through an inner relationship between all its phenomena. Now this reveals itself in the higher grades of the objectification of will, where the whole phenomenon is more distinct, thus in the vegetable and animal kingdoms, through the universally prevailing analogy of all forms, the fundamental type which recurs in all phenomena. . . . To discover this fundamental type has been the chief concern, or at any rate the praiseworthy endeavor, of the natural philosophers of the school of Schelling, who have in this respect considerable merit, although in many cases their hunt after analogies in nature degenerated into mere conceits. They have, however, rightly shown that that general relationship and family likeness exists also in the ideas of unorganized nature; for example, between electricity and magnetism, the identity of which was afterwards established; between chemical attraction and gravitation, and so forth. They specially called attention to the fact that *polarity*, that is, the sundering of a force into two qualitatively different and opposed activities striving after reunion, which also shows itself for the most part in space as a dispersion in opposite directions, is a fundamental type of almost all the phenomena of nature, from the magnet and the crystal to man himself. Yet this knowledge has been current in China from the earliest times, in the doctrine of opposition of Yin and Yang. . . .

According to the view I have expressed, the traces of chemical and physical modes of operation will indeed be found in the organism, but it can never be explained from them; because it is by no means a phenomenon even accidentally brought about through the united actions of such forces, but a higher Idea which has overcome these lower Ideas by *subduing assimilation*; for the *one* will which objectifies itself in all Ideas always seeks the highest possible objectification, and has therefore in this case given up the lower grades of its manifestation after a conflict, in order to appear in a higher grade, and one so much the more powerful. No victory without conflict: since the higher Idea or objectification of will can only appear through the conquest of the lower, it endures the opposition of these lower Ideas, which, although brought into subjection, still constantly strive to obtain an independent and complete expression of their being. The magnet that has attracted a piece of iron carries on a perpetual conflict with gravitation, which, as the lower objectification of will, has a prior right to the matter of the iron; and in this constant battle the magnet indeed grows stronger, for the opposition excites it, as it were, to greater effort. In the same way every manifestation of the will, including that which expresses itself in the human organism, wages a constant war against the many physical and chemical forces which, as lower Ideas, have a prior right to that matter. Thus the arm falls which for a while, overcoming gravity, we have held stretched out; thus the pleasing sensation of health, which proclaims the victory of the Idea of the self-conscious organism over the physical and chemical laws, which originally governed the humors of the body, is so often interrupted, and is indeed always accompanied by greater or less discomfort, which arises from the resistance of these forces, and on account of which the vegetative part of our life is constantly attended by slight pain. Thus also digestion weakens all the animal functions, because it requires the whole vital force to overcome the chemical forces of nature by assimilation. Hence also in general the burden of physical life, the necessity of sleep, and, finally, of death; for at last these subdued forces of nature, assisted by circumstances, win back from the organism, wearied even by the constant victory, the matter it took from them, and attain to an unimpeded expression of their being. We may therefore say that every organism expresses the Idea of which it is the image, only after we have subtracted the part of its force which is expended in subduing the lower Ideas that strive with it for matter. This seems to have been running in the mind of Jacob Böhme when he says somewhere that all the bodies of men and animals, and even all plants, are really half dead. According as the subjection in the organism of these forces of nature, which express the lower grades of the objectification of will, is more or less successful, the more or the less completely does it attain to the expression of its Idea; that is to say, the nearer it is to the *ideal* or the further from it—the *ideal* of beauty in its species.

Thus everywhere in nature we see strife, conflict, and alternation of victory, and in it we shall come to recognise more distinctly that variance with itself which is essential to the will. . . . Thus the will to live everywhere preys upon itself, and in different forms is its own nourishment, till finally the human race, because it subdues all the others, regards nature as a manufactory for its use. Yet even the human race, as we shall see in Book IV, reveals in itself with most terrible distinctness this conflict, this variance with itself of the will, and we find *homo homini lupus*. Meanwhile we can recognize this strife, this subjugation, just as well in the lower grades of the objectification of will. Many insects (especially ichneumonflies) lay their eggs on the skin, and even in the body of the larvae of other insects, whose slow destruction is the first work of the newly hatched brood. . . . But the bulldog ant of Australia affords us the most extraordinary example of this kind; for if it is cut in two, a battle begins between the head and the tail. The head seizes the tail with its teeth and the tail defends itself bravely by stinging the head: the battle may last for half an hour, until they die or are dragged away by other ants. This contest takes place every time the experiment is tried. On the banks of the Missouri one sometimes sees a mighty oak the stem and branches of which are so encircled, fettered, and interlaced by a gigantic wild vine, that it withers as if choked. . . .

Thus knowledge generally, rational as well as merely sensuous, proceeds originally from the will itself, belongs to the inner being of the higher grades of its objectification as a mere means of supporting the individual and the species, just like any organ of the body. Originally destined for the service of the will for the accomplishment of its aims, it remains almost throughout entirely subjected to its service: it is so in all brutes and in almost all men. . . .

BOOK III: THE WORLD AS IDEA

Second Aspect. The Idea Independent of the Principle of Sufficient Reason: The Platonic Idea: The Object of Art

32.

It follows from our consideration of the subject, that, for us, Idea and thing-in-itself are not entirely one and the same, in spite of the inner agreement between Kant and Plato, and the identity of the aim they had before them or the conception of the world which roused them and led them to philosophize. The Idea is for us rather the direct, and therefore adequate, objectivity of the thing-in-itself, which is, however, itself the *will*—the will as not yet objectified, not yet become idea. For the thing-in-itself must, even according to Kant, be free from all the forms connected with knowing as such; and it is merely an error on his part that he did not count among these forms, before all others, that of being object for a subject, for it is the first and most universal form of all phenomena, that is, of all idea; he should therefore have distinctly denied objective existence to this thing-in-itself, which would have saved him from a great inconsistency that was soon discovered. The Platonic Idea, on the other hand, is necessarily object, something known, an idea, and in that respect is different from the thing-in-itself, but in that respect only. It has merely laid aside the subordinate forms of the phenomenon, all of which we include in the principle of sufficient reason, or rather it has not yet assumed them; but it has retained the first and most universal form, that of the idea in general, the form of being object for a subject. It is the forms which are subordinate to this (whose general expression is the principle of sufficient reason) that multiply the Idea in particular transitory individuals, whose number is a matter of complete indifference to the Idea. The principle of sufficient reason is thus again the form into which the Idea centers when it appears in the knowledge of the subject as individual. The particular thing that manifests itself in accordance with the principle of sufficient reason is thus only an indirect objectification of the thing-in-itself (which is the will), for between it and the thing-in-itself stands the Idea as the only direct objectivity of the will, because it has assumed none of the special forms of knowledge as such, except that of the idea in general, that is, the form of being object for a subject. Therefore it alone is the most *adequate objectivity* of the will or thing-in-itself which is possible; indeed it is the whole thing-in-itself, only under the form of the idea; and here lies the ground of the great agreement between Plato and Kant, although, in strict accuracy, that of which they speak is not the same. But the particular things are no really adequate objectivity of the will, for in them it is obscured by those forms whose general expression is the principle of sufficient reason, but which are condi-

tions of the knowledge which belongs to the individual as such. If it is allowable to draw conclusions from an impossible presupposition, we would, in fact, no longer know particular things, not events, nor change, nor multiplicity, but would comprehend only Ideas— only the grades of the objectification of that one will, of the thing-in-itself, in pure unclouded knowledge. Consequently our world would be a *nunc stans*, if it were not that, as knowing subjects, we are also individuals, that is, our perceptions come to us through the medium of a body, from the affections of which they proceed, and which is itself only concrete willing, objectivity of the will, and thus is an object among objects, and as such comes into the knowing consciousness in the only way in which an object can, through the forms of the principle of sufficient reason, and consequently already presupposes, and therefore brings in, time, and all other forms which that principle expresses. Time is only the broken and piecemeal view which the individual being has of the Ideas, which are outside time, and consequently *eternal*. Therefore Plato says time is the moving picture of eternity.

33.

Since now, as individuals, we have no other knowledge than that which is subject to the principle of sufficient reason, and this form of knowledge excludes the Ideas, it is certain that if it is possible for us to raise ourselves from the knowledge of particular things to that of the Ideas, this can only happen by an alteration taking place in the subject which is analogous and corresponds to the great change of the whole nature of the object, and by virtue of which the subject, so far as it knows an Idea, is no more individual.

It will be remembered from the preceding book that knowledge in general belongs to the objectification of will at its higher grades, and sensibility, nerves, and brain, just like the other parts of the organised being, are the expression of the will at this stage of its objectivity, and therefore the idea which appears through them is also in the same way bound to the service of will as a means for the attainment of its now complicated aims for sustaining a being of manifold requirements. Thus originally, and according to its nature, knowledge is completely subject to the will, and, like the immediate object which, by means of the application of the law of causality, is its starting point, all knowledge which proceeds in accordance with the principle of sufficient reason remains in a closer or more distant relation to the will. For the individual finds his body as an object among objects, to all of which it is related and connected according to the principle of sufficient reason. Thus all investigations of these relations and connections lead back to his body, and consequently to his will. Since it is the principle of sufficient reason which places the objects in this relation to the body, and, through it, to the will, the one endeavor of the knowledge which is subject to this principle will be to find out the relations in which objects are placed to each other through this principle, and thus to trace their innumerable connections in space, time, and causality. For only through these is the object *interesting* to the individual, that is, related to the will. Therefore the knowledge which is subject to the will knows nothing further of objects than their relations, knows the objects only so far as they exist at this time, in this place, under these circumstances, from these causes, and with these effects—in a word, as particular things; and if all these relations were to be taken away, the objects would also have disappeared for it, because it knew nothing more about them. We must not disguise the fact that what the sciences consider in things is also in reality nothing more than this; their relations, the connections of time and space, the causes of natural changes, the resemblance of forms, the motives of actions—thus merely relations. What distinguishes science from ordinary knowledge is merely its systematic form, the facilitating of knowledge by the comprehension of all particulars in the universal, by means of the subordination of concepts, and completeness of knowledge which is thereby attained. . . .

Knowledge now, as a rule, remains always subordinate to the service of the will, as indeed it originated for this service, and grew, so to speak, to the will, as the head to the body. In the case of the brutes this subjection of knowledge to the will can never be abolished. In the case of men it can be abolished only in exceptional cases, which we shall presently consider more closely. This distinction between man and brute is outwardly expressed by the difference of the relation of the head to the body. In the case of the lower brutes both are deformed: in all brutes the head

is directed towards the earth, where the objects of its will lie: even in the higher species the head and the body are still far more one than in the case of man, whose head seems freely set upon his body, as if only carried by and not serving it. . . .

34.

The transition which we have referred to as possible, but yet to be regarded as only exceptional, from the common knowledge of particular things to the knowledge of the Idea, takes place suddenly; for knowledge breaks free from the service of the will, by the subject ceasing to be merely individual, and thus becoming the pure will-less subject of knowledge, which no longer traces relations in accordance with the principle of sufficient reason, but rests in fixed contemplation of the object presented to it, out of its connection with all others, and rises into it. . . .

If, raised by the power of the mind, a man relinquishes the common way of looking at things, gives up tracing, under the guidance of the forms of the principle of sufficient reason, their relations to each other, the final goal of which is always a relation to his own will; if he thus ceases to consider the where, the when, the why, and the whither of things, and looks simply and solely at the *what*; if, further, he does not allow abstract thought, the concepts of the reason, to take possession of his consciousness, but, instead of all this, gives the whole power of his mind to perception, sinks himself entirely in this, and lets his whole consciousness be filled with the quiet contemplation of the natural object actually present, whether a landscape, a tree, a mountain, a building, or whatever it may be, inasmuch as he *loses* himself in this object (to use a pregnant German idiom), that is forgets even his individuality, his will, and only continues to exist as the pure subject, the clear mirror of the object, so that it is as if the object alone were there, without any one to perceive it, and he can no longer separate the perceiver from the perception, but both have become one, because the whole consciousness is filled and occupied with one single sensuous picture; if thus the object has to such an extent passed out all relation to something outside it, and the subject out of all relation to the will, then that which is so known is no longer the particular thing as such; but it is the *Idea*, the eternal form, the immediate objectivity of the will at this grade; and, therefore, he who is sunk in this perception is no longer individual, for in such perception the individual has lost himself; but he is *pure, will-less, painless, timeless subject of knowledge.*

35.

In order to gain a deeper insight into the nature of the world, it is absolutely necessary that we should learn to distinguish the will as thing-in-itself from its adequate objectivity, and also the different grades in which this appears more and more distinctly and fully, that is the Ideas themselves, from the merely phenomenal existence of these Ideas in the forms of the principle of sufficient reason, the restricted method of knowledge of the individual. We shall then agree with Plato when he attributes actual being only to the Ideas, and allows only an illusive, dream-like existence to things in space and time, the real world for the individual. Then we shall understand how one and the same Idea reveals itself in so many phenomena, and presents its nature only bit by bit to the individual, one side after another. Then we shall also distinguish the Idea itself from the way in which its manifestation appears in the observation of the individual, and recognise the former as essential and the latter as unessential. Let us consider this with the help of examples taken from the most insignificant things, and also from the greatest. When the clouds move, the figures which they form are not essential, but indifferent to them; but that as elastic vapor they are pressed together, drifted along, spread out, or torn asunder by the force of the wind: this is their nature, the essence of the forces which objectify themselves in them, the Idea; their actual forms are only for the individual observer. To the brook that flows over stones, the eddies, the waves, the foam-flakes which it forms are indifferent and unessential; but that it follows the attraction of gravity, and behaves as inelastic, perfectly mobile, formless, transparent fluid: this is its nature; this, *if known through perception*, is its Idea; these accidental forms are only for us so long as we know as individuals. The ice on the windowpane forms itself into crystals according to the laws of crystallisation, which reveal the essence of the force of nature that appears here, exhibit the Idea; but the trees and flowers which it traces on the pane are

unessential, and are only there for us. What appears in the clouds, the brook, and the crystal is the weakest echo of that will which appears more fully in the plant, more fully still in the beast, and most fully in man. But only the essential in all these grades of its objectification constitutes the Idea; on the other hand, its unfolding or development, because broken up in the forms of the principle of sufficient reason into a multiplicity of many-sided phenomena, is unessential to the Idea, lies merely in the kind of knowledge that belongs to the individual and has reality only for this. The same thing necessarily holds good of the unfolding of that Idea which is the completest objectivity of will. Therefore, the history of the human race, the throng of events, the change of times, the various forms of human life in different lands and countries, all this is only the accidental form of the manifestation of the Idea, does not belong to the Idea itself, in which alone lies the adequate objectivity of the will, but only to the phenomenon which appears in the knowledge of the individual, and is just as foreign, unessential, and indifferent to the Idea itself as the figures which they assume are to the clouds, the form of its eddies and foam-flakes to the brook, or its trees and flowers to the ice.

To him who has thoroughly grasped this, and can distinguish between the will and the Idea, and between the Idea and its manifestation, the events of the world will have significance only so far as they are the letters out of which we may read the Idea of man, but not in and for themselves. He will not believe with the vulgar that time may produce something actually new and significant; that through it, or in it, something absolutely real may attain to existence, or indeed that it itself as a whole has beginning and end, plan and development, and in some way has for its final aim the highest perfection (according to their conception) of the last generation of man, whose life is a brief thirty years. Therefore he will just as little, with Homer, people a whole Olympus with gods to guide the events of time, as, with Ossian, he will take the forms of the clouds for individual beings; for, as we have said, both have just as much meaning as regards the Idea which appears in them. In the manifold forms of human life and in the unceasing change of events, he will regard the Idea only as the abiding and essential, in which the will to live has its fullest objectivity, and which shows its different sides in the capacities, the passions, the errors and the excellences of the human race; in self-interest, hatred, love, fear, boldness, frivolity, stupidity, slyness, wit, genius, and so forth, all of which crowding together and combining in thousands of forms (individuals), continually create the history of the great and the little world, in which it is all the same whether they are set in motion by nuts or by crowns. Finally, he will find that in the world it is the same as in the dramas of Dozzi, in all of which the same persons appear, with like intention, and with a like fate; the motives and incidents are certainly different in each piece, but the spirit of the incidents is the same; the actors in one piece know nothing of the incidents of another, although they performed in it themselves; therefore, after all experience of former pieces, Pantaloon has become no more agile or generous, Tartaglia no more conscientious, Brighella no more courageous, and Columbine no more modest.

Suppose we were allowed for once a clearer glance into the kingdom of the possible, and over the whole chain of causes and effects; if the earth spirit appeared and showed us in a picture all the greatest men, enlighteners of the world, and heroes, that chance destroyed before they were ripe for their work; then the great events that would have changed the history of the world and brought in periods of the highest culture and enlightenment, but which the blindest chance, the most insignificant accident, hindered at the outset; lastly, the splendid powers of great men, that would have enriched whole ages of the world, but which, either misled by error or passion, or compelled by necessity, they squandered uselessly on unworthy or unfruitful objects, or even wasted in play. If we saw all this, we would shudder and lament at the thought of the lost treasures of whole periods of the world. But the earth spirit would smile and say, "the source from which the individuals and their powers proceed is inexhaustible and unending as time and space; for, like these forms of all phenomena, they also are only phenomena, visibility of the will. No finite measure can exhaust that infinite source; therefore an undiminished eternity is always open for the return of any event or work that was nipped in the bud. In this world of phenomena true loss is just as little possible as true gain. The will alone is; it is the thing-in-itself,

and the source of all these phenomena. Its self knowledge and its assertion or denial, which is then decided upon, is the only event in-itself."

36.

History follows the thread of events; it is pragmatic so far as it deduces them in accordance with the law of motivation, a law that determines the self-manifesting will wherever it is enlightened by knowledge. At the lowest grades of its objectivity, where it still acts without knowledge, natural science, in the form of etiology, treats of the laws of the changes of its phenomena, and, in the form of morphology, of what is permanent in them. This almost endless task is lightened by the aid of concepts, which comprehend what is general in order that we may deduce what is particular from it. Lastly, mathematics treats of the mere forms, time and space, in which the Ideas, broken up into multiplicity, appear for the knowledge of the subject as individual. All these, of which the common name is science, proceed according to the principle of sufficient reason in its different forms, and their theme is always the phenomenon, its laws, connections, and the relations which result from them. But what kind of knowledge is concerned with that which is outside and independent of all relations, that which alone is really essential to the world, the true content of its phenomena, that which is subject to no change, and therefore is known with equal truth for all time, in a word, the *Ideas*, which are the direct and adequate objectivity of the thing-in-itself, the will? We answer, *Art*, the work of genius. It repeats or reproduces the eternal Ideas grasped through pure contemplation, the essential and abiding in all the phenomena of the world; and according to what the material is in which it reproduces, it is sculpture or painting, poetry or music. Its one source is the knowledge of Ideas; its one aim the communication of this knowledge. While science, following the unresting and inconstant stream of the fourfold forms of reason and consequent, with each end attained sees further, and can never reach a final goal nor attain full satisfaction, any more than by running we can reach the place where the clouds touch the horizon; art, on the contrary, is everywhere at its goal. For it plucks the object of its contemplation out of the stream of the world's course, and has it isolated before it. And this particular thing, which in that stream was a small perishing part, becomes to art the representative of the whole, an equivalent of the endless multitude in space and time. It therefore pauses at this particular thing; the course of time stops; the relations vanish for it; only the essential, the Idea, is its object. We may, therefore, accurately define it as the *way of viewing things independent of the principle of sufficient reason,* in opposition to the way of viewing them which proceeds in accordance with that principle, and which is the method of experience and of science. This last method of considering things may be compared to a line infinitely extended in a horizontal direction, and the former to a vertical line which cuts it at any point. The method of viewing things which proceeds in accordance with the principle of sufficient reason is the rational method, and it alone is valid and of use in practical life and in science. The method which looks away from the content of this principle is the method of genius, which is only valid and of use in art. The first is the method of Aristotle; the second is, on the whole, that of Plato. The first is like the mighty storm, that rushes along without beginning and without aim, bending, agitating, and carrying away everything before it; the second is like the silent sunbeam, that pierces through the storm quite unaffected by it. The first is like the innumerable showering drops of the waterfall, which, constantly changing, never rest for an instant; the second is like the rainbow, quietly resting on this raging torrent. Only through the pure contemplation described above, which ends entirely in the object, can Ideas be comprehended; and the nature of *genius* consists in pre-eminent capacity for such contemplation. Now, as this requires that a man should entirely forget himself and the relations in which he stands, *genius* is simply the completest *objectivity,* that is, the objective tendency of the mind, as opposed to the subjective, which is directed to one's own self—in other words, to the will. Thus genius is the faculty of continuing the state of pure perception, of losing oneself in perception, and of enlisting in this service the knowledge which originally existed only for the service of the will; that is to say, genius is the power of leaving one's own interests, wishes, and aims entirely out of sight, thus of entirely renouncing one's own personality for a time, so as to remain *pure knowing subject,* clear vision of the world; and this not merely at moments, but for a sufficient length of time, and with

sufficient consciousness, to enable one to reproduce by deliberate art what has thus been apprehended, and "to fix in lasting thoughts the wavering images that float before the mind." It is as if, when genius appears in an individual, a far larger measure of the power of knowledge falls to his lot than is necessary for the service of an individual will; and this superfluity of knowledge, being free, now becomes subject purified from will, a clear mirror of the inner nature of the world. This explains the activity, amounting even to disquietude, of men of genius, for the present can seldom satisfy them, because it does not fill their consciousness. This gives them that restless aspiration, that unceasing desire for new things, and for the contemplation of lofty things, and also that longing that is hardly ever satisfied, for men of similar nature and of like stature, to whom they might communicate themselves; while the common mortal, entirely filled and satisfied by the common present, ends in it, and finding everywhere his like, enjoys that peculiar satisfaction in daily life that is denied to genius.

✦ ✦ ✦

BOOK IV: THE WORLD AS WILL

Second Aspect. The Assertion and Denial of the Will to Live, When Self-Consciousness has Been Attained

54.

. . . The will, which, considered purely in itself, is without knowledge, and is merely a blind incessant impulse, as we see it appear in unorganized and vegetable nature and their laws, and also in the vegetative part of our own life, receives through the addition of the world as idea, which is developed in subjection to it, the knowledge of its own willing and of what it is that it wills. And this is nothing else but the world as idea, life, precisely as it exists. Therefore we called the phenomenal world the mirror of the will, its objectivity. And since what the will wills is always life, just because life is nothing but the representation of that willing for the idea, it is all one and a mere pleonasm if, instead of simply saying "the will," we say "the will to live." . . .

Above all things, we must distinctly recognise that the form of the phenomenon of will, the form of life or reality, is really only the *present,* not the future nor the past. The latter are only in the conception, exist only in the connection of knowledge, so far as it follows the principle of sufficient reason. No man has ever lived in the past, and none will live in the future; the *present* alone is the form of all life, and is its sure possession which can never be taken from it. . . . The present is the form essential to the objectification of the will. It cuts time, which extends infinitely in both directions, as a mathematical point, and stands immovably fixed, like an everlasting mid-day with no cool evening, as the actual sun burns without intermission, while it only seems to sink into the bosom of night. Therefore, if a man fears death as his annihilation, it is just as if he were to think that the sun cries out at evening, "Woe is me! for I go down into eternal night." And conversely, whoever is oppressed with the burdens of life, whoever desires life and affirms it, but abhors its torments, and especially can no longer endure the hard lot that has fallen to himself, such a man has no deliverance to hope for from death, and cannot right himself by suicide. The cool shades of Orcus allure him only with the false appearance of a haven of rest. The earth rolls from day into night, the individual dies, but the sun itself shines without intermission, an eternal noon. Life is assured to the will to live; the form of life is an endless present, no matter how the individuals, the phenomena of the Idea, arise and pass away in time, like fleeting dreams. . . .

But this that we have brought to clearest consciousness, that although the particular phenomenon of the will has a temporal beginning and end, the will itself as thing-in-itself is not affected by it, nor yet the correlative of all object, the knowing but never known subject, and that life is always assured to the will to live—this is not to be numbered with the doctrines of immortality. For permanence has no more to do with the will or with the pure subject of knowing, the eternal eye of the world, than transitoriness, for both are predicates that are only valid in time, and the will and the pure subject of knowing lie outside time. Therefore the egoism of the individual (this particular phenomenon of will enlightened by the subject of knowing) can extract as little nourishment and consolation for his wish to endure through endless time from the view we have expressed, as he could from the knowledge that after his death the rest

of the eternal world would continue to exist, which is just the expression of the same view considered objectively, and therefore temporally. For every individual is transitory only as phenomenon, but as thing-in-itself is timeless, and therefore endless. But it is also only as phenomenon that an individual is distinguished from the other things of the world; as thing-in-itself he is the will which appears in all, and death destroys the illusion which separates his consciousness from that of the rest: this is immortality. . . . What we fear in death is the end of the individual which it openly professes itself to be, and since the individual is a particular objectification of the will to live itself, its whole nature struggles against death. Now when feeling thus exposes us helpless, reason can yet step in and for the most part overcome its adverse influence, for it places us upon a higher standpoint, from which we no longer contemplate the particular but the whole. Therefore a philosophical knowledge of the nature of the world, which extended to the point we have now reached in this work but went no farther, could even at this point of view overcome the terror of death in the measure in which reflection had power over direct feeling in the given individual. A man who had thoroughly assimilated the truths we have already advanced, but had not come to know, either from his own experience or from a deeper insight, that constant suffering is essential to life, who found satisfaction and all that he wished in life, and could calmly and deliberately desire that his life, as he had hitherto known it, should endure for ever or repeat itself ever anew, and whose love of life was so great that he willingly and gladly accepted all the hardships and miseries to which it is exposed for the sake of its pleasures—such a man would stand "with firm-knit bones on the well-rounded, enduring earth," and would have nothing to fear. Armed with the knowledge we have given him, he would await with indifference the death that hastens towards him on the wings of time. He would regard it as a false illusion, an impotent specter, which frightens the weak but has no power over him who knows that he is himself the will of which the whole world is the objectification or copy, and that therefore he is always certain of life, and also of the present, the peculiar and only form of the phenomenon of the will. He could not be terrified by an endless past or future in which he would not be, for this he would regard as the empty delusion of the web of Mâyâ. Thus he would no more fear death than the sun fears the night. In the *Bhagavad-Gita,* Krishna thus raises the mind of his young pupil Arjuna, when, seized with compunction at the sight of the arrayed hosts (somewhat as Xerxes was), he loses heart and desires to give up the battle in order to avert the death of so many thousands. Krishna leads him to this point of view, and the death of those thousands can no longer restrain him; he gives the sign for battle. . . .

57.

At every grade that is enlightened by knowledge, the will appears as an individual. The human individual finds himself as finite in infinite space and time, and consequently as a vanishing quantity compared with them. He is projected into them, and, on account of their unlimited nature, he has always a merely relative, never absolute *when* and *where* of his existence; for his place and duration are finite parts of what is infinite and boundless. His real existence is only in the present, whose unchecked flight into the past is a constant transition into death a constant dying. For his past life, apart from its possible consequences for the present, and the testimony regarding the will that is expressed in it, is now entirely done with, dead, and no longer anything; and, therefore, it must be, as a matter of reason, indifferent to him whether the content of that past was pain or pleasure. But the present is always passing through his hands into the past; the future is quite uncertain and always short. Thus his existence, even when we consider only its formal side, is a constant hurrying of the present into the dead past, a constant dying. But if we look at it from the physical side, it is clear that, as our walking is admittedly merely a constantly prevented falling, the life of our body is only a constantly prevented dying, an ever-postponed death: finally, in the same way, the activity of our mind is a constantly deferred ennui. Every breath we draw wards off the death that is constantly intruding upon us. In this way we fight with it every moment, and again, at longer intervals, through every meal we eat, every sleep we take, every time we warm ourselves, etc. In the end, death must conquer, for we became subject to him through birth, and he

only plays for a little while with his prey before he swallows it up. We pursue our life, however, with great interest and much solicitude as long as possible, as we blow out a soap bubble as long and as large as possible, although we know perfectly well that it will burst.

We saw that the inner being of unconscious nature is a constant striving without end and without rest. And this appears to us much more distinctly when we consider the nature of brutes and man. Willing and striving is its whole being, which may be very well compared to an unquenchable thirst. But the basis of all willing is need, deficiency, and thus pain. Consequently, the nature of brutes and man is subject to pain originally and through its very being. If, on the other hand, it lacks objects of desire, because it is at once deprived of them by a too easy satisfaction, a terrible void and ennui comes over it, that is, its being and existence itself becomes an unbearable burden to it. Thus its life swings like a pendulum backwards and forwards between pain and ennui. This has also had to express itself very oddly in this way; after man had transferred all pain and torments to hell, there then remained nothing over for heaven but ennui.

But the constant striving which constitutes the inner nature of every manifestation of will obtains its primary and most general foundation at the higher grades of objectification, from the fact that here the will manifests itself as a living body, with the iron command to nourish it; and what gives strength to this command is just that this body is nothing but the objectified will to live itself. Man, as the most complete objectification of that will, is in like measure also the most necessitous of all beings: he is through and through concrete willing and needing; he is a concretion of a thousand necessities. With these he stands upon the earth, left to himself, uncertain about everything except his own need and misery. Consequently the care for the maintenance of that existence under exacting demands, which are renewed every day, occupies, as a rule, the whole of human life. To this is directly related the second claim, that of the propagation of the species. At the same time he is threatened from all sides by the most different kinds of dangers, from which it requires constant watchfulness to escape. With cautious steps and casting anxious glances round him he pursues his path, for a thousand accidents and a thousand enemies lie in wait for him. Thus he went while yet a savage, thus he goes in civilized life; there is no security for him. . . .

The life of the great majority is only a constant struggle for this existence itself, with the certainty of losing it at last. But what enables them to endure this wearisome battle is not so much the love of life as the fear of death, which yet stands in the background as inevitable, and may come upon them at any moment. Life itself is a sea, full of rocks and whirlpools, which man avoids with the greatest care and solicitude, although he knows that even if he succeeds in getting through with all his efforts and skill, he yet by doing so comes nearer at every step to the greatest, the total, inevitable, and irremediable shipwreck, death; nay, even steers right upon it: this is the final goal of the laborious voyage, and worse for him than all the rocks from which he has escaped.

Now it is well worth observing that, on the one hand, the suffering and misery of life may easily increase to such an extent that death itself, in the flight from which the whole of life consists, becomes desirable, and we hasten towards it voluntarily; and again, on the other hand, that as soon as want and suffering permit rest to a man, ennui is at once so near that he necessarily requires diversion. The striving after existence is what occupies all living things and maintains them in motion. But when existence is assured, then they know not what to do with it; thus the second thing that sets them in motion is the effort to get free from the burden of existence, to make it cease to be felt, "to kill time," that is, to escape from ennui. Accordingly we see that almost all men who are secure from want and care, now that at last they have thrown off all other burdens, become a burden to themselves, and regard as a gain every hour they succeed in getting through, and thus every diminution of the very life which, till then, they have employed all their powers to maintain as long as possible. Ennui is by no means an evil to be lightly esteemed; in the end it depicts on the countenance real despair. It makes beings who love each other so little as men do, seek each other eagerly, and thus becomes the source of social intercourse. Moreover, even from motives of policy, public precautions are everywhere taken against it, as against other universal calamities. For this evil may drive men to the greatest excesses, just as much as its opposite extreme, famine: the people

require *panem et circenses*. The strict penitentiary system of Philadelphia makes use of ennui alone as a means of punishment, through solitary confinement and idleness, and it is found so terrible that it has even led prisoners to commit suicide. As want is the constant scourge of the people, so ennui is that of the fashionable world. In middle-class life ennui is represented by the Sunday, and want by the six weekdays.

Thus between desiring and attaining all human life flows on throughout. The wish is, in its nature, pain; the attainment soon begets satiety: the end was only apparent; possession takes away the charm; the wish, the need, presents itself under a new form; when it does not, then follows desolateness, emptiness, ennui, against which the conflict is just as painful as against want. That wish and satisfaction should follow each other neither too quickly nor too slowly reduces the suffering which both occasion to the smallest amount, and constitutes the happiest life. For that which we might otherwise call the most beautiful part of life, its purest joy, if it were only because it lifts us out of real existence and transforms us into disinterested spectators of it—that is, pure knowledge, which is foreign to all willing, the pleasure of the beautiful, the true delight in art—this is granted only to a very few, because it demands rare talents, and to these few only as a passing dream. And then, even these few, on account of their higher intellectual power, are made susceptible of far greater suffering than duller minds can ever feel, and are also placed in lonely isolation by a nature which is obviously different from that of others; thus here also accounts are squared. But to the great majority of men purely intellectual pleasures are not accessible. They are almost quite incapable of the joys which lie in pure knowledge. They are entirely given up to willing. If, therefore, anything is to win their sympathy, to be *interesting* to them, it must (as is implied in the meaning of the word) in some way excite their *will*, even if it is only through a distant and merely problematical relation to it; the will must not be left altogether out of the question, for their existence lies far more in willing than in knowing— action and reaction is their one element. We may find in trifles and everyday occurrences that naïve expressions of this quality. Thus, for example, at any place worth seeing they may visit, they write their names, in order thus to react, to affect the place since it does not affect them. Again, when they see a strange, rare animal, they cannot easily confine themselves to merely observing it; they must rouse it, tease it, play with it, merely to experience action and reaction; but this need for excitement of the will manifests itself very specially in the discovery and support of card-playing, which is quite peculiarly the expression of the miserable side of humanity.

But whatever nature and fortune may have done, whoever a man be and whatever he may possess, the pain which is essential to life cannot be thrown off.... The ceaseless efforts to banish suffering accomplish no more than to make it change its form. It is essentially deficiency, want, care for the maintenance of life. If we succeed, which is very difficult, in removing pain in this form, it immediately assumes a thousand others, varying according to age and circumstances, such as lust, passionate love, jealousy, envy, hatred, anxiety, ambition, covetousness, sickness, etc. If at last it can find entrance in no other form, it comes in the sad, grey garments of tediousness and ennui, against which we then strive in various ways. If finally we succeed in driving this away, we shall hardly do so without letting pain enter in one of its earlier forms, and the dance begin again from the beginning; for all human life is tossed backwards and forwards between pain and ennui.

◆ ◆ ◆

58.

All satisfaction, or what is commonly called happiness, is always really and essentially only *negative*, and never positive. It is not an original gratification coming to us of itself, but must always be the satisfaction of a wish. The wish, that is, some want, is the condition which precedes every pleasure. But with the satisfaction the wish and therefore the pleasure cease. Thus the satisfaction or the pleasing can never be more than the deliverance from a pain, from a want; for such is not only every actual, open sorrow, but every desire the importunity of which disturbs our peace, and, indeed, the deadening ennui also that makes life a burden to us. It is, however, so hard to attain or achieve anything; difficulties and troubles without end are opposed to every purpose, and at every step hindrances accumulate. But when finally everything is overcome and attained, nothing can ever be gained but deliverance from some sorrow or desire,

so that we find ourselves just in the same position as we occupied before this sorrow or desire appeared. All that is even directly given us is merely the want, that is, the pain. The satisfaction and the pleasure we can only know indirectly through the remembrance of the preceding suffering and want, which ceases with its appearance. Hence it arises that we are not properly conscious of the blessings and advantages we actually possess, nor do we prize them, but think of them merely as a matter of course, for they gratify us only negatively by restraining suffering. Only when we have lost them do we become sensible of their value; for the want, the privation, the sorrow, is the positive, communicating itself directly to us. Thus also we are pleased by the remembrances of past need, sickness, want, and such like, because this is the only means of enjoying the present blessings. And, further, it cannot be denied that in this respect, and from this standpoint of egoism, which is the form of the will to live, the sight or the description of the sufferings of others affords us satisfaction and pleasure.... Yet we shall see farther on that this kind of pleasure, through knowledge of our own well-being obtained in this way, lies very near the source of real, positive wickedness.

That all happiness is only of a negative not a positive nature, that just on this account it cannot be lasting satisfaction and gratification, but merely delivers us from some pain or want which must be followed either by a new pain, or by languor, empty longing, and ennui; this finds support in art, that true mirror of the world and life, and especially in poetry. Every epic and dramatic poem can only represent a struggle, an effort, and fight for happiness, never enduring and complete happiness itself. It conducts its heroes through a thousand difficulties and dangers to the goal; as soon as this is reached, it hastens to let the curtain fall; for now there would remain nothing for it to do but to show that the glittering goal in which the hero expected to find happiness had only disappointed him, and that after its attainment he was no better off than before. Because a genuine enduring happiness is not possible, it cannot be the subject of art. Certainly the aim of the idyll is the description of such a happiness, but one also sees that the idyll as such cannot continue. The poet always finds that it either becomes epical in his hands, and in this case it is a very insignificant epic, made up of trifling sorrows, trifling delights, and trifling efforts—this is the commonest case—or else it becomes a merely descriptive poem, describing the beauty of nature, that is, pure knowing free from will, which certainly, as a matter of fact, is the only pure happiness, which is neither preceded by suffering or want, nor necessarily followed by repentance, sorrow, emptiness, or satiety; but this happiness cannot fill the whole life, but is only possible at moments. What we see in poetry we find again in music; in the melodies of which we have recognised the universal expression of the inmost history of the self-conscious will, the most secret life, longing, suffering, and delight; the ebb and flow of the human heart. Melody is always a deviation from the keynote through a thousand capricious wanderings, even to the most painful discord, and then a final return to the keynote which expresses the satisfaction and appeasing of the will, but with which nothing more can then be done, and the continuance of which any longer would only be a wearisome and unmeaning monotony corresponding to ennui.

All that we intend to bring out clearly through these investigations, the impossibility of attaining lasting satisfaction and the negative nature of all happiness, finds its explanation in what is shown at the conclusion of Book II: that the will, of which human life, like every phenomenon, is the objectification, is a striving without aim or end. We find the stamp of this endlessness imprinted upon all the parts of its whole manifestation, from its most universal form, endless time and space, up to the most perfect of all phenomena, the life and efforts of man. We may theoretically assume three extremes of human life, and treat them as elements of actual human life. First, the powerful will, the strong passions (Radscha-Guna). It appears in great historical characters; it is described in the epic and the drama. But it can also show itself in the little world, for the size of the objects is measured here by the degree in which they influence the will, not according to their external relations. Secondly, pure knowing, the comprehension of the Ideas, conditioned by the freeing of knowledge from the service of will: the life of genius (Satwa-Guna). Thirdly and lastly, the greatest lethargy of the will, and also of the knowledge attaching to it, empty longing, life-benumbing languor (Tama-Guna). The life of the individual, far from becoming permanently fixed in

one of these extremes, seldom touches any of them, and is for the most part only a weak and wavering approach to one or the other side, a needy desiring of trifling objects, constantly recurring, and so escaping ennui. It is really incredible how meaningless and void of significance when looked at from without, how dull and unenlightened by intellect when felt from within, is the course of the life of the great majority of men. It is a weary longing and complaining, a dream-like staggering through the four ages of life to death, accompanied by a series of trivial thoughts. Such men are like clockwork, which is wound up, and goes it knows not why; and every time a man is begotten and born, the clock of human life is wound up anew, to repeat the same old piece it has played innumerable times before, passage after passage, measure after measure, with insignificant variations. Every individual, every human being and his course of life, is but another short dream of the endless spirit of nature, of the persistent will to live; is only another fleeting form, which it carelessly sketches on its infinite page, space and time; allows to remain for a time so short that it vanishes into nothing in comparison with these, and then obliterates to make new room. And yet, and here lies the serious side of life, every one of these fleeting forms, these empty fancies, must be paid for by the whole will to live, in all its activity, with many and deep sufferings, and finally with a bitter death, long feared and coming at last. This is why the sight of a corpse makes us suddenly so serious.

The life of every individual, if we survey it as a whole and in general, and only lay stress upon its most significant features, is really always a tragedy, but gone through in detail, it has the character of a comedy. For the deeds and vexations of the day, the restless irritation of the moment, the desires and fears of the week, the mishaps of every hour, are all through chance, which is ever bent upon some jest, scenes of a comedy. But the never satisfied wishes, the frustrated efforts, the hopes unmercifully crushed by fate, the unfortunate errors of the whole life, with increasing suffering and death at the end, are always a tragedy. Thus, as if fate would add derision to the misery of our existence, our life must contain all the woes of tragedy, and yet we cannot even assert the dignity of tragic characters, but in the broad detail of life must inevitably be the foolish characters of a comedy.

But however much great and small trials may fill human life, they are not able to conceal its insufficiency to satisfy the spirit; they cannot hide the emptiness and superficiality of existence, nor exclude ennui, which is always ready to fill up every pause that care may allow. Hence it arises that the human mind, not content with the cares, anxieties, and occupations which the actual world lays upon it, creates for itself an imaginary world also in the form of a thousand different superstitions, then finds all manner of employment with this, and wastes time and strength upon it, as soon as the real world is willing to grant it the rest which it is quite incapable of enjoying. This is accordingly most markedly the case with nations for which life is made easy by the congenial nature of the climate and the soil, most of all with the Hindus, then with the Greeks, the Romans, and later with the Italians, the Spaniards, etc. Demons, gods, and saints man creates in his own image; and to them he must then unceasingly bring offerings, prayers, temple decorations, vows and their fulfilment, pilgrimages, salutations, ornaments for their images, etc. Their service mingles everywhere with the real, and, indeed, obscures it. Every event of life is regarded as the work of these beings; the intercourse with them occupies half the time of life, constantly sustains hope, and by the charm of illusion often becomes more interesting than intercourse with real beings. It is the expression and symptom of the actual need of mankind, partly for help and support, partly for occupation and diversion; and if it often works in direct opposition to the first need, because when accidents and dangers arise valuable time and strength, instead of being directed to warding them off, are uselessly wasted on prayers and offerings; it serves the second end all the better by this imaginary converse with a visionary spirit world; and this is the by no means contemptible gain of all superstitions.

68.

All suffering, since it is a mortification and a call to resignation, has potentially a sanctifying power. This is the explanation of the fact that every great misfortune or deep pain inspires a certain awe. But the sufferer only really becomes an object of reverence when, surveying the course of his life as a chain of sorrows, or mourning some great and incurable misfortune, he does not really look at the special combination of circumstances which has plunged his own life into suffering, nor stops at the single great misfortune that has befallen him; for in so doing his knowledge still follows the principle of sufficient reason, and clings to the particular phenomenon; he still wills life, only not under the conditions which have happened to him; but only then, I say, is he truly worthy of reverence when he raises his glance from the particular to the universal, when he regards his suffering as merely an example of the whole, and for him, since in a moral regard he partakes of genius, one case stands for a thousand, so that the whole of life conceived as essentially suffering brings him to resignation. Therefore it inspires reverence when in Goethe's "Torquato Tasso" the princess speaks of how her own life and that of her relations has always been sad and joyless, and yet regards the matter from an entirely universal point of view.

A very noble character we always imagine with a certain trace of quiet sadness, which is anything but a constant fretfulness at daily annoyances (this would be an ignoble trait, and lead us to fear a bad disposition), but is a consciousness derived from knowledge of the vanity of all possessions, of the suffering of all life, not merely of his own. But such knowledge may primarily be awakened by the personal experience of suffering, especially some one great sorrow, as a single unfulfilled wish brought Petrarch to that state of resigned sadness concerning the whole of life which appeals to us so pathetically in his works; for the Daphne he pursued had to flee from his hands in order to leave him, instead of herself, the immortal laurel. When through some such great and irrevocable denial of fate the will is to some extent broken, almost nothing else is desired, and the character shows itself mild, just, noble, and resigned. When, finally, grief has no definite object, but extends itself over the whole of life, then it is to a certain extent a going into itself, a withdrawal, a gradual disappearance of the will, whose visible manifestation, the body, it imperceptibly but surely undermines, so that a man feels a certain loosening of his bonds, a mild foretaste of that death which promises to be the abolition at once of the body and of the will. Therefore a secret pleasure accompanies this grief, and it is this, as I believe, which the most melancholy of all nations has called "the joy of grief." But here also lies the danger of *sentimentality*, both in life itself and in the representation of it in poetry; when a man is always mourning and lamenting without courageously rising to resignation. In this way we lose both earth and heaven, and retain merely a watery sentimentality. Only if suffering assumes the form of pure knowledge, and this, acting as a *quieter of the will*, brings about resignation, is it worthy of reverence. In this regard, however, we feel a certain respect at the sight of every great sufferer which is akin to the feeling excited by virtue and nobility of character, and also seems like a reproach of our own happy condition. We cannot help regarding every sorrow, both our own and those of others, as at least a potential advance towards virtue and holiness, and, on the contrary, pleasures and worldly satisfactions as a retrogression from them. This goes so far, that every man who endures a great bodily or mental suffering, indeed every one who merely performs some physical labor which demands the greatest exertion, in the sweat of his brow and with evident exhaustion, yet with patience and without murmuring, every such man, I say, if we consider him with close attention, appears to us like a sick man who tries a painful cure, and who willingly, and even with satisfaction, endures the suffering it causes him, because he knows that the more he suffers the more the cause of his disease is affected, and that therefore the present suffering is the measure of his cure.

According to what has been said, the denial of the will to live, which is just what is called absolute, entire resignation, or holiness, always proceeds from that quieter of the will which the knowledge of its inner conflict and essential vanity, expressing themselves in the suffering of all living things, becomes. The difference, which we have represented as two paths, consists in whether that knowledge is called

up by suffering which is merely and purely *known*, and is freely appropriated by means of the penetration of the *principium individuationis*, or by suffering which is directly *felt* by a man himself. True salvation, deliverance from life and suffering, cannot even be imagined without complete denial of the will. Till then, every one is simply this will itself, whose manifestation is an ephemeral existence, a constantly vain and empty striving, and the world full of suffering we have represented, to which all irrevocably and in like manner belong. For we found above that life is always assured to the will to live, and its one real form is the present, from which they can never escape, since birth and death reign in the phenomenal world. The Indian mythos expresses this by saying "they are born again." The great ethical difference of character means this, that the bad man is infinitely far from the attainment of the knowledge from which the denial of the will proceeds, and therefore he is in truth *actually* exposed to all the miseries which appear in life as *possible*; for even the present fortunate condition of his personality is merely a phenomenon produced by the *principium individuationis*, and a delusion of Mâyâ, the happy dream of a beggar. The sufferings which in the vehemence and ardour of his will he inflicts upon others are the measure of the suffering, the experience of which in his own person cannot break his will, and plainly lead it to the denial of itself. All true and pure love, on the other hand, and even all free justice, proceed from the penetration of the *principium individuationis*, which, if it appears with its full power, results in perfect sanctification and salvation, the phenomenon of which is the state of resignation described above, the unbroken peace which accompanies it, and the greatest delight in death.

STUDY QUESTIONS: SCHOPENHAUER, *THE WORLD AS WILL AND IDEA*

1. What does Schopenhauer mean by "The world is my idea?" Why does this truth hold for everything? How is consciousness related to this truth?
2. What is the one truth that can be asserted a priori?
3. In what way is empirical reality compatible with transcendental ideality?
4. Why should "the world is my will" strike you as awful?
5. What is Schopenhauer's view of Descartes, Berkeley, and Kant, respectively, regarding the proposition, "the world is idea?"
6. In what way is Schopenhauer's view related to the Vedanta philosophy of India?
7. What does Schopenhauer mean by "matter?" Does he deny its existence? Why?

8. What major mistake did Kant make in his philosophy?

9. What is the principle merit of Kant's philosophy?

10. What is "the subject?" What is its relationship to the world, and to phenomena?

11. What does Schopenhauer mean by "immediate object?" What is an example of one, in your experience?

12. Why is the controversy about the reality of the outer world "foolish?"

13. Why do subject and object precede all knowledge?

14. What is empirical reality? In what does it consist?

15. What is the role of causality? How is it related to the understanding?

16. What was Kant's mistake about dreams?

17. What does Schopenhauer mean by the difference between "long" and "short" dreams?

18. Is life a dream? In what sense? Why can't you directly control your dreams?

19. What is the relationship between the body and knowledge?

20. What is the knowledge peculiar to the reason as distinguished from the understanding?

21. How does Schopenhauer show that the will is knowledge a priori of the body, and that the body is knowledge *a posteriori* of the will? What is the significance of this distinction?

22. Can knowledge of the will be separated from knowledge of the body? Why?

23. How does Schopenhauer prove the identity of the will and the body?

24. Can each individual know everything? Why? What is the significance of this for the role and nature of philosophy?

25. What are the *principium individuationis?*

26. What is Schopenhauer's view of God?

27. What is Schopenhauer's view of Plato's Ideas? Is the word "idea" as used by Kant the same as Plato's use? What is the difference? Whom does Schopenhauer side with on this issue, and why?

28. What is the role of the Chinese *Yin* and *Yang* to Schopenhauer's view?

29. What is the *pure knowing subject?*

30. What is Schopenhauer's view of the *Bhagavad-Gita?*

31. What is ennui? What role does it play in his view of life?

32. Why is art so important? How does it achieve its aim? What is the relation between art and philosophy, in Schopenhauer's view?

33. What does Schopenhauer mean by the "sanctifying power" of suffering?

34. What is the danger of sentimentality?

Philosophical Bridges: Schopenhauer's Influence

Schopenhauer's philosophy has been immensely influential. Among philosophers, he had a deep and lasting influence, most notably on Nietzsche, Bergson, James, and Dewey. Even Wittgenstein, who discovered Schopenhauer's works while still a teenager, said that with only a few minor adjustments, Schopenhauer's philosophy was fundamentally right. (Apparently, Wittgenstein kept a copy of The World as Will and Idea at his bedside.) No less profound was Schopenhauer's influence on Sigmund Freud, who through reading Schopenhauer and Kant discovered how the insights of these great philosophers could be applied to create the new science of psychiatry—the key being that the body itself, along with all its ailments, was a manifestation of the will and that, ultimately, a causal relationship between them could be honed for therapeutic purposes that would eventually achieve cures to human psychological suffering nothing short of miraculous.

Among twentieth century writers and artists, Schopenhauer's influence was as great as Nietzsche's. The great novelist Thomas Mann regarded his philosophy as essential to the future evolution of humanity: "Schopenhauer is first the philosopher of the will and second the philosopher of pessimism. But actually there is no first and second, for they are one and the same, and he was the second by virtue of his being the first; he was necessarily pessimist because he was the philosopher and psychologist of the will. Will, as the opposite pole of inactive satisfaction, is naturally a fundamental unhappiness. It is unrest, a striving for something—it is want, craving, avidity, demand, suffering; and a world of will can be nothing else but a world of suffering."

Leo Tolstoy, too, found similar inspiration in Schopenhauer, whom he regarded as one of the greatest philosophers of all time and had his works translated into Russian. And Richard Wagner was deeply influenced by his thought, which scholars (e.g. Bryan Magee) have claimed found its way directly into Wagner's music.

Philosophical Bridges: The Influence of the German Idealists

The golden age of German idealism, which had evolved from the Kantian transcendental idealism of the previous century into the objective idealism of Fichte, the subjective idealism of Schelling, the absolute idealism of Hegel, and the representational idealism of Schopenhauer, produced a philosophical maelstrom unseen since the golden age of Greece. The full extent of its significance and influence is still not readily apparent. Even though in England John McTaggart, T. H. Green and F. H. Bradley, B. Bosanquet in France, and Josiah Royce in the United States developed very similar idealist views of reality, the prevalent view among many philosophers today, particularly those trained in the analytic tradition, is that all varieties of such idealisms were refuted in the twentieth century or at least died out or fell out of favor, when in fact the German idealism of nineteenth century crossed over in the twentieth century into quantum physics via Niels Bohr and Werner Heisenberg. According to quantum physics, mind and world are so intimately connected that, as Bohr puts it, "an independent reality in the ordinary physical sense can neither be ascribed to the phenomena nor to the agencies of observations." And the great American physicist John Archibald Wheeler calls his "participatory universe" model a revolutionary upgrade of "essentially the objective idealism of Schelling." At the quantum level, the essential properties of subatomic particles to not exist until the conscious mind brings it into existence. In this way the German idealist philosophies of the nineteenth century became the quantum physics of the twentieth century.

BIBLIOGRAPHY

FICHTE
Primary
Fichte: Early Philosophical Writings, ed. and trans. by D. Breazeale, Ithaca, NY: Cornell University Press, 1988

The Popular Works of J.G. Fichte, trans. by W. Smith, London, 1848

The Science of Knowledge, trans. by B. Rand, Berline: Sammtlichte Werke, 1845

Secondary
Adamson, R. *Fichte*, Books for Libraries Press, 1969

Breazeale, D. and Rockmore, T., eds., *Fichte: Historical Contexts/Contemporary Controversies*, Humanities Press, 1994

Hegel, G. W. F., *The Difference Between Fichte's and Schelling's System of Philosophy*, trans. by H.S. Harris and A. Cerf, SUNY Press, 1977

Neuhouser, F., *Fichte's Theory of Subjectivity*, Cambridge University Press, 1990

SCHELLING
Primary
The Ages of the World, trans., with notes, by F. Bolton, Columbia University Press, 1942

Of Human Freedom, trans. by J. Gutmann, Open Court, 1936

System of Transcendental Idealism, trans. by P. Heath, University Press of Virginia, 1978.

Secondary
Beach, E. A., *The Potencies of the God(s): Schelling's Philosophy of Mythology*, SUNY Press, 1994

Bowie, A., *Schelling and Modern European Philosophy: An Introduction*, Routledge, 1993

Marx, W., *The Philosophy of F. W. J. Schelling: History, System, Freedom*, Indiana University Press, 1984

Sandkühler, H. J. *Friedrich Wilhelm Joseph Schelling*, Metzler, 1970.

Snow, D. E., *Schelling and the End of Idealism*, SUNY Press, 1996

White, A. *Schelling: Introduction to the System of Freedom*, Yale University Press, 1983

HEGEL
Primary
Introductory Lectures on Aesthetics, translated by B. Bosanquet. Penguin Books, 1993

Lectures on the History of Philosophy: Plato and the Platonists, vol., 2, trans. by E.S. Haldane and F. H. Simson., University of Nebraska Press, 1995

Logic, trans. by W. Wallace, Clarendon Press, 1975

Philosophy of History, trans. by J. Sibree, Dover, 1956

Philosophy of Mind, trans. by A.V. Miller, Clarendon Press, 1971

Philosophy of Right, trans. by T.M. Knox, Oxford University Press, 1952

Phenomenology of Spirit, trans. by A.V. Miller, Clarendon Press, 1977

Secondary
Barnett, S. ed., *Hegel After Derrida*, Routledge, 1998

Beiser, F., *The Cambridge Companion to Hegel*, Cambridge University Press, 1993

Brown, A. L., *On Hegel*, Wadsworth, 2001

Inwood, M., *A Hegel Dictionary*, Blackwell, 1992

Kainz, H., *G. W. F. Hegel: The Philosophical System*, Ohio University Press, 1996

Kaufmann, W., *Hegel: Texts and Commentary*, Anchor Books, 1966

Kojeve, A., *Introduction to the Reading of Hegel*, Cornell University Press, 1969

Kolb, D., *The Critique of Pure Modernity: Hegel, Heidegger, and After*, University of Chicago Press, 1986

Taylor, C., *Hegel*, Cambridge University Press, 1975

Zizek, S., *Tarrying with the Negative: Kant, Hegel, and the Critique of Ideology*, Duke University Press, 1993

SCHOPENHAUER
Primary
The Fourfold Root of the Principle of Sufficient Reason, trans. by E. F. J. Payne, Open Court, 1974

"On the Suffering of the World," reprinted in *The Meaning of Life*, ed. S. Sanders and D. R. Cheney, Prentice-Hall, 1980, pp. 25–32

On the Basis of Morality, trans. by E. F. J. Payne, Bobbs-Merrill, 1965

The World as Will and Representation, trans. by E. F. J. Payne, Dover, 1969

Secondary
Fox, M., *Schopenhauer: His Philosophical Achievement*, Oxford University Press, 1980

Hamlyn, D. W., *Schopenhauer*, Routledge & Kegan Paul, 1980

Maggee, B., *The Philosophy of Schopenhauer*, Oxford University Press, 1983

Odell, S. J., *On Schopenhauer*, Wadsworth, 2001

SECTION III

◆ THE EXISTENTIALISTS ◆

PROLOGUE

Although Platonic and Aristotelian philosophies evolved along different, sometimes opposing, paths, both accepted—either overtly or covertly—as fundamental an absolute presupposition that we can state as follows: *essence precedes existence*. Plato's ideas, found nowhere in experience, are eternal and abstract, beyond space and time, and are ultimate essences that precede the existence of objects in the world. The triangle you draw is a copy, or representation, of the eternal idea, or form, of the ideal triangle that existed before you drew it. Nothing can exist in the world of appearances without its ideal form preceding its arrival, as it were, on the scene. Similarly, for Aristotle, everything that exists does so with a purpose for which it was by nature designed to strive. In existentialist philosophies, this fundamental proposition is turned on its head. Rather, as the great twentieth century French philosopher Jean-Paul Sartre would eventually put it, *existence precedes essence*.

The roots of this philosophically revolutionary idea can be found in Schopenhauer, who replaced the notion of *reason* with purposeless *will*. But existentialism, as a philosophy, would not be named as such for decades to come. In the works of Kierkegaard and Nietzche the existentialist ideal found its first, original and some would argue primordial force.

KIERKEGAARD (1813–1855)

Biographical History

Søren Kierkegaard was born in Copenhagen, Denmark. He studied theology, literature and philosophy at the University of Copenhagen. Like most European universities of the time, Copenhagen was deeply under the influence of Hegel's philosophy. Kierkegaard's initial fascination with Hegel's elaborate system became a sounding board against which the young genius rebelled: "If Hegel had written the whole of his Logic and then said . . . that it was merely a joke, then he could certainly have been the greatest thinker who ever lived. As it is, he is himself merely a joke." The problem with then-contemporary Hegelian philosophy, in Kierkegaard's eyes, was that it not only failed to address the unique and fundamental true nature of human existence, but denied it—namely *subjectivity*. Kierkegaard developed this criticism brilliantly in his master's thesis, *The Concept of Irony*. He went on to publish many highly influential and original books, in which he argued for the primacy of subjectivity as the essential aspect of individual human existence.

He was only 42 when he died. On his tombstone is inscribed *Enkelte*, the unique category of the individual central to Kierkegaard's unique philosophy.

Philosophical Overview

Kierkegaard was deeply critical of traditional philosophy as it was practiced within academic institutions, and even more so of all institutional religions, especially the official Danish state church. In his view, such systems stifle human individuality and deny the human any possibility of living the authentic life of a true individual. Authentic engagement with the world, with others, and even with oneself, requires the individual to make original choices. What makes this so difficult, and rare, is that making choices requires that we live in an abyss of unknowing, in perpetual despair and dread. Neither logic nor reason can help; they are themselves tools of avoiding responsibility. "Why did you do X?" To answer, "Because it was the right thing," or "It was rational," is a way of avoiding the responsibility of having to choose. "Because I chose X," is the only legitimate, authentic way to be, self-existence through self-actualization. The process involves experiencing directly the awareness of existence within oneself, to see it as an ultimate unknowable unknown. Despair affirms one's own individual existence as subjectivity.

According to Kierkegaard, thought cannot relate to existence. This is in marked contrast to Hegel, for whom thought and existence are identical. Kierkegaard has a Platonic view of meaning: existence is unthinkable, and thought is an abstraction that is limited, as such, to general categories and the concepts derived therein. Thinking does not connect us to existence but stands in the way of a direct engagement; it removes us from the directness of experience and imprisons us in language and abstract theories. Which is not to say that thought is irrelevant. In one of Kierkegaard's most important works, *Concluding Unscientific Postscript* (1846), he distinguishes *subjective* thought, which concerns itself with the *how*, from objective thought, which concerns itself with the *what*. This distinction, central to Kierkegaard's philosophy, makes deliberating and choosing the primary function of thought.

Kierkegaard acknowledges Descartes' contribution to philosophy for basing his epistemology in the self. But he criticizes Descartes on the same grounds as he criticizes Hegel. The problem is that Descartes, like Hegel, identifies the self with thought. It is a grave philosophical mistake to go from "I think, therefore I am," to "I am a thinking thing." All thinking about ourselves is just another manifestation of outwardness and the misguided craving for objectivity. All thinking about ourselves obscures the true experience of our own existence; thinking is a moving away from the true existential core of our own being, it is theoretical, an abstraction. Existence must be experienced directly, without theory or ordinary thinking. Because passion, decision, and action are at the core of Kierkegaard's existentialist vision, he is widely regarded as the originating founder of existentialism.

The paradox is that although thought cannot grasp pure existence, thought must nevertheless be used to *interpret* existence. That is how what he calls *subjective thought* allows us to create ourselves. This is the existentialist, subjective thinker, defined not by studying or observing truth but by living it. The authentic individual *becomes* truth, the truth *exists* as that individual.

Hegel's objective view of history, his objective view of reflection, and his emphasis on objective existence, are sounding boards against which Kierkegaard constructs his own contrarian philosophy. The Hegelian individual is defined by the state. The Hegelian individual exists, as such, within a system of objective thought. The individual's own existence is excluded because all the individual has been given by the education system for self-understanding are abstract, universal, timeless categories. The individual's own concrete, particular existence in time is appropriated by the system; he becomes a member of a group, absorbed until the individual as such exists no more. By contrast, Kierkegaard's individual is radically subjective. Since in his view no truly objective system is possible, the subjective thinker must exist in perpetual uncertainty. We must recognize this as our fate; only then can we lead an authentic life.

Kierkegaard applied his philosophy to his own works. Not only does he avoid building any philosophical systems, he avoids directly attributing his own works to himself. Unlike virtually all other philosophers, Kierkegaard presents his works through the individual eyes of characters distinct from the author. Indeed, in some ways he anticipates the twentieth-century deconstructionists (e.g. Derrida) according to whom the view of an author as an objective, external observer is itself viewed as an artificial construction. Kierkegaard's vivid characters write in their own voice, they have their own distinctive psychologies, and their ideas and beliefs are in each case different. It is as if different individuals wrote his books, each with his own subjective voice. *Either/Or,* for instance, is written as a series of correspondences between a young aesthete and an older mentor named Judge Wilhelm. The correspondence of the young man is lyrical, poetic, romantic; the correspondence of the old man is pedantic and dry. But even this is an oversimplification, for Kierkegaard puts the book within the persona of yet another pseudonym, Victor Eremita, an imaginary editor of the letters! Johannes de Silentio, Constantin Constantius, Johannes Climacus, Nicolaus Notabene, Vigilius Hafniensis, are some of the other pseudonyms created by Kierkegaard for his works.

EITHER/OR
An Ecstatic Lecture
Kierkegaard

Kierkegaard's views arose in opposition to Hegel's. *Either/Or* (1843) is actually a satire of what Kierkegaard regarded as the depersonalization of human existence brought about by Hegel's departure from traditional Aristotelian logic. The foundation of Aristotle's logic was built on three axioms:

1. *the principle of identity,*
2. *the principle of noncontradiction, and*
3. *the principle of the excluded middle.*

According to the first, everything is identical to itself. According to the second, nothing both is and is not the case. Consider the proposition, "George Washington was the first president of the United States." It cannot be the case that this proposition is both true and false. According to the third, anything either is or is not the case; for instance, "George Washington was the first president of the United States" is either true or false. In so far as Hegel's dialectical logic rejects these three principles, it makes everything be, or contain, its own opposite. This means that Hegel's system invalidates the second and third Aristotelian axioms, both of which are derived from the more basic principle of identity. Such a departure from traditional Aristotelian logic is, in Kierkegaard's view, unacceptable because, without the principle of identity, the authentic individual as such no longer exists. This is because without the excluded middle there can be no freedom of choice, and all decision making becomes superfluous. This leads to the absurd state described in *Either/Or*.

If you marry, you will regret it; if you do not marry, you will also regret it; if you marry or do not marry, you will regret both; whether you marry or do not marry, you will regret both. Laugh at the world's follies, you will regret it; weep over them, you will also regret that; laugh at the world's follies or weep over them, you will regret both; whether you laugh at the world's follies or weep over them, you will regret both. Believe a woman, you will regret it, believe her not, you will also regret that; believe a woman, or believe her not, you will regret both; whether you believe a woman or believe her not, you will regret both. Hang yourself, you will regret it; do not hang yourself, and you will also regret that; hang yourself or do not hang yourself, you will regret both; whether you hang yourself or do not hang yourself, you will regret both. This, gentlemen, is the sum and substance of all philosophy. It is not only at certain moments that I view everything *aeterno modo*, as Spinoza says, but I live constantly *aeterno modo*. There are many who think that they live thus, because after having done the one or the other, they combine or mediate the opposites. But this is a misunderstanding; for the true eternity does not lie behind either/or, but before it. Hence, their eternity will be a painful succession of temporal moments, for they will be consumed by a twofold regret. My philosophy is at least easy to understand, for I have only one principle, and I do not even proceed from that. It is necessary to distinguish between the successive dialectic in either/or, and the eternal dialectic here set forth. Thus, when I say that I do not proceed from my principle, this must not be understood in opposition to a proceeding forth from it, but

is rather a negative expression for the principle itself, through which it is apprehended in equal opposition to a proceeding or a non-proceeding from it. I do not proceed from my principle, for if I did, I would regret it, and if I did not, I would also regret that. If it seems, therefore, to one or another of my respected hearers that there is anything in what I say, it only proves that he has no talent for philosophy; if my argument seems to have any forward movement, this also proves the same. But for those who can follow me, although I do not make any progress, I shall now unfold the eternal truth, by virtue of which this philosophy remains within itself, and admits of no higher philosophy. For if I proceeded from my principle, I should find it impossible to stop, for if I stopped, I should regret it, and if I did not stop, I should also regret that, and so forth. But since I never start, so can I never stop; my eternal departure is identical with my eternal cessation. Experience has shown that it is by no means difficult for philosophy to begin. Far from it. It begins with nothing, and consequently can always begin. But the difficulty, both for philosophy and for philosophers, is to stop. This difficulty is obviated in my philosophy, for if anyone believes that when I stop now, I really stop, he proves himself lacking in the speculative insight. For I do not stop now, I stopped at the time when I began. Hence my philosophy has the advantage of brevity, and it is also impossible to refute; for if anyone were to contradict me, I should undoubtedly have the right to call him mad. Thus it is seen that the philosopher lives continuously *aeterno modo*, and has not, . . . only certain hours which are lived for eternity.

Kierkegaard, from *Either/Or*, translated by David F. Swenson, and William Marvin Swenson, Princeton: Princeton University Press 1944.

STUDY QUESTIONS: KIERKEGAARD, *EITHER/OR*

1. What is the difference between viewing versus living everything *aeterno modo*?
2. Why is it important to distinguish the successive dialectic from the eternal dialectic? What is the difference and what is its significance?
3. Why is the philosophy of the either/or impossible to refute?
4. Why has the narrator of the either/or never been happy?
5. Why, if you were to contradict the narrator's statements, would he have the right to call you mad?
6. What is the one principle of the narrator's philosophy, from which he says he does not even proceed?
7. Does he claim that his philosophy is easy to understand? Why?

CONCLUDING UNSCIENTIFIC POSTSCRIPT
The Subjective Truth, Inwardness; Truth is Subjectivity

Like Augustine, Kierkegaard presents a view of faith as being primary, and even superior to, reason. The greatest virtue that an individual can attain is not rationality but faith, which brings about a deep and profound existential connection within oneself to an authentic relationship with spirituality and God. But the faith Kierkegaard here presents is sharply contrasted with conformity with an organized, social institution such as one finds in organized religious institutions where the emphasis is on obedience to authority. According to Kierkegaard, subjectivity, not objectivity, is the authentic path to human goodness and salvation. Any objective, rational arguments for religion or the existence of God are not only false but antithetical to the true quest for spiritual enlightenment, which is not collective but individualistic.

Whether truth is defined more empirically, as the conformity of thought and being, or more idealistically, as the conformity of being with thought, it is, in either case, important to note carefully what is meant by being. And in formulating the answer to this question it is likewise important to take heed lest the knowing spirit be tricked into losing itself in the indeterminate, so that it fantastically becomes a something that no existing human being ever was or can be, a sort of phantom with which the individual occupies himself upon occasion, but without making it clear to himself in terms of dialectical intermediaries how he happens to get into this fantastic realm, what significance being there has for him, and whether the entire activity that goes on out there does not resolve itself into a tautology within a recklessly fantastic venture of thought.

If being, in the two indicated definitions, is understood as empirical being, truth is at once transformed into a *desideratum*, and everything must be understood in terms of becoming; for the empirical object is unfinished and the existing cognitive spirit is itself in process of becoming. Thus the truth becomes an approximation whose beginning cannot be posited absolutely, precisely because the conclusion is lacking, the effect of which is retroactive. Whenever a beginning is *made*, on the other hand, unless through being unaware of this the procedure stamps itself as arbitrary, such a beginning is not the consequence of an immanent movement of thought, but is effected through a resolution of the will, essentially in the strength of faith. That the knowing spirit is an existing individual spirit, and that every human being is such an entity existing for himself, is a truth I cannot

---

Kierkegaard, from *Concluding Unscientific Postscript*, translated by David Swenson, Princeton University Press 1941.

too often repeat; for the fantastic neglect of this is responsible for much confusion. Let no one misunderstand me. I happen to be a poor existing spirit like all other men; but if there is any lawful and honest manner in which I could be helped into becoming something extraordinary, like the pure I-am-I for example, I always stand ready gratefully to accept the gift and the benefaction. But if it can only be done in the manner indicated, by saying *ein zwei drei kokolorum,* or by tying a string around the little finger, and then when the moon is full, hiding it in some secret place—in that case I prefer to remain what I am, a poor existing human being.

The term "being," as used in the above definitions, must therefore be understood (from the systematic standpoint) much more abstractly, presumably as the abstract reflection of, or the abstract prototype for, what being is as concrete empirical being. When so understood there is nothing to prevent us from abstractly determining the truth as abstractly finished and complete, for the correspondence between thought and being is, from the abstract point of view, always finished. Only with the concrete does becoming enter in, and it is from the concrete that abstract thought abstracts.

But if being is understood in this manner, the formula becomes a tautology. Thought and being mean one and the same thing, and the correspondence spoken of is merely an abstract self-identity. Neither formula says anything more than that the truth is, so understood as to accentuate the copula: the truth *is,* that is the truth is a reduplication. Truth is the subject of the assertion, but the assertion that it is, is the same as the subject, for this being that the truth is said to have is never its own abstract form. In this manner we give expression to the fact that truth is not something simple, but is in a wholly abstract sense a reduplication, a reduplication which is nevertheless instantly revoked.

Abstract thought may continue as long as it likes to rewrite this thought in varying phraseology, but it will never get any farther. As soon as the being which corresponds to the truth comes to be empirically concrete, the truth is put in process of becoming, and is again by way of anticipation the conformity of thought with being. This conformity is actually realized for God, but it is not realized for any existing spirit, who is himself existentially in process of becoming.

For an existing spirit *qua* existing spirit, the question of the truth will again exist. The abstract answer has significance only for the abstraction into which an existing spirit is transformed when he abstracts from himself qua existing individual. This can be done only momentarily, and even in such moments of abstraction the abstract thinker pays his debt to existence by existing in spite of all abstraction. It is therefore an existing spirit who is now conceived as raising the question of truth, presumably in order that he may exist in it; but in any case the question is raised by someone who is conscious of being a particular existing human being. In this way I believe I can render myself intelligible to every Greek, as well as to every reasonable human being. If a German philosopher wishes to indulge a passion for making himself over, and, just as alchemists and necromancers were wont to garb themselves fantastically, first makes himself over into a superrational something for the purpose of answering this question of the truth in an extremely satisfactory manner, the affair is no concern of mine, nor is his extremely satisfactory answer, which is no doubt very satisfactory indeed—when you are fantastically transformed. On the other hand, whether it is or is not the case that a German professor behaves in this manner can be readily determined by anyone who will concentrate enthusiastically upon seeking guidance at the hands of such a sage, without criticism but seeking merely to assimilate the wisdom in a docile spirit by proposing to shape his own life in accordance with it. Precisely when thus enthusiastically attempting to learn from such a German professor, one would realize the most apt of epigrams upon him. For such a speculative philosopher could hardly be more embarrassed than by the sincere and enthusiastic zeal of a learner who proposes to express and to realize his wisdom by appropriating it existentially. For this wisdom is something that the Herr Professor has merely imagined, and written books about, but never himself tried. Aye, it has never even occurred to him that this should be done. Like the custom clerk who writes what he could not himself read, satisfied that his responsibilities ended with the writing, so there are speculative philosophers who write what, when it is to be read in the light of action, shows itself to be nonsense, unless it is, perhaps, intended only for fantastic beings.

In that the question of truth is thus raised by an existing spirit qua existing, the above abstract reduplication that is involved in it again confronts him. But existence itself, namely, existence as it is in the individual who raises the question and himself exists, keeps the two moments of thought and being apart, so that reflection presents him with two alternatives. For an objective reflection the truth becomes an object, something objective, and thought must be pointed away from the subject. For a subjective reflection the truth becomes a matter of appropriation, of inwardness, of subjectivity, and thought must probe more and more deeply into the subject and his subjectivity.

But then what? Shall we be compelled to remain in this disjunction, or may we not here accept the offer of benevolent assistance from the principle of mediation, so that the truth becomes an identity of subject and object? Well, why not? But can the principle of mediation also help the existing individual while still remaining in existence himself to become the mediating principle, which is *sub specie aeterni,* whereas the poor existing individual is confined to the straitjacket of existence? Surely it cannot do any good to mock a man, luring him on by dangling before his eyes the identity of subject and object, when his situation prevents him from making use of this identity, since he is in process of becoming in consequence of being an existing individual. How can it help to explain to a man how the eternal truth is to be understood eternally, when the supposed user of the explanation is prevented from so understanding it through being an existing individual, and merely becomes fantastic when he imagines himself to be sub specie aeterni? What such a man needs instead is precisely an explanation of how the eternal truth is to be understood in determinations of time by one who as existing is himself in time, which even the worshipful Herr Professor concedes, if not always, at least once a quarter when he draws his salary.

The identity of subject and object posited through an application of the principle of mediation merely carries us back to where we were before, to the abstract definition of the truth as an identity of thought and being, for to determine the truth as an identity of thought and object is precisely the same

thing as saying that the truth *is,* that is that the truth is a reduplication. The lofty wisdom has thus again merely been absent-minded enough to forget that it was an existing spirit who asked about the truth. Or is the existing spirit himself the identity of subject and object, the subject-object? In that case I must press the question of where such an existing human being is, when he is thus at the same time also a subject-object? Or shall we perhaps here again first transform the existing spirit into something in general, and there-upon explain everything except the question asked, namely, how an existing subject is related to the truth *in concreto;* explain everything except the question that must in the next instance be asked, namely, how a particular existing spirit is related to this something in general, which seems to have not a little in common with a paper kite, or with the lump of sugar which the Dutch used to hang up under the loft for all to lick at.

So we return to the two ways of reflection, and we have not forgotten that it is an existing spirit who asks the question, a wholly individual human being. Nor can we forget that the fact that he exists is precisely what will make it impossible for him to proceed along both ways at once, while his earnest concern will prevent him from frivolously and fantastically becoming subject-object. Which of these two ways is now the way of truth for an existing spirit? For only the fantastic I-am-I is at once finished with both ways, or proceeds methodically along both ways simultaneously, a mode of ambulation which for an existing human is so inhuman that I dare not recommend it.

Since the inquirer stresses precisely the fact that he is an existing individual, then one of the above two ways which especially accentuates existence would seem to be especially worthy of commendation.

The way of objective reflection makes the subject accidental, and thereby transforms existence into something indifferent, something vanishing. Away from the subject the objective way of reflection leads to the objective truth, and while the subject and his subjectivity become indifferent, the truth also becomes indifferent, and this indifference is precisely its objective validity, for all interest, like all decisiveness, is rooted in subjectivity. The way of objective reflection leads to abstract thought, to mathematics, to historical knowledge of different kinds; and always it leads away from the subject, whose existence or non-existence, and from the objective point of view quite rightly, becomes infinitely indifferent. Quite rightly, since as Hamlet says, existence and nonexistence have only subjective significance. At its maximum this way will arrive at a contradiction, and in so far as the subject does not become wholly indifferent to himself, this merely constitutes a sign that his objective striving is not objective enough. At its maximum this way will lead to the contradiction that only the objective has come into being, while the subjective has gone out; that is to say, the existing subjectivity has vanished, in that it has made an attempt to become what in the abstract sense is called subjectivity, the mere abstract form of an abstract objectivity. And yet, the objectivity which has thus come into being is, from the subjective point of view at the most, either an hypothesis or an approximation, because all eternal decisiveness is rooted in subjectivity.

However, the objective way deems itself to have a security which the subjective way does not have (and, of course, existence and existing cannot be thought in combination with objective security); it thinks to escape a danger which threatens the subjective way, and this danger is at its maximum: madness. In a merely subjective determination of the truth, madness and truth become in the last analysis indistinguishable, since they may both have inwardness.[1] Nevertheless, perhaps I may here venture to offer a little remark, one which would seem to be not wholly superfluous in an objective age. The absence of inwardness is also madness. The objective truth as such, is by no means adequate to determine that whoever utters it is sane; on the contrary, it may even betray the fact that he is mad, although what he says may be entirely true, and especially objectively true. I shall here permit myself to tell a story, which without any sort of adaptation on my part comes direct from an asylum. A patient in such an institution seeks to escape, and actually succeeds in effecting his purpose by leaping out of a window, and prepares to start on the road to freedom, when the thought strikes him (shall I say sanely enough or madly enough?): "When you come to town you will be recognized, and you will at once be brought back here again; hence you need to prepare yourself fully to convince everyone by the objective truth of what you say, that all is in order as far as your sanity is concerned." As he walks along and thinks about this, he sees a ball lying on the ground, picks it up, and puts it into the tail pocket of his coat. Every step he takes the ball strikes him, politely speaking, on his hinder parts, and every time it thus strikes him he says: "Bang, the earth is round." He comes to the city, and at once calls on one of his friends; he wants to convince him that he is not crazy, and therefore walks back and forth, saying continually: "Bang, the earth is round!" But is not the earth round? Does the asylum still crave yet another sacrifice for this opinion, as in the time when all men believed it to be flat as a pancake? Or is a man who hopes to prove that he is sane, by uttering a generally accepted and generally respected objective truth, insane? And yet it was clear to the physician that the patient was not yet cured; though it is not to be thought that the cure would consist in getting him to accept the opinion that the earth is flat. But all men are not physicians, and what the age demands seems to have a considerable influence upon the question of what madness is. Aye, one could almost be tempted sometimes to believe that the modern age, which has modernized Christianity has also modernized the question of Pontius Pilate, and that its urge to find something in which it can rest proclaims itself in the question: What is madness? When a *Privatdocent*, every time his scholastic gown reminds him that he ought to say something, says *de omnibus dubitandum est*, and at the same time writes away at a system which offers abundant internal evidence in every other sentence that the man has never doubted anything at all: he is not regarded as mad.

Don Quixote is the prototype for a subjective madness, in which the passion of inwardness embraces

---

[1] Even this is not really true, however, for madness never has the specific inwardness of the infinite. Its fixed idea is precisely some sort of objectivity, and the contradiction of madness consists in embracing this with passion. The critical point in such madness is thus again not the subjective, but the little finitude which has become a fixed idea, which is something that can never happen to the infinite.

a particular finite fixed idea. But the absence of inwardness gives us on the other hand the prating madness, which is quite as comical; and it might be a very desirable thing if an experimental psychologist would delineate it by taking a handful of such philosophers and bringing them together. In the type of madness which manifests itself as an aberrant inwardness, the tragic and the comic is that the something which is of such infinite concern to the unfortunate individual is a particular fixation which does not really concern anybody. In the type of madness which consists in the absence of inwardness, the comic is that though the something which the happy individual knows really is the truth, the truth which concerns all men, it does not in the slightest degree concern the much respected prater. This type of madness is more inhuman than the other. One shrinks from looking into the eyes of a madman of the former type lest one be compelled to plumb there the depths of his delirium; but one dares not look at a madman of the latter type at all, from fear of discovering that he has eyes of glass and hair made from carpet-rags; that he is, in short, an artificial product. If you meet someone who suffers from such a derangement of feeling, the derangement consisting in his not having any, you listen to what he says in a cold and awful dread, scarcely knowing whether it is a human being who speaks, or a cunningly contrived walking stick in which a talking machine has been concealed. It is always unpleasant for a proud man to find himself unwittingly drinking a toast of brotherhood with the public hangman, but to find oneself engaged in rational and philosophical conversation with a walking stick is almost enough to make a man lose his mind.

The subjective reflection turns its attention inwardly to the subject, and desires in this intensification of inwardness to realize the truth. And it proceeds in such fashion that, just as in the preceding objective reflection, when the objectivity had come into being, the subjectivity had vanished; so here the subjectivity of the subject becomes the final stage, and objectivity a vanishing factor. Not for a single moment is it forgotten that the subject is an existing individual, and that existence is a process of becoming, and that therefore the notion of the truth as identity of thought and being is a chimera of abstraction, in its truth only an expectation of the creature; not because the truth is not such an identity, but because

the knower is an existing individual for whom the truth cannot be such an identity as long as he lives in time. Unless we hold fast to this, speculative philosophy will immediately transport us into the fantastic realism of the I-am-I, which modern speculative thought has not hesitated to use without explaining how a particular individual is related to it; and God knows, no human being is more than such a particular individual.

If an existing individual were really able to transcend himself, the truth would be for him something final and complete; but where is the point at which he is outside himself? The I-am-I is a mathematical point which does not exist, and in so far there is nothing to prevent everyone from occupying this standpoint; the one will not be in the way of the other. It is only momentarily that the particular individual is able to realize existentially a unity of the infinite and the finite which transcends existence. This unity is realized in the moment of passion. Modern philosophy has tried anything and everything in the effort to help the individual to transcend himself objectively, which is a wholly impossible feat; existence exercises its restraining influence, and if philosophers nowadays had not become mere scribblers in the service of a fantastic thinking and its preoccupation, they would long ago have perceived that suicide was the only tolerable practical interpretation of its striving. But the scribbling modern philosophy holds passion in contempt; and yet passion is the culmination of existence for an existing individual—and we are all of us existing individuals. In passion the existing subject is rendered infinite in the eternity of the imaginative representation, and yet he is at the same time most definitely himself. The fantastic I-am-I is not an identity of the infinite and the finite, since neither the one nor the other is real; it is a fantastic rendezvous in the clouds, an unfruitful embrace, and the relationship of the individual self to this mirage is never indicated.

All essential knowledge relates to existence, or only such knowledge as has an essential relationship to existence is essential knowledge. All knowledge which does not inwardly relate itself to existence, in the reflection of inwardness, is, essentially viewed, accidental knowledge; its degree and scope is essentially indifferent. That essential knowledge is essentially related to existence does not mean the abovementioned identity which abstract thought postulates between thought and being; nor does it signify, objectively, that knowledge corresponds to something existent as its object. But it means that knowledge has a relationship to the knower, who is essentially an existing individual, and that for this reason all essential knowledge is essentially related to existence. Only ethical and ethico-religious knowledge has an essential relationship to the existence of the knower.

Mediation is a mirage, like the I-am-I. From the abstract point of view everything is and nothing comes into being. Mediation can therefore have no place in abstract thought, because it presupposes *movement*. Objective knowledge may indeed have the existent for its object; but since the knowing subject is an existing individual, and through the fact of his existence in process of becoming, philosophy must first explain how a particular existing subject is related to a knowledge of mediation. It must explain what he is in such a moment, if not pretty nearly *distrait*; where he is, if not in the moon? There is constant talk of mediation and mediation; is mediation then a man, as Peter Deacon believes that *Imprimatur* is a man? How does a human being manage to become something of this kind? Is this dignity, this great *philosophicum*, the fruit of study, or does the magistrate give it away, like the office of deacon or grave-digger? Try merely to enter into these and other such plain questions of a plain man, who would gladly become mediation if it could be done in some lawful and honest manner, and not either by saying *ein zwei drei kokolorum*, or by forgetting that he is himself an existing human being, for whom existence is therefore something essential, and an ethico-religious existence a suitable *quantum satis*. A speculative philosopher may perhaps find it in bad taste to ask such questions. But it is important not to direct the polemic to the wrong point, and hence not to begin in a fantastic objective manner to discuss *pro* and *contra* whether there is a mediation or not, but to hold fast what it means to be a human being.

In an attempt to make clear the difference of way that exists between an objective and a subjective reflection, I shall now proceed to show how a subjective reflection makes its way inwardly in inwardness.

Inwardness in an existing subject culminates in passion; corresponding to passion in the subject the truth becomes a paradox; and the fact that the truth becomes a paradox is rooted precisely in its having a relationship to an existing subject. Thus the one corresponds to the other. By forgetting that one is an existing subject, passion goes by the board and the truth is no longer a paradox; the knowing subject becomes a fantastic entity rather than a human being, and the truth becomes a fantastic object for the knowledge of this fantastic entity.

When the question of truth is raised in an objective manner, reflection is directed objectively to the truth, as an object to which the knower is related. Reflection is not focused upon the relationship, however, but upon the question of whether it is the truth to which the knower is related. If only the object to which he is related is the truth, the subject is accounted to be in the truth. When the question of the truth is raised subjectively, reflection is directed subjectively to the nature of the individual's relationship; if only the mode of this relationship is in the truth, the individual is in the truth even if he should happen to be thus related to what is not true.[1] Let us take as an example the knowledge of God. Objectively, reflection is directed to the problem of whether this object is the true God; subjectively, reflection is directed to the question whether the individual is related to a something in such a manner that his relationship is in truth a God-relationship. On which side is the truth now to be found? Ah, may we not here resort to a mediation, and say: it is on neither side, but in the mediation of both? Excellently well-said, provided we might have it explained how an existing individual manages to be in a state of mediation. For to be in a state of mediation is to be finished, while to exist is to become. Nor can an existing individual be in two places at the same time—he cannot be an identity of subject and object. When he is nearest to being in two places at the same time he is in passion; but passion is momentary, and passion is also the highest expression of subjectivity.

The existing individual who chooses to pursue the objective way enters upon the entire approximation process by which it is proposed to bring God to light objectively. But this is in all eternity impossible, because God is a subject, and therefore exists only for

---

[1]The reader will observe that the question here is about essential truth, or about the truth which is essentially related to existence, and that it is precisely for the sake of clarifying it as inwardness or as subjectivity that this contrast is drawn.

subjectivity in inwardness. The existing individual who chooses the subjective way apprehends instantly the entire dialectical difficulty involved in having to use some time, perhaps a long time, in finding God objectively; and he feels this dialectical difficulty in all its painfulness, because every moment is wasted in which he does not have God.[1] That very instant he has God, not by virtue of any objective deliberation, but by virtue of the infinite passion of inwardness. The objective inquirer, on the other hand, is not embarrassed by such dialectical difficulties as are involved in devoting an entire period of investigation to finding God—since it is possible that the inquirer may die tomorrow; and if he lives he can scarcely regard God as something to be taken along if convenient, since God is precisely that which one takes *a tout prix*, which in the understanding of passion constitutes the true inward relationship to God.

It is at this point, so difficult dialectically, that the way swings off for everyone who knows what it means to think, and to think existentially; which is something very different from sitting at a desk and writing about what one has never done, something very different from writing *de omnibus dubitandum* and at the same time being as credulous existentially as the most sensuous of men. Here is where the way swings off, and the change is marked by the fact that while objective knowledge rambles comfortably on by way of the long road of approximation without being impelled by the urge of passion, subjective knowledge counts every delay a deadly peril, and the decision so infinitely important and so instantly pressing that it is as if the opportunity had already passed.

Now when the problem is to reckon up on which side there is most truth, whether on the side of one who seeks the true God objectively, and pursues the approximate truth of the God-idea; or on the side of one who, driven by the infinite passion of his need of God, feels an infinite concern for his own relationship to God in truth (and to be at one and the same time on both sides equally, is as we have noted not possible for an existing individual, but is merely the happy delusion of an imaginary I-am-I): the answer cannot be in doubt for anyone who has not been demoralized with the aid of science. If one who lives in the midst of Christendom goes up to the house of God, the house of the true God, with the true conception of God in his knowledge, and prays, but prays in a false spirit; and one who lives in an idolatrous community prays with the entire passion of the infinite, although his eyes rest upon the image of an idol: where is there most truth? The one prays in truth to God though he worships an idol; the other prays falsely to the true God, and hence worships in fact an idol.

When one man investigates objectively the problem of immortality, and another embraces an uncertainty with the passion of the infinite: where is there most truth, and who has the greater certainty? The one has entered upon a never-ending approximation, for the certainty of immortality lies precisely in the subjectivity of the individual; the other is immortal, and fights for his immortality by struggling with the uncertainty. Let us consider Socrates. Nowadays everyone dabbles in a few proofs; some have several such proofs, others fewer. But Socrates! He puts the question objectively in a problematic manner: *if* there is an immortality. He must therefore be accounted a doubter in comparison with one of our modern thinkers with the three proofs? By no means. On this "if" he risks his entire life, he has the courage to meet death, and he has with the passion of the infinite so determined the pattern of his life that it must be found acceptable—*if* there is an immortality. Is any better proof capable of being given for the immortality of the soul? But those who have the three proofs do not at all determine their lives in conformity therewith; if there is an immortality it must feel disgust over their manner of life: can any better refutation be given of the three proofs? The bit of uncertainty that Socrates had, helped him because he himself contributed the passion of the infinite; the three proofs that the others have do not profit them at all, because they are dead to spirit and enthusiasm, and their three proofs, in lieu of proving anything

---

[1]In this manner God certainly becomes a postulate, but not in the otiose manner in which this word is commonly understood. It becomes clear rather that the only way in which an existing individual comes into relation with God, is when the dialectical contradiction brings his passion to the point of despair, and helps him to embrace God with the "category of despair" (faith). Then the postulate is so far from being arbitrary that it is precisely a life-necessity. It is then not so much that God is a postulate, as that the existing individual's postulation of God is a necessity.

else, prove just this. A young girl may enjoy all the sweetness of love on the basis of what is merely a weak hope that she is beloved, because she rests everything on this weak hope; but many a wedded matron more than once subjected to the strongest expressions of love, has in so far indeed had proofs, but strangely enough has not enjoyed *quod erat demonstrandum*. The Socratic ignorance, which Socrates held fast with the entire passion of his inwardness, was thus an expression for the principle that the eternal truth is related to an existing individual, and that this truth must therefore be a paradox for him as long as he exists; and yet it is possible that there was more truth in the Socratic ignorance as it was in him, than in the entire objective truth of the System, which flirts with what the times demand and accommodates itself to *Privatdocents*.

The objective accent falls on WHAT is said, the subjective accent on HOW it is said. This distinction holds even in the aesthetic realm, and receives definite expression in the principle that what is in itself true may in the mouth of such and such a person become untrue. In these times this distinction is particularly worthy of notice, for if we wish to express in a single sentence the difference between ancient times and our own, we should doubtless have to say: *In ancient times only an individual here and there knew the truth;*

now all know it, except that the inwardness of its appropriation stands in an inverse relationship to the extent of its dissemination.[1] Aesthetically the contradiction that truth becomes untruth in this or that person's mouth, is best construed comically: in the ethico-religious sphere, accent is again on the "how." But this is not to be understood as referring to demeanor, expression, or the like; rather it refers to the relationship sustained by the existing individual, in his own existence, to the content of his utterance. Objectively the interest is focussed merely on the thought content, subjectively on the inwardness. At its maximum this inward "how" is the passion of the infinite, and the passion of the infinite is the truth. But the passion of the infinite is precisely subjectivity, and thus subjectivity becomes the truth. Objectively there is no infinite decisiveness, and hence it is objectively in order to annul the difference between good and evil, together with the principle of contradiction, and therewith also the infinite difference between the true and the false. Only in subjectivity is there decisiveness, to seek objectivity is to be in error. It is the passion of the infinite that is the decisive factor and not its content, for its content is precisely itself. In this manner subjectivity and the subjective "how" constitute the truth.

STUDY QUESTIONS: KIERKEGAARD, CONCLUDING UNSCIENTIFIC POSTSCRIPT

1. In Kierkegaard's definition of truth, what does he mean by *being*? What is the relationship between truth and being?
2. Why is truth always merely an approximation?
3. What is extraordinary about the "pure I-am-I?"
4. What keeps the two moments of thought and being apart?
5. Does Kierkegaard agree on the identity of subject and object?
6. What does Kierkegaard mean by the "wholly individual human being"?
7. Why is all eternal decisiveness rooted in subjectivity? What is the significance of this?

---

[1] *Stages on Life's Way*, Note on p. 426. Though ordinarily not wishing an expression of opinion on the part of reviewers, I might at this point almost desire it, provided such opinions, so far from flattering me, amounted to an assertion of the daring truth that what I say is something that everybody knows, even every child, and that the cultured know infinitely much better. If it only stands fast that everyone knows it, my standpoint is in order, and I shall doubtless make shift to manage with the unity of the comic and the tragic. If there were anyone who did not know it I might perhaps be in danger of being dislodged from my position of equilibrium by the thought that I might be in a position to communicate to someone the needful preliminary knowledge. It is just this which engages my interest so much, this that the cultured are accustomed to say: that everyone knows what the highest is. This was not the case in paganism, nor in Judaism, nor in the seventeen centuries of Christianity. Hail to the nineteenth century! Everyone knows it. What progress has been made since the time when only a few knew it. To make up for this, perhaps, we must assume that no one nowadays does it.

8. What is the relationship between madness and truth?
9. What is the absence of inwardness?
10. What is the point of the Don Quixote example?
11. Why does Kierkegaard say that the "I-am-I is a mathematical point that does not exist"?
12. What aspect of the finite an infinite transcends existence?
13. What does Kierkegaard mean by "essential knowledge"? How is it related to inwardness?
14. How is the I-am-I a mirage?
15. In what does inwardness in an existing subject culminate?
16. How are truth and paradox related?

Philosophical Bridges: Kierkegaard's Influence

Because he so vividly made the case that philosophy, with all its trials and tribulations and even darkness, not only matters to our lives, but is the fulcrum of human individuality, Kierkegaard is generally regarded as the "father of existentialism." His books caused a tremendous stir throughout the philosophical and literary world. In a letter to Hans Christian Andersen, one reviewer laments:

> A new literary comet . . . has soared in the heavens here . . . It is so demonic that one reads and reads it, puts it aside in dissatisfaction, but always takes it up again, because one can neither let it go nor hold onto it. 'But what is it?' I can hear you say. It is *Either/Or* by Søren Kierkegaard. You have no idea what sensation it has caused. I think that no book has caused such a stir with the reading public since Rousseau placed his *Confessions* on the altar (quoted in *On Kierkegaard*, Susan Leigh Anderson).

In making his case that faith may require the individual to act not only irrationally but unethically, as a test of authenticity and spirituality, Kierkegaard continues to inspire generations of writers and philosophers who regard him, as H. J. Blackman so aptly puts it, as "the boldest and the greatest of existentialist thinkers" (*Six Existentialist Thinkers*). Although Kierkegaard wrote in Danish, his works have been translated into nearly every language, and his audience today is worldwide and cuts across many disciplines, such as the Spanish philosopher Migue de Unamuno, the Swiss theologian Karl Barth, German theologian Paul Tillich, and the American philosopher Reinhold Niebuhr. All the great existentialists—Jaspers, Heidegger, Sartre, Camus—acknowledge Kierkegaard as their founder, without whom existentialism would probably never have existed.

NIETZSCHE (1844–1900)
Biographical History

Friedrich Nietzsche, the son and grandson of devout Lutheran ministers, was born in Röcken, Prussia. His father died when Nietzsche was 4 and his mother, grandmother, and aunts raised him. At school he excelled in all disciplines, but especially loved classic literature and philosophy, particularly Plato. He was admitted to the University of Bonn but found both the students and professors too superficial for his liking, and he transferred to Leipzig. There he encountered his two greatest inspirations: the philosophy of Schopenhauer and the music of Richard Wagner. After publishing a few highly regarded articles, he finished his doctorate at Leipzig, and then accepted a professorship at the University of Basel, Switzerland. He was still only 24.

Nietzsche became one of Richard Wagner's closest friends and confidants. With the success and acclaim of his books, he resigned from the university and became a full-time writer, producing over a dozen brilliant works, including *Thus Spake Zarathustra* (1883–1885), *Beyond Good and Evil* (1886), *The Genealogy of Morals* (1887), *The Antichrist* (1895), and *The Will to Power* (1901).

Philosophical Overview

Nietzsche's philosophy, like that of many other nineteenth-century thinkers who reacted against Hegel, springs from the idea that there are no things-in-themselves, no noumenal realm. But in Nietzsche's view neither is there any phenomenal reality. Like Kierkegaard, he discards as complete myth the notion of Platonic ideas. Nothing exists but a Heraclitean flux, an underlying and ceaselessly turbulent, ever-changing chaos upon which our will acts. And the will, as in Schopenhauer, is not bound by reason; the Logos, too, is an ancient unreality. Epistemology is dead. Even God is dead, by which Nietzsche means that the idea has ceased to perform any positive function. Nietzsche thus seeks a return of philosophy to its Sophist form. In a way reminiscent of Thrasymachus, he argues that might is right: the powerful must impose their will upon the weak.

Avowals of knowledge are pure invention; the only authentic way to be, then, is to lie with a purpose. That purpose is power. Nietzsche is opposed, however, to traditional forms of the lie, which he identifies as the chief function and domain of all religious, political, and educational institutions. Such lies are but elaborate forms of self-deception. Rather, Nietzsche espouses an *authentic* form of lying, which is fundamentally creative, and the purpose of which is to subjugate the will of others to one's own. This is what he calls "the will to power." This molding can only be done by the brave and powerful who have survived the educational system of lies imposed through institutions that in his view are but the dead remnants of previous acts of will to power. Such institutions are the corruptive means for what he calls the *transvaluation of values*, where what is truly good is made to appear bad, and what is truly bad is made to appear good.

Language, in Nietzsche's view, is also a mask, imposed from without upon the individual as a "condition of life." However, because language is, necessarily, a type of deception or lie, it is also the source of our freedom to create. For the will, language becomes a "mobile army of metaphors, metonyms and anthropomorphisms." Metaphors are figures of speech wherein terms are transposed from their original meaning to a new meaning. This creates a false likeness or analogy that does not exist in reality but only in our description. Metonyms, on the other hand, are figures of speech by which names are used as substitutes for something that the name is associated with. Such associations, in Nietzsche's view, are merely linguistic—they have no reality beyond the language. According to Nietzsche, the metaphoric, metonymic, and anthropomorphic nature of language gives a primal power to poetry as expression of truth. He does not accept the standard sort of distinction between "literal" or "scientific" language and "metaphoric" or "figurative" language. Both are essentially poetic. The division between the two forms is not only false and artificial but the source of confusion among philosophers. Nietzsche wants to return to philosophy the function of language as poetry; his own major philosophical works he called "poems." They are his poetical interpretations of being and, as such, expressions of the artistic force of his own acts of self-creation.

BEYOND GOOD AND EVIL
Nietzsche

In *Beyond Good and Evil* Nietzsche shows how the concepts "good" and "bad" are prime examples of the transvaluation of values. The weak use institutions of power to subvert the biological and psychological urges that he regards as fundamental aspects of authentic existence. The subversion worms itself into the structure of thought and language, which thus becomes the vehicle not of truth but of self-deception.

Language, in Nietzsche's view, is a form of lying. Words by their very nature deny what is truly real, namely, the perpetual Heraclitean flux. This is because words, as names, stand for things that persist in space and time. But nothing does—words and language help the mind to ignore the flux of the appearances and to imagine a constancy that is merely fictitious.

Nietzsche asks us to consider our learned desire to identify ourselves with a particular political, racial, national, or religious group. It may give us a sense of security, but it also imprisons us in a false social identity imposed by educational, political, and religious institutions. Thus, like Kierkegaard, Nietzsche wants us instead to achieve, through an act of willful self-creation, our own individual identity. But unlike Kierkegaard, who finds in the individual a true, authentic, personal being, this according to Nietzsche is also but a type of lie and deception, a mask.

Nietzsche distinguishes the noble, poetic lies that in his view affirm life from the common lies that he attributes to religions such as Christianity, which he regards as ignoble and life-denying. Christianity according to Nietzsche denies the chaotic nature of reality, the flux that exists only to be molded by the will to power. He sees the overt hope and longing for a world beyond this one as but an overt desire for nothingness and death. Religion is in that sense life-denying.

By the famous phrase "God is dead," Nietzsche does not mean that God is a being who once was alive and has since died; rather, he means that the idea, the notion, the concept of God, is no longer viable. As a result, religion turns values upside down. He uses Christianity as an example of how what he calls *slave morality* takes over *master morality*. He calls Christianity the most "fatal and seductive lie that has ever yet existed" and declares "open war on it."

PREFACE

Supposing that Truth is a woman—what then? Is there not ground for suspecting that all philosophers, in so far as they have been dogmatists, have failed to understand women—that the terrible seriousness and clumsy importunity with which they have usually paid their addresses to Truth, have been unskilled and unseemly methods for winning a woman? Certainly she has never allowed herself to be won; and at pres- ent every kind of dogma stands with sad and discour- aged mien—*if*, indeed, it stands at all! For there are scoffers who maintain that it has fallen, that all dogma lies on the ground—nay more, that it is at its last gasp. But to speak seriously, there are good grounds for hop- ing that all dogmatising in philosophy, whatever solemn, whatever conclusive and decided airs it has assumed, may have been only a noble puerilism and tyronism; and probably the time is at hand when it will

Nietzsche, from *Beyond Good and Evil*, translated by Helen Zimmern, Edinburgh, 1911.

be once and again understood *what* has actually sufficed for the basis of such imposing and absolute philosophical edifices as the dogmatists have hitherto reared: perhaps some popular superstition of immemorial time (such as the soul-superstition, which, in the form of subject and ego-superstition, has not yet ceased doing mischief); perhaps some play upon words, a deception on the part of grammar, or an audacious generalisation of very restricted, very personal, very human—all-too-human facts. The philosophy of the dogmatists, it is to be hoped, was only a promise for thousands of years afterwards, as was astrology in still earlier times, in the service of which probably more labor, gold, acuteness, and patience have been spent than on any actual science hitherto: we owe to it, and to its "super-terrestrial" pretensions in Asia and Egypt, the grand style of architecture. It seems that in order to inscribe themselves upon the heart of humanity with everlasting claims, all great things have first to wander about the earth as enormous and awe-inspiring caricatures—dogmatic philosophy has been a caricature of this kind. For instance, the Vedanta doctrine in Asia, and Platonism in Europe. Let us not be ungrateful to it, although it must certainly be confessed that the worst, the most tiresome, and the most dangerous of errors hitherto has been a dogmatist error—namely, Plato's invention of Pure Spirit and the Good in Itself. But now when it has been surmounted, when Europe, rid of this nightmare, can again draw breath freely and at least enjoy a healthier—sleep, we, *whose duty is wakefulness itself*, are the heirs of all the strength which the struggle against this error has fostered. It amounted to the very inversion of truth, and the denial of the *perspective*—the fundamental condition—of life, to speak of Spirit and the Good as Plato spoke of them; indeed one might ask, as a physician: "How did such a malady attack that finest product of antiquity, Plato? Had the wicked Socrates really corrupted him? Was Socrates after all a corrupter of youths, and deserved his hemlock?" But the struggle against Plato, or—to speak plainer, and for the "people"—the struggle against the ecclesiastical oppression of millenniums of Christianity (for Christianity is Platonism for the "people"), produced in Europe a magnificent tension of soul, such as had not existed anywhere previously; with such a tensely strained bow one can now aim at the furthest goals. As a matter of fact, the European feels this tension as a state of distress, and twice attempts have been made in grand style to unbend the bow: once by means of Jesuitism, and the second time by means of democratic enlightenment—which, with the aid of liberty of the press and newspaper-reading, might, in fact, bring it about that the spirit would not so easily find itself in "distress"! (The Germans invented gunpowder—all credit to them! But they again made things square—they invented printing.) But we, who are neither Jesuits, nor democrats, nor even sufficiently Germans, we *good Europeans*, and free, *very* free spirits—we have it still, all the distress of spirit and all the tension of its bow! And perhaps also the arrow, the duty, and, who knows? *The goal to aim at. . . .*

Sils-Maria, Upper Engadine, June 1885

PREJUDICES OF PHILOSOPHERS

The Will to Truth, which is to tempt us to many a hazardous enterprise, the famous Truthfulness of which all philosophers have hitherto spoken with respect, what questions has this Will to Truth not laid before us! What strange, perplexing, questionable questions! It is already a long story; yet it seems as if it were hardly commenced. Is it any wonder if we at last grow distrustful, lose patience, and turn impatiently away? That this Sphinx teaches us at last to ask questions ourselves? *Who* is it really that puts questions to us here? *What* really is this "Will to Truth" in us? In fact we made a long halt at the question as to the origin of this Will—until at last we came to an absolute standstill before a yet more fundamental question. We inquired about the *value* of this Will. Granted that we want the truth: *why not rather* untruth? And uncertainty? Even ignorance? The problem of the value of truth presented itself before us—or was it we who presented ourselves before the problem? Which of us is the Oedipus here? Which the Sphinx? It would seem to be a rendezvous of questions and notes of interrogation. And could it be believed that it at last seems to us as if the problem had never been propounded before, as if we were the first to discern it, get a sight of it, and *risk raising* it. For there is risk in raising it, perhaps there is no greater risk.

"*How could* anything originate out of its opposite? For example, truth out of error? Or the Will to

Truth out of the will to deception? Or the generous deed out of selfishness? Or the pure sun bright vision of the wise man out of covetousness? Such genesis is impossible; whoever dreams of it is a fool, nay, worse than a fool; things of the highest value must have a different origin, an origin of *their own*—in this transitory, seductive, illusory, paltry world, in this turmoil of delusion and cupidity, they cannot have their source. But rather in the lap of Being, in the intransitory, in the concealed God, in the 'thing-in-itself'—*there* must be their source, and nowhere else!" This mode of reasoning discloses the typical prejudice by which metaphysicians of all times can be recognized, this mode of valuation is at the back of all their logical procedure; through this "belief" of theirs, they exert themselves for their "knowledge," for something that is in the end solemnly, christened "the Truth." The fundamental belief of metaphysicians is *the belief in antitheses of values*. It never occurred even to the wariest of them to doubt here on the very threshold (where doubt, however, was most necessary); though they had made a solemn vow, "*de omnibus dubitandum.*" For it may be doubted, firstly, whether antitheses exist at all; and secondly, whether the popular valuations and antitheses of value upon which metaphysicians have set their seal, are not perhaps merely superficial estimates, merely provisional perspectives, besides being probably made from some corner, perhaps from below—"frog perspectives," as it were, to borrow an expression current among painters. In spite of all the value which may belong to the true, the positive, and the unselfish, it might be possible that a higher and more fundamental value for life generally should be assigned to pretence, to the will to delusion, to selfishness, and cupidity. It might even be possible that *what* constitutes the value of those good and respected things, consists precisely in their being insidiously related, knotted, and crocheted to these evil and apparently opposed things—perhaps even in being essentially identical with them. Perhaps! But who wishes to concern himself with such dangerous "Perhapses"? For that investigation one must await the advent of a new order of philosophers, such as will have other tastes and inclinations, the reverse of those hitherto prevalent—philosophers of the dangerous "Perhaps" in every sense of the term. And to speak in all seriousness, I see such new philosophers beginning to appear.

Having kept a sharp eye on philosophers, and having read between their lines long enough, I now say to myself that the greater part of conscious thinking must be counted amongst the instinctive functions, and it is so even in the case of philosophical thinking; one has here to learn anew, as one learned anew about heredity and "innateness." As little as the act of birth comes into consideration in the whole process and procedure of heredity, just as little is "being-conscious" *opposed* to the instinctive in any decisive sense; the greater part of the conscious thinking of a philosopher is secretly influenced by his instincts, and forced into definite channels. And behind all logic and its seeming sovereignty of movement, there are valuations, or to speak more plainly, physiological demands, for the maintenance of a definite mode of life. For example, that the certain is worth more than the uncertain, that illusion is less valuable than "truth": such valuations, in spite of their regulative importance for *us*, might notwithstanding be only superficial valuations, special kinds of *niaiserie*, such as may be necessary for the maintenance of beings such as ourselves. Supposing, in effect, that man is not just the "measure of things.". . .

The falseness of an opinion is not for us any objection to it: it is here, perhaps, that our new language sounds most strangely. The question is, how far an opinion is life-furthering, life-preserving, species preserving, perhaps species-rearing; and we are fundamentally inclined to maintain that the falsest opinions (to which the synthetic judgments a priori belong), are the most indispensable to us; that without a recognition of logical fictions, without a comparison of reality with the purely *imagined* world of the absolute and immutable, without a constant counterfeiting of the world by means of numbers, man could not live—that the renunciation of false opinions would be a renunciation of life, a negation of life. *To recognize untruth as a condition of life*; that is certainly to impugn the traditional ideas of value in a dangerous manner, and a philosophy which ventures to do so, has thereby alone placed itself beyond good and evil.

That which causes philosophers to be regarded half-distrustfully and half-mockingly, is not the oft-repeated discovery how innocent they are—how often and easily they make mistakes and lose their way in short, how childish and childlike they are—but that there is not enough honest dealing with them, whereas they all raise a loud and virtuous out-cry when the problem of truthfulness is even hinted at in the remotest manner. They all pose as though their real opinions had been discovered and attained through the self-evolving of a cold, pure divinely indifferent dialectic (in contrast to all sorts of mystics who fairer and foolisher, talk of "inspiration"), whereas, in fact, a prejudiced proposition idea, or "suggestion" which is generally their heart's desire abstracted and refined is defended by them with argu-ments sought out after the event. They are all advo-cates who do not wish to be regarded as such, generally astute defenders, also, of their prejudices, which they dub "truths"—and *very* far from having the conscience which bravely admits this to itself; very far from having the good taste of the courage which goes so far as to let this be understood, perhaps to warn friend or foe, or in cheerful confidence and self-ridicule. The spectacle of the Tartuffery of old Kant, equally stiff and decent, with which he entices us into the dialectic byways that lead (more correctly mislead) to his "categorical imperative"—makes us fastidious ones smile, we who find no small amuse-ment in spying out the subtle tricks of old moralists and ethical preachers. Or, still more so, the hocus-pocus in mathematical form, by means of which Spin-oza has as it were clad his philosophy in mail and mask—in fact, the "love of *his* wisdom," to translate the term fairly and squarely—in order thereby to strike terror at once into the heart of the assailant who should dare to cast a glance on that invincible maiden, that Pallas Athene—how much of personal timidity and vulnerability does this masquerade of a sickly recluse betray!

It has gradually become clear to me what every great philosophy up till now has consisted of—namely, the confession of its originator, and a species of involuntary and unconscious auto-biography; and moreover that the moral (or immoral) purpose in every philosophy has constituted the true vital germ out of which the entire plant has always grown. Indeed, to understand how the abstrusest metaphysi-cal assertions of a philosopher have been arrived at, it is always well (and wise) to first ask oneself, "What morality do they (or does he) aim at?" Accordingly, I do not believe that an "impulse to knowledge" is the father of philosophy, but that another impulse, here as elsewhere, has only made use of knowledge (and

mistaken knowledge!) as an instrument. But whoever considers the fundamental impulses of man with a view to determining how far they may have here acted as *inspiring* genii (or as demons and kobolds), will find that they have all practised philosophy at one time or another, and that each one of them would have been only too glad to look upon itself as the ultimate end of existence and the legitimate *lord* over all the other impulses. For every impulse is impe-rious, and as *such*, attempts to philosophize. To be sure, in the case of scholars, in the case of really scien-tific men, it may be otherwise— "better," if you will; there may really be such a thing as an "impulse to knowledge," some kind of small, independent clock-work, which, when well wound up, works away indus-triously to that end, *without* the rest of the scholarly impulses taking any material part therein. The actual "interests" of the scholar, therefore, are generally in quite another direction—in the family, perhaps, or in money-making, or in politics, it is, in fact, almost indifferent at what point of research his little machine is placed, and whether the hopeful young worker becomes a good philologist, a mushroom specialist, or a chemist; he is not *characterized* by becoming this or that. In the philosopher, on the contrary, there is absolutely nothing impersonal; and above all, his morality furnishes a decided and decisive testimony as to *who he is*—that is to say, in what order the deepest impulses of his nature stand to each other.

You desire to *live* "according to Nature"? Oh, you noble Stoics, what fraud of words! Imagine to your-selves a being like Nature, boundlessly extravagant, boundlessly indifferent, without purpose or considera-tion, without pity or justice, at once fruitful and bar-ren and uncertain, imagine to yourselves *indifference* as a power—how *could* you live in accordance with such indifference? To live—is not that just endeavor-ing to be otherwise than this Nature? Is not living valuing, preferring, being unjust, being limited, endeavoring to be different? And granted that your imperative, "living according to Nature," means actu-ally the same as "living according to life"—how could you do *differently*? Why should you make a principle out of what you yourselves are, and must be? In real-ity, however, it is quite otherwise with you: while you pretend to read with rapture the canon of your law in Nature, you want something quite the contrary, you extraordinary stage-players and self-deluders! In your pride you wish to dictate your morals and ideals to Nature, to Nature herself, and to incorporate them therein; you insist that it shall be Nature "according to the Stoa," and would like everything to be made after your own image, as a vast, eternal glorification and generalisation of Stoicism! With all your love for truth, you have forced yourselves so long, so persistently, and with such hypnotic rigidity to see Nature *falsely*, that is to say, Stoically, that you are no longer able to see it otherwise—and to crown all, some unfathomable superciliousness gives you the bedlamite hope that *because* you are able to tyrannize over yourselves—Stoicism is self-tyranny—Nature will also allow herself to be tyrannized over: is not the Stoic a *part* of Nature? . . . But this is an old and everlasting story: what happened in old times with the Stoics still happens today, as soon as ever a philosophy begins to believe in itself. It always creates the world in its own image; it cannot do otherwise; philosophy is this tyrannical impulse itself, the most spiritual Will to Power, the will to "creation of the world," the will to the *causa prima*.

The eagerness and subtlety, I should even say craftiness, with which the problem of "the real and the apparent world" is dealt with at present throughout Europe, furnishes food for thought and attention, and he who hears only a "Will to Truth" in the background, and nothing else, cannot certainly boast of the sharpest ears. In rare and isolated cases, it may really have happened that such a Will to Truth—a certain extravagant and adventurous pluck, a metaphysician's ambition of the forlorn hope—has participated therein: that which in the end always prefers a handful of "certainty" to a whole cartload of beautiful possibilities; there may even be puritanical fanatics of conscience, who prefer to put their last trust in a sure nothing, rather than in an uncertain something. But that is Nihilism, and the sign of a despairing, mortally wearied soul, notwithstanding the courageous bearing such a virtue may display. It seems, however, to be otherwise with stronger and livelier thinkers who are still eager for life. In that they side *against* appearance, and speak superciliously of "perspective," in that they rank the credibility of their own bodies about as low as the credibility of the ocular evidence that "the earth stands still," and thus, apparently, allowing with complacency their securest possession to escape (for what does one at present believe in more firmly than

in one's body?)—who knows if they are not really trying to win back something which was formerly an even *securer* possession, something of the old domain of the faith of former times, perhaps the "immortal soul," perhaps "the old God," in short, ideas by which they could live better—that is to say, more vigorously and more joyously—than by "modern ideas"? There is *distrust* of these modern ideas in this mode of looking at things, a disbelief in all that has been constructed yesterday and today; there is perhaps some slight admixture of satiety and scorn, which can no longer endure the bric-a-brac of ideas of the most varied origin, such as so-called Positivism at present throws on the market; a disgust of the more refined taste at the village fair motleyness and patchiness of all these reality-philosophasters, in whom there is nothing either new or true, except this motleyness. Therein it seems to me that we should agree with those skeptical anti-realists and knowledge microscopists of the present day, their instinct, which repels them from *modern* reality, is unrefuted . . . what do their retrograde bypaths concern us! The main thing about them is *not* that they wish to go back, but that they wish to get *away* therefrom. A little *more* strength, swing, courage, and artistic power, and they would be *off*—and not back!

It seems to me that there is everywhere an attempt at present to divert attention from the actual influence which Kant exercised on German philosophy, and especially to ignore prudently the value which he set upon himself. Kant was first and foremost proud of his Table of Categories; with it in his hand he said "This is the most difficult thing that could ever be undertaken on behalf of metaphysics." Let us only understand this "could be"! He was proud of having *discovered* a new faculty in man, the faculty of synthetic judgment a priori. Granting that he deceived himself in this matter; the development and rapid flourishing of German philosophy depended nevertheless on his pride, and on the eager rivalry of the younger generation to discover if possible something—at all events "new faculties"—of which to be still prouder! But let us reflect for a moment—it is high time to do so. "How are synthetic judgments a priori *possible?*" Kant asks himself—and what is really his answer? "By *means of a means* (faculty)," but unfortunately not in five words, but so circumstantially, imposingly, and with such display of German profundity and verbal flourishes, that one altogether loses sight of the comical *niaiserie alle-mande* involved in such an answer. People were beside themselves with delight over this new faculty, and the jubilation reached its climax when Kant further discovered a moral faculty in man—for at that time Germans were still moral, not yet dabbling in the "Politics of hard fact." Then came the honeymoon of German philosophy. All the young theologians of the Tübingen institution went immediately into the groves—all seeking for "faculties." And what did they not find in that innocent, rich, and still youthful period of the German spirit, to which Romanticism, the malicious fairy, piped and sang, when one could not yet distinguish between "finding" and "invent-ing"! Above all a faculty for the "transcendental"; Schelling christened it, intellectual intuition, and thereby gratified the most earnest longings of the nat-urally piety-inclined Germans. One can do no greater wrong to the whole of this exuberant and eccentric movement (which was really youthfulness, notwith-standing that it disguised itself so boldly in hoary and senile conceptions), than to take it seriously, or even treat it with moral indignation. Enough, however—the world grew older, and the dream vanished. A time came when people rubbed their foreheads, and they still rub them today. People had been dreaming, and first and foremost—old Kant. "By means of a means (faculty)," he had said, or at least meant to say. But is that an answer? An explanation? Or is it not rather merely a repetition of the question? How does opium induce sleep? "By means of a means (fac-ulty)," namely the *virtus dormitiva*, replies the doctor in Molière,

> *Quia est in eo virtus dormitiva,*
> *Cujus est natura sensus assoupire.*

But such replies belong to the realm of comedy, and it is high time to replace the Kantian question, "How are synthetic judgments *a priori* possible?" by another question. "Why is belief in such judgments *necessary*?" In effect it is high time that we should understand that such judgments must be *believed* to be true, for the sake of the preservation of creatures like ourselves; though they still might naturally be *false* judgments! Or, more plainly spoken, and roughly and readily—synthetic judgments *a priori* should not "be possible" at all we have no right to them; in our mouths they are nothing but false judgments. Only, of course, the belief in their truth is necessary as plausi-ble belief and ocular evidence belonging to the per-spective view of life. And finally, to call to mind the enormous influence which "German philosophy"—I hope you understand its right to inverted commas (goosefeet)—has exercised throughout the whole of Europe, there is no doubt that a certain *virtus dormi-tiva* had a share in it; thanks to German philosophy, it was a delight to the noble idlers the virtuous, the mystics, the artists, the three-fourths Christians, and the political obscurantists of all nations, to find an antidote to the still overwhelming sensualism which overflowed from the last century into this, in short—*"sensus assoupire."*

As regards materialistic atomism, it is one of the best refuted theories that have been advanced, and in Europe there is now perhaps no one in the learned world so unscholarly as to attach serious signification to it, except for convenient everyday use (as an abbreviation of the means of expression) thanks chiefly to the Creation Boscovich: he and the Pole Copernicus have hitherto been the greatest and most successful opponents of ocular evidence. For while Copernicus has persuaded us to believe, contrary to all the senses, that the earth does *not* stand fast, Boscovich has taught us to abjure the belief in the last thing that "stood fast" of the earth—the belief in "substance," in "matter," in the earth-residuum, and particle-atom. It is the greatest triumph over the senses that has hitherto been gained on earth. One must, however, go still further, and also declare war, relentless war to the knife, against the "atomistic requirements" which still lead a dangerous afterlife in places where no one suspects them, like the more cel-ebrated "metaphysical requirements". One must also above all give the finishing stroke to that other and more portentous atomism which Christianity has taught best and longest, the *soul atomism*. Let it be permitted to designate by this expression the belief which regards the soul as something indestructible, eternal, indivisible, as a monad, as an *atomon: this* belief ought to be expelled from science! Between ourselves, it is not at all necessary to get rid of "the soul" thereby, and thus renounce one of the oldest and most venerated hypotheses—as happens fre-quently to the clumsiness of naturalists, who can hardly touch on the soul without immediately losing it. But the way is open for new acceptations and refinements of the soul hypothesis; and such conceptions as "mortal soul," and "soul as subjective multiplicity," and "soul as social structure of the instinct and passions," want henceforth to have legitimate rights in science. In that the *new* psychologist is about to put an end to the superstitions which have hitherto flourished with almost tropical luxuriance around the idea of the soul, he is really, as it were, thrusting himself into a new desert and a new distrust. It is possible that the older psychologists had a merrier and more comfortable time of it; eventually, however, he finds that precisely thereby he is also condemned to *invent*—and, who knows, perhaps to *discover* the new.

Psychologists should bethink themselves before putting down the instinct of self-preservation as the cardinal instinct of an organic being. A living thing seeks above all to *discharge* its strength—life itself is *Will to Power*; self-preservation is only one of the indirect and most frequent *results* thereof. In short, here, as everywhere else, let us beware of *superfluous* teleological principles—one of which is the instinct of self-preservation (we owe it to Spinoza's inconsistency). It is thus, in effect, that method ordains, which must be essentially economy of principles.

It is perhaps just dawning on five or six minds that natural philosophy is only a world exposition and world arrangement (according to us, if I may say so!) and *not* a world explanation; but in so far as it is based on belief in the senses, it is regarded as more, and for a long time to come must be regarded as more—namely, as an explanation. It has eyes and fingers of its own, it has ocular evidence and palpableness of its own: this operates fascinatingly, persuasively, and *convincingly* upon an age with fundamentally plebeian tastes—in fact, it follows instinctively the canon of truth of eternal popular sensualism. What is clear, what is, "explained"? Only that which can be seen and felt—one must pursue every problem thus far. Obversely, however, the charm of the Platonic mode of thought, which was an *aristocratic* mode, consisted precisely in *resistance to* obvious sense-evidence—perhaps among men who enjoyed even stronger and more fastidious senses than our contemporaries, but who knew how to find a higher triumph in remaining masters of them, and this by means of pale, cold, grey conceptional networks which they threw over the motley whirl of the senses—the mob of the senses, as Plato said. In this overcoming of the world, and interpreting of the world in the manner of Plato, there was an *enjoyment* different from that which the physicists of today offer us, and likewise the Darwinists and antiteleologists among the physiological workers, with their principles of the "smallest possible effort," and the greatest possible blunder. "Where there is nothing more to see or to grasp, there is also nothing more for men to do" is certainly an imperative different from the Platonic one, but it may notwithstanding be the right imperative for a hardy, laborious race of machinists and bridge-builders of the future, who have nothing but *rough* work to perform.

To study physiology with a clear conscience, one must insist on the fact that the sense-organs are *not* phenomena in the sense of the idealistic philosophy; as such they certainly could not be causes! Sensualism, therefore, at least as regulative hypothesis, if not as heuristic principle. What? And others say even that the external world is the work of our organs? But then our body, as a part of this external world, would be the work of our organs? But then our body, as a part of this external world, would be the work of our organs! But then our organs themselves would be the work of our organs! It seems to me that this is a complete *reduction ad absurdum,* if the conception *causa sui* is something fundamentally absurd. Consequently, the external world is *not* the work of our organs?

There are still harmless self-observers who believe that there are "immediate certainties"; for instance, "I think," or as the superstition of Schopenhauer puts it, "I will"; as though cognition here got hold of its object purely and simply as "the thing-in-itself," without any falsification taking place either on the part of the subject or the object. I would repeat it, however, a hundred times, that "immediate certainty," as well as "absolute knowledge" and the "thing-in-itself," involve a *contradictio in adjecto;* we really ought to free ourselves from the misleading significance of words! The people on their part may think that cognition is knowing all about things, but the philosopher must say to himself "When I analyze the process that is expressed in the sentence, 'I think,' I find a whole series of daring assertions, the argumentative proof of which would be difficult, perhaps impossible: for instance, that it is *I* who think, that there must necessarily be something that thinks, that thinking is an activity and operation on the part of a being who is thought of as a cause, that there is an 'ego,' and finally, that it is already determined what is to be designated by thinking—that I *know* what thinking is. For if I had not already decided within myself what it is, by what standard could I determine whether that which is just happening is not perhaps 'willing' or 'feeling'? In short, the assertion. 'I think,' assumes that I *compare* my state at the present moment with other states of myself which I know, in order to determine what it is; on account of this retrospective connection with further 'knowledge,' it has at any rate no immediate certainty for me."—In place of the "immediate certainty" in which the people may believe in the special case, the philosopher thus finds a series of metaphysical questions presented to him, veritable conscience questions of the intellect, to wit, "From whence did I get the notion of 'thinking'? Why do I believe in cause and effect? What gives me the right to speak of an 'ego,' and even of an 'ego' as cause, and finally of an 'ego' as cause of thought?" He who ventures to answer these metaphysical questions at once by an appeal to a sort of *intuitive* perception, like the person who says, "I think, and know that this, at least, is true, actual, and certain" will encounter a smile and two notes of interrogation in a philosopher nowadays. "Sir," the philosopher will perhaps give him to understand "it is improbable that you are not mistaken, but why should it be the truth?"

With regard to the superstitions of logicians, I shall never tire of emphasising a small, terse fact which is unwillingly recognized by these credulous minds—namely that a thought comes when "it" wishes and not when "I" wish, so that it is a *perversion* of the facts, of the case to say that the subject "I" is the condition of the predicate "think". *One*, thinks; but that this "one" is precisely the famous old "ego" is, to put it mildly, only a supposition, an assertion, and assuredly not an "immediate certainty." After all, one has even gone too far with this "one thinks"—even the "one" contains an *interpretation* of the process, and does not belong to the process itself. One infers here according to the usual grammatical formula, "To think is an activity; every activity requires an agency that is active; consequently". . . . It was pretty much on the same lines that the older atomism sought,

besides the operating "power," the material particle wherein it resides and our of which it operates—the atom. More rigorous minds, however, learned at last to get along without this "earth residuum," and perhaps some day we shall accustom ourselves, even from the logician's point of view, to get along without the little "one" (to which the worthy old "ego" has refined itself).

It is certainly not the least charm of a theory that it is refutable, it is precisely thereby that it attracts the more subtle minds. It seems that the hundred-times-refuted theory of the "free will" owes its persistence to this charm alone; some one is always appearing who feels himself strong enough to refute it.

Philosophers are accustomed to speak of the will as though it were the best-known thing in the world; indeed, Schopenhauer has given us to understand that the will alone is really known to us, absolutely and completely known, without deduction or addition. But it again and again seems to me that in this case Schopenhauer also only did what philosophers are in the habit of doing—he seems to have adopted a *popular prejudice* and exaggerated it. Willing seems to me to be above all something *complicated*, something that is a unity only in name, and it is precisely in a name that popular prejudice lurks, which has got the mastery over the inadequate precautions of philosophers in all ages. So let us for once be more cautious, let us be "unphilosophical": let us say that in all willing there is firstly a plurality of sensations, namely, the sensation of the condition *"away from which we go,"* the sensation of the condition *"towards which we go,"* the sensation of this *"from"* and *"towards"* itself, and then besides, an accompanying muscular sensation, which, even without our putting in motion "arms and legs," commences its action by force of habit, directly we "will" anything. Therefore, just as sensations (and indeed many kinds of sensations) are to be recognized as ingredients of the will, so, in the second place, thinking is also to be recognized as ingredients of the will, so, in the second place, thinking is also to be recognized; in every act of the will there is a ruling thought—and let us not imagine it possible to sever this thought from the "willing," as if the will would then remain over! In the third place, the will is not only a complex of sensation and thinking, but it is above all an *emotion*, and in fact the emotion of the command. That which is termed "freedom of the will" is essentially the emotion of supremacy in respect to him who must obey: "I am free, 'he' must obey." This consciousness is inherent in every will; and equally so the straining of the attention, the straight look which fixes itself exclusively on one thing, the unconditional judgment that "this and nothing else is necessary now," the inward certainty that obedience will be rendered—and whatever else pertains to the position of the commander. A man who *wills* commands something within himself which renders obedience, or which he believes renders obedience. But now let us notice what is the strangest thing about the will, this affair so extremely complex, for which the people have only one name. Inasmuch as in the given circumstances we are at the same time the commanding *and* the obeying parties, and as the obeying party we know the sensations of constraint, impulsion, pressure, resistance, and motion, which usually commence immediately after the act of will; inasmuch as, on the other hand, we are accustomed to disregard this duality, and to deceive ourselves about it by means of the synthetic term "I" a whole series of erroneous conclusions, and consequently of false judgments about the will itself, has become attached to the act of willing to such a degree that he who wills believes firmly that willing *suffices* for action. Since in the majority of cases there has only been exercise of will when the effect of the command—consequently obedience, and therefore action—was to be *expected,* the *appearance* has translated itself into the sentiment, as if there were there a *necessity of effect;* in a word, he who wills believes with a fair amount of certainty that will and action are somehow one; he ascribes the success, the carrying out of the willing, to the will itself, and thereby enjoys an increase of the sensation of power which accompanies all success. "Freedom of Will," that is, the expression for the complex state of delight of the person exercising volition, who commands and at the same time identifies himself with the executor of the order who, as such, enjoys also the triumph over obstacles, but thinks within himself that it was really his own will that overcame them. In this way the person exercising volition adds the feelings of delight of his successful executive instruments, the useful "underwills" or under-souls—indeed, our body is but a social structure composed of many souls—to his feelings of delight as commander. *L'effet c'est moi:*

what happens here is what happens in every well-constructed and happy commonwealth, namely, that the governing class identifies itself with the successes of the commonwealth. In all willing it is absolutely a question of commanding and obeying, on the basis, as already said, of a social structure composed of many "souls" on which account a philosopher should claim the right to include willing-as-such within the sphere of morals regarded as the doctrine of the relations of supremacy under which the phenomenon of "life" manifests itself.

That the separate philosophical ideas are not anything optional or autonomously evolving, but grow up in connection and relationship with each other; that, however suddenly and arbitrarily they seem to appear in the history of thought, they nevertheless belong just as much to a system as the collective members of the fauna of a Continent—is betrayed in the end by the circumstance: how unfailingly the most diverse philosophers always fill in again a definite fundamental scheme of *possible* philosophies. Under an invisible spell, they always revolve once more in the same orbit; however independent of each other they may feel themselves with their critical or systematic wills, something within them leads them, something impels them in definite order the one after the other—to wit, the innate methodology and relationship of their ideas. Their thinking is in fact far less a discovery than a re-recognizing, a remembering, a return and a homecoming to a far-off, ancient common household of the soul, out of which those ideas formerly grew: philosophizing is so far a kind of atavism of the highest order. The wonderful family resemblance of all Indian, Greek, and German philosophizing is easily enough explained. In fact, where there is affinity of language, owing to the common philosophy of grammar—I mean owing to the unconscious domination and guidance of similar grammatical functions—it cannot but be that everything is prepared at the outset for a similar development and succession of philosophical system; just as the way seems barred against certain other possibilities of world-interpretation. It is highly probable that philosophers within the domain of the Ural-Altaic languages (where the conception of the subject is least developed) look otherwise "into the world," and will be found on paths of thought different from those of the Indo-Germans and Muslims, the spell of certain grammatical functions is ultimately also the spell of *physiological* valuations and racial conditions—so much by way of rejecting Locke's superficiality with regard to the origin of ideas.

The *causa sui* is the best self-contradiction that has yet been conceived it is a sort of logical violation and unnaturalness, but the extravagant pride of man has managed to entangle itself profoundly and frightfully with this very folly. The desire for "freedom of will" in the superlative, metaphysical sense, such as still holds sway, unfortunately, in the minds of the half-educated, the desire to bear the entire and ultimate responsibility for one's actions oneself, and to absolve God, the world, ancestors, chance, and society therefrom, involves nothing less than to be precisely this *causa sui*, and with more than Munchausen daring, to pull oneself up into existence by the hair, out of the slough of nothingness. If any one should find out in this manner the crass stupidity of the celebrated conception of "free will" and put it out of his head altogether, I beg of him to carry his "enlightenment" a step further, and also put out of his head the contrary of this monstrous conception of "free will": I mean "non-free will," which is tantamount to a misuse of cause and effect. One should not wrongly *materialize* "cause" and "effect," as the natural philosophers do (and whoever like them naturalise in thinking at present), according to the prevailing mechanical doltishness which makes the cause press and push until it "effects" its end; one should use "cause" and "effect" only as pure *conceptions*, that is to say, as conventional fictions for the purpose of designation and mutual understanding, *not* for explanation. In "being-in-itself" there is nothing of "causal-connection," of "necessity," or of "psychological non-freedom;" there the effect does *not* follow the cause, there "law" does not obtain. It is *we* alone who have devised cause, sequence, reciprocity, relativity, constraint, number, law, freedom, motive, and purpose; and when we interpret and intermix this symbol world, as "being in itself," with things, we act once more as we have always acted—*mythologically*. The "non-free will" is mythology; in real life it is only a question of *strong* and *weak* wills. It is almost always a symptom of what is lacking in himself, when a thinker, in every "causal-connection" and "psychological necessity," manifests something of compulsion, indigence, obsequiousness, oppression, and non-freedom; it is suspicious to have such feelings—the person betrays himself. And in general, if I have observed correctly, the "non-freedom of the will" is regarded as a problem from two entirely opposite standpoints, but always in a profoundly *personal* manner; some will not give up their "responsibility," their belief in *themselves*, the personal right to *their* merits, at any price (the vain races belong to this class); others on the contrary, do not wish to be answerable for anything, or blamed for anything, and owing to an inward self-contempt, seek *to get out of the business*, no matter how. The latter, when they write books, are in the habit at present of taking the side of criminals; a sort of socialistic sympathy is their favorite disguise. And as a matter of fact, the fatalism of the weak-willed embellishes itself surprisingly when it can pose as "*La religion de la souf-france humaine*"; that is its "good taste."

Let me be pardoned, as an old philologist who cannot desist from the mischief of putting his finger on bad modes of interpretation, but "Nature's conformity to law," of which you physicists talk so proudly, as though—why, it exists only owing to your interpretation and bad "philology." It is no matter of fact, no "text," but rather just a naively humanitarian adjustment and perversion of meaning, with which you make abundant concessions to the democratic instincts of the modern soul! "Everywhere equality before the law—Nature is not different in that respect, nor better than we" a fine instance of secret motive, in which the vulgar antagonism to everything privileged and autocratic—likewise a second and more refined atheism—is once more disguised. "*Ni dieu, ni maitre*," that, also, is what you want, and therefore "Cheers for natural law!" Is it not so? But, as has, been said, that is interpretation, not text, and somebody might come along, who, with opposite intentions and modes of interpretation, could read out of the same "Nature," and with regard to the same phenomena, just the tyrannically inconsiderate and relentless enforcement of the claims of power—an interpreter who should so place the unexceptionalness and unconditionalness of all "Will to Power" before your eyes, that almost every word, and the word "tyranny" itself, would eventually seem unsuitable, or like a weakening and softening, metaphor—as being too human; and who should, nevertheless, end by asserting the same about this world as you do namely that it has a "necessary" and "calculable" course, *not*, however, because laws obtain in it but because they are absolutely *lacking,* and every power effects its ultimate consequences every moment. Granted that this also is only interpretation—and you will be eager enough to make this objection? Well, so much the better.

All psychology hitherto has run aground on moral prejudices and timidities, it has not dared to launch out into the depths. In so far as it is allowable to recognise in that which has hitherto been written, evidence of that which has hitherto been kept silent, it seems as if nobody had yet harbored the notion of psychology as the Morphology and *Development-doctrine of the Will to Power,* as I conceive of it. The power of moral prejudices has penetrated deeply into the most intellectual world, the world apparently most indifferent and unprejudiced, and has obviously operated in an injurious, obstructive, blinding, and distorting manner. A proper physio-psychology has to contend with unconscious antagonism in the heart of the investigator, it has "the heart" against it: even a doctrine of the reciprocal conditionalness of the "good" and the "bad" impulses, causes (as refined immorality) distress and aversion in a still strong and manly conscience—still more so, a doctrine of the derivation of all good impulses from bad ones: If, however, a person should regard even the emotions of hatred, envy, covetousness, and imperiousness as life-conditioning emotions, as factors which must be present, fundamentally and essentially, in the general economy of life (which must, therefore, be further developed if life is to be further developed), he will suffer from such a view of things as from seasickness. And yet this hypothesis is far from being the strangest and most painful in this immense and almost new domain of dangerous knowledge; and there are in fact a hundred good reasons why every one should keep away from it who *can* do so! On the other hand, if one has once drifted hither with one's bark, well! Very good! Now let us set our teeth firmly! Let us open our eyes and keep our hand fast on the helm! We sail away right *over* morality, we crush out, we destroy perhaps the remains of our own morality by daring to make our voyage thither—but what do *we* matter! Never yet did a *profounder* world of insight reveal itself to daring travellers and adventurers, and the psychologist who thus "makes a sacrifice"—it is *not* the *sacrifizio dell' intelletto,* on the contrary—will at least be entitled to demand in return that psychol-

ogy shall once more be recognized as the queen of the sciences, for whose service and equipment the other sciences exist. For psychology is once more the path to the fundamental problems.

THE FREE SPIRIT

It is the business of the very few to be independent; it is a privilege of the strong. And whoever attempts it, even with the best right, but without being *obliged* to do so; proves that he is probably not only strong, but also daring beyond measure. He enters into a labyrinth, he multiplies a thousandfold the dangers which life in itself already brings with it; not the least of which is that no one can see how and where he loses his way, becomes isolated, and is torn piecemeal by some minotaur of conscience. Supposing such a one comes to grief, it is so far from the comprehension of men that they neither feel it, nor sympathize with it. And he cannot any longer go back! He cannot even go back again to the sympathy of men!

Our deepest insights must—and should—appear as follies; and under certain circumstances as crimes, when they come unauthorisedly to the ears of those who are not disposed and predestined for them. The exoteric and the esoteric, as they were formerly distinguished by philosophers—among the Indians, as among the Greeks, Persians, and Muslims, in short, wherever people believed in gradations of rank and *not* in equality and equal rights—are not so much in contradistinction to one another in respect to the exoteric class, standing without, and viewing, estimating, measuring, and judging from the outside, and not from the inside; the more essential distinction is that the class in question views things from below upwards—while the esoteric class views things *from above downwards.* There are heights of the soul from which tragedy itself no longer appears to operate tragically; and if all the woe in the world were taken together, who would dare to decide whether the sight of it would *necessarily* seduce and constrain to sympathy, and thus to a doubling of the woe? . . . That which serves the higher class of men for nourishment or refreshment, must be almost poison to an entirely different and lower order of human beings. The virtues of the common man would perhaps mean vice and weaknesses in a philosopher; it might be possible for a highly developed man, supposing him to degenerate and go to ruin, to acquire qualities thereby alone, for the sake of which he would have to be honoured as a saint in the lower world into which he had sunk. There are books which have an inverse value for the soul and the health according as the inferior soul and the lower vitality, or the higher and more powerful, makes use of them. In the former case they are dangerous, disturbing, unsettling books, in the latter case they are herald-calls which summon the bravest to *their* bravery. Books for the general reader are always ill-smelling books, the odor of paltry people clings to them. Where the populace eat and drink, and even where they reverence, it is accustomed to stink. One should not go into churches if one wishes to breathe *pure* air. . . .

It cannot be helped: the sentiment of surrender, of sacrifice for one's neighbor, and all self-renunciation-morality, must be mercilessly called to account, and brought to judgment; just as the aesthetics of "disinterested contemplation," under which the emasculation of art nowadays seeks insidiously enough to create itself a good conscience. There is far too much witchery and sugar in the sentiments "for others" and "*not* for myself," for one not needing to be doubly distrustful here, and for one asking promptly: "Are they not perhaps *deceptions?*" That they *please* him who has them, and him who enjoys their fruit, and also the mere spectator—that is still no argument in their *favor*, but just calls for caution. Let us therefore be cautious!

At whatever standpoint of philosophy one may place oneself nowadays, seen from every position, the *erroneousness* of the world in which we think we live is the surest and most certain thing our eyes can light upon: we find proof after proof thereof, which would fain allure us into surmises concerning a deceptive principle in the "nature of things." He, however, who makes thinking itself, and consequently "the spirit," responsible for the falseness of the world—an honorable exit, which every conscious or unconscious *advocatus dei* avails himself of—he who regards this world, including space, time, form, and movement, as falsely *deduced*, would have at least good reason in the end to become distrustful also of all thinking; has it not hitherto been playing upon us the worst of scurvy tricks? And what guarantee would it give that it would not continue to do what it has always been doing? In all seriousness, the innocence of thinkers has something touching and respect-inspiring in it, which even nowadays permits them to wait upon consciousness with the request that it will give them *honest* answers: for example, whether it be "real" or not, and why it keeps the outer world so resolutely at a distance, and other questions of the same description. The belief in "immediate certainties" is a *moral naiveté* which does honor to us philosophers; but we have now to cease being "*merely* moral" men! Apart from morality, such belief is a folly which does little honor to us! If in middle-class life an ever-ready distrust is regarded as the sign of a "bad character," and consequently as an imprudence here amongst us, beyond the middle-class world and its Yeas and Nays, what should prevent us being imprudent and saying: the philosopher has at length a *right* to "bad character," as the being who has hitherto been most befooled on earth. He is now under *obligation* to distrustfulness, to the wickedest squinting out of every abyss of suspicion. Forgive me the joke of this gloomy grimace and turn of expression, for I myself have long ago learned to think and estimate differently with regard to deceiving, and being deceived, and I keep at least a couple of pokes in the ribs ready for the blind rage with which philosophers struggle against being deceived. Why *not?* It is nothing more than a moral prejudice that truth is worth more than semblance; it is, in fact, the worst proved supposition in the world. *So* much must be conceded. There could have been no life at all except upon the basis of perspective estimates and semblances; and if, with the virtuous enthusiasm and stupidity of many philosophers, one wished to do away altogether with the "seeming world"—well, granted that *you* could do that—at least nothing of your "truth" would thereby remain! Indeed, what is it that forces us in general to the supposition that there is an essential opposition of "true" and "false"? Is it not enough to suppose degrees of seemingness, and as it were lighter and darker shades and tones of semblance—different *valeurs*, as the painters say? Why might not the world *which concerns us* be a fiction? And to anyone who suggested: "But to a fiction belongs an originator," might it not be bluntly replied: *Why?* May not this "belong" also belong to the fiction? Is it not at length permitted to be a little ironical towards the subject, just as towards the predicate and object? Might not the philosopher elevate himself above faith in grammar? All respect to governesses, but is it not time that philosophy should renounce governess-faith?

O Voltaire! O humanity! O idiocy! There is something ticklish in "the truth," and in the *search* for the truth; and if man goes about it too humanely—"*il ne cherche le vrai que pour faire le bien*"—I wager he finds nothing!

Supposing that nothing else is "given" as real but our world of desires and passions, that we cannot sink or rise to any other "reality" but just that of our impulses—for thinking is only a relation of these impulses to one another—are we not permitted to make the attempt and to ask the question whether this which is "given" does not *suffice*, by means of our counterparts, for the understanding even of the so-called mechanical (or "material") world? I do not mean as an illusion, a "semblance," a "representation" (in the Berkeleyan and Schopenhauerian sense), but as possessing the same degree of reality as our emotions themselves, as a more primitive form of the world of emotions, in which everything still lies locked in a mighty unity, which afterwards branches off and develops itself in organic processes (naturally also, refines and debilitates), as a kind of instinctive life in which all organic functions, including self-regulation, assimilation, nutrition, secretion, and change of matter, are still synthetically united with one another—as a *primary form* of life? In the end, it is not only permitted to make this attempt, it is commanded by the conscience of *logical method*. Not to assume several kinds of causality, so long as the attempt to get along with a single one has not been pushed to its furthest extent (to absurdity; if I may be allowed to say so): that is a morality of method which one may not repudiate nowadays—it follows "from its definition," as mathematicians say. The question is ultimately whether we really recognise the will as *operating*, whether we believe in the causality of the will; if we do so—and fundamentally our belief *in this* is just our belief in causality itself—we *must* make the attempt to posit hypothetically the causality of the will as the only causality. "Will" can naturally only operate on "will," and not on "matter" (not on "nerves," for instance): in short, the hypothesis must be hazarded whether will does not operate on will wherever "effects" are recognised, and whether all mechanical action, inasmuch as a power operates therein, is not just the power of will, the effect of will.

Granted, finally, that we succeeded in explaining our entire instinctive life as the development and ramification of one fundamental form of will—namely, the Will to Power, as *my* thesis puts it; granted that all organic functions could be traced back to this Will to Power, and that the solution of the problem of generation and nutrition—it is one problem—could also be found therein: one would thus have acquired the right to define *all* active force unequivocally as *Will to Power*. The world seen from within, the world defined and designated according to its "intelligible character"—it would simply be "Will to Power," and nothing else.

"What? Does not that mean in popular language: God is disproved, but not the devil?" On the contrary! On the contrary, my friends! And who the devil also compels you to speak popularly! A mind might be measured by the amount of "truth" it could endure—or to speak more plainly, by the extent to which it *required* truth attenuated, veiled, sweetened, damped, and falsified. But there is no doubt that for the discovery of certain *portions* of truth the wicked and unfortunate are more favourably situated and have a greater likelihood of success; not to speak of the wicked who are happy, a species about whom moralists are silent. Perhaps severity and craft are more favorable conditions for the development of strong independent spirits and philosophers than the gentle, refined, yielding good nature, and habit of taking things easily, which are prized, and rightly prized in a learned man. Presupposing always, to begin with, that the term "philosopher" be not confined to the philosopher who writes books, or even introduces *his* philosophy into books! Stendhal furnishes a last feature of the portrait of the free-spirited philosopher, which for the sake of German taste I will not omit to underline—for it is *opposed* to German taste. "*Pour être bon philosophe*," says this last great psychologist, "*il faut être sec, clair, sans illusion. Un banquier, qui a fait fortune, a une partie du caractère requis pour faire des découvertes en philosophie, c'est-à-dire pour voir clair dans ce qui est.*"

Everything that is profound loves the mask; the profoundest things have a hatred even of figure and likeness. Should not the *contrary* only be the right disguise for the shame of a God to go about in? A question worth asking! It would be strange if some mystic has not already ventured on the same kind of thing. There are proceedings of such a delicate nature that it is well to overwhelm them with coarseness and make them unrecognisable; there are actions of love and of an extravagant magnanimity after which nothing can be wiser than to take a stick and thrash the witness soundly: one thereby obscures his recollection. Many a one is able to obscure and abuse his own memory, in order at least to have vengeance on this sole party in the secret shame is inventive. They are not the worst things of which one is most ashamed: there is not only deceit behind a mask—there is so much goodness in craft. I could imagine that a man with something costly and fragile to conceal, would roll through life clumsily and rotundly like an old, green, heavily hooped wine-cask: the refinement of his shame requiring it to be so. A man who has depths in his shame meets his destiny and his delicate decisions upon paths which few ever reach, and with regard to the existence of which his nearest and most intimate friends may be ignorant; his mortal danger conceals itself from their eyes, and equally so his regained security. Such a hidden nature, which instinctively employs speech for silence and concealment, and is inexhaustible in evasion of communication, *desires* and insists that a mask of himself shall occupy his place in the hearts and heads of his friends; and supposing he does not desire it, his eyes will some day be opened to the fact that there is nevertheless a mask of him there—and that it is well to be so. Every profound spirit needs a mask; nay, more around every profound spirit there continually grows a mask, owing to the constantly false, that is to say, *superficial* interpretation of every word he utters, every step he takes, every sign of life he manifests.

One must subject oneself to one's own tests that one is destined for independence and command, and do so at the right time. One must not avoid one's tests, although they constitute perhaps the most dangerous game one can play, and are in the end tests made only before ourselves and before no other judge. Not to cleave to any person; be it even the dearest—every person is a prison and also a recess. Not to cleave to a fatherland, be it ever the most suffering and necessitous—it is even less difficult to detach one's heart from a victorious fatherland. Not to cleave to a sympathy, be it even for higher men, into whose peculiar torture and helplessness chance has given us an insight. Not to cleave to a science, though it tempt one with the most valuable discover-

ies, apparently specially reserved for *us*. Not to cleave to one's own liberation, to the voluptuous distance and remoteness of the bird, which always flies further aloft in order always to see more under it—the danger of the flier. Not to cleave to our own virtues, nor become as a whole a victim to any of our specialities, to our "hospitality" for instance, which is the danger of dangers for highly developed and wealthy souls, who deal prodigally, almost indifferently with themselves, and push the virtue of liberality so far that it becomes a vice. One must know how *to conserve oneself*—the best test of independence.

A new order of philosophers is appearing; I shall venture to baptize them by a name not without danger. As far as I understand them, as far as they allow themselves to be understood—for it is their nature to *wish* to remain something of a puzzle—these philosophers of the future might rightly, perhaps also wrongly, claim to be designated as "*tempters*". This name itself is after all only: an attempt, or, if it be preferred, a temptation.

Will they be new friends of "truth," these coming philosophers? Very probably, for, all philosophers hitherto have loved their, truths: But assuredly they will not be dogmatists: It must be contrary to their pride, and also contrary to their taste; that their truth should still be truth for every one—that which has hitherto been the secret wish and ultimate purpose of all dogmatic efforts. "My opinion is *my* opinion: another person has not easily a right to it," such a philosopher of the future will say, perhaps. One must renounce the bad taste of wishing to agree with many people. "Good" is no longer good when one's neighbor takes it into his mouth. And how could there be a "common good"! The expression contradicts itself; that which can be common is always of small value. In the end things must be as they are and have been—the great things remain for the profound, the delicacies and thrills for the refined, and, to sum up shortly, everything rare for the rare.

Need I say expressly after all this that they will be free, *very* free spirits, these philosophers of the future—as certainly also they will not be merely free spirits, but something more, higher, greater, and fundamentally different, which does not wish to be misunderstood and mistaken? But while I say this, I feel under *obligation* almost as much to them as to ourselves (we free spirits who are their heralds and forerunners), to sweep away from ourselves altogether a stupid old prejudice and misunderstanding, which, like a fog, has too long made the conception of "free spirit" obscure. In every country of Europe, and the same in America, there is at present something which makes an abuse of this name a very narrow, prepossessed, enchained class of spirits, who desire almost the opposite of what our intentions and instincts prompt—not to mention that in respect to the *new* philosophers who are appearing, they must still more be closed windows and bolted doors. Briefly and regrettably, they belong to the *levellers*, these wrongly named "free spirits," as glib-tongued and scribe-fingered slaves of the democratic taste and its "modern ideas": all of them men without solitude, without personal solitude, blunt honest fellows to whom neither courage nor honorable conduct ought to be denied; only, they are not free, and are ludicrously superficial, especially in their innate partiality for seeing the cause of almost *all* human misery and failure in the old forms in which society has hitherto existed—a notion which happily inverts the truth entirely! What they would fain attain with all their strength, is the universal, green-meadow happiness of the herd, together with security, safety, comfort, and alleviation of life for every one; their two most frequently chanted songs and doctrines are called "Equality of Rights" and "Sympathy with all Sufferers," and suffering itself is looked upon by them as something which must be *done away with*. We opposite ones, however, who have opened our eye and conscience to the question how and where the plant "man" has hitherto grown most vigorously, believe that this has always taken place under the opposite conditions, that for this end the dangerousness of his situation had to be increased enormously, his inventive faculty and dissembling power (his "spirit") had to develop into subtlety and daring under long oppression and compulsion, and his Will to Life had to be increased to the unconditioned Will to Power. We believe that severity, violence, slavery, danger in the street and in the heart, secrecy, Stoicism, tempter's art and devilry of every kind, that everything wicked, terrible, tyrannical, predatory, and serpentine in man, serves as well for the elevation of the human species as its opposite—we do not even say enough when we only say *this much*; and in any case we find ourselves here, both with our speech and our silence, at the *other* extreme of all modern ideology and gregarious desir-

ability, as their antipodes perhaps? What wonder that we "free spirits" are not exactly the most communicative spirits? That we do not wish to betray in every respect *what* a spirit can free itself from, and *where* perhaps it will then be driven? And as to the import of the dangerous formula, "beyond good and evil," with which we at least avoid confusion, we *are* something else than "*libres-penseurs*," "*liberi pensatori*," "free-thinkers," and whatever these honest advocates of "modern ideas" like to call themselves. Having been at home, or at least guests, in many realms of the spirit; having escaped again and again from the gloomy, agreeable nooks in which preferences and prejudices, youth, origin, the accident of men and books, or even the weariness of travel seemed to confine us; full of malice against the seductions of dependency which lie concealed in honours, money, positions, or exaltation of the senses; grateful even for distress and the vicissitudes of illness, because they always free us from some rule, and its "prejudice," grateful to the God, devil, sheep, and worm in us, inquisitive to a fault, investigators to the point of cruelty, with unhesitating fingers for the intangible, with teeth and stomachs for the most indigestible, ready for any business that requires sagacity and acute senses, ready for every adventure, owing to an excess of "free will" with anterior and posterior souls, into the ultimate intentions of which it is difficult to pry, with foregrounds and backgrounds to the end of which no foot may run hidden ones under the mantles of light, appropriators, although we resemble heirs and spendthrifts, arrangers and collectors from morning till night, misers of our wealth and our full-crammed drawers, economical in learning and forgetting, inventive in scheming; sometimes proud of tables of categories, sometimes pendants, sometimes night-owls of work even in full day; yea, if necessary, even scarecrows—and it is necessary nowadays, that is to say inasmuch as we are the born, sworn, jealous friends of *solitude*, of our own profoundest midnight and midday solitude—such kind of men are we, we free spirits! And perhaps *ye* are also something of the same kind, ye coming ones? Ye *new* philosophers?

WHAT IS NOBLE?

Every elevation of the type "man," has hitherto been the work of an aristocratic society, and so will it always be, a society believing in a long scale of gradations of rank and differences of worth among human beings, and requiring slavery in some form or other. Without the *pathos of distance*, such as grows out of the incarnated difference of classes, out of the constant outlooking and downlooking of the ruling caste on subordinates and instruments, and out of their equally constant practice of obeying and commanding, of keeping down and keeping at a distance—that other more mysterious pathos could never have arisen, the longing for an ever new widening of distance within the soul itself, the formation of ever higher, rarer, further, more extended, more comprehensive states, in short, just the elevation of the type "man," the continued "self-surmounting of man," to use a moral formula in a supermoral sense. To be sure, one must not resign oneself to any humanitarian illusions about the history of the origin of an aristocratic society (that is to say, of the preliminary condition for the elevation of the type "man"): the truth is hard. Let us acknowledge unprejudicedly how every higher civilisation hitherto has *originated!* Men with a still natural nature, barbarians in every terrible sense of the word, men of prey, still in possession of unbroken strength of will and desire for power, threw themselves upon weaker, more moral, more peaceful races (perhaps trading or cattle-rearing communities), or upon old mellow civilizations in which the final vital force was flickering out in brilliant fireworks of wit and depravity. At the commencement, the noble caste was always the barbarian caste: their superiority did not consist first of all in their physical, but in their psychical power—they were more *complete* men (which at every point also implies the same as "more complete beasts").

Corruption—as the indication that anarchy threatens to break out among the instincts, and that the foundation of the emotions, called "life," is convulsed—is something radically different according to the organization in which it manifests itself. When, for instance, an aristocracy like that of France at the beginning of the Revolution, flung away its privileges with sublime disgust and sacrificed itself to an excess of its moral sentiments, it was corruption—it was really only the closing act of the corruption which had existed for centuries, by virtue of which that aristocracy had abdicated step by step its lordly prerogatives and lowered itself to a *function* of royalty (in the end even to its decoration and parade dress). The

essential thing, however, is a good and healthy aristocracy is that it should *not* regard itself as a function either of the kingship or the commonwealth, but as the *significance* and highest justification thereof—that it should therefore accept with a good conscience the sacrifice of a legion of individuals, who, *for its sake*, must be suppressed and reduced to imperfect men, to slaves and instruments. Its fundamental belief must be precisely that society is *not* allowed to exist for its own sake, but only as a foundation and scaffolding, by means of which a select class of beings may be able to elevate themselves to their higher duties, and in general to a higher *existence*: like those sun-seeking climbing plants in Java—they are called *Sipo Matador*—which encircle an oak so long and so often with their arms, until at last, high above it, but supported by it, they can unfold their tops in the open light, and exhibit their happiness.

To refrain mutually from injury, from violence, from exploitation, and put one's will on a par with that of others: this may result in a certain rough sense in good conduct among individuals when the necessary conditions are given (namely the actual similarity of the individuals in amount of force and degree of worth, and their co-relation within one organization). As soon, however, as one wished to take this principle more generally and if possible even as *the fundamental principle of society*, it would immediately disclose what it really is—namely, a Will to the *denial* of life, a principle of dissolution and decay. Here one must think profoundly to the very basis and resist all sentimental weakness: life itself is *essentially* appropriation, injury, conquest of the strange and weak, suppression, severity, obtrusion of peculiar forms, incorporation, and at the least, putting it mildest, exploitation—but why should one for ever use precisely these words on which for ages a disparaging purpose has been stamped? Even the organization within which, as was previously supposed, the individuals treat each other as equal—it takes place in every healthy aristocracy—must itself, if it be a living and not a dying organization, do all that towards other bodies, which the individuals within it refrain from doing to each other: it will have to be the incarnated Will to Power, it will endeavor to grow, to gain ground, attract to itself and acquire ascendency—not owing to any morality or immorality, but because it *lives*, and because life is precisely Will to Power. On no point, however, is the ordinary consciousness of Europeans more unwilling to be cor-rected than on this matter; people now rave every-where, even under the guise of science, about coming conditions of society in which "the exploiting charac-ter" is to be absent—that sounds to my ears as if they promised to invent a mode of life which should refrain from all organic functions. "Exploitation" does not belong to a depraved, or imperfect and primitive soci-ety: it belongs to the *nature* of the living being as a pri-mary organic function; it is a consequence of the intrinsic Will to Power, which is precisely the Will to Life. Granting that as a theory this is a novelty—as a reality it is the *fundamental fact* of all history: let us be so far honest towards ourselves!

In a tour through the many finer and coarser moralities which have hitherto prevailed or still pre-vail on the earth, I found certain traits recurring regu-larly together, and connected with one another, until finally two primary types revealed themselves to me, and a radical distinction was brought to light. There is *master morality* and *slave morality*—I would at once add, however, that in all higher and mixed civilisa-tions, there are also attempts at the reconciliation of the two moralities; but one finds still oftener the con-fusion and mutual misunderstanding of them, indeed, sometimes their close juxtaposition, even in the same man, within one soul. The distinctions of moral val-ues have either originated in a ruling caste, pleasantly conscious of being different from the ruled, or among the ruled class, the slaves and dependents of all sorts. In the first case, when it is the rulers who determine the conception "good," it is the exalted, proud dispo-sition which is regarded as the distinguishing feature, and that which determines the order of rank. The noble type of man separates from himself the beings in whom the opposite of this exalted, proud disposi-tion displays itself he despises them. Let it at once be noted that in this first kind of morality the antithesis "good" and "bad" means practically the same as "noble" and "despicable"—the antithesis "good" and "*evil*" is of a different origin. The cowardly, the timid, the insignificant, and those thinking merely of narrow utility are despised, moreover, also, the distrustful, with their constrained glances, the self-abasing, the doglike kind of men who let themselves be abused, the mendicant flatterers, and above all the liars—it is a fundamental belief of all aristocrats that the com-mon people are untruthful. "We truthful ones," the

nobility in ancient Greece called themselves. It is obvious that everywhere the designations of moral value were at first applied to *men*, and were only derivatively and at a later period applied to *actions* it is a gross mistake, therefore, when historians of morals start with questions like, "Why have sympathetic actions been praised?" The noble type of man regards *himself* as a determiner of values, he does not require to be approved of; he passes the judgment: "What is injurious to me is injurious to itself" he knows that it is he himself only who confers honor on things; he is a *creator of values*. He honors whatever he recognizes in himself such morality is self-glorification. In the foreground there is the feeling of plenitude; of power, which seeks to overflow, the happiness of high ten-sion, the consciousness of a wealth which would fain give and bestow—the noble man also helps the unfor-tunate, but not, or scarcely out of pity, but rather from an impulse generated by the superabundance of power. The noble man honors in himself the powerful one him also who has power over himself, who knows how to speak and how to keep silence, who takes pleasure in subjecting himself to severity and hard-ness, and has reverence for all that is severe and hard. "Wotan placed a hard heart in my breast," says an old Scandinavian saga: it is thus rightly expressed from the soul of a proud Viking. Such a type of man is even proud of *not* being made for sympathy; the hero of the saga therefore adds warningly: "He who has not a hard heart when young, will never have one." The noble and brave who think thus are the furthest removed from the morality which sees precisely in sympathy, or in acting for the good of others, or in *désintéressement*, the characteristic of the moral; faith in oneself, pride in oneself, a radical enmity and irony towards "selflessness," belong as definitely to noble morality, as do a careless scorn and precaution in presence of sympathy and the "warm heart." It is the powerful who *know* how to honor, it is their art, their domain for invention. The profound reverence for age and for tradition—all law rests on this double reverence—the belief and prejudice in favor of ancestors and unfavorable to newcomers, is typical in the morality of the powerful; and if, reversely, men of "modern ideas" believe almost instinctively in "progress" and the "future," and are more and more lacking in respect for old age, the ignoble origin of these "ideas" has complacently betrayed itself thereby.

A morality of the ruling class, however, is more especially foreign and irritating to present-day taste in the sternness of its principle that one has duties only to one's equals; that one may act towards beings of a lower rank, towards all that is foreign, just as seems good to one, or "as the heart desires," and in any case "beyond good and evil": it is here that sympathy and similar sentiments can have a place. The ability and obligation to exercise prolonged gratitude and prolonged revenge—both only within the circle of equals—artfulness in retaliation, *raffinement* of the idea in friendship, a certain necessity to have enemies (as outlets for the emotions of envy, quarrelsomeness, arrogance—in fact, in order to be a good *friend*): all these are typical characteristics of the noble morality, which, as has been pointed out, is not the morality of "modern ideas," and is therefore at present difficult to realize; and also to unearth and disclose, It is otherwise with the second type of morality, *slave morality*. Supposing that the abused, the oppressed, the suffering, the unemancipated, the weary, and those uncertain of themselves, should moralize, what will be the common element in their moral estimates? Probably a pessimistic suspicion with regard to the entire situation of man will find expression, perhaps a condemnation of man, together with his situation. The slave has an unfavorable eye for the virtues of the powerful; he has a skepticism and distrust, a refinement of distrust of everything "good" that is there honored—he would fain persuade himself that the very happiness there is not genuine. On the other hand, *those* qualities which serve to alleviate the existence of sufferers are brought into prominence and flooded with light; it is here that sympathy, the kind, helping hand, the warm heart, patience, diligence, humility, and friendliness attain to honor; for here these are the most useful qualities, and almost the only means of supporting the burden of existence. Slave morality is essentially the morality of utility. Here is the seat of the origin of the famous antithesis "good" and "*evil*": power and dangerousness are assumed to reside in the evil, a certain dreadfulness, subtlety, and strength, which do not admit of being despised. According to slave morality, therefore, the "evil" man arouses fear; according to master morality, it is precisely the "good" man who arouses fear and seeks to arouse it, while the bad man is regarded as the despicable being. The contrast attains its maximum when, in accordance with the logical consequences of slave morality, a shade of depreciation—it may be slight and well-intentioned—at last attaches itself even to the "good" man of this morality; because, according to the servile mode of thought, the good man must in any case be the *safe* man: he is good-natured, easily deceived perhaps a little stupid, *unbonhomme*. Everywhere that slave morality gains the ascendency, language shows a tendency to approximate the significations of the words "good" and "stupid." A last fundamental difference the desire for *freedom*, the instinct for happiness and the refinements of the feeling of liberty belong as necessarily to slave morals and morality, as artifice and enthusiasm in reverence and devotion are the regular symptoms of an aristocratic mode of thinking and estimating. Hence we can understand without further detail why love *as a passion*—it is our European speciality—must absolutely be of noble origin; as is well known, its invention is due to the Provencal poet-cavaliers those brilliant ingenious men of the "*gai saber*," to whom Europe owes so much; and almost owes itself.

Vanity is one of the things which are perhaps most difficult for a noble man to understand: he will be tempted to deny it, where another kind of man thinks he sees it self-evidently. The problem for him is to represent to his mind beings who seek to arouse a good opinion of themselves which they themselves do not possess—and consequently also do not "deserve"—and who yet *believe* in this good opinion afterwards. This seems to him on the one hand such bad taste and so self-disrespectful, and on the other hand so grotesquely unreasonable, that he would like to consider vanity an exception, and is doubtful about it in most cases when it is spoken of. He will say, for instance, "I may be mistaken about my value, and on the other hand may nevertheless demand that my value should be acknowledged by others precisely as I rate it. That, however, is not vanity (but self-conceit, or, in most cases, that which is called, 'humility,' and also 'modesty')." Or he will even say, "For many reasons I can delight in the good opinion of others, perhaps because I love and honor them, and rejoice in all their joys, perhaps also because their good opinion endorses and strengthens my belief in my own good opinion, perhaps because the good opinion of others, even in cases where I do not share it, is useful to me, or gives promise of usefulness—all this, however, is not vanity." The man of noble character must first bring it home forcibly to his mind, especially with the aid of history, that, from time immemorial, in all social strata in any way dependent, the ordinary man *was* only that which he *passed for*—not being at all accustomed to fix values, he did not assign even to himself any other value than that which his master assigned to him (it is the peculiar *right of masters* to create values). It may be looked upon as the result of an extraordinary atavism, that the ordinary man, even at present, is still always *waiting* for an opinion about himself, and then instinctively submitting himself to it; yet by no means only to a "good" opinion, but also to a bad and unjust one (think, for instance, of the greater part of the self-appreciations and self-depreciations which believing women learn from their confessors, and which in general the believing Christian learns from his Church), In fact, conformably to the slow rise of the democratic social order (and its cause, the blending of the blood of masters and slaves), the originally noble and rare impulse of the masters to assign a value to themselves and to "think well" of themselves, will now be more and more encouraged and extended; but it has at all times an older, ampler, and more radically ingrained propensity opposed to it—and in the phenomenon of "vanity" this older propensity overmasters the younger. The vain person rejoices over *every* good opinion which he hears about himself (quite apart from the point of view of its usefulness, and equally regardless of its truth or falsehood), just as he suffers from every bad opinion: for he subjects himself to both, he *feels* himself subjected to both, by that oldest instinct of subjection which breaks forth in him. It is "the slave" in the vain mans blood, the remains of the slave's craftiness—and how much of the "slave" is still left in woman, for instance!—which seeks to *seduce* to good opinions of itself; it is the slave, too, who immediately afterwards falls prostrate himself before these opinions, as though he had not called them forth. And to repeat it again: vanity is an atavism. . . .

At the risk of displeasing innocent ears, I submit that egoism belongs to the essence of a noble soul, I mean the unalterable belief that to a belief such as "we," other beings must naturally be in subjection, and have to sacrifice themselves. The noble soul accepts the fact of his egoism without question, and also without consciousness of harshness, constraint,

or arbitrariness therein, but rather as something that may have its basis in the primary law of things. If he sought a designation for it he would say, "It is justice itself." He acknowledges under certain circumstances, which made him hesitate at first, that there are other equally privileged ones; as soon as he has settled this question of rank, he moves among those equals and equally privileged ones with the same assurance, as regards modesty and delicate respect, which he enjoys in intercourse with himself, in accordance with an innate heavenly mechanism which all the stars understand. It is an *additional* instance of his egoism, this artfulness and self-limitation in intercourse with his equals—every star is a similar egoist; he honors *himself* in them, and in the rights which he concedes to them, he has no doubt that the exchange of honors and rights, as the *essence* of all intercourse, belongs also to the natural condition of things. The noble soul gives as he takes, prompted by the passionate and sensitive instinct of requital, which is at the root of his nature. The notion of "favour" has, *inter pares*, neither significance nor good repute; there may be a sublime way of letting gifts as it were light upon one from above; and of drinking them thirstily like dew-drops; but for those arts and displays the noble soul has no aptitude. His egoism hinders him here: in general, he looks "aloft" unwillingly. He looks either *forward*, horizontally and deliberately, or downwards—he *knows that he is on a height.* . . .

What is noble? What does the word "noble" still mean for us nowadays? How does the noble man betray himself, how is he recognized under this heavy overcast sky of the commencing plebeianism, by which everything is rendered opaque and leaden? It is not his actions which establish his claim—actions are always ambiguous, always inscrutable; neither is it his "works." One finds nowadays among artists and scholars plenty of those who betray by their works that a profound longing for nobleness impels them; but this very *need of* nobleness is radically different from the needs of the noble soul itself, and is in fact the eloquent and dangerous sign of the lack thereof. It is not the works, but the *belief* which is here decisive and determines the order of rank—to employ once more an old religious formula with a new and deeper meaning—it is some fundamental certainty which a noble soul has about itself, something which is not to be sought, is not to be found, and perhaps, also, is not to be lost. *The noble soul has reverence for itself.* . . .

. . . Every philosophy also *conceals* a philosophy; every opinion is also a *lurking-place*, every word is also a *mask*.

Every deep thinker is more afraid of being understood than of being misunderstood. The latter perhaps wounds his vanity; but the former wounds his heart; his sympathy, which always says: "Ah, why would *you* also have as hard a time of it as I have?"

Man, a *complex*, mendacious, artful, and inscrutable animal, uncanny to the other animals by his artifice and sagacity, rather than by his strength, has invented the good conscience in order finally to enjoy his soul as something *simple*; and the whole of morality is a long, audacious falsification, by virtue of which generally enjoyment at the sight of the soul becomes possible. From this point of view there is perhaps much more in the conception of "art" than is generally believed.

A philosopher: that is a man who constantly experiences, sees, hears, suspects, hopes, and dreams extraordinary things; who is struck by his own thoughts as if they came from the outside, from above and below, as a species of events and lightning flashes *peculiar to him*; who is perhaps himself a storm pregnant with new lightnings; a portentous man, around whom there is always rumbling and mumbling and gaping and something uncanny going on. A philosopher: alas, a being who often runs away from himself, is often afraid of himself, but whose curiosity always makes him "come to himself" again.

A man who says: "I like that, I take it for my own, and mean to guard and protect it from every one"; a man who can conduct a case, carry out a resolution, remain true to an opinion, keep hold of a woman; punish and overthrow insolence; a man who has his indignation and his sword, and to whom the weak, the suffering, the oppressed, and even the animals willingly submit and naturally belong; in short, a man who is a *master* by nature—when such a man has sympathy, well! *That* sympathy has value! But of what account is the sympathy of those who suffer! Or of those even who preach sympathy! There is nowadays, throughout almost the whole of Europe, a sickly irritability and sensitiveness towards pain, and also a repulsive irrestrainableness in complaining, an effem-

inizing, which, with the aid of religion and philosophical nonsense, seeks to deck itself out as something superior—there is a regular cult of suffering. The *unmanliness* of that which is called "sympathy" by such groups of visionaries, is always, I believe, the first thing that strikes the eye. One must resolutely and radically taboo this latest form of bad taste; and finally, I wish people to put the good amulet, *"gai saber"* ("gay science," in ordinary language), on heart and neck, as a protection against it.

The Olympian Vice. Despite the philosopher who, as a genuine Englishman, tried to bring laughter into bad repute in all thinking minds—"Laughing is a bad infirmity of human nature, which every thinking mind will strive to overcome" (Hobbes)—I would even allow myself to rank philosophers according to the quality of their laughing, up to those who are capable of *golden* laughter. And supposing that Gods also philosophize, which I am strongly inclined to believe, owing to many reasons—I have no doubt that they also know how to laugh thereby in an overman-like and new fashion—and at the expense of all serious things! Gods are fond of ridicule: it seems that they cannot refrain from laughter even in holy matters.

The genius of the heart, as that great mysterious one possesses it, the tempter god and born rat catcher of consciences, whose voice can descend into the netherworld of every soul, who neither speaks a word nor casts a glance in which there may not be some motive or touch of allurement, to whose perfection it pertains that he knows how to appear—not as he is, but in a guise which acts as an *additional* constraint on his followers to press ever closer to him; to follow him more cordially and thoroughly—the genius of the heart, which imposes silence and attention on everything loud and self-conceited, which smooths rough souls and makes them taste a new longing—to lie placid as a mirror, that the deep heavens may be reflected in them—the genius of the heart, which teaches the clumsy and too hasty hand to hesitate, and to grasp more delicately; which scents the hidden and forgotten treasure, the drop of goodness and sweet spirituality under thick dark ice, and is a divining-rod for every grain of gold, long buried and imprisoned in mud and sand; the genius of the heart, from contact with which every one goes away richer; not favored or surprised, not as though gratified and oppressed by the good things of others; but richer in himself, newer than before, broken up, blown upon, and sounded by a thawing wind; more uncertain perhaps, more delicate; more fragile, more bruised, but full of hopes which as yet lack names; full of a new will and current, full of a new ill will and counter-current . . . but what am I doing, my friends? Of whom am I talking to you? Have I forgotten myself so far that I have not even told you his name? Unless it be that you have already divined of your own accord who this questionable? God and spirit is, that wishes to be *praised* in such a manner? For, as it happens to every one who from childhood onward has always been on his legs, and in foreign lands, I have also encountered on my path many strange and dangerous spirits; above all, however, and again and again, the one of whom I have just spoken: in fact, no less a personage than the *God Dionysus*, the great equivocator and tempter, to whom, as you know, I once offered in all secrecy and reverence my first fruits—the last, as it seems to me, who has offered a *sacrifice* to him, for I have found no one who could understand what I was then doing. In the meantime, however, I have learned much, far too much, about the philosophy of this God, and, as I said, from mouth to mouth—I, the last disciple and initiate of the God Dionysus: and perhaps I might at last begin to give you, my friends, as far as I am allowed, a little taste of this philosophy? In a hushed voice, as is but seemly, for it has to do with much that is secret, new, strange, wonderful, and uncanny. The very fact that Dionysus is a philosopher, and that therefore Gods also philosophize, seems to me a novelty which is not unensnaring, and might perhaps arouse suspicion precisely amongst philosophers. Amongst you, my friends, there is less to be said against it, except that it comes too late and not at the right time; for, as it has been disclosed to me, you are loth nowadays to believe in God and gods. It may happen, too, that in the frankness of my story I must go further than is agreeable to the strict usages of your ears? Certainly the God in question went further, very much further, in such dialogues, and was always many paces ahead of me. . . . Indeed, if it were allowed, I should have to give him, according to human usage, fine ceremonious titles of luster and merit, I should have to extol his courage as investigator and discoverer, his fearless honesty, truthfulness, and love of wisdom. But such a God does not know

what to do with all that respectable trumpery and pomp. "Keep that," he would say, "for thyself and those like thee, and whoever else require it! I have no reason to cover my nakedness!" One suspects that this kind of divinity and philosopher perhaps lacks shame? He once said: "Under certain circumstances I love mankind," and referred thereby to Ariadne, who was present, "in my opinion man is an agreeable, brave, inventive animal, that has not his equal upon earth, he makes his way even through all labyrinths. I like man, and often think how I can still further advance him, and make him stronger, more evil, and more profound." "Stronger, more evil, and more profound?" I asked in horror. "Yes," he said again, "stronger, more evil, and more profound; also more beautiful" and thereby the tempter god smiled with his halcyon smile, as though he had just paid some charming compliment. One here sees at once that it is not only shame that this divinity lacks, and in general there are good grounds for supposing that in some things the Gods could all of them come to us men for instruction. We men are more human.

Alas! what are you, after all, my written and painted thoughts! Not long ago you were so variegated, young, and malicious, so full of thorns and secret spices, that you made me sneeze and laugh—and now? You have already doffed your novelty, and some of you, I fear, are ready to become truths, so immortal do they look, so pathetically honest, so tedious! And was it ever otherwise? What then do we write and paint, we mandarins with Chinese brush, we immortalizers of things which *lend* themselves to writing, what are we alone capable of painting? Alas, only that which is just about to fade and begins to lose its odor! Alas, only exhausted and departing storms and belated yellow sentiments! Alas, only birds strayed and fatigued by flight, which now let themselves be captured with the hand—with *our* hand! We immortalize what cannot live and fly much longer, things only which are exhausted and mellow! And it is only for your *afternoon*, you, my written and painted thoughts, for which alone I have colors, many colors perhaps, many variegated softenings, and fifty yellows and browns and greens and reds—but nobody will divine thereby how ye looked in your morning, you sudden sparks and marvels of my solitude, you, my old, beloved—*evil* thoughts!

STUDY QUESTIONS: NIETZSCHE, *BEYOND GOOD AND EVIL*

1. Why have philosophers, according to Nietzsche, failed to understand women? What is the significance of this?
2. What is the Will to Truth?
3. How is untruth a condition of life? What does Nietzsche mean by this? How does he make the case?
4. What does Nietzsche make of Kant's Table of Categories?
5. What is the "honeymoon of German philosophy?"
6. How does Nietzsche use Moliere to satirize Kant?
7. What is Nietzsche view of atomism? Of materialism?
8. What is meant by the *aristocratic* mode of Platonic thought?
9. What are the "superstitions" of the logicians?
10. What is Nietzsche's view of Schopenhauer?
11. How does Nietzsche regard the phrase, "I think?" What role does it play in his philosophy?
12. Is "I" according to Nietzsche a synthetic term? Why?
13. In what way is Locke's theory of the origin of ideas superficial?
14. What most distinguishes master morality from slave morality? What is the significance of this distinction for Nietzsche's overall view of morality?
15. What is vanity? Why is it so difficult for a noble person to understand?
16. Why does every philosophy, in his view, conceal a philosophy?
17. Why is every word a mask?
18. Why are deep thinkers more afraid of being understood than of being misunderstood?
19. How does Nietzsche regard the personality of the god Dionysus? What is the function of this characteristic in his philosophy?

THE WILL TO POWER

What is life-affirming Nietzsche calls *true;* what is life-denying he calls *false.* But by these words he does not mean what, for instance, a logician means. He means poetic, aesthetic truth. Like Schopenhauer and Kierkegaard, Nietzsche sees rationality itself, each and every aspect of thought, as a sublimated manifestation of the will to power. Rationality is but rationalization, ultimately a form of self-deception. If we accept this notion of truth and falsehood, then our lies, pretensions, and self-deceptions are not bad but the source of our possible greatness, making possible our willing the chaotic flux like a great work of art, within which we, the artists, create ourselves through the Will to Power.

Thus, in marked contrast to Schopenhauer's dark vision of the will as a blind and ultimately destructive force that must be transcended, Nietzsche sees the will as having an essentially Dionysian character. Its positive, life-affirming force culminates in the "Superman," an enlightened self-affirming individual.

Nietzsche, from *The Will to Power,* tramslated by A.M. Ludovici.

I regard Christianity as the most fatal and seductive lie that has ever yet existed—as the greatest and most *impious* lie. I can discern the last sprouts and branches of its ideal beneath every form of disguise, I decline to enter into any compromise or false position in reference to it. I urge people to declare open war with it.

The morality of paltry people as the measure of all things: this is the most repugnant kind of degeneracy that civilization has ever yet brought into existence. And this *kind of ideal* is hanging still, under the name of "God," over men's heads!

However modest one's demands may be concerning intellectual cleanliness, when one touches the New Testament one cannot help experiencing a sort of inexpressible feeling of discomfort; for the unbounded cheek with which the least qualified people will have their say in its pages, in regard to the greatest problems of existence, and claim to sit in judgment on such matters, exceeds all limits. The impudent levity with which the most unwieldy problems are spoken of here (life, the world, God, the purpose of life), as if they were not problems at all, but the most simple things which these little bigots *know all about!!!*

This was the most fatal form of insanity that has ever yet existed on earth—when these little lying abortions of bigotry begin laying claim to the words "God," "Last Judgment," "truth," "love," "wisdom," "Holy Spirit," and thereby distinguishing themselves from the rest of the world; when such men begin to transvalue values to suit themselves, as though they were the sense, the salt, the standard, and the measure of all things; then all that one should do is this: build lunatic asylums for their incarceration. To *persecute* them was an egregious act of antique folly: this was taking them too seriously; it was making them serious.

The whole fatality was made possible by the fact that a similar form of megalomania was already *in existence,* the *Jewish* form (once the gulf separating the Jews from the Christian-Jews was bridged, the Christian-Jews *were compelled* to employ those self-preservative measures afresh which were discovered by the Jewish instinct, for their own self-preservation, after having accentuated them); and again through the fact that Greek moral philosophy had done every-thing that could be done to prepare the way for moral-fanaticism, even among Greeks and Romans, and to render it palatable. . . . Plato, the great importer of corruption, who was the first who refused to see Nature in morality, and who had already deprived the Greek gods of all their worth by his notion "*good*," was already tainted with *Jewish bigotry* (in Egypt?). . . .

The *law* which is the fundamentally realistic formula of certain self preservative measures of a community forbids certain actions that have a definite tendency to jeopardize the welfare of that community it does *not* forbid the attitude of mind which gives rise to these actions—for in the pursuit of other ends the community requires these forbidden actions, namely, when it is a matter of opposing its *enemies.* The moral idealist now steps forward and says: "God sees into mens hearts: the action itself counts for nothing; the reprehensible attitude of mind from which it proceeds must be extirpated. . . ." In normal conditions men laugh at such things; it is only in exceptional cases, when a community lives *quite* beyond the need of waging war in order to maintain itself, that an ear is lent to such things. Any attitude of mind is abandoned, the utility of which cannot be conceived.

This was the case, for example, when Buddha appeared among a people that was both peaceable and afflicted with great intellectual weariness.

This was also the case in regard to the first Christian community (as also the Jewish), the primary condition of which was the absolutely *unpolitical* Jewish society. Christianity could grow only upon the soil of Judaism—that is to say, among a people that had already renounced the political life, and which led a sort of parasitic existence within the Roman sphere of government. Christianity goes a step *farther:* it allows men to "emasculate" themselves even more; the circumstances actually favor their doing so. *Nature* is *expelled* from morality when it is said, "Love ye your enemies," for *Nature's* injunction, "Ye shall *love* your neighbor and *hate* your enemy," has now become senseless in the law (in instinct); now, even *the love a man feels for his neighbor* must first be based upon something (*a sort of love of God*). *God* is introduced everywhere, and *utility* is withdrawn; the natural *origin* of morality is denied everywhere: the *veneration* of Nature, which lies in *acknowledging a natural morality, is destroyed* to the roots. . . .

Whence comes the *seductive charm* of this emasculate ideal of man? Why are we not *disgusted* by it, just as we are disgusted at the thought of a eunuch? . . . The answer is obvious: it is not the voice of the eunuch that revolts us, despite the cruel mutilation of which it is the result; for, as a matter of fact, it has grown sweeter. . . . And owing to the very fact that the "male organ" has been amputated from virtue, its voice now has a feminine ring, which, formerly, was not to be discerned.

On the other hand, we have only to think of the terrible hardness, dangers, and accidents to which a life of manly virtues leads—the life of a Corsican, even at the present day, or that of a heathen Arab (which resembles the Corsican's life even to the smallest detail: the Arab's songs might have been written by Corsicans)—in order to perceive how the most robust type of man was fascinated and moved by the voluptuous ring of this "goodness" and "purity." . . . A pastoral melody . . . an idyll . . . the "good man": such things have most effect in ages when tragedy is abroad.

The *Astuteness of moral castration*. How is war waged against the virile passions and valuations? No violent physical means are available; the war must therefore be one of ruses, spells, and lies—in short, a "spiritual war."

First recipe: one appropriates virtue in general, and makes it the main feature of one's ideal; the older ideal is denied and declared to be *the reverse of all ideals*. Slander has to be carried to a fine art for this purpose.

Second recipe: one's own type is set up as a general *standard*; and this is projected into all things, behind all things, and behind the destiny of all things—as God.

Third recipe: the opponents of one's ideal are declared to be the opponents of God; one arrogates to oneself a *right* to great pathos, to power, and a right to curse and to bless.

Fourth recipe: all suffering, all gruesome, terrible, and fatal things are declared to be the results of opposition to *one's* ideal—all suffering is *punishment* even in the case of one's adherents (except it be a trial, etc.).

Fifth recipe: one goes so far as to regard Nature as the reverse of one's ideal and the lengthy sojourn amid natural conditions is considered a great trial of patience—a sort of martyrdom; one studies contempt, both in one's attitudes and one's looks towards all "natural things."

Sixth recipe: the triumph of anti-naturalism and ideal castration, the triumph of the world of the pure, good, sinless, and blessed, is projected into the future as the consummation, the finale, the great hope, and the "Coming of the Kingdom of God."

I hope that one may still be allowed to laugh at this artificial hoisting up of a small species of man to the position of an absolute standard of all things?

To what extent psychologists have been corrupted by the moral idiosyncrasy! Not one of the ancient philosophers had the courage to advance the theory of the non-free will (that is to say, the theory that denies morality); not one had the courage to identify the typical feature of happiness of every kind of happiness ("pleasure"), with the will to power: for the pleasure of power was considered immoral; not one had the courage to regard virtue as a *result of immorality* (as a result of a will to power) in the service of a species (or of a race, or of a *polis*); for the will to power was considered immoral.

In the whole of moral evolution, there is no sign of truth: all the conceptual elements which come into play are fictions; all the psychological tenets are false; all the forms of logic employed in this department of prevarication are Sophisms. The chief feature of all moral philosophers is their total lack of intellectual cleanliness and self-control: they regard "fine feelings" as arguments: their heaving breasts seem to them the bellows of godliness. . . . Moral philosophy is the most suspicious period in the history of the human intellect.

The first great example in the name of morality and under its patronage, a great wrong was committed, which as a matter of fact was in every respect an act of decadence. Sufficient stress cannot be laid upon this fact, that the great Greek philosophers not only represented the decadence of *every kind of Greek ability*, but also made it *contagious*. . . . This "virtue" made wholly abstract was the highest form of seduction; to make oneself abstract means to *turn one's back on the world*.

The moment is a very remarkable one: the Sophists are within sight of the first *criticism* of morality, the first *knowledge* of morality: they classify the majority of moral valuations (in view of their dependence upon local conditions) together, they lead one to understand that every form of morality is capable of being upheld dialectically—that is to say, they guessed that all the fundamental principles of a morality must be *sophistical*—a proposition which was afterwards proved in the grandest possible style by the ancient philosophers from Plato onwards (up to Kant); they postulate the primary truth that there is no such thing as a "moral per se," a good per se, and that it is madness to talk of "truth" in this respect.

Wherever was *intellectual uprightness* to be found in those days?

The Greek culture of the Sophists had grown out of all the Greek instincts; it belongs to the culture of the age of Pericles as necessarily as Plato does not it has its predecessors in Heraclitus, Democritus, and in the scientific types of the old philosophy at finds expression in the elevated culture of Thucydides, for instance. And it has ultimately shown itself to be right every step in the science of epistemology and morality has *confirmed the attitude* of the Sophists. Our modern attitude of mind is, to a great extent. Heraclitean, Democritean and Protagorean . . . to say that it is *Protagorean* is even sufficient: because Protagoras was in himself a synthesis of the two men Heraclitus and Democritus.

(*Plato: a great Cagliostro*—let us think of how Epicurus judged him; how Timon, Pyrrho's friend, judged him. Is Plato's integrity by any chance beyond question? . . . But we at least know what he wished to have *taught* as absolute truth—namely, things which were to him not even relative truths the separate and immortal life of "souls.") . . .

Of all the interpretations of the world attempted heretofore the *mechanical* one seems today to be most prominent. Apparently it has a clean conscience on its side; for no science believes inwardly in progress and success unless it be with the help of mechanical procedures. Everyone knows these procedures: "reason" and purpose are kept out of consideration as far as possible; it is shown that, provided a sufficient amount of time be allowed to elapse, everything can evolve out of everything else, and no one attempts to suppress his malicious satisfaction, when the "apparent design in the fate" of a plant or of the yolk of an egg, may be traced to stress and thrust—in short, people are heartily glad to pay respect to this principle of profoundest stupidity, if I may be allowed to pass a playful remark concerning these serious matters. Meanwhile, among the most select intellects to be found in this movement, some presentiment of evil, some anxiety is noticeable, as if the theory had a rent in it that sooner or later might be its last: I mean the sort of rent that denotes the end of all balloons inflated with such theories.

Stress and thrust themselves cannot be "explained," one cannot get rid of the *actio in distans*. The belief even in the ability to explain is now lost, and people peevishly admit that one can only describe, not explain, that the dynamic interpretation of the world, with its denial of "empty space" and its little agglomerations of atoms, will soon get the better of physicists: although in this way *Dynamis* is certainly granted an inner quality.

The triumphant concept *energy*, with which our physicists created God and the world, needs yet to be completed: it must be given an inner will which I characterize as the "*Will to Power*"—that is to say, as an insatiable desire to manifest power; or the application and exercise of power as a creative instinct, etc. Physicists cannot get rid of the "*actio in distans*" in their principles; any more than they can a repelling force (or an attracting one). There is no help for it, all movements, all "appearances," all "laws" must be understood as *symptoms* of an *inner* phenomenon, and the analogy of man must be used for this purpose. It is possible to trace all the instincts of an animal to the will to power; as also all the functions of organic life to this one source.

Is the "Will to Power" a kind of will, or is it identical with the concept will? Is it equivalent to desiring or commanding; is it the Will that Schopenhauer says is the essence of things?

My proposition is that the will of psychologists hitherto has been an unjustifiable generalization, and there is no such thing as this sort of will, that instead of the development of one will into several forms being taken as a fact, the character of will has been cancelled owing to the fact that its content, its "whither," was subtracted from it. In Schopenhauer this is so in the highest degree; what he calls "Will" is merely an empty word. There is even less plausibility in the Will to Live, for life is simply one of the manifestations of the Will to Power; it is quite arbitrary and ridiculous to suggest that everything is striving to enter into this particular form of the Will to Power.

How is it that the fundamental article of faith in all psychologies is a piece of most outrageous contortion and fabrication? "Man strives after happiness," for instance—how much of this is true? In order to understand what life is, and what kind of striving and tenseness life contains, the formula should hold good not only of trees and plants but of animals also. "What does the plant strive after?" But here we have already invented a false entity that does not exist—concealing and denying the fact of an infinitely variegated growth, with individual and semi-individual starting points—when we give it the clumsy title "plant" as if it were a unit. It is very obvious that the ultimate and smallest "individuals" cannot be understood in the sense of metaphysical individuals or atoms; their sphere of power is continually shifting its ground: but with all these changes, can it be said that any of them strives after happiness? All this expanding, this incorporation and growth, is a search for resistance; movement is essentially related to states of pain the driving power here must represent some other desire if it leads to such continual willing and seeking of pain. To what end do the trees of a virgin forest contend with each other? "For happiness"? For power! . . .

Man is now master of the forces of nature, and master too of his own wild and unbridled feelings (the passions have followed suit, and have learned to become useful)—in comparison with primeval man, the man of today represents an enormous quantum of power, but not an increase in happiness! How can one maintain, then, that he has striven after happiness? . . .

The new concept of the universe. The universe exists; it is nothing that grows into existence and that passes out of existence. Or, better still, it develops, it passes away, but it never began to develop, and has never ceased from passing away; it *maintains* itself in both states. . . . It lives on itself, its excrements are its nourishment.

We need not concern ourselves for one instant with the hypothesis of a *created* world. The concept "create" is today utterly indefinable and unrealizable; it is but a word that hails from superstitious ages; nothing can be explained with a word. The last attempt to conceive of a world that *began* was recently made in diverse ways, with the help of logical reasoning chiefly, as you will guess, with an ulterior theological motive.

Several attempts have been made lately to show that the concept that "the universe has an infinite past" (*regressus in infinitum*) is contradictory in fact, it was even demonstrated, at the price of confounding the head with the tail. Nothing can prevent me from calculating backward from this moment of time, and of saying: "I shall never reach the end"; just as I can calculate without end in a forward direction, from the same moment. It is only when I wish to commit the error—I shall be careful to avoid it—of reconciling this correct concept of a *regressus in infinitum* with the absolutely unrealizable concept of an infinite *progressus* up to the present; only when I consider the direction (forward or backward) as logically indifferent that I take hold of the head—this very moment—and think I hold the tail: this pleasure I leave to you. . . .

I have come across this thought in other thinkers before me, and every time I found that it was determined by other ulterior motives (chiefly theological; in favor of a *creator spiritus*). If the universe were in any way able to congeal to dry up, to perish; or if it were capable of attaining to a state of equilibrium; or if it had any kind of goal at all which a long lapse of time, immutability, and finality reserved for it (in short, to speak metaphysically, if becoming could resolve itself into being or into nonentity), this state ought already to have been reached. But it has not been reached it therefore follows. . . . This is the only certainty we can grasp, which can serve as a corrective to a host of cosmic hypotheses possible in themselves. If, for instance, materialism cannot consistently escape the conclusion of a final state, . . . then materialism is thereby refuted.

If the universe may be conceived as a definite quantity of energy, as a definite number of centers of energy—and every other concept remains indefinite and therefore useless—it follows that the universe must go through a calculable number of combinations in the great game of chance that constitutes its existence. In infinity at some moment or other, every possible combination must have been realized; not only this, but it must have been realized an infinite number of times. And inasmuch as between every one of these combinations and its next recurrence every other possible combination would necessarily have been undergone, and since every one of these combinations would determine the whole series in the same order, a circular movement of absolutely identical series is thus demonstrated: the universe is shown to be a circular movement that has already repeated itself an infinite number of times, and that plays its game for all eternity. This conception is not simply materialistic; for if it were this, it would not involve an infinite recurrence of identical cases, but a final state. Owing to the fact that the universe has not reached this final state, materialism shows itself to be but an imperfect and provisional hypothesis.

And do you know what "the universe" is to my mind? Shall I show it to you in my mirror? This universe is a monster of energy, without beginning or end; a fixed and brazen quantity of energy that grows neither bigger nor smaller, does not consume itself, but only alters its face; as a whole its bulk is immutable, it is a household without either losses or gains, but likewise without increase and without sources of revenue, surrounded by nonentity as by a frontier. It is nothing vague or wasteful, it does not stretch into infinity; but is a definite quantum of energy located in limited space, and not in space that would be anywhere empty. It is rather energy everywhere, the play of forces and force-waves, at the same time one and many, agglomerating here and diminishing there, a sea of forces storming and raging in itself, forever changing, forever rolling back over incalculable ages to recurrence, with an ebb and flow of its forms, producing the most complicated things out of the most simple structures; producing the most ardent, most savage, and most contradictory things out of the quietest, most rigid, and most frozen material, and then returning from multifariousness to uniformity, from the play of contradictions back into the delight of consonance, saying Yea unto itself, even in this homogeneity of its courses and ages; forever blessing itself as something which recurs for all eternity—a becoming that knows not satiety, or disgust, or weariness—this, my Dionysian world of eternal self-creation, of eternal self-destruction, this mysterious world of twofold voluptuousness; this, my "Beyond Good and Evil," without aim, unless there is an aim in the bliss of the circle, without will, unless a ring must by nature keep good will to itself—would you have a name for my world? A *solution* of all your riddles? Do you also want a light, you most concealed, strongest and most undaunted men of the blackest midnight? *This world is the Will to Power—and nothing else!* And even you yourselves are this Will to Power—and nothing else!

. . . He, however, who has reflected deeply concerning the question, how and where the plant man his hitherto grown most vigorously, is forced to believe that this has always taken place under the opposite conditions; that to this end the danger of the situation has to increase enormously, his inventive faculty and dissembling powers have to fight their way up under long oppression and compulsion, and his Will to Life has to be increased to the unconditioned Will to Power, to *over power*: he believes that danger, severity, violence, peril in the street and in the heart, inequality of rights, secrecy, Stoicism, seductive art, and devilry of every kind—in short, the opposite of all gregarious desiderata—are necessary for the elevation of man. Such a morality with opposite designs, which would rear man upwards instead of to comfort and mediocrity; such a morality, with the intention of producing a ruling caste—the future lords of the earth—must, in order to be taught at all, introduce itself as if it were in some way correlated to the prevailing moral law, and must come forward under the cover of the latter's words and forms. But seeing that, to this end, a host of transitionary and deceptive measures must be discovered, and that the life of a single individual stands for almost nothing compared to the accomplishment of such lengthy tasks and aims, the first thing that must be done is to tear *a new kind* of man in whom the duration of the necessary will and the necessary instincts is guaranteed for many generations. This must be a new kind of ruling species and caste—this ought to be quite as clear as the somewhat lengthy and not easily expressed consequences of this thought. The aim should be to prepare a *transvaluation of values* for a particularly strong kind of man, most highly gifted in intellect and will, and, to this end, slowly and cautiously to liberate in him a whole host of slandered instincts hitherto held in check: whoever meditates about this problem belongs to us, the free spirits. . . .

From now henceforward there will be such favorable first conditions for greater ruling powers as have never yet been found on earth. And this is by no means the most important point. The establishment has been made possible of international race unions which will set themselves the task of rearing a ruling race, the future "lords of the earth," a new, vast aristocracy based upon the most severe self-discipline, in which the will of philosophical men of power and artist-tyrants will be stamped upon thousands of years: a higher species of men who, thanks to their preponderance of will, knowledge, riches, and influence, will avail themselves of democratic Europe as the most suitable and supple instrument they can have for taking the fate of the earth into their own hands, and working as artists upon man himself. Enough! The time is coming for us to transform all our views on politics.

I fancy I have divined some of the things that lie hidden in the soul of the highest man; perhaps every man who has divined so much must go to ruin. But he who has seen the highest man must do all he can to make him *possible*.

Fundamental thought: we must make the future the standard of all our valuations—and not seek the laws for our conduct behind us.

Not "mankind," but *Superman*, is the goal. . . .

STUDY QUESTIONS: NIETZSCHE, *THE WILL TO POWER*

1. Why is Christianity, according to Nietzsche, a lie?
2. Does Nietzsche see Christianity and Judaism as significantly different or alike? Why?
3. What is Nietzsche's view of Greek moral philosophy?
4. What does Nietzsche think of religious laws? Why?
5. What does Nietzsche mean by "moral castration"?
6. What does Nietzsche think of the Sophists?
7. Is the Will to Power a kind of will?
8. What is the world?
9. How are the world and the Will to Power related?
10. Why is the will, as used by psychologists, an "unjustifiable generalization?" What does Nietzsche mean by this? How should the will be regarded instead?
11. Did the universe, according to Nietzsche, have a beginning time? Was it created? Why is this important for his overall view?
12. What is the goal of Nietzsche's philosophy?

THE GENEALOGY OF MORALS

Originally published in 1887, *The Genealogy of Morals* is Nietzsche's least aphoristic and most analytic work. He presents his famous distinction between master and slave morality, itself based on an analysis of the master-slave relationship between self-consciousness and 'the other' in Hegel (see the Hegel section). The difference between the two moralities is that master morality is positive and affirms itself in its own terms, not in relation to anyone or anything else, such that the term "good" is equated with nobility and power, and beauty accorded the highest value. Slave morality, on the other hand, is fundamentally negative and defined in terms of what is extrinsic to oneself, most often couched in some sort of spiritual or metaphysical authority such as God. The good is defined in terms of sentimental emotions such as humility, pity, and self-effacement, and the bad is defined, as in Christianity, with some metaphysical notion of *evil*. The problem with slave morality is that it is life-denying and affirms only what is worst and weakest about the human race.

The whole function of philosophy, according to Nietzsche, is to turn this base morality on its head, so that humanity can transcend these limitations and raise up to create and re-create itself in a new and more powerful vision in which we take responsibility for ourselves and the world.

Notice the homage he pays in the Preface to his teacher Schopenhauer, and how he views the system of his other teacher, Hegel. The Preface explains what he is trying to do in the work, and how he sees the terms "good and evil" and "good and bad." The work is full of clever, lyrical writing and plenty of irony.

PREFACE

1.

We are unknown, we knowers, ourselves to ourselves: this has its own good reason. We have never searched for ourselves—how should it then come to pass, that we should ever *find* ourselves? Rightly has it been said, "Where your treasure is, there will your heart be also." *Our* treasure is there, where stand the hives of our knowledge. It is to those hives that we are always striving; as born creatures of flight, and as the honey-gatherers of the spirit, we care really in our hearts only for one thing—to bring something "home to the hive"!

As far as the rest of life with its so-called "experiences" is concerned, which of us has even sufficient serious interest? Or sufficient time? In our dealings with such points of life, we are, I fear, never properly to the point; to be precise, our heart is not there, and certainly not our ear. Rather like one who, delighting in a divine distraction, or sunken in the seas of his own soul, in whose ear the clock has just thundered with all its force its 12 strokes of noon, suddenly wakes up, and asks himself, "What has in point of fact just struck?" so do we at times rub afterwards, as it were, our puzzled ears, and ask in complete astonishment and complete embarrassment, "Through what have we in point of fact just lived?" further, "Who are we in point of fact?" and count, *after they have struck,* as I have explained, all the twelve throbbing beats of the clock of our experience, of our life, of our being—ah!—and count wrong in the endeavor. Of necessity we remain strangers to ourselves, we understand ourselves not, in ourselves we are bound to be mistaken, for of us holds good to all eternity the motto, "Each one is the farthest away from himself"—as far as ourselves are concerned we are not "knowers."

2.

My thoughts concerning the *genealogy* of our moral prejudices—for they constitute the issue in this polemic—have their first, bald, and provisional expression in that collection of aphorisms entitled *Human, All-Too-Human, a Book for Free Minds,* the writing of which was begun in Sorrento, during a winter which allowed me to gaze over the broad and dangerous territory through which my mind had up to that time wandered. This took place in the winter of 1876–1877; the thoughts themselves are older.

They were in their substance already the same thoughts which I take up again in the following treatises—we hope that they have derived benefit from the long interval, that they have grown riper, clearer, stronger, more complete. The fact, however, that I still cling to them even now, that in the meanwhile they have always held faster by each other, have, in fact, grown out of their original shape and into each other, all this strengthens in my mind the joyous confidence that they must have been originally neither separate disconnected capricious nor sporadic phenomena, but have sprung from a common root from a fundamental *"fiat"* of knowledge, whose empire reached to the soul's depth, and that grew ever more definite in its voice, and more definite in its demands. That is the only state of affairs that is proper in the case of a philosopher.

We have no right to be "*disconnected*"; we must neither err "disconnectedly" nor strike the truth "disconnectedly." Rather with the necessity with which a

---

Nietzsche, from *The Genealogy of Morals,* "Preface" and "First Essay: 'Good and Evil' and 'Good and Bad,'" translated by Horace B. Samuel, 1913.

tree bears its fruit, so do our thoughts, our values, our Yes's and No's and If's and Whether's, grow connected and interrelated, mutual witnesses of *one* will, *one* health, *one* kingdom, *one* sun—as to whether they are to *your* taste, these fruits of ours? But what matters that to the trees? What matters that to us, us the philosophers?

3.

Owing to a scrupulosity peculiar to myself, which I confess reluctantly—it concerns indeed *morality*—a scrupulosity, which manifests itself in my life at such an early period, with so much spontaneity, with so chronic a persistence and so keen an opposition to environment, epoch, precedent, and ancestry that I should have been almost entitled to style it my a priori—my curiosity and my suspicion felt themselves betimes bound to halt at the question, of what in point of actual fact was the *origin* of our "Good" and of our "Evil." Indeed, at the boyish age of 13 the problem of the origin of Evil already haunted me: at an age "when games and God divide one's heart," I devoted to that problem my first childish attempt at the literary game, my first philosophic essay—and as regards my infantile solution of the problem, well, I gave quite properly the honor to God, and made him the *father* of evil. Did my own a priori demand that precise solution from me? That new, immoral, or at least "amoral" a priori and that "categorical imperative" which was its voice (but, oh! how hostile to the Kantian article, and how pregnant with problems!), to which since then I have given more and more attention, and indeed what is more than attention. Fortunately I soon learned to separate theological from moral prejudices, and I gave up looking for a *supernatural* origin of evil. A certain amount of historical and philological education, to say nothing of an innate faculty of psychological discrimination *par excellence* succeeded in transforming almost immediately my original problem into the following one: under what conditions did Man invent for himself those judgments of values, "Good" and "Evil"? *And what intrinsic value do they possess in themselves?* Have they up to the present hindered or advanced human well-being? Are they a symptom of the distress, impoverishment, and degeneration of Human Life? Or, conversely, is it in them that is manifested the fulness, the strength, and the will of Life, its courage, its self-confidence, its future? On this point I found and hazarded in my mind the most diverse answers, I established distinctions in periods, peoples, and castes, I became a specialist in my problem, and from my answers grew new questions, new investigations, new conjectures, new probabilities; until at last I had a land of my own and a soil of my own, a whole secret world growing and flowering, like hidden gardens of whose existence no one could have an inkling—oh, how happy are we, we finders of knowledge, provided that we know how to keep silent sufficiently long.

4.

My first impulse to publish some of my hypotheses concerning the origin of morality I owe to a clear, well-written, and even precocious little book, in which a perverse and vicious kind of moral philosophy (your real *English* kind) was definitely presented to me for the first time; and this attracted me—with that magnetic attraction, inherent in that which is diametrically opposed and antithetical to one's own ideas. The title of the book was *The Origin of the Moral Emotions*; its author, Dr. Paul Rée; the year of its appearance, 1877. I may almost say that I have never read anything in which every single dogma and conclusion has called forth from me so emphatic a negation as did that book, albeit a negation untainted by either pique or intolerance. I referred accordingly both in season and out of season in the previous works, at which I was then working, to the arguments of that book, not to refute them—for what have I got to do with mere refutations—but substituting, as is natural to a positive mind, for an improbable theory one which is more probable, and occasionally no doubt for one philosophic error another. In that early period I gave, as I have said, the first public expression to those theories of origin to which these essays are devoted, but with a clumsiness which I was the last to conceal from myself, for I was as yet cramped, being still without a special language for these special subjects, still frequently liable to relapse and to vacillation. To go into details, compare what I say in *Human, All-Too-Human*, part i., about the parallel early history of Good and Evil, Aph. 45 (namely, their origin from the castes of the aristocrats and the slaves); similarly, Aph. 136 et seq., concerning the birth and value of ascetic morality; similarly, Aphs. 96, 99, vol. ii., Aph. 89, concerning the Morality of Custom, that far older and more original kind of morality which is *toto cœlo* different from the altruistic ethics (in which Dr. Ree, like all the English moral philosophers, sees the ethical "Thing-in-itself"); finally, Aph. 92. Similarly, Aph. 26 in *Human, All-Too-Human,* part ii., and Aph. 112, the *Dawn of Day,* concerning the origin of Justice as a balance between persons of approximately equal power (equilibrium as the hypothesis of all contract, consequently of all law); similarly, concerning the origin of Punishment, *Human, All-Too-Human,* part ii., Aphs. 22, 23, in regard to which the deterrent object is neither essential nor original (as Dr. Rée thinks—rather is it that this object is only imported, under certain definite conditions, and always as something extra and additional).

5.

In reality I had set my heart at that time on something much more important than the nature of the theories of myself or others concerning the origin of morality (or, more precisely, the real function from my view of these theories was to point an end to which they were one among many means). The issue for me was the value of morality, and on that subject I had to place myself in a state of abstraction, in which I was almost alone with my great teacher Schopenhauer, to whom that book, with all its passion and inherent contradiction (for that book also was a polemic), turned for present help as though he were still alive. The issue was, strangely enough, the value of the "unegoistic" instincts, the instincts of pity, self-denial, and self-sacrifice which Schopenhauer had so persistently painted in golden colours, deified and etherealised, that eventually they appeared to him, as it were, high and dry, as "intrin[sgrave]ic values in themselves," on the strength of which he uttered both to Life and to himself his own negation. But against *these very* instincts there voiced itself in my soul a more and more fundamental mistrust, a skepticism that dug ever deeper and deeper: and in this very instinct I saw the *great* danger of mankind, its most sublime temptation and seduction—seduction to what? To nothingness? In these very instincts I saw the beginning of the end, stability, the exhaustion that gazes backwards, the will turning *against* Life, the

last illness announcing itself with its own mincing melancholy: I realized that the morality of pity which spread wider and wider, and whose grip infected even philosophers with its disease, was the most sinister symptom of our modern European civilization; I realized that it was the route along which that civilization slid on its way to a new Buddhism? A European Buddhism? *Nihilism?* This exaggerated estimation in which modern philosophers have held pity, is quite a new phenomenon. Up to that time philosophers were absolutely unanimous as to the *worthlessness* of pity. I need only mention Plato, Spinoza, La Rochefoucauld, and Kant—four minds as mutually different as is possible, but united on one point; their contempt of pity.

6.

This problem of the value of pity and of the pity-morality (I am an opponent of the modern infamous emasculation of our emotions) seems at the first blush a mere isolated problem, a note of interrogation for itself; he, however, who once halts at this problem, and learns how to put questions, will experience what I experienced—a new and immense vista unfolds itself before him, a sense of potentiality seizes him like a vertigo, every species of doubt, mistrust, and fear springs up, the belief in morality, nay, in all morality, totters—finally a new demand voices itself. Let us speak out this *new demand:* we need a *critique* of moral values, *the value of these values* is for the first time to be called into question, and for this purpose a knowledge is necessary of the conditions and circumstances out of which these values grew, and under which they experienced their evolution and their distortion (morality as a result, as a symptom, as a mask, as Tartuffism, as disease, as a misunderstanding, but also morality as a cause, as a remedy, as a stimulant, as a fetter, as a drug), especially as such a knowledge has neither existed up to the present time nor is even now generally desired. The value of these "values" was taken for granted as an indisputable fact, which was beyond all question. No one has, up to the present, exhibited the faintest doubt or hesitation in judging the "good man" to be of a higher value than the "evil man," of a higher value with regard specifically to human progress, utility, and prosperity generally, not forgetting the future. What? Suppose the converse were the truth! What? Suppose there lurked in the "good man" a symptom of retrogression, such as a danger, a temptation, a poison, a *narcotic,* by means of which the present *battened on the future!* More comfortable and less risky perhaps than its opposite, but also pettier, meaner! So that morality would really be saddled with the guilt, if the *maximum potentiality of the power and splendor* of the human species were never to be attained? So that really morality would be the danger of dangers?

7.

Enough, that after this vista had disclosed itself to me, I myself had reason to search for learned, bold, and industrious colleagues (I am doing it even to this very day). It means traversing with new clamorous questions, and at the same time with new eyes, the immense, distant, and completely unexplored land of morality—of a morality which has actually existed and been actually lived! And is this not practically equivalent to first *discovering* that land? If, in this context, I thought, amongst others, of the aforesaid Dr. Rée, I did so because I had no doubt that from the very nature of his questions he would be compelled to have recourse to a truer method, in order to obtain his answers. Have I deceived myself on that score? I wished at all events to give a better direction of vision to an eye of such keenness and such impartiality. I wished to direct him to the real *history of morality,* and to warn him, while there was yet time, against a world of English theories that culminated *in the blue vacuum of heaven.* Other colors, of course, rise immediately to one's mind as being a hundred times more potent than blue for a genealogy of morals, for instance, *grey,* by which I mean authentic facts capable of definite proof and having actually existed, or, to put it shortly, the whole of that long hieroglyphic script (which is so hard to decipher) about the past history of human morals. This script was unknown to Dr. Rée; but he had read Darwin, and so in his philosophy the Darwinian beast and that pink of modernity, the demure weakling and dilettante, who "bites no longer," shake hands politely in a fashion that is at least instructive, the latter exhibiting a certain facial expression of refined and good-humored indolence, tinged with a touch of pessimism and exhaustion; as if it really did not pay to take all these things—I mean moral problems—so seriously. I, on the other hand, think that there are no subjects which *pay* better for being taken seriously; part of this payment is, that perhaps eventually they admit of being taken *gaily.* This gaiety, indeed, or, to use my own language, this *joyful wisdom,* is a payment; a payment for a protracted, brave, laborious, and burrowing seriousness, which, it goes without saying, is the attribute of but a few. But on that day on which we say from the fullness of our hearts, "Forward! Our old morality too is fit material *for Comedy,*" we shall have discovered a new plot, and a new possibility for the Dionysian drama entitled *The Soul's Fate*—and he will speedily utilize it, one can wager safely, he, the great ancient eternal dramatist of the comedy of our existence.

8.

If this writing be obscure to any individual, and jar on his ears, I do not think that it is necessarily I who am to blame. It is clear enough, on the hypothesis which I presuppose, namely, that the reader has first read my previous writings and has not grudged them a certain amount of trouble. It is not, indeed, a simple matter to get really at their essence. Take, for instance, my *Zarathustra;* I allow no one to pass muster as knowing that book, unless every single word therein has at some time wrought in him a profound wound, and at some time exercised on him a profound enchantment. Then and not till then can he enjoy the privilege of participating reverently in the halcyon element, from which that work is born, in its sunny brilliance, its distance, its spaciousness, its certainty. In other cases the aphoristic form produces difficulty, but this is only because this form is treated *too casually.* An aphorism properly coined and cast into its final mould is far from being "deciphered" as soon as it has been read; on the contrary, it is then that it first requires *to be expounded*—of course for that purpose an art of exposition is necessary. The third essay in this book provides an example of what is offered, of what in such cases I call exposition: an aphorism is prefixed to that essay, the essay itself is its commentary. Certainly one *quality* which nowadays has been best forgotten—and that is why it will take some time yet for my writings to become readable—is essential in order to practice reading as an art, a quality for the exercise of which it is necessary to be a cow, and under *no circumstances* a modern man: *rumination*.

Sils-Maria, Upper Engadine, *July*, 1887.

FIRST ESSAY

"Good and Evil," "Good and Bad"

1.

Those English psychologists, who up to the present are the only philosophers who are to be thanked for any endeavor to get as far as a history of the origin of morality—these men, I say, offer us in their own personalities no paltry problem. They even have, if I am to be quite frank about it, in their capacity of living riddles, an advantage over their books—*they themselves are interesting!* These English psychologists—what do they really mean? We always find them voluntarily or involuntarily at the same task of pushing to the front the *partie honteuse* of our inner world, and looking for the efficient, governing, and decisive principle in that precise quarter where the intellectual self-respect of the race would be the most reluctant to find it (for example, in the *vis inertiœ* of habit, or in forgetfulness, or in a blind and fortuitous mechanism and association of ideas, or in some factor that is purely passive, reflex, molecular, or fundamentally stupid). What is the real motivating power which always impels these psychologists in precisely *this* direction? Is it an instinct for human disparagement somewhat sinister, vulgar, and malignant, or perhaps in comprehensible even to itself? Or perhaps a touch of pessimistic jealousy, the mistrust of disillusioned idealists who have become gloomy, poisoned, and bitter? Or a petty subconscious enmity and rancor against Christianity (and Plato), that has conceivably never crossed the threshold of consciousness? Or just a vicious taste for those elements of life which are bizarre, painfully paradoxical, mystical, and illogical? Or, as a final alternative, a dash of each of these motives—a little vulgarity, a little gloominess, a little anti-Christianity, a little craving for the necessary piquancy?

But I am told that it is simply a case of old frigid and tedious frogs crawling and hopping around men and inside men, as if they were as thoroughly at home there, as they would be in a swamp.

I am opposed to this statement, nay, I do not believe it; and if, in the impossibility of knowledge, one is permitted to wish, so do I wish from my heart that just the converse metaphor should apply, and that these analysts with their psychological microscopes should be, at bottom, brave, proud, and magnanimous animals who know how to bridle both their hearts and their smarts, and have specifically trained themselves to sacrifice what is desirable to what is true, *any* truth in fact, even the simple, bitter, ugly, repulsive, unchristian, and immoral truths—for there are truths of that description.

2.

All honor, then, to the noble spirits who would fain dominate these historians of morality. But it is certainly a pity that they lack the *historical sense* itself, that they themselves are quite deserted by all the beneficent spirits of history. The whole train of their thought runs, as was always the way of old-fashioned philosophers, on *thoroughly* unhistorical lines: there is no doubt on this point. The crass ineptitude of their genealogy of morals is immediately apparent when the question arises of ascertaining the origin of the idea and judgment of "good." "Man had originally," so speaks their decree, "praised and called 'good' altruistic acts from the standpoint of those on whom they were conferred, that is, those to whom they were *useful*; subsequently the origin of this praise was *forgotten*, and altruistic acts, simply because, as a sheer matter of habit, they were praised as good, came also to be felt as good—as though they contained in themselves some intrinsic goodness." The thing is obvious—this initial derivation contains already all the typical and idiosyncratic traits of the English psychologists—we have "utility," "forgetting," "habit," and finally "error," the whole assemblage forming the basis of a system of values, on which the higher man has up to the present prided himself as though it were a kind of privilege of man in general. This pride *must* be brought low, this system of values *must* lose its values; is that attained?

Now the first argument that comes ready to my hand is that the real homestead of the concept "good" is sought and located in the wrong place: the judgment "good" did *not* originate among those to whom goodness was shown. Much rather has it been the good themselves, that is, the aristocratic, the powerful, the high-stationed, the high-minded, who have felt that they themselves were good, and that their actions were good, that is to say of the first order, in contradistinction to all the low, the low-minded, the vulgar, and the plebeian. It was out of this pathos of distance that they first arrogated the right to create values for their own profit, and to coin the names of such values—what had they to do with utility? The standpoint of utility is as alien and as inapplicable as it could possibly be, when we have to deal with so volcanic an effervescence of supreme values, creating and demarcating as they do a hierarchy within themselves. It is at this juncture that one arrives at an appreciation of the contrast to that tepid temperature, which is the presupposition on which every combination of worldly wisdom and every calculation of practical expediency is always based—and not for one occasional, not for one exceptional instance, but chronically. The pathos of nobility and distance, as I have said, the chronic and despotic *esprit de corps* and fundamental instinct of a higher dominant race coming into association with a meaner race, an "under race," this is the origin of the antithesis of good and bad. (The masters' right of giving names goes so far that it is permissible to look upon language itself as the expression of the power of the masters: they say "this *is* that, and that," and seal finally every object and every event with a sound, and thereby at the same time take possession of it.) It is because of this origin that the word "good" is far from having any necessary connection with altruistic acts, in accordance with the superstitious belief of these moral philosophers. On the contrary, it is on the occasion of the *decay* of aristocratic values, that the antitheses between "egoistic" and "altruistic" presses more and more heavily on the human conscience—it is, to use my own language, the *herd instinct* which finds in this antithesis an expression in many ways. And even then it takes a considerable time for this instinct to become sufficiently dominant, for the valuation to be inextricably dependent on this antithesis (as is the case in contemporary Europe); for today the prejudice is predominant, which, acting even now with all the intensity of an obsession and brain disease, holds that "moral," "altruistic," and "*désintéressé*" are concepts of equal value.

3.

In the second place, quite apart from the fact that this hypothesis as to the genesis of the value "good" cannot be historically upheld, it suffers from an inherent psychological contradiction. The utility of altruistic conduct has presumably been the origin of its being praised, and this origin has become *forgotten*. But in what conceivable way is this forgetting *possible?* Has perchance the utility of such conduct ceased at some given moment? The contrary is the case. This utility has rather been experienced every day at all times, and is consequently a feature that obtains a new and regular emphasis with every fresh day; it follows that, so far from vanishing from the consciousness, so far indeed from being forgotten, it must necessarily become impressed on the consciousness with ever-increasing distinctness. How much more logical is that contrary theory (it is not the truer for that) which is represented, for instance, by Herbert Spencer, who places the concept "good" as essentially similar to the concept "useful," "purposive," so that in the judgments "good" and "bad" mankind is simply summarizing and investing with a sanction its *unforgotten* and *unforgettable experiences* concerning the "useful-purposive" and the "mischievous-non-purposive." According to this theory, "good" is the attribute of that which has previously shown itself useful; and so is able to claim to be considered "valuable in the highest degree," "valuable in itself." This method of explanation is also, as I have said, wrong, but at any rate the explanation itself is coherent, and psychologically tenable.

4.

The guidepost which first put me on the *right* track was this question—what is the true etymological significance of the various symbols for the idea "good" which have been coined in the various languages? I then found that they all led back to *the same evolution of the same idea*—that everywhere "aristocrat," "noble" (in the social sense), is the root idea, out of which have necessarily developed "good" in the sense of "with aristocratic soul," "noble," in the sense of "with a soul of high calibre," "with a privileged soul"—a development which invariably runs parallel with that other evolution by which "vulgar," "plebeian," "low," are made to change finally into "bad." The most eloquent proof of this last contention is the German word "*schlecht*" itself: this word is identical with "*schlicht*" (compare "*schlechtweg*" and "*schlechterdings*")—which, originally and as yet without any sinister innuendo, simply denoted the plebeian man in contrast to the aristocratic man. It is at the sufficiently late period of the Thirty Years' War that this sense becomes changed to the sense now current. From the standpoint of the Genealogy of Morals this discovery seems to be substantial: the lateness of it is to be attributed to the retarding influence exercised in the modern world by democratic prejudice in the sphere of all questions of origin. This extends, as will shortly be shown, even to the province of natural science and physiology, which *prima facie* is the most objective. The extent of the mischief which is caused by this prejudice (once it is free of all trammels except those of its own malice), particularly to Ethics and History, is shown by the notorious case of Buckle. It was in Buckle that that *plebeianism* of the modern spirit, which is of English origin, broke out once again from its malignant soil with all the violence of a slimy volcano, and with that salted, rampant, and vulgar eloquence with which up to the present time all volcanoes have spoken.

5.

With regard to *our* problem, which can justly be called an *intimate* problem, and which elects to appeal to only a limited number of ears, it is of no small interest to ascertain that in those words and roots which denote "good" we catch glimpses of that archtrait, on the strength of which the aristocrats feel themselves to be beings of a higher order than their fellows. Indeed, they call themselves in perhaps the most frequent instances simply after their superiority in power (*e.g.* "the powerful," "the lords," "the commanders"), or after the most obvious sign of their superiority, as for example "the rich," "the possessors" (that is the meaning of *arya*; and the Iranian and Slav languages correspond). But they also call themselves after some *characteristic idiosyncrasy;* and this is the case which now concerns us. They name themselves, for instance, "the truthful": this is first done by the Greek nobility whose mouthpiece is found in Theognis, the Megarian poet. The word ἐσθλός, which is coined for the purpose, signifies etymologically "one who *is*," who has reality, who is real, who is true; and then with a subjective twist, the "true," as the "truthful": at this stage in the evolution of the idea, it becomes the motto and party cry of the nobility, and quite completes the transition to the meaning "noble,"

so as to place outside the pale the lying, vulgar man, as Theognis conceives and portrays him—till finally the word after the decay of the nobility is left to delineate psychological *noblesse*, and becomes as it were ripe and mellow. In the word κακός as in δειλός (the plebeian in contrast to the ἀγαθός) the cowardice is emphasized. This affords perhaps an inkling on what lines the etymological origin of the very ambiguous ἀγαθός is to be investigated. In the Latin *malus* (which I place side by side with μέλας) the vulgar man can be distinguished as the dark-colored, and above all as the black-haired ("*hic niger est*"), as the pre-Aryan inhabitants of the Italian soil, whose complexion formed the clearest feature of distinction from the dominant blondes, namely, the Aryan conquering race. At any rate Gaelic has afforded me the exact analogue—*Fin* (for instance, in the name *Fin-Gal*), the distinctive word of the nobility, finally—good, noble, clean, but originally the blonde-haired man in contrast to the dark black-haired aboriginals. The Celts, if I may make a parenthetic statement, were throughout a blonde race; and it is wrong to connect, as Virchow still connects, those traces of an essentially dark-haired population which are to be seen on the more elaborate ethnographical maps of Germany with any Celtic ancestry or with any admixture of Celtic blood. In this context it is rather the *pre-Aryan* population of Germany which surges up to these districts. (The same is true substantially of the whole of Europe. In point of fact, the subject race has finally again obtained the upper band, in complexion and the shortness of the skull, and perhaps in the intellectual and social qualities. Who can guarantee that modern democracy, still more modern anarchy, and indeed that tendency to the "commune," the most primitive form of society, which is now common to all the Socialists in Europe, does not in its real essence signify a monstrous reversion, and that the conquering and *master* race—the Aryan race—is not also becoming inferior physiologically?) I believe that I can explain the Latin *bonus* as the "warrior": my hypothesis is that I am right in deriving *bonus* from an older *duonus* (compare *bellum-duellum* = *duen-lum*, in which the word *duonus* appears to me to be contained). *Bonus* accordingly as the man of discord, of variance, "entzweiung" (*duo*), as the warrior: one sees what in ancient Rome "the good" meant for a man.

Must not our actual German word *gut* mean "*the god-like, the man of godlike race*"? and be identical with the national name (originally the nobles' name) of the *Goths?*

The grounds for this supposition do not appertain to this work.

6.

Above all, there is no exception (though there are opportunities for exceptions) to this rule, that the idea of political superiority always resolves itself into the idea of psychological superiority, in those cases where the highest caste is at the same time the *priestly* caste, and in accordance with its general characteristics confers on itself the privilege of a title which alludes specifically to its priestly function. It is in these cases, for instances, that "clean" and "unclean" confront each other for the first time as badges of class distinction; here again there develops a "good" and a "bad," in a sense which has ceased to be merely social. Moreover, care should be taken not to take these ideas of "clean" and "unclean" too seriously, too broadly, or too symbolically: all the ideas of ancient man have, on the contrary, got to be understood in their initial stages, in a sense which is, to an almost inconceivable extent, crude, coarse, physical, and narrow, and above all essentially *unsymbolical*. The "clean man" is originally only a man who washes himself, who abstains from certain foods which are conducive to skin diseases, who does not sleep with the unclean women of the lower classes, who has a horror of blood—not more, not much more! On the other hand, the very nature of a priestly aristocracy shows the reasons why just at such an early juncture there should ensue a really dangerous sharpening and intensification of opposed values: it is, in fact, through these opposed values that gulfs are cleft in the social plane, which a veritable Achilles of free thought would shudder to cross. There is from the outset a certain *diseased taint* in such sacerdotal aristocracies, and in the habits which prevail in such societies—habits which, *averse* as they are to action, constitute a compound of introspection and explosive emotionalism, as a result of which there appears that introspective morbidity and neurasthenia, which adheres almost inevitably to all priests at all times. With regard, however, to the remedy which they

themselves have invented for this disease—the philosopher has no option but to state, that it has proved itself in its effects a hundred times more dangerous than the disease, from which it should have been the deliverer. Humanity itself is still diseased from the effects of the naïvetés of this priestly cure. Take, for instance, certain kinds of diet (abstention from flesh), fasts, sexual continence, flight into the wilderness (a kind of Weir-Mitchell isolation, though of course without that system of excessive feeding and fattening which is the most efficient antidote to all the hysteria of the ascetic ideal); consider too the whole metaphysic of the priests, with its war on the senses, its enervation, its hair-splitting; consider its self-hypnotism on the fakir and Brahman principles (it uses Brahman as a glass disc and obsession), and that climax which we can understand only too well of an unusual satiety with its panacea of *nothingness* (or God—the demand for a *unio mystica* with God is the demand of the Buddhist for nothingness, nirvana—and nothing else!). In sacerdotal societies *every* element is on a more dangerous scale, not merely cures and remedies, but also pride, revenge, cunning, exaltation, love, ambition, virtue, morbidity—further, it can fairly be stated that it is on the soil of this *essentially dangerous* form of human society, the sacerdotal form, that man really becomes for the first time an *interesting animal*, that it is in this form that the soul of man has in a higher sense attained *depths* and become *evil*—and those are the two fundamental forms of the superiority which up to the present man has exhibited over every other animal.

7.

The reader will have already surmised with what ease the priestly mode of valuation can branch off from the knightly aristocratic mode, and then develop into the very antithesis of the latter: special impetus is given to this opposition, by every occasion when the castes of the priests and warriors confront each other with mutual jealousy and cannot agree over the prize. The knightly-aristocratic "values" are based on a careful cult of the physical, on a flowering, rich, and even effervescing healthiness, that goes considerably beyond what is necessary for maintaining life, on war, adventure, the chase, the dance, the tourney—on everything, in fact, which is contained in strong, free, and joyous action. The priestly-aristocratic mode of valuation is—we have seen—based on other hypotheses: it is bad enough for this class when it is a question of war! Yet the priests are, as is notorious, *the worst enemies*—why? Because they are the weakest. Their weakness causes their hate to expand into a monstrous and sinister shape, a shape which is most crafty and most poisonous. The really great haters in the history of the world have always been priests, who are also the cleverest haters—in comparison with the cleverness of priestly revenge, every other piece of cleverness is practically negligible. Human history would be too fatuous for anything were it not for the cleverness imported into it by the weak—take at once the most important instance. All the world's efforts against the "aristocrats," the "mighty," the "masters," the "holders of power," are negligible by comparison with what has been accomplished against those classes by *the Jews*—the Jews, that priestly nation which eventually realised that the one method of effecting satisfaction on its enemies and tyrants was by means of a radical transvaluation of values, which was at the same time an act of the *cleverest revenge*. Yet the method was only appropriate to a nation of priests, to a nation of the most jealously nursed priestly revengefulness. It was the Jews who, in opposition to the aristocratic equation (good = aristocratic = beautiful = happy = loved by the gods), dared with a terrifying logic to suggest the contrary equation, and indeed to maintain with the teeth of the most profound hatred (the hatred of weakness) this contrary equation, namely, "the wretched are alone the good; the poor, the weak, the lowly, are alone the good; the suffering, the needy, the sick, the loathsome, are the only ones who are pious, the only ones who are blessed, for them alone is salvation—but you, on the other hand, you aristocrats, you men of power, you are to all eternity the evil, the horrible, the covetous, the insatiate, the godless; eternally also shall you be the unblessed, the cursed, the damned!" We know who it was who reaped the heritage of this Jewish transvaluation. In the context of the monstrous and inordinately fateful initiative which the Jews have exhibited in connection with this most fundamental of all declarations of war, I remember the passage which came to my pen on another occasion (*Beyond Good and Evil*, Aph. 195)—that it was, in fact, with

the Jews that the *revolt of the slaves* begins in the sphere *of morals*; that revolt which has behind it a history of two millennia, and which at the present day has only moved out of our sight, because it has achieved victory.

8.

But you understand this not? You have no eyes for a force which has taken two thousand years to achieve victory? There is nothing wonderful in this; all *lengthy* processes are hard to see and to realize. But *this* is what took place: from the trunk of that tree of revenge and hate, Jewish hate—that most profound and sublime hate, which creates ideals and changes old values to new creations, the like of which has never been on earth—there grew a phenomenon which was equally incomparable, *a new love*, the most profound and sublime of all kinds of love—and from what other trunk could it have grown? But beware of supposing that this love has soared on its upward growth, as in any way a real negation of that thirst for revenge, as an antithesis to the Jewish hate! No, the contrary is the truth! This love grew out of that hate, as its crown, as its triumphant crown, circling wider and wider amid the clarity and fullness of the sun, and pursuing in the very kingdom of light and height its goal of hatred, its victory, its spoil, its strategy, with the same intensity with which the roots of that tree of hate sank into everything which was deep and evil with increasing stability and increasing desire. This Jesus of Nazareth, the incarnate gospel of love, this "Redeemer" bringing salvation and victory to the poor, the sick, the sinful—was he not really temptation in its most sinister and irresistible form, temptation to take the tortuous path to those very *Jewish* values and those very Jewish ideals? Has not Israel really obtained the final goal of its sublime revenge, by the tortuous paths of this "Redeemer," for all that he might pose as Israel's adversary and Israel's destroyer? Is it not due to the black magic of a really *great* policy of revenge, of a far-seeing, burrowing revenge, both acting and calculating with slowness, that Israel himself must repudiate before all the world the actual instrument of his own revenge and nail it to the cross, so that all the world—that is, all the enemies of Israel—could nibble without suspicion at this very bait? Could, moreover, any human mind with all its elaborate ingenuity invent a bait that was more truly *dangerous*? Anything that was even equivalent in the power of its seductive, intoxicating, defiling, and corrupting influence to that symbol of the holy cross, to that awful paradox of a "god on the cross," to that mystery of the unthinkable, supreme, and utter horror of the self-crucifixion of a god for the *salvation of man*? It is at least certain that *sub hoc signo* Israel, with its revenge and transvaluation of all values, has up to the present always triumphed again over all other ideals, over all more aristocratic ideals.

9.

"But why do you talk of nobler ideals? Let us submit to the facts; that the people have triumphed—or the slaves, or the populace, or the herd, or whatever name you care to give them—if this has happened through the Jews, so be it! In that case no nation ever had a greater mission in the world's history. The 'masters' have been done away with; the morality of the vulgar man has triumphed. This triumph may also be called a blood-poisoning (it has mutually fused the races)—I do not dispute it; but there is no doubt but that this intoxication has succeeded. The 'redemption' of the human race (that is, from the masters) is progressing swimmingly; everything is obviously becoming Judaized, or Christianized, or vulgarized (what is there in the words?). It seems impossible to stop the course of this poisoning through the whole body politic of mankind—but its *tempo* and pace may from the present time be slower, more delicate, quieter, more discreet—there is time enough. In view of this context has the Church nowadays any necessary purpose? Has it, in fact, a right to live? Or could man get on without it? *Quoeritur.* It seems that it fetters and retards this tendency, instead of accelerating it. Well, even that might be its utility. The Church certainly is a crude and boorish institution, that is repugnant to an intelligence with any pretence at delicacy, to a really modern taste. Should it not at any rate learn to be somewhat more subtle? It alienates nowadays, more than it allures. Which of us would be a freethinker if there were no Church? It is the Church which repels us, *not* its poison—apart from the Church we like the poison." This is the epilogue of a freethinker to my discourse, of an honorable animal (as he has given abundant proof), and a democrat to boot; he had up

to that time listened to me, and could not endure my silence, but for me, indeed, with regard to this topic there is much on which to be silent.

10.

The revolt of the slaves in morals begins in the very principle of *resentment* becoming creative and giving birth to values—a resentment experienced by creatures who, deprived as they are of the proper outlet of action, are forced to find their compensation in an imaginary revenge. While every aristocratic morality springs from a triumphant affirmation of its own demands, the slave morality says "no" from the very outset to what is "outside itself," "different from itself," and "not itself": and this "no" is its creative deed. This volte-face of the valuing standpoint—this *inevitable* gravitation to the objective instead of back to the subjective—is typical of "resentment": the slave morality requires as the condition of its existence an external and objective world, to employ physiological terminology, it requires objective stimuli to be capable of action at all—its action is fundamentally a reaction. The contrary is the case when we come to the aristocrat's system of values: it acts and grows spontaneously, it merely seeks its antithesis in order to pronounce a more grateful and exultant "yes" to its own self. Its negative conception, "low," "vulgar," "bad," is merely a pale late-born foil in comparison with its positive and fundamental conception (saturated as it is with life and passion), of "we aristocrats, we good ones, we beautiful ones, we happy ones."

When the aristocratic morality goes astray and commits sacrilege on reality, this is limited to that particular sphere with which it is *not* sufficiently acquainted—a sphere, in fact, from the real knowledge of which it disdainfully defends itself. It misjudges, in some cases, the sphere which it despises, the sphere of the common vulgar man and the low people: on the other hand, due weight should be given to the consideration that in any case the mood of contempt, of disdain, of superciliousness, even on the supposition that it *falsely* portrays the object of its contempt, will always be far removed from that degree of falsity which will always characterize the attacks—in effigy, of course—of the vindictive hatred and revengefulness of the weak in onslaughts on their enemies. In point of fact, there is in contempt too strong an admixture of nonchalance, of casualness, of boredom, of impatience, even of personal exultation, for it to be capable of distorting its victim into a real caricature or a real monstrosity. Attention again should be paid to the almost benevolent *nuances* which, for instance, the Greek nobility imports into all the words by which it distinguishes the common people from itself; note how continuously a kind of pity, care, and consideration imparts its honeyed *flavor*, until at last almost all the words which are applied to the vulgar man survive finally as expressions for "unhappy," "worthy of pity" (compare δειλός, δείλαιος, πονηρός, μοχϑηρός; the latter two names really denoting the vulgar man as labor-slave and beast of burden), and how, conversely, "bad," "low," "unhappy" have never ceased to ring in the Greek ear with a tone in which "unhappy" is the predominant note: this is a heritage of the old noble aristocratic morality, which remains true to itself even in contempt (let philologists remember the sense in which ὀϊζυρός, ἄνολδος, τλήμων, δυστυχεῖν, ξυμφορά used to be employed. The "wellborn" simply *felt* themselves the "happy" they did not have to manufacture their happiness artificially through looking at their enemies, or in cases to talk and lie themselves into happiness (as is the custom with all resentful men); and similarly, complete men as they were, exuberant with strength, and consequently *necessarily* energetic, they were too wise to dissociate happiness from action—activity becomes in their minds necessarily counted as happiness (that is the etymology of εὐπράττειν)—all in sharp contrast to the "happiness" of the weak and the oppressed, with their festering venom and malignity, among whom happiness appears essentially as a narcotic, a deadening, a quietude, a peace, a "Sabbath," an enervation of the mind and relaxation of the limbs—in short, a purely *passive* phenomenon. While the aristocratic man lived in confidence and openness with himself (γενναῖος, "noble-born," emphasises the nuance "sincere," and perhaps also "naïf"), the resentful man, on the other hand, is neither sincere nor naïve, nor honest and candid with himself. His soul *squints;* his mind loves hidden crannies, tortuous paths and backdoors, everything secret appeals to him as *his* world, *his* safety, *his* balm; he is past master in silence, in not forgetting, in waiting, in provisional self-depreciation and self-abasement. A race of such *resentful* men will of

necessity eventually prove more *prudent* than any aristocratic race, it will honor prudence on quite a distinct scale, as, in fact, a paramount condition of existence, while prudence among aristocratic men is apt to be tinged with a delicate flavor of luxury and refinement; so among them it plays nothing like so integral a part as that complete certainty of function of the governing *unconscious* instincts, or as indeed a certain lack of prudence, such as a vehement and valiant charge, whether against danger or the enemy, or as those ecstatic bursts of rage, love, reverence, gratitude, by which at all times noble souls have recognized each other. When the resentment of the aristocratic man manifests itself, it fulfils and exhausts itself in an immediate reaction, and consequently instills no *venom.* On the other hand, it never manifests itself at all in countless instances, when in the case of the feeble and weak it would be inevitable. An inability to take seriously for any length of time their enemies, their disasters, their *misdeeds*—that is the sign of the full strong natures who possess a superfluity of molding plastic force, that heals completely and produces forgetfulness. A good example of this in the modern world is Mirabeau, who had no memory for any insults and meannesses which were practiced on him, and who was only incapable of forgiving because he forgot. Such a man indeed shakes off with a shrug many a worm which would have buried itself in another; it is only in characters like these that we see the possibility (supposing, of course, that there is such a possibility in the world) of the real "*love* of one's enemies." What respect for his enemies is found, in an aristocratic man—and such a reverence is already a bridge to love! He insists on having his enemy to himself as his distinction. He tolerates no other enemy but a man in whose character there is nothing to despise and *much* to honor! On the other hand, imagine the "enemy" as the resentful man conceives him, and it is here exactly that we see his work, his creativeness; he has conceived "the evil enemy," the "evil one," and indeed that is the root idea from which he now evolves as a contrasting and corresponding figure a "good one," himself—his very self!

11.

The method of this man is quite contrary to that of the aristocratic man, who conceives the root idea "good" spontaneously and straight away, that is to say, out of himself, and from that material then creates for himself a concept of "bad"! This "bad" of aristocratic origin and that "evil" out of the cauldron of unsatisfied hatred—the former an imitation, an "extra," an additional nuance; the latter, on the other hand, the original, the beginning, the essential act in the conception of a slave morality—these two words "bad" and "evil," how great a difference do they mark, in spite of the fact that they have an identical contrary in the idea "good." But the idea "good" is *not* the same: much rather let the question be asked, "Who is really evil according to the meaning of the morality of resentment?" In all sternness let it be answered thus: *just* the good man of the other morality, just the aristocrat, the powerful one, the one who rules, but who is distorted by the venomous eye of resentfulness, into a new color, a new signification, a new appearance. This particular point we would be the last to deny: the man who learnt to know those "good" ones only as enemies, learnt at the same time not to know them only as "*evil enemies*," and the same men who *inter pares* were kept so rigorously in bounds through convention, respect, custom, and gratitude, though much more through mutual vigilance and jealousy *inter pares*, these men who in their relations with each other find so many new ways of manifesting consideration, self-control, delicacy, loyalty, pride, and friendship, these men are in reference to what is outside their circle (where the foreign element, a *foreign* country, begins), not much better than beasts of prey, which have been let loose. They enjoy there freedom from all social control, they feel that in the wilderness they can give vent with impunity to that tension which is produced by enclosure and imprisonment in the peace of society, they *revert* to the innocence of the beast-of-prey conscience, like jubilant monsters, who perhaps come from a ghostly bout of murder, arson, rape, and torture, with bravado and a moral equanimity, as though merely some wild student's prank had been played, perfectly convinced that the poets have now an ample theme to sing and celebrate. It is impossible not to recognize at the core of all these aristocratic races the beast of prey; the magnificent *blonde brute*, avidly rampant for spoil and victory; this hidden core needed an outlet from time to time, the beast must get loose again, must return into the wilderness—the Roman, Arabic, German, and Japanese nobility, the Homeric heroes, the Scandinavian Vikings, are all alike in this need. It is the aristocratic races who have left the idea "Barbarian" on all the tracks in which they have marched; nay, a consciousness of this very barbarianism, and even a pride in it, manifests itself even in their highest civilisation (for example, when Pericles says to his Athenians in that celebrated funeral oration, "Our audacity has forced a way over every land and sea, rearing everywhere imperishable memorials of itself for *good* and for *evil*"). This audacity of aristocratic races, mad, absurd, and spasmodic as may be its expression; the incalculable and fantastic nature of their enterprises—Pericles sets in special relief and glory the ραθυμία of the Athenians, their nonchalance and contempt for safety, body, life, and comfort, their awful joy and intense delight in all destruction, in all the ecstasies of victory and cruelty—all these features become crystallized, for those who suffered thereby in the picture of the "barbarian," of the "evil enemy," perhaps of the "Goth" and of the "Vandal." The profound, icy mistrust which the German provokes, as soon as he arrives at power—even at the present time—is always still an aftermath of that inextinguishable horror with which for whole centuries Europe has regarded the wrath of the blonde Teuton beast (although between the old Germans and ourselves there exists scarcely a psychological, let alone a physical, relationship). I have once called attention to the embarrassment of Hesiod, when he conceived the series of social ages, and endeavored to express them in gold, silver, and bronze. He could only dispose of the contradiction, with which he was confronted, by the Homeric world, an age magnificent indeed, but at the same time so awful and so violent, by making two ages out of one, which he henceforth placed one behind the other—first, the age of the heroes and demigods, as that world had remained in the memories of the aristocratic families, who found therein their own ancestors; secondly, the bronze age, as that corresponding age appeared to the descendants of the oppressed, spoiled, ill-treated, exiled, enslaved; namely, as an age of bronze, as I have said, hard, cold, terrible, without feelings and without conscience, crushing everything, and bespattering everything with blood. Granted the truth of the theory now believed to be true, that the very *essence of all civilization* is to *train* out of man, the beast of prey, a tame and civilized animal, a domesticated animal, it follows indubitably that we must regard as the real *tools of civilization* all those instincts of reaction and resentment, by the help of which the aristocratic races, together with their ideals, were finally degraded and overpowered; though that has not yet come to be synonymous with saying that the bearers of those tools also *represented* the civilization. It is rather the contrary that is not only probable—nay, is *palpable* today; these bearers of vindictive instincts that have to be bottled up, these descendants of all European and non-European slavery, especially of the pre-Aryan population—these people, I say, represent the *decline* of humanity! These "tools of civilization" are a disgrace to humanity, and constitute in reality more of an argument against civilization, more of a reason why civilization should be suspected. One may be perfectly justified in being always afraid of the blonde beast that lies at the core of all aristocratic races, and in being on one's guard: but who would not a hundred times prefer to be afraid, when one at the same time admires, than to be immune from fear, at the cost of being perpetually obsessed with the loathsome spectacle of the distorted, the dwarfed, the stunted, the envenomed? And is that not our fate? What produces today our repulsion towards "man"? For we *suffer* from "man," there is no doubt about it. It is not fear; it is rather that we have nothing more to fear from men; it is that the worm "man" is in the foreground and pullulates; it is that the "tame man," the wretched mediocre and unedifying creature, has learnt to consider himself a goal and a pinnacle, an inner meaning, a historic principle, a "higher man"; yes, it is that he has a certain right so to consider himself, in so far as he feels that in contrast to that excess of deformity, disease, exhaustion, and effeteness whose odor is beginning to pollute present-day Europe, he at any rate has achieved a relative success, he at any rate still says "yes" to life.

12.

I cannot refrain at this juncture from uttering a sigh and one last hope. What is it precisely which I find intolerable? That which I alone cannot get rid of, which makes me choke and faint? Bad air! Bad air! That something misbegotten comes near me; that I must inhale the odor of the entrails of a misbegotten soul! That excepted, what can one not endure in the way of need, privation, bad weather, sickness, toil, solitude? In point of fact, one manages to get over everything, born as one is to a burrowing and battling existence; one always returns once again to the light, one always lives again one's golden hour of victory, and then one stands as one was born, unbreakable, tense, ready for something more difficult, for something more distant, like a bow stretched but the tauter by every strain. But from time to time do you grant me—assuming that "beyond good and evil" there are goddesses who can grant—one glimpse, grant me but one glimpse only, of something perfect, fully realized, happy, mighty, triumphant, of something that still gives cause for fear! A glimpse of a man that justifies the existence of man, a glimpse of an incarnate human happiness that realizes and redeems, for the sake of which one may hold fast to *the belief in man!* For the position is this: in the dwarfing and levelling of the European man lurks *our* greatest peril, for it is this outlook which fatigues—we see today nothing which wishes to be greater, we surmise that the process is always still backwards, still backwards towards something more attentuated, more inoffensive, more cunning, more comfortable, more mediocre, more indifferent, more Chinese, more Christian—man, there is no doubt about it, grows always "better"—the destiny of Europe lies even in this—that in losing the fear of man, we have also lost the hope in man, yea, the will to be man. The sight of man now fatigues. What is present-day Nihilism if it is not *that?* We are tired of *man.*

13.

But let us come back to it; the problem of *another* origin of the good—of the good, as the resentful man has thought it out—demands its solution. It is not surprising that the lambs should bear a grudge against the great birds of prey, but that is no reason for blaming the great birds of prey for taking the little lambs. And when the lambs say among themselves, "Those birds of prey are evil, and he who is as far removed from being a bird of prey, who is rather its opposite, a lamb, is he not good?" then there is nothing to cavil at in the setting up of this ideal, though it may also be that the birds of prey will regard it a little sneeringly, and perchance say to themselves, "*We* bear no grudge against them, these good lambs, we even like them; nothing is tastier than a tender lamb." To require of strength that it should *not* express itself as strength, that it should not be a wish to overpower, a wish to overthrow, a wish to become master, a thirst for enemies and antagonisms and triumphs, is just as absurd as to require of weakness that it should express itself as strength. A quantum of force is just such a quantum of movement, will, action—rather it is nothing else than just those very phenomena of moving, willing, acting, and can only appear otherwise in the misleading errors of language (and the fundamental fallacies of reason which have become petrified therein), which understands, and understands wrongly,, all working as conditioned by a worker, by a "subject." And just exactly as the people separate the lightning from its flash, and interpret the latter as a thing done, as the working of a subject which is called lightning, so also does the popular morality separate strength from the expression of strength, as though behind the strong man there existed some indifferent neutral *substratum*, which enjoyed a *caprice and option* as to whether or not it should express strength. But there is no such *substratum*, there is no "being" behind doing, working, becoming; "the doer" is a mere appanage to the action. The action is everything. In point of fact, the people duplicate the doing, when they make the lightning lighten, that is a "doing-doing"; they make the same phenomenon first a cause, and then, secondly, the effect of that cause. The scientists fail to improve matters when they say, "Force moves, force causes," and so on. Our whole science is still, in spite of all its coldness, of all its freedom from passion, a dupe of the tricks of language, and has never succeeded in getting rid of that superstitious changeling "the subject" (the atom, to give another instance, is such a changeling, just as the Kantian "thing-in-itself"). What wonder, if the suppressed and stealthily simmering passions of revenge and hatred exploit for their own advantage their belief, and indeed hold no belief with a more steadfast enthusiasm than this—"that the strong has the *option* of being weak, and the bird of prey of being a lamb." Thereby do they win for themselves the right of attributing to the birds of prey the *responsibility* for being birds of prey: when the oppressed, downtrodden, and overpowered say to themselves with the vindictive guile of weakness, "Let us be otherwise than the evil, namely, good! And good is every one who does not oppress, who hurts no one who does not attack, who does not pay back, who hands over revenge to God, who holds himself, as we do, in hiding; who goes out of the way of evil, and demands, in short, little from life; like ourselves the patient, the meek, the just." Yet all this, in its cold and unprejudiced interpretation, means nothing more than "once for all, the weak are weak; it is good to do *nothing for which we are not strong enough*"; but this dismal state of affairs, this prudence of the lowest order which even insects possess (which in a great danger are fain to sham death so as to avoid doing "too much'"), has, thanks to the counterfeiting and self-deception of weakness, come to masquerade in the pomp of an ascetic, mute, and expectant virtue, just as though the *very* weakness of the weak—that is its *being*, its working, its whole unique inevitable inseparable reality—were a voluntary result, something wished, chosen, a deed, an act of *merit*. This kind: of man finds the belief in a neutral, free-choosing "subject" *necessary* from an instinct of self-preservation, of self-assertion, in which every lie is fain to sanctify itself. The subject (or, to use popular language, the *soul*) has perhaps proved itself the best dogma in the world simply because it rendered possible to the horde of mortal, weak, and oppressed individuals of every, kind, that most sublime specimen of self-deception, the interpretation of weakness as freedom, of being this, or being that, as *merit*.

14.

Will anyone look a little into—right into—the mystery of how *ideals* are *manufactured* in this world? Who has the courage to do it? Come!

Here we have a vista opened into these grimy workshops. Wait just a moment, dear Mr. Inquisitive and Foolhardy; your eye must first grow accustomed to this false, changing light—Yes! Enough! Now speak! What is happening below down yonder? Speak out! Tell what you see, man of the most dangerous curiosity, for now *I* am the listener.

"I see nothing, I hear the more. It is a cautious, spiteful, gentle whispering and muttering together in all the corners and crannies. It seems to me that they are lying; a sugary softness adheres to every sound.

Weakness is turned to *merit*, there is no doubt about it—it is just as you say."

Further!

"And the impotence which requites not, is turned to 'goodness,' craven baseness to meekness, submission to those whom one hates, to obedience (namely, obedience to one of whom they say that he ordered this submission—they call him God). The inoffensive character of the weak, the very cowardice in which he is rich, his standing at the door, his forced necessity of waiting, gain here fine names, such as 'patience,' which is also called 'virtue'; not being able to avenge one's self, is called not wishing to avenge one's self, perhaps even forgiveness (for *they* know not what they do—we alone know what they do). They also talk of the 'love of their enemies' and sweat thereby."

Further!

"They are miserable, there is no doubt about it, all these whisperers and counterfeiters in the corners, although they try to get warm by crouching close to each other, but they tell me that their misery is a favor and distinction given to them by God, just as one beats the dogs one likes best; that perhaps this misery is also a preparation, a probation, a training; that perhaps it is still more something which will one day be compensated and paid back with a tremendous interest in gold, nay in happiness. This they call 'Blessedness.'"

Further!

"They are now giving me to understand, that not only are they better men than the mighty, the lords of the earth, whose spittle they have got to lick (*not out of fear, not at all out of fear!* But because God ordains that one should honor all authority)—not only are they better men, but that they also have a 'better time,' at any rate, will one day have a 'better time.' But enough! Enough! I can endure it no longer. Bad air! Bad air! These workshops *where ideals are manufactured*—verily they reek with the crassest lies."

Nay. Just one minute! You are saying nothing about the masterpieces of these virtuosos of black magic, who can produce whiteness, milk, and innocence out of any black you like. Have you not noticed what a pitch of refinement is attained by their *chef d'oeuvre*, their most audacious, subtle, ingenious, and

lying artist trick? Take care! These cellar-beasts, full of revenge and hate—what do they make out of their revenge and hate? Do you hear these words? Would you suspect, if you trusted only their words, that you are among men of resentment and nothing else?

"I understand, I prick my ears up again (ah! ah! ah! and I hold my nose). Now do I hear for the first time that which they have said so often—'We good, *we are the righteous*'—what they demand they call not revenge but 'the triumph of *righteousness*'; what they hate is not their enemy, no, they hate 'unrighteousness,' 'godlessness'; what they believe in and hope is not the hope of revenge, the intoxication of sweet revenge ("sweeter than honey," did Homer call it?), but the victory of God, of the *righteous* God over the 'godless'; what is left for them to love in this world is not their brothers in hate, but their 'brothers in love,' as they say, all the good and righteous on the earth."

And how do they name that which serves them as a solace against all the troubles of life—their phantasmagoria of their anticipated future blessedness?

"How? Do I hear right? They call it 'the Last Judgment,' the advent of *their* kingdom, 'the kingdom of God,' but *in the meanwhile* they live 'in faith,' 'in love,' 'in hope.'"

Enough! Enough!

15.

In the faith in what? In the love for what? In the hope of what? These weaklings! They also wish to be strong some time: there is no doubt about it, some time *their* kingdom also must come—"the kingdom of God" is their name for it, as has been mentioned—they are so meek in everything! Yet in order to experience *that* kingdom it is necessary to live long, to live beyond death—yes, *eternal* life is necessary so that one can make up forever for that earthly life "in faith," "in love," and "in hope." Make up for what? Make up by what? Dante, as it seems to me, made a crass mistake when with awe-inspiring ingenuity he placed that inscription over the gate of his hell, "Me too made eternal love". At any rate the following inscription would have a much better right to stand over the gate of the Christian Paradise and its "eternal blessedness"—"Me too made eternal hate"—granted of course that a truth may rightly stand over the gate to a lie! For what is the blessedness of that Paradise? Possibly we could quickly surmise it; but it is better that it should be explicitly attested by an authority who in such matters is not to be disparaged, Thomas of Aquinas, the great teacher and saint. "*Beati in regno celesti*," says he, as gently as a lamb, "*videbunt poenas damnatorum, ut beatitudo illis magis complaceat*." Or if we wish to hear a stronger tone, a word from the mouth of a triumphant father of the Church, who warned his disciples against the cruel ecstasies of the public spectacles—but why? Faith offers us much more, says he (*de Spectac.*, c. 29 ss), something much stronger; thanks to the redemption, joys of quite another kind stand at our disposal; instead of athletes we have our martyrs.

16.

Let us come to a conclusion. The two *opposing values*, "good and bad," "good and evil," have fought a dreadful, thousand-year fight in the world, and though indubitably the second value has been for a long time in the preponderance, there are not wanting places where the fortune of the fight is still undecisive. It can almost be said that in the meanwhile the fight reaches a higher and higher level, and that in the meanwhile it has become more and more intense, and always more and more psychological; so that nowadays there is perhaps no more decisive mark of the *higher nature*, of the more psychological nature, than to be in that sense self-contradictory, and to be actually still a battleground for those two opposites. The symbol of this fight, written in a writing which has remained worthy of perusal throughout the course of history up to the present time, is called "Rome against Judæa, Judæa against Rome." Hitherto there has been no greater event *than* that fight, the putting of *that* question, *that* deadly antagonism. Rome found in the Jew the incarnation of the unnatural, as though it were its diametrically opposed monstrosity, and in Rome the Jew was held to be *convicted of hatred* of the whole human race: and rightly so, in so far as it is right to link the well-being and the future of the human race to the unconditional mastery of the aristocratic values, of the Roman values. What, conversely, did the Jews feel against Rome? One can surmise it from a thousand symptoms, but it is sufficient to carry one's mind back to the Johannian

Apocalypse, that most obscene of all the written outbursts, which has revenge on its conscience. (One should also appraise at its full value the profound logic of the Christian instinct, when over this very book of hate it wrote the name of the Disciple of Love, that self-same disciple to whom it attributed that impassioned and ecstatic Gospel—therein lurks a portion of truth, however much literary forging may have been necessary for this purpose.) The Romans were the strong and aristocratic; a nation stronger and more aristocratic has never existed in the world, has never even been dreamed of; every relic of them, every inscription enraptures, granted that one can divine *what* it is that writes the inscription. The Jews, conversely, were that priestly nation of resentment *par excellence*, possessed by a unique genius for popular morals—just compare with the Jews the nations with analogous gifts, such as the Chinese or the Germans, so as to realize afterwards what is first rate, and what is fifth rate.

Which of them has been provisionally victorious, Rome or Judæa? But there is not a shadow of doubt; just consider to whom in Rome itself nowadays you bow down, as though before the quintessence of all the highest values—and not only in Rome, but almost over half the world, everywhere where man has been tamed or is about to be tamed—to *three Jews*, as we know, and *one Jewess* (to Jesus of Nazareth, to Peter the fisher, to Paul the tentmaker, and to the mother of the aforesaid Jesus, named Mary). This is very remarkable: Rome is undoubtedly defeated. At any rate there took place in the Renaissance a brilliantly sinister revival of the classical ideal, of the aristocratic valuation of all things. Rome herself, like a man waking up from a trance, stirred beneath the burden of the new Judaised Rome that had been built over her, which presented the appearance of an œcumenical synagogue and was called the "Church": but immediately Judœa triumphed again, thanks to that fundamentally popular (German and English) movement of revenge, which is called the Reformation, and taking also into account its inevitable corollary, the restoration of the Church, the restoration also of the ancient graveyard peace of classical Rome. Judæa proved yet once more victorious over the classical ideal in the French Revolution, and in a sense which was even more crucial and even more profound: the last political aristocracy that existed in Europe, that of the *French* seventeenth and eighteenth centuries, broke into pieces beneath the instincts of a resentful populace—never had the world heard a greater jubilation, a more uproarious enthusiasm. Indeed, there took place in the midst of it the most monstrous and unexpected phenomenon; the ancient ideal *itself* swept before the eyes and conscience of humanity with all its life and with unheard of splendor, and in opposition to resentment's lying war cry of *the prerogative of the most,* in opposition to the will to lowliness, abasement, and equalisation, the will to a retrogression and twilight of humanity, there rang out once again, stronger, simpler, more penetrating than ever, the terrible and enchanting counter war cry of *the prerogative of the few!* Like a final signpost to other ways, there appeared Napoleon, the most unique and violent anachronism that ever existed, and in him the incarnate problem *of the aristocratic ideal in itself.* Consider well what a problem it is: Napoleon, that synthesis of Monster and Superman.

17.

Was it therewith over? Was that greatest of all antitheses of ideals thereby relegated *ad acta* for all time? Or only postponed, postponed for a long time? May there not take place at some time or other a much more awful, much more carefully prepared flaring up of the old conflagration? Further! Should not one wish *that* consummation with all one's strength? Will it one's self? Demand it one's self? He who at this juncture begins, like my readers, to reflect, to think further, will have difficulty in coming quickly to a conclusion, ground enough for me to come myself to a conclusion, taking it for granted that for some time past what I mean has been sufficiently clear, what I exactly *mean* by that dangerous motto which is inscribed on the body of my last book, *Beyond Good and Evil*—at any rate that is not the same as "Beyond Good and Bad."

NOTES

I avail myself of the opportunity offered by this treatise to express, openly and formally, a wish which up to the present has only been expressed in occasional conversations with scholars, namely, that some faculty of philosophy should, by means of a series of prize essays, gain the glory of having promoted the further study of the *history of morals.* Perhaps this book may serve to give a forcible impetus in such a direction. With regard to a possibility of this character, the following question deserves consideration. It merits quite as much the attention of philologists and historians as of actual professional philosophers.

    "What indication of the history of the evolution of the moral ideas is afforded by philology, and especially by etymological investigation?"

    On the other hand, it is, of course, equally necessary to induce physiologists and doctors to be interested in these problems (*of the value* of the *valuations* which have prevailed up to the present). In this connection the professional philosophers may be trusted to act as the spokesmen and intermediaries in these particular instances, after, of course, they have quite succeeded in transforming the relationship between philosophy and physiology and medicine, which is originally one of coldness and suspicion, into the most friendly and fruitful reciprocity. In point of fact, all tables of values, all the "thou shalts" known to history and ethnology, need primarily a *physiological,* at any rate in preference to a psychological, elucidation and interpretation; all equally require a critique from medical science. The question, "What is the *value* of this or that table of 'values' and morality?" will be asked from the most varied standpoints. For instance, the question of "valuable *for what*" can never be analyzed with sufficient nicety. That, for instance, which would evidently have value with regard to promoting in a race the greatest possible powers of endurance (or with regard to increasing its adaptability to a specific climate, or with regard to the preservation of the greatest number) would have nothing like the same value, if it were a question of evolving a stronger species. In gauging values, the good of the majority and the good of the minority are opposed standpoints, we leave it to the naïveté of English biologists to regard the former standpoint as *intrinsically* superior. *All the sciences have now to pave the way for the future task of the philosopher; this task being understood to mean, that he must solve the problem of* value*, that he has to fix the* hierarchy of value*s.*

STUDY QUESTIONS: NIETZSCHE, *THE GENEALOGY OF MORALS*

1. What is Nietzsche's view of the British moral philosophers?
2. What is Nietzsche's view of British psychologists? What was their chief contribution?
3. How important is the master's right of giving names? What function does it serve?
4. What is the source of the decay of aristocratic values?
5. What is etymology and how important is it in Nietzsche's philosophy?
6. What is *our* problem, what Nietzsche also calls our *intimate* problem?
7. What is Nietzsche's view of the Brahman (Hindu) principles of mystical union with God?
8. How does Nietzsche's view the Buddhist tradition of attaining *nirvana*?
9. What do Buddhism and Hindusim have in common, in Nietzsche's view?
10. What role does *resentment* play in slave revolts?
11. What is Nietzsche's view of Christianity? Of Judaism? What do these two religions have in common?
12. What sort of man does a synthesis of Monster and Superman produce? Does Nietzsche give any examples?

THUS SPAKE ZARATHUSTRA

This literary masterpiece was, in the words of his sister, Mrs. Forster-Nietzsche,

> My brother's most personal work; it is the history of his most individual experience, of his friendships, ideals, raptures, bitterest disappointments and sorrows. Above it all, however, there soars, transfiguring it, the image of his greatest hopes and remotest aims. My brother had the figure of Zarathustra in his mind from his very earliest youth. He once told me that even as a child he had dreamt of him. . . . All Zarathustra's views, as also his personality, were early conceptions of my brother's mind.

Here we encounter Nietzche's ideal Superman, and his lyrical philosophizing on life, death, and virtue. Zarathustra is a fictional character created by Nietzche as a visionary spokesman-prophet for his philosophy, but the name itself is the German version of *Zoroaster*, a Persian prophet who founded Zoroastrianism. Niezsche himself wrote that "I had to do a *Persian* the honor of identifying him with this creature of my fancy. Persians were the first to take a broad and comprehensive view of history. Every series of evolutions, according to them, was presided over by a prophet; and every prophet had his "Hazar," his dynasty of a thousand years." Zarathustra, then, is Nietasche's would-be avatar of a new philosophical dynasty.

Nietzsche, from *Thus Spake Zarathustra*, translated by Thomas Caramon, Tulle, 1909.

ZARATHUSTRA'S PROLOGUE

1.

WHEN Zarathustra was 30 years old, he left his home and the lake of his home, and went into the mountains. There he enjoyed his spirit and his solitude, and for ten years did not weary of it. But at last his heart changed, and rising one morning with the rosy dawn, he went before the sun, and spake thus unto it:

Thou great star! What would be thy happiness if thou hadst not those for whom thou shinest!

For ten years hast thou climbed hither unto my cave; thou wouldst have wearied of thy light and of the journey; had it not been for me, mine eagle, and my serpent.

But we awaited thee every morning, took from thee thine overflow, and blessed thee for it.

Lo! I am weary of my wisdom, like the bee that hath gathered too much honey; I need hands outstretched to take it.

I would fain bestow and distribute, until the wise have once more become joyous in their folly, and the poor happy in their riches.

Therefore must I descend into the deep: as thou doest in the evening, when thou goest behind the sea, and givest light also to the nether-world, thou exuberant star!

Like thee must I *go down*, as men say, to whom I shall descend.

Bless me, then, thou tranquil eye, that canst behold even the greatest happiness without envy!

Bless the cup that is about to overflow, that the water may flow golden out of it, and carry everywhere the reflection of thy bliss!

Lo! This cup is again going to empty itself, and Zarathustra is again going to be a man.

Thus began Zarathustra's descent.

2.

Zarathustra went down the mountain alone, no one meeting him. When he entered the forest, however, there suddenly stood before him an old man, who had left his holy cot to seek roots. And thus spake the old man to Zarathustra:

"No stranger to me is this wanderer: many years ago passed he by. Zarathustra he was called; but he hath altered.

Then thou carriedst thine ashes into the mountains: wilt thou now carry thy fire into the valleys? Fearest thou not the incendiary's doom?

Yea, I recognise Zarathustra. Pure is his eye, and no loathing lurketh about his mouth. Goeth he not along like a dancer?

Altered is Zarathustra; a child hath Zarathustra become; an awakened one is Zarathustra: what wilt thou do in the land of the sleepers?

As in the sea hast thou lived in solitude, and it hath borne thee up. Alas, wilt thou now go ashore? Alas, wilt thou again drag thy body thyself?"

Zarathustra answered, "I love mankind."

"Why," said the saint, "did I go into the forest and the desert? Was it not because I loved men far too well?

Now I love God; men, I do not love. Man is a thing too imperfect for me. Love to man would be fatal to me."

Zarathustra answered, "What spake I of love! I am bringing gifts unto men."

"Give them nothing," said the saint. "Take rather part of their load, and carry it along with them—that will be most agreeable unto them, if only it be agreeable unto thee!

If, however, thou wilt give unto them, give them no more than an alms, and let them also beg for it!"

"No," replied Zarathustra, "I give no alms. I am not poor enough for that."

The saint laughed at Zarathustra, and spake thus: "Then see to it that they accept thy treasures! They are distrustful of anchorites, and do not believe that we come with gifts.

The fall of our footsteps ringeth too hollow through their streets. And just as at night, when they are in bed and hear a man abroad long before sunrise, so they ask themselves concerning us, 'Where goeth the thief?'

Go not to men, but stay in the forest! Go rather to the animals! Why not be like me, a bear amongst bears, a bird amongst birds?"

"And what doeth the saint in the forest?" asked Zarathustra.

The saint answered, "I make hymns and sing them; and in making hymns I laugh and weep and mumble. Thus do I praise God.

With singing, weeping, laughing, and mumbling do I praise the God who is my God. But what dost thou bring us as a gift?"

When Zarathustra had heard these words, he bowed to the saint and said, "What should I have to give thee! Let me rather hurry hence lest I take aught away from thee!" And thus they parted from one another, the old man and Zarathustra, laughing like schoolboys.

When Zarathustra was alone, however, he said to his heart, "Could it be possible! This old saint in the forest hath not yet heard of it, that *God is dead!*"

3.

When Zarathustra arrived at the nearest town which adjoineth the forest, he found many people assembled in the marketplace; for it had been announced that a rope dancer would give a performance. And Zarathustra spake thus unto the people:

I teach you the Superman. Man is something that is to be surpassed. What have ye done to surpass man?

All beings hitherto have created something beyond themselves, and ye want to be the ebb of that great tide, and would rather go back to the beast than surpass man?

What is the ape to man? A laughingstock, a thing of shame. And just the same shall man be to the Superman: a laughingstock, a thing of shame.

Ye have made your way from the worm to man, and much within you is still worm. Once were ye apes, and even yet man is more of an ape than any of the apes.

Even the wisest among you is only a disharmony and hybrid of plant and phantom. But do I bid you become phantoms or plants?

Lo, I teach you the Superman!

The Superman is the meaning of the earth. Let your will say, 'The Superman *shall be* the meaning of the earth!'

I conjure you, my brethren, *remain true to the earth*, and believe not those who speak unto you of superearthly hopes! Poisoners are they, whether they know it or not.

Despisers of life are they, decaying ones and poisoned ones themselves, of whom the earth is weary; so away with them!

Once blasphemy against God was the greatest blasphemy; but God died, and therewith also those blasphemers. To blaspheme the earth is now the most dreadful sin, and to rate the heart of the unknowable higher than the meaning of the earth!

Once the soul looked contemptuously on the body, and then that contempt was the supreme thing—the soul wished the body meager, ghastly, and famished. Thus it thought to escape from the body and the earth.

Oh, that soul was itself meager, ghastly, and famished; and cruelty was the delight of that soul!

But ye, also, my brethren, tell me: what doth your body say about your soul? Is your soul not poverty and pollution and wretched self-complacency?

Verily, a polluted stream is man. One must be a sea, to receive a polluted stream without becoming impure.

Lo, I teach you the Superman: he is that sea; in him can your great contempt be submerged.

What is the greatest thing ye can experience? It is the hour of great contempt. The hour in which even your happiness becometh loathsome unto you, and so also your reason and virtue.

The hour when ye say, "What good is my happiness! It is poverty and pollution and wretched self-complacency. But my happiness should justify existence itself!"

The hour when ye say, "What good is my reason! Doth it long for knowledge as the lion for his food? It is poverty and pollution and wretched self-complacency!"

The hour when ye say, "What good is my virtue! As yet it hath not made me passionate. How weary I am of my good and my bad! It is all poverty and pollution and wretched self-complacency!"

The hour when ye say, "What good is my justice! I do not see that I am fervor and fuel. The just, however, are fervor and fuel!"

The hour when we say, "What good is my pity! Is not pity the cross on which he is nailed who loveth man? But my pity is not a crucifixion."

Have ye ever spoken thus? Have ye ever cried thus? Ah! Would that I had heard you crying thus!

It is not your sin—it is your self-satisfaction that crieth unto heaven; your very sparingness in sin crieth unto heaven!

Where is the lightning to lick you with its tongue? Where is the frenzy with which ye should be inoculated?

Lo, I teach you the Superman: he is that lightning, he is that frenzy!

When Zarathustra had thus spoken, one of the people called out, "We have now heard enough of the rope dancer; it is time now for us to see him!" And all the people laughed at Zarathustra. But the rope dancer, who thought the words applied to him, began his performance.

4.

Zarathustra, however, looked at the people and wondered. Then he spake thus:

Man is a rope stretched between the animal and the Superman—a rope over an abyss.

A dangerous crossing, a dangerous wayfaring, a dangerous looking-back, a dangerous trembling and halting.

What is great in man is that he is a bridge and not a goal: what is lovable in man is that he is an *over-going* and a *down-going*.

I love those that know not how to live except as down-goers, for they are the over-goers.

I love the great despisers, because they are the great adorers, and arrows of longing for the other shore.

I love those who do not first seek a reason beyond the stars for going down and being sacrifices, but sacrifice themselves to the earth, that the earth of the Superman may hereafter arrive.

I love him who liveth in order to know, and seeketh to know in order that the Superman may hereafter live. Thus seeketh he his own down-going.

I love him who laboreth and inventeth, that he may build the house for the Superman, and prepare for him earth, animal, and plant: for thus seeketh he his own down-going.

I love him who loveth his virtue, for virtue is the will to down-going, and an arrow of longing.

I love him who reserveth no share of spirit for himself, but wanteth to be wholly the spirit of his virtue, thus walketh he as spirit over the bridge.

I love him who maketh his virtue his inclination and destiny, thus, for the sake of his virtue, he is willing to live on, or live no more.

I love him who desireth not too many virtues. One virtue is more of a virtue than two, because it is more of a knot for one's destiny to cling to.

I love him whose soul is lavish, who wanteth no thanks and doth not give back: for he always bestoweth, and desireth not to keep for himself.

I love him who is ashamed when the dice fall in his favor, and who then asketh: "Am I a dishonest player?"—for he is willing to succumb.

I love him who scattereth golden words in advance of his deeds, and always doeth more than he promiseth, for he seeketh his own down-going.

I love him who justifieth the future ones, and redeemeth the past ones, for he is willing to succumb through the present ones.

I love him who chasteneth his God, because he loveth his God, for he must succumb through the wrath of his God.

I love him whose soul is deep even in the wounding, and may succumb through a small matter, thus goeth he willingly over the bridge.

I love him whose soul is so overfull that he forgetteth himself, and all things are in him, thus all things become his down-going.

I love him who is of a free spirit and a free heart: thus is his head only the bowels of his heart; his heart, however, causeth his down-going.

I love all who are like heavy drops falling one by one out of the dark cloud that lowereth over man; they herald the coming of the lightning, and succumb as heralds.

Lo, I am a herald of the lightning, and a heavy drop out of the cloud. The lightning, however, is the *Superman*.

5.

When Zarathustra had spoken these words, he again looked at the people, and was silent. "There they stand," said he to his heart, "there they laugh—they understand me not; I am not the mouth for these ears.

Must one first batter their ears, that they may learn to hear with their eyes? Must one clatter like kettledrums and penitential preachers? Or do they only believe the stammerer?

They have something whereof they are proud. What do they call it, that which maketh them proud? Culture, they call it; it distinguisheth them from the goatherds.

They dislike, therefore, to hear of 'contempt' of themselves. So I will appeal to their pride.

I will speak unto them of the most contemptible thing that, however, is *the last man!*"

And thus spake Zarathustra unto the people:

It is time for man to fix his goal. It is time for man to plant the germ of his highest hope.

Still is his soil rich enough for it. But that soil will one day be poor and exhausted, and no lofty tree will any longer be able to grow thereon.

Alas! There cometh the time when man will no longer launch the arrow of his longing beyond man—and the string of his bow will have unlearned to whizz!

I tell you: one must still have chaos in one, to give birth to a dancing star. I tell you: ye have still chaos in you.

Alas! There cometh the time when man will no longer give birth to any star. Alas! There cometh the time of the most despicable man, who can no longer despise himself.

Lo! I show you *the last man*.

"What is love? What is creation? What is longing? What is a star?" So asketh the last man and blinketh.

The earth hath then become small, and on it there hoppeth the last man who maketh everything small. His species is ineradicable like that of the ground flea; the last man liveth longest.

"We have discovered happiness," say the last men, and blink thereby.

They have left the regions where it is hard to live, for they need warmth. One still loveth one's neighbor and rubbeth against him, for one needeth warmth.

Turning ill and being distrustful, they consider sinful; they walk warily. He is a fool who still stumbleth over stones or men!

A little poison now and then; that maketh pleasant dreams. And much poison at last for a pleasant death.

One still no worketh, for work is a pastime. But one is careful lest the pastime should hurt one.

One no longer becometh poor or rich; both are too burdensome. Who still wanteth to rule? Who still wanteth to obey? Both are too burdensome.

No shepherd, and one herd! Every one wanteth the same; every one is equal: he who hath other sentiments goeth voluntarily into the madhouse.

"Formerly all the world was insane"—say the subtlest of them, and blink thereby.

They are clever and know all that hath happened, so there is no end to their raillery. People still fall out, but are soon reconciled—otherwise it spoileth their stomachs.

They have their little pleasures for the day, and their little pleasures for the night, but they have a regard for health.

"We have discovered happiness," say the last men, and blink thereby.

And here ended the first discourse of Zarathustra, which is also called "The Prologue", for at this point the shouting and mirth of the multitude interrupted him. "Give us this last man, O Zarathustra," they called out, "make us into these last men! Then will we make thee a present of the Superman!" And all the people exulted and smacked their lips. Zarathustra, however, turned sad, and said to his heart:

"They understand me not. I am not the mouth for these ears.

Too long, perhaps, have I lived in the mountains; too much have I hearkened unto the brooks and trees. Now do I speak unto them as unto the goatherds.

Calm is my soul, and clear, like the mountains in the morning. But they think me cold, and a mocker with terrible jests.

And now do they look at me and laugh; and while they laugh they hate me too. There is ice in their laughter."

6.

Then, however, something happened which made every mouth mute and every eye fixed. In the meantime, of course, the rope dancer had commenced his performance: he had come out at a little door, and was going along the rope which was stretched between two towers, so that it hung above the marketplace and the people. When he was just midway across, the little door opened once more, and a gaudily dressed fellow like a buffoon sprang out, and went rapidly after the first one. "Go on, halt-foot," cried his frightful voice, "go on, lazybones, interloper, sallow-face!—lest I tickle thee with my heel! What dost thou here between the towers? In the tower is the place for thee, thou shouldst be locked up; to one better than thyself thou blockest the way!" And with every word he came nearer and nearer the first one. When, however, he was but a step behind, there happened the frightful thing which made every mouth mute and every eye fixed: he uttered a yell like a devil, and jumped over the other who was in his way. The latter, however, when he thus saw his rival triumph, lost at the same time his head and his footing on the rope; he threw his pole away, and shot downwards faster than it, like an eddy of arms and legs, into the depth. The marketplace and the people were like the sea when the storm cometh on: they all flew apart and in disorder, especially where the body was about to fall.

Zarathustra, however, remained standing, and just beside him fell the body, badly injured and disfigured, but not yet dead. After a while consciousness returned to the shattered man, and he saw Zarathustra kneeling beside him. "What art thou doing there?" said he at last, "I knew long ago that the devil would trip me up. Now he draggeth me to hell. Wilt thou prevent him?"

"On mine honor, my friend," answered Zarathustra, "there is nothing of all that whereof thou speakest: there is no devil and no hell. Thy soul will be dead even sooner than thy body. Fear, therefore, nothing any more!"

The man looked up distrustfully. "If thou speakest the truth," said he, "I lose nothing when I lose my life. I am not much more than an animal which hath been taught to dance by blows and scanty fare."

"Not at all," said Zarathustra, "thou hast made danger thy calling; therein there is nothing contemptible. Now thou perishest by thy calling; therefore will I bury thee with mine own hands."

When Zarathustra had said this the dying one did not reply further; but he moved his hand as if he sought the hand of Zarathustra in gratitude.

7.

Meanwhile the evening came on, and the marketplace veiled itself in gloom. Then the people dispersed, for even curiosity and terror become fatigued. Zarathustra, however still sat beside the dead man on the ground, absorbed in thought and forgot the time. But at last it became night, and a cold wind blew upon the lonely one. Then arose Zarathustra and said to his heart:

Verily, a fine catch of fish hath Zarathustra made today! It is not a man he hath caught, but a corpse.

Somber is human life, and as yet without meaning: a buffoon may be fateful to it.

I want to teach men the sense of their existence, which is the Superman, the lightning out of the dark cloud—man.

But still am I far from them, and my sense speaketh not unto their sense. To men I am still something between a fool and a corpse.

Gloomy is the night, gloomy are the ways of Zarathustra. Come, thou cold and stiff companion! I carry thee to the place where I shall bury thee with mine own hands.

8.

When Zarathustra had said this to his heart, he put the corpse upon his shoulders and set out on his way. Yet had he not gone a hundred steps, when there stole a man up to him and whispered in his ear—and lo! he that spake was the buffoon from the tower. "Leave this town, O Zarathustra," said he, "there are too many here who hate thee. The good and just hate thee, and call thee their enemy and despiser; the believers in the orthodox belief hate thee, and call thee a danger to the multitude. It was thy good fortune to be laughed at; and verily thou spakest like a buffoon. It was thy good fortune to associate with the dead dog; by so humiliating thyself thou hast saved thy life today. Depart, however, from this town, or tomorrow I shall jump over thee, a living man over a dead one." And when he had said this, the buffoon vanished; Zarathustra, however, went on through the dark streets.

At the gate of the town the gravediggers met him. They shone their torch on his face, and, recognizing Zarathustra, they sorely derided him. "Zarathustra is carrying away the dead dog; a fine thing that Zarathustra hath turned a gravedigger! For our hands are too cleanly for that roast. Will Zarathustra steal the bite from the devil? Well then, good luck to the repast! If only the devil is not a better thief than Zarathustra! He will steal them both, he will eat them both!" And they laughed among themselves, and put their heads together.

Zarathustra made no answer thereto, but went on his way. When he had gone on for two hours, past forests and swamps, he had heard too much of the hungry howling of the wolves, and he himself became hungry. So he halted at a lonely house in which a light was burning.

"Hunger attacketh me," said Zarathustra, "like a robber. Among forests and swamps my hunger attacketh me, and late in the night.

"Strange humors hath my hunger. Often it cometh to me only after a repast, and all day it hath failed to come: where hath it been?"

And thereupon Zarathustra knocked at the door of the house. An old man appeared, who carried a light, and asked, "Who cometh unto me and my bad sleep?"

"A living man and a dead one," said Zarathustra. "Give me something to eat and drink, I forgot it during the day. He that feedeth the hungry refresheth his own soul, saith wisdom."

The old man withdrew, but came back immediately and offered Zarathustra bread and wine. "A bad country for the hungry," said he, "that is why I live here. Animal and man come unto me, the anchorite. But bid thy companion eat and drink also, he is wearier than thou." Zarathustra answered, "My companion is dead; I shall hardly be able to persuade him to eat." "That doth not concern me," said the old man sullenly, "he that knocketh at my door must take what I offer him. Eat, and fare ye well!"

Thereafter Zarathustra again went on for two hours, trusting to the path and the light of the stars: for he was an experienced night walker, and liked to look into the face of all that slept. When the morning dawned, however, Zarathustra found himself in a thick forest, and no path was any longer visible. He then put the dead man in a hollow tree at his head—for he wanted to protect him from the wolves—and laid himself down on the ground and moss. And immediately he fell asleep, tired in body, but with a tranquil soul.

9.

Long slept Zarathustra, and not only the rosy dawn passed over his head, but also the morning. At last however, his eyes opened, and amazedly he gazed into the forest and the stillness; amazedly he gazed into himself. Then he arose quickly, like a seafarer who all at once seeth the land; and he shouted for joy, for he saw a new truth. And he spake thus to his heart:

A light hath dawned upon me: I need companions—living ones, not dead companions and corpses, which I carry with me where I will.

But I need living companions, who will follow me because they want to follow themselves—and to the place where I will.

A light hath dawned upon me. Not to the people is Zarathustra to speak, but to companions! Zarathustra shall not be the herd's herdsman and hound!

To allure many from the herd—for that purpose have I come. The people and the herd must be angry with me: a robber shall Zarathustra be called by the herdsmen.

Herdsmen, I say, but they call themselves the good and just. Herdsmen, I say, but they call themselves the believers in the orthodox belief.

Behold the good and just! Whom do they hate most? Him who breaketh up their tables of values, the breaker, the lawbreaker—he, however, is the creator.

Behold the believers of all beliefs! Whom do they hate most? Him who breaketh up their tables of values, the breaker, the lawbreaker—he, however, is the creator.

Companions, the creator seeketh, not corpses—and not herds or believers either. Fellow creators the creator seeketh—those who grave new values on new tables.

Companions, the creator seeketh, and fellow reapers: for everything is ripe for the harvest with him. But he lacketh the hundred sickles, so he plucketh the ears of corn and is vexed.

Companions, the creator seeketh, and such as know how to whet their sickles. Destroyers, will they be called, and despisers of good and evil. But they are the reapers and rejoicers.

Fellow creators, Zarathustra seeketh; fellow reapers and fellow rejoicers, Zarathustra seeketh: what hath he to do with herds and herdsmen and corpses!

And thou, my first companion, rest in peace! Well have I buried thee in thy hollow tree; well have I hid thee from the wolves.

But I part from thee; the time hath arrived. Twixt rosy dawn and rosy dawn there came unto me a new truth.

I am not to be a herdsman, I am not to be a gravedigger. Not any more will I discourse unto the people; for the last time have I spoken unto the dead.

With the creators, the reapers, and the rejoicers will I associate: the rainbow will I show them, and all the stairs to the Superman.

To the lone dwellers will I sing my song, and to the twain dwellers; and unto him who hath still ears for the unheard, will I make the heart heavy with my happiness.

I make for my goal, I follow my course; over the loitering and tardy will I leap. Thus let my on-going be their down-going!

10.

This had Zarathustra said to his heart when the sun stood at noon-tide. Then he looked inquiringly aloft, for he heard above him the sharp call of a bird. And behold! An eagle swept through the air in wide circles, and on it hung a serpent, not like a prey, but like a friend, for it kept itself coiled round the eagle's neck.

"They are mine animals," said Zarathustra, and rejoiced in his heart.

"The proudest animal under the sun, and the wisest animal under the sun—they have come out to reconnoiter.

They want to know whether Zarathustra still liveth. Verily, do I still live?

More dangerous have I found it among men than among animals; in dangerous paths goeth Zarathustra. Let mine animals lead me!"

When Zarathustra had said this, he remembered the words of the saint in the forest. Then he sighed and spake thus to his heart:

"Would that I were wiser! Would that I were wise from the very heart, like my serpent!

But I am asking the impossible. Therefore do I ask my pride to go always with my wisdom!

And if my wisdom should some day forsake me—alas! it loveth to fly away!—may my pride then fly with my folly!"

Thus began Zarathustra's decent.

PART I

XXII.—The Bestowing Virtue

1.

When Zarathustra had taken leave of the town to which his heart was attached, the name of which is "The Pied Cow," there followed him many people who called themselves his disciples, and kept him company. Thus came they to a crossroad. Then Zarathustra told them that he now wanted to go alone; for he was fond of going alone. His disciples, however, presented him at his departure with a staff, on the golden handle of which a serpent twined round the sun. Zarathustra rejoiced on account of the staff, and supported himself thereon; then spake he thus to his disciples:

Tell me, pray: how came gold to the highest value? Because it is uncommon, and unprofiting, and beaming, and soft in luster; it always bestoweth itself.

Only as image of the highest virtue came gold to the highest value. Goldlike, beameth the glance of the bestower. Gold luster maketh peace between moon and sun.

Uncommon is the highest virtue, and unprofiting, beaming is it, and soft of luster: a bestowing virtue is the highest virtue.

Verily, I divine you well, my disciples: ye strive like me for the bestowing virtue. What should ye have in common with cats and wolves?

It is your thirst to become sacrifices and gifts yourselves: and therefore have ye the thirst to accumulate all riches in your soul.

Insatiably striveth your soul for treasures and jewels, because your virtue is insatiable in desiring to bestow.

Ye constrain all things to flow towards you and into you, so that they shall flow back again out of your fountain as the gifts of your love.

Verily, an appropriator of all values must such bestowing love become; but healthy and holy, call I this selfishness.

Another selfishness is there, an all-too-poor and hungry kind, which would always steal—the selfishness of the sick, the sickly selfishness.

With the eye of the thief it looketh upon all that is lustrous; with the craving of hunger it measureth him who hath abundance; and ever doth it prowl round the tables of bestowers.

Sickness speaketh in such craving, and invisible degeneration; of a sickly body, speaketh the larcenous craving of this selfishness.

Tell me, my brother, what do we think bad, and worst of all? Is it not *degeneration*? And we always suspect degeneration when the bestowing soul is lacking.

Upward goeth our course from genera on to super genera. But a horror to us is the degenerating sense, which saith, "All for myself."

Upward soareth our sense: thus is it a simile of our body, a simile of an elevation. Such similes of elevations are the names of the virtues.

Thus goeth the body through history, a becomer and fighter. And the spirit—what is it to the body? Its fights' and victories' herald, its companion and echo.

Similes, are all names of good and evil; they do not speak out, they only hint. A fool who seeketh knowledge from them!

Give heed, my brethren, to every hour when your spirit would speak in similes: there is the origin of your virtue.

Elevated is then your body, and raised up; with its delight, enraptureth it the spirit, so that it becometh creator, and valuer, and lover, and everything's benefactor.

When your heart overfloweth broad and full like the river, a blessing and a danger to the lowlanders: there is the origin of your virtue.

When ye are exalted above praise and blame, and your will would command all things, as a loving one's will; there is the origin of your virtue.

When ye despise pleasant things, and the effeminate couch, and cannot couch far enough from the effeminate: there is the origin of your virtue.

When ye are willers of one will, and when that change of every need is needful to you: there is the origin of your virtue.

Verily, a new good and evil is it! Verily, a new deep murmuring, and the voice of a new fountain!

Power is it, this new virtue; a ruling thought is it, and around it a subtle soul, a golden sun, with the serpent of knowledge around it.

2.

Here paused Zarathustra awhile, and looked lovingly on his disciples. Then he continued to speak thus—and his voice had changed:

Remain true to the earth, my brethren, with the power of your virtue! Let your bestowing love and your knowledge be devoted to be the meaning of the earth! Thus do I pray and conjure you.

Let it not fly away from the earth and beat against eternal walls with its wings! Ah, there hath always been so much flown-away virtue!

Lead, like me, the flown-away virtue back to the earth—yea, back to body and life, that it may give to the earth its meaning, a human meaning!

A hundred times hitherto hath spirit as well as virtue flown away and blundered. Alas! In our body

dwelleth still all this delusion and blundering: body and will hath it there become.

A hundred times hitherto hath spirit as well as virtue attempted and erred. Yea, an attempt hath man been. Alas, much ignorance and error hath become embodied in us!

Not only the rationality of millenniums—also their madness, breaketh out in us. Dangerous is it to be an heir.

Still fight we step by step with the giant Chance, and over all mankind hath hitherto ruled nonsense, the lack of sense.

Let your spirit and your virtue be devoted to the sense of the earth, my brethren; let the value of everything be determined anew by you! Therefore shall ye be fighters! Therefore shall ye be creators!

Intelligently doth the body purify itself; attempting with intelligence it exalteth itself; to the discerners all impulses sanctify themselves; to the exalted the soul becometh joyful.

Physician, heal thyself: then wilt thou also heal thy patient. Let it be his best cure to see with his eyes him who maketh himself whole.

A thousand paths are there which have never yet been trodden, a thousand salubrities and hidden islands of life. Unexhausted and undiscovered is still man and man's world.

Awake and hearken, ye lonesome ones! From the future come winds with stealthy pinions, and to fine ears good tidings are proclaimed.

Ye lonesome ones of today, ye seceding ones, ye shall one day be a people. Out of you who have chosen yourselves, shall a chosen people arise—and out of it the Superman.

Verily, a place of healing shall the earth become! And already is a new odor diffused around it, a salvation-bringing odor—and a new hope!

3.

When Zarathustra had spoken these words, he paused, like one who had not said his last word; and long did he balance the staff doubtfully in his hand. At last he spake thus—and his voice had changed:

I now go alone, my disciples! Ye also now go away, and alone! So will I have it.

Verily, I advise you: depart from me, and guard yourselves against Zarathustra! And better still: be ashamed of him! Perhaps he hath deceived you.

The man of knowledge must be able not only to love his enemies, but also to hate his friends.

One requiteth a teacher badly if one remain merely a scholar. And why will ye not pluck at my wreath?

Ye venerate me; but what if your veneration should some day collapse? Take heed lest a statue crush you!

Ye say, ye believe in Zarathustra? But of what account is Zarathustra! Ye are my believers, but of what account are all believers!

Ye had not yet sought yourselves, then did ye find me. So do all believers; therefore all belief is of so little account.

Now do I bid you lose me and find yourselves; and only when ye have all denied me, will I return unto you.

Verily, with other eyes, my brethren, shall I then seek my lost ones; with another love shall I then love you.

And once again shall ye have become friends unto me, and children of one hope: then will I be with you for the third time, to celebrate the great noontide with you.

And it is the great noontide, when man is in the middle of his course between animal and Superman, and celebrateth his advance to the evening as his highest hope, for it is the advance to a new morning.

At such time will the down-goer bless himself, that he should be an over-goer; and the sun of his knowledge will be at noontide.

"Dead are all the Gods: now do we desire the Superman to live." Let this be our final will at the great noontide!

Thus spake Zarathustra.

STUDY QUESTIONS: NIETESCHE, *THUS SPAKE ZARATHUSTRA*

1. How does Nietzsche announce the death of the Gods? How then does he say he loves God?
2. What role does the Superman play in the death of the Gods?
3. Why must humanity surpass itself?
4. How does happiness become loathsome?
5. Zarathustra claims humanity will view him as something between a fool and a corpse. Why?
6. What does Zarathustra mean by virtue?
7. How is virtue attained?
8. Can everyone attain virtue? Why?

Philosophical Bridges: Nietzsche's Influence

Nietzsche inspired many subsequent philosophers, writers, and literary theorists, from existentialists to deconstructionists such as Jacques Derrida. His perspectival theory of truth and instrumentalist theory of knowledge influenced a wide range of philosophers, including philosophers of science such as Thomas Kuhn and Paul Feyerabend who, like Nietzsche, argue that facts cannot be separated from values, that even the most rigorous scientific method involves interpretation, and that even the most precise observation is theory-laden.

Nietzsche's books continue to inspire a broad and influential following of admirers across the disciplines. George Bernard Shaw, Thomas Mann, and Hermann Hesse are among the writers who drew great inspiration from his works. Among philosophers, Karl Jaspers, Martin Heidegger, and Jean-Paul Sartre were all influenced by him, as were Jacques Derrida and Michel Foucault. Sigmund Freud also found in Nietzsche great insights into the nature of human psychology and the forces of the will that structure it.

Philosophical Bridges: The Existentialist Influence

The existentialist movement that grew out of the ideas planted in the nineteenth century by Kierkegaard, Nietzche, and others produced some of the greatest existentialist thinkers of the twentieth century: Karl Jaspers, Martin Heidegger, and Jean-Paul Sartre, who helped propel existentialism into one of the most widely influential and best known philosophies in the world. Their influence went not only beyond philosophy into literature and art, inspiring writers, painters, playwrights, and filmmakers, but also spawned other, related movements, even among scientists, most notably two leading nineteenth century physicists, Gustav Kirchhoff (1824–1887) and Ernst Mach (1838–1916). Through Richard Avenarius (1843–1896), who helped influence Mach and also William James, the ideas were picked up by research psychologists such as Wilhelm Wundt (1832–1920), founder of the first psychological laboratory. Charles Peirce, William James and to a lesser degree John Dewey drew upon the same sources for their development of pragmatism, while F. S. C. Schiller used them as the foundation for his moral theory. But the most enduring existentialist philosophy as such was the crowning achievement of the French school, led by monumental figures such as Jean-Paul Sartre, Camus, and Simone de Beauvoir. In the United States existentialism thrives mainly in literature and film—Hemingway is arguably the most famous existential literary figure, and many Hollywood directors, writers, and actors today continue to give prominent voice to existentialist themes.

BIBLIOGRAPHY

GENERAL

Gill, R. and Sherman, E. *The Fabric of Existentialism: Philosophical and Literary Sources*, Prentice Hall, 1973

Kaufmann, W., ed., *Existentialism from Dostoevsky to Sartre*, World Publishing Concept, 1956

Spanos, W. *A Casebook on Existentialism*, Crowell, 1966

Wahl, J. *A Short History of Existentialism*, Philosophical Library, 1949

KIERKEGAARD

Primary

Bretall, R., ed., *A Kierkegaard Anthology*, Princeton University Press, 1946

Lowrie, W., *Fear and Trembling and the Sickness Unto Death*, Princeton University Press, 1973

Kierkegaard's Writings, vols. I–XXV, Princeton University Press, 1978–

Secondary

Anderson, S. L. *On Kierkegaard*, Wadsworth, 2000

Bretall, R. ed., *A Kierkegaard Anthology*, Modern Library, 1936

Evans, S. *Kierkegaard's "Fragments" and "Postscript,"* Humanities Press, 1983

Gardiner, P. *Kierkegaard*, Oxford University Press, 1988

Kierkegaard, Søren, *Fear and Trembling Unto Death*, trans. W. Lowrie, Princeton University Press, 1974

Kirmmse, B., ed., *Encounters with Kierkegaard: A Life as Seen by His Contemporarires*, Princeton University Press, 1966

Kirmmse, B., *Kierkegaard in Golden Age Denmark*, Indiana University Press, 1990

Lowrie, W. *A Short Life of Kierkegaard*, Princeton University Press, 1970

Thomson, J. ed., *Kierkegaard: A Collection of Critical Essays*, Anchor Books, 1972

NIETZSCHE

Primary

Human All too Human, translated by Hollingdale, R. J., Cambridge University Press, 1986

The Gay Science, translated by Kaufmann, W., Random House, 1974

Thus Spake Zarathustra, trans. R. J. Hollingdale, Penguin Books, 1969

Beyond Good and Evil, trans. W. Kaufmann, Random House, 1966

The Geneology of Morals, trans. F. Golffing, Doubleday, 1956

Twilight of the Idols, trans. R. J. Hollingdale, Penguin, 1984

The Antichrist, trans. R. J. Hollingdale, Penguin, 1984

Ecce Homo, trans. R. J. Hollingdale, Penguin, 1983

The Will to Power, translated by Kaufmann, W. and Hollingdale, R. J., Random House, 1968

Secondary

Copleston, F. C., *Friedrich Nietzsche: A Philosopher of Culture,* Barnes & Noble, 1975

Danto, A., *Nietzsche As Philosopher,* Macmillan, 1965

Hollingdale, R. J., *Nietzsche,* Routledge & Kegan Paul, 1973

Kaufmann, W., *Nietzsche, Philosopher, Psychologist, Anti-Christ,* Princeton University Press, 1968

Nietzsche, F., *The Complete Works of Nietzsche,* ed. O. Levy, Foulis, 1910

Richardson, J., *Nietzsche's System,* Oxford University Press, 1996

Solomon, R., and Higgins, K., eds., *Reading Nietasche,* Oxford University Press, 1988

Steinhart, E., *On Nietzsche,* Wadsworth, 2000

SECTION IV

THE SOCIAL PHILOSOPHERS

PROLOGUE

Most people believe in a mind-independent real world that is directly experienced. Let us call this, the view that children unprompted by philosophers naturally come to, "naïve realism." There are two components to naïve realism:

1. there exists a mind-independent real world, and
2. the mind-independent real world is directly experienced.

Among the philosophers presented thus far in this volume who have taken a stand for or against (1), none yet have accepted (2), though in subsequent chapters we will see some who accept (2). Various idealist responses to (1) deny the existence of a mind-independent world, whereas various representationalist responses, most notably the neo-Kantians, accept (1) but argue that the real world is in part created by the mind (the phenomenal world) and in part created by things-in-themselves (the noumenal world). This is an oversimplification, of course, but the point is that the views thus far considered have all been built on the notion that any two-way relation between the real world and the mind is predicated on the notion of individual minds affecting one and the same public reality. In other words, only one world exists within which we are each individuals participating in the same reality. That is, reality is itself an objective phenomenon. Now, we've seen how Schopenhauer moves in a new direction, followed by Kierkegaard and Nietzsche. In Shopenhauer's view, the thing-in-itself behind the phenomenal world is *the will*, which he equates with the body, implying that subjectivity can be transcended by seeing to what extent different minds agree about whether an experience is real. And given the active view of the mind's powers by Kant, Hegel, Fichte, Schelling, Kierkegaard and Nietzsche, the verification of what is and what is not real occurs in some sort of social arena.

Many of the subsequent philosophers were influenced by this line of thought. Comte's positivism and the logical positivism of the twentieth century are both based on the notion that public, that is, social, verification is a necessary condition for truth and meaning. These new socially minded philosophies coincided with what has come to be known as the

Industrial Revolution, a term coined by the English economic historian Arnold Toynbee (1889–1975) to describe Europe's economic development from 1760 to 1840, is the backdrop for a philosophical shift in thought from epistemology and metaphysics toward social engineering that occurred during this time. Traditionally, the "product" of philosophy, its "end goal," so to speak, was *thought*, in the following sense: the philosophical enlightenment process takes you from one set of thoughts to another, from the false to the true. This of course has some obvious exceptions, such as during the Epicurean and Stoic periods, when the emphasis was not on the having of correct or sound judgments but, rather, the attainment of certain sorts of emotional states and the promotion of psychological well-being. Such a shift of philosophy into the social arena during the latter part of the nineteenth century is evident in the shift in Kierkegaard, Nietzsche, and Marx from the search for new and better epistemologies and metaphysical systems to building, instead, a new kind of human individual. The shift is achieved not with new critiques of reason but, rather, especially in the works of Nietzsche and Marx, on critiques of society and its institutions.

COMTE (1798–1857)

Biographical History

Isidore Auguste Marie Françoise Comte was born in Montpelier, France. His father was the local tax collector. In his second year at the famous École Polytechnique in Paris he took part in a huge student rebellion that ended up closing the school. Mathematically gifted, he used his natural skills to tutor students in mathematics while he continued studying philosophy on his own and privately with various philosophers around town. He befriended Count Henri de Saint-Simon, a brilliant intellectual who inspired many of Comte's later ideas. In 1826 Comte had begun to unveil a new philosophy he was developing in a series of lectures in Paris when he suffered a nervous breakdown and abandoned the project. When in 1833 the École Polytechnique reopened he applied for and got the position of entrance examiner. When the administration discovered two years later that he had taken a major part in the revolution that had closed the school, he argued with them over all the issues against which he had protested, and they fired him. By then, however, Comte had become well-known as a brilliant and gifted mind, admired by many famous figures including, in England, John Stuart Mill, who called him an "original and bold new thinker" and provided him with a series of grants and financial support, as did many other figures, such as Maximilien Littré, one of the most famous philologists and lexicographers of the time.

Comte is one of the founders of the philosophical movement known as positivism (see below), and more or less single-handedly created the discipline of social science, or *sociology*, the term he coined for the systematic study of society.

Comte married, but it was not a happy union. It ended after eighteen bitter years in divorce; he then suddenly found the love of his life, Clotilde de Vaux, another brilliant mind, and their relationship was as deep and profound as it was unfortunately short-lived; she died within a year. He idolized her and she influenced his later development of the positivist society, particularly the important role of women within it, a radical idea for the time, championed also by his patron Mill. He continued to write and develop his ideas until his death in Paris in 1857.

Philosophical Overview

Comte's first published work, *A Plan for the Scientific Works Necessary to Reorganize Society* (1822), lays out a bold plan for reorganizing society and planning for the future betterment of humanity. Four years later, his *Consideration on the Spiritual Power* (1826) outlines what would later become his "religion of humanity," a secular spiritual society based on human values that rejects church authority and otherworldly spiritual ideas of traditional religious orthodoxies. His major work, the *Course of the Positive Philosophy* (in six volumes, 1842–1854) presents his theory and methods of sociology and lays out a plan for the ideal human society.

Comte was a major force behind the nineteenth-century shift from metaphysical to scientific philosophy. Science, then and now, is predicated on a method of acquiring knowledge based on some sort of social verification, what we might think of as "social epistemology." Think of public verification of evidence, reproducibility of results by others, independent teams of researchers cross-checking each other's results, and so on. In that sense science is a social, not an individual, activity. In many ways this is just the opposite of the Cartesian certainty (as propounded by René Descartes) of, say, "I think, therefore I am," wherein knowledge is grounded in the individual's own internal relation to truth. The "scientific" meaning of truth is something akin to "publicly verified."

In Comte's view, the physical world itself is defined with what can be sensed immediately in experience. Think of it this way: the "im" of *immediate* has the same meaning as in *immoral*, meaning, "not." Thus *immediate* means "not mediated." Perception in his view is thus not a middleman between the external physical world and conscious experience but the direct apprehension of physical reality, the source of knowledge in so far as sense experience does not have to pass through any other medium, no additional stems, no symbolic, theoretic, or inferential construction necessary. To distinguish it from *representialism*, let us call this sort of view *presentationalism*. Thus, according to Comte's presentationalist view of perception, knowledge is given in terms of whatever is directly and immediately present in experience. If one is a naïve realist (see previous, in the Prologue), then what is immediately present to the mind are *physical presentations* and one is a *physical presentationalist*. If, as for instance Schopenhauer argues, what is immediately present to the mind are phenomenal objects, then one is a *phenomenal presentationalist*. Typically, the idealists we studied in Section II, then, are all phenomenal presentationalists. Whereas Materialists, such as Comte but also Marx are *physical* presentationalists.

One can think of a number of obvious objections, the very sorts of arguments that idealists put forth, for instance, but in Comte's view, the search for the underlying causes of anything, up to and including experience, is in vain and doomed to failure. (Recall Kant's antinomies of reason.) Comte thus simply rejects any allusion to causes as agents or forces (recall Hume's criticism of causality). The question, then, is what the phenomena in our experience are, namely, to what they refer: what do phenomena denote? Comte's profound answer may come as a surprise: *mathematical functions* or *equations*. These are the actual designated objects of our phenomenal conscious states. Now, mathematical functions and equations are, themselves, not physical entities. Rather, they are conceptual, abstract. Many physicists before and since have either held this sort of view or alluded to it, from the great Isaac Newton to contemporary quantum physicists. What is before the conscious mind, the phenomena in experience, refer to or denote are not some sort of Kantian unknowable objects, things-in-themselves forever and utterly beyond experience, but mathematically knowable structures. This move turns away from the introspective philosophies that put psychological states as the epistemological bearers of truth, in favor of a public, sociological realm of cross-verification, "social facts," and the birth of a new science of sociology. For in Comte's view his methods don't just apply to the worlds but also to the social realm.

Comte is radically opposed to religion, especially organized religion, just as much as Nietzsche, Kierkegaard, and Marx, and calls for the eradication of all religion basically because he sees religion as standing in the way of human progress. He argues that in education we should replace religious conditioning with a new and improved "calendar of saints," consisting of philosophers and scientists, businessmen and politicians, and artists, a list that would include people like John Stuart Mill, Adam Smith, Dante, and Shakespeare.

To grasp fully the profundity and completeness of Comte's vast philosophical system, one must work through his last published work, *The Philosophy of Mathematics*. Unfortunately, this work has been systematically ignored, not just by his contemporaries but by many of his followers, especially those who have since come to call themselves sociologists. The reason is that this work integrates the social aspects of his thinking with his overall philosophy of reality and theory of knowledge, with a call to a return of philosophy in particular and the knowledge seeking enterprise in general to the Pythagorean mysteries, and calls upon all intellectuals, but especially philosophers—as Plato had from the very beginning—to properly learn and understand mathematics.

COURSE OF THE POSITIVE PHILOSOPHY

In this work Comte presents his law of three theoretical conditions necessary for the proper intellectual development of human thought. The first, "theological or fictitious" stage is the most primitive because it relies on supernatural beings, supernatural explanations, and a commitment through faith to a system of beliefs derived not by testing of hypotheses but, rather, by rigid indoctrination into an orthodoxy. The second, "metaphysical" stage is better than the first stage, in so far as the supernatural entities are replaced with abstract ones. In the third, "positive" stage, the mind frees itself from the vain search for abstract or "absolute" notions by relying on reason and experience.

Before we can proceed in trying to understand ourselves and the world, Comte argues, we must first eradicate the error that we can know anything more than phenomena and their relations. This is in accord with the idealists. But he goes further, which in some ways anticipates the subsequent development of the "science" of phenomenology by other philosophers, most notably, Husserl (who also was a mathematician). For Comte claims that just as we cannot know the essence of phenomena, we cannot know their first causes nor their ultimate ends; all that the control of phenomena by experiment and observation reveals are the constant relations between the phenomena themselves, uniformities which we call laws. Therefore absolute knowledge in any realm is impossible because things-in-themselves, the essence of facts, and what is behind or behind experience, is beyond reach of the mind. Thus, while rejecting metaphysics, he avoids both idealism and empiricism.

Comte, from the *Cours de Philosophie positive*, Paris, 1830–1842, translated by Harriet Martineau. Reprinted from A. Comte's *The Positive Philosophy* (London, 1853).

INTRODUCTION

Chapter I: View of the Nature and Importance of the Positive Philosophy

. . . From the study of the development of the human mind, in all directions, and through all times, the discovery arises of a great fundamental law, to which it is necessarily subject, and which has a solid foundation of proof, both in the facts of our organization and in our historical experience. The law is this: that each of our leading conceptions, each branch of our knowledge, passes successively through three different theoretical conditions: the theological, or fictitious; the metaphysical, or abstract; and the scientific, or positive. In other words, the human mind, by its nature, employs in its progress three methods of philosophizing, the character of which is essentially different, and even radically opposed: namely, the theological method, the metaphysical, and the positive. Hence arise three philosophies, or general systems of conceptions on the aggregate of phenomena, each of which excludes the others. The first is the necessary point of departure of the human understanding; and the third is its fixed and definitive state. The second is merely a state of transition.

In the theological state, the human mind, seeking the essential nature of beings, the first and final causes (the origin and purpose) of all effects—in short, absolute knowledge—supposes all phenomena to be produced by the immediate action of supernatural beings.

In the metaphysical state, which is only a modification of the first, the mind supposes, instead of supernatural beings, abstract forces, veritable entities (that is, personified abstractions) inherent in all beings, and capable of producing all phenomena. What is called the explanation of phenomena is, in this stage, a mere reference of each to its proper entity.

In the final, the positive state, the mind has given over the vain search after absolute notions, the origin and destination of the universe, and the causes of phenomena, and applies itself to the study of their laws—that is, their invariable relations of succession and resemblance. Reasoning and observation, duly combined, are the means of this knowledge. What is now understood when we speak of an explanation of facts is simply the establishment of a connection between single phenomena and some general facts, the number of which continually diminishes with the progress of science.

The theological system arrived at the highest perfection of which it is capable when it substituted the providential action of a single Being for the varied operations of the numerous divinities which had been before imagined. In the same way, in the last stage of the metaphysical system, men substitute one great entity (nature) as the cause of all phenomena, instead of the multitude of entities at first supposed. In the same way, again, the ultimate perfection of the positive system would be (if such perfection could be hoped for) to represent all phenomena as particular aspects of a single general fact, such as gravitation, for instance.

The importance of the working of this general law will be established hereafter. At present, it must suffice to point out some of the grounds of it.

There is no science which, having attained the positive stage, does not bear marks of having passed through the others. Some time since it was (whatever it might be) composed, as we can now perceive, of metaphysical abstractions; and, further back in the course of time, it took its form from theological conceptions. We shall have only too much occasion to see, as we proceed, that our most advanced sciences still bear very evident marks of the two earlier periods through which they have passed.

The progress of the individual mind is not only an illustration, but an indirect evidence of that of the general mind. The point of departure of the individual and of the race being the same, the phases of the mind of a man correspond to the epochs of the mind of the race. Now, each of us is aware, if he looks back upon his own history, that he was a theologian in his childhood, a metaphysician in his youth, and a natural philosopher in his manhood. All men who are up to their age can verify this for themselves.

Besides the observation of facts, we have theoretical reasons in support of this law.

The most important of these reasons arises from the necessity that always exists for some theory to which to refer our facts, combined with the clear impossibility that, at the outset of human knowledge, men could have formed theories out of the observation of facts. All good intellects have repeated, since Bacon's time, that there can be no real knowledge but that which is based on observed facts. This is incontestable, in our present advanced stage; but, if we look back to the primitive stage of human knowledge, we shall see that it must have been otherwise then. If it is true that every theory must be based upon observed facts, it is equally true that facts cannot be observed without the guidance of some theory. Without such guidance, our facts would be desultory and fruitless; we could not retain them: for the most part we could not even perceive them.

Thus, between the necessity of observing facts in order to form a theory, and having a theory in order to observe facts, the human mind would have been entangled in a vicious circle, but for the natural opening afforded by theological conceptions. This is the fundamental reason for the theological character of the primitive philosophy. This necessity is confirmed by the perfect suitability of the theological philosophy to the earliest researches of the human mind. It is remarkable that the most inaccessible questions—those of the nature of beings, and the origin and purpose of phenomena—should be the first to occur in a primitive state, while those which are really within our reach are regarded as almost unworthy of serious study. The reason is evident enough: that experience alone can teach us the measure of our powers; and if men had not begun by an exaggerated estimate of what they can do, they would never have done all that they are capable of. Our organization requires this. At such a period there could have been no reception of a positive philosophy, whose function is to discover the laws of phenomena, and whose leading characteristic it is to regard as interdicted to human reason those sublime mysteries which theology explains, even to their minutest details, with the most attractive facility. It is just so under a practical view of the nature of the researches with which men first occupied themselves. Such inquiries offered the powerful charm of unlimited empire over the external world, a world destined wholly for our use, and involved in every way with our existence. The theological philosophy, presenting this view, administered exactly the stimulus necessary to incite the human mind to the irksome labour without which it could make no progress. We can now scarcely conceive of such a state of things, our reason having become sufficiently mature to enter upon laborious scientific researches, without needing any such stimulus as wrought upon the imaginations of astrologers and

alchemists. We have motive enough in the hope of discovering the laws of phenomena, with a view to the confirmation or rejection of a theory. But it could not be so in the earliest days; and it is to the chimeras of astrology and alchemy that we owe the long series of observations and experiments on which our positive science is based. Johannes Kepler felt this on behalf of astronomy, and Claude Louis Berthollet on behalf of chemistry. Thus was a spontaneous philosophy, the theological, the only possible beginning, method, and provisional system, out of which the positive philosophy could grow. It is easy, after this, to perceive how metaphysical methods and doctrines must have afforded the means of transition from the one to the other.

The human understanding, slow in its advance, could not step at once from the theological into the positive philosophy. The two are so radically opposed, that an intermediate system of conceptions has been necessary to render the transition possible. It is only in doing this, that metaphysical conceptions have any utility whatever. In contemplating phenomena, men substitute for supernatural direction a corresponding entity. This entity may have been supposed to be derived from the supernatural action: but it is more easily lost sight of, leaving attention free for the facts themselves, till, at length, metaphysical agents have ceased to be anything more than the abstract names of phenomena. It is not easy to say by what other process than this our minds could have passed from supernatural considerations to natural; from the theological system to the positive.

The law of human development being thus established, let us consider what is the proper nature of the positive philosophy.

As we have seen, the first characteristic of the positive philosophy is that it regards all phenomena as subjected to invariable natural *laws*. Our business is—seeing how vain is any research into what are called *causes*, whether first or final—to pursue an accurate discovery of these laws, with a view to reducing them to the smallest possible number. By speculating upon causes, we could solve no difficulty about origin and purpose. Our real business is to analyze accurately the circumstances of phenomena, and to connect them by the natural relations of succession and resemblance. The best illustration of this is in the case of the doctrine of gravitation. We say that the general phenomena of the universe are *explained* by it, because it connects under one head the whole immense variety of astronomical facts, exhibiting the constant tendency of atoms towards each other in direct proportion to their masses, and in inverse proportion to the squares of their distances, while the general fact itself is a mere extension of one which is perfectly familiar to us, and which we therefore say that we know—the weight of bodies on the surface of the earth. As to what weight and attraction are, we have nothing to do with that, for it is not a matter of knowledge at all. Theologians and metaphysicians may imagine and refine about such questions; but positive philosophy rejects them. When any attempt has been made to explain them, it has ended only in saying that attraction is universal weight, and that weight is terrestrial attraction: that is, that the two orders of phenomena are identical; which is the point from which the question set out. Again, Charles Fourier, in his fine series of researches on heat, has given us all the most important and precise laws of the phenomena of heat, and many large and new truths, without once inquiring into its nature, as his predecessors had done when they disputed about calorific matter and the action of an universal ether. In treating his subject in the positive method, he finds inexhaustible material for all his activity of research, without betaking himself to insoluble questions.

Before ascertaining the stage which the positive philosophy has reached, we must bear in mind that the different kinds of our knowledge have passed through the three stages of progress at different rates, and have not therefore arrived at the same time. The rate of advance depends on the nature of the knowledge in question, so distinctly that, as we shall see hereafter, this consideration constitutes an accessory to the fundamental law of progress. Any kind of knowledge reaches the positive stage early in proportion to its generality, simplicity, and independence of other departments. Astronomical science, which is above all made up of facts that are general, simple, and independent of other sciences, arrived first; then terrestrial physics; then chemistry; and, at length, physiology.

It is difficult to assign any precise date to this revolution in science. It may be said, like everything else, to have been always going on, and especially since the labours of Aristotle and the school of Alexandria, and then from the introduction of natural science into the west of Europe by the Arabs. But, if we must fix upon some marked period, to serve as a rallying point, it must be that, about two centuries ago, when the human mind was astir under the precepts of Bacon, the conceptions of Descartes, and the discoveries of Galileo. Then it was that the spirit of the positive philosophy rose up in opposition to that of the superstitious and scholastic systems which had hitherto obscured the true character of all science. Since that date, the progress of the positive philosophy, and the decline of the other two, have been so marked that no rational mind now doubts that the revolution is destined to go on to its completion—every branch of knowledge being, sooner or later, brought within the operation of positive philosophy. This is not yet the case. Some are still lying outside, and not till they are brought in will the positive philosophy possess that character of universality which is necessary to its definitive constitution.

In mentioning just now the four principal categories of phenomena—astronomical, physical, chemical, and physiological—there was an omission which will have been noticed. Nothing was said of social phenomena. Though involved with the physiological, social phenomena demand a distinct classification, both on account of their importance and of their difficulty. They are the most individual, the most complicated, the most dependent on all others; and therefore they must be the latest, even if they had no special obstacle to encounter. This branch of science has not hitherto entered into the domain of positive philosophy. Theological and metaphysical methods, exploded in other departments, are as yet exclusively applied, both in the way of inquiry and discussion, in all treatment of social subjects, though the best minds are heartily weary of eternal disputes about divine right and the sovereignty of the people. This is the great, while it is evidently the only gap which has to be filled, to constitute, solid and entire, the positive philosophy. Now that the human mind has grasped celestial and terrestrial physics—mechanical and chemical; organic physics, both vegetable and animal—there remains one science, to fill up the series of sciences of observation—social physics. This is what men have now most need of: and this it is the principal aim of the present work to establish.

It would be absurd to pretend to offer this new science at once in a complete state. Others, less new, are in very unequal conditions of forwardness. But the same character of positivity which is impressed on all the others will be shown to belong to this. This once done, the philosophical system of the moderns will be in fact complete, as there will then be no phenomenon which does not naturally enter into some one of the five great categories. All our fundamental conceptions having become homogeneous, the positive state will be fully established. It can never again change its character, though it will be for ever in course of development by additions of new knowledge. Having acquired the character of universality which has hitherto been the only advantage resting with the two preceding systems, it will supersede them by its natural superiority, and leave to them only a historical existence.

We have stated the special aim of this work. Its secondary and general aim is this: to review what has been effected in the sciences, in order to show that they are not radically separate, but all branches from the same trunk. If we had confined ourselves to the first and special object of the work, we should have produced merely a study of social physics; whereas, in introducing the second and general we offer a study of positive philosophy, passing in review all the positive sciences already formed.

The purpose of this work is not to give an account of the natural sciences. Besides that it would be endless, and that it would require a scientific preparation such as no one man possesses, it would be apart from our object, which is to go through a course of not positive science, but positive philosophy. We have only to consider each fundamental science in its relation to the whole positive system, and to the spirit which characterizes it; that is, with regard to its methods and its chief results.

The two aims, though distinct, are inseparable; for, on the one hand, there can be no positive philosophy without a basis of social science, without which it could not be all-comprehensive; and, on the other hand, we could not pursue social science without having been prepared by the study of phenomena less complicated than those of society, and furnished with a knowledge of laws and anterior facts which have a bearing upon social science. Though the fundamental

sciences are not all equally interesting to ordinary minds, there is no one of them that can be neglected in an inquiry like the present; and, in the eye of philosophy, all are of equal value to human welfare. Even those which appear the least interesting have their own value, either on account of the perfection of their methods, or as being the necessary basis of all the others.

Lest it should be supposed that our course will lead us into a wilderness of such special studies as are at present the bane of a true positive philosophy, we will briefly advert to the existing prevalence of such special pursuit. In the primitive state of human knowledge there is no regular division of intellectual labor. Every student cultivates all the sciences. As knowledge accrues, the sciences part off; and students devote themselves each to some one branch. It is owing to this division of employment, and concentration of whole minds upon a single department, that science has made so prodigious an advance in modern times; and the perfection of this division is one of the most important characteristics of the positive philosophy. But, while admitting all the merits of this change, we cannot be blind to the eminent disadvantages which arise from the limitation of minds to a particular study. It is inevitable that each should be possessed with exclusive notions, and be therefore incapable of the general superiority of ancient students, who actually owed that general superiority to the inferiority of their knowledge. We must consider whether the evil can be avoided without losing the good of the modern arrangement; for the evil is becoming urgent. We all acknowledge that the divisions established for the convenience of scientific pursuit are radically artificial; and yet there are very few who can embrace in idea the whole of any one science; each science moreover being itself only a part of a great whole. Almost every one is busy about his own particular section, without much thought about its relation to the general system of positive knowledge. We must not be blind to the evil, nor slow in seeking a remedy. We must not forget that this is the weak side of the positive philosophy, by which it may yet be attacked, with some hope of success, by the adherents of the theological and metaphysical systems. As to the remedy, it certainly does not lie in a return to the ancient confusion of pursuits, which would be mere retrogression, if it were possible, which it is not. It lies in perfecting the division of employments itself, in carrying it one degree higher, in constituting one more specialty from the study of scientific generalities. Let us have a new class of students, suitably prepared, whose business it shall be to take the respective sciences as they are, determine the spirit of each, ascertain their relations and mutual connection, and reduce their respective principles to the smallest number of general principles, in conformity with the fundamental rules of the positive method. At the same time, let other students be prepared for their special pursuit by an education which recognizes the whole scope of positive science, so as to profit by the labours of the students of generalities, and so as to correct reciprocally, under that guidance, the results obtained by each. We see some approach already to this arrangement. Once established, there would be nothing to apprehend from many extent of division of employments. When we once have a class of learned men, at the disposal of all others, whose business it shall be to connect each new discovery with the general system, we may dismiss all fear of the great whole being lost sight of in the pursuit of the details of knowledge. The organization of scientific research will then be complete; and it will henceforth have occasion only to extend its development, and not to change its character. After all, the formation of such a new class as is proposed would be merely an extension of the principle which has created all the classes we have. While science was narrow, there was only one class: as it expanded, more were instituted. With a further advance a fresh need arises, and this new class will be the result.

The general spirit of a course of positive philosophy having been thus set forth, we must now glance at the chief advantages which may be derived, on behalf of human progression, from the study of it. . . .

The study of the positive philosophy affords the only rational means of exhibiting the logical laws of the human mind, which have hitherto been sought by unfit methods. To explain what is meant by this, we may refer to a saying of de Blainville, in his work on comparative anatomy, that every active, and especially every living being, may be regarded under two relations—the statical and the dynamical; that is, under conditions or in action. It is clear that all con-

siderations range themselves under the one or the other of these heads. Let us apply this classification to the intellectual functions.

If we regard these functions under their statical aspect—that is, if we consider the conditions under which they exist—we must determine the organic circumstances of the case, which inquiry involves it with anatomy and physiology. If we look at the dynamic aspect, we have to study simply the exercise and results of the intellectual powers of the human race, which is neither more nor less than the general object of the positive philosophy. In short, looking at all scientific theories as so many great logical facts, it is only by the thorough observation of these facts that we can arrive at the knowledge of logical laws. These being the only means of knowledge of intellectual phenomena, the illusory psychology, which is the last phase of theology, is excluded. It pretends to accomplish the discovery of the laws of the human mind by contemplating it in itself. . . .

The present exclusive specialty of our pursuits, and the consequent isolation of the sciences, spoils our teaching. If any student desires to form an idea of natural philosophy as a whole, he is compelled to go through each department as it is now taught, as if he were to be only an astronomer, or only a chemist; so that, be his intellect what it may, his training must remain very imperfect. And yet his object requires that he should obtain general positive conceptions of all the classes of natural phenomena. It is such an aggregate of conceptions, whether on a great or on a small scale, which must henceforth be the permanent basis of all human combinations. It will constitute the mind of future generations. In order to this regeneration of our intellectual system, it is necessary that the sciences, considered as branches from one trunk, should yield us, as a whole, their chief methods and their most important results. The specialities of science can be pursued by those whose vocation lies in that direction. They are indispensable; and they are not likely to be neglected; but they can never of themselves renovate our system of education; and, to be of their full use, they must rest upon the basis of that general instruction which is a direct result of the positive philosophy.

The same special study of scientific generalities must also aid the progress of the respective positive sciences, and this constitutes our third head of advantages.

The divisions which we establish between the sciences are, though not arbitrary, essentially artificial. The subject of our researches is one: we divide it for our convenience, in order to deal the more easily with its difficulties. But it sometimes happens—and especially with the most important doctrines of each science—that we need what we cannot obtain under the present isolation of the sciences—a combination of several special points of view; and for want of this, very important problems wait for their solution much longer than they otherwise need do. To go back into the past for an example: Descartes' grand conception with regard to analytical geometry is a discovery which has changed the whole aspect of mathematical science, and yielded the germ of all future progress; and it issued from the union of two sciences which had always before been separately regarded and pursued. The case of pending questions is yet more impressive; as, for instance, in chemistry, the doctrine of definite proportions. Without entering upon the discussion of the fundamental principle of this theory, we may say with assurance that, in order to determine it—in order to determine whether it is a law of nature that atoms should necessarily combine in fixed numbers—it will be indispensable that the chemical point of view should be united with the physiological. The failure of the theory with regard to organic bodies indicates that the cause of this immense exception must be investigated; and such an inquiry belongs as much to physiology as to chemistry. Again, it is as yet undecided whether azoth is a simple or a compound body. It was concluded by almost all chemists that azoth is a simple body; the illustrious Berzelius hesitated, on purely chemical considerations; but he was also influenced by the physiological observation that animals which receive no azoth in their food have as much of it in their tissues as carnivorous animals. From this we see how physiology must unite with chemistry to inform us whether azoth is simply or compound, and to institute a new series of researches upon the relation between the composition of living bodies and their mode of alimentation.

Such is the advantage which, in the third place, we shall owe to positive philosophy—the elucidation of the respective sciences by their combination. In the fourth place:

IV. The positive philosophy offers the only solid basis for that social reorganization which must succeed the critical condition in which the most civilized nations are now living.

It cannot be necessary to prove to anybody who reads this work that ideas govern the world, or throw it into chaos; in other words, that all social mechanism rests upon opinions. The great political and moral crisis that societies are now undergoing is shown by a rigid analysis to arise out of intellectual anarchy. While stability in fundamental maxims is the first condition of genuine social order, we are suffering under an utter disagreement which may be called universal. Till a certain number of general ideas can be acknowledged as a rallying point of social doctrine, the nations will remain in a revolutionary state, whatever palliatives may be devised; and their institutions can be only provisional. But whenever the necessary agreement on first principles can be obtained, appropriate institutions will issue from them, without shock or resistance; for the causes of disorder will have been arrested by the mere fact of the agreement. It is in this direction that those must look who desire a natural and regular, a normal state of society.

Now, the existing order is abundantly accounted for by the existence, all at once, of three incompatible philosophies—the theological, the metaphysical, and the positive. Any one of these might alone secure some sort of social order; but while the three coexist, it is impossible for us to understand one another upon any essential point whatever. If this is true, we have only to ascertain which of the philosophies must, in the nature of things, prevail; and, this ascertained, every man, whatever may have been his former views, cannot but concur in its triumph. The problem once recognized cannot remain long unsolved; for all considerations whatever point to the positive philosophy as the one destined to prevail. It alone has been advancing during a course of centuries, throughout which the others have been declining. The fact is incontestable. Some may deplore it, but none can destroy it, nor therefore neglect it but under penalty of being betrayed by illusory speculations. This general revolution of the human mind is nearly accomplished. We have only to complete the positive philosophy by bringing social phenomena within its comprehension, and afterwards consolidating the whole into one body of homogeneous doctrine. The marked preference which almost all minds, from the highest to the commonest, accord to positive knowledge over vague and mystical conceptions, is a pledge of what the reception of this philosophy will be when it has acquired the only quality that it now wants—a character of due generality. When it has become complete, its supremacy will take place spontaneously, and will reestablish order throughout society. There is, at present, no conflict but between the theological and the metaphysical philosophies. They are contending for the task of reorganizing society; but it is a work too mighty for either of them. The positive philosophy has hitherto intervened only to examine both, and both are abundantly discredited by the process. It is time now to be doing something more effective, without wasting our forces in needless controversy. It is time to complete the vast intellectual operation begun by Bacon, Descartes, and Galileo, by constructing the system of general ideas which must henceforth prevail among the human race. This is the way to put an end to the revolutionary crisis which is tormenting the civilized nations of the world.

Leaving these four points of advantage, we must attend to one precautionary reflection.

Because it is proposed to consolidate the whole of our acquired knowledge into one body of homogeneous doctrine, it must not be supposed that we are going to study this vast variety as proceeding from a single principle, and as subjected to a single law. There is something so chimerical in attempts at universal explanation by a single law, that it may be as well to secure this work at once from any imputation of the kind, though its development will show how unde-

served such an imputation would be. Our intellectual resources are too narrow, and the universe is too complex, to leave any hope that it will ever be within our power to carry scientific perfection to its last degree of simplicity. Moreover, it appears as if the value of such an attainment, supposing it possible, were greatly overrated. The only way, for instance, in which we could achieve the business, would be by connecting all natural phenomena with the most general law we know, which is that of gravitation, by which astronomical phenomena are already connected with a portion of terrestrial physics. Pierre-Simon Laplace has indicated that chemical phenomena may be regarded as simple atomic effects of the Newtonian attraction, modified by the form and mutual position of the atoms. But supposing this view proveable (which it cannot be while we are without data about the constitution of bodies), the difficulty of its application would doubtless be found so great that we must still maintain the existing division between astronomy and chemistry, with the difference that we now regard as natural that division which we should then call artificial. Laplace himself presented his idea only as a philosophic device, incapable of exercising any useful influence over the progress of chemical science. Moreover, supposing this insuperable difficulty overcome, we should be no nearer to scientific unity, since we then should still have to connect the whole of physiological phenomena with the same law, which certainly would not be the least difficult part of the enterprise. Yet, all things considered, the hypothesis we have glanced at would be the most favorable to the desired unity.

STUDY QUESTIONS: COMTE, *COURSE OF THE POSITIVE PHILOSOPHY*

1. What is the "fundamental law" arising from the study and development of the human mind?
2. What are the "three philosophies" as Comte characterizes them?
3. Is the metaphysical stage necessary?
4. Why can one not go directly from the theological to the positive stage of understanding?
5. What is a law of nature?
6. What makes a law invariable?
7. What is the significance of the example of the great mathematician Fourier?
8. What role did "the precepts of Bacon, the conceptions of Descartes, and the discoveries of Galileo" play in the development of Comte's philosophy?
9. What does Comte mean by "social phenomena?"
10. What does he mean by "social physics?"

11. What is the chief advantage of the course of positive philosophy?
12. Are the divisions between the sciences artificial? Why?
13. What is the vast "intellectual operation" begun by Bacon, Descartes, and Galileo?

Philosophical Bridges: Comte's Influence

Toward the end of the nineteenth century, Comte's books and essays provided a major source of inspiration for the subsequent shift in philosophy from a metaphysical to a scientific orientation where, as we explained earlier, "scientific" is broadly construed within its implicit, albeit convert, social aspects (i.e., "social epistemology"). Comte directly influenced the moral, political and social philosophy of John Stuart Mill, scientism of the logical positivists (the early twentieth century movement that started in Vienna), and the radical break of philosophers such as Nietzsche and Marx with traditional religion. Today, sociology, the thriving discipline of study initiated by Comte, has a wide influence on all the various of social inquiry under its auspices, both from the perspective of the study of the society of individuals and the social institutions by which human beings conduct their political, religious, educational, and economic institutions.

FEUERBACH (1804–1872)

Biographical History

Karl Marx had this to say about his contemporary Feuerbach: "Feuerbach is the only one who has a serious, critical attitude to the Hegelian dialectic and who has made genuine discoveries in this field. He is in fact the true conqueror of the old philosophy."

Ludwig Feuerbach was born in Landshut, Bavaria, to a prominent family of lawyers and legal scholars. He started out quite religious in the Christian tradition, and was influenced by the Hegelian Christian theology of his professor Karl Daub at Heidelberg University, which he entered in 1823. He had a falling out over it with his father, a well-known professor of jurisprudence who hated Hegel's philosophy. In spite of this his father allowed him to go transfer to the University of Berlin, where Hegel was professor and there he immediately began to study with the master. But there he came under surveillance by the authorities, aided probably by his father, for being either a member of or sympathetic to the Burschenshaft, a subversive group, which prolonged his graduation. Karl went to prison; Ludwig did not.

Studying with Hegel proved to be the pivotal experience of his life. After earning his doctorate Feuerbach became a lecturer in philosophy specializing in logic, metaphysics, and history. Two of his first books, *The History of Modern Philosophy from Bacon to Spinoza* (1833) and *The Presentation and Development and Criticism of Leibniz's Philosophy*, earned him a solid if unexciting reputation. Meanwhile, he had published, anonymously, *Thoughts on Death and Immortality,* in which he argued that there is no individual afterlife and that any belief in God or religion was but egoistic wish-fulfillment. Christianity, in particular, he argued, is a religion of pure selfish egoism. Moreover, he infused the book with aphorisms that poked fun at his religious contemporaries and their vain, superstitious, beliefs.

People suspected that he was the author and he was arrested. He refused to deny that he was the author and lost his teaching position.

In the meantime, however, he married the wealthy heiress Berthe Löw. They settled in Bruckberg, a lovely town in Bavaria, where he lived the rich life of an independent scholar whose fame quickly spread throughout Europe. In 1841, his book, *The Essence of Christianity,* from which our excerpt is taken, established him one of the leading intellectual forces of the Left Hegelians, among them Karl Marx.

In 1860, after the revolutions throughout Europe that had begun in 1848, his wife's factory went bankrupt and the couple, virtually penniless overnight, moved near Nürnberg, where friends and supporters from the new Social Democratic Workers Party supported them. He died and was buried in Nüremberg.

Philosophical Overview

Like Marx (as well as Kierkegaard and Nietzsche), Ludwig Feuerbach was a philosophical rebel, an outsider to the academy, institutions and culture of his time. In his dissertation, *On the Infinitude, Unity and Commonality of Reason*, he argues that all human beings are unified under one principle that is the ground of all being: reason. This is in the spirit of the Hegelian fundamental proposition that evaluates the real with the rational and the rational with the real. But the significance of Feuerbach's thinking comes from his early break with Hegel, wherein he equates the real not with anything mental (rationality itself being, in his view, a mental faculty) but with the material world of space, time and matter. There is nothing above and beyond the material universe. The question, then, is what role if any religion should play in the moral, psychological, spiritual, and social development of mankind.

Feuerbach's answer is that religion and God are not merely inventions of the human mind but are, themselves, aspects of our own human natures objectified. All notions of divinity, of divine attributes, and so on, are but mere objectifications of human nature. Thus whereas in Hegel, who identifies God with the Absolute, God is most real, in Feuerbach human subjectivity becomes the most real, fundamental ground of all being. In so far as religion (and Hegel) subverts human subjectivity to the notion of God, it is but a mere and foolish fantasy. Its only saving grace is that, like good fiction and art, it may allow us to overcome our limitations.

THE ESSENCE OF CHRISTIANITY

This book rattled Germany and the rest of Europe in the 1840s. When George Eliot (the pseudonym of Mary Ann Evans, 1819—1880), famed English novelist, translated it into English, its influence reached all corners of the globe. It angered and inspired many, and became the bible of many leading intellectuals and artists throughout Europe, such as Marx, Engels, Nietsche, and Wagner. Feuerbach argues that religion, as an institution, is identical with self-consciousness, by which he means not merely self-awareness but the consciousness we have "of our own nature." And that nature is *infinite*. Thus there is in his view no such thing as partial or finite consciousness. All consciousness, he argues from the start, is necessarily infinite consciousness, which helps in part explain the infinite nature the human mind attributes to its own conjured-up objectification of itself, namely, God.

Feuerbach, from *The Essence of Christianity*, translated by George Eliot, 1854.

CHAPTER 1: INTRODUCTION

1. The Essential Nature of Man

Religion has its basis in the essential difference between man and the brute—the brutes have no religion . . . But what is this essential difference between man and the brute? The most simple, general, and also the most popular answer to this question is consciousness, but consciousness in the strict sense; for the consciousness implied in the feeling of self as an individual, in discrimination by the senses, in the perception and even judgment of outward things according to definite sensible signs, cannot be denied to the brutes. Consciousness in the strictest sense is present only in a being to whom his species, his essential nature, is an object of thought. The brute is indeed conscious of himself as an individual, and he has accordingly the feeling of self as the common center of successive sensations, but not as a species; hence, he is without that consciousness which in its nature, as in its name, is akin to science. Where there is this higher consciousness there is a capability of science. Science is the cognizance of species. In practical life we have to do with individuals; in science, with species. But only a being to whom his own species, his own nature, is an object of thought, can make the essential nature of other things or beings an object of thought.

Hence the brute has only a simple, man a twofold life: in the brute, the inner life is one with the outer; man has both an inner and an outer life. The inner life of man is the life which has relation to his species, to his general, as distinguished from his individual, nature. Man thinks—that is, he converses with himself. The brute can exercise no function which has relation to its species without another individual external to itself; but man can perform the functions of thought and speech, which strictly imply such a relation, apart from another individual. Man is himself at once I and thou; he can put himself in the place of another, for this reason, that to him his species, his essential nature, and not merely his individuality, is an object of thought.

Religion being identical with the distinctive characteristic of man, is then identical with self-consciousness—with the consciousness which man has of his nature. But religion, expressed generally, is consciousness of the infinite; thus it is and can be nothing else than the consciousness which man has of his own—not finite and limited, but infinite nature. A really finite being has not even the faintest adumbration, still less consciousness, of an infinite for the limit of the nature is also the limit of the consciousness. The consciousness of the caterpillar, whose life is confined to a particular species of plant, does not extend itself beyond this narrow domain. It does, indeed, discriminate between this plant and other plants, but more it knows not. A consciousness so limited, but on account of that very limitation so infallible, we do not call consciousness, but instinct. Consciousness, in the strict or proper sense, is identical with consciousness of the infinite; a limited consciousness is no consciousness; consciousness is essentially infinite in its nature. The consciousness of the infinite is nothing else than the consciousness of the infinity of the consciousness; or, in the consciousness of the infinite, the conscious subject has for his object the infinity of his own nature.

What, then, *is* the nature of man, of which he is conscious, or what constitutes the specific distinction, the proper humanity of man?[1] Reason, will, affection. To a complete man belong the power of thought, the power of will, the power of affection. The power of thought is the light of the intellect, the power of will is energy of character, the power of affection is love. Reason, love, force of will, are perfections—the perfections of the human being— nay, more, they are absolute perfections of being. To will, to love, to think, are the highest powers, are the absolute nature of man as man, and the basis of his existence. Man exists to think, to love, to will. Now that which is the end, the ultimate aim, is also the true basis and principle of a being. But what is the end of reason? Reason. Of love? Love. Of will? Freedom of the will. We think for the sake of thinking; love for the sake of loving; will for the sake of

---

[1]The obtuse Materialist says: "Man is distinguished from the brute *only* by consciousness—he is an animal with consciousness superadded" not reflecting, that in a being which awakes to consciousness, there takes place a qualitative change, a differentiation of the entire nature. For the rest, our words are by no means intended to depreciate the nature of the lower animals. This is not the place to enter further into that question.

willing—that is, that we may be free. True existence is thinking, loving, willing existence. That alone is true, perfect, divine, which exists for its own sake. But such is love, such is reason, such is will. The divine trinity in man, above the individual man, is the unity of reason, love, will. Reason, will, love, are not powers which man possesses, for he is nothing without them, he is what he is only by them; they are the constituent elements of his nature, which he neither has nor makes, the animating, determining, governing powers—divine, absolute powers—to which he can oppose no resistance.

How can the feeling man resist feeling, the loving one love, the rational one reason? Who has not experienced the overwhelming power of melody? And what else is the power of melody but the power of feeling? Music is the language of feeling; melody is audible feeling—feeling communicating itself. Who has not experienced the power of love, or at least heard of it? Which is the stronger—love or the individual man? Is it man that possesses love, or is it not much rather love that possesses man? When love impels a man to suffer death even joyfully for the beloved one, is this death-conquering power his own individual power, or is it not rather the power of love? And who that ever truly thought has not experienced that quiet, subtle power—the power of thought? When thou sinkest into deep reflection, forgetting thyself and what is around thee, dost thou govern reason, or is it not reason which governs and absorbs thee? Scientific enthusiasm—is it not the most glorious triumph of intellect over thee? The desire of knowledge—is it not a simply irresistible, and all-conquering power? And when thou suppressest a passion, renouncest a habit, in short, achievest a victory over thyself, is this victorious power thy own personal power, or is it not rather the energy of will, the force of morality, which seizes the mastery of thee, and fills thee with indignation against thyself and thy individual weaknesses?

Man is nothing without an object. The great models of humanity, such men as reveal to us what man is capable of, have attested the truth of this proposition by their lives. They had only one dominant passion—the realisation of the aim which was the essential object of their activity. But the object to which a subject essentially, necessarily relates, is nothing else than this subject's own, but objective, nature. If it be an object common to several individuals of the same species, but under various conditions, it is still, at least as to the form tinder which it presents itself to each of them according to their respective modifications, their own, but objective, nature.

Thus the Sun is the common object of the planets, but it is an object to Mercury, to Venus, to Saturn, to Uranus, under other conditions than to the Earth. Each planet has its own sun. The Sun which lights and warms Uranus has no physical (only an astronomical, scientific) existence for the Earth; and not only does the Sun appear different, but it really is another sun on Uranus than on the Earth. The relation of the Sun to the Earth is therefore at the same time a relation of the Earth to itself, or to its own nature, for the measure of the size and of the intensity of light which the Sun possesses as the object of the Earth is the measure of the distance which determines the peculiar nature of the Earth. Hence each planet has in its sun the mirror of its own nature.

In the object which he contemplates, therefore, man becomes acquainted with himself; consciousness of the objective is the self-consciousness of man. We know the man by the object, by his conception of what is external to himself; in it his nature becomes evident; this object is his manifested nature, his true objective *ego*. And this is true not merely of spiritual, but also of sensuous objects. Even the objects which are the most remote from man, because they are objects to him, and to the extent to which they are so, are revelations of human nature. Even the moon, the Sun, the stars, call to man (*Gnosi seautov*) ["Know yourself"]. That he sees them, and so sees them, is an evidence of his own nature. The animal is sensible only of the beam which immediately affects life; while man perceives the ray, to him physically indifferent, of the remotest star. Man alone has purely intellectual, disinterested joys and passions; the eye of man alone keeps theoretic festivals. The eye which looks into the starry heavens, which gazes at that light, alike useless and harmless, having nothing in common with the earth and its necessities—this eye sees in that light its own nature, its own origin. The eye is heavenly in its nature. Hence man elevates himself above the earth only with the eye; hence theory begins with the contemplation of the heavens. The first philosophers were astronomers. It is the heavens that admonish man of his destination, and remind him that he is destined not merely to action, but also to contemplation.

The *absolute* to man is his own nature. The power of the object over him is therefore the power of his own nature. Thus the power of the object of feeling is the power of feeling itself; the power of the object of the intellect is the power of the intellect itself; the power of the object of the will is the power of the will itself. The man who is affected by musical sounds is governed by feeling; by the feeling, that is, which finds its corresponding element in musical sounds. But it is not melody as such, it is only melody pregnant with meaning and emotion, which has power over feeling. Feeling is only acted on by that which conveys feeling, that is, by itself, its own nature. Thus also the will; thus, and infinitely more, the intellect. Whatever kind of object, therefore, we are at any time conscious of, we are always at the same time conscious of our own nature; we can affirm nothing without affirming ourselves. And since to will, to feel, to think, are perfections, essences, realities, it is impossible that intellect, feeling, and will should feel or perceive themselves as limited, finite powers, that is, as worthless, as nothing. For finiteness and nothingness are identical; finiteness is only a euphemism for nothingness. Finiteness is the metaphysical, the theoretical—nothingness the pathological, practical expression. What is finite to the understanding is nothing to the heart. But it is impossible that we should be conscious of will, feeling, and intellect, as finite powers, because every perfect existence, every original power, and essence, is the immediate verification and affirmation of itself. It is impossible to love, will, or think, without perceiving these activities to be perfections—impossible to feel that one is a loving, willing, thinking being, without experiencing an infinite joy therein. Consciousness consists in a being becoming objective to itself; hence it is nothing apart, nothing distinct from the being which is conscious of itself. How could it otherwise become conscious of itself? It is therefore impossible to be conscious of a perfection as an imperfection, impossible to feel feeling limited, to think thought limited.

Consciousness is self-verification, self-affirmation, self-love, joy in one's own perfection. Consciousness is the characteristic mark of a perfect nature; it exists only in a self-sufficing, complete being. Even human

vanity attests this truth. A man looks in the glass—he has complacency in his appearance. This complacency is a necessary, involuntary consequence of the completeness, the beauty of his form. A beautiful form is satisfied in itself; it has necessarily joy in itself in self-contemplation. This complacency becomes vanity only when a man piques himself on his form as being his individual form, not when he admires it as a specimen of human beauty in general. It is fitting that he should admire it thus: he can conceive no form more beautiful, more sublime than the human. Assuredly every being loves itself, its existence, and fitly so. To exist is a good . . . Everything that exists has value, is a being of distinction—at least this is true of the species: hence it asserts, maintains itself. But the highest form of self-assertion, the form which is itself a superiority, a perfection, a bliss, a good, is consciousness.

Every limitation of the reason, or in general of the nature of man, rests on a delusion, an error. It is true that the human being, as an individual, can and must—herein consists his distinction from the brute—feel and recognize himself to be limited; but he can become conscious of his limits, his finiteness, only because the perfection, the infinitude of his species, is perceived by him, whether as an object of feeling of conscience, or of the thinking consciousness. If he makes his own limitations the limitations of the species, this arises from the mistake that he identifies himself immediately with the species—a mistake which is intimately connected with the individual's love of ease, sloth, vanity, and egoism. For a limitation which I know to be merely mine humiliates, shames, and perturbs me. Hence to free myself from this feeling of shame, from this state of dissatisfaction, I convert the limits of my individuality into the limits of human nature in general. What is incomprehensible to me is incomprehensible to others; why should I trouble myself further? It is no fault of mine; my understanding is not to blame, but the understanding of the race. But it is a ludicrous and even culpable error to define as finite and limited what constitutes the essence of man, the nature of the species, which is the absolute nature of the individual. Every being is sufficient to itself. No being can deny itself, that is, its own nature; no being is a limited one to itself. Rather, every being is in and by itself infinite—has its God, its highest conceivable being, in itself. Every limit of a being is cognizable only by another being out of and above him. The life of the ephemera is extraordinarily short in comparison with that of longer-lived creatures; but nevertheless, for the ephemera this short life is as long as a life of years to others. The leaf on which the caterpillar lives is for it a world, an infinite space.

That which makes a being what it is, is its talent, its power, its wealth, its adornment. How can it possibly hold its existence nonexistence, its wealth poverty, its talent incapacity? If the plants had eyes, taste, and judgment, each plant would declare its own flower the most beautiful; for its comprehension, its taste, would reach no farther than its natural power of production. What the productive power of its nature has brought forth as the highest, that must also its taste, its judgment, recognise and affirm as the highest. What the nature affirms, the understanding, the taste, the judgment, cannot deny; otherwise the understanding, the judgment, would no longer be the understanding and judgment of this particular being, but of some other. The measure of the nature is also the measure of the understanding. If the nature is limited, so also is the feeling, so also is the understanding. But to a limited being its limited understanding is not felt to be a limitation; on the contrary, it is perfectly happy and contented with this understanding; it regards it, praises and values it, as a glorious, divine power; and the limited understanding, on its part, values the limited nature whose understanding it is. Each is exactly adapted to the other; how should they be at issue with each other? A being's understanding is its sphere of vision. As far as thou seest, so far extends thy nature; and conversely. The eye of the brute reaches no farther than its needs, and its nature no farther than its needs. And so far as thy nature reaches, so far reaches thy unlimited self-consciousness, so far art thou God. The discrepancy between the understanding and the nature, between the power of conception and the power of production in the human consciousness, on the one hand, is merely of individual significance and has not a universal application; and, on the other hand, it is only apparent. He who, having written a bad poem, knows it to be bad, is in his intelligence, and therefore in his nature, not so limited as he who, having written a bad poem, admires it and thinks it good.

It follows that if thou thinkest the infinite, thou perceivest and affirmest the infinitude of the power of thought; if thou feelest the infinite, thou feelest and affirmest the infinitude of the power of feeling. The object of the intellect is intellect objective to itself; the object of feeling is feeling objective to itself. If thou hast no sensibility, no feeling for music, thou perceivest in the finest music nothing more than in the wind that whistles by thy ear, or than in the brook which rushes past thy feet. What, then, is it which acts on thee when thou art affected by melody? What dost thou perceive in it? What else than the voice of thy own heart? Feeling speaks only to feeling; feeling is comprehensible only by feeling, that is, by itself—for this reason, that the object of feeling is nothing else than feeling. Music is a monologue of emotion. But the dialogue of philosophy also is in truth only a monologue of the intellect; thought speaks only to thought. The splendors of the crystal charm the sense, but the intellect is interested only in the laws of crystallization. The intellectual only is the object of the intellect.

All therefore which, in the point of view of metaphysical, transcendental speculation and religion, has the significance only of the secondary, the subjective, the medium, the organ—has in truth the significance of the primary, of the essence, of the object itself. If, for example, feeling is the essential organ of religion, the nature of God is nothing else than an expression of the nature of feeling. The true but latent sense of the phrase, "Feeling is the organ of the divine," is, feeling is the noblest, the most excellent, that is, the divine, in man. How couldst thou perceive the divine by feeling, if feeling were not itself divine in its nature? The divine assuredly is known only by means of the divine—God is known only by himself. The divine nature which is discerned by feeling is in truth nothing else than feeling enraptured, in ecstasy with itself—feeling intoxicated with joy, blissful in its own plenitude.

It is already clear from this that where feeling is held to be the organ of the infinite, the subjective essence of religion, the external data of religion lose their objective value. And thus, since feeling has been held the cardinal principle in religion, the doctrines of Christianity, formerly so sacred, have lost their importance. If, from this point of view, some value is still conceded to Christian ideas, it is a value springing entirely from the relation they bear to feeling; if another object would excite the same emotions, it would be just as welcome. But the object of religious feeling is become a matter of indifference, only because when once feeling has been pronounced to be the subjective essence of religion, it in fact is also the objective essence of religion, though it may not be declared, at least directly, to be such. I say directly, for indirectly this is certainly admitted, when it is declared that feeling, as such, is religious, and thus the distinction between specifically religious and irreligious, or at least non-religious, feelings is abolished—a necessary consequence of the point of view in which feeling only is regarded as the organ of the divine. For on what other ground than that of its essence, its nature, dost thou hold feeling to be the organ of the infinite, the divine being? And is not the nature of feeling in general also the nature of every special feeling, be its object what it may? What, then, makes this feeling religious? A given object? Not at all; for this object is itself a religious one only when it is not an object of the cold understanding or memory, but of feeling. What then? The nature of feeling—a nature of which every special feeling, without distinction of objects, partakes. Thus, feeling is pronounced to be religious, simply because it is feeling; the ground of its religiousness is its own nature, lies in itself. But is not feeling thereby declared to be itself the absolute, the divine? If feeling in itself is good, religious, that is, holy, divine, has not feeling its God in itself?

But if, notwithstanding thou wilt posit an object of feeling, but at the same time seekest to express thy feeling truly, without introducing by thy reflection any foreign element, what remains to thee but to distinguish between thy individual feeling and the general nature of feeling—to separate the universal in feeling from the disturbing, thy adulterating influences with which feeling is bound up in thee, under thy individual conditions? Hence what thou can alone contemplate, declare to be the infinite, and define as its essence, is merely the nature of feeling. Thou hast thus no other definition of God than this: God is pure, unlimited, free feeling. Every other God, whom thou supposest, is a God thrust upon thy feeling from without. Feeling is atheistic in the sense of the orthodox belief, which attaches religion to an exter-

nal object; it denies an objective God—it is itself God. In this point of view only the negation of feeling is the negation of God. Thou art simply too cowardly or too narrow to confess in words what thy feeling tacitly affirms. Fettered by outward considerations, still in bondage to vulgar empiricism, incapable of comprehending the spiritual grandeur of feeling thou art terrified before the religious atheism of thy heart. By this fear thou destroyest the unity of thy feeling with itself, in imagining to thyself an objective being distinct from thy feeling, and thus necessarily sinking back into the old questions and doubts—is there a God or not?—questions and doubts which vanish, nay, are impossible, where feeling is defined as the essence of religion. Feeling is thy own inward power, but at the same time a power distinct from thee, and independent of thee; it is in thee, above thee; it is itself that which constitutes the objective in thee—thy own which impresses thee as another being; in short, thy God. How wilt thou, then, distinguish from this objective being within thee another objective being? How wilt thou get beyond thy feeling?

But feeling has here been adduced only as an example. It is the same with every other power, faculty, potentiality, reality, activity—the name is indifferent—which is defined as the essential organ of any object. Whatever is a subjective expression of a nature is simultaneously also its objective expression. Man cannot get beyond his true nature. He may indeed by means of the imagination conceive individuals of another so-called higher kind, but he can never get loose from his species, his nature; the conditions of being the positive final predicates which he gives to these other individuals, are always determinations or qualities drawn from his own nature—qualities in which he in truth only images and projects himself. There may certainly be thinking beings besides men on the other planets of our solar system. But by the supposition of such beings we do not change our standing point—we extend our conceptions *quantitatively* not *qualitatively*. For as surely as all the other planets there are the same laws of motion, so surely are there the same laws of perception and thought as here. In fact, we people the other planets, not that we may place there different beings from ourselves, but more beings of our own or of a similar nature.

STUDY QUESTIONS: FEUERBACH, *THE ESSENCE OF CHRISTIANITY*

1. Why do human beings create religion and animals not? What is the significance of this fact?
2. How does Feuerbach try to establish his key proposition, that "religion is identical with self-consciousness?"
3. How are reason, will, and affection related?
4. In what sense are reason, love, and force of will *perfections*?
5. What does Feuerbach mean by the proposition, "man is nothing without an object?"
6. Why does Feuerbach consider the concept *nothingness* to be pathological?
7. Why are talent, power, wealth, and adornment so important, from a *metaphysical* point of view?

Philosophical Bridges: Feuerbach's Influence

First as a leader of the Young Hegelians, then the Left Hegelians, Feuerbach was one of the pivotal forces for philosophical and social revolution throughout the latter part of the nineteenth century. He signaled the turning away from idealism and the hold of Hegel's elaborate system. As a precursor of what has since come to be known as *projection theories* of religion (in which religions are viewed as projections of the human ego) he was a pivotal influence on figures such as Marx, Nietzsche, Wagner, and on the founder of psychoanalysis, Sigmund Freud. Indeed, it would be difficult to imagine Freud's analysis of religion and religious psychoses as unhealthy projections of the human ego without Feuerbach's works. Even many theologians, such as, most notably, Martin Buber and Karl Barth, would go on to agree with much of the substance of Feuerbach's criticisms of religion as practiced in the cultural institutions that can themselves become subtle or not-so-subtle forces of repression.

BENTHAM (1748–1832)

Biographical History

Jeremy Bentham was born in London. His father, a leading attorney, and his mother recognized early on that their son was a prodigy: by 3 he was reading the works of history in their library (most notably, Paul de Rapin's *History*) and spoke Latin fluently. He was accepted to Queen's College, Oxford, at the age of 12; the work that most impressed him there was Robert Sanderson's *Logic*. He earned his B.A. in three years, at the age of 15, his M.A. by 17. His father wanted him to go to law school and he did, he even passed the bar, but never practiced. He was more interested in the philosophical foundations of ethics and trying to reform the legal system; his main interest was in trying to see all the various ways that morality in general connects with legal theory. His first book, *Fragment on Government* (1776) is a searing criticism of the lack of reform in the commentaries on leading politicians and judges of the time; it was the beginning of what would come to be called his *philosophic radicalism*. He founded a group called the Philosophical Radicals, which eventually evolved into the British Liberal Party.

He did not particularly like Great Britain and traveled around throughout Europe. His first essay, on the philosophy of economics, *Defence of Usury* (1787) was written and published in Russia. He became a citizen of France in 1792. In *Defense of Usury*, he argues that we are each as individuals the best judges about what is good and bad for us, and that politicians and lawyers should as much as possible stop meddling in people's affairs. In his *Introduction to the Principles of Morals and Legislation* (1789), which made him an influential international figure, he lays the groundwork for utilitarianism that, as further developed by his most illustrious student, John Stuart Mill, became one of the leading moral theories in the world. He had many devoted followers and students, and he helped found University College, London. When he died he left explicit instructions that his body remain, dressed in his clothes, in a glass case and regularly displayed. He sits there still.

Philosophical Overview

Bentham defines his "principle of utility" as

> that property in any object whereby it tends to produce pleasure, good, or happiness, or to prevent the happening of mischief, pain, evil, or unhappiness to the party whose interest is considered.

This principle, according to Bentham, explains the two main motives for all human action: pain and pleasure. Social, political, and legal institutions should follow the greatest happiness principle: choose that course of action that leads to the greatest happiness for the greatest number of people. In this way utilitarianism was supposed to free people from oppressive laws, make governing bodies moral, and provide a solid foundation for democracy. Leaders no less so than individuals in a utilitarian society are morally bound to follow the same universal principle, readily accessible to everyone. Everyone knows what pain and pleasure are; this cannot be manipulated. Moreover, we are each our own best judge as to how best to live and attain happiness. Utilitarianism was thus designed to break the repressive structure of laws imposed by leaders, under the false banner of morality, on their people. As Bentham put it, "all government is in itself one vast evil." The only justification for putting such evil into place would be to prevent some greater evil; governments should therefore never stray from the principle of utility—the greatest good for the greatest number.

AN INTRODUCTION TO THE PRINCIPLES OF MORALS AND LEGISLATION

Bentham

CHAPTER I: OF THE PRINCIPLE OF UTILITY

1.

Nature has placed mankind under the governance of two sovereign masters, *pain* and *pleasure*. It is for them alone to point out what we ought to do, as well as to determine what we shall do. On the one hand the standard of right and wrong, on the other the chain of causes and effects, are fastened to their throne. They govern us in all we do, in all we say, in all we think; every effort we can make to throw off our subjection will serve but to demonstrate and confirm it. In words a man may pretend to abjure their empire, but in reality he will remain subject to it all the while. The *principle of utility* recognizes this subjection, and assumes it for the foundation of that system, the object of which is to rear the fabric of felicity by the hands of reason and of law. Systems which attempt to question it, deal in sounds instead of sense, in caprice instead of reason, in darkness instead of light.

But enough of metaphor and declamation; it is not by such means that moral science is to be improved.

2.

The principle of utility is the foundation of the present work—it will be proper therefore at the outset to give an explicit and determinate account of what is meant by it. By the principle of utility is meant that principle which approves or disapproves of every action whatsoever, according to the tendency which it appears to have to augment or diminish the happiness of the party whose interest is in question, or, what is the same thing in other words, to promote or to oppose that happiness. I say of every action whatsoever; and therefore not only of every action of a private individual, but of every measure of government.

3.

By utility is meant that property in any object, whereby it tends to produce benefit, advantage, pleasure, good, or happiness (all this in the present case comes to the same thing), or (what comes again to the same thing) to prevent the happening of mischief, pain, evil, or unhappiness to the party whose interest is considered: if that party be the community in general, then the happiness of the community; if a particular individual, then the happiness of that individual.

4.

The interest of the community is one of the most general expressions that can occur in the phraseology of morals: no wonder that the meaning of it is often lost. When it has a meaning, it is this: the community is a fictitious *body*, composed of the individual persons who are considered as constituting as it were its *members*. The interest of the community then is, what? The sum of the interests of the several members who compose it.

5.

It is in vain to talk of the interest of the community without understanding what is the interest of the individual. A thing is said to promote the interest, or to be *for* the interest, of an individual, when it tends to add to the sum total of his pleasures, or, what comes to the same thing, to diminish the sum total of his pains.

6.

An action then may be said to be conformable to the principle of utility, or for shortness sake, to utility (meaning with respect to the community at large), when the tendency it has to augment the happiness of the community is greater than any it has to diminish it.

7.

A measure of government (which is but a particular kind of action, performed by a particular person or persons) may be said to be conformable to or dictated by the principle of utility, when in like manner the tendency which it has to augment the happiness of the community is greater than any which it has to diminish it.

8.

When an action, or in particular a measure of government, is supposed by a man to be conformable to the principle of utility, it may be convenient, for the purposes of discourse, to imagine a kind of law or dictate, called a law or dictate of utility: and to speak of the action in question, as being conformable to such law or dictate.

9.

A man may be said to be a partisan of the principle of utility, when the approbation or disapprobation he annexes to any action, or to any measure, is determined, by and proportioned to the tendency which he conceives it to have to augment or to diminish the happiness of the community: or in other words, to its conformity or unconformity to the laws or dictates of utility.

10.

Of an action that is conformable to the principle of utility, one may always say either that it is one that ought to be done, or at least that it is not one that ought not to be done. One may say also, that it is right it should be done, that it is a right action—at least that it is not a wrong action. When thus interpreted, the words *ought*, and *right* and *wrong*, and others of that stamp, have a meaning; when otherwise, they have none.

11.

Has the rectitude of this principle been ever formally contested? It should seem that it had, by those who have not known what they have been meaning. Is it susceptible of any direct proof? It should seem not, for that which is used to prove every thing else, cannot itself be proved: a chain of proofs must have their commencement somewhere. To give such proof is as impossible as it is needless.

12.

Not that there is or ever has been that human creature breathing, however stupid or perverse, who has not on many, perhaps on most occasions of his life, deferred to it. By the natural constitution of the human frame, on most occasions of their lives men in general embrace this principle, without thinking of it: if not for the ordering of their own actions, yet for the trying of their own actions, as well as of those of other men. There have been, at the same time, not many, perhaps, even of the most intelligent, who have been disposed to embrace it purely and without reserve. There are even few who have not taken some occasion or other to quarrel with it, either on account of their not understanding always how to apply it, or on account of some prejudice or other which they were afraid to examine into, or could not bear to part with. For such is the stuff that man is made of: in principle and in practice, in a right track and in a wrong one, the rarest of all human qualities is consistency.

13.

When a man attempts to combat the principle of utility, it is with reasons drawn, without his being aware of it, from that very principle itself. His arguments, if they prove any thing, prove not that the principle is *wrong*, but that, according to the applications he supposed to be made of it, it is *misapplied*. Is it possible for a man to move the earth? Yes; but he must first find out another earth to stand upon.

14.

To disprove the propriety of it by arguments is impossible; but, from the causes that have been mentioned, or from some confused or partial view of it, a man may happen to be disposed not to relish it. Where this is the case, if he thinks the settling of his opinions on such a subject worth the trouble, let him take the following steps, and at length, perhaps he may come to reconcile himself to it.

1. Let him settle with himself, whether he would wish to discard this principle altogether; if so, let him consider what it is that all his reasonings (in matters of politics especially) can amount to.

2. If he would, let him settle with himself, whether he would judge and act without any principle, or whether there is any other he would judge and act by.

3. If there be, let him examine and satisfy himself whether the principle he thinks he has found is really any separate intelligible principle, or whether it be not a mere principle in words, a kind of phrase, which at bottom expresses neither more nor less than the mere averment of his own unfounded sentiments: that is, what in another person he might be apt to call caprice.

4. If he is inclined to think that his own approbation or disapprobation, annexed to the idea of an act, without any regard to its consequences, is a sufficient foundation for him to judge and act upon, let him ask himself whether his sentiment is to be a standard of right and wrong, with respect to every other man, or whether every man's sentiment has the same privilege of being a standard in itself.

5. In the first case, let him ask himself whether his principle is not despotical, and hostile to all the rest of [the] human race.

6. In the second case, whether it is not anarchical, and whether at this rate there are not as many different standards of right and wrong as there are men. And whether even in the same man, the same thing, which is right today, may not (without the least change in its nature) be wrong tomorrow. And whether the same thing is not right and wrong in the same place at the same time. And in either case, whether all argument is not at an end. And whether, when two men have said, "I like this," and "I don't like it," they can (upon such a principle) have any thing more to say.

7. If he should have said to himself, no, for that the sentiment which he proposes as a standard must be grounded on reflection, let him say on what particulars the reflection is to turn. If on

particulars having relation to the utility of the act, then let him say whether this is not deserting his own principle, and borrowing assistance from that very one in opposition to which he sets it up—or if not on those particulars, on what other particulars.

8. If he should be for compounding the matter, and adopting his own principle in part, and the principle of utility in part, let him say how far he will adopt it.

9. When he has settled with himself where he will stop, then let him ask himself how he justifies to himself the adopting it so far and why he will not adopt it any farther.

10. Admitting any other principle than the principle of utility to be a right principle, a principle that it is right for a man to pursue—admitting (what is not true) that the word *right* can have a meaning without reference to utility, let him say whether there is any such thing as a *motive* that a man can have to pursue the dictates of it. If there is, let him say what that motive is, and how it is to be distinguished from those which enforce the dictates of utility; if not, then lastly let him say what it is this other principle can be good for.

CHAPTER II: OF PRINCIPLES ADVERSE TO THAT OF UTILITY

1.

If the principle of utility be a right principle to be governed by, and that in all cases, it follows from what has been just observed, that whatever principle differs from it in any case must necessarily be a wrong one. To prove any other principle, therefore, to be a wrong one, there needs no more than just to show it to be what it is, a principle of which the dictates are in some point or other different from those of the principle of utility: to state it is to confute it.

2.

A principle may be different from that of utility in two ways: (1) By being constantly opposed to it: this is the case with a principle which may be termed the principle of asceticism. (2) By being sometimes opposed to it, and sometimes not, as it may happen: this is the case with another, which may be termed the principle of *sympathy* and *antipathy*.

3.

By the principle of asceticism I mean that principle, which, like the principle of utility, approves or disapproves of any action, according to the tendency which it appears to have to augment or diminish the happiness of the party whose interest is in question; but in an inversive manner: approving of actions in as far as they tend to diminish his happiness: disapproving of them in as far as they tend to augment it.

9.

The principle of asceticism seems originally to have been the reverie of certain hasty speculators, who having perceived, or fancied, that certain pleasures, when reaped in certain circumstances, have, at the long run, been attended with pains more than equivalent to them, took occasion to quarrel with every thing that offered itself under the name of pleasure. Having then got thus far, and having forgot the point which they set out from, they pushed on, and went so much further as to think it meritorious to fall in love with pain. Even this, we see, is at bottom but the principle of utility misapplied.

10.

The principle of utility is capable of being consistently pursued; and it is but tautology to say, that the more consistently it is pursued, the better it must ever be for humankind. The principle of asceticism never was, nor ever can be, consistently pursued by any living creature. Let but one-tenth part of the inhabitants of this earth pursue it consistently, and in a day's time they will have turned it into a hell.

11.

Among principles adverse to that of utility, that which at this day seems to have most influence in matters of government, is what may be called the principle of sympathy and antipathy. By the principle of sympathy and antipathy, I mean that principle which approves or disapproves of certain actions, not on account of their tending to augment the happiness, nor yet on account of their tending to diminish the happiness of the party whose interest is in question, but merely because a man finds himself disposed to approve or disapprove of them: holding up that approbation or disapprobation as a sufficient reason for itself, and disclaiming the necessity of looking out for any extrinsic ground. Thus far in the general department of morals: and in the particular department of politics, measuring out the quantum (as well as determining the ground) of punishment, by the degree of the disapprobation.

14.

The various systems that have been formed concerning the standard of right and wrong, may all be reduced to the principle of sympathy and antipathy. One account may serve for all of them. They consist all of them in so many contrivances for avoiding the obligation of appealing to any external standard, and for prevailing upon the reader to accept of the author's sentiment or opinion as a reason, and that a sufficient one, for itself. The phrases are different, but the principle the same.

CHAPTER III: OF THE FOUR SANCTIONS OF SOURCES OF PAIN AND PLEASURE

1.

It has been shown that the happiness of the individuals, of whom a community is composed, that is, their pleasures and their security, is the end and the sole end which the legislator ought to have in view: the sole standard, in conformity to which each individual ought, as far as depends upon the legislator, to be *made* to fashion his behavior. But whether it be this or any thing else that is to be *done*, there is nothing by which a man can ultimately be *made* to do it, but either pain or pleasure. Having taken a general view of these two grand objects (namely pleasure, and what comes to the same thing, immunity from pain) in the character of *final* causes; it will be necessary to take a view of pleasure and pain itself, in the character of *efficient* causes or means.

2.

There are four distinguishable sources from which pleasure and pain are in use to flow—considered separately, they may be termed the *physical*, the *political*, the *moral*, and the *religious*—and inasmuch as the pleasures and pains belonging to each of them are capable of giving a binding force to any law or rule of conduct, they may all of them be termed sanctions.

3.

If it be in the present life, and from the ordinary course of nature, not purposely modified by the interposition of the will of any human being, nor by any extraordinary interposition of any superior invisible being, that the pleasure or pain takes place or is expected, it may be said to issue from, or to belong to, the *physical sanction*.

4.

If at the hands of a *particular* person or set of persons in the community, who under names correspondent to that of *judge*, are chosen for the particular purpose of dispensing it, according to the will of the sovereign or supreme ruling power in the state, it may be said to issue from the *political sanction*.

5.

If at the hands of such chance persons in the community, as the party in question may happen in the course of his life to have concerns with, according to each man's spontaneous disposition, and not according to any settled or concerted rule, it may be said to issue from the *moral* or *popular sanction*.

6.

If from the immediate hand of a superior invisible being, either in the present life, or in a future, it may be said to issue from the *religious sanction*.

7.

Pleasures or pains which may be expected to issue from the *physical*, *political*, or *moral* sanctions, must all of them be expected to be experienced, if ever, in the present life: those which may be expected to issue from the *religious* sanctions, may be expected to be experienced either in the *present* life or in a *future*.

8.

Those which can be experienced in the present life, can of course be no others than such as human nature in the course of the present life is susceptible of: and from each of these sources may flow all the pleasures or pains of which, in the course of the present life, human nature is susceptible. With regard to these, then (with which alone we have in this place any concern), those of them which belong to any one of those sanctions differ not ultimately in mind from those which belong to any one of the other three: the only difference there is among them lies in the circumstances that accompany their production. A suffering which befalls a man in the natural and spontaneous course of things, shall be styled, for instance, a *calamity*; in which case, if it be supposed to befall him through any imprudence of his, it may be styled a punishment issuing from the physical sanction. Now this same suffering, if inflicted by the law, will be what is commonly called a *punishment*; if incurred for want of any friendly assistance, which the misconduct, or supposed misconduct, of the sufferer has occasioned to be withholden, a punishment issuing from the *moral* sanction; if through the immediate interposition of a particular providence, a punishment issuing from the religious sanction.

9.

A man's goods, or his person, are consumed by fire. If this happened to him by what is called an accident, it was a calamity; if by reason of his own imprudence (for instance, from his neglecting to put his candle out), it may be styled a punishment of the physical sanction; if it happened to him by the sentence of the political magistrate, a punishment belonging to the political sanction—that is, what is commonly called a punishment; if for want of any assistance which his *neighbor* withheld from him out of some dislike to his *moral* character, a punishment of the *moral* sanction; if by an immediate act of *God's* displeasure, manifested on account of some sin committed by him, or through any distraction of mind, occasioned by the dread of such displeasure, a punishment of the *religious* sanction.

10.

As to such of the pleasures and pains belonging to the religious sanction, as regard a future life, of what kind these may be, we cannot know. These lie not open to our observation. During the present life they are matter only of expectation; and, whether that expectation be derived from natural or revealed religion, the particular kind of pleasure or pain, if it be different from all those which lie open to our observation, is what we can have no idea of. The best ideas we can obtain of such pains and pleasures are altogether unliquidated in point of reality. In what other respects our ideas of them may be liquidated, will be considered in another place.

11.

Of these four sanctions, the physical is altogether, we may observe, the groundwork of the political and the moral; so is it also of the religious, in as far as the latter bears relation to the present life. It is included in each of these other three. This may operate in any case (that is, any of the pains or pleasures belonging to it may operate) independently of *them*—none of *them* can operate but by means of this. In a word, the powers of nature may operate of themselves; but neither the magistrate, nor men at large, *can* operate, nor is God in the case in question *supposed* to operate, but through the powers of nature.

12.

For these four objects, which in their nature have so much in common, it seemed of use to find a common name. It seemed of use, in the first place, for the convenience of giving a name to certain pleasures and pains, for which a name equally characteristic could hardly otherwise have been found; in the second place, for the sake of holding up the efficacy of certain moral forces, the influence of which is apt not to be sufficiently attended to. Does the political sanction exert an influence over the conduct of mankind? The moral, the religious sanctions, do so too. In every inch of his career are the operations of the political magistrate liable to be aided or impeded by these two foreign powers: who, one or other of them, or both, are sure to be either his rivals or his allies. Does it happen to him to leave them out in his calculations? He will be sure almost to find himself mistaken in the result. Of all this we shall find abundant proofs in the sequel of this work. It behooves him, therefore, to have them continually before his eyes; and that under such a name as exhibits the relation they bear to his own purposes and designs.

CHAPTER IV: VALUE OF A LOT OF PLEASURE OR PAIN, HOW TO BE MEASURED

1.

Pleasures then, and the avoidance of pains are the *ends* which the legislator has in view: it behooves him therefore to understand their *value*. Pleasures and pains are the *instruments* he has to work with. It behooves him therefore to understand their force, which is again, in another point of view, their value.

2.

To a person considered *by himself* the value of a pleasure or pain considered *by itself* will be greater or less, according to the four following circumstances:

1. Its *intensity*.
2. Its *duration*.
3. Its *certainty* or *uncertainty*.
4. Its *propinquity* or *remoteness*.

3.

These are the circumstances which are to be considered in estimating a pleasure or a pain considered each of them by itself. But when the value of any pleasure or pain is considered for the purpose of estimating the tendency of any act by which it is produced, there are two other circumstances to be taken into the account; these are,

5. Its *fecundity*, or the chance it has of being followed by sensations of the *same* kind—that is, pleasures, if it be a pleasure; pains, if it be a pain.
6. Its *purity*, or the chance it has of *not* being followed by sensations of the *opposite* kind: that is, pains, if it be a pleasure: pleasures, if it be a pain.

These two last, however, are in strictness scarcely to be deemed properties of the pleasure or the pain itself; they are not, therefore, in strictness to be taken into the account of the value of that pleasure or that pain. They are in strictness to be deemed properties only of the act, or other event, by which such pleasure or pain has been produced; and accordingly are only to be taken into the account of the tendency of such act or such event.

4.

To a *number* of persons, with reference to each of whom the value of a pleasure or a pain is considered, it will be greater or less, according to seven circumstances: to wit, the six preceding ones; namely

1. Its *intensity*.
2. Its *duration*.
3. Its *certainty* or *uncertainty*.
4. Its *propinquity* or *remoteness*.

5. Its *fecundity*.
6. Its *purity*.

And one other, to wit:

7. Its *extent*; that is, the number of persons to whom it *extends*; or (in other words) who are affected by it.

5.

To take an exact account, then, of the general tendency of any act, by which the interests of a community are affected, proceed as follows. Begin with any one person of those whose interests seem most immediately to be affected by it, and take an account,

1. Of the value of each distinguishable *pleasure* which appears to be produced by it in the *first* instance.
2. Of the value of each *pain* which appears to be produced by it in the *first* instance.
3. Of the value of each pleasure which appears to be produced by it *after* the first. This constitutes the *fecundity* of the first *pleasure* and the *impurity* of the first *pain*.
4. Of the value of each *pain* which appears to be produced by it after the first. This constitutes the *fecundity* of the first *pain*, and *impurity* of the first pleasure.
5. Sum up all the values of all the *pleasures* on the one side, and those of all the pains on the other. The balance, if it be on the side of pleasure, will give the *good* tendency of the act upon the whole, with respect to the interests of that *individual* person; if on the side of pain, the *bad* tendency of it upon the whole.
6. Take an account of the *number* of persons whose interests appear to be concerned; and repeat the above process with respect to each. *Sum up* the numbers expressive of the degrees of *good* tendency, which the act has, with respect to each individual, in regard to whom the tendency of it is *good* upon the whole. Do this again with respect to each individual, in regard to whom the tendency of it is *bad* upon the whole. Take the *balance*; which, if on the side of *pleasure*. will give the general *good tendency* of the act, with respect to the total number or community of

individuals concerned; if on the side of pain, the general *evil tendency*, with respect to the same community.

6.

It is not to be expected that this process should be strictly pursued previously to every moral judgment, or to every legislative or judicial operation. It may, however, be always kept in view, and as near as the process actually pursued on these occasions approaches to it, so near will such process approach to the character of an exact one.

7.

The same process is alike applicable to pleasure and pain, in whatever shape they appear; and by whatever denomination they are distinguished: to pleasure, whether it be called *good* (which is properly the cause or instrument of pleasure), or *profit* (which is distant pleasure, or the cause or instrument of distant pleasure), or *convenience*, or *advantage, benefit, emolument, happiness,* and so forth: to pain, whether it be called *evil* (which corresponds to good), or *mischief* or *inconvenience,* or *disadvantage,* or *loss,* or *unhappiness,* and so forth.

8.

Nor is this a novel and unwarranted, any more than it is a useless theory. In all this there is nothing but what the practice of mankind, wheresoever they have a clear view of their own interest, is perfectly conformable to. An article of property, an estate in land, for instance, is valuable—on what account? On account of the pleasures of all kinds which it enables a man to produce, and, what comes to the same thing, the pains of all kinds which it enables him to avert. But the value of such an article of property is universally understood to rise or fall according to the length or shortness of the time which a man has in it: the certainty or uncertainty of its coming into possession: and the nearness or remoteness of the time at which, if at all, it is to come into possession. As to the *intensity* of the pleasures which a man may derive from it, this is never thought of, because it depends upon the use which each particular person may come to make of it; which cannot be estimated till the particular pleasures he may come to derive from it, or

the particular pains he may come to exclude by means of it, are brought to view. For the same reason, neither does he think of the *fecundity* or *purity* of those pleasures.

CHAPTER X

Of Motives

No motives either constantly good or constantly bad

9.

In all this chain of motives, the principal or original link seems to be the last internal motive in prospect: it is to this that all the other motives in prospect owe their materiality: and the immediately acting motive its existence. This motive in prospect, we see is always some pleasure, or some pain; some pleasure, which the act in question is expected to be a means of continuing or producing: some pain which it is expected to be a means of discontinuing of preventing. A motive is substantially nothing more than pleasure or pain, operating in a certain manner.

10.

Now, pleasure is in *itself* a good—nay, even setting aside immunity from pain, the only good—pain is in itself an evil—and, indeed, without exception, the only evil—or else the words good and evil have no meaning. And this is alike true of every sort of pain, and of every sort of pleasure. It follows, therefore, immediately and incontestably, that *there is no such thing as any sort of motive that is in itself a bad one.*

11.

It is common, however, to speak of actions as proceeding from *good* or *bad* motives, in which case the motives meant are such as are internal. The expression is far from being an accurate one, and as it is apt to occur in the consideration of almost every kind of offence, it will be requisite to settle the precise meaning of it, and observe how far it quadrates with the truth of things.

12.

With respect to goodness and badness, as it is with everything else that is not itself either pain or pleasure, so is it with motives. If they are good or bad, it is only on account of their effects; good, on account of their tendency to produce pleasure, or avert pain: bad, on account of their tendency to produce pain, or avert pleasure. Now the case is, that from one and the same motive, and from every kind of motive, may proceed actions that are good, others that are bad, and others that are indifferent.

STUDY QUESTIONS: BENTHAM, *AN INTRODUCTION TO THE PRINCIPLES OF MORALS AND LEGISLATION*

1. What are the two "sovereign masters" under which nature has placed humanity?
2. What are the means by which moral science can be improved?
3. What is the principle of utility? How is it the foundation for the present work?
4. What does Bentham mean by *utility*?
5. Can the interest of the community be understood without the interest of the individual? Why?
6. How are the words *ought*, *right* and *wrong* to be interpreted? What do they have in common?
7. Is Bentham a moral relativist? That is, does he think that any other but the principle of utility can be a right principle to govern humanity? Why?
8. What is the principle of sympathy and antipathy? How is it related to the principle of utility?
9. What are the main sources of pain and pleasure?
10. When is political sanction justified?
11. Is pleasure a derivative (instrumental) value or a value in and of itself? Why?

Philosophical Bridges: Bentham's Influence

Utilitarianism today, in its various evolutionary offshoots from Bentham's original formulation, is one of the leading moral theories in the world. His *Principles* drew both praise and protest throughout Europe and the United States, influencing just about all moral thinkers since, whether they agree or disagree. His work in trying to establish a code of law that could apply to all countries provided the sounding board for later international laws and institutions. His searing criticism of his own tradition of law and politics was so outrageously provocative that it has inspired many a rebel, then and since. He lashes out, for instance, at judges who "made the common law. Do you know how they make it? Just as a man makes laws for his dog. When your dog does anything you want to break him of, you wait till he does it and then beat him . . . this is the way judges make laws for you and me." Utilitarianism, because it is a theory that, ultimately, is not theoretical but practical, sanctioned not by church or political authority but based on a utility widely accessible to all, namely, pleasure, was Bentham's guided missile against the repressive structure of laws, under the guise of morality, on people by corrupt and exploitive leaders. To have a leading political and moral figure come out and not only reject all monarchies and established religion but to proclaim "all government is in itself one vast evil," unleashed a moral revolution against authority reaching all the way back to Socrates, ongoing to the present day.

MILL (1806–1873)

Biographical History

Born in London, England, John Stuart Mill was educated at home by a prominent philosopher, historian, and economist devoted to his upbringing: his father. At the age of 3 he began studying Greek and five years later he had read all the works of Plato in the original. By 12 he had read Aristotle's logical treatises, Euclid's elements, and mastered logic, mathematics, and world history. Mill said that "through the training bestowed on me by my father, I started, I may fairly say, with an advantage of a quarter century over my contemporaries." However, at the age of 25, Mill suffered an emotional breakdown. He writes that

> The habit of analysis has a tendency to wear away the feelings . . . I was thus, as I said to myself, left stranded at the commencement of my voyage, with a well equipped ship and a rudder, but no sail.

Mill had one great love in his life, in Mrs. Harriet Taylor; they did not marry, however, until after her husband died. She not only inspired him emotionally; Mill credited her as coauthor of his most important works: A *System of Logic* (1843), *The Principles of Political Economy* (1848), and *On Liberty* (1859).

  Mill was not a professional academician. He spent most of his working life as an employee of the East India Company, from which he retired in 1865 to run for Parliament. He won the election and achieved sweeping reforms on behalf of the working classes, including exploited immigrant workers. He applied his philosophical theories to many practical causes. In *The Subjection of Women* (1861), he argues that women should be given the power to vote, to have careers, and to take positions of political and social leadership. He helped found the first women's suffrage society and was among the first to advocate birth control being openly available to all.

Philosophical Overview

Besides his work in moral and political theory, Mill wrote a new and groundbreaking account of logic incorporating induction and what has since come to be known as "Mill's Method." The book, *System of Logic* (1843), is still widely used today. In it, he provides inductive methods for discovering causal relations among and between phenomena.

  Mill's moral and political philosophy grew out of a profound reaction to his greatest philosophical inspiration, Jeremy Bentham. He explains the nature of the "personal transformation" he experienced studying Bentham:

> Bentham passed judgment on the common modes of reasoning in morals and legislation, deduced from phrases like "law of nature," "right reason," "the moral sense," "natural rectitude," and the like, and characterized them as dogmatism in disguise, imposing its sentiments on others. . . . It had not struck me before, that Bentham's principles put an end to all this. The feeling rushed upon me, that all previous moralists were superseded, and that here indeed was the commencement of a new era in thought. This impression was strengthened by the manner in which Bentham put into scientific form the application of the happiness principle to the morality of actions. . . . there seemed to be added to this intellectual clearness, the most inspiring prospects of practical improvements in human affairs. . . . When I laid down the last

volume of the *Traité*, I had become a different being. . . . I now had opinions: a creed, a doctrine, a philosophy, in one of the best senses of the word, a religion. . . . And I had a grand conception laid before me of changes to be effected in the condition of mankind through that doctrine . . . sufficiently large and brilliant to light up my life, as well as to give definite shape to my aspirations.

(Quoted in *On Mill*, Susan Leigh Anderson)

UTILITARIANISM
Mill

In this groundbreaking work, instead of defining the utility principle in terms of avoiding pain and securing pleasure, as Bentham did, Mill argues that such blatant self-interest is inadequate for moral goodness. Bentham's calculus, in Mill's view, fails because it does not provide a qualitative distinction between pleasures. Bentham defined pains and pleasures using seven categories: (1) intensity, (2) duration, (3) certainty, (4) proximity, (5) fecundity, (6) purity, and (7) extent. This moral calculus allows us to make appropriate judgments. Say a decision to do X would produce brief, intense pleasure for a few, and long, intense pain for many. It is then a bad decision. Bentham's calculus does not distinguish between types of pleasure and pains, saying "quantity of pleasure being equal, pushpin is as good as poetry." Mill disagrees. In *Utilitarianism*, he distinguishes pains and pleasures with respect to their quality, which he adds to the list as an eighth category. As he famously put it, "better to be Socrates dissatisfied than a fool satisfied." The problem, then becomes one of who should decide among these qualities and how. Mill's answer bridges moral theory with political theory; such questions must be settled democratically, by majority rule.

The creed which accepts as the foundation of morals "utility" or the "greatest happiness principle" holds that actions are right in proportion as they tend to promote happiness, wrong as they tend to produce the reverse of happiness. By happiness is intended pleasure, and the absence of pain; by unhappiness, pain, and the privation of pleasure. To give a clear view of the moral standard set up by the theory, much more requires to be said; in particular, what things it includes in the ideas of pain and pleasure; and to what extent this is left an open question. But these supplementary explanations do not affect the theory of life on which this theory of morality is grounded—namely, that pleasure and freedom from pain are the only things desirable as ends; and that all desirable things (which are as numerous in the utilitarian as in any other scheme) are desirable either for the pleasure inherent in themselves, or as means to the promotion of pleasure and the prevention of pain.

Now such a theory of life excites in many minds, and among them in some of the most estimable in feeling and purpose, inveterate dislike. To suppose that life has (as they express it) no higher end than pleasure—no better and nobler object of desire and pursuit—they designate as utterly mean and groveling; as a doctrine worthy only of swine, to whom the followers of Epicurus were, at a very early period, contemptuously likened; and modern holders of the doctrine are occasionally made the subject of equally polite comparisons by its German, French, and English assailants.

Mill, from *Utilitarianism*, 1863.

When thus attacked, the Epicureans have always answered that it is not they, but their accusers, who represent human nature in a degrading light, since the accusation supposes human beings to be capable of no pleasures except those of which swine are capable. If this supposition were true, the charge could not be gainsaid, but would then be no longer an imputation; for if the sources of pleasure were precisely the same to human beings and to swine, the rule of life which is good enough for the one would be good enough for the other. The comparison of the Epicurean life to that of beasts is felt as degrading, precisely because a beast's pleasures do not satisfy a human being's conceptions of happiness. Human beings have faculties more elevated than the animal appetites and, when once made conscious of them, do not regard anything as happiness which does not include their gratification. I do not, indeed, consider the Epicureans to have been by any means faultless in drawing out their scheme of consequences from the utilitarian principle. To do this in any sufficient manner, many Stoic, as well as Christian, elements require to be included. But there is no known Epicurean theory of life which does not assign to the pleasures of the intellect, of the feelings and imagination, and of the moral sentiments, a much higher value as pleasures than to those of mere sensation. It must be admitted, however, that utilitarian writers in general have placed the superiority of mental over bodily pleasures chiefly in the greater permanency, safety, uncostliness, etc., of the former—that is, in their circumstantial advantages rather than in their intrinsic nature. And on all these points utilitarians have fully proved their case; but they might have taken the other and, as it may be called, higher ground with entire consistency. It is quite compatible with the principle of utility to recognize the fact that some kinds of pleasure are more desirable and more valuable than others. It would be absurd that, while, in estimating all other things, quality is considered as well as quantity, the estimation of pleasures should be supposed to depend on quantity alone.

If I am asked what I mean by difference of quality in pleasures, or what makes one pleasure more valuable than another, merely as a pleasure, except its being greater in amount, there is but one possible answer. Of two pleasures, if there be one to which all or almost all who have experience of both give a decided preference, irrespective of any feeling of moral obligation to prefer it, that is the more desirable pleasure. If one of the two is, by those who are competently acquainted with both, placed so far above the other that they prefer it, even though knowing it to be attended with a greater amount of discontent, and would not resign it for any quantity of the other pleasure which their nature is capable of, we are justified in ascribing to the preferred enjoyment a superiority in quality so far outweighing quantity as to render it, in comparison, of small account.

Now it is an unquestionable fact that those who are equally acquainted with and equally capable of appreciating and enjoying both, do give a most marked preference to the manner of existence which employs their higher faculties. Few human creatures would consent to be changed into any of the lower animals for a promise of the fullest allowance of a beast's pleasures; no intelligent human being would consent to be a fool, no instructed person would be an ignoramus, no person of feeling and conscience would be selfish and base, even though they should be persuaded that the fool, the dunce, or the rascal is better satisfied with his lot than they are with theirs. They would not resign what they possess more than he for the most complete satisfaction of all the desires which they have in common with him. If they ever fancy they would, it is only in cases of unhappiness so extreme that to escape from it they would exchange their lot for almost any other, however undesirable in their own eyes. A being of higher faculties requires more to make him happy, is capable probably of more acute suffering, and certainly accessible to it at more points, than one of an inferior type; but in spite of these liabilities, he can never really wish to sink into what he feels to be a lower grade of existence. We may give what explanation we please of this unwillingness; we may attribute it to pride, a name which is given indiscriminately to some of the most and to some of the least estimable feelings of which mankind are capable; we may refer it to the love of liberty and personal independence, an appeal to which was with the Stoics one of the most effective means for the inculcation of it; to the love of power or to the love of excitement, both of which do really enter into and contribute to it; but its most appropriate appellation is a sense of dignity, which all human beings possess in one form or other, and in some, though by no means in exact, proportion to their higher faculties, and which is so essential a part of the happiness of those in whom it is strong that nothing which conflicts with it could be otherwise than momentarily an object of desire to them. Whoever supposes that this preference takes place at a sacrifice of happiness—that the superior being, in anything like equal circumstances, is not happier than the inferior—confounds the two very different ideas of happiness and content. It is undisputable that the being whose capacities of enjoyment are low has the greatest chance of having them fully satisfied; and a highly endowed being will always feel that any happiness which he can look for, as the world is constituted, is imperfect. But he can learn to bear its imperfections, if they are at all bearable; and they will not make him envy the being who is indeed unconscious of the imperfections, but only because he feels not at all the good which those imperfections qualify. It is better to be a human being dissatisfied than a pig satisfied; better to be Socrates dissatisfied than a fool satisfied. And if the fool, or the pig, are of a different opinion, it is because they only know their own side of the question. The other party to the comparison knows both sides.

It may be objected that many who are capable of the higher pleasures occasionally, under the influence of temptation, postpone them to the lower. But this is quite compatible with a full appreciation of the intrinsic superiority of the higher. Men often, from infirmity of character, make their election for the nearer good, though they know it to be the less valuable; and this no less when the choice is between two bodily pleasures than when it is between bodily and mental. They pursue sensual indulgences to the injury of health, though perfectly aware that health is the greater good. It may be further objected that many who begin with youthful enthusiasm for everything noble, as they advance in years, sink into indolence and selfishness. But I do not believe that those who undergo this very common change voluntarily choose the lower description of pleasures in preference to the higher. I believe that, before they devote themselves exclusively to the one, they have already become incapable of the other. Capacity for the nobler feelings is in most natures a very tender plant, easily killed, not only by hostile influences, but by mere

want of sustenance; and in the majority of young persons it speedily dies away if the occupations to which their position in life has devoted them and the society into which it has thrown them, are not favorable to keeping that higher capacity in exercise. Men lose their high aspirations as they lose their intellectual tastes, because they have not time or opportunity for indulging them; and they addict themselves to inferior pleasures, not because they deliberately prefer them, but because they are either the only ones to which they have access, or the only ones which they are any longer capable of enjoying. It may be questioned whether any one who has remained equally susceptible to both classes of pleasures, ever knowingly and calmly preferred the lower, though many, in all ages, have broken down in an ineffectual attempt to combine both.

From this verdict of the only competent judges, I apprehend there can be no appeal. On a question which is the best worth having of two pleasures, or which of two modes of existence is the most grateful to the feelings, apart from its moral attributes and from its consequences, the judgment of those who are qualified by knowledge of both, or, if they differ, that of the majority of them, must be admitted as final. And there needs to be less hesitation to accept this judgment respecting the quality of pleasures, since there is no other tribunal to be referred to even on the question of quantity. What means are there of determining which is the acutest of two pains, or the intensest of two pleasurable sensations, except the general suffrage of those who are familiar with both? Neither pains nor pleasures are homogeneous, and pain is always heterogeneous with pleasure. What is there to decide whether a particular pleasure is worth purchasing at the cost of a particular pain, except the feelings and judgment of the experienced? When, therefore, those feelings and judgment declare the pleasures derived from the higher faculties to be preferable *in kind,* apart from the question of intensity, to those of which the animal nature, disjointed from the higher faculties, is susceptible, they are entitled on this subject to the same regard.

I have dwelt on this point, as being a necessary part of a perfectly just conception of utility or happiness considered as the directive rule of human conduct. But it is by no means an indispensable condition to the acceptance of the utilitarian standard; for that standard is not the agent's own greatest happiness, but the greatest amount of happiness altogether; and if it may possibly be doubted whether a noble character is always the happier for its nobleness, there can be no doubt that it makes other people happier, and that the world in general is immensely a gainer by it. Utilitarianism, therefore, could only attain its end by the general cultivation of nobleness of character, even if each individual were only benefited by the nobleness of others, and his own, so far as happiness is concerned, were a sheer deduction from the benefit. But the bare enunciation of such an absurdity as this last renders refutation superfluous.

According to the greatest happiness principle, as above explained, the ultimate end, with reference to and for the sake of which all other things are desirable—whether we are considering our own good or that of other people—is an existence exempt as far as possible from pain, and as rich as possible in enjoyments, both in point of quantity and quality; the test of quality and the rule for measuring it against quantity being the preference felt by those who, in their opportunities of experience, to which must be added their habits of self-consciousness and self-observation, are best furnished with the means of comparison. This being, according to the utilitarian opinion, the end of human action, is necessarily also the standard of morality, which may accordingly be defined "the rules and precepts for human conduct," by the observance of which an existence such as has been described might be, to the greatest extent possible, secured to all mankind; and not to them only, but, so far as the nature of things admits, to the whole sentient creation. . . .

The happiness which forms the utilitarian standard of what is right in conduct is not the agent's own happiness but that of all concerned. As between his own happiness and that of others, utilitarianism requires him to be as strictly impartial as a disinterested and benevolent spectator. In the golden rule of Jesus of Nazareth, we read the complete spirit of the ethics of utility. "To do as you would be done by," and "to love your neighbor as yourself," constitute the ideal perfection of utilitarian morality. As the means of making the nearest approach to this ideal, utility would enjoin, first, that laws and social arrangements should place the happiness or (as, speaking practically, it may be called) the interest of every individual as nearly as possible in harmony with the interest of the whole, and, secondly, that education and opinion, which have so vast a power over human character, should so use that power as to establish in the mind of every individual an indissoluble association between his own happiness and the good of the whole, especially between his own happiness and the practice of such modes of conduct, negative and positive, as regard for the universal happiness prescribes; so that not only he may be unable to conceive the possibility of happiness to himself, consistently with conduct opposed to the general good, but also that a direct impulse to promote the general good may be in every individual one of the habitual motives of action, and the sentiments connected therewith may fill a large and prominent place in every human being's sentient existence. If the impugners of the utilitarian morality represented it to their own minds in this its true character, I know not what recommendation possessed by any other morality they could possibly affirm to be wanting to it; what more beautiful or more exalted developments of human nature any other ethical system can be supposed to foster, or what springs of action, not accessible to the utilitarian, such systems rely on for giving effect to their mandates.

. . . The corollaries from the principle of utility, like the precepts of every practical art, admit of indefinite improvement, and, in a progressive state of the human mind, their improvement is perpetually going on. But to consider the rules of morality as improvable is one thing; to pass over the intermediate generalization entirely and endeavor to test each individual action directly by the first principle is another. It is a strange notion that the acknowledgment of a first principle is inconsistent with the admission of secondary ones. To inform a traveler respecting the place of his ultimate destination is not to forbid the use of landmarks and direction posts on the way. The proposition that happiness is the end and aim of morality does not mean that no road ought to be laid down to that goal, or that persons going thither should not be advised to take one direction rather than another. Men really ought to leave off talking a kind of nonsense on this subject, which they would neither talk nor listen to on other matters of practical concernment. Nobody argues that the art of navigation is not founded on astronomy because sailors cannot wait to calculate the nautical almanac. Being rational creatures, they go to sea with it ready calculated; and all rational creatures go out upon the sea of life with their minds made up on the common questions of right and wrong, as well as on many of the far more difficult questions of wise and foolish. And this, as long as foresight is a human quality, it is to be presumed they will continue to do. Whatever we adopt as the fundamental principle of morality, we require subordinate principles to apply it by; the impossibility of doing without them, being common to all systems, can afford no argument against any one in particular; but gravely to argue as if no such secondary principles could be had, and as if mankind had remained till now, and always must remain, without drawing any general conclusions from the experience of human life, is as high a pitch, I think, as absurdity has ever reached in philosophical controversy. . . .

OF WHAT SORT OF PROOF THE PRINCIPLE OF UTILITY IS SUSCEPTIBLE

Questions of ultimate ends do not admit of proof, in the ordinary acceptation of the term. To be incapable of proof by reasoning is common to all first principles, to the first premises of our knowledge, as well as to those of our conduct. But the former, being matters of fact, may be the subject of a direct appeal to the faculties which judge of fact—namely, our senses and our internal consciousness. Can an appeal be made to the same faculties on questions of practical ends? Or by what other faculty is cognizance taken of them?

Questions about ends are in other words, questions what things are desirable. The utilitarian doctrine is that happiness is desirable, and the only thing desirable, as an end; all other things being only desirable as means to that end. What ought to be required of this doctrine, what conditions is it requisite that the doctrine should fulfill—to make good its claim to be believed?

The only proof capable of being given that an object is visible is that people actually see it. The only proof that a sound is audible is that people hear it; and so of the other sources of our experience. In like manner, I apprehend, the sole evidence it is possible to produce that anything is desirable is that people do actually desire it. If the end which the utilitarian doctrine proposes to itself were not, in theory and in practice, acknowledged to be an end, nothing could ever convince any person that it was so. No reason can be given why the general happiness is desirable, except that each person, so far as he believes it to be attainable, desires his own happiness. This, however, being a fact, we have not only all the proof which the case admits of, but all which it is possible to require, that happiness is a good; that each person's happiness is a good to that person, and the general happiness; therefore, a good to the aggregate of all persons. Happiness has made out its title as *one* of the ends of conduct, and consequently one of the criteria of morality.

But it has not, by this alone, proved itself to be the sole criterion. To do that, it would seem, by the same rule, necessary to show, not only that people desire happiness, but that they never desire anything else. Now it is palpable that they do desire things which, in common language, are decidedly distinguished from happiness. They desire, for example, virtue and the absence of vice, no less really than pleasure and the absence of pain. The desire of virtue is not as universal, but it is as authentic a fact as the desire of happiness. And hence the opponents of the utilitarian standard deem that they have a right to infer that there are other ends of human action besides happiness, and that happiness is not the standard of approbation and disapprobation.

But does the utilitarian doctrine deny that people desire virtue, or maintain that virtue is not a thing to be desired? The very reverse. It maintains not only that virtue is to be desired, but that it is to be desired disinterestedly, for itself. Whatever may be the opinion of utilitarian moralists as to the original conditions by which virtue is made virtue, however they may believe (as they do) that actions and dispositions are only virtuous because they promote another end than virtue, yet this being granted, and it having been decided, from considerations of this description, what *is* virtuous, they not only place virtue at the very head of the things which are good as means to the ultimate end, but they also recognize as a psychological fact the possibility of its being, to the individual, a good in itself; without looking to any end beyond it; and hold that the mind is not in a right state, not in a state conformable to utility, not in the state most conducive to the general happiness, unless it does love virtue in this manner—as a thing desirable in itself, even although, in the individual instance, it should not produce those other desirable consequences which it tends to produce, and on account of which it is held to be virtue. This opinion is not, in the smallest degree, a departure from the happiness principle. The ingredients of happiness are very various, and each of them is desirable in itself, and not merely when considered as swelling an aggregate. The principle of utility does not mean that any given pleasure, as music, for instance, or any given exemption from pain, for example, health, is to be looked upon as means to a collective something termed happiness, and to be desired on that account. They are desired and desirable in and for themselves; besides being means, they are a part of the end. Virtue, according to the utilitarian doctrine, is not naturally and originally part of the end, but it is capable of becoming so; and in those who love it disinterestedly it has become so, and is desired and cherished, not as a means to happiness, but as a part of their happiness.

To illustrate this further, we may remember that virtue is not the only thing originally a means, and which if it were not a means to anything else would be and remain indifferent, but which by association with what it is a means to comes to be desired for itself, and that too with the utmost intensity. What, for example, shall we say of the love of money? There is nothing originally more desirable about money than about any heap of glittering pebbles. Its worth is solely that of the things which it will buy; the desires for other things than itself, which it is a means of gratifying. Yet the love of money is not only one of the strongest moving forces of human life, but money is, in many cases, desired in and for itself; the desire to possess it is often stronger than the desire to use it, and goes on increasing when all the desires which point to ends beyond it, to be compassed by it, are falling off. It may, then, be said truly that money is desired not for the sake of an end, but as part of the end. From being a means to happiness, it has come to be itself a principal ingredient of the individual's con-

ception of happiness. The same may be said of the majority of the great objects of human life: power, for example, or fame, except that to each of these there is a certain amount of immediate pleasure annexed, which has at least the semblance of being naturally inherent in them—a thing which cannot be said of money. Still, however, the strongest natural attraction, both of power and of fame, is the immense aid they give to the attainment of our other wishes; and it is the strong association thus generated between them and all our objects of desire which gives to the direct desire of them the intensity if other assumes, so as in some characters to surpass in strength all other desires. In these cases the means have become a part of the end, and a more important part of it than any of the things which they are means to. What was once desired as an instrument for the attainment of happiness has come to be desired for its own sake. In being desired for its own sake it is, however, desired as *part* of happiness. The person is made, or thinks he would be made, happy by its mere possession; and is made unhappy by failure to obtain it. The desire of it is not a different thing from the desire of happiness any more than the love of music or the desire of health. They are included in happiness. They are some of the elements of which the desire of happiness is made up. Happiness is not an abstract idea but a concrete whole; and these are some of its parts. And the utilitarian standard sanctions and approves their being so. Life would be a poor thing, very ill provided with sources of happiness, if there were not this provision of nature by which things originally indifferent, but conductive to, or otherwise associated with, the satisfaction of our primitive desires, become in themselves sources of pleasure more valuable than the primitive pleasures; both in permanency, in the space of human existence that they are capable of covering, and even in intensity.

Virtue, according to the utilitarian conception, is a good of this description. There was no original desire of it, or motive to it, save its conduciveness to pleasure, and especially to protection from pain. But through the association thus formed it may be felt a good in itself, and desired as such with as great intensity as any other good; and with this difference between it and the love of money, of power, or of fame, that all of these may, and often do, render the individual noxious to the other members of the society to which he belongs, whereas there is nothing which makes him so much a blessing to them as the cultivation of the disinterested love of virtue. And consequently, the utilitarian standard, while it tolerates and approves those other acquired desires, up to the point beyond which they would be more injurious to the general happiness than promotive of it, enjoins and requires the cultivation of the love of virtue up to the greatest strength possible, as being above all things important to the general happiness.

It results from the preceding considerations that there is in reality nothing desired except happiness. Whatever is desired otherwise than as a means to some end beyond itself, and ultimately to happiness, is desired as itself a part of happiness, and is not desired for itself until it has become so. Those who desire virtue for its own sake desire it either because the consciousness of it is a pleasure, or because the consciousness of being without it is a pain, or for both reasons united; as in truth the pleasure and pain seldom exist separately, but almost always together—the same person feeling pleasure in the degree of virtue attained, and pain in not having attained more. If one of these gave him no pleasure, and the other no pain, he would not love or desire virtue, or would desire it only for the other benefits which it might produce to himself or to persons whom he cared for.

We have now, then, an answer to the question, of what sort of proof the principle of utility is susceptible. If the opinion which I have now stated is psychologically true—if human nature is so constituted as to desire nothing which is not either a part of happiness or a means of happiness, we can have no other proof, and we require no other, that these are the only things desirable. If so, happiness is the sole end of human action, and the promotion of it the test by which to judge of all human conduct; from whence it necessarily follows that it must be the criterion of morality, since a part is included in the whole.

And now to decide whether this is really so, whether mankind do desire nothing for itself but that which is a pleasure to them, or of which the absence is a pain, we have evidently arrived at a question of fact and experience, dependent, like all similar questions, upon evidence. It can only be determined by practised self-consciousness and self-observation, assisted by observation of others. I believe that these sources of evidence, impartially consulted, will declare that desiring a thing and finding it pleasant, aversion to it and thinking of it as painful, are phenomena entirely inseparable or rather two parts of the same phenomenon; in strictness of language, two different modes of naming the same psychological fact; that to think of an object as desirable (unless for the sake of its consequences) and to think of it as pleasant are one and the same thing; and that to desire anything except in proportion as the idea of it is pleasant, is a physical and metaphysical impossibility.

So obvious does this appear to me that I expect it will hardly be disputed; and the objection made will be, not that desire can possibly be directed to anything ultimately except pleasure and exemption from pain, but that the will is a different thing from desire; that a person of confirmed virtue or any other person whose purposes are fixed carries out his purposes without any thought of the pleasure he has in contemplating them or expects to derive from their fulfillment, and persists in acting on them, even though these pleasures are much diminished by changes in his character or decay of his passive sensibilities, or are outweighed by the pains which the pursuit of the purposes may bring upon him. All this I fully admit and have stated it elsewhere as positively and emphatically as anyone. Will, the active phenomenon, is a different thing from desire, the state of passive sensibility, and, though originally an offshoot from it, may in time take root and detach itself from the parent stock, so much so that in the case of an habitual purpose, instead of willing the thing because we desire it, we often desire it only because we will it. This, however, is but an instance of that familiar fact, the power of habit, and is nowise confined to the case of virtuous actions. Many indifferent things which men originally did from a motive of some sort, they continue to do from habit. Sometimes this is done unconsciously; the consciousness coming only after the action; at other times with conscious volition, but volition which has become habitual and is put in operation by the force of habit, in opposition perhaps to the deliberate preference, as often happens with those who have contracted habits of vicious or hurtful indulgence. Third and last comes the case in which the habitual act of will in the individual instance is not in contradiction to the general intention prevailing at other times, but in fulfillment of it; as in the case of the person of confirmed virtue and of all who pursue deliberately and consistently any determinate end. The distinction between will and desire thus understood is an authentic and highly important psychological fact; but the fact consists solely in this—that will, like all other parts of our constitution, is amenable to habit, and that we may will from habit what we no longer desire for itself, or desire only because we will it. It is not the less true that will, in the beginning, is entirely produced by desire; including in that term the repelling influence of pain as well as the attractive one of pleasure. Let us take into consideration no longer the person who has a confirmed will to do right, but him in whom that virtuous will is still feeble, conquerable by temptation, and not to be fully relied on; by what means can it be strengthened? How can the will to be virtuous, where it does not exist in sufficient force, be implanted or awakened? Only by making the person *desire* virtue—by making him think of it in a pleasurable light, or of its absence in a painful one. It is by associating the doing right with pleasure, or the doing wrong with pain, or by eliciting and impressing and bringing home to the person's experience the pleasure naturally involved in the one or the pain in the other, that it is possible to call forth that will to be virtuous which, when confirmed, acts without any thought of either pleasure or pain. Will is the child of desire, and passes out of the dominion of its parent only to come under that of habit. That which is the result of habit affords no presumption of being intrinsically good; and there would be no reason for wishing that the purpose of virtue should become independent of pleasure and pain were it not that the influence of the pleasurable and painful associations which prompt to virtue is not sufficiently to be depended on for unerring constancy of action until it has acquired the support of habit. Both in feeling and in conduct, habit is the only thing which imparts certainty; and it is because of the importance to others of being able to rely absolutely on one's feelings and conduct, and to oneself of being able to rely on one's own, that the will to do right ought to be cultivated into this habitual independence. In other words, this state of the will is a means to good, not intrinsically a good; and does not contradict the doctrine that nothing is a good to human beings but in so far as it is either itself pleasurable or a means of attaining pleasure or averting pain.

But if this doctrine be true, the principle of utility is proved. Whether it is so or not, must now be left to the consideration of the thoughtful reader.

STUDY QUESTIONS: MILL, *UTILITARIANISM*

1. What is "happiness," according to Mill? How does his view differ from his predecessors?
2. How does Mill view the Epicureans?
3. How does Mill distinguish qualities of pleasures?
4. Is everyone equally capable of "higher" pleasures? Why?
5. What does Mill make of Jesus' golden rule?
6. Is the principle of utility susceptible to proof?
7. What is the utilitarian conception of *virtue*?
8. How are will and desire related?

ON LIBERTY

In *On Liberty* Mill argues that the basic utilitarian principle—the greatest happiness for the greatest number—is best achieved by letting everyone have virtually unrestricted freedom, not only of thought but also of action. The only stipulation is that one's thoughts and actions must not cause actual harm to others.

The lessons of the past should teach us, he argues, that no one person, no one system of philosophy, is sufficient for a healthy society. Since no one has a monopoly on absolute

Mill, from *On Liberty*, first published in London in 1859.

truth and all anyone ever has are, at best, partial truths, there should always be a plurality of voices. Moreover, the wisest should not become rulers, for then the ordinary citizens will look up to them and by growing accustomed to following leaders, in the long run stagnate. When official truths are passed down from generation to generation, there is no attempt to generate the new. A society should thus encourage individuality, because that is the wellspring of originality, through which new ideas are born. It is therefore in the interest of the majority of a society to be tolerant of all its minorities. Only then can the greatest happiness for the greatest number be achieved.

CHAPTER I

Introductory

. . . The object of this essay is to assert one very simple principle, as entitled to govern absolutely the dealings of society with the individual in the way of compulsion and control, whether the means used be physical force in the form of legal penalties, or the moral coercion of public opinion. That principle is, that the sole end for which mankind are warranted, individually or collectively, in interfering with the liberty of action of any of their number, is self-protection. That the only purpose for which power can be rightfully exercised over any member of a civilized community, against his will, is to prevent harm to others. His own good, either physical or moral, is not a sufficient warrant. He cannot rightfully be compelled to do or forbear because it will be better for him to do so, because it will make him happier, because, in the opinions of others, to do so would be wise, or even right. These are good reasons for remonstrating with him, or reasoning with him, or persuading him, or entreating him, but not for compelling him, or visiting him with any evil in case he do otherwise. To justify that, the conduct from which it is desired to deter him must be calculated to produce evil to some one else. The only part of the conduct of anyone, for which he is amenable to society, is that which concerns others. In the part which merely concerns himself, his independence is, of right, absolute. Over himself, over his own body and mind, the individual is sovereign.

It is perhaps hardly necessary to say that this doctrine is meant to apply only to human beings in the maturity of their faculties. We are not speaking of children, or of young persons below the age which the law may fix as that of manhood or womanhood.

Those who are still in a state to require being taken care of by others, must be protected against their own actions as well as against external injury. . . .

It is proper to state that I forego any advantage which could be derived to my argument from the idea of abstract right, as a thing independent of utility. I regard utility as the ultimate appeal on all ethical questions; but it must be utility in the largest sense, grounded on the permanent interests of a man as a progressive being. Those interests, I contend, authorized the subjection of individual spontaneity to external control, only in respect to those actions of each which concern the interest of other people. If anyone does an act hurtful to others, there is a *prima facie* case for punishing him, by law, or, where legal penalties are not safely applicable, by general disapprobation. There are also many positive acts for the benefit of others, which he may rightfully be compelled to perform: such as to give evidence in a court of justice; to bear his fair share in the common defense, or in any other joint work necessary to the interest of the society of which he enjoys the protection; and to perform certain acts of individual beneficence, such as saving a fellow creature's life, or interposing to protect the defenseless against ill usage, things which wherever it is obviously a man's duty to do, he may rightfully be made responsible to society for not doing. A person may cause evil to others not only by his actions but by his inaction, and in either case he is justly accountable to them for the injury. The latter case, it is true, requires a much more cautious exercise of compulsion than the former. To make anyone answerable for doing evil to others is the rule; to make him answerable for not preventing evil is, comparatively speaking, the exception. Yet there are many cases clear enough and grave enough to justify that exception. In all things which regard the external relations of the individual, he is *de jure* amenable to those whose interests are concerned, and, if need be, to society as their protector. There are often good reasons for not holding him to the responsibility; but these reasons must arise from the special expediencies of the case: either because it is a kind of case in which he is on the whole likely to act better, when left to his own discretion, than when controlled in any way in which society have it in their power to control him; or because the attempt to exercise control would produce other evils, greater than those which it would prevent. When such reasons as these preclude the enforcement of responsibility, the conscience of the agent himself should step into the vacant judgment seat, and protect those interests of others which have no external protection; judging himself all the more rigidly, because the case does not admit of his being made accountable to the judgment of his fellow creatures.

But there is a sphere of action in which society, as distinguished from the individual, has, if any, only an indirect interest; comprehending all that portion of a person's life and conduct which affects only himself, or if it also affects others, only with their free, voluntary, and undeceived consent and participation. When I say only himself, I mean directly, and in the first instance; for whatever affects himself, may affect others through himself; and the objection which may be grounded on this contingency, will receive consideration in the sequel. This, then, is the appropriate region of human liberty. It comprises, *first*, the inward domain of consciousness; demanding liberty of conscience in the most comprehensive sense; liberty of thought and feeling; absolute freedom of opinion and sentiment on all subjects, practical or speculative, scientific, moral or theological. The liberty of expressing and publishing opinions may seem to fall under a different principle, since it belongs to that part of the conduct of an individual which concerns other people; but, being almost of as much importance as the liberty of thought itself, and resting in great part on the same reasons, is practically inseparable from it. *Secondly*, the principle requires liberty of tastes and pursuits; of framing the plan of our life to suit our own character; of doing as we like, subject to such consequences as may follow: without impediment from our fellow creatures, so long as what we do does not harm them, even though they should think our conduct foolish, perverse, or wrong.

Thirdly, from this liberty of each individual, follows the liberty, within the same limits, of combination among individuals; freedom to unite, for any purpose not involving harm to others: the persons combining being supposed to be of full age, and not forced or deceived.

No society in which these liberties are not, on the whole, respected, is free, whatever may be its form of government; and none is completely free in which they do not exist absolute and unqualified. The only freedom which deserves the name, is that of pursuing our own good in our own way, so long as we do not attempt to deprive others of theirs, or impede their efforts to obtain it. Each is the proper guardian of his own health, whether bodily, or mental and spiritual. Mankind are greater gainers by suffering each other to live as seems good to themselves, than by compelling each to live as seems good to the rest.

Though this doctrine is anything but new, and, to some persons, may have the air of a truism, there is no doctrine which stands more directly opposed to the general tendency of existing opinion and practice. . . . There is . . . an inclination to stretch unduly the powers of society over the individual, both by the force of opinion and even by that of legislation; and as the tendency of all the changes taking place in the world is to strengthen society, and diminish the power of the individual, this encroachment is not one of the evils which tend spontaneously to disappear, but, on the contrary, to grow more and more formidable. The disposition of mankind, whether as rulers or as fellow citizens, to impose their own opinions and inclinations as a rule of conduct on others, is so energetically supported by some of the best and by some of the worst feelings incident to human nature, that it is hardly ever kept under restraint by anything but want of power; and as the power is not declining, but growing, unless a strong barrier of moral conviction can be raised against the mischief, we must expect, in the present circumstances of the world, to see it increase. . . .

CHAPTER II

Of the Liberty of Thought and Discussion

The time, it is to be hoped, is gone by, when any defence would be necessary of the "liberty of the press" as one of the securities against corrupt or tyrannical government. . . . Speaking generally, it is not, in constitutional countries, to be apprehended that the government, whether completely responsible to the people or not, will often attempt to control the expression of opinion, except when in doing so it makes itself the organ of the general intolerance of the public. Let us suppose, therefore, that the government is entirely at one with the people, and never thinks of exerting any power of coercion unless in agreement with what it conceives to be their voice. But I deny the right of the people to exercise such coercion, either by themselves or by their government. The power itself is illegitimate. The best government has no more title to it than the worst. It is as noxious, or more noxious, when exerted in accordance with public opinion, than when in opposition to it. If all mankind minus one were of one opinion, and only one person were of the contrary opinion, mankind would be no more justified in silencing that one person, than he, if he had the power, would be justified in silencing mankind. Were an opinion a personal possession of no value except to the owner; if to be obstructed in the enjoyment of it were simply a private injury, it would make some difference whether the injury was inflicted only on a few persons or on many. But the peculiar evil of silencing the expression of an opinion is, that it is robbing the human race: posterity as well as the existing generation; those who dissent from the opinion, still more than those who hold it. If the opinion is right, they are deprived of the opportunity of exchanging error for truth; if wrong, they lose, what is almost as great a benefit, the clearer perception and livelier impression of truth, produced by its collision with error.

It is necessary to consider separately these two hypotheses, each of which has a distinct branch of the argument corresponding to it. We can never be sure that the opinion we are endeavoring to stifle is a false opinion; and if we were sure, stifling it would be an evil still.

First, the opinion which it is attempted to suppress by authority may possibly be true. Those who desire to suppress it, of course deny its truth; but they are not infallible. They have no authority to decide the question for all mankind, and exclude every other person from the means of judging. To refuse a hearing to an opinion, because they are sure that it is false, is to assume that *their* certainty is the same thing as *absolute* certainty. All silencing of discussion is an assumption of infallibility. Its condemnation may be allowed to rest on this common argument, not the worse for being common.

Unfortunately for the good sense of mankind, the fact of their fallibility is far from carrying the weight in their practical judgment which is always allowed to it in theory; for while everyone well knows himself to be fallible, few think it necessary to take any precautions against their own fallibility, or admit the supposition that any opinion of which they feel very certain, may be one of the examples of the error to which they acknowledge themselves to be liable. Absolute princes, or others who are accustomed to unlimited deference, usually feel this complete confidence in their own opinions on nearly all subjects. People more happily situated, who sometimes hear their opinions disputed, and are not wholly unused to be set right when they are wrong, place the same unbounded reliance only on such of their opinions as are shared by all who surround them, or to whom they habitually defer; for in proportion to a man's want of confidence in his own solitary judgment, does he usually repose, with implicit trust, on the infallibility of "the world" in general. And the world, to each individual, means the part of it with which he comes in contact—his party, his sect, his church, his class of society—the man may be called, by comparison, almost liberal and large-minded to whom it means anything so comprehensive as his own country or his own age. Nor is his faith in this collective authority at all shaken by his being aware that other ages, countries, sects, churches, classes, and parties have thought, and even now think, the exact reverse. He devolves upon his own world the responsibility of being in the right against the dissentient worlds of other people; and it never troubles him that mere accident has decided which of these numerous worlds is the object of his reliance, and that the same causes which make him a churchman in London, would have made him a Buddhist or a Confucian in Peking. Yet it is as evident in itself as any amount of argument can make it, that ages are no more infallible than individuals; every age having held many opinions which subsequent ages have deemed not only false but absurd; and it is as certain that many opinions now general will be rejected by future ages, as it is that many, once general, are rejected by the present.

The objection likely to be made to this argument would probably take some such form as the following. There is no greater assumption of infallibility in forbidding the propagation of error, than in any other thing which is done by public authority on its own judgment and responsibility. Judgment is given to men that they may use it. Because it may be used erroneously, are men to be told that they ought not to use it at all? To prohibit what they think pernicious, is not claiming exemption from error, but fulfilling the duty incumbent on them, although fallible, of acting on their conscientious conviction. If we were never to act on our opinions, because those opinions may be wrong, we should leave all our interests uncared for, and all our duties unperformed. An objection which applies to all conduct can be no valid objection to any conduct in particular. It is the duty of governments, and of individuals, to form the truest opinions they can; to form them carefully, and never impose them upon others unless they are quite sure of being right. But when they are sure (such reasoners may say), it is not conscientiousness but cowardice to shrink from acting on their opinions, and allow doctrines which they honestly think dangerous to the welfare of mankind, either in this life or in another, to be scattered abroad without restraint, because other people, in less enlightened times, have persecuted opinions now believed to be true. Let us take care, it may be said, not to make the same mistake; but governments and nations have made mistakes in other things, which are not denied to be fit subjects for the exercise of authority: they have laid on bad taxes, made unjust wars. Ought we therefore to lay on no taxes, and, under whatever provocation, make no wars? Men, and governments, must act to the best of their ability. There is no such thing as absolute certainty, but there is assurance sufficient for the purposes of human life. We may, and must, assume our opinion to be true for the guidance of our own conduct, and it is assuming no more when we forbid bad men to pervert society by the propagation of opinions which we regard as false and pernicious.

I answer that it is assuming very much more. There is the greatest difference between presuming an opinion to be true because, with every opportunity for contesting it, it has not been refuted, and assuming its truth for the purpose of not permitting its refutation. Complete liberty of contradicting and disproving our opinion is the very condition which justifies us in assuming its truth for purposes of action; and on no other terms can a being with human faculties have any rational assurance of being right.

When we consider either the history of opinion, or the ordinary conduct of human life, to what is it to be ascribed that the one and the other are no worse than they are? Not certainly to the inherent force of the human understanding; for, on any matter not self-evident, there are 99 persons totally incapable of judging of it for one who is capable; and the capacity of the hundredth person is only comparative: for the majority of the eminent men of every past generation held many opinions now known to be erroneous, and did or approved numerous things which no one will now justify. Why is it, then, that there is on the whole a preponderance among mankind of rational opinions and rational conduct? If there really is this preponderance—which there must be unless human affairs are, and have always been, in an almost desperate state—it is owing to a quality of the human mind, the source of everything respectable in man either as an intellectual or as a moral being, namely, that his errors are corrigible. He is capable of rectifying his mistakes, by discussion and experience. Not by experience alone. There must be discussion, to show how experience is to be interpreted. Wrong opinions and practices gradually yield to fact and argument; but facts and arguments, to produce any effect on the mind, must be brought before it. Very few facts are able to tell their own story, without comments to bring out their meaning. The whole strength and value, then, of human judgment, depending on the one property, that it can be set right when it is wrong, reliance can be placed on it only when the means of setting it right are kept constantly at hand. In the case of any person whose judgment is really deserving of confidence, how has it become so? Because he has kept his mind open to criticism of his opinions and conduct. Because it has been his practice to listen to all that could be said against him; to profit by as much of it as was just, and expound to himself, and upon occasion to others, the fallacy of what was fallacious. Because he has felt that the only way in which a human being can make some approach to knowing the whole of a subject, is by hearing what can be said about it by persons of every variety of opinion, and studying all modes in which it can be looked at by every character of mind. No wise man ever acquired his wisdom in any mode but this; not is it in the nature of human intellect to become wise in any other manner. The steady habit of correcting and completing his own opinion by collating it with those of others, so far from causing doubt and hesitation in carrying it into practice, is the only stable foundation for a just reliance on it for, being cognizant of all that can, at least obviously, be said against him, and having taken up his position against all gainsayers— knowing that he has sought for objections and difficulties, instead of avoiding them, and has shut out no light which can be thrown upon the subject from any quarter—he has a right to think his judgment better than that of any person, or any multitude, who have not gone through a similar process.

It is not too much to require that what the wisest of mankind, those who are best entitled to trust their own judgment, find necessary to warrant their relying on it, should be submitted to by that miscellaneous collection of a few wise and many foolish individuals, called the public. The most intolerant of churches, the Roman Catholic Church, even at the canonization of a saint, admits, and listens patiently to, a "devil's advocate." The holiest of men, it appears, cannot be admitted to posthumous honors, until all that the devil could say against him is known and weighed. If even the Newtonian philosophy were not permitted to be questioned, mankind could not feel as complete assurance of its truth as they now do. The beliefs which we have most warrant for, have no safeguard to rest on but a standing invitation to the whole world to prove them unfounded. If the challenge is not accepted; or is accepted and the attempt fails, we are far enough from certainty still; but we have done the best that the existing state of human reason admits of; we have neglected nothing that could give the truth a chance of reaching us: if the lists are kept open, we may hope that if there be a better truth, it will be found when the human mind is capable of

receiving it; and in the meantime we may rely on having attained such approach to truth as is possible in our own day. This is the amount of certainty attainable by a fallible being, and this the sole way of attaining it.

Strange it is that men should admit the validity of the arguments for free discussion, but object to their being "pushed to an extreme"; not seeing that unless the reasons are good for an extreme case, they are not good for any case. Strange that they should imagine that they are not assuming infallibility, when they acknowledge that there should be free discussion on all subjects which can possibly be *doubtful*, but think that some particular principle or doctrine should be forbidden to be questioned because it is so *certain*, that is, because *they are certain* that it is certain. To call any proposition certain while there is anyone who would deny its certainty if permitted, but who is not permitted, is to assume that we ourselves, and those who agree with us, are the judges of certainty, and judges without hearing the other side.

In the present age—which has been described as "destitute of faith, but terrified at skepticism"—in which people feel sure, not so much that their opinions are true, as that they should not know what to do without them—the claims of an opinion to be protected from public attack are rested not so much on its truth, as on its importance to society. There are, it is alleged, certain beliefs so useful, not to say indispensable, to well-being that it is as much the duty of governments to uphold those beliefs, as to protect any other of the interests of society. In a case of such necessity, and so directly in the line of their duty, something less than infallibility may, it is maintained, warrant, and even bind governments to act on their own opinion, confirmed by the general opinion of mankind. It is also often argued, and still oftener thought, that none but bad men would desire to weaken these salutary beliefs; and there can be nothing wrong, it is thought, in restraining bad men, and prohibiting what only such men would wish to practice. This mode of thinking makes the justification of restraints on discussion not a question of the truth of doctrines, but of their usefulness; and flatters itself by that means to escape the responsibility of claiming to be an infallible judge of opinions. But those who thus satisfy themselves, do not perceive that the assumption of infallibility is merely shifted from one point to another. The usefulness of an opinion is itself matter of opinion: as disputable, as open to discussion, and requiring discussion as much as the opinion itself. There is the same need of an infallible judge of opinions to decide an opinion to be noxious, as to decide it to be false, unless the opinion condemned has full opportunity of defending itself. And it will not do to say that the heretic may be allowed to maintain the utility or harmlessness of his opinion, though forbidden to maintain its truth. The truth of an opinion is part of its utility. If we would know whether or not it is desirable that a proposition should be believed, is it possible to exclude the consideration of whether or not it is true? In the opinion, not of bad men, but of the best men, no belief which is contrary to truth can be really useful; and can you prevent such men from urging that plea, when they are charged with culpability for denying some doctrine which they are told is useful, but which they believe to be false? Those who are on the side of received opinions never fail to take all possible advantages of this plea: you do not find *them* handling the question of utility as if it could be completely abstracted from that of truth; on the contrary, it is, above all, because their doctrine is "the truth," that the knowledge or the belief of it is held to be so indispensable. There can be no fair discussion of the question of usefulness when an argument so vital may be employed on one side, but not on the other. And in point of fact, when law or public feeling do not permit the truth of an opinion to be disputed, they are just as little tolerant of a denial of its usefulness. The utmost they allow is an extenuation of its absolute necessity, or of the positive guilt of rejecting it.

In order more fully to illustrate the mischief of denying a hearing to opinions because we, in our own judgment, have condemned them, it will be desirable to fix down the discussion to a concrete case; and I choose, by preference, the cases which are least favorable to me—in which the argument against freedom of opinion, both on the score of truth and on that of utility, is considered the strongest. Let the opinions impugned be the belief in a God and in a future state, or any of the commonly received doctrines of morality. To fight the battle on such ground gives a great advantage to an unfair antagonist; since he will be sure to say (and many who have no desire to be unfair will say it internally), "Are these the doctrines which you do not deem sufficiently certain to be taken under the protection of laws? Is the belief in a God one of the opinions to feel sure of which you hold to be assuming infallibility?" But I must be permitted to observe that it is not the feeling sure of a doctrine (be it what it may) which I call an assumption of infallibility. It is the undertaking to decide that question *for others;* without allowing them to hear what can be said on the contrary side. And I denounce and reprobate this pretension not the less if put forth on the side of my most solemn convictions. However positive anyone's persuasion may be, not only of the falsity but of the pernicious consequences—not only of the pernicious consequences, but (to adopt expressions which I altogether condemn) the immorality and impiety of an opinion; yet if, in pursuance of that private judgment, though backed by the public judgment of his country or his contemporaries, he prevents the opinion from being heard in its defense, he assumes infallibility. And so far from the assumption being less objectionable or less dangerous because the opinion is called immoral or impious, this is the case of all others in which it is most fatal. These are exactly the occasions on which the men of one generation commit those dreadful mistakes which excite the astonishment and horror of posterity. It is among such that we find the instances memorable in history, when the arm of the law has been employed to root out the best men and the noblest doctrines; with deplorable success as to the men, though some of the doctrines have survived to be (as if in mockery) invoked in defense of similar conduct toward those who dissent from *them,* or from their received interpretation.

Mankind can hardly be too often reminded, that there was once a man named Socrates, between whom and the legal authorities and public opinion of his time there took place a memorable collision. Born in an age and country abounding in individual greatness, this man has been handed down to us by those who best knew both him and the age, as the most virtuous man in it; while *we* know him as the head and prototype of all subsequent teachers of virtue, the source equally of the lofty inspiration of Plato and the judicious utilitarianism of Aristotle . . . the two headsprings of ethical as of all other philosophy. This acknowledged master of all the eminent thinkers who have since lived—whose fame, still growing after more than two thousand years, all but outweighs the whole remainder of the names which make his native city illustrious—was put to death by his countrymen, after a judicial conviction, for impiety and immorality. Impiety, in denying the gods recognized by the State; indeed his accuser asserted (see the *Apology*) that he believed in no gods at all, immorality, in being, by his doctrines and instructions, a "corruptor of youth." Of these charges the tribunal, there is every ground for believing, honestly found him guilty, and condemned the man who probably of all then born had deserved best of mankind to be put to death as a criminal.

To pass from this to the only other instance of judicial iniquity, the mention of which, after the condemnation of Socrates, would not be an anticlimax: the event which took place on Calvary rather more than eighteen hundred years ago. The man who left on the memory of those who witnessed his life and conversation such an impression of his moral grandeur that eighteen subsequent centuries have done homage to him as the Almighty in person, was ignominiously put to death, as what? As a blasphemer. Men did not merely mistake their benefactor; they mistook him for the exact contrary of what he was, and treated him as that prodigy of impiety which they themselves are now held to be for their treatment of him. The feelings with which mankind now regard these lamentable transactions, especially the later of the two, render them extremely unjust in their judgment of the unhappy actors. These were, to all appearance, not bad men—not worse than men commonly are, but rather the contrary; men who possessed in a full, or somewhat more than a full measure, the religious, moral, and patriotic feelings of their time and people: the very kind of men who, in all times, our own included, have every chance of passing through life blameless and respected. The high priest who rent his garments when the words were pronounced which, according to all the ideas of his country, constituted the blackest guilt, was in all probability quite as sincere in his horror and indignation as the generality of respectable and pious men now are in the religious and moral sentiments they profess; and most of those who now shudder at his conduct, if they had lived in his time, and been born Jews, would have acted precisely as he did. Orthodox Christians who are tempted to think that those who stoned to death the first martyrs must have been worse men than they themselves are, ought to remember that one of those persecutors was Saint Paul. . . .

Let us now pass to the second division of the argument, and dismissing the supposition that any of the received opinions may be false, let us assume them to be true, and examine into the worth of the manner in which they are likely to be held, when their truth is not freely and openly canvassed. However unwilling a person who has a strong opinion may admit the possibility that his opinion may be false, he ought to be moved by the consideration that, however true it may be, if it is not fully, frequently, and fearlessly discussed, it will be held as a dead dogma, not a living truth.

There is a class of persons (happily not quite so numerous as formerly) who think it enough if a person assents undoubtingly to what they think true, though he has no knowledge whatever of the grounds of the opinion, and could not make a tenable defense of it against the most superficial objections. Such persons, if they can once get their creed taught from authority, naturally think that no good, and some harm, comes of its being allowed to be questioned. Where their influence prevails, they make it nearly impossible for the received opinion to be rejected wisely and considerately, though it may still be rejected rashly and ignorantly; for to shut out discussion entirely is seldom possible, and when it once gets in, beliefs not grounded on conviction are apt to give way before the slightest semblance of an argument. Waiving, however, this possibility—assuming that the true opinion abides in the mind, but abides as a prejudice, a belief independent of, and proof against, argument—this is not the way in which truth ought to be held by a rational being. This is not knowing the truth. Truth, thus held, is but one superstition the more, accidentally clinging to the words which enunciate a truth.

If the intellect and judgment of mankind ought to be cultivated, a thing which Protestants at least do not deny, on what can these faculties be more appropriately exercised by anyone, than on the things which concern him so much that it is considered necessary for him to hold opinions on them? If the cultivation of the understanding consists in one thing more than in another, it is surely in learning the grounds of one's own opinions. Whatever people believe, on subjects on which it is of the first importance to believe rightly, they ought to be able to defend against at least the common objections. But, some one may say, "Let them be *taught* the grounds of their opinions. It does not follow that opinions must be merely parroted because they are never heard controverted. Persons who learn geometry do not simply commit the theorems to memory, but understand and learn likewise the demonstrations; and it would be absurd to say that they remain ignorant of the grounds of geometrical truths, because they never hear any one deny, and attempt to disprove them." Undoubtedly: and such teaching suffices on a subject like mathematics, where there is nothing at all to be said on the wrong side of the question. The peculiarity of the evidence of mathematical truths is that all the argument is on one side. There are no objections, and no answers to objections. But on every subject on which difference of opinion is possible, the truth depends on a balance to be struck between two sets of conflicting reasons. Even in natural philosophy, there is always some other explanation possible of the same facts—some geocentric theory instead of heliocentric, some phlogiston instead of oxygen—and it has to be shown why that other theory cannot be the true one; and until this is shown, and until we know how it is shown, we do not understand the grounds of our opinion. But when we turn to subjects infinitely more complicated, to morals, religion, politics, social relations, and the business of life, three-fourths of the arguments for every disputed opinion consist in dispelling the appearances which favor some opinion different from it. The greatest orator, save one, of antiquity, has left it on record that he always studied his adversary's case with as great, if not still greater, intensity than even his own. What Cicero practiced as the means of forensic success requires to be imitated by all who study any subject in order to arrive at the truth. He who knows only his own side of the case, knows little of that. His reasons may be good, and no one may have been able to refute them. But if he is equally unable to refute the reasons on the opposite side; if he does not so much as know what they are, he has no ground for preferring either opinion.

The rational position for him would be suspension of judgment, and unless he contents himself with that, he is either led by authority, or adopts, like the generality of the world, the side to which he feels most inclination. Nor is it enough that he should hear the arguments of adversaries from his own teachers, presented as they state them, and accompanied by what they offer as refutations. That is not the way to do justice to the arguments, or bring them into real contact with his own mind. He must be able to hear them from persons who actually believe them; who defend them in earnest, and do their very utmost for them. He must know them in their more plausible and persuasive form; he must feel the whole force of the difficulty which the true view of the subject has to encounter and dispose of; else he will never really possess himself of the portion of truth which meets and removes that difficulty. Ninety-nine in a hundred of what are called educated men are in this condition; even of those who can argue fluently for their opinions. Their conclusion may be true, but it might be false for anything they know: they have never thrown themselves into the mental position of those who think differently from them, and considered what such persons may have to say; and consequently they do not, in any proper sense of the word, know the doctrine which they themselves profess. They do not know those parts of it which explain and justify the remainder; the considerations which show that a fact which seemingly conflicts with another is reconcilable with it, or that, of two apparently strong reasons, one and not the other ought to be preferred. All that part of the truth which turns the scale, and decides the judgment of a completely informed mind, they are strangers to; nor is it ever really known but to those who have attended equally and impartially to both sides, and endeavored to see the reasons of both in the strongest light. So essential is this discipline to a real understanding of moral and human subjects, that if opponents of all important truths do not exist, it is indispensable to imagine them, and supply them with the strongest arguments which the most skilful devil's advocate can conjure up. . . .

If however, the mischievous operation of the absence of free discussion, when the received opinions are true, were confined to leaving men ignorant of the grounds of those opinions, it might be thought that this, if an intellectual, is no moral evil, and does not affect the worth of the opinions, regarded in their influence on the character. The fact, however, is that not only the grounds of the opinion are forgotten in the absence of discussion, but too often the meaning of the opinion itself. The words which convey it cease to suggest ideas, or suggest only a small portion of those they were originally employed to communicate. Instead of a vivid conception and a living belief, there remain only a few phrases retained by rote; or, if any part, the shell and husk only of the meaning is retained, the finer essence being lost. The great chapter in human history which this fact occupies and fills, cannot be too earnestly studied and meditated on. . . .

The same thing holds true, generally speaking, of all traditional doctrines—those of prudence and knowledge of life, as well as of morals or religion. All languages and literatures are full of general observations on life, both as to what it is, and how to conduct oneself in it; observations which everybody knows, which everybody repeats, or hears with acquiescence, which are received as truisms, yet of which most people first truly learn the meaning when experience, generally of a painful kind, has made it a reality to them. How often, when smarting under some unforeseen misfortune or disappointment, does a person call to mind some proverb or common saying, familiar to him all his life, the meaning of which, if he had ever before felt it as he does now, would have saved him from the calamity. There are indeed reasons for this, other than the absence of discussion; there are many truths of which the full meaning *cannot* be realized until personal experience has brought it home. But much more of the meaning even of these would have been understood, and what was understood would have been far more deeply impressed on the mind, if the man had been accustomed to hear it argued *pro* and *con* by people who did understand it. The fatal tendency of mankind to leave off thinking about a thing when it is no longer doubtful, is the cause of half their errors. A contemporary author has well spoken of "the deep slumber of a decided opinion."

But what! (it may be asked). Is the absence of unanimity an indispensable condition of true knowledge? Is it necessary that some part of mankind should persist in error to enable any to realize the truth? Does a belief cease to be real and vital as soon as it is generally received; and is a proposition never thoroughly understood and felt unless some doubt of it remains? As soon as mankind have unanimously accepted a truth, does the truth perish within them? The highest aim and best result of improved intelligence, it has hitherto been thought, is to unite mankind more and more in the acknowledgment of all important truths; and does the intelligence only last as long as it has not achieved its object? Do the fruits of conquest perish by the very completeness of the victory?

I affirm no such thing. As mankind improves, the number of doctrines which are no longer disputed or doubted will be constantly on the increase: and the well-being of mankind may almost be measured by the number and gravity of the truths which have reached the point of being uncontested. The cessation, on one question after another, of serious controversy, is one of the necessary incidents of the consolidation of opinion; a consolidation as salutary in the case of true opinions, as it is dangerous and noxious when the opinions are erroneous. But though this gradual narrowing of the bounds of diversity of opinion is necessary in both senses of the term, being at once inevitable and indispensable, we are not therefore obliged to conclude that all its consequences must be beneficial. The loss of so important an aid to the intelligent and living apprehension of a truth, as is afforded by the necessity of explaining it to, or defending it against, opponents, though not sufficient to outweigh, is no trifling drawback from, the benefit of its universal recognition. Where this advantage can no longer be had, I confess I should like to see the teachers of mankind endeavoring to provide a substitute for it; some contrivance for making the difficulties of the question as present to the learner's consciousness, as if they were pressed upon him by a dissentient champion, eager for his conversion. . . .

It is the fashion of the present time to disparage negative logic—that which points out weaknesses in theory or errors in practice, without establishing positive truths. Such negative criticism would indeed be poor enough as an ultimate result; but as a means to attaining any positive knowledge or conviction worthy the name, it cannot be valued too highly; and until people are again systematically trained to it, there will be few greater thinkers, and a low general average of intellect, in any but the mathematical and physical departments of speculation. On any other subject no one's opinions deserve the name of knowledge, except so far as he has either had forced upon him by others, or gone through of himself, the same mental process which would have been required of him in carrying on an active controversy with opponents. That, therefore, which when absent, it is so indispensable, but so difficult, to create, how worse than absurd it is to forego, when spontaneously offering itself! If there are any persons who contest a received opinion, or who will do so if law or opinion will let them, let us thank them for it, open our minds to listen to them, and rejoice that there is some one to do for us what we otherwise ought, if we have any regard for either the certainty or the vitality of our convictions, to do with much greater labor for ourselves.

It still remains to speak of one of the principal causes which make diversity of opinion advantageous, and will continue to do so until mankind shall have entered a stage of intellectual advancement which at present seems at an incalculable distance. We have hitherto considered only two possibilities: that the received opinion may be false, and some other opinion consequently true; or that, the received opinion being true, a conflict with the opposite error is essential to a clear apprehension and deep feeling of its truth. But there is a commoner case than either of these: when the conflicting doctrines, instead of being one true and the other false, share the truth between them, and the nonconforming opinion is needed to supply the remainder of the truth, of which the received doctrine embodies only a part. Popular opinions, on subjects not palpable to sense, are often true, but seldom or never the whole truth. They are a part of the truth; sometimes a greater, sometimes a smaller part, but exaggerated, distorted, and disjointed from the truths by which they ought to be accompanied and limited. Heretical opinions, on the other hand, are generally some of these suppressed and neglected truths, bursting the bonds which kept them down, and neither seeking reconciliation with the truth contained in the common opinion, or fronting it as

enemies, and setting themselves up, with similar exclusiveness, as the whole truth. The latter case is hitherto the most frequent, as, in the human mind, one-sidedness has always been the rule, and many-sidedness the exception. Hence, even in revolutions of opinion, one part of the truth usually sets while another rises. Even progress, which ought to super-add, for the most part only substitutes, one partial and incomplete truth for another; improvement consisting chiefly in this, that the new fragment of truth is more wanted, more adapted to the needs of the time, than that which it displaces. Such being the partial character of prevailing opinions, even when resting on a true foundation, every opinion which embodies somewhat of the portion of truth which the common opinion omits, ought to be considered precious, with whatever amount of error and confusion that truth may be blended. No sober judge of human affairs will feel bound to be indignant because those who force on our notice truths which we should otherwise have overlooked, overlook some of those which we see. Rather, he will think that so long as popular truth is one-sided, it is more desirable than otherwise that unpopular truth should have one-sided assertors too; such being usually the most energetic, and the most likely to compel reluctant attention to the fragment of wisdom which they proclaim as if it were the whole.

Thus, in the eighteenth century, when nearly all the instructed, and all those of the uninstructed who were led by them, were lost in admiration of what is called civilization, and of the marvels of modern science, literature, and philosophy, and while greatly overrating the amount of unlikeness between the men of modern and those of ancient times, indulged the belief that the whole of the difference was in their own favor; with what a salutary shock did the paradoxes of Rousseau explode like bombshells in the midst, dislocating the compact mass of one-sided opinion, and forcing its elements to recombine in a better form and with additional ingredients. Not that the current opinions were on the whole farther from the truth than Rousseau's were: on the contrary, they were nearer to it: they contained more of positive truth, and very much less of error. Nevertheless there lay in Rousseau's doctrine, and has floated down the stream of opinion along with it, a considerable amount of exactly those truths which the popular opinion wanted; and these are the deposit which was left behind when the flood subsided. The superior worth of simplicity of life, the enervating and demoralizing effect of the trammels and hypocrisies of artificial society, are ideas which have never been entirely absent from cultivated minds since Rousseau wrote; and they will in time produce their due effect, though at present needing to be asserted as much as ever, and to be asserted by deeds, for words, on their subject, have nearly exhausted their power.

In politics, again, it is almost a commonplace, that a party of order or stability, and a party of progress or reform, are both necessary elements of a healthy state of political life; until the one or the other shall have so enlarged its mental grasp as to be a party equally of order and of progress, knowing and distinguishing what is fit to be preserved from what ought to be swept away. Each of these modes of thinking derives its utility from the deficiencies of the other; but it is in a great measure the opposition of the other that keeps each within the limits of reason and sanity. Unless opinions favorable to democracy and to aristocracy, to property and to equality, to cooperation and to competition, to luxury and to abstinence, to sociality and individuality, to liberty and discipline, and all the other standing antagonisms of practical life, are expressed with equal freedom, and enforced and defended with equal talent and energy, there is no chance of both elements obtaining their due: one scale is sure to go up, and the other down. Truth, in the great practical concerns of life, is so much a question of the reconciling and combining of opposites, that very few have minds sufficiently capacious and impartial to make the adjustment with an approach to correctness, and it has to be made by the rough process of a struggle between combatants fighting under hostile banners. On any of the great open questions just enumerated, if either of the two opinions has a better claim than the other, not merely to be tolerated, but to be encouraged and countenanced; it is the one which happens at the particular time and place to be in a minority. That is the opinion which, for the time being, represents the neglected interests, the side of human well-being which is in danger of obtaining less than its share. I am aware that there is not, in this country, any intolerance of differences of opinion on most of these top-

ics. They are adduced to show, by admitted and multiplied examples, the universality of the fact that only through diversity of opinion is there, in the existing state of human intellect, a chance of fair play to all sides of the truth. When there are persons to be found who form an exception to the apparent unanimity of the world on any subject, even if the world is in the right, it is always probable that dissentients have something worth hearing to say for themselves, and that truth would lose something by their silence. . . .

We have now recognized the necessity to the mental well-being of mankind (on which all their other well-being depends) of freedom of opinion, and freedom of the expression of opinion, on four distinct grounds; which we will now briefly recapitulate.

First, if any opinion is compelled to silence, that opinion may, for aught we can certainly know, be true. To deny this is to assume our own infallibility.

Secondly, though the silenced opinion be an error, it may, and very commonly does, contain a portion of truth; and since the general or prevailing opinion on any subject is rarely or never the whole truth; it is only by the collision of adverse opinions that the remainder of the truth has any chance of being supplied.

Thirdly, even if the received opinion be not only true, but the whole truth; unless it is suffered to be, and actually is, vigorously and earnestly contested, it will, by most of those who receive it, be held in the manner of a prejudice, with little comprehension or feeling of its rational grounds. And not only this, but, fourthly, the meaning of the doctrine itself will be in danger of being lost, or enfeebled, and deprived of its vital effect on the character and conduct: the dogma becoming a mere formal procession, inefficacious for good, but cumbering the ground, and preventing the growth of any real and heartfelt conviction, from reason or personal experience. . . .

CHAPTER III

Of Individuality, As One of the Elements of Well-Being

Such being the reasons which make it imperative that human beings should be free to form opinions, and to express their opinions without reserve; and such the baneful consequences to the intellectual, and through that to the moral nature of man, unless this liberty is either conceded, or asserted in spite of prohibition; let us next examine whether the same reasons do not require that men should be free to act upon their opinions—to carry these out in their lives, without hindrance, either physical or moral, from their fellow men, so long as it is at their own risk and peril. This last proviso is of course indispensable. No one pretends that actions should be as free as opinions. On the contrary, even opinions lose their immunity when the circumstances in which they are expressed are such as to constitute their expression a positive instigation to some mischievous act. An opinion that corn dealers are starvers of the poor, or that private property is robbery, ought to be unmolested when simply circulated through the press, but many justly incur punishment when delivered orally to an excited mob assembled before the house of a corn dealer, or when handed about among the same mob in the form of a placard. Acts, of whatever kind, which without justifiable cause do harm to others, may be, and in the more important cases absolutely require to be, controlled by the unfavorable sentiments, and, when needful, by the active interference of mankind. The liberty of the individual must be thus far limited; he must not make himself a nuisance to other people. But if he refrains from molesting others in what concerns them, and merely acts according to his own inclination and judgment in things which concern himself, the same reasons which show that opinion should be free, without molestation, to carry his opinions into practice at his own cost. That mankind are not infallible; that their truths, for the most part, are only half-truths; that unity of opinion, unless resulting from the fullest and freest comparison of opposite opinions, is not desirable, and diversity not an evil, but a good, until mankind are much more capable than at present of recognizing all sides of the truth, are principles applicable to men's modes of action, not less than to their opinions. As it is useful that while mankind are imperfect there should be different opinions, so it is that there should be different experiments of living; that free scope should be given to varieties of character, short of injury to others, and that the worth of different modes of life should be proved practically, when any one thinks fit to try them. It is desirable, in short, that in things which do not primarily concern others, individuality should assert itself. Where not the person's own character, but the traditions or customs of other people are the rule of conduct, there is wanting one of the principal ingredients of human happiness; and quite the chief ingredient of individual and social progress.

In maintaining this principle, the greatest difficulty to be encountered does not lie in the appreciation of means toward an acknowledged end, but in the indifference of persons in general to the end in itself. If it were felt that the free development of individuality is one of the leading essentials of well-being; that it is not only a coordinate element with all that is designated by the terms civilization, instruction, education, culture, but is itself a necessary part and condition of all those things there would be no danger that liberty should be undervalued, and the adjustment of the boundaries between it and social control would present no extraordinary difficulty. But the evil is, that individual spontaneity is hardly recognized by the common modes of thinking as having any intrinsic worth, or deserving any regard on its own account. The majority, being satisfied with the ways of mankind as they now are (for it is they who make them what they are), cannot comprehend why those ways should not be good enough for everybody; and what is more, spontaneity forms no part of the ideal of the majority of moral and social reformers, but is rather looked on with jealousy, as a troublesome and perhaps rebellious obstruction to the general acceptance of what these reformers, in their own judgment, think would be best for mankind.

. . . No one's idea of excellence in conduct is that people should do absolutely nothing but copy one another. No one would assert that people ought not to put into their mode of life, and into the conduct of their concerns, any impress whatever of their own judgment, or of their own individual character. On the other hand, it would be absurd to pretend that people ought to live as if nothing whatever had been known in the world before they came into it; as if experience had as yet done nothing toward showing that one mode of existence, or of conduct, is preferable to another. Nobody denies that people should be so taught and trained in youth as to know and benefit by the ascertained results of human experience. But it is the privilege and proper condition of a human being, arrived at the maturity of his faculties, to use and interpret experience in his own way. It is for him to find out what part of recorded experience is properly applicable to his own circumstances and character. The traditions and customs of other people are to a certain extent, evidence of what their experience has taught *them:* presumptive evidence, and as such, have a claim to his deference. But in the first place, their experience may be too narrow, or they may not have interpreted it rightly. Secondly, their interpretation of experience may be correct, but unsuitable to him. Customs are made for customary circumstances and customary characters, and his circumstances or his character may be uncustomary. Thirdly, though the customs be both good as customs, and suitable to him, yet to conform to custom, merely *as* custom, does not educate or develop in him any of the qualities which are the distinctive endowment of a human being. The human faculties of perception, judgment, discriminative feeling, mental activity, and even moral preference, are exercised only in making a choice. He who does anything because it is the custom makes no choice. He gains no practice either in discerning or in desiring what is best. The mental and moral, like the muscular powers, are improved only by being used. The faculties are called into no exercise by doing a thing merely because others do it, no more than by believing a thing only because others believe it. If the grounds of an opinion are not conclusive to the person's own reason, his reason cannot be strengthened, but is likely to be weakened, by his adopting it; and if the inducements to an act are not such as are consentaneous to his own feelings and character (where affection, or the rights of others, are not concerned) it is so much done toward rendering his feelings and character inert and torpid, instead of active and energetic.

He who lets the world, or his own portion of it, choose his plan of life for him, has no need of any other faculty than the ape-like one of imitation. He who chooses his plan for himself, employs all his faculties. He must use observation to see, reasoning and judgment to foresee, activity to gather materials for decision, discrimination to decide, and when he has decided, firmness and self-control to hold to his deliberate decision. And these qualities he requires and exercises exactly in proportion as the part of his conduct which he determines according to his own judgment and feelings is a large one. It is possible that he might be guided in some good path, and kept out of harm's way, without any of these things. But what will be his comparative worth as a human being? It really is of importance, not only what men do, but also what manner of men they are that do it. Among the works of man which human life is rightly employed in perfecting and beautifying, the first in importance surely is man himself. Supposing it were possible to get houses built, corn grown, battles fought, causes tried, and even churches erected and prayers said, by machinery—by automatons in human form—it would be a considerable loss to exchange for these automatons even the men and women who at present inhabit the more civilized parts of the world, and who assuredly are but starved specimens of what nature can and will produce. Human nature is not a machine to be built after a model, and set to do exactly the work prescribed for it, but a tree, which requires to grow and develop itself on all sides, according to the tendency of the inward forces which make it a living thing.

It will probably be conceded that it is desirable people shall exercise their understandings, and that an intelligent following of custom, or even occasionally an intelligent deviation from custom, is better than a blind and simply mechanical adhesion to it. To a certain extent it is admitted that our understanding should be our own: but there is not the same willingness to admit that our desires and impulses should be our own likewise; or that to possess impulses of our own, and of any strength, is anything but a peril and a snare. Yet desires and impulses are as much a part of a perfect human being as beliefs and restraints; and strong impulses are only perilous when not properly balanced—when one set of aims and inclinations is developed into strength, while others, which ought to coexist with them, remain weak and inactive. It is not because men's desires are strong that they act ill; it is because their consciences are weak. There is no natural connection between strong impulses and a weak conscience. The natural connection is the other way. To say that one person's desires and feelings are stronger and more various than those of another, is merely to say that he has more of the raw material of human nature, and is therefore capable, perhaps of more evil, but certainly of more good. Strong impulses are but another name for energy. Energy may be turned to bad uses; but more good may always be made of an energetic nature than of an indolent and impassive one. Those who have most natural feeling are always those whose cultivated feelings may be made the strongest. The same strong susceptibilities which make the personal impulses vivid and powerful, are also the source from whence are generated the most passionate love of virtue, and the sternest self-control. It is through the cultivation of these that society both does its duty and protects its interests; not by rejecting the stuff of which heroes are made because it knows not how to make them. A person whose desires and impulses are his own—are the expression of his own nature, as it has been developed and modified by his own culture—is said to have a character. One whose desires and impulses are not his own, has no character, no more than a steam engine has a character. If, in addition to being his own, his impulses are strong, and are under the government of a strong will, he has an energetic character. Whoever thinks that individuality of desires and impulses should not be encouraged to unfold itself, must maintain that society has no need of strong natures—is not the better for containing many persons who have much character—and that a high general average of energy is not desirable.

It is not by wearing down into uniformity all that is individual in themselves, but by cultivating it, and calling it forth, within the limits imposed by the rights and interests of others, that human beings become a noble and beautiful object of contemplation; and as the works partake the character of those who do them, by the same process human life also becomes rich, diversified, and animating, furnishing more abundant aliment to high thoughts and elevating feelings, and strengthening the tie which binds every individual to the race, by making the race infinitely better worth belong to. In proportion to the development of his individuality, each person becomes more valuable to himself, and is therefore capable of being more valuable to others. There is a greater fullness of life about his own existence, and when there is more life in the units there is more in the mass which is composed of them. As much compression as is necessary to prevent the stronger specimens of human nature from encroaching on the rights of others cannot be dispensed with; but for this there is ample compensation even in the point of view of human development. The means of development which the individual loses by being prevented from gratifying his inclinations to the injury of others, are chiefly obtained at the expense of the development of other people. And even to himself there is a full equivalent in the better development of the social part of his nature, rendered possible by the restraint put upon the selfish part. To be held to rigid rules of justice for the sake of others, develops the feelings and capacities which have the good of others for their object. But to be restrained in things not affecting their good, by their mere displeasure, develops nothing valuable, except such force of character as may unfold itself in resisting the restraint. If acquiesced in, it dulls and blunts the whole nature. To give any fair play to the nature of each, it is essential that different persons should be allowed to lead different lives. In proportion as this latitude has been exercised in any age, has that age been noteworthy to posterity. Even despotism does not produce its worst effects, so long as individuality exists under it; and whatever crushes individuality is despotism, by whatever name it may be called, and whether it professes to be enforcing the will of God or the injunctions of men.

Having said that the individuality is the same thing with development, and that it is only the cultivation of individuality which produces, or can produce, well-developed human beings, I might here close the argument: for what more or better can be said of any condition of human affairs than that it brings human beings themselves nearer to the best thing they can be? or what worse can be said of any obstruction to good than that it prevents this? Doubtless, however, these considerations will not suffice to convince those who most need convincing; and it is necessary further to show that these developed human beings are of some use to the undeveloped—to point out to those who do not desire liberty, and would not avail themselves of it, that they may be in some intelligible manner rewarded for allowing other people to make use of it without hindrance.

In the first place, then, I would suggest that they might possibly learn something from them. It will not be denied by anybody that originality is a valuable element in human affairs. There is always need of persons not only to discover new truths, and point out when what were once truths are true no longer, but also to commence new practices, and set the example of more enlightened conduct, and better taste and sense in human life. This cannot well be gainsaid by anybody who does not believe that the world has already attained perfection in all its ways and practices. It is true that this benefit is not capable of being rendered by everybody alike; there are but few persons, in comparison with the whole of mankind, whose experiments, if adopted by others, would be likely to be any improvement on established practice. But these few are the salt of the earth; without them, human life would become a stagnant pool. Not only is it they who introduce good things which did not before exist; it is they who keep the life in those which already exist. If there were nothing new to be done, would human intellect cease to be necessary? Would it be a reason why those who do the old things should forget why they are done, and do them like cattle, not like human beings? There is only too great a tendency in the best beliefs and practices to degenerate into the mechanical; and unless there were a succession of persons whose over-recurring originality prevents the grounds of those beliefs and practices from becoming merely traditional, such dead matter would not resist the smallest shock from anything really alive, and there would be no reason why civilization should not die out, as in the Byzantine Empire. Persons of genius, it is true, are, and are always likely to be, a small minority; but in order to have them, it is necessary to preserve the soil in which they grow. Genius can only breathe freely in an *atmosphere* of freedom. Persons of genius are, *ex vi termini* [by the force of the phraseology], more individual than any other people—less capable, consequently, of fitting themselves, without hurtful compression, into any of the small number of molds which society provides in order to save its members the trouble of forming their own character. If from timidity they consent to be forced into one of these molds, and to let all that part of themselves which cannot expand under the pressure remain unexpanded, society will be little the better for their genius. If they are of a strong character, and break their fetters, they become a mark for

the society which has not succeeded in reducing them to commonplace, to point out with solemn warning as "wild," "erratic," and the like; much as if one should complain of the Niagara river for not flowing smoothly between its banks like a Dutch canal.

I insist thus emphatically on the importance of genius, and the necessity of allowing it to unfold itself freely both in thought and in practice, being well aware that no one will deny the position in theory, but knowing also that almost everyone, in reality, is totally indifferent to it. People think genius a fine thing if it enables a man to write an exciting poem, or paint a picture. But in its true sense, that of originality in thought and action, though no one says that it is not a thing to be admired, nearly all, at heart, think that they can do very well without it. Unhappily this is too natural to be wondered at. Originality is the one thing which unoriginal minds cannot feel the use of. They cannot see what it is to do for them: how should they? If they could see what it would do for them, it would not be originality. The first service which originality has to render them, is that of opening their eyes: which being once fully done, they would have a chance of being themselves original. Meanwhile, recollecting that nothing was ever yet done which someone was not the first to do, and that all good things which exist are the fruits of originality, let them be modest enough to believe that there is something still left for it to accomplish; and assure themselves that they are more in need of originality, the less they are conscious of the want.

In sober truth, whatever homage may be professed, or even paid, to real or supposed mental superiority, the general tendency of things throughout the world is to render mediocrity the ascendant power among mankind. In ancient history, in the Middle Ages, and in a diminishing degree through the long transition from feudality to the present time, the individual was a power in himself, and if he had either great talents or a high social position, he was a considerable power. At present individuals are lost in the crowd. In politics it is almost a triviality to say that public opinion now rules the world. The only power deserving the name is that of masses and of governments while they make themselves the organ of the tendencies and instincts of masses. This is as true in the moral and social relations of private life as in public transactions. Those whose opinions go by the name of public opinion are not always the same sort of public: in America they are the whole white population; in England, chiefly the middle class. But they are always a mass, that is to say, collective mediocrity. And what is a still greater novelty, the mass do not now take their opinions from dignitaries in church or state, from ostensible leaders, or from books. Their thinking is done for them by men much like themselves, addressing them or speaking in their name; on the spur of the moment, through the newspapers. I am not complaining of all this. I do not assert that anything better is compatible, as a general rule, with the present low state of the human mind. But that does not hinder the government of mediocrity from being mediocre government. No government by a democracy or a numerous aristocracy, either in its political acts or in the opinions, qualities, and tone of mind which it fosters, ever did or could rise above mediocrity, except in so far as the sovereign Many have let themselves be guided (which in their best times they always have done) by the counsels and influence of a more highly gifted and instructed one or few. The initiation of all wise or noble things comes and must come from individuals; generally at first from some one individual. The honor and glory of the average man is that he is capable of following that initiative; that he can respond internally to wise and noble things, and be led to them with his eyes open. I am not countenancing the sort of "hero worship" which applauds the strong man of genius for forcibly seizing on the government of the world and making it do his bidding in spite of itself. All he can claim is, freedom to point out the way. The power of compelling others into it is not only inconsistent with the freedom and development of all the rest, but corrupting to the strong man himself. It does seem, however, that when the opinions of masses of merely average men are everywhere become or becoming the dominant power, the counterpoise and corrective to that tendency would be the more and more pronounced individuality of those who stand on the higher eminences of thought. It is in these circumstances most especially, that exceptional individuals, instead of being deterred, should be encouraged in acting differently from the mass. In other times there was no advantage in their doing so, unless they acted not only differently but better. In this age, the mere example of nonconformity, the mere refusal to bend the knee to custom, is itself a service. Precisely because the tyranny of opinion is such as to make eccentricity a reproach, it is desirable, in order to break through that tyranny, that people should be eccentric. Eccentricity has always abounded when and where strength of character has abounded; and the amount of eccentricity in a society has generally been proportional to the amount of genius, mental vigor, and moral courage it contained. That so few now dare to be eccentric marks the chief danger of the time.

I have said that it is important to give the freest scope possible to uncustomary things, in order that it may in time appear which of these are fit to be converted into customs. But independence of action, and disregard of custom, are not solely deserving of encouragement for the chance they afford that better modes of action, and customs more worthy of general adoption, may be struck out; nor is it only persons of decided mental superiority who have a just claim to carry on their lives in their own way. There is no reason that all human existence should be constructed on some one or some small number of patterns. If a person possesses any tolerable amount of common sense and experience, his own mode of laying out his existence is the best, not because it is the best in itself, but because it is his own mode. Human beings are not like sheep; and even sheep are not undistinguishably alike. A man cannot get a coat or a pair of boots to fit him unless they are either made to his measure, or he has a whole warehouseful to choose from: and is it easier to fit him with a life than with a coat, or are human beings more like one another in their whole physical and spiritual conformation than in the shape of their feet? If it were only that people have diversities of taste, that is reason enough for not attempting to shape them all after one model. But different persons also require different conditions for their spiritual development; and can no more exist healthily in the same moral, than all the variety of plants can in the same physical, atmosphere and climate. The same things which are helps to one person towards the cultivation of his higher nature are hindrances to another. The same mode of life is a healthy excitement to one, keeping all his faculties of action and enjoyment in their best order, while to another it is a distracting burden, which suspends or crushes all internal life. Such are the differences among human beings in their sources of pleasure, their susceptibilities of pain, and the operation on them of different physical and moral agencies, that unless there is a corresponding diversity in their modes of life, they neither obtain their fair share of happiness, nor grow up to the mental, moral, and aesthetic stature of which their nature is capable. . . .

There is one characteristic of the present direction of public opinion peculiarly calculated to make it intolerant of any marked demonstration of individuality. The general average of mankind are not only moderate in intellect, but also moderate in inclinations: they have no tastes or wishes strong enough to incline them to do anything unusual, and they consequently do not understand those who have, and class all such with the wild and intemperate whom they are accustomed to look down upon. Now, in addition to this fact which is general, we have only to suppose that a strong movement has set in towards the improvement of morals, and it is evident what we have to expect. In these days such a movement has set in; much has actually been effected in the way of increased regularity of conduct and discouragement of excesses; and there is a philanthropic spirit abroad, for the exercise of which there is no more inviting field than the moral and prudential improvement of our fellow creatures. These tendencies of the times cause the public to be more disposed than at most former periods to prescribe general rules of conduct, and endeavor to make every one conform to the approved standard. And that standard, express or tacit, is to desire nothing strongly. Its ideal of character is to be without any marked character; to maim by compression, like a Chinese lady's foot, every part of human nature which stands out prominently, and tends to make the person markedly dissimilar in outline to commonplace humanity.

As is usually the case with ideals which exclude one-half of what is desirable, the present standard of approbation produces only an inferior imitation of the other half. Instead of great energies guided by vigorous reason, and strong feelings strongly controlled by a conscientious will, its result is weak feelings, and weak energies, which therefore can be kept in outward conformity to rule without any strength either of will or of reason. Already energetic characters on any large scale are becoming merely traditional. There is now scarcely any outlet for energy in this country except business. The energy expended in this may still be regarded as considerable. What little is left from that employment is expended on some hobby; which may be a useful, even a philanthropic hobby, but is always some one thing, and generally a thing of small dimensions. The greatness of England is now all collective; individually small, we only appear capable of anything great by our habit of combining; and with this our moral and religious philanthropists are perfectly contented. But it was men of another stamp than this that made England what it has been; and men of another stamp will be needed to prevent its decline.

The despotism of custom is everywhere the standing hindrance to human advancement, being in unceasing antagonism to that disposition to aim at something better than customary, which is called, according to circumstances, the spirit of liberty, or that of progress or improvement. The spirit of improvement is not always a spirit of liberty, for it may aim at forcing improvements on an unwilling people; and the spirit of liberty, in so far as it resists such attempts, may ally itself locally and temporarily with the opponents of improvement; but the only unfailing and permanent source of improvement is liberty, since by it there are as many possible independent centers of improvement as there are individuals. The progressive principle, however, in either shape, whether as the love of liberty or of improvement, is antagonistic to the sway of custom, involving at least emancipation from that yoke; and the contest between the two constitutes the chief interest of the history of mankind. . . .

What has made the European family of nations an improving, instead of a stationary portion of mankind? Not any superior excellence in them, which, when it exists, exists as the effect not as the cause; but their remarkable diversity of character and culture. Individuals, classes, nations, have been extremely unlike one another; they have struck out a great variety of paths, each leading to something valuable; and although at every period those who traveled in different paths have been intolerant of one another, and each would have thought it an excellent thing if all the rest could have been compelled to travel his road, their attempts to thwart each other's development have rarely had any permanent success, and each has in time endured to receive the good which the others have offered. Europe is, in my judgment, wholly indebted to this plurality of paths for its progressive and many-sided development. But it already begins to possess this benefit in a considerably less degree. . . .

Formerly, different ranks, different neighborhoods, different trades and professions, lived in what might be called different worlds; at present to a great degree in the same. Comparatively speaking, they now read the same things, listen to the same things, see the same things, go to the same places, have their hopes and fears directed to the same objects, have the same rights and liberties, and the same means of asserting them. Great as are the differences of position which remain, they are nothing to those which have ceased. And the assimilation is still proceeding. All the political changes of the age promote it, since they all tend to raise the low and to lower the high. Every extension of education promotes it, because education brings people under common influences, and gives them access to the general stock of facts and sentiments. Improvement in the means of communication promotes it, by bringing the inhabitants of distant places into personal contact, and keeping up a rapid flow of changes of residence between one place and another. The increase of commerce and manufactures promotes it, by diffusing more widely the advantages of easy circumstances, and opening all objects of ambition, even the highest, to general competition, whereby the desire of rising becomes no longer the character of a particular class, but of all classes. A more powerful agency than even all these, in bringing about a general similarity among mankind, is the complete establishment, in this and other free countries, of the ascendancy of public opinion in the state. As the various social eminences which enabled persons entrenched on them to disregard the opinion of the multitude gradually become leveled; as the very idea of resisting the will of the public, when it is positively known that they have a will, disappears more and more from the minds of practical politicians: there ceases to be any social support for nonconformity—any substantive power in society which, itself opposed to the ascendancy of numbers, is interested in taking under its protection opinions and tendencies at variance with those of the public.

The combination of all these causes forms so great a mass of influences hostile to individuality, that it is not easy to see how it can stand its ground. It will do so with increasing difficulty, unless the intelligent part of the public can be made to feel its value—to see that it is good there should be differences, even though not for the better, even though, as it may appear to them, some should be for the worse. If the claims of individuality are ever to be asserted, the time is now, while much is still wanting to complete the enforced assimilation. It is only in the earlier stages that any stand can be successfully made against the encroachment. The demand that all other people shall resemble ourselves grows by what it feeds on. If resistance waits till life is reduced *nearly* to one uniform type, all deviations from that type will come to be considered impious, immoral, even monstrous and contrary to nature. Mankind speedily become unable to conceive diversity, when they have been for some time unaccustomed to see it.

STUDY QUESTIONS: MILL, ON *LIBERTY*

1. What does Mill mean by "liberty?"
2. What is "liberty of action?"
3. Does everyone desire liberty equally? Why?
4. Does Mill believe in abstract rights? Why?
5. How are conflicts of interest between society and an individual to be resolved, in Mill's view?
6. What does Mill mean by "the inward domain of consciousness?" How is it related to liberty?
7. What is Mill's view of freedom of the press?
8. Does the government have the right to coerce an individual against his will? Why?
9. Which church does Mill's regard as the most intolerant? Why?

10. What is Mill's view of Socrates, and of the impiety with which he was charged?
11. What does Mill's mean by "negative logic?" Does he value it? Why?
12. How does Mills regard Rousseau?
13. What does Mill's mean by *individuality*, and why is it so important?
14. What does individuality have to do with personal well-being?

Philosophical Bridges: Mill's Influence

Utilitarianism became one of the most influential movements of late nineteenth and early twentieth century ethical and political thought, both in Europe and the United States. Mill helped initiate the nineteenth century debate over justice, equality, and the moral imperative of social, political, and religious institutions. His view of a healthy society as one that grows and changes with the times and encourages individuality, even eccentricity, among its citizenry, is deeply influential to this day.

There is hardly a moral or political philosopher today who has not been either directly or indirectly influenced by Mill. Two important improvements over his original formulation of utilitarianism have kept the theory as a viable force among contemporary debates. These two newer versions of utilitarianism, called *act utilitarianism* and *rule utilitarianism,* were central to the ethical debates in philosophy during the latter part of the twentieth century. More recently, *preference utilitarianism* and *cost-benefit analysis* have emerged as the latest state of the art in utilitarianism.

As a philosopher, he has been called, by Eugene August, (in his book *John Stuart Mill, A Mind At Large*) "the last great 'Renaissance mind' of western thought, imperially taking all knowledge for his province. He was also the first great interdisciplinary mind of the modern world, forging links among the various fields of learning to which he contributed so brilliantly. To a world beset by multiplicity of knowledge and narrow specialisms, Mill remains the grand instructive example of intellectual integration."

Marx (1818–1883)

Biographical History

Karl Marx was born in the town of Trèves, Prussia (now Trier, Germany). He attended the universities of Berlin and Bonn, where he studied history and philosophy, and earned his doctorate in philosophy at the University of Jena. In his doctoral dissertation he contrasted the Greek atomist views of Democritus and Epicurus.

After receiving his doctorate, he could not find a teaching position, due to his radical leftist views. He got a job as a newspaper editor at the *Rheinische Zeitung* in Cologne, and as a foreign correspondent in London for the *New York Tribune*. He lost his job at the *Rheinische Zeitung* after writing an inflammatory article deeply critical of poverty and the government's repression of workers. He moved to Paris, where he got a job as coeditor of a journal in Paris, and married his college sweetheart Jenny von Westphalen. But the journal went bankrupt and Marx was again unemployed, as he remained for most of his life. He was so poor that several of their children died of malnutrition. His friend and collaborator, economist Friedrich Engels, the son of a wealthy industrialist, supported him for many years, and together they wrote the *Communist Manifesto* (1848), one of the most influential books of all time.

In 1845, having been expelled from France for his involvement with the newly formed communist party, he moved to Brussels, where he wrote *The German Ideology* (1846) and *The Poverty of Philosophy* (1847). After attending the Communist League in London that same year, he went to Cologne and tried to start up a communist newspaper but was expelled by the government. He moved to London, where he became a foreign correspondent for the *New York Tribune*. He remained in London, studying in the reading room of the British Museum, where he wrote his *Critique of Political Economy* (1859) and *Das Kapital* (1867), his most important work, for which he is generally regarded as the most important figure in the history of socialist thought.

Philosophical Overview

Philosophy during Marx's university days in Germany was dominated entirely by Hegel and his works. Philosophers divided themselves into two camps. The Hegelian right consisted of older, conservative professors. They tended to give orthodox interpretations of Hegel's views of religion and morality. The Hegelian left consisted of younger, radical philosophers. As a member of "the Young Hegelians," Marx belonged to the latter. The Young Hegelians regarded Hegel's views on social and political issues as false but pregnant with deep, hidden insights that revealed, under closer scrutiny, the very opposite of Hegel's philosophy. Thus Marx in the end claimed that his own philosophy of dialectic materialism was an upside-down, inside-out version of Hegel's dialectic idealism.

Most of the Young Hegelians who rejected Hegel's system did so in philosophical rebellion against transcendental entities like Hegel's concept of the Absolute world-mind. The biggest early influence on the young Marx was Ludwig Feuerbach's *Essence of Christianity*, in which Feuerbach argues that the human mind is corrupted by its idealized images of universal values that, in reality, cannot be attained. Seduced by its own idealizations into craving what it cannot have, consciousness is thus *alienated*, not just from the world but even more so from itself. Its desires are transferred onto a surrogate ideal and purely imaginary being, God. In so doing, consciousness denies itself the possibility of its own ascension to the ideal. Instead consciousness imprisons itself in the false ideal of God. In this way Feuerbach argued, and Marx followed suit, that all religious imagery should be erased from the human psyche. Like the Stoics and Epicurians, the Young Hegelians, inspired by Feuerbach and led by Marx, argued that peace and happiness cannot be achieved unless first we do away with religion. Marx did not merely repeat Feuerbach's arguments but improved and strengthened them. His *Theses on Feuerbach* (1886) is a brilliant criticism of Feuerbach's notion that change can be brought about simply by changing or manipulating ideas and images. Thus, in marked contrast to Feuerbach's "speculative" materialism, the purpose of Marx's "practical materialism" is to force a change in the actual material relationships in which human social, political, and psychological structures consist.

Thus, in his own way, Marx not only turned Hegel upside down and inside out, he reversed Descartes' apocryphal statement from *Meditations*. According to Descartes, the purpose of philosophy is not to change the world but to change yourself. According to Marx, because consciousness is itself a byproduct of society and the world, the purpose of philosophy is to change the world: "The philosophers have only *interpreted* the world in various ways, the point however is to *change* it."

COMMUNIST MANIFESTO
Marx and Engels

BOURGEOIS AND PROLETARIANS

The history of all hitherto existing society is the history of class struggles.

Free man and slave, patrician and plebeian, lord and serf, guild master and journeyman, in a word, oppressor and oppressed, stood in constant opposition to one another, carried on an uninterrupted, now hidden, now open fight, a fight that each time ended either in a revolutionary reconstitution of society at large or in the common ruin of the contending classes.

In the earlier epochs of history we find almost everywhere a complicated arrangement of society into various orders, a manifold gradation of social rank. In ancient Rome we have patricians, knights, plebeians, slaves; in the Middle Ages, feudal lords, vassals, guild masters, journeymen, apprentices, serfs; in almost all of these classes, again, subordinate gradations.

The modern bourgeois society that has sprouted from the ruins of feudal society has not done away with class antagonisms. It has but established new classes, new conditions of oppression, new forms of struggle in place of the old ones.

Our epoch, the epoch of the bourgeoisie, possesses, however, this distinctive feature: it has simplified the class antagonisms. Society as a whole is more and more splitting up into two great hostile camps, into two great classes directly facing each other: bourgeoisie and proletariat.

From the serfs of the Middle Ages sprang the chartered burghers of the earliest towns. From these burgesses the first elements of the bourgeoisie were developed.

The discovery of America, the rounding of the Cape, opened up fresh ground for the rising bourgeoisie. The East Indian and Chinese markets, the colonization of America, trade with the colonies, the increase in the means of exchange and in commodities generally, gave to commerce, to navigation, to industry an impulse never before known, and thereby, to the revolutionary element in the tottering feudal society, a rapid development.

The feudal system of industry, under which industrial production was monopolized by closed guilds, now no longer sufficed for the growing wants of the new markets. The manufacturing system took its place. The guild masters were pushed on one side by the manufacturing middle class; division of labor between the different corporate guilds vanished in the face of division of labor in each single workshop.

Meantime the markets kept ever growing, the demand ever rising. Even manufacture no longer sufficed. Thereupon steam and machinery revolutionized industrial production. The place of manufacture was taken by the giant, modern industry, the place of the industrial middleclass by industrial millionaires, the leaders of whole industrial armies, the modern bourgeois.

Modern industry has established the world market, for which the discovery of America paved the way. This market has given an immense development to commerce, to navigation, to communication by land. This development has, in its turn, reacted on the extension of industry; and in proportion as industry, commerce, navigation, railways extended, in the same proportion the bourgeoisie developed, increased its capital, and pushed into the background every class handed down from the Middle Ages.

We see, therefore, how the modern bourgeoisie is itself the product of a long course of development, of

Marx and Engels, from *Communist Manifesto*, translated by Samuel Moore, 1888, with emendations by Daniel Kolak.

a series of revolutions in the modes of production and of exchange.

Each step in the development of the bourgeoisie was accompanied by a corresponding political advance of that class. An oppressed class under the sway of the feudal nobility, an armed and self-governing association in the medieval commune; here independent urban republic (as in Italy and Germany), there taxable "third estate" of the monarchy (as in France), afterward, in the period of manufacture proper, serving either the semi-feudal or the absolute monarchy as a counterpoise against the nobility, and, in fact, cornerstone of the great monarchies in general, the bourgeoisie has at last, since the establishment of Modern Industry and of the world market, conquered for itself, in the modern representative State, exclusive political sway. The executive of the modern state is but a committee for managing the common affairs of the whole bourgeoisie.

The bourgeoisie, historically, has played a most revolutionary part.

The bourgeoisie, wherever it has got the upper hand, has put an end to all feudal, patriarchal, idyllic relations. It has pitilessly torn asunder the motley feudal ties that bound man to his "natural superiors," and has left remaining no other nexus between man and man than naked self-interest, than callous "cash payment." It has drowned the most heavenly ecstasies of religious fervor, of chivalrous enthusiasm, of philistine sentimentalism, in the icy water of egotistical calculation. It has resolved personal worth into exchange value, and in place of the numberless indefeasible chartered freedoms has set up that single, unconscionable freedom—free trade. In one word, for exploitation, veiled by religious and political illusions, it has substituted naked, shameless, direct, brutal exploitation.

The bourgeoisie has stripped of its halo every occupation hitherto honored and looked up to with reverent awe. It has converted the physician, the lawyer, the priest, the poet, the man of science, into its paid wage laborers.

The bourgeoisie has torn away from the family its sentimental veil, and has reduced the family relation to a mere money relation.

The bourgeoisie has disclosed how it came to pass that the brutal display of vigor in the Middle Ages, which reactionists so much admire, found its fitting complement in the most slothful indolence. It has been the first to show what man's activity can bring about. It has accomplished wonders far surpassing Egyptian pyramids, Roman aqueducts and Gothic cathedrals; it has conducted expeditions that put in the shade all former exoduses of nations and crusades.

The bourgeoisie cannot exist without constantly revolutionizing the instruments of production, and thereby the relations of production, and with them the whole relations of society. Conservation of the old modes of production in unaltered form was, on the contrary, the first condition of existence for all earlier industrial classes. Constant revolutionizing of production, uninterrupted disturbance of all social conditions, everlasting uncertainty and agitation distinguish the bourgeois epoch from all earlier ones. All fixed, fast-frozen relations, with their train of ancient and venerable prejudices and opinions, are swept away, all new-formed ones become antiquated before they can ossify. All that is solid melts into air, all that is holy is profaned, and man is at last compelled to face with sober senses his real conditions of life and his relations with his kind.

The need of a constantly expanding market for its products chases the bourgeoisie over the whole surface of the globe. It must nestle everywhere, settle everywhere, establish connections everywhere.

The bourgeoisie has through its exploitation of the world market given a cosmopolitan character to production and consumption in every country. To the great chagrin of reactionists, it has drawn from under the feet of industry the national ground on which it stood. All old-established national industries have been destroyed or are daily being destroyed. They are dislodged by new industries, whose introduction becomes a life and death question for all civilized nations, by industries that no longer work up indigenous raw material but raw material drawn from the remotest zones; industries whose products are consumed, not only at home, but in every quarter of the globe. In place of the old wants, satisfied by the production of the country, we find new wants, requiring for their satisfaction the products of distant lands and climes. In place of the old local and national seclusion and self-sufficiency, we have intercourse in every direction, universal interdependence of nations. And as in material, so also in intellectual production. The intellectual creations of individual nations become common property. National one-sidedness and narrow-mindedness become more and more impossible, and from the numerous national and local literatures there arises a world literature.

The bourgeoisie, by the rapid improvement of all instruments of production, by the immensely facilitated means of communication, draws all, even the most barbarian, nations into civilization. The cheap prices of its commodities are the heavy artillery with which it batters down all Chinese walls, with which it forces the barbarians' intensely obstinate hatred of foreigners to capitulate. It compels all nations, on pain of extinction, to adopt the bourgeois mode of production; it compels them to introduce what it calls civilization into their midst, that is, to become bourgeois themselves. In a word, it creates a world after its own image.

The bourgeoisie has subjected the country to the rule of the towns. It has created enormous cities, has greatly increased the urban population as compared with the rural, and has thus rescued a considerable part of the population from the idiocy of rural life. Just as it has made the country dependent on the towns, so it has made barbarian and semi-barbarian countries dependent on the civilized ones, nations of peasants on nations of bourgeois, the East on the West.

The bourgeoisie keeps doing away more and more with the scattered state of the population, of the means of production, and of property. It has agglomerated population, centralized means of production, and has concentrated property in a few hands. The necessary consequence of this was political centralization. Independent or but loosely connected provinces with separate interests, laws, governments, and systems of taxation became lumped together into one nation, with one government, one code of laws, one national class interest, one frontier and one customs tariff.

The bourgeoisie during its rule of scarce one hundred years has created more massive and more colossal productive forces than have all preceding generations together. Subjection of nature's forces to man, machinery, application of chemistry to industry and agriculture, steam navigation, railways, electric telegraphs, clearing of whole continents for cultiva-

tion, canalization of rivers, whole populations conjured out of the ground—what earlier century had even a presentiment that such productive forces slumbered in the lap of social labor?

We see then: the means of production and of exchange, on the foundation of which the bourgeoisie built itself up, were generated in feudal society. At a certain stage in the development of these means of production and of exchange, the conditions under which feudal society produced and exchanged, the feudal organization of agriculture and manufacturing industry, in a word, the feudal relations of property became no longer compatible with the already developed productive forces; they became so many fetters. They had to be burst asunder; they were burst asunder.

Into their place stepped free competition, accompanied by a social and political constitution adapted to it and by the economic and political sway of the bourgeois class.

A similar movement is going on before our own eyes. Modern bourgeois society with its relations of production, of exchange and of property, a society that has conjured up such gigantic means of production and of exchange, is like the sorcerer who is no longer able to control the powers of the nether world whom he has called up by his spells. For many a decade past the history of industry and commerce is but the history of the revolt of modern productive forces against modern conditions of production, against the property relations that are the conditions for the existence of the bourgeoisie and of its rule. It is enough to mention the commercial crises that by their periodical return put on trial, each time more threateningly, the existence of the entire bourgeois society. In these crises a great part not only of the existing products, but also of the previously created productive forces, are periodically destroyed. In these crises there breaks out an epidemic that in all earlier epochs would have seemed an absurdity—the epidemic of over-production. Society suddenly finds itself put back into a state of momentary barbarism; it appears as if a famine, a universal war of devastation had cut off the supply of every means of subsistence; industry and commerce seem to be destroyed; and why? Because there is too much civilization, too much means of subsistence, too much industry, too much commerce. The productive forces at the disposal of society no longer tend to further the development of the conditions of bourgeois property; on the contrary, they have become too powerful for these conditions, by which they are fettered, and as soon as they overcome these fetters, they bring disorder into the whole of bourgeois society, endanger the existence of bourgeois property. The conditions of bourgeois society are too narrow to comprise the wealth created by them. And how does the bourgeoisie get over these crises? On the one hand by enforced destruction of a mass of productive forces, on the other, by the conquest of new markets and by the more thorough exploitation of the old ones. That is to say, by paving the way for more extensive and more destructive crises and by diminishing the means whereby crises are prevented.

The weapons with which the bourgeoisie felled feudalism to the ground are now turned against the bourgeoisie itself.

But not only has the bourgeoisie forged the weapons that bring death to itself; it has also called into existence the people who are to wield those weapons—the modern working class, the proletarians.

In proportion as the bourgeoisie, that is, capital, is developed, in the same proportion is the proletariat, the modern working class, developed—a class of laborers who live only as long as they find work, and who find work only as long as their labor increases capital. These laborers, who must sell themselves piecemeal, are a commodity like every other article of commerce, and are consequently exposed to all the vicissitudes of competition, to all the fluctuations of the market.

Owing to the extensive use of machinery and to division of labor, the work of the proletarians has lost all individual character and, consequently, all charm for the workman. He becomes an appendage of the machine, and it is only the most simple, most monotonous, and most easily acquired knack that is required of him. Hence, the cost of production of a workman is restricted almost entirely to the means of subsistence that he requires for his maintenance and for the propagation of his race. But the price of a commodity, and therefore also of labor, is equal to its cost of production. In proportion, therefore, as the repulsiveness of the work increases, the wage decreases. Nay more, in proportion as the use of machinery and division of labor increase, in the same proportion the burden of toil also increases, whether by prolongation of the working hours, by increase of the work exacted in a given time or by increased speed of the machinery, etc.

Modern industry has converted the little workshop of the patriarchal master into the great factory of the industrial capitalist. Masses of laborers, crowded into the factory, are organized like soldiers. As privates of the industrial army they are placed under the command of a perfect hierarchy of officers and sergeants. Not only are they slaves of the bourgeois class and of the bourgeois State; they are daily and hourly enslaved by the machine, by the overseer and, above all, by the individual bourgeois manufacturer himself. The more openly this despotism proclaims gain to be its end and aim, the more petty, the more hateful and the more embittering it is.

The less the skill and exertion of strength implied in manual labor, in other words, the more modern industry becomes developed, the more is the labor of men superseded by that of women. Differences of age and sex no longer have any distinctive social validity for the working class. All are instruments of labor, more or less expensive to use, according to their age and sex.

No sooner is the exploitation of the laborer by the manufacturer so far at an end that he receives his wages in cash, than he is set upon by the other portions of the bourgeoisie, the landlord, the shopkeeper, the pawnbroker, etc.

The lower strata of the middleclass—the small tradespeople, shopkeepers, and retired tradesmen generally, the handicraftsmen, and peasants—all these sink gradually into the proletariat, partly because their diminutive capital does not suffice for the scale on which Modern Industry is carried on and is swamped in the competition with the large capitalists, partly because their specialized skill is rendered worthless by new methods of production. Thus the proletariat is recruited from all classes of the population.

The proletariat goes through various stages of development. With its birth begins its struggle with the bourgeoisie. At first the contest is carried on by individual laborers, then by the work people of the factory, then by the operatives of one trade in one locality against the individual bourgeois who directly exploits them. They direct their attacks not against the bourgeois conditions of production, but against the instruments of production themselves; they destroy imported wares that compete with their labor, they smash machinery to pieces, they set factories ablaze, they seek to restore by force the vanished status of the workman of the Middle Ages.

At this stage the laborers still form an incoherent mass scattered over the whole country and broken up by their mutual competition. If anywhere they unite to form more compact bodies, this is not yet the consequence of their own active union but of the bourgeoisie, which class, in order to attain its own political ends, is compelled to set the whole proletariat in motion and, moreover is, for a time, yet able to do so. At this stage, therefore, the proletarians do not fight their enemies, but the enemies of their enemies, the remnants of absolute monarchy, the landowners, the non-industrial bourgeois, the petty bourgeoisie. Thus the whole historical movement is concentrated in the hands of the bourgeoisie; every victory so obtained is a victory for the bourgeoisie.

But with the development of industry the proletariat not only increases in number; it becomes concentrated in greater masses, its strength grows, and it feels that strength more. The various interests and conditions of life within the ranks of the proletariat are more and more equalized in proportion as machinery obliterates all distinctions of labor and nearly everywhere reduces wages to the same low level. The growing competition among the bourgeois, and the resulting commercial crises, make the wages of the workers ever more fluctuating. The unceasing improvement of machinery, ever more rapidly developing, makes their livelihood more and more precarious; the collisions between individual workmen and individual bourgeois take more and more the character of collisions between two classes. Thereupon the workers begin to form combinations (trade unions) against the bourgeois; they club together in order to keep up the rate of wages; they found permanent associations in order to make provision beforehand for these occasional revolts. Here and there the contest breaks out into riots.

Now and then the workers are victorious, but only for a time. The real fruit of their battles lies, not in the immediate result, but in the ever expanding union of the workers. This union is helped on by the improved means of communication that are created by modern industry and that place the workers of different localities in contact with one another. It was just this contact that was needed to centralize the numerous local struggles, all of the same character, into one national struggle between classes. But every class struggle is a political struggle. And that union, to attain which the burghers of the Middle Ages with their miserable highways required centuries, the modern proletarians, thanks to railways, achieve in a few years.

This organization of the proletarians into a class and consequently into a political party is continually being upset again by the competition between the workers themselves. But it ever rises up again, stronger, firmer, mightier. It compels legislative recognition of particular interests of the workers, by taking advantage of the divisions among the bourgeoisie itself. Thus the ten hours' bill in England was carried.

Altogether, collisions between the classes of the old society in many ways further the course of development of the proletariat. The bourgeoisie finds itself involved in a constant battle. At first with the aristocracy; later on, with those portions of the bourgeoisie itself whose interests have become antagonistic to the progress of industry; at all times with the bourgeoisie of foreign countries. In all these battles it sees itself compelled to appeal to the proletariat, to ask for its help, and thus to drag it into the political arena. The bourgeoisie itself, therefore, supplies the proletariat with its own elements of political and general education; in other words, it furnishes the proletariat with weapons for fighting the bourgeoisie.

Further, as we have already seen, entire sections of the ruling classes are precipitated into the proletariat by the advance of industry, or are at least threatened in their conditions of existence. These also supply the proletariat with fresh elements of enlightenment and progress.

Finally, in times when the class struggle nears the decisive hour, the process of dissolution going on within the ruling class, in fact within the whole range of old society, assumes such a violent, glaring character that a small section of the ruling class cuts itself adrift and joins the revolutionary class, the class that holds the future in its hands. Therefore, just as, at an earlier period a section of the nobility went over to the bourgeoisie, so now a portion of the bourgeoisie goes over to the proletariat, and in particular a portion of the bourgeois ideologists who have raised themselves to the level of comprehending theoretically the historical movement as a whole.

Of all the classes that stand face to face with the bourgeoisie today, the proletariat alone is a really revolutionary class. The other classes decay and finally disappear in the face of modern industry; the proletariat is its special and essential product.

The lower middleclass, the small manufacturer, the shopkeeper, the artisan, the peasant, all these fight against the bourgeoisie to save from extinction their existence as fractions of the middle class. They are therefore not revolutionary, but conservative. Nay more, they are reactionary, for they try to roll back the wheel of history. If by chance they are revolutionary, they are so only in view of their impending transfer into the proletariat; they thus defend not their present, but their future interests; they desert their own standpoint to place themselves at that of the proletariat.

The "dangerous class," the social scum, that passively rotting mass thrown off by the lowest layers of the old society may here and there be swept into the movement by a proletariat revolution; its conditions of life, however, prepare it far more for the part of a bribed tool of reactionary intrigue.

In the conditions of the proletariat, those of the old society at large are already virtually swamped. The proletarian is without property; his relation to his wife and children has no longer anything in common with the bourgeois family relations; modern industrial labor, modern subjection to capital, the same in England as in France, in America as in Germany, has stripped him of every trace of national character. Law, morality, and religion are to him so many bourgeois prejudices behind which lurk in ambush just as many bourgeois interests.

All the preceding classes that got the upper hand sought to fortify their already acquired status by subjecting society at large to their conditions of appropriation. The proletarians cannot become masters of the productive forces of society except by abolishing their own previous mode of appropriation, and thereby also every other previous mode of appropriation. They have nothing of their own to secure and to fortify; their mission is to destroy all previous securities for, and insurances of, individual property.

All previous historical movements were movements of minorities or in the interest of minorities. The proletarian movement is the self-conscious, independent movement of the immense majority in the interest of the immense majority. The proletariat, the lowest stratum of our present society, cannot stir, cannot raise itself up, without the whole superincumbent strata of official society being sprung into the air.

Though not in substance, yet in form; the struggle of the proletariat with the bourgeoisie is at first a national struggle. The proletariat of each country must, of course, first of all settle matters with its own bourgeoisie.

In depicting the most general phases of the development of the proletariat, we traced the more or less veiled civil war raging within existing society up to the point where that war breaks out into open revolution, and where the violent overthrow of the bourgeoisie lays the foundation for the sway of the proletariat.

Hitherto, every form of society has been based, as we have already seen, on the antagonism of oppressing and oppressed classes. But in order to oppress a class certain conditions must be assured to it under which it can, at least, continue its slavish existence. The serf, in the period of serfdom, raised himself to membership in the commune, just as the petty bourgeois, under the yoke of feudal absolutism, managed to develop into a bourgeois. The modern laborer, on the contrary; instead of rising with the progress of industry sinks deeper and deeper below the conditions of existence of his own class. He becomes a pauper, and pauperism develops more rapidly than population and wealth. And here it becomes evident that the bourgeoisie is unfit any longer to be the ruling class in society and to impose its conditions of existence upon society as an overriding law. It is unfit to rule because it is incompetent to assure an existence to its slave within his slavery, because it cannot help letting him sink into such a state that it has to feed him instead of being fed by him. Society can no longer live under this bourgeoisie, in other words, its existence is no longer compatible with society.

The essential condition for the existence and for the sway of the bourgeois class is the formation and augmentation of capital; the condition for capital is wage labor. Wage labor rests exclusively on competition between the laborers. The advance of industry, whose involuntary promoter is the bourgeoisie, replaces the isolation of the laborers, due to competition, by their revolutionary combination due to association. The development of Modern Industry therefore cuts from under its feet the very foundation on which the bourgeois produces and appropriates products. What the bourgeoisie therefore produces, above all, are its own gravediggers. Its fall and the victory of the proletariat are equally inevitable.

PROLETARIANS AND COMMUNISTS

In what relation do the communists stand to the proletarians as a whole?

The communists do not form a separate party opposed to other working-class parties.

They have no interests separate and apart from those of the proletariat as a whole.

They do not set up any sectarian principles of their own, by which to shape and mold the proletarian movement.

The communists are distinguished from the other working class parties by this only: (1) In the national struggles of the proletarians of the different countries they point out and bring to the front the common interests of the entire proletariat, independent of all nationality. (2) In the various stages of development which the struggle of the working class against the bourgeoisie has to pass through, they always and everywhere represent the interests of the movement as a whole.

The communists, therefore, are on the one hand, practically, the most advanced and resolute section of the working-class parties of every country, that section which pushes forward all others; on the other hand, theoretically, they have over the great mass of the proletariat the advantage of clearly understanding the line of march, the conditions, and the ultimate general results of the proletarian movement.

The immediate aim of the communists is the same as that of all the other proletarian parties: formation of the proletariat into a class, overthrow of the bourgeois supremacy, conquest of political power by the proletariat.

The theoretical conclusions of the communists are in no way based on ideas or principles that have

been invented, or discovered, by this or that would-be universal reformer.

They merely express, in general terms, actual relations springing from an existing class struggle, from a historical movement going on under our very eyes. The abolition of existing property relations is not at all a distinctive feature of communism.

All property relations in the past have continually been subject to historical change consequent upon the change in historical conditions.

The French Revolution, for example, abolished feudal property in favor of bourgeois property.

The distinguishing feature of communism is not the abolition of property generally, but the abolition of bourgeois property. But modern bourgeois private property is the final and most complete expression of the system of producing and appropriating products that is based on class antagonisms, on the exploitation of the many by the few.

In this sense the theory of the communists may be summed up in the single sentence: Abolition of private property.

We communists have been reproached with the desire of abolishing the right of personally acquiring property as the fruit of a man's own labor, which property is alleged to be the groundwork of all personal freedom, activity, and independence.

Hard-won, self-acquired, self-earned property! Do you mean the property of the petty artisan and of the small peasant, a form of property that preceded the bourgeois form? There is no need to abolish that; the development of industry has to a great extent already destroyed it, and is still destroying it daily.

Or do you mean modern bourgeois private property?

But does wage labor create any property for the laborer? Not a bit. It creates capital, that is, that kind of property which exploits wage labor, and which cannot increase except upon condition of begetting a new supply of wage labor for fresh exploitation. Property, in its present form, is based on the antagonism of capital and wage labor. Let us examine both sides of this antagonism.

To be a capitalist is to have not only a purely personal but a social *status* in production. Capital is a collective product, and only by the united action of many members, nay, in the last resort only by the united action of all members of society, can it be set in motion.

Capital is, therefore, not a personal, but a social power.

When, therefore, capital is converted into common property, into the property of all members of society, personal property is not thereby transformed into social property. It is only the social character of the property that is changed. It loses its class character.

Let us now take wage labor.

The average price of wage labor is the minimum wage, that is, that quantum of the means of subsistence which is absolutely requisite to keep the laborer in bare existence as a laborer. What, therefore, the wage laborer appropriates by means of his labor merely suffices to prolong and reproduce a bare existence. We by no means intend to abolish this personal appropriation of the products of labor, an appropriation that is made for the maintenance and reproduction of human life, and that leaves no surplus wherewith to command the labor of others. All that we want to do away with is the miserable character of this appropriation, under which the laborer lives merely to increase capital, and is allowed to live only insofar as the interest of the ruling class requires it.

In bourgeois society living labor is but a means to increase accumulated labor. In communist society accumulated labor is but a means to widen, to enrich, to promote the existence of the laborer.

In bourgeois society, therefore, the past dominates the present; in communist society the present dominates the past. In bourgeois society capital is independent and has individuality, while the living person is dependent and has no individuality.

And the abolition of this state of things is called by the bourgeois abolition of individuality and freedom! And rightly so. The abolition of bourgeois individuality, bourgeois independence, and bourgeois freedom is undoubtedly aimed at.

By freedom is meant, under the present bourgeois conditions of production, free trade, free selling and buying.

But if selling and buying disappear, free selling and buying disappear also. This talk about free selling and buying, and all the other "brave words" of our bourgeoisie about freedom in general, have a meaning, if any, only in contrast with restricted selling and buying, with the fettered traders of the Middle Ages, but have no meaning when opposed to the communistic abolition of buying and selling, of the bourgeois conditions of production, and of the bourgeoisie itself.

You are horrified at our intending to do away with private property. But in your existing society private property is already done away with for nine-tenths of the population; its existence for the few is solely due to its non-existence in the hands of those nine tenths. You reproach us, therefore, with intending to do away with a form of property the necessary condition for whose existence is the non-existence of any property for the immense majority of society.

In one word, you reproach us with intending to do away with your property. Precisely so; that is just what we intend.

From the moment when labor can no longer be converted into capital, money, or rent, into a social power capable of being monopolized, that is, from the moment when individual property can no longer be transformed into bourgeois property, into capital, from that moment, you say, individuality vanishes.

You must, therefore, confess that by "individual" you mean no other person than the bourgeois, than the middle-class owner of property. This person must, indeed, be swept out of the way and made impossible.

Communism deprives no man of the power to appropriate the products of society; all that it does is to deprive him of the power to subjugate the labor of others by means of such appropriation.

It has been objected that upon the abolition of private property all work will cease and universal laziness will overtake us.

According to this, bourgeois society ought long ago have gone to the dogs through sheer idleness, for those of its members who work acquire nothing and those who acquire anything do not work. The whole of this objection is but another expression of the tautology that there can no longer be any wage labor when there is no longer any capital.

All objections urged against the communistic mode of producing and appropriating material products have, in the same way, been urged against the communistic modes of producing and appropriating intellectual products. Just as, to the bourgeois, the disappearance of class property is the disappearance of production itself, so the disappearance of class culture is to him identical with the disappearance of all culture.

That culture, the loss of which he laments, is, for the enormous majority, a mere training to act as a machine.

But don't wrangle with us so long as you apply, to our intended abolition of bourgeois property, the standard of your bourgeois notions of freedom, culture, law, etc. Your very ideas are but the outgrowth of the conditions of your bourgeois production and bourgeois property, just as your jurisprudence is but the will of your class made into a law for all, a will whose essential character and direction are determined by the economic conditions of existence of your class.

The selfish misconception that induces you to transform into eternal laws of nature and of reason the social forms springing from your present mode of production and form of property—historical relations that rise and disappear in the progress of production—this misconception you share with every ruling class that has preceded you. What you see clearly in the case of ancient property, what you admit in the case of feudal property you are of course forbidden to admit in the case of your own bourgeois form of property.

Abolition of the family! Even the most radical flare up at this infamous proposal of the communists.

On what foundation is the present family, the bourgeois family, based? On capital, on private gain. In its completely developed form this family exists only among the bourgeoisie. But this state of things finds its complement in the practical absence of the family among the proletarians, and in public prostitution.

The bourgeois family will vanish as a matter of course when its complement vanishes, and both will vanish with the vanishing of capital.

Do you charge us with wanting to stop the exploitation of children by their parents? To this crime we plead guilty.

But, you will say, we destroy the most hallowed of relations when we replace home education by social.

And your education! Is not that also social, and determined by the social conditions under which you educate, by the intervention, direct or indirect, of society, by means of schools, etc.? The communists have not invented the intervention of society in education; they do but seek to alter the character of that intervention, and to rescue education from the influence of the ruling class.

The bourgeois claptrap about the family and education, about the hallowed co-relation of parent and child, becomes all the more disgusting, the more, by the action of modern industry, all family ties among the proletarians are torn asunder and their children transformed into simple articles of commerce and instruments of labor.

"But you communists would introduce community of women," screams the whole bourgeoisie in chorus.

The bourgeois sees in his wife a mere instrument of production. He hears that the instruments of production are to be exploited in common and, naturally, can come to no other conclusion than that the lot of being common to all will likewise fall to the women.

He has not even a suspicion that the real point aimed at is to do away with the status of women as mere instruments of production.

For the rest, nothing is more ridiculous than the virtuous indignation of our bourgeois at the community of women which, they pretend, is to be openly and officially established by the communists. The communists have no need to introduce community of women; it has existed almost from time immemorial.

Our bourgeois, not content with having the wives and daughters of their proletarians at their disposal, not to speak of common prostitutes, take the greatest pleasure in seducing each other's wives.

Bourgeois marriage is in reality a system of wives in common and thus, at the most, what the communists might possibly be reproached with is that they desire to introduce, in substitution for a hypocritically concealed, an openly legalized community of women. For the rest, it is self-evident that the abolition of the present system of production must bring with it the abolition of the community of women springing from that system, that is, of prostitution, both public and private.

The communists are further reproached with desiring to abolish countries and nationality.

The workingmen have no country. We cannot take from them what they have not got. Since the proletariat must first of all acquire political supremacy, must rise to be the leading class of the nation, must constitute itself *the* nation, it is, so far, itself national, though not in the bourgeois sense of the word.

National differences and antagonisms between peoples are daily more and more vanishing, owing to the development of the bourgeoisie, to freedom of commerce, to the world market, to uniformity in the mode of production and in the conditions of life corresponding thereto.

The supremacy of the proletariat will cause them to vanish still faster. United action, of the leading civilized countries at least, is one of the first conditions for the emancipation of the proletariat.

In proportion as the exploitation of one individual by another is put to an end, the exploitation of one nation by another will also be put to an end. In proportion as the antagonism between classes within the nation vanishes, the hostility of one nation to another will come to an end.

The charges against communism made from a religious, a philosophical, and, generally, from an ideological standpoint are not deserving of serious examination.

Does it require deep intuition to comprehend that man's ideas, views, and conceptions, in one word, man's consciousness, change with every change in the conditions of his material existence, in his social relations, and in his social life?

What else does the history of ideas prove than that the intellectual production changes its character in proportion as material production is changed? The ruling ideas of each age have ever been the ideas of its ruling class.

When people speak of ideas that revolutionize society they do but express the fact that within the old society the elements of a new one have been created, and that the dissolution of the old ideas keeps even pace with the dissolution of the old conditions of existence.

When the ancient world was in its last throes, the ancient religions were overcome by Christianity. When Christian ideas succumbed in the eighteenth century to nationalist ideas, feudal society fought its death battle with the then revolutionary bourgeoisie. The ideas of religious liberty and freedom of conscience merely gave expression to the sway of free competition within the domain of knowledge.

"Undoubtedly," it will be said, "religious, moral, philosophical, and juridical ideas have been modified in the course of historical development. But religion, morality, philosophy, political science, and law constantly survived this change.

"There are, besides, eternal truths, such as freedom, justice, etc., that are common to all states of society. But communism abolishes eternal truths, it abolishes all religion, and all morality, instead of constituting them on a new basis; it therefore acts in contradiction to all past historical experience."

What does this accusation reduce itself to? The history of all past society has consisted in the development of class antagonisms, antagonisms that assumed different forms at different epochs.

But whatever form they may have taken, one fact is common to all past ages, viz., the exploitation of one part of society by the other. No wonder then that the social consciousness of past ages, despite all the multiplicity and variety it displays, moves within certain common forms, or general ideas, which cannot completely vanish except with the total disappearance of class antagonisms.

The communist revolution is the most radical rupture with traditional property relations; no wonder that its development involves the most radical rupture with traditional ideas.

But let us have done with the bourgeois objections to communism.

We have seen above that the first step in the revolution by the working class is to raise the proletariat to the position of ruling class, to win the battle of democracy.

The proletariat will use its political supremacy to wrest, by degrees, all capital from the bourgeoisie, to centralize all instruments of production in the hands of the state, that is, of the proletariat organized as the ruling class, and to increase the total of productive forces as rapidly as possible.

Of course, in the beginning this cannot be effected except by means of despotic inroads on the rights of property and on the conditions of bourgeois production; by means of measures, therefore, which appear economically insufficient and untenable, but which, in the course of the movement outstrip themselves, necessitate further inroads upon the old social order, and are unavoidable as a means of entirely revolutionizing the mode of production.

These measures will of course be different in different countries.

Nevertheless, in the most advanced countries the following will be pretty generally applicable:

1. Abolition of property in land and application of all rents of land to public purposes.
2. A heavy progressive or graduated income tax.
3. Abolition of all right of inheritance.
4. Confiscation of the property of all emigrants and rebels.
5. Centralization of credit in the hands of the state, by means of a national bank with state capital and an exclusive monopoly.
6. Centralization of the means of communication and transport in the hands of the state.
7. Extension of factories and instruments of production owned by the state; the bringing into cultivation of wastelands, and the improvement of the soil generally in accordance with a common plan.
8. Equal liability of all to labor. Establishment of industrial armies, especially for agriculture.
9. Combination of agriculture with manufacturing industries; gradual abolition of the distinction between town and country, by a more equable distribution of the population over the country.
10. Free education for all children in public schools. Abolition of children's factory labor in its present form. Combination of education with industrial production, etc.

When, in the course of development, class distinctions have disappeared and all production has been concentrated in the hands of a vast association of the whole nation, the public power will lose its political character. Political power, properly so called, is merely the organized power of one class for oppressing another. If the proletariat during its contest with the bourgeoisie is compelled, by the force of circumstances, to organize itself as a class, if, by means of a revolution, it makes itself the ruling class and, as such, sweeps away by force the old conditions of production, then it will, along with these conditions, have swept away the conditions for the existence of class antagonisms and of classes generally, and will thereby have abolished its own supremacy as a class.

In place of the old bourgeois society, with its classes and class antagonisms, we shall have an association in which the free development of each is the condition for the free development of all. . . .

In short, the communists everywhere support every revolutionary movement against the existing social and political order of things.

In all these movements they bring to the front, as the leading question in each, the property question, no matter what its degree of development at the time.

Finally, they labor everywhere for the union and agreement of the democratic parties of all countries.

The communists disdain to conceal their views and aims. They openly declare that their ends can be attained only by the forcible overthrow of all existing social conditions. Let the ruling classes tremble at a communistic revolution. The proletarians have nothing to lose but their chains. They have a world to win.

Workers of the World, unite!

STUDY QUESTIONS: MARX AND ENGELS, COMMUNIST MANIFESTO

1. In what ways is modern society according to Marx like Rome and the Middle Ages? What has changed? What has stayed the same?
2. What is the bourgeoisie?
3. What is the "third estate?"
4. How do the bourgeoisie exploit the world market?
5. What is the proletariat?
6. What is Marx's view of trade unions? What is their significance and what role do they play?
7. What is the "dangerous class?"
8. What is the relation of wage later to capital?
9. To which class do communists belong?
10. What are the types of private property and how are they distinguished? What is Marx's view of this?

11. In modern capitalist society, what is meant by "freedom?"
12. Does the elimination of private property, in Marx's view, eliminate the individual? Why?
13. Is communism in Marx's view individualistic, or anti-individualistic? Why? How does he make his case?
14. What is Marx's criticism of the role of women in bourgeois society? How are they exploited?
15. What is Marx's view of Christianity? Of religion in general?

ALIENATION

The relationship between Marx's view of the key relationship between alienation and human consciousness, resulting in that consciousness is not the cause of social process but an effect, is central throughout his work. In his *Contribution to the Critique of Political Economy*, he writes:

> In the social production of their life, men enter into definite relations that are indispensable and independent of their will, relations of production, which correspond to a definite stage of development of their material productive forces. The sum total of these relations of production constitutes the economic structure of society, the real foundation, on which rises a legal and political superstructure and to which correspond definite forms of social consciousness. The mode of production of material life conditions the social, political, and intellectual life process in general. It is not the consciousness of men that determines their social being, but, on the contrary, their social being that determines their consciousness.

That is why, according to Marx, removing greed and competition from society would by liberating consciousness from alienation allow us to evolve into a more enlightened state in which individuals are freed from the cocoon of oppressive society. Without alienated labor the world according to Marx would be a utopia.

In "Alienation," he argues that consciousness itself, because it is not a cause of society but its effect, is imprisoned by capitalism. The only way to liberate consciousness, according to Marx, is by removing the competition inherent in capitalist systems.

We have proceeded from the premises of political economy. We have accepted its language and its laws. We presupposed private property, the separation of labor, capital and land, and of wages, profit of capital, and rent of land—likewise division of labor, competition, the concept of exchange value, etc. On the basis of political economy itself, in its own words, we have shown that the worker sinks to the level of a commodity and becomes indeed the most wretched of commodities; that the wretchedness of the worker is in inverse proportion to the power and magnitude of his production; that the necessary result of competition is the accumulation of capital in a few hands, and thus the restoration of monopoly in a more terrible form; that finally the distinction between capitalist and land-renter, like that between the tiller of the soil and the factory worker, disappears and that the whole of society must fall apart into the two classes—the property *owners* and the propertyless *workers*.

Political economy proceeds from the fact of private property, but it does not explain it to us. It expresses in general, abstract formulae the *material* process through which private property actually passes, and these formulae it then takes for *laws*. It does not *comprehend* these laws—that is, it does not demonstrate how they arise from the very nature of private property. Political economy does not disclose the source of the division between labor and capital, and between capital and land. When, for example, it

---

Marx, from *Economic and Philosophic Manuscripts of 1844*, translated by Martin Milligan, with emendations by Daniel Kolak.

defines the relationship of wages to profit, it takes the interest of the capitalists to be the ultimate cause; that is, it takes for granted what it is supposed to evolve. Similarly, competition comes in everywhere. It is explained from external circumstances. As to how far these external and apparently fortuitous circumstances are but the expression of a necessary course of development, political economy teaches us nothing. We have seen how, to it, exchange itself appears to be a fortuitous fact. The only wheels which political economy sets in motion are *avarice* and the *war among the avaricious—competition*.

Precisely because political economy does not grasp the connections within the movement, it was possible to counterpose, for instance, the doctrine of competition to the doctrine of monopoly, the doctrine of craft liberty to the doctrine of the corporation, the doctrine of the division of landed property to the doctrine of the big estate—for competition, craft liberty and the division of landed property were explained and comprehended only as fortuitous, premeditated and violent consequences of monopoly, the corporation, and feudal property, not as their necessary, inevitable and natural consequences.

Now, therefore, we have to grasp the essential connection between private property, avarice, and the separation of labor, capital, and landed property; between exchange and competition, value and the devaluation of men, monopoly and competition, etc.; the connection between this whole estrangement and the *money* system.

Do not let us go back to a fictitious primordial condition as the political economist does, when he tries to explain. Such a primordial condition explains nothing. He merely pushes the question away into a gray nebulous distance. He assumes in the form of fact, of an event, what he is supposed to deduce—namely, the necessary relationship between two things—between, for example, division of labor and exchange. Theology in the same way explains the origin of evil by the fall of man; that is, it assumes as a fact, in historical form, what has to be explained.

We proceed from an *actual* economic fact.

The worker becomes all the poorer the more wealth he produces, the more his production increases in power and range. The worker becomes an ever cheaper commodity the more commodities he creates.

With the *increasing value* of the world of things proceeds in direct proportion the *devaluation* of the world of men. Labor produces not only commodities: it produces itself and the worker as a *commodity*—and does so in the proportion in which it produces commodities generally.

This fact expresses merely the object which labor produces—labor's product—confronts it as *something alien*, as a *power independent* of the producer. The product of labor is labor which has been congealed in an object, which has become material: it is the *objectification* of labor. Labor's realization is its objectification. In the conditions dealt with by political economy this realization of labor appears as *loss of reality* for the workers; objectification as *loss of the object* and *object bondage*; appropriation as *estrangement*, as *alienation*.

So much does labor's realization appear as loss of reality that the worker loses reality to the point of starving to death. So much does objectification appear as loss of the object that the worker is robbed of the objects most necessary not only for his life but for his work. Indeed, labor itself becomes an object which he can get hold of only with the greatest effort and with the most irregular interruptions. So much does the appropriation of the object appear as estrangement that the more objects the worker produces the fewer can he possess and the more he falls under the dominion of his product, capital.

All these consequences are contained in the definition that the worker is related to the *product of his labor* as to an *alien* object. For on this premise it is clear that the more the worker spends himself, the more powerful the alien objective world becomes which he creates over-against himself, the poorer he himself—his inner world—becomes, the less belongs to him as his own. It is the same in religion. The more man puts into God, the less he retains in himself. The worker puts his life into the object; but now his life no longer belongs to him but to the object. Hence, the greater this activity, the greater is the worker's lack of objects. Whatever the product of his labor is, he is not. Therefore the greater this product, the less is he himself. The *alienation* of the worker in his product means not only that his labor becomes an object, an *external* existence, but that it exists *outside him*, independently, as something alien to him, and that it becomes a power on its own confronting him; it means that the life which he has conferred on the object confronts him as something hostile and alien.

Let us now look more closely at the *objectification*, at the production of the worker; and therein at the alienation, the *loss* of the object, his product.

The worker can create nothing without *nature*, without the *sensuous external world*. It is the material on which his labor is manifested, in which it is active, from which and by means of which it produces.

But just as nature provides labor with the *means of life* in the sense that labor cannot *live* without objects on which to operate, on the other hand, it also provides the *means of life* in the more restricted sense—that is, the means for the physical subsistence of the *worker* himself.

Thus the more the worker by his labor *appropriates* the external world, sensuous nature, the more he deprives himself of *means of life* in the double respect: first, that the sensuous external world more and more ceases to be an object belonging to his labor—to be his labor's *means of life*; and secondly, that it more and more ceases to be *means of life* in the immediate sense, means for the physical subsistence of the worker.

Thus in this double respect the worker becomes a slave of his object, first, in that he receives an *object of labor*, that is, in that he receives *work*; and secondly, in that he receives *means of subsistence*. Therefore, it enables him to exist, first, as a *worker*; and, second, as a *physical subject*. The extremity of this bondage is that it is only as a *worker* that he continues to maintain himself as a *physical subject*, and that it is only as a *physical subject* that he is a *worker*. (The laws of political economy express the estrangement of the worker in his object thus: the more the worker produces, the less he has to consume; the more values he creates, the more valueless, the more unworthy he becomes; the better formed his product, the more deformed becomes the worker; the more civilized his object, the more barbarous becomes the worker; the mightier labor becomes, the more powerless becomes the worker; the more ingenious labor becomes, the duller becomes the worker and the more he becomes nature's bondsman.)

Political economy conceals the estrangement inherent in the nature of labor by not considering the direct relationship between the worker (labor) and production.

It is true that labor produces for the rich wonderful things—but for the worker it produces privation. It produces palaces—but for the worker, hovels. It produces beauty—but for the worker, deformity. It replaces labor by machines—but some of the workers it throws back to a barbarous type of labor, and the other workers it turns into machines. It produces intelligence—but for the worker idiocy, cretinism.

The direct relationship of labor to its produce is the relationship of the worker to the objects of his production. The relationship of the man of means to the objects of production and to production itself is only a *consequence* of the first relationship—and confirms it. We shall consider this other aspect later.

When we ask, then, what is the essential relationship of labor we are asking about the relationship of the *worker* to production.

Till now we have been considering the estrangement, the alienation of the worker only in one of its aspects, that is, the worker's *relationship to the products of his labor*. But the estrangement is manifested not only in the result but in the *act of production*—within the *producing activity* itself. How would the worker come to face the product of his activity as a stranger, were it not that in the very act of production he was estranging himself from himself? The product is after all but the summary of the activity, of production. If then the product of labor is alienation, production itself must be active alienation, the alienation of activity, the activity of alienation. In the estrangement of the object of labor is merely summarized the estrangement, the alienation, in the activity of labor itself.

What, then, constitutes the alienation of labor?

First, the fact that labor is *external* to the worker, that is, it does not belong to his essential being; that in his work, therefore, he does not affirm himself but denies himself, does not feel content but unhappy, does not develop freely his physical and mental energy but mortifies his body and ruins his mind. The worker therefore only feels himself outside his work, and in his work feels outside himself. He is at home when he is not working, and when he is working he is not at home. His labor is therefore not voluntary, but coerced; it is *forced labor*. It is therefore not the satisfaction of a need; it is merely a *means* to satisfy needs external to it. Its alien character emerges clearly in the fact that as soon as no physical or other compulsion exists, labor is shunned like the plague. External labor, labor in which man alienates himself, is a labor of self-sacrifice, of mortification. Lastly, the external character of labor for the worker appears in the fact that it is not his own, but someone else's, that it does not belong to him, that in it he belongs, not to himself, but to another. Just as in religion the spontaneous activity of the human imagination, of the human brain and the human heart, operates independently of the individual—that is, operates on him as an alien, divine, or diabolical activity—in the same way the worker's activity is not his spontaneous activity. It belongs to another; it is the loss of his self.

As a result, therefore, man (the worker) no longer feels himself to be freely active in any but his animal functions—eating, drinking, procreating, or at most in his dwelling and in dressing up, etc.; and in his human functions he no longer feels himself to be anything but an animal. What is animal becomes human and what is human becomes animal.

Certainly drinking, eating, procreating, etc., are also genuinely human functions. But in the abstraction which separates them from the sphere of all other human activity and turns them into sole and ultimate ends, they are animal.

We have considered the act of estranging practical human activity, labor, in two of its aspects: (1) The relation of the worker to the *product of labor* as an alien object exercising power over him. This relation is at the same time the relation to the sensuous external world, to the objects of nature as an alien world antagonistically opposed to him. (2) The relation of labor to the *act of production* within the *labor* process. This relation is the relation of the worker to his own activity as an alien activity not belonging to him; it is activity as suffering, strength as weakness, begetting as emasculating, the worker's *own* physical and mental energy, his personal life or what is life other than activity—as an activity which is turned against him, neither depends on nor belongs to him. Here we have *self-alienation*, as we had previously the estrangement of the *thing*.

We have yet a third aspect of alienated *labor* to deduce from the two already considered.

Man is a species being, not only because in practice and in theory he adopts the species as his object (his own as well as those of other things), but—and this is only another way of expressing it—but also because he treats himself as the actual, living species; because he treats himself as a *universal* and therefore a free being.

The life of the species, both in man and in animals, consists physically in the fact that man (like the animal) lives on inorganic nature; and the more universal man is compared with an animal, the more universal is the sphere of inorganic nature on which he lives. Just as plants, animals, stones, the air, light, etc., constitute a part of human consciousness in the realm of theory, partly as objects of natural science, partly as objects of art—his spiritual inorganic nature, spiritual nourishment which he must first prepare to make it palatable and digestable—so too in the realm of practice they constitute a part of human life and human activity. Physically man lives only on these products of nature, whether they appear in the form of food, heating, clothes, a dwelling, or whatever it may be. The universality of man is in practice manifested precisely in the universality which makes all nature his *inorganic* body—both inasmuch as nature is (1) his direct means of life, and (2) the material, the object, and the instrument of his life activity. Nature is man's *inorganic body*—nature, that is, insofar as it is not itself the human body. Man *lives* on nature—means that nature is his *body*, with which he must remain in continuous intercourse if he is not to die. That man's physical and spiritual life is linked to nature means simply that nature is linked to itself, for man is a part of nature.

In alienating from man (1) nature, and (2) himself, his own active functions, his life activity, estranged labor estranges the *species* from man. It turns for him the *life of the species* into a means of individual life. First it estranges the life of the species and individual life, and secondly it makes individual life in its abstract form the purpose of the life of the species, likewise in its abstract and estranged form.

For in the first place labor, *life activity, productive life* itself, appears to man merely as a *means* of satisfying a need—the need to maintain the physical existence. Yet the productive life is the life of the species. It is life-engendering life. The whole character of a species—its species character—is contained in the character of its life activity; and free, conscious activity is man's species character. Life itself appears only as a *means to life*.

The animal is immediately identical with its life activity. It does not distinguish itself from it. It is *its life activity*. Man makes his life activity itself the object of his will and of his consciousness. He has conscious life activity. It is not a determination with which he directly merges. Conscious life activity directly distinguishes man from animal life activity. It is just because of this that he is a species being. Or it is only because he is a species being that he is a conscious being, that is, that his own life is an object for him. Only because of that is his activity free activity. Estranged labor reverses this relationship, so that it is just because man is a conscious being that he makes his life activity, his *essential* being, a mere means to his *existence*.

In creating an *objective world* by his practical activity, in *working up* inorganic nature, man proves himself a conscious species being, that is, as a being that treats the species as its own essential being, or that treats itself as a species being. Admittedly animals also produce. They build themselves nests, dwellings, like the bees, beavers, ants, etc. But an animal only produces what it immediately needs for itself or its young. It produces one-sidedly, while man produces universally. It produces only under the dominion of immediate physical need, while man produces even when he is free from physical need and only truly produces in freedom therefrom. An animal produces only itself, while man reproduces the whole of nature. An animal's product belongs immediately to its physical body, while man freely confronts his product. An animal forms things in accordance with the standard and the need of the species to which it belongs, while man knows how to produce in accordance with the standard of every species, and knows how to apply everywhere the inherent standard to the object. Man therefore also forms things in accordance with the laws of beauty.

It is just in the working up of the objective world, therefore, that man first really proves himself to be a *species being*. This production is his active species life. Through and because of this production, nature appears as *his* work and his reality. The object of labor is, therefore, the *objectification of man's species life*: for he duplicates himself not only, as in consciousness, intellectually, but also actively, in reality, and therefore he contemplates himself in a world that he has created. In tearing away from man the object of his production, therefore, estranged labor tears from him his *species life*, his real species objectivity, and transforms his advantage over animals into the disadvantage that his inorganic body, nature, is taken from him.

Similarly, in degrading spontaneous activity, free activity, to a means, estranged labor makes man's species life a means to his physical existence.

The consciousness which man has of his species is thus transformed by estrangement in such a way that the species life becomes for him a means.

Estranged labor turns thus: (3) *Man's species being*, both nature and his spiritual species property, into a being *alien* to him, into a *means* to his *individual existence*. It estranges man's own body from him, as it does external nature and his spiritual essence, his *human being*. (4) An immediate consequence of the fact that man is estranged from the product of his labor, from his life activity, from his species being is the *alienation of man* from man. If a man is confronted by himself, he is confronted by the *other* man. What applies to a man's relation to his work, to the product of his labor and to himself, also holds of a man's relation to the other man, and to the other man's labor and object of labor.

In fact, the proposition that man's species nature is alienated from him means that one man is alienated from the other, as each of them is from man's essential nature.

The alienation of man, and in fact every relationship in which man stands to himself, is first realized and expressed in the relationship in which a man stands to other men.

Hence within the relationship of alienated labor each man views the other in accordance with the standard and the position in which he finds himself as a worker.

We took our departure from a fact of political economy—the alienation of the worker and his production. We have formulated the concept of this fact—*estranged, alienated* labor. We have analyzed this concept—hence analyzing merely a fact of political economy.

Let us now see, further, how in real life the concept of estranged, alienated labor must express and present itself.

If the product of labor is alien to me, if it confronts me as an alien power, to whom, then, does it belong?

To a being *other* than me.

Who is this being?

The *gods?* To be sure, in the earliest times the principal production (for example, the building of temples, etc., in Egypt, India and Mexico) appears to be in the service of the gods, and the product belongs to the gods. However, the gods on their own were never the lords of labor. No more was *nature*. And what a contradiction it would be if, the more man subjugated nature by his labor and the more the miracles of the gods were rendered superfluous by the miracles of industry, the more man were to renounce the joy of production and the enjoyment of the produce in favor of these powers.

The *alien* being, to whom labor and the produce of labor belongs, in whose service labor is done and for whose benefit the produce of labor is provided, can only be *man* himself.

If the product of labor does not belong to the worker, if it confronts him as an alien power, this can only be because it belongs to some *other man than the worker*. If the worker's activity is a torment to him, to another it must be *delight* and his life's joy. Not the gods, not nature, but only man himself can be this alien power over man.

We must bear in mind the above-stated proposition that man's relation to himself only becomes *objective* and *real* for him through his relation to the other man. Thus, if the product of his labor, his labor *objectified*, is for him an *alien*, hostile, powerful object independent of him, then his position towards it is such that someone else is master of this object, someone who is alien, hostile, powerful, and independent of him. If his own activity is to him an unfree activity, then he is treating it as activity performed in the service, under the dominion, the coercion and the yoke of another man.

Every self-alienation of man from himself and from nature appears in the relation in which he places himself and nature to men other than and differentiated from himself. For this reason religious self-alienation necessarily appears in the relationship of the layman to the priest, or again to a mediator, etc., since we are here dealing with the intellectual world. In the real practical world self-alienation can only become manifest through the real practical relationship to other men. The medium through which alienation takes place is itself *practical*. Thus through alienated labor man not only engenders his relationship to the object and to the act of production as to powers that are alien and hostile to him; he also engenders the relationship in which other men stand to his production and to his product, and the relationship in which he stands to these other men. Just as he begets his own production as the loss of his reality, as his punishment; just as he begets his own product as a loss, as a product not belonging to him; so he begets the dominion of the one who does not produce over production and over the product. Just as he estranges from himself his own activity, so he confers to the stranger activity which is not his own.

Till now we have only considered this relationship from the standpoint of the worker and later we shall be considering it also from the standpoint of the nonworker.

Through *estranged, alienated labor,* then, the worker produces the relationship to this labor of a man alien to labor and standing outside it. The relationship of the worker to labor engenders the relation to it of the capitalist, or whatever one chooses to call the master of labor. *Private property* is thus the product, the result, the necessary consequence, of *alienated labor,* of the external relation of the worker to nature and to himself.

Private property thus results by analysis from the concept of *alienated labor*—that is, of *alienated man*, of estranged labor, of estranged life, of *estranged* man.

True, it is as a result of the *movement of private property* that we have obtained the concept of *alienated labor (of alienated life)* from political economy. But on analysis of this concept it becomes clear that though private property appears to be the source, the cause of alienated labor, it is really its consequence, just as the gods *in the beginning* are not the cause but the effect of man's intellectual confusion. Later this relationship becomes reciprocal.

Only at the very culmination of the development of private property does this, its secret, re-emerge, namely, that on the one hand it is the *product* of alienated labor, and that secondly it is the *means* by which labor alienates itself, the *realization of this alienation*.

This exposition immediately sheds light on various hitherto unsolved conflicts.

1. Political economy starts from labor as the real soul of production; yet to labor it gives nothing, and to private property everything. From this contradiction Proudhon has concluded in favor of labor and against private property. We understand, however, that this apparent contradiction is the contradiction of *alienated labor* with itself, and that political economy has merely formulated the laws of estranged labor.

We also understand, therefore, that *wages* and *private property* are identical: where the product, the object of labor pays for labor itself, the wage is but a necessary consequence of labor's estrangement, for after all in the wage of labor, labor does not appear as an end in itself but as the servant of the wage. We shall develop this point later, and meanwhile will only deduce some conclusions.

A *forcing up of wages* (disregarding all other difficulties, including the fact that it would only be by force, too, that the higher wages, being an anomaly, could be maintained) would therefore be nothing but *better payment for the slave*, and would not conquer either for the worker or for labor their human status and dignity.

Indeed, even the *equality of wages* demanded by Proudhon only transforms the relationship of the present-day worker to his labor into the relationship of all men to labor. Society is then conceived as an abstract capitalist.

Wages are a direct consequence of estranged labor, and estranged labor is the direct cause of private property. The downfall of the one aspect must therefore mean the downfall of the other.

2. From the relationship of alienated labor to private property it further follows that the emancipation of society from private property, etc., from servitude, is expressed in the *political* form of the *emancipation of the workers*; not that *their* emancipation alone was at stake but because the emancipation of the workers contains universal human emancipation—and it contains this, because the whole of human servitude is involved in the

relation of the worker to production, and every relation of servitude is but a modification and consequence of this relation.

Just as we have found the concept of *private property* from the concept of *estranged, alienated labor* by analysis, in the same way every *category* of political economy can be evolved with the help of these two factors; and we shall find again in each category, for example, trade, competition, capital, money, only a *definite* and *developed expression* of the first foundations.

Before considering this configuration, however, let us try to solve two problems.

1. To define the general *nature of private property*, as it has arisen as a result of estranged labor, in its relation to *truly human, social property*.

2. We have accepted the *estrangement of labor*, its *alienation*, as a fact, and we have analyzed this fact. How, we now ask, does *man* come to *alienate*, to estrange, *his labor*? How is this estrangement rooted in the nature of human development? We have already gone a long way to the solution of this problem by *transforming* the question as to the *origin of private property* into the question as to the relation of *alienated labor* to the course of humanity's development. For when one speaks of *private property*, one thinks of being concerned with something external to man. When one speaks of labor, one is directly concerned with man himself. This new formulation of the question already contains its solution.

As to (1). *The general nature of private property and its relation to truly human property.*

Alienated labor has resolved itself for us into two elements which mutually condition one another, or which are but different expressions of one and the same relationship. *Appropriation* appears as *estrangement*, as *alienation*, and *alienation* appears as *appropriation*, estrangement as true *enfranchisement*.

We have considered the one side—*alienated* labor in relation to the *worker* himself, that is, the *relation of alienated labor to itself*. The *property-relation of the non-worker to the worker and to labor* we have found as the product, the necessary outcome of this relation of alienated labor. *Private property*, as the material, summary expression of alienated labor, embraces both relations—the *relation of the worker to work, to the product of his labor and to the non-worker*, and the relation of the *non-worker to the worker and to the product of his labor.*

Having seen that in relation to the worker who *appropriates* nature by means of his labor, this appropriation appears as estrangement, his own spontaneous activity as activity for another and as an activity of another, vitality as a sacrifice of life, production of the object as loss of the object to an alien power, to an *alien* person—we shall now consider the relation to the worker, to labor and its object of this person who is *alien* to labor and the worker.

First it has to be noted, that everything which appears in the worker as an *activity of alienation, of estrangement*, appears in the nonworker as a *state of alienation, of estrangement.*

Secondly, that the worker's *real, practical attitude* in production and to the product (as a state of mind) appears in the non-worker confronting him as a *theoretical* attitude.

Thirdly, the nonworker does everything against the worker which the worker does against himself; but he does not do against himself what he does against the worker.

STUDY QUESTIONS: MARX, *ALIENATION*

1. Why does the worker become poorer the more wealth he produces?
2. What does Marx mean by the *objectification of labor*?
3. What do religion and alienated labor have in common?
4. What does Marx mean by *physical subject*?
5. "What is human becomes animal, and what is animal becomes human." How does this happen, according to Marx? What are we supposed to do about it?
6. What is *self-alienation*?
7. What is species character? What is species being? How are the two related?
8. What does Marx mean by *life activity*?
9. How is religious self-alienation related to economic self-alienation?
10. How are private property and alienated labor related? Is this a good or bad thing? Why?
11. What do private property and servitude have in common?

THE POWER OF MONEY

Here Marx argues that the power of money is mainly negative. The problem as he sees it is that money perverts our natural needs, turns them upside down. The weak and unattractive male becomes powerful and attractive in virtue not of his own strength and beauty but through sheer buying power. He hires lawyers and thinkers, the way he employs technology, to wield a power that, without money, he would never have. Thus the ugliest and most petty billionaire, for instance, will in capitalist society be perceived as the most attractive and sought-after person. The natural order is thus corrupted and perverted.

If man's *feelings*, passions, etc., are not merely anthropological phenomena in the [narrower] sense, but truly *ontological* affirmations of essential being (of nature), and if they are only really affirmed because their *object* exists for them as an object of *sense*, then it is clear:

1. That they have by no means merely one mode of affirmation, but rather that the distinctive character of their existence, of their life, is constituted by the distinctive mode of their affirmation. In what manner the object exists for them, is the characteristic mode of their *gratification*.

Marx, from *Economic and Philosophic Manuscripts of 1844*, translated by Martin Milligan.

2. Wherever the sensuous affirmation is the direct annulment of the object in its independent form (as in eating, drinking, working up of the object, etc.), this is the affirmation of the object.

3. Insofar as man, and hence also his feeling, etc., are *human*, the affirmation of the object by another is likewise his own enjoyment.

4. Only through developed industry—that is, through the medium of private property—does the ontological essence of human passion come to be both in its totality and in its humanity; the science of man is therefore itself a product of man's establishment of himself by practical activity.

5. The meaning of private property—liberated from its estrangement—is the *existence of essential objects* for man, both as objects of enjoyment and as objects of activity.

By possessing the *property* of buying everything, by possessing the property of appropriating all objects, *money* is thus the *object* of eminent possession. The universality of its *property* is the omnipotence of its being. It therefore functions as the almighty being. Money is the *pimp* between man's need and the object, between his life and his means of life. But *that which* mediates *my* life for me, also *mediates* the existence of other people *for me*. For me it is the *other* person.

> *What, man! confound it, hands and feet*
> *And head and backside, are all yours!*
> *And what we take while life is sweet,*
> *Is that to be declared not ours?*
> *Six stallions, say, I can afford,*
> *Is not their strength my property?*
> *I tear along, a sporting lord,*
> *As if their legs belonged to me.*
> (Goethe: *Faust*—Mephistopheles)

Shakespeare in *Timon of Athens*:

> *Gold? Yellow, glittering, precious gold? No, Gods,*
> *I am no idle votarist! . . . Thus much of this will make*
>   *black white, foul fair,*
> *Wrong, right, base noble, old young, coward valiant.*
> *. . . Why, this*
> *Will lug your priests and servants from your sides,*
> *Pluck stout men's pillows from below their heads:*
> *This yellow slave*

> *Will knit and break religions, bless the accursed;*
> *Make the hoar leprosy adored, place thieves*
> *And give them title, knee and approbation*
> *With senators on the bench: This is it*
> *That makes the wappen'd widow wed again;*
> *She, whom the spital-house and ulcerous sores*
> *Would cast the gorge at, this embalms and spices*
> *To the April day again. . . . Damned earth,*
> *Thou common whore of mankind, that putt'st odds*
> *Among the rout of nations.*

And also later:

> *O thou sweet king-killer, and dear divorce*
> *Twixt natural son and sire! thou bright defiler*
> *of Hymen's purest bed! thou valiant Mars!*
> *Thou ever young, fresh, loved and delicate wooer,*
> *Whose blush doth thaw the consecrated snow*
> *That lies on Dian's lap! Thou visible God!*
> *That solder'st close impossibilities,*
> *And maest them kiss! That speak'st with every tongue,*
> *To every purpose! O thou touch of hearts!*
> *Think, thy slave man rebels, and by thy virtue*
> *Set them into confounding odds, that beasts*
> *May have the world in empire!*

Shakespeare excellently depicts the real nature of *money*. To understand him, let us begin, first of all, by expounding the passage from Goethe.

That which is for me through the medium of *money*—that for which I can pay (i.e., which money can buy)—that am *I*, the possessor of the money. The extent of the power of money is the extent of my power. Money's properties are my properties and essential powers—the properties and powers of its possessor. Thus, what I *am* and *am capable* of is by no means determined by my individuality. I am ugly, but I can buy for myself the most *beautiful* of women. Therefore I am not *ugly* for the effect of *ugliness*—its deterrent power—is nullified by money. I, in my character as an individual, am *lame*, but money furnishes me with 24 feet. Therefore I am not lame. I am bad, dishonest, unscrupulous, stupid; but money is honored, and therefore so is its possessor. Money is the supreme good, therefore its possessor is good. Money, besides, saves me the trouble of being dishonest: I am therefore presumed honest. I am *stupid*, but money is the *real mind* of all things and how then should its possessor be stupid? Besides, he can buy talented people for himself, and is he who has power over the talented not more talented than the talented? Do not I, who thanks to money am capable of *all* that the human heart longs for, possess all human capacities? Does not my money therefore transform all my incapacities into their contrary?

If *money* is the bond binding me to *human* life, binding society to me, binding me and nature and man, is not money the bond of all *bonds*? Can it not dissolve and bind all ties? Is it not, therefore, the universal *agent of divorce*? It is the true *agent of divorce* as well as the true *binding agent*—the [universal] *galvano-chemical* power of society.

Shakespeare stresses especially two properties of money: (1) It is the visible divinity—the transformation of all human and natural properties into their contraries, the universal confounding and overturning of things: it makes brothers of impossibilities. (2) It is the common whore, the common pimp of people and nations.

The overturning and confounding of all human and natural qualities, the fraternization of impossibilities—the *divine* power of money—lies in its *character* as men's estranged, alienating and self-disposing *species-nature*. Money is the alienated *ability of mankind*.

That which I am unable to do as a *man*, and of which therefore all my individual essential powers are incapable, I am able to do by means of *money*. Money thus turns each of these powers into something which in itself it is not—turns it, that is, into its *contrary*.

If I long for a particular dish or want to take the mail coach because I am not strong enough to go by foot, money fetches me the dish and the mail coach: that is, it converts my wishes from something in the realm of imagination, translates them from their meditated, imagined or willed existence into their *sensuous, actual* existence—from imagination to life, from imagined being into real being. In effecting this mediation, money is the *truly creative* power.

No doubt *demand* also exists for him who has no money, but his demand is a mere thing of the imagination without effect or existence for me, for a third party, for the others, and which therefore remains for me *unreal* and *objectless*. The difference between effective demand based on a money and ineffective demand based on my need, my passion, my wish, etc., is the difference between *being* and *thinking*, between the imagined which *exists* merely within me and the imagined as it is for me outside me as a *real object*.

If I have no money for travel, I have no *need*—that is, no real and self-realizing need—to travel. If I have the *vocation* for study but no money for it, I have *no* vocation for study—that is, no *effective*, no *true* vocation. On the other hand, if I have really *no* vocation for study but have the will *and* the money for it, I have an *effective* vocation for it. Being the external, common *medium* and *faculty* for turning an *image* into *reality* and *reality* into a mere *image* (a faculty not springing from man as man or from human society as society), *money* transforms the *real essential powers of man and nature* into what are merely abstract conceits and therefore *imperfections*—into tormenting chimeras—just as it transforms *real imperfections and chimeras*—essential powers which are really impotent, which exist only in the imagination of the individual—into *real powers* and *faculties*.

In the light of this characteristic alone, money is thus the general overturning of *individualities* which turns them into their contrary and adds contradictory attributes to their attributes.

Money, then, appears as this *overturning* power both against the individual and against the bonds of society, etc., which claim to be *essences* in themselves. It transforms fidelity into infidelity, love into hate, hate into love, virtue into vice, vice into virtue, servant into master, master into servant, idiocy into intelligence and intelligence into idiocy.

Since money, as the existing and active concept of value, confounds and exchanges all things, it is the general *confounding* and *compounding* of all things—the world upside down—the confounding and compounding of all natural and human qualities.

He who can buy bravery is brave; though a coward. As money is not exchanged for any one specific quality, for any one specific thing, or for any particular human essential power, but for the entire objective world of man and nature, from the standpoint of its possessor it therefore serves to exchange every property for every other, even contradictory, property and object: it is the fraternization of impossibilities. It makes contradictions embrace.

Assume *man* to be *man* and his relationship to the world to be a human one: then you can exchange love only for love, trust for trust, etc. If you want to enjoy art, you must be an artistically cultivated person; if you want to exercise influence over other people, you must be a person with a stimulating and encouraging effect on other people. Every one of your relations to man and to nature must be a *specific expression*, corresponding to the object of your will, of your *real individual* life. If you love without evoking love in return—that is, if your loving as loving does not produce reciprocal love; if through a *living expression* of yourself as a loving person you do not make yourself a *loved person*, then your love is impotent—a misfortune.

STUDY QUESTIONS: MARX, *THE POWER OF MONEY*

1. How does Marx relate Goethe's and Shakespeare's depictions of what money is?
2. How is money at the same time both the agent of divorce and binding agent of society?
3. What does Marx mean by "affirmation of the object?"
4. What role does developed industry play in Marx's view?
5. How does money bond you to a *human* life?
6. How are money and greed related?

Philosophical Bridges: Marx's Influence

There are few names in philosophy with which as many people have claimed association as with that of Karl Marx. Even that is an understatement; entire countries, comprising of hundreds of millions of people, have identified themselves as Marxist. This holds for instance for the former Soviet Union and eastern European countries, the former Yugoslavia, and present-day China. That the predicate "former" applies to so many of these countries suggests that Marx's influence is over; but many so-called Marxist forms of government, synonymous with the communism that seems to have collapsed under its own weight from so many places around the globe, comprised of systems containing elements that Marx would never have accepted. Many have argued that communism as practiced in the former Soviet Union and Eastern Block countries, for example, was a distortion of his actual philosophy. In any case, the influence of Marx on the political scene in the twentieth century, however one wants to interpret it, is gargantuan.

More recently, there has been a great resurgence in Marx scholarship, due in part perhaps to the demise of communism that may have had a liberating affect on the actual philosophy that bears his name. For instance, there are various movements in the United States and Europe under the rubric of Marxist feminism, Marxist ecology, and so on. Many see a new relevance of Marx to contemporary problems in the economic, political, ethical, and social arena where political power struggles wax and wane between collectives and individuals, conservatives and liberals. Ecofeminist philosophers such as Carolyn Merchant, for instance, claim that dialectical materialism is the philosophy of choice on questions of the environment. Perhaps because feminists today see women as an oppressed class, the significance of Marx for philosophers such as Gwyn Kirk, Chris Cuomo, and others, is that he provides the means by which an oppressed class can not only express its concerns but change the environment and end the oppression.

BIBLIOGRAPHY

COMTE
Primary
The Positive Philosophy, trans. H. Martineau, London, 1853

Secondary
Evans-Pritchard, E. E., *The Sociology of Comte: An Appreciation*, Manchester University Press, 1970

Harp, G. J., *The Positivist Republic: Auguste Comte and the Reconstruction of American Liberalism, 1865–1920*, Pennsylvania State University Press, 1995

Martin, F. S., *Comte: The Founder of Sociology*, Russell & Russell, 1965

Pickering, M., *Auguste Comte: An Intellectual Biography*, Cambridge University Press, 1993

Simon, W. M., *European Positivism in the Nineteenth Century*, Cornell University Press, 1963

Standley, A. R., *Auguste Comte*, Twayne, 1981

Style, J. M., *Auguste Comte: Thinker and Lover*, Kegan Paul, 1928

BENTHAM
Primary
An Introduction to the Principles of Morals and Legistlation, first published in 1789, new edition, Oxford 1823

Secondary
Albee, E., *A History of English Utilitarianism* Swan Sonnenschein, 1902

Atkinson, C. M., *Jeremy Bentham: His Life and Works*, Methuen, 1905

Baumgardt, D., *Bentham and the Ethics of Today*, Princeton University Press, 1952

Dinwiddy, *Bentham*, Oxford University Press, 1989

Long, D. G., *Bentham on Liberty: Jeremy Bentham's Idea of Liberty in Relation to His Utilitarianism*, University of Toronto Press, 1977

Lyons, D., *In the Interest of the Governed: A Study in Bentham's Philosophy of Utility and Law*, Clarendon Press, 1973

Manning, D. J., *The Mind of Jeremy Bentham*, Barnes & Noble, 1968

Plamenatz, J., *The English Utilitarians*, Blackwell, 1966

Steintrager, J., *Bentham*, Cornell University Press, 1977

Stephen, L., *The English Utilitarians*, Duckworth, 1900

MILL
Primary
Autobiography, The Library of Liberal Arts, 1957

Collected Works of John Stuart Mill, University of Toronto Press, 1989

On Liberty and Other Essays, ed. J. Gray, Oxford University Press, 1998

Utilitarianism and Other Writings, ed. M. Warnock, New American Library, 1974

Secondary
Anderson, S. L., *On Mill*, Wadsworth, 2000

Anschutz, R. P., *The Philosophy of John Stuart Mill*, Oxford University Press, 1953

August, E., *John Stuart Mill, A Mind At Large*, Charles Scribner's Sons, 1975

Britton, K., *John Stuart Mill*, Dover, 1969

Donner, W., *The Liberal Self: John Stuart Mill's Moral and Political Philosophy*, Cornell University Press, 1991

Himmelfarb, G., *On Liberty and Liberalism: the Case of John Stuart Mill*, Knopf, 1974

Mill, J. S., *Autobiography*, The Library of Liberal Arts, 1957

McCloskey, H. J., *John Stuart Mill: A Critical Study*, Macmillan, 1971

Ryan, A., *J.S. Mill*, Routledge and Kegan Pau, 1974

Schneewind, J., ed., *Mill: A Collecton of Critical Essays*, Anchor Doubleday, 1968

Smart, J. J. C., and Williams, B., *Utilitarianism: For and Against*, Cambridge University Press, 1973

MARX
Primary
The Economic and Philosophic Manuscripts of 1844, trans. M. Milligan, International Publishers, 1964

The German Ideology, ed. C. J. Arthur, International Publishers, 1981

The Communist Manifesto, ed. M. Malia, Penguin, 1998

Karl Marx: Early Writings, trans. T. B. Bottomore, McGraw-Hill 1963

Karl Marx: Selected Writings, ed. D. McLellan, Oxford University Pres 1977

Secondary

Berlin, I., *Karl Marx: His Life and Environment*, Oxford University Press, 1963

Bottomore, T., ed., *Karl Marx: Early Writings*, C.A. Watts, 1963

Cuomo, C., *Feminism and Ecological Communities: An Ethic of Flourishing*, Taylor & Francis, 2001.

Eagelton, T., *Marx*, Routledge, 1999

Elster, J., *An Introduction to Karl Marx*, Cambridge University Press, 1986

Engels, F., *The Origin of the Family, Private Property, and the State*, International Publishers, 1942

Lee, W. L., *On Marx*, Wadsworth, 2002

Lichtheim, G., *Marxism: An Historical and Critical Study*, Routledge & Kegan Paul, 1961

McLellan, D., *Karl Marx: His Life and Thought*, Harper & Row, 1973

Merchant, C., *Radical Ecology: The Search for a Livable World*, Pontlady's Chapman & Hall, 1992

Singer, P., *Marx*, Oxford University Press, 1980

Stein, G., *Three Lives*, Dover Publications, 1994

SECTION V

◆ THE AMERICAN PRAGMATISTS AND IDEALISTS

PROLOGUE

Except for the brilliant and widely influential literary philosophical works of Emerson and Thoreau, there was little philosophy to speak of in the United States. Thus, the sudden and extraordinary philosophical contributions of Charles Peirce (1839–1914), his pupil William James (1842–1910), Josiah Royce (1855–1916), and John Dewey (1859–1952), are all the more remarkable, no less so than their proliferation throughout American colleges and universities ever since. It is now called "the golden age of American philosophy," and rightfully so, which is all the more remarkable given that in America there was neither a bronze nor stone age. As one observer of the early American philosophy scene, Andrew Reck, put it, "A sprawling company of farmers, engineers, politicians and businessmen, Americans on the whole have entrusted the care of their spiritual life to preachers, lawyers, and soldiers. The very term "culture" arouses mental associations with ladies' clubs, in isolation from the masculine world where work gets done." If part of the explanation of the previous paucity of philosophy in America does indeed lie in the dominant role played at the time by pious, faith-based theology, certainly part of the explanation of its subsequent renaissance is the simultaneous arrival on the scene of these four brilliant, original thinkers, any one of whom would have been sufficient to galvanize the process.

To get a philosophical education at the time one had to go to Europe, and it is no surprise that all four of these great minds had strong associations, either direct or indirect, with philosophy as it was flourishing at the time in Germany. Kant, after all, was the first philosopher to use the word *pragmatishe* in the sense employed by Peirce and James, as well as Dewey. The strong influence of Kant and neo-Kantian German thought on Peirce, James, Royce, and Dewey, is evident not only in their formative years but throughout their work. James spent a year studying in Germany. Peirce studied Kant and Hegel. Dewey, who was inspired by the German rational idealism of Leibniz, Kant, and Hegel, considered himself a Hegelian and wrote his doctoral dissertation on Leibniz. Josiah Royce, who went from the newly formed University of California to study philosophy in Germany, was a self-styled Hegelian idealist. And yet, the philosophy produced by these four thinkers in their own right is anything but derivative. It is profoundly new and original, and today continues to influence philosophers not just in the United States and Europe but throughout the world.

Peirce (1839–1914)

Biographical History

Charles Sanders Peirce was born in Cambridge, Massachusetts. His father was a mathematician and professor of mathematics at Harvard University. Peirce went to Harvard and graduated at the bottom of his class. In 1870 he formed a discussion group, called the "Metaphysical Club," in Cambridge, Massachusetts, which included students such as William James and Oliver Wendell Holmes. Except for teaching logic at the Johns Hopkins University as an adjunct from 1879 to 1884, and some lectures that he gave at Harvard and the Lowell Institute in Boston, he could not find a permanent teaching position. He later joined the United States Coast and Geodetic Survey.

Philosophical Overview

Peirce's philosophy developed from a close study of Kant and Hegel, infused with the then-new and extremely radical evolutionary theory of Charles Darwin (1809–1882). Peirce is generally credited as being the founder of American pragmatism. Starting with insights weaned from his reading of Leibniz, Kant and Hegel, Peirce developed a new concept of truth based on the practical significance of propositions from the standpoint of personal experience. It involves the clarification of thought using his *pragmatic principle*:

> Consider what effects, that conceivably might have practical bearings, we conceive the object of our conception to have. Then our conception of these effects is the whole of our conception of the object.

Beliefs in Peirce's view are *habits* predisposing us to behave in certain ways, depending on the situation, by causing either a physical movement in our bodies or a psychological expectation in our minds. But not all beliefs are created equal. The most common and worst way to form beliefs is the method of tenacity: you hold firm to whatever you think or feel is true, and simply ignore any evidence or argument to the contrary. The second, slightly less worse but still philosophically impoverished way is through conditioning by *authority*. This is the oldest and most traditional way of getting people to accept received, "official" theological and political opinions as their own; it results from our governmental, church, and military institutions conditioning us to be obedient to authority. The third, a priori, method is the one accepted by rationalists such as, most notably, Plato and Descartes. It is preferable to the first two but ultimately is no better. The reason why reason fails, in Peirce's view, is that it is but an elaborate form of rationalization. Thus the best way, and the only truly reliable method, is what he calls *scientific* method, which is necessarily self-correcting. The key is that we must not be biased or prejudiced in any way, which amounts to not knowing in advance what it is that we are looking for or where we are going. This, after all, is how evolution works. Nature is not teleological, and neither should be our quest for certainty.

Peirce puts high value, therefore, on spontaneity. Instead of starting with universal doubt, as Descartes did, we start by learning everything we can; our beliefs then occur in response to something independent of ourselves. In this way, the proper method for acquiring beliefs is independent of personal prejudices. It does not require any sort of unique experiences had by the special few who then become the philosophical authorities, the epistemological masters. The process is democratic, brutally egalitarian, and leads to a pragmatic sort of truth. Ideally, we should all be affected, or affectable, in the same way as a result of applying his method.

Peirce is not denying the reality of the world as something independent of thought, belief, or will. Nor is he denying that we can form correct beliefs. On the contrary; the aim of his philosophical method is to make us see that our beliefs are "not a momentary code of consciousness." Let 'S' Stand for any individual and 'A' for any proposition. For S tò believe that A behaviorally predisposes S to act as if A were true. By thus providing S with psychological confidence, S is allowed to behave in and interact with the world in certain ways. For S to truly doubt A, on the other hand, means that S is in a psychologically uncertain state with regard to A. S then does not know what to do when some situation involving A requires S to reach a decision. Peirce's brilliant insight here is that it is for this reason that we are predisposed by nature to avoid doubt at all costs: doubt is psychologically painful, it is an anxious state, and makes us unfit to interact well with our environment. The process of philosophical inquiry is therefore essential if we are to escape doubt. Inquiry according to Peirce requires (1) a stimulus, in the form of the psychological experience of doubt described above; (2) an end, which means that an opinion is settled, there is some closure; and (3) a *method*, by which he means the scientific, "self-correcting" method. The key to this whole process, which became a sort of philosophical foundation for all the pragmatists, is that inquiry is not some purely intellectual activity of thought but must occur in the form of a problem felt directly in experience. If S feels there is no problem, which means that S is not genuinely concerned, puzzled, or irritated, S is not capable of true inquiry. Intellectual doubt is not sufficient; the doubt must be experientially felt. Without real doubt the mind is closed to inquiry.

THE FIXATION OF BELIEF
Peirce

"The Fixation of Belief" is one of Peirce's most famous articles. This is where Peirce most clearly identifies the four methods by which our habits, customs, traditions, and beliefs, be they personal convictions or of great metaphysical import, take hold of our minds, to which we become fixed. They are *tenacity*, *authority*, the *a priori method*, and the *method of science*. He explains why the first three are from a pragmatic point of view deeply and fundamentally misguided—even the third, though rationalist philosophers have accepted it. The fourth is the way to go, without knowing or even expecting in advance where the inquiry will lead.

Few persons care to study logic, because everybody conceives himself to be proficient enough in the art of reasoning already. But I observe that this satisfaction is limited to one's own ratiocination, and does not extend to that of other men.

We come to the full possession of our power of drawing inferences, the last of all our faculties, for it is not so much a natural gift as a long and difficult art. The history of its practice would make a grand subject for a book.

We are, doubtless, in the main logical animals, but we are not perfectly so. Most of us, for example, are naturally more sanguine and hopeful than logic would justify. We seem to be so constituted that, in the absence of any facts to go upon, we are happy and self-satisfied; so that the effect of experience is continually to counteract our hopes and aspirations. Yet a lifetime of the application of this corrective does not usually eradicate our sanguine disposition. Where hope is unchecked by any experience, it is likely that our optimism is extravagant. Logicality in regard to practical matters is the most useful quality an animal can possess, and might, therefore, result from the action of natural selection; but outside of these, it is probably of more advantage to the animal to have his mind filled with pleasing and encouraging visions, independently of their truth; and thus, upon impractical subjects, natural selection might occasion a fallacious tendency of thought.

That which determines us, from given premises, to draw one inference rather than another, is some habit of mind, whether it be constitutional or acquired. The habit is good or otherwise, according as it produces true conclusions from true premises or not; and an inference is regarded as valid or not, without reference to the truth or falsity of its conclusion specially, but according as the habit which determines it is such as to produce true conclusions in general or not. The particular habit of mind which governs this or that inference may be formulated in a proposition whose truth depends on the validity of the inferences which the habit determines; and such a formula is called a *guiding principle* of inference.

We generally know when we wish to ask a question and when we wish to pronounce a judgment, for there is a dissimilarity between the sensation of doubting and that of believing.

But this is not all which distinguishes doubt from belief. There is a practical difference. Our beliefs guide our desires and shape our actions. The Assassins, or followers of the Old Man of the Mountain, used to rush into death at his least command, because they believed that obedience to him would insure everlasting felicity. Had they doubted this, they would not have acted as they did. So it is with every belief, according to its degree. The feeling of believing is a more or less sure indication of there being established in our nature some habit which will determine our actions. Doubt never has such an effect.

Nor must we overlook a third point of difference. Doubt is an uneasy and dissatisfied state from which we struggle to free ourselves and pass into the state of belief; while the latter is a calm and satisfactory state which we do not wish to avoid, or to change to a belief in anything else. On the contrary, we cling tenaciously, not merely to believing, but to believing just what we do believe.

Thus, both doubt and belief have positive effects upon us, though very different ones. Belief does not make us act at once, but puts us into such a condition that we shall behave in a certain way, when the occasion arises. Doubt has not the least effect of this sort, but stimulates us to action until it is destroyed. This reminds us of the irritation of a nerve and the reflex action produced thereby; while for the analogue of belief, in the nervous system, we must look to what are called nervous associations—for example, to that habit of the nerves in consequence of which the smell of peach will make the mouth water.

The irritation of doubt causes a struggle to attain a state of belief. I shall term this struggle *inquiry*, though it must be admitted that this is sometimes not a very apt designation.

The irritation of doubt is the only immediate motive for the struggle to attain belief. It is certainly best for us that our beliefs should be such as may truly guide our actions so as to satisfy our desires; and this reflection will make us reject any belief which does not seem to have been so formed as to insure this result. But it will only do so by creating doubt in the place of that belief. With the doubt, therefore, the

Peirce, from "The Fixation of Belief," *Popular Science Monthly*, 1877.

struggle begins, and with the cessation of doubt it ends. Hence, the sole object of inquiry is the settlement of opinion. We may fancy that this is not enough for us, and that we seek, not merely an opinion, but a true opinion. But put this fancy to the test, and it proves groundless; for as soon as a firm belief is reached we are entirely satisfied, whether the belief be false or true. And it is clear that nothing out of the sphere of our knowledge can be our object, for nothing which does not affect the mind can be a motive for mental effort. The most that can be maintained is that we seek for a belief that we shall *think* to be true. But we think each one of our beliefs to be true, and, indeed, it is mere tautology to say so.

That the settlement of opinion is the sole end of inquiry is a very important proposition. It sweeps away, at once, various vague and erroneous conceptions of proof. A few of these may be noticed here.

1. Some philosophers have imagined that to start an inquiry it was only necessary to utter a question or set it down on paper, and have even recommended us to begin our studies with questioning everything! But the mere putting of a proposition into the interrogative form does not stimulate the mind to any struggle after belief. There must be a real and living doubt, and without this all discussion is idle.

2. It is a very common idea that a demonstration must rest on some ultimate and absolutely indubitable propositions. These, according to one school, are first principles of a general nature; according to another, are first sensations. But, in point of fact, an inquiry, to have that completely satisfactory result called demonstration, has only to start with propositions perfectly free from all actual doubt. If the premises are not in fact doubted at all, they cannot be more satisfactory than they are.

3. Some people seem to love to argue a point after all the world is fully convinced of it. But no further advance can be made. When doubt ceases, mental action on the subject comes to an end; and, if it did go on, it would be without a purpose.

If the settlement of opinion is the sole object of inquiry, and if belief is of the nature of a habit, why should we not maintain the desired end by taking any answer to a question, which we may fancy, and constantly reiterating it to ourselves, dwelling on all

which may be conducive to that belief, and learning to turn with contempt and hatred from anything which might disturb it? This simple and direct method is really pursued by many men. I remember once being entreated not to read a certain newspaper lest it might change my opinion upon free trade. "Lest I might be entrapped by its fallacies and misstatements," was the form of expression. "You are not," my friend said, "a special student of political economy. You might, therefore, easily be deceived by fallacious arguments upon the subject. You might, then, if you read this paper, be led to believe in protection. But you admit that free trade is the true doctrine; and you do not wish to believe what is not true." I have often known this system to be deliberately adopted. Still oftener, the instinctive dislike of an undecided state of mind, exaggerated into a vague dread of doubt, makes men cling spasmodically to the views they already take. The man feels that, if he only holds to his belief without wavering, it will be entirely satisfactory. Nor can it be denied that a steady and immovable faith yields great peace of mind. It may, indeed, give rise to inconveniences, as if a man should resolutely continue to believe that fire would not burn him, or that he would be eternally damned if he received his *ingesta* otherwise than through a stomach pump. But then the man who adopts this method will not allow that its inconveniences are greater than its advantages. He will say, "I hold steadfastly to the truth and the truth is always wholesome." And in many cases it may very well be that the pleasure he derives from his calm faith overbalances any inconveniences resulting from its deceptive character. Thus, if it be true that death is annihilation, then the man who believes that he will certainly go straight to heaven when he dies, provided he has fulfilled certain simple observances in this life, has a cheap pleasure which will not be followed by the least disappointment. A similar consideration seems to have weight with many persons in religious topics, for we frequently hear it said, "Oh, I could not believe so-and-so, because I should be wretched if I did." When an ostrich buries its head in the sand as danger approaches, it very likely takes the happiest course. It hides the danger, and then calmly says there is no danger; and, if it feels perfectly sure there is none, why should it raise its head to see? A man may go through life systematically keeping out of view all that might cause a change in his opinions, and if he only succeeds—basing his method, as he does, on two fundamental psychological laws—I do not see what can be said against his doing so. It would be an egotistical impertinence to object that his procedure is irrational, for that only amounts to saying that his method of settling belief is not ours. He does not propose to himself to be rational, and, indeed, will often talk with scorn of man's weak and illusive reason. So let him think as he pleases.

But this method of fixing belief, which may be called the method of tenacity, will be unable to hold its ground in practice. The social impulse is against it. The man who adopts it will find that other men think differently from him, and it will be apt to occur to him in some saner moment that their opinions are quite as good as his own, and this will shake his confidence in his belief. This conception, that another man's thought or sentiment may be equivalent to one's own, is a distinctly new step, and a highly important one. It arises from an impulse too strong in man to be suppressed without danger of destroying the human species. Unless we make ourselves hermits, we shall necessarily influence each other's opinions, so that the problem becomes how to fix belief, not in the individual merely, but in the community.

Let the will of the state act, then, instead of that of the individual. Let an institution be created which shall have for its object to keep correct doctrines before the attention of the people, to reiterate them perpetually, and to teach them to the young; having at the same time power to prevent contrary doctrines from being taught, advocated, or expressed. Let all possible causes of a change of mind be removed from men's apprehensions. Let them be kept ignorant, lest they should learn of some reason to think otherwise than they do. Let their passions be enlisted, so that they may regard private and unusual opinions with hatred and horror. Then, let all men who reject the established belief be terrified into silence. Let the people turn out and tar and feather such men, or let inquisitions be made into the manner of thinking of suspected persons, and, when they are found guilty of forbidden beliefs, let them be subjected to some signal punishment. When complete agreement could not otherwise be reached, a general massacre of all who have not thought in a certain way has proved a very effective means of settling opinion in a country. If the power to do this be wanting, let a list of opinions be drawn up, to which no man of the least independence of thought can assent, and let the faithful be required to accept all these propositions, in order to segregate them as radically as possible from the influence of the rest of the world.

This method has, from the earliest times, been one of the chief means of upholding correct theological and political doctrines, and of preserving their universal or catholic character. In Rome, especially, it has been practiced from the days of Numa Pompilius to those of Pius Nonus. This is the most perfect example in history; but wherever there is a priesthood—and no religion has been without one—this method has been more or less made use of. Wherever there is an aristocracy, or a guild, or any association of a class of men whose interests depend, or are supposed to depend, on certain propositions, there will be inevitably found some traces of this natural product of social feeling. Cruelties always accompany this system; and when it is consistently carried out, they become atrocities of the most horrible kind in the eyes of any rational man. Nor should this occasion surprise, for the officer of a society does not feel justified in surrendering the interests of that society for the sake of mercy, as he might his own private interests. It is natural, therefore, that sympathy and fellowship should thus produce a most ruthless power.

In judging this method of fixing belief, which may be called the method of authority, we must, in the first place, allow its immeasurable mental and moral superiority to the method of tenacity. Its success is proportionately greater; and, in fact, it has over and over again worked the most majestic results. The mere structures of stone which it has caused to be put together—in Siam, for example, in Egypt, and in Europe—have many of them a sublimity hardly more than rivalled by the greatest works of Nature. And, except the geological epochs, there are no periods of time so vast as those which are measured by some of these organized faiths. If we scrutinize the matter closely, we shall find that there has not been one of their creeds which has remained always the same; yet the change is so slow as to be imperceptible during one person's life, so that individual belief remains sensibly fixed. For the mass of mankind, then, there is perhaps no better method than this. If it is their highest impulse to be intellectual slaves, then slaves they ought to remain.

But no institution can undertake to regulate opinions upon every subject. Only the most important ones can be attended to, and on the rest men's minds must be left to the action of natural causes. This imperfection will be no source of weakness so long as men are in such a state of culture that one opinion does not influence another—that is, so long as they cannot put two and two together. But in the most priest-ridden states some individuals will be found who are raised above that condition. These men possess a wider sort of social feeling; they see that men in other countries and in other ages have held to very different doctrines from those which they themselves have been brought up to believe; and they cannot help seeing that it is the mere accident of their having been taught as they have, and of their having been surrounded with the manners and associations they have, that has caused them to believe as they do and not far differently. Nor can their candor resist the reflection that there is no reason to rate their own views at a higher value than those of other nations and other centuries; thus giving rise to doubts in their minds.

They will further perceive that such doubts as these must exist in their minds with reference to every belief which seems to be determined by the caprice either of themselves or of those who originated the popular opinions. The willful adherence to a belief, and the arbitrary forcing of it upon others, must, therefore, both be given up. A different new method of settling opinions must be adopted, that shall not only produce an impulse to believe, but shall also decide what proposition it is which is to be believed. Let the action of natural preferences be unimpeded, then, and under their influence let men, conversing together and regarding matters in different lights, gradually develop beliefs in harmony with natural causes. This method resembles that by which conceptions of art have been brought to maturity. The most perfect example of it is to be found in the history of metaphysical philosophy. Systems of this sort have not usually rested upon any observed facts, at least not in any great degree. They have been chiefly adopted because their fundamental propositions seemed "agreeable to reason." This is an apt expression; it does not mean that which agrees with experience, but that which we find ourselves inclined to believe. Plato, for example, finds it agreeable to reason that the distances of the celestial spheres from one another should be proportional to the different lengths of strings which produce harmonious chords. Many philosophers have been led to their main conclusions by considerations like this; but this is the lowest and least developed from which the method takes, for it is clear that another man might find Kepler's theory, that the celestial spheres are proportional to the inscribed and circumscribed spheres of the different regular solids, more agreeable to *his* reason. But the shock of opinions will soon lead men to rest on preferences of a far more universal nature. Take, for example, the doctrine that man only acts selfishly—that is, from the consideration that acting in one way will afford him more pleasure than acting in another. This rests on no fact in the world, but it has had a wide acceptance as being the only reasonable theory.

This method is far more intellectual and respectable from the point of view of reason than either of the others which we have noticed. But its failure has been the most manifest. It makes of inquiry something similar to the development of taste; but taste, unfortunately, is always more or less a matter of fashion, and accordingly metaphysicians have never come to any fixed agreement, but the pendulum has swung backward and forward between a more material and a more spiritual philosophy, from the earliest times to the latest. And so from this, which has been called the a priori method, we are driven, in Lord Bacon's phrase, to a true induction. We have examined this a priori method as something which promised to deliver our opinions from their accidental and capricious element. But development, while it is a process which eliminates the effect of some casual circumstances, only magnifies that of others. This method, therefore, does not differ in a very essential way from that of authority. The government may not have lifted its finger to influence my convictions; I may have been left outwardly quite free to choose, we will say, between monogamy and polygamy, and appealing to my conscience only, I may have concluded that the latter practice is in itself licentious. But when I come to see that the chief obstacle to the spread of Christianity among a people of as high culture as the Hindus has been a conviction of the immorality of our way of treating women, I cannot help seeing that, though governments do not interfere, sentiments in their development will be very greatly determined by accidental causes. Now, there are some people, among whom I must suppose that my reader is to be found, who, when they see that any belief of theirs is determined by any circumstance extraneous to the facts, will from that moment not merely admit in words that that belief is doubtful, but will experience a real doubt of it, so that it ceases in some degree to be a belief.

To satisfy our doubts, therefore, it is necessary that a method should be found by which our beliefs may be caused by nothing human, but by some external permanency—by something upon which our thinking has no effect. Some mystics imagine that they have such a method in a private inspiration from on high. But that is only a form of the method of tenacity, in which the conception of truth as something public is not yet developed. Our external permanency would not be external, in our sense, if it was restricted in its influence to one individual. It must be something which affects, or might affect, every man. And, though these affections are necessarily as various as are individual conditions, yet the method must be such that the ultimate conclusion of every man shall be the same. Such is the method of science. Its fundamental hypothesis, restated in more familiar language, is this: There are Real things, whose characters are entirely independent of our opinions about them; those realities affect our senses according to regular laws, and, though our sensations are as different as are our relations to the objects, yet, by taking advantage of the laws of perception, we can ascertain by reasoning how things really are; and any man, if we have sufficient experience and he reason enough about it, will be led to the one true conclusion. The new conception here involved is that of Reality. It may be asked how I know that there are any realities. If this hypothesis is the sole support of my method of inquiry, my method of inquiry must not be used to support my hypothesis. The reply is this: (1) If investigation cannot be regarded as proving that there are Real things, it at least does not lead to a contrary conclusion; but the method and the conception on which it is based remain ever in harmony. No doubts of the method, therefore, necessarily arise from its practice, as is the case with all the others. (2) The feeling which gives rise to any method of fixing belief is a dissatisfaction at two repugnant propositions. But here already is a vague concession that there is some *one* thing to which a proposition should conform. Nobody, therefore, can really doubt that there are realities, for, if he did, doubt would not be a source of dissatisfaction. The hypothesis, therefore, is one which every mind admits. So that the social impulse does not cause men to doubt it. (3) Everybody uses the scientific method about a great many things, and only ceases to use it when he does not know how to apply it. (4) Experience of the method has not led us to doubt it, but, on the contrary, scientific investigation has had the most wonderful triumphs in the way of settling opinion. These afford the explanation of my not doubting the method or the hypothesis which it supposes; and not having any doubt, nor believing that anybody else whom I could influence has, it would be the merest babble for me to say more about it. If there be anybody with a living doubt upon the subject, let him consider it. . . .

This is the only one of the four methods which presents any distinction of a right and a wrong way. If I adopt the method of tenacity, and shut myself out from all influences, whatever I think necessary to doing this, is necessary according to that method. So with the method of authority: the state may try to put down heresy by means which, from a scientific point of view, seem very ill-calculated to accomplish its purposes; but the only test *on that method* is what the state thinks; so that it cannot pursue the method wrongly. So with the a priori method. The very essence of it is to think as one is inclined to think. All metaphysicians will be sure to do that, however they may be inclined to judge each other to be perversely wrong. Hegel's system of Nature represents tolerably the science of that day; and one may be sure that whatever scientific investigation has put out of doubt will presently receive a priori demonstration on the part of the metaphysicians. But with the scientific method the case is different. I may start with known and observed facts to proceed to the unknown; and yet the rules which I follow in doing so may not be such as investigation would approve. The test of whether I am truly following the method is not an immediate appeal to my feelings and purposes, but, on the contrary, itself involves the application of the method. Hence it is that bad reasoning as well as good reasoning is possible; and this fact is the foundation of the practical side of logic.

It is not to be supposed that the first three methods of settling opinion present no advantage whatever over the scientific method. On the contrary, each has some peculiar convenience of its own. The a priori method is distinguished for its comfortable conclusions. It is the nature of the process to adopt whatever belief we are inclined to, and there are certain flatteries to the vanity of man which we all believe by nature, until we are awakened from our pleasing dream by rough facts. The method of authority will always govern the mass of mankind; and those who wield the various forms of organized force in the state will never be convinced that dangerous reasoning ought not to be suppressed in some way. If liberty of speech is to be untrammelled from the grosser forms of constraint, then uniformity of opinion will be secured by a moral terrorism to which the respectability of society will give its thorough approval. Following the method of authority is the path of peace. Certain nonconformities are permitted; certain others (considered unsafe) are forbidden. These are different in different countries and in different ages; but, wherever you are, let it be known that you seriously hold a tabooed belief, and you may be perfectly sure of being treated with a cruelty less brutal but more refined than hunting you like a wolf. Thus, the greatest intellectual benefactors of mankind have never dared, and dare not now, to utter the whole of their thought; and thus a shade of *prima facie* doubt is cast upon every proposition which is considered essential to the security of society. Singularly enough, the persecution does not all come from without; but a man torments himself and is oftentimes more distressed at finding himself believing propositions which he has been brought up to regard with aversion. The peaceful and sympathetic man will, therefore, find it hard to resist the temptation to submit his opinions to authority. But most of all I admire the method of tenacity for its strength, simplicity, and directness. Men who pursue it are distinguished for their decision of character, which becomes very easy with such a mental rule. They do not waste time in trying to make up their minds what they want, but, fastening like lightning upon whatever

alternative comes first, they hold it to the end, whatever happens, without an instant's irresolution. This is one of the splendid qualities which generally accompany brilliant, unlasting success. It is impossible not to envy the man who can dismiss reason, although we know how it must turn out at last.

Such are the advantages which the other methods of settling opinion have over scientific investigation. A man should consider well of them; and then he should consider that, after all, he wishes his opinions to coincide with the fact and that there is no reason why the result of those three methods should do so. To bring about this effect is the prerogative of the method of science. Upon such considerations he has to make his choice—a choice which is far more than the adoption of any intellectual opinion, which is one of the ruling decisions of his life, to which, when once made, he is bound to adhere. The force of habit will sometimes cause a man to hold on to old beliefs, after he is in a condition to see that they have no sound basis. But reflection upon the state of the case will overcome these habits, and he ought to allow reflection its full weight. People sometimes shrink from doing this, having an idea that beliefs are wholesome which they cannot help feeling rest on nothing. But let such persons suppose an analogous though different case from their own. Let them ask themselves what they would say to a reformed Muslim who should hesitate to give up his old notions in regard to the relations of the sexes; or to a reformed Catholic who should still shrink from reading the Bible. Would they not say that these persons ought to consider the matter fully, and clearly understand the new doctrine, and then ought to embrace it, in its entirety? But, above all, let it be considered that what is more wholesome than any particular belief is integrity of belief, and that to avoid looking into the support of any belief from a fear that it may turn out rotten is quite as immoral as it is disadvantageous. The person who confesses that there is such a thing as truth, which is distinguished from falsehood simply by this, that if acted on it will carry us to the point we aim at and not astray, and then, though convinced of this, dares not know the truth and seeks to avoid it, is in a sorry state of mind indeed.

Yes, the other methods do have their merits: a clear logical conscience does cost something—just as any virtue, just as all that we cherish, costs us dear.

But we should not desire it to be otherwise. The genius of a man's logical method should be loved and reverenced as his bride, whom he has chosen from all the world. He need not condemn the others; on the contrary, he may honor them deeply, and in doing so he only honors her the more. But she is the one that he has chosen, and he knows that he was right in making that choice. And having made it, he will work and fight for her, and will not complain that there are blows to take, hoping that there may be as many and as hard to give, and will strive to be the worthy knight and champion of her from the blaze of whose splendors he draws his inspiration and his courage.

STUDY QUESTIONS: PEIRCE, *THE FIXATION OF BELIEF*

1. Why are so few people interested in studying logic?
2. What does Peirce mean by "habit of mind?"
3. What is doubt? In what terms does Peirce define it? What function does doubt serve?
4. What is the sole end of inquiry?
5. How does Peirce use the ostrich example?
6. What is Peirce's view of authority?
7. What is Peirce's view of Plato?
8. What is the point of the Kepler example?
9. Why must we seek a cause for our beliefs that is "nothing human?"
10. What does Peirce think of mystics? What is the significance of the example of mysticism?
11. What is the "path of peace?" Is it a good path to follow? Why?

HOW TO MAKE OUR IDEAS CLEAR

"How to Make Our Ideas Clear" is a follow-up to Peirce's "Fixation of Belief," and begins with a criticism of Descartes' notion of clear and distinct ideas, which he claims is *itself* not clear and distinct. The problem is that Descartes, by relying solely on the method a priori, relies in the end on what is ultimately unverifiable "self-evidence." This is the first and lowest level of clarity, insufficient for knowledge. He also criticizes Leibniz's method of abstract definition on similar grounds, namely, that "nothing new can ever be learned by analyzing definitions." This is a slightly higher, second level of clarity, but also insufficient for knowledge. Peirce argues on behalf of a third level of clearness, which he states in terms of his pragmatic maxim: any concepts or terms that reaching beyond the possible effects on observable objects are neither true nor false but meaningless. Beliefs must, therefore, be judged solely by the habits they produce, the practical rules of action that they govern. His system thus comes full circle and completes itself.

When Descartes set about the reconstruction of philosophy, his first step was to (theoretically) permit skepticism and to discard the practice of the schoolmen of looking to authority as the ultimate source of truth. That done, he sought a more natural fountain of true principles, and professed to find it in the human mind; thus passing, in the directest way, from the method of authority to that of a priority, as described in my first paper. Self-consciousness was to furnish us with our fundamental truths, and to decide what was agreeable to reason. But since, evidently, not all ideas are true, he was led to note, as the first condition of infallibility, that they must be clear. The distinction between an idea *seeming* clear and really being so, never occurred to him. Trusting to intro-spection, as he did, even for a knowledge of external things, why should he question its testimony in respect to the contents of our own minds? But then, I suppose, seeing men, who seemed to be quite clear and positive, holding opinions upon fundamental principles, he was further led to say that clearness of ideas is not sufficient, but that they need also to be distinct, that is, to have nothing unclear about them. What he probably meant by this (for he did not explain himself with precision) was, that they must sustain the test of dialectical examination; that they must not only seem clear at the outset, but that dis-cussion must never be able to bring to light points of obscurity connected with them.

Such was the distinction of Descartes, and one sees that it was precisely on the level of his philoso-phy. It was somewhat developed by Leibniz. This great and singular genius was as remarkable for what he failed to see as for what he saw. That a piece of mechanism could not do work perpetually without being fed with power in some form, was a thing per-fectly apparent to him; yet he did not understand that the machinery of the mind can only transform knowl-edge, but never originate it, unless it be fed with facts of observation. He thus missed the most essential point of the Cartesian philosophy, which is, that to accept propositions which seem perfectly evident to us is a thing which, whether it be logical or illogical, we cannot help doing. Instead of regarding the matter in this way, he sought to reduce the first principles of science to formulas which cannot be denied without self-contradiction, and was apparently unaware of the great difference between his position and that of Descartes. So he reverted to the old formalities of logic, and, above all, abstract definitions played a great part in his philosophy. It was quite natural, therefore, that on observing that the method of Descartes labored under the difficulty that we may seem to ourselves to have clear apprehensions of ideas which in truth are very hazy, no better remedy occurred to him than to require an abstract definition of every important term. Accordingly, in adopting the distinction of *clear* and *distinct* notions, he described the latter quality as the clear apprehension of everything contained in the definition; and the books have ever since copied his words. There is no danger that his chimerical scheme will ever again be overvalued. Nothing new can ever be learned by ana-lyzing definitions. Nevertheless, our existing beliefs can be set in order by this process, and order is an essential element of intellectual economy, as of every other. It may be acknowledged, therefore, that the books are right in making familiarity with a notion the first step toward clearness of apprehension, and the defining of it the second. But in omitting all men-tion of any higher perspicuity of thought, they simply mirror a philosophy which was exploded a hundred years ago. That much-admired "ornament of logic"— the doctrine of clearness and distinctness—may be pretty enough, but it is high time to relegate to our cabinet of curiosities the antique *bijou* and to wear about us something better adapted to modern uses.

The very first lesson that we have a right to demand that logic shall teach us is, how to make our ideas clear; and a most important one it is, depreci-ated only by minds who stand in need of it. To know what we think, to be masters of our own meaning, will make a solid foundation for great and weighty thought. It is most easily learned by those whose ideas are meager and restricted; and far happier they than such as wallow helplessly in a rich mud of concep-tions. A nation, it is true, may, in the course of gener-ations, overcome the disadvantage of an excessive wealth of language and its natural concomitant, a vast, unfathomable deep of ideas. We may see it in history, slowly perfecting its literary forms, sloughing at length its metaphysics, and, by virtue of the untirable patience which is often a compensation, attaining great excellence in every branch of mental acquirement.

. . . The action of thought is excited by the irrita-tion of doubt, and ceases when belief is attained; so that the production of belief is the sole function of thought. All these words, however, are too strong for my purpose. It is as if I had described the phenomena as they appear under a mental microscope. Doubt and Belief, as the words are commonly employed, relate to religious or other grave discussions. But here I use them to designate the starting of any question, no matter how small or how great, and the resolution of it. If, for instance, in a horsecar, I pull out my purse and find a five-cent nickel and five coppers, I decide, while my hand is going to the purse, in which way I will pay my fare. To call such a question Doubt, and my decision Belief, is certainly to use words very disproportionate to the occasion. To speak of such a doubt as causing an irritation which needs to be appeased, suggests a temper which is uncomfortable to the verge of insanity. Yet, looking at the matter minutely, it must be admitted that, if there is the least hesitation as to whether I shall pay the five coppers or the nickel (as there will be sure to be, unless I act from some previously contracted habit in the matter), though irritation is too strong a word, yet I am excited to such small mental activity as may be necessary to deciding how I shall act. Most frequently doubts arise from some indecision, however momentary, in our action. Sometimes it is not so. I have, for example, to wait in a railway station, and to pass the time I read the advertisements on the walls, I compare the advantages of different trains and different routes which I never expect to take, merely fancying myself to be in a state of hesitancy, because I am bored with having nothing to trouble me. Feigned hesitancy, whether feigned for mere amusement or with a lofty purpose, plays a great par in the production of scientific inquiry. However the doubt may originate, it stimulates the mind to an activity which may be slight or energetic, calm or turbulent. Images pass rapidly through consciousness, one incessantly melting into another, until at last, when all is over— it may be in a fraction of a second, in an hour, or after long years—we find ourselves decided as to how we should act under such circumstances as those which occasioned our hesitation. In other words, we have attained belief. . . .

And what, then, is belief? It is the demicadence which closes a musical phrase in the symphony of our intellectual life. We have seen that it has just three properties: first, it is something that we are aware of; second, it appeases the irritation of doubt; and, third, it involves the establishment in our nature of a rule of action, or, say, for short, a *habit*. As it appeases the irritation of doubt, which is the motives for thinking, thought relaxes, and comes to rest for a moment when belief is reached. But, since belief is a rule for action, the application of which involves further doubt and further thought, at the same time that it is a stopping place, it is also a new starting place for thought. That is why I have permitted myself to call it thought at rest, although thought is essentially an action. The *final* upshot of thinking is the exercise of volition; and of this thought no longer forms a part; but belief

is only a stadium of mental action, an effect upon our nature due to thought, which will influence future thinking.

The essence of belief is the establishment of a habit, and different beliefs are distinguished by the different modes of action to which they give rise. If beliefs do not differ in this respect, if they appease the same doubt by producing the same rule of action, then no mere differences in the manner of consciousness of them can make them different beliefs; any more than playing a tune in different keys is playing different tunes. Imaginary distinctions are often drawn between beliefs which differ only in their mode of expression—the wrangling which ensues is real enough, however. To believe that any objects are arranged as in Figure 1, and to believe that they are arranged [as] in Figure 2, are one and the same belief; yet it is conceivable that a man should assert one proposition and deny the other. Such false distinctions do as much harm as the confusion of beliefs really different, and are among the pitfalls of which

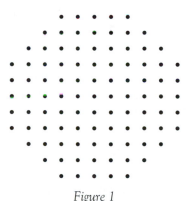

Figure 1

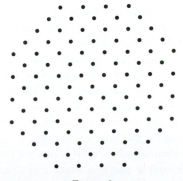

Figure 2

we ought constantly to beware, especially when we are upon metaphysical ground. One singular deception of this sort, which often occurs, is to mistake the sensation produced by our own unclearness of thought for a character of the object we are thinking. Instead of perceiving that the obscurity is purely subjective, we fancy that we contemplate a quality of the object which is essentially mysterious; and if our conception be afterward presented to us in a clear form we do not recognize it as the same, owing to the absence of the feeling of unintelligibility. So long as this deception lasts, it obviously puts an impassable barrier in the way of perspicuous thinking; so that it equally interests the opponent of rational thought to perpetuate it, and its adherents to guard against it.

Another such deception is to mistake a mere difference in the grammatical construction of two words for a distinction between the ideas they express. In this pedantic age, when the general mob of writers attend so much more to words than to things, this error is common enough. When I just said that thought is an *action,* and that it consists in a relation, although a person performs an action, but not a relation, which can only be the result of an action, yet there was no inconsistency in what I said, but only a grammatical vagueness.

From all these sophisms we shall be perfectly safe so long as we reflect that the whole function of thought is to produce habits of action; and that whatever there is connected with a thought, but irrelevant to its purpose, is an accretion to it, but no part of it. If there be a unity among our sensations which has no reference to how we shall act on a given occasion, as when we listen to a piece of music, why, we do not call that thinking. To develop its meaning, we have, therefore, simply to determine what habits it produces, for what a thing means is simply what habits it involves. Now, the identity of a habit depends on how it might lead us to act, not merely under such circumstances as are likely to arise, but under such as might possibly occur, no matter how improbable they may be. What the habit is depends on *when* and *how* it causes us to act. As for the when, every stimulus to action is derived from perception; as for the how, every purpose of action is to produce some sensible result. Thus, we come down to what is tangible and conceivably practical, as the root of every real distinction of thought, no matter

how subtle it may be; and there is no distinction of meaning so fine as to consist in anything but a possible difference of practice.

Let us now approach the subject of logic, and consider a conception which particularly concerns it, that of *reality.* Taking clearness in the sense of familiarity, no idea could be clearer than this. Every child uses it with perfect confidence, never dreaming that he does not understand it. As for clearness in its second grade, however, it would probably puzzle most men, even among those of a reflective turn of mind, to give an abstract definition of the real. Yet such a definition may perhaps be reached by considering the points of difference between reality and its opposite, fiction. A figment is a product of somebody's imagination; it has such characters as his thought impresses upon it. That whose characters are independent of how you or I think is an external reality. There are, however, phenomena within our own minds, dependent upon our thought, which are at the same time real in the sense that we really think them. But though their characters depend on how we think, they do not depend on what we think those characters to be. Thus, a dream has a real existence as a menu phenomenon, if somebody has really dreamt it; that he dreamt so and so does not depend on what anybody thinks was dreamt, but is completely independent of all opinion on the subject. On the other hand, considering not the fact of dreaming but the thing dreamt, it retains its peculiarities by virtue of no other fact than that it was dreamt to possess them. Thus we may define the real as that whose characters are independent of what anybody may think them to be.

But, however satisfactory such a definition may be found, it would be a great mistake to suppose that it makes the idea of reality perfectly clear. Here, then, let us apply our rules. According to them, reality, like every other quality, consists in the peculiar sensible effects which things partaking of it produce. The only effect which real things have is to cause belief, for all the sensations which they excite emerge into consciousness in the form of beliefs. The question therefore is, how is true belief (or belief in the real) distinguished from false belief (or belief in fiction).

. . . Now, as we have seen in the former paper, the ideas of truth and falsehood, in their full development, appertain exclusively to the scientific method of settling opinion. A person who arbitrarily chooses the propositions which he will adopt can use the word truth only to emphasize the expression of his determination to hold on to his choice. Of course, the method of tenacity never prevailed exclusively; reason is too natural to men for that. But in the literature of the dark ages we find some fine examples of it. When Scotus Erigena is commenting upon a poetical passage in which Helleborus is spoken of as having caused the death of Socrates, he does not hesitate to inform the inquiring reader that Helleborus and Socrates were two eminent Greek philosophers, and that the latter having been overcome in argument by the former took the matter to heart and died of it! . . .

The real spirit of Socrates, who I hope would have been delighted to have been "overcome in argument," because he would have learned something by it, is in curious contrast with the naïve idea of the glossist, for whom discussion would seem to have been simply a struggle. When philosophy began to awake from its long slumber, and before theology completely dominated it, the practice seems to have been for each professor to seize upon any philosophical position he found unoccupied and which seemed a strong one, to intrench himself in it, and to sally forth from time to time to give battle to the others.

. . . Since the time of Descartes, the defect in the conception of truth has been less apparent. Still, it will sometimes strike a scientific man that the philosophers have been less intent on finding out what the facts are, than on inquiring what belief is most in harmony with their system. It is hard to convince a follower of the a priori method by adducing facts; but show him that an opinion he is defending is inconsistent with what he has laid down elsewhere, and he will be very apt to retract it. These minds do not seem to believe that disputation is ever to cease; they seem to think that the opinion which is natural for one man is not so for another, and that belief will, consequently, never be settled. In contenting themselves with fixing their own opinions by a method which would lead another man to a different result, they betray their feeble hold of the conception of what truth is. . . .

They may at first obtain different results, but, as each perfects his method and his processes, the results will move steadily together toward a destined center. So with all scientific research. Different minds may set out with the most antagonistic views, but the progress of investigation carries them by a force outside of themselves to one and the same conclusion. This activity of thought by which we are carried, not where we wish, but to a foreordained goal, is like the operation of destiny. No modification of the point of view taken, no selection of other facts for study, no natural bent of mind even, can enable a man to escape the predestinate opinion. This great law is embodied in the conception of truth and reality. The opinion which is fated to be ultimately agreed to by all who investigate, is what we mean by the truth, and the object represented in this opinion is the real. That is the way I would explain reality . . . Though the object of the final opinion depends on what that opinion is, yet what that opinion is does not depend on what you or I or any man thinks. Our perversity and that of others may indefinitely postpone the settlement of opinion; it might even conceivably cause an arbitrary proposition to be universally accepted as long as the human race should last. Yet even that would not change the nature of the belief, which alone could be the result of investigation carried sufficiently far; and if, after the extinction of our race, another should arise with faculties and disposition for investigation, that true opinion must be the one which they would ultimately come to. "Truth crushed to earth shall rise again," and the opinion which would finally result from investigation does not depend on how anybody may actually think. But the reality of that which is real does depend on the real fact that investigation is destined to lead, at last, if continued long enough, to a belief in it.

STUDY QUESTIONS: PEIRCE, *HOW TO MAKE OUR IDEAS CLEAR*

1. Why is Peirce critical of Descartes' "clear and distinct ideas?" What is his criticism? What is the significance of it for Peirce's overall view?
2. Is Leibniz's method better than Descartes'? Why?
3. What is the "ornament of logic?"

4. What is the action of thought excited by?
5. What is a belief?
6. What is the purpose of a belief? What function does it serve?
7. What is Peirce's view of *reality*? What is the relationship between reality and logic?
8. How is true belief distinguished from false belief?
9. What is the point of the Scotus Erigena and Socrates example?
10. What does Peirce mean by "the real spirit of Socrates?"
11. What is the main defect of the concept of truth since the time of Descartes?

Philosophical Bridges: Peirce's Influence

We have already mentioned that William James, himself one of the most influential figures in American thought, was Peirce's pupil. Peirce's conception of meaning as inseperable from experimental evidence—the meaning of a sentence consists in the conditions under which we are warranted in asserting it—remains a widely accepted canon in many philosophical circles to this day. His insistence that any belief system is fallible and open to revision and that a true theory is one that would be verified in the long run by the scientific community, has become part of a tradition in which metaphysical theories are seen as inseparable from common sense. His influence on John Dewey was no less profound, as well as on Josiah Royce, and thus Peirce can be seen as the avatar not only of American pragmatism but also of American instrumentalism and American idealism.

William James (1842–1910)

Biographical History

William James was born in New York City, the first of five children. His grandfather, the Calvinist entrepreneur known as "Wiliam of Albany," who helped develop the Erie Canal between the Hudson River and the Great Lakes, left the family a sizeable fortune. His father and mother, well-connected intellectuals and supporters of the arts, inspired by French socialist Charles Fourier and Swedish mystic Emanuel Swedenborg, took a great personal interest in the children's education, providing them the best private tutors in Europe and in the United States. His father believed that God is incarnated within and identical with each human being. Regular houseguests included Ralph Waldo Emerson and Henry David Thoreau. William's younger brother became the world-famous novelist Henry James. William studied first art, with the great American painter William Morris Hunt, then medicine and natural science at the Lawrence Scientific School; he received his M.D. (1869) from Harvard Medical School. He was as interested in the natural world as he was in the workings of the human being; an avid naturalist, he joined zoologist Louis Agassiz on an expedition to unknown parts of the Amazon jungle in Brazil. His interest in German psychophysics took him for an additional year of study in Germany, after which he returned to Harvard as an instructor in comparative physiology.

James had various bouts of depression and what was then called "melancholia," throughout his early life. In 1870, these vague and troublesome psychological states co-alesced into what he would later describe as his first and most profound "mystical" experience, which launched his lifelong philosophical quest for understanding the meaning and nature of the human soul and the existence of the world:

> I went one evening into a dressing room in the twilight to procure some article that was there; when suddenly there fell upon me without any warning, just as if it came out of the darkness, a horrible fear of my own existence. . . . it was as if something hitherto solid within my breast gave way entirely, and I became a mass of quivering fear. After this the universe was changed for me altogether. I awoke morning after morning with a horrible dread at the pit of my stomach, and with a sense of the insecurity of life that I never knew before, and that I have never felt since. It was like a revelation. . . for months I was unable to go out into the dark alone. In general I dreaded to be left alone. I remember wondering how other people could live, how I myself had ever lived, so unconscious of that pit of insecurity beneath the surface of life.

James made lasting contributions both to psychology and to philosophy, especially philosophy of mind, epistemology, and the philosophy of religion. He left Harvard to teach physiology and psychology at Johns Hopkins University in Baltimore, but returned to Harvard in 1880 as a member of its new illustrious philosophy department that included Josiah Royce and graduate student George Santayana (1863–1952). James directed Santayana's doctoral thesis, which apparently he was not very happy with, calling it "the perfection of rottenness."

In 1890 James published the first textbook on psychology, his famous and widely influential *Principles of Psychology,* which provided the philosophical foundation for the newly developing science of psychology. James also helped found the American Psychological Association and served as its first president.

Philosophical Overview

Inspired by Peirce and Dewey, James developed his own version of a pragmatic theory of truth, which he also called pragmatic, but which Peirce and Dewey both disassociated themselves from. The difference, often glossed over, is quite significant. For both Peirce and Dewey, pragmatism is rooted in scientific thinking and scientific method. For James, on the other hand, there is much more emphasis on personal, religious, and moral considerations: "an idea is 'true,'" he wrote, "so long as to believe it is profitable to our lives." James was rebelling against a representational or correspondence theory of truth, according to which an idea or proposition "represents" or "corresponds" to reality and is true if and only if it is a copy of objective reality. Even Bertrand Russell, who admired James for his psychology and especially his analysis of consciousness, called James's theory of truth "subjectivist madness." Ignoring all his critics, James spent five years writing his *Varieties of Religious Experience* (1902). It is a scholarly and popular blend of philosophy, psychology, religion, and most importantly mysticism, which he tried to make philosophically acceptable. It is to this today the definitive study of mystical experience. James next tried to make his version of a pragmatic theory of truth respectable and, in 1907, succeeded with the publication of *Pragmatism: A New Name for Some Old Ways of Thinking.* James' more broad approach surprised many because of its solid grounding in the works of European philosophers, who also took interest in his work. This method spread among other American pragmatists; so while James dedicated his book to John Stuart Mill, Dewey expressed a fondness for Hegel, as did Royce, and Peirce acknowledged Kant's influence.

James went on to develop his ideas into a new theory of mind with a startling analysis of consciousness. He cleverly applied the introspective techniques he had acquired in his work with mysticism to a subtle and precise analysis of percepts and concepts. This aspect of his work culminated with a radical new approach to philosophical problems, which he called radical empiricism, and is today regarded as James's crowning achievement in philosophy. A psychologically sophisticated version of logical positivism, radical empiricism is a marriage between pragmatism and the analysis of experience. James altered his earlier pragmatic theory of truth and meaning, so that his view became that whether a proposition was true was determined not by whether it makes the right sort of difference to a person but, rather, on whether it succeeds to predict new sense experience. This move transformed James's earlier philosophical system and, by tying it closely with the nature of experience, led to a revolutionary version of idealism, according to which the world itself consists entirely of experience, with some elements of logical positivism: propositions that do not successfully make predictions one way or the other are neither true nor false but *meaningless*. In the end, James' view transcended both traditional idealism and materialism, in favor of *neutral monism*, a worldview in which neither matter *nor* consciousness as such exists. James's theory involves both phenomenalism (all that is and can be known are phenomena) and, because of its pragmatic foundations, a philosophical versions of naïve realism that is still highly influential among many American schools of philosophy. His innovation involves the subtle notion that the only givens in existence are ideas but they are not *mental*. James thus brings to the American philosophical scene certain aspects of absolute idealism while at the same time rejecting the notion of the reality of an independent, subjective consciousness, while espousing both naturalism and realism—an extraordinary philosophical balancing act.

THE WILL TO BELIEVE
William James

1.

Let us give the name of *hypothesis* to anything that may be proposed to our belief; and just as the electricians speak of live and dead wires, let us speak of any hypothesis as either *live* or *dead*. A live hypothesis is one which appeals as a real possibility to him to whom it is proposed. If I ask you to believe in the Mahdi, the notion makes no electric connection with your nature—it refuses to scintillate with any credibility at all. As an hypothesis it is completely dead. To an Arab, however (even if he be not one of the Mahdi's followers), the hypothesis is among the mind's possibilities: it is alive. This shows that deadness and liveness in an hypothesis are not intrinsic properties, but relations to the individual thinker. They are measured by his willingness to act. The maximum of liveness in an hypothesis means willingness to act irrevocably. Practically, that means belief; but there is some believing tendency wherever there is willingness to act at all.

Next, let us call the decision between two hypotheses an *option*. Options may be of several kinds. They may be—first, *living* or *dead*; secondly, *forced* or *avoidable*; thirdly, *momentous* or *trivial*; and for our purposes we may call an option a genuine option when it is of the forced, living, and momentous kind.

1. A living option is one in which both hypotheses are live ones. If I say to you: "Be a theosophist or be a Mohammedan," it is probably a dead option, because for you neither hypothesis is likely to be alive. But if I say, "Be an agnostic or be a Christian," it is otherwise: trained as you are, each hypothesis makes some appeal, however small, to your belief.

James, from An Address to the Philosophical Clubs of Yale and Brown Universities. Published in the *New World*, June 1896.

2. Next, if I say to you: "Choose between going out with your umbrella or without it," I do not offer you a genuine option, for it is not forced. You can easily avoid it by not going out at all. Similarly, if I say, "Either love me or hate me," "Either call my theory true or call it false," your option is avoidable. You may remain indifferent to me, neither loving nor hating, and you may decline to offer any judgment as to my theory. But if I say, "Either accept this truth or go without it," I put on you a forced option, for there is no standing place outside of the alternative. Every dilemma based on a complete logical disjunction, with no possibility of not choosing, is an option of this forced kind.

3. Finally, if I were Dr. Nansen and proposed to you to join my north pole expedition, your option would be momentous; for this would probably be your only similar opportunity, and your choice now would either exclude you from the north pole sort of immortality altogether or put at least the chance of it into your hands. He who refuses to embrace a unique opportunity loses the prize as surely as if he tried and failed. *Per contra*, the option is trivial when the opportunity is not unique, when the stake is insignificant, or when the decision is reversible if it later prove unwise. Such trivial options abound in the scientific life. A chemist finds an hypothesis live enough to spend a year in its verification: he believes in it to that extent. But if his experiments prove inconclusive either way, he is quit for his loss of time, no vital harm being done.

It will facilitate our discussion if we keep all these distinctions well in mind.

2.

The next matter to consider is the actual psychology of human opinion. When we look at certain facts, it seems as if our passional and volitional nature lay at the root of all our convictions. When we look at others, it seems as if they could do nothing when the intellect had once said its say. Let us take the latter facts up first.

Does it not seem preposterous on the very face of it to talk of our opinions being modifiable at will? Can our will either help or hinder our intellect in its perceptions of truth? Can we, by just willing it, believe that Abraham Lincoln's existence is a myth, and that the portraits of him in *McClure's Magazine* are all of some one else? Can we, by any effort of our will, or by any strength of wish that it were true, believe ourselves well and about when we are roaring with rheumatism in bed, or feel certain that the sum of the two one-dollar bills in our pocket must be a hundred dollars? We can *say* any of these things, but we are absolutely impotent to believe them; and of just such things is the whole fabric of the truths that we do believe in made up—matters of fact, immediate or remote, as Hume said, and relations between ideas, which are either there or not there for us if we see them so, and which if not there cannot be put there by any action of our own.

In Pascal's *Thoughts* there is a celebrated passage known in literature as Pascal's wager. In it he tries to force us into Christianity by reasoning as if our concern with truth resembled our concern with the stakes in a game of chance. Translated freely his words are these: You must either believe or not believe that God is—which will you do? Your human reason cannot say. A game is going on between you and the nature of things which at the day of judgment will bring out either heads or tails. Weigh what your gains and your losses would be if you should stake all you have on heads, or God's existence: if you win in such case, you gain eternal beatitude; if you lose, you lose nothing at all. If there were an infinity of chances, and only one for God in this wager, still you ought to stake your all on God; for though you surely risk a finite loss by this procedure, any finite loss is reasonable, even a certain one is reasonable, if there is but the possibility of infinite gain. Go, then, and take holy water, and have masses said; belief will come and stupefy your scruples—*Cela vous fera croire et vous abêtira.* Why should you not? At bottom, what have you to lose?

You probably feel that when religious faith expresses itself thus, in the language of the gaming table, it is put to its last trumps. Surely Pascal's own personal belief in masses and holy water had far other springs; and this celebrated page of his is but an argument for others, a last desperate snatch at a weapon against the hardness of the unbelieving heart. We feel that a faith in masses and holy water adopted wilfully after such a mechanical calculation would lack the inner soul of faith's reality; and if we were ourselves in the place of the Deity, we should probably take particular pleasure in cutting off believers of this pattern from their infinite reward. It is evident that unless there be some pre-existing tendency to believe in masses and holy water, the option offered to the will by Pascal is not a living option. Certainly no Turk ever took to masses and holy water on its account; and even to us Protestants these means of salvation seem such foregone impossibilities that Pascal's logic, invoked for them specifically, leaves us unmoved. As well might the Mahdi write to us, saying, "I am the Expected One whom God has created in his effulgence. You shall be infinitely happy if you confess me; otherwise you shall be cut off from the light of the sun. Weigh, then, your infinite gain if I am genuine against your finite sacrifice if I am not!" His logic would be that of Pascal; but he would vainly use it on us, for the hypothesis he offers us is dead. No tendency to act on it exists in us to any degree.

The talk of believing by our volition seems, then, from one point of view, simply silly. From another point of view it is worse than silly, it is vile. When one turns to the magnificent edifice of the physical sciences, and sees how it was reared; what thousands of disinterested moral lives of men lie buried in its mere foundations; what patience and postponement, what choking down of preference, what submission to the icy laws of outer fact are wrought into its very stones and mortar; how absolutely impersonal it stands in its vast augustness—then how besotted and contemptible seems every little sentimentalist who comes blowing his voluntary smoke-wreaths, and pretending to decide things from out of his private dream! Can we wonder if those bred in the rugged and manly school of science should feel like spewing such subjectivism out of their mouths? The whole system of loyalties which grow up in the schools of science go dead against its toleration; so that it is only natural that those who have caught the scientific fever should pass over to the opposite extreme, and write sometimes as if the incorruptibly truthful intellect ought positively to prefer bitterness and unacceptableness to the heart in its cup.

It fortifies my soul to know
That though I perish, Truth is so—

sings Clough, while Huxley exclaims, "my only consolation lies in the reflection that, however bad our posterity may become, so far as they hold by the plain rule of not pretending to believe what they have no reason to believe, because it may be to their advantage so to pretend [the word 'pretend' is surely here redundant], they will not have reached the lowest depth of immorality." And that delicious *enfant terrible* Clifford writes: "Belief is desecrated when given to unproved and unquestioned statements for the solace and private pleasure of the believer.... Whoso would deserve well of his fellows in this matter will guard the purity of his belief with a very fanaticism of jealous care, lest at any time it should rest on an unworthy object, and catch a stain which can never be wiped away.... If [a] belief has been accepted on insufficient evidence [even though the belief be true, as Clifford on the same page explains] the pleasure is a stolen one.... It is sinful because it is stolen in defiance of our duty to mankind. That duty is to guard ourselves from such beliefs as from a pestilence which may shortly master our own body and then spread to the rest of the town.... It is wrong always, everywhere, and for every one, to believe anything upon insufficient evidence."

3.

All this strikes one as healthy, even when expressed, as by Clifford, with somewhat too much of robustious pathos in the voice. Free will and simple wishing do seem, in the matter of our credences, to be only fifth wheels to the coach. Yet if any one should thereupon assume that intellectual insight is what remains after wish and will and sentimental preference have taken wing, or that pure reason is what then settles our opinions, he would fly quite as directly in the teeth of the facts.

It is only our already dead hypotheses that our willing nature is unable to bring to life again. But what has made them dead for us is for the most part a previous action of our willing nature of an antagonistic kind. When I say "willing nature," I do not mean only such deliberate volitions as may have set up habits of belief that we cannot now escape from— I mean all such factors of belief as fear and hope, prejudice and passion, imitation and partisanship, the circumpressure of our caste and set. As a matter of fact we find ourselves believing, we hardly know how or why. Mr. Balfour gives the name of "authority" to all those influences, born of the intellectual climate, that make hypotheses possible or impossible for us, alive or dead. Here in this room, we all of us believe in molecules and the conservation of energy, in democracy and necessary progress, in Protestant Christianity and the duty of fighting for "the doctrine of the immortal Monroe," all for no reasons worthy of the name. We see into these matters with no more inner clearness, and probably with much less, than any disbeliever in them might possess. His unconventionality would probably have some grounds to show for its conclusions; but for us, not insight, but the *prestige* of the opinions, is what makes the spark shoot from them and light up our sleeping magazines of faith. Our reason is quite satisfied, in nine hundred and ninety-nine cases out of every thousand of us, if it can find a few arguments that will do to recite in case our credulity is criticized by some one else. Our faith is faith in some one else's faith, and in the greatest matters this is most the case. Our belief in truth itself, for instance, that there is a truth, and that our minds and it are made for each other—what is it but a passionate affirmation of desire, in which our social system backs us up? We want to have a truth; we want to believe that our experiments and studies and discussions must put us in a continually better and better position towards it; and on this line we agree to fight out our thinking lives. But if a Pyrrhonistic sceptic asks us *how we know* all this, can our logic find a reply? No! Certainly it cannot. It is just one volition against another—we willing to go in for life upon a trust or assumption which he, for his part, does not care to make.

As a rule we disbelieve all facts and theories for which we have no use. Clifford's cosmic emotions find no use for Christian feelings. Huxley belabors the bishops because there is no use for sacerdotalism in his scheme of life. Newman, on the contrary, goes over to Romanism, and finds all sorts of reasons good for staying there, because a priestly system is for him an organic need and delight. Why do so few "scientists" even look at the evidence for telepathy, so called? Because they think, as a leading biologist, now dead, once said to me, that even if such a thing were true, scientists ought to band together to keep it suppressed and concealed. It would undo the uniformity of Nature and all sorts of other things without which scientists cannot carry on their pursuits. But if this very man had been shown something which as a scientist he might *do* with telepathy, he might not

only have examined the evidence but even have found it good enough. This very law which the logicians would impose upon us—if I may give the name of logicians to those who would rule out our willing nature here—is based on nothing but their own natural wish to exclude all elements for which they, in their professional quality of logicians, can find no use.

Evidently, then, our non-intellectual nature does influence our convictions. There are passional tendencies and volitions which run before and others which come after belief, and it is only the latter that are too late for the fair; and they are not too late when the previous passional work has been already in their own direction. Pascal's argument, instead of being powerless, then seems a regular clincher, and is the last stroke needed to make our faith in masses and holy water complete. The state of things is evidently far from simple; and pure insight and logic, whatever they might do ideally, are not the only things that really do produce our creeds.

4.

Our next duty, having recognized this mixed-up state of affairs, is to ask whether it be simply reprehensible and pathological, or whether, on the contrary, we must treat it as a normal element in making up our minds. The thesis I defend is, briefly stated, this: *Our passional nature not only lawfully may, but must, decide an option between propositions, whenever it is a genuine option that cannot by its nature be decided on intellectual grounds; for to say, under such circumstances, "Do not decide, but leave the question open," is itself a passional decision—just like deciding yes or no—and is attended with the same risk of losing the truth.* The thesis thus abstractly expressed will, I trust, soon become quite clear. But I must first indulge in a bit more of preliminary work.

5.

It will be observed that for the purposes of this discussion we are on "dogmatic" ground—ground, I mean, which leaves systematic philosophical scepticism altogether out of account. The postulate that there is truth, and that it is the destiny of our minds to attain it, we are deliberately resolving to make, though the sceptic will not make it. We part company with him, therefore, absolutely, at this point. But the faith that truth exists, and that our minds can find it, may be held in two ways. We may talk of the *empiricist* way and of the *absolutist* way of believing in truth. The absolutists in this matter say that we not only can attain to knowing truth, but we can *know when* we have attained to knowing it; while the empiricists think that although we may attain it, we cannot infallibly know when. To *know* is one thing, and to know for certain *that* we know is another. One may hold to the first being possible without the second; hence the empiricists and the absolutists, although neither of them is a skeptic in the usual philosophic sense of the term, show very different degrees of dogmatism in their lives.

If we look at the history of opinions, we see that the empiricist tendency has largely prevailed in science, while in philosophy the absolutist tendency has had everything its own way. The characteristic sort of happiness, indeed, which philosophies yield has mainly consisted in the conviction felt by each successive school or system that by it bottom certitude had been attained. "Other philosophies are collections of opinions, mostly false; *my* philosophy gives standing ground forever"—who does not recognize in this the keynote of every system worthy of the name? A system, to be a system at all, must come as a *closed* system, reversible in this or that detail, perchance, but in its essential features never!

Scholastic orthodoxy, to which one must always go when one wishes to find perfectly clear statement, has beautifully elaborated this absolutist conviction in a doctrine which it calls that of "objective evidence." If, for example, I am unable to doubt that I now exist before you, that two is less than three, or that if all men are mortal then I am mortal too, it is because these things illumine my intellect irresistibly. The final ground of this objective evidence possessed by certain propositions is the *adaequatio intellectûs nostri cum rê.* The certitude it brings involves an *aptitudinem ad extorquendum certum assensum* on the part of the truth envisaged, and on the side of the subject a *quietem in cognitione,* when once the object is mentally received, that leaves no possibility of doubt behind; and in the whole transaction nothing operates but the *entitas ipsa* of the object and the *entitas ipsa* of the mind. We slouchy modern thinkers dislike to talk in Latin—indeed, we dislike to talk in

set terms at all; but at bottom our own state of mind is very much like this whenever we uncritically abandon ourselves: You believe in objective evidence, and I do. Of some things we feel that we are certain: we know, and we know that we do know. There is something that gives a click inside of us, a bell that strikes twelve, when the hands of our mental clock have swept the dial and meet over the meridian hour. The greatest empiricists among us are only empiricists on reflection: when left to their instincts, they dogmatize like infallible popes. When the Cliffords tell us how sinful it is to be Christians on such "insufficient evidence," insufficiency is really the last thing they have in mind. For them the evidence is absolutely sufficient, only it makes the other way. They believe so completely in an anti-Christian order of the universe that there is no living option: Christianity is a dead hypothesis from the start.

6.

But now, since we are all such absolutists by instinct, what in our quality of students of philosophy ought we to do about the fact? Shall we espouse and endorse it? Or shall we treat it as a weakness of our nature from which we must free ourselves, if we can?

I sincerely believe that the latter course is the only one we can follow as reflective men. Objective evidence and certitude are doubtless very fine ideals to play with, but where on this moonlit and dreamvisited planet are they found? I am, therefore, myself a complete empiricist so far as my theory of human knowledge goes. I live, to be sure, by the practical faith that we must go on experiencing and thinking over our experience, for only thus can our opinions grow more true; but to hold any one of them—I absolutely do not care which—as if it never could be reinterpretable or corrigible, I believe to be a tremendously mistaken attitude, and I think that the whole history of philosophy will bear me out. There is but one indefectibly certain truth, and that is the truth that Pyrrhonistic Skepticism itself leaves standing— the truth that the present phenomenon of consciousness exists. That, however, is the bare starting point of knowledge, the mere admission of a stuff to be philosophized about. The various philosophies are but so many attempts at expressing what this stuff really is. And if we repair to our libraries what disagreement do we discover! Where is a certainly true answer found? Apart from abstract propositions of comparison (such as two and two are the same as four), propositions which tell us nothing by themselves about concrete reality, we find no proposition ever regarded by any one as evidently certain that has not either been called a falsehood, or at least had its truth sincerely questioned by some one else. The transcending of the axioms of geometry, not in play but in earnest, by certain of our contemporaries (as Zöllner and Charles H. Hinton), and the rejection of the whole Aristotelian logic by the Hegelians, are striking instances in point.

No concrete test of what is really true has ever been agreed upon. Some make the criterion external to the moment of perception, putting it either in revelation, the *consensus gentium*, the instincts of the heart, or the systematized experience of the race. Others make the perceptive moment its own test—Descartes, for instance, with his clear and distinct ideas guaranteed by the veracity of God; Reid with his "common sense"; and Kant with his forms of synthetic judgment a priori. The inconceivability of the opposite; the capacity to be verified by sense; the possession of complete organic unity or self-relation, realized when a thing is its own other—are standards which, in turn, have been used. The much lauded objective evidence is never triumphantly there; it is a mere aspiration or *Grenzbegriff*, marking the infinitely remote ideal of our thinking life. To claim that certain truths now possess it, is simply to say that when you think them true and they *are* true, then their evidence is objective, otherwise it is not. But practically one's conviction that the evidence one goes by is of the real objective brand, is only one more subjective opinion added to the lot. For what a contradictory array of opinions have objective evidence and absolute certitude been claimed! The world is rational through and through—its existence is an ultimate brute fact; there is a personal God—a personal God is inconceivable; there is an extra mental physical world immediately known—the mind can only know its own ideas; a moral imperative exists—obligation is only the resultant of desires; a permanent spiritual principle is in every one—there are only shifting states of mind; there is an endless chain of causes—there is an absolute first cause; an eternal necessity—a freedom; a purpose—no purpose; a primal One—a primal Many; a universal continuity—an essential discontinuity in things; an infinity—no infinity. There is this—there is that; there is indeed nothing which some one has not thought absolutely true, while his neighbor deemed it absolutely false; and not an absolutist among them seems ever to have considered that the trouble may all the time be essential, and that the intellect, even with truth directly in its grasp, may have no infallible signal for knowing whether it be truth or no. When, indeed, one remembers that the most striking practical application to life of the doctrine of objective certitude has been the conscientious labors of the Holy Office of the Inquisition, one feels less tempted than ever to lend the doctrine a respectful ear.

But please observe, now, that when as empiricists we give up the doctrine of objective certitude, we do not thereby give up the quest or hope of truth itself. We still pin our faith on its existence, and still believe that we gain an ever better position towards it by systematically continuing to roll up experiences and think. Our great difference from the scholastic lies in the way we face. The strength of his system lies in the principles, the origin the *terminus a quo* of his thought; for us the strength is in the outcome, the upshot, the *terminus ad quem*. Not where it comes from but what it leads to is to decide. It matters not to an empiricist from what quarter an hypothesis may come to him: he may have acquired it by fair means or by foul; passion may have whispered or accident suggested it; but if the total drift of thinking continues to confirm it, that is what he means by its being true.

7.

One more point, small but important, and our preliminaries are done. There are two ways of looking at our duty in the matter of opinion—ways entirely different, and yet ways about whose difference the theory of knowledge seems hitherto to have shown very little concern. *We must know the truth*; and *we must avoid error*—these are our first and great commandments as would-be knowers; but they are not two ways of stating an identical commandment, they are two separable laws. Although it may indeed happen that when we believe the truth A, we escape as an incidental consequence from believing the falsehood B, it hardly ever happens that by merely disbelieving

B we necessarily believe *A*. We may in escaping *B* fall into believing other falsehoods, *C* or *D*, just as bad as *B*; or we may escape *B* by not believing anything at all, not even *A*.

Believe truth! Shun error! These, we see, are two materially different laws; and by choosing between them we may end by coloring differently our whole intellectual life. We may regard the chase for truth as paramount, and the avoidance of error as secondary; or we may, on the other hand, treat the avoidance of error as more imperative, and let truth take its chance. Clifford, in the instructive passage which I have quoted, exhorts us to the latter course. Believe nothing, he tells us, keep your mind in suspense forever, rather than by closing it on insufficient evidence incur the awful risk of believing lies. You, on the other hand, may think that the risk of being in error is a very small matter when compared with the blessings of real knowledge, and be ready to be duped many times in your investigation rather than postpone indefinitely the chance of guessing true. I myself find it impossible to go with Clifford. We must remember that these feelings of our duty about either truth or error are in any case only expressions of our passional life. Biologically considered, our minds are as ready to grind out falsehood as veracity, and he who says, "Better go without belief forever than believe a lie!" merely shows his own preponderant private horror of becoming a dupe. He may be critical of many of his desires and fears, but this fear he slavishly obeys. He cannot imagine any one questioning its binding force. For my own part, I have also a horror of being duped; but I can believe that worse things than being duped may happen to a man in this world: so Clifford's exhortation has to my ears a thoroughly fantastic sound. It is like a general informing his soldiers that it is better to keep out of battle forever than to risk a single wound. Not so are victories either over enemies or over nature gained. Our errors are surely not such awfully solemn things. In a world where we are so certain to incur them in spite of all our caution, a certain lightness of heart seems healthier than this excessive nervousness on their behalf. At any rate, it seems the fittest thing for the empiricist philosopher.

8.

And now, after all this introduction, let us go straight at our question. I have said, and now repeat it, that

not only as a matter of fact do we find our passional nature influencing us in our opinions, but that there are some options between opinions in which this influence must be regarded both as an inevitable and as a lawful determinant of our choice.

I fear here that some of you my hearers will begin to scent danger, and lend an inhospitable ear. Two first steps of passion you have indeed had to admit as necessary—we must think so as to avoid dupery, and we must think so as to gain truth; but the surest path to those ideal consummations, you will probably consider, is from now onwards to take no further passionate step.

Well, of course, I agree as far as the facts will allow. Wherever the option between losing truth and gaining it is not momentous, we can throw the chance of *gaining truth* away, and at any rate save ourselves from any chance of *believing falsehood*, by not making up our minds at all till objective evidence has come. In scientific questions, this is almost always the case; and even in human affairs in general, the need of acting is seldom so urgent that a false belief to act on is better than no belief at all. Law courts, indeed, have to decide on the best evidence attainable for the moment, because a judge's duty is to make law as well as to ascertain it, and (as a learned judge once said to me) few cases are worth spending much time over: the great thing is to have them decided on *any* acceptable principle, and got out of the way. But in our dealings with objective nature we obviously are recorders, not makers, of the truth; and decisions for the mere sake of deciding promptly and getting on to the next business would be wholly out of place. Throughout the breadth of physical nature facts are what they are quite independently of us, and seldom is there any such hurry about them that the risks of being duped by believing a premature theory need be faced. The questions here are always trivial options, the hypotheses are hardly living (at any rate not living for us spectators), the choice between believing truth or falsehood is seldom forced. The attitude of skeptical balance is, therefore, the absolutely wise one if we would escape mistakes. What difference, indeed, does it make to most of us whether we have or have not a theory of the Röntgen rays, whether we believe or not in mind-stuff, or have a conviction about the causality of conscious states? It makes no difference. Such options are not forced on us. On every account it is better not to make them, but still keep weighing reasons *pro et contra* with an indifferent hand.

I speak, of course, here of the purely judging mind. For purposes of discovery such indifference is to be less highly recommended, and science would be far less advanced than she is if the passionate desires of individuals to get their own faiths confirmed had been kept out of the game. See for example the sagacity which Spencer and Weismann now display. On the other hand, if you want an absolute duffer in an investigation, you must, after all, take the man who has no interest whatever in its results: he is the warranted incapable, the positive fool. The most useful investigator, because the most sensitive observer, is always he whose eager interest in one side of the question is balanced by an equally keen nervousness lest he become deceived. Science has organized this nervousness into a regular *technique,* her so-called method of verification; and she has fallen so deeply in love with the method that one may even say she has ceased to care for truth by itself at all. It is only truth as technically verified that interests her. The truth of truths might come in merely affirmative form, and she would decline to touch it. Such truth as that, she might repeat with Clifford, would be stolen in defiance of her duty to mankind. Human passions, however, are stronger than technical rules. "*Le coeur a ses raisons,*" as Pascal says, "*que la raison ne connaît pas*" ("The heart has its reasons which reason does not know."); and however indifferent to all but the bare rules of the game the umpire, the abstract intellect, may be, the concrete players who furnish him the materials to judge of are usually, each one of them, in love with some pet "live hypothesis" of his own. Let us agree, however, that wherever there is no forced option, the dispassionately judicial intellect with no pet hypothesis, saving us, as it does, from dupery at any rate, ought to be our ideal.

The question next arises: are there not somewhere forced options in our speculative questions, and can we (as men who may be interested at least as much in positively gaining truth as in merely escaping dupery) always wait with impunity till the coercive evidence shall have arrived? It seems a priori improbable that the truth should be so nicely adjusted to our needs and powers as that. In the great boardinghouse of nature, the cakes and the butter and the syrup seldom come out so even and leave the plates so clean. Indeed, we should view them with scientific suspicion if they did.

9.

Moral questions immediately present themselves as questions whose solution cannot wait for sensible proof. A moral question is a question not of what sensibly exists, but of what is good, or would be good if it did exist. Science can tell us what exists; but to compare the *worths,* both of what exists and of what does not exist, we must consult not science, but what Pascal calls our heart. Science herself consults her heart when she lays it down that the infinite ascertainment of fact and correction of false belief are the supreme goods for man. Challenge the statement, and science can only repeat it oracularly, or else prove it by showing that such ascertainment and correction bring man all sorts of other goods which man's heart in turn declares. The question of having moral beliefs at all or not having them is decided by our will. Are our moral preferences true or false, or are they only odd biological phenomena, making things good or bad for *us,* but in themselves indifferent? How can your pure intellect decide? If your heart does not *want* a world of moral reality, your head will assuredly never make you believe in one. Mephistophelian skepticism, indeed, will satisfy the head's play instincts much better than any rigorous idealism can. Some men (even at the student age) are so naturally cool-hearted that the moralistic hypothesis never has for them any pungent life, and in their supercilious presence the hot young moralist always feels strangely ill at ease. The appearance of knowingness is on their side, of *naïveté* and gullibility on his. Yet, in the inarticulate heart of him, he clings to it that he is not a dupe, and that there is a realm in which (as Emerson says) all their wit and intellectual superiority is no better than the cunning of a fox. Moral skepticism can no more be refuted or proved by logic than intellectual skepticism can. When we stick to it that there *is* truth (be it of either kind), we do so with our whole nature, and resolve to stand or fall by the results. The skeptic with his whole nature adopts the doubting attitude; but which of us is the wiser, Omniscience only knows.

Turn now from these wide questions of good to a certain class of questions of fact, questions concerning personal relations, states of mind between one man and another. For example, *Do you like me or not?* Whether you do or not depends, in countless instances, on whether I meet you halfway, am willing to assume that you must like me, and show you trust and expectation. The previous faith on my part in your liking's existence is in such cases what makes your liking come. But if I stand aloof, and refuse to budge an inch until I have objective evidence, until you shall have done something apt, as the absolutists say, *ad extorquendum assensum meum*, ten to one your liking never comes. How many women's hearts are vanquished by the mere sanguine insistence of some man that they *must* love him! He will not consent to the hypothesis that they cannot. The desire for a certain kind of truth here brings about that special truth's existence; and so it is in innumerable cases of other sorts. Who gains promotions, boons, appointments, but the man in whose life they are seen to play the part of live hypotheses, who discounts them, sacrifices other things for their sake before they have come, and takes risks for them in advance? His faith acts on the powers above him as a claim, and creates its own verification.

A social organism of any sort whatever, large or small, is what it is because each member proceeds to his own duty with a trust that the other members will simultaneously do theirs. Wherever a desired result is achieved by the cooperation of many independent persons, its existence as a fact is a pure consequence of the precursive faith in one another of those immediately concerned. A government, an army, a commercial system, a ship, a college, an athletic team, all exist on this condition, without which not only is nothing achieved, but nothing is even attempted. A whole train of passengers (individually brave enough) will be looted by a few highwaymen, simply because the latter can count on one another, while each passenger fears that if he makes a movement of resistance, he will be shot before any one else backs him up. If we believed that the whole car-full would rise at once with us, we should each severally rise, and train-robbing would never even be attempted. There are, then, cases where a fact cannot come at all unless a preliminary faith exists in its coming. *And where faith in a fact can help create the fact,* that would be an insane logic which should say that faith running ahead of scientific evidence is the "lowest kind of immorality" into which a thinking being can fall. Yet such is the logic by which our scientific absolutists pretend to regulate our lives!

10.

In truths dependent on our personal action, then, faith based on desire is certainly a lawful and possibly an indispensable thing.

But now, it will be said, these are all childish human cases, and have nothing to do with great cosmical matters, like the question of religious faith. Let us then pass on to that. Religions differ so much in their accidents that in discussing the religious question we must make it very generic and broad. What then do we now mean by the religious hypothesis? Science says things are; morality says some things are better than other things; and religion says essentially two things.

First, she says that the best things are the more eternal things, the overlapping things, the things in the universe that throw the last stone, so to speak, and say the final word. "Perfection is eternal"—this phrase of Charles Secrétan seems a good way of putting this first affirmation of religion, an affirmation which obviously cannot yet be verified scientifically at all.

The second affirmation of religion is that we are better off even now if we believe her first affirmation to be true.

Now, let us consider what the logical elements of this situation are *in case the religious hypothesis in both its branches be really true.* (Of course, we must admit that possibility at the outset. If we are to discuss the question at all, it must involve a living option. If for any of you religion be a hypothesis that cannot, by any living possibility, be true, then you need go no farther. I speak to the "saving remnant" alone.) So proceeding, we see, first, that religion offers itself as a *momentous* option. We are supposed to gain, even now, by our belief, and to lose by our disbelief, a certain vital good. Secondly, religion is a *forced* option, so far as that good goes. We cannot escape the issue by remaining skeptical and waiting for more light, because, although we do avoid error in that way *if religion be untrue,* we lose the good, *if it be true,* just as certainly as if we positively chose to disbelieve. It is as if a man should hesitate indefinitely to ask a certain woman to marry him because he was not perfectly sure that she would prove an angel after he brought her home. Would he not cut himself off from that particular angel possibility as decisively as if he went and married some one else? Skepticism, then, is not avoidance of option; it is option of a certain particular kind of risk. *Better risk loss of truth than chance of error*—that is your faith vetoer's exact position. He is actively playing his stake as much as the believer is; he is backing the field against the religious hypothesis, just as the believer is backing the religious hypothesis against the field. To preach skepticism to us as a duty until "sufficient evidence" for religion be found, is tantamount therefore to telling us, when in presence of the religious hypothesis, that to yield to our fear of its being error is wiser and better than to yield to our hope that it may be true. It is not intellect against all passions, then; it is only intellect with one passion laying down its law. And by what, forsooth, is the supreme wisdom of this passion warranted? Dupery for dupery, what proof is there that dupery through hope is so much worse than dupery through fear? I, for one, can see no proof; and I simply refuse obedience to the scientist's command to imitate his kind of option, in a case where my own stake is important enough to give me the right to choose my own form of risk. If religion be true and the evidence for it be still insufficient, I do not wish, by putting your extinguisher upon my nature (which feels to me as if it had after all some business in this matter), to forfeit my sole chance in life of getting upon the winning side—that chance depending, of course, on my willingness to run the risk of acting as if my passionate need of taking the world religiously might be prophetic and right.

All this is on the supposition that it really may be prophetic and right, and that, even to us who are discussing the matter, religion is a live hypothesis which may be true. Now, to most of us religion comes in a still further way that makes a veto on our active faith even more illogical. The more perfect and more eternal aspect of the universe is represented in our religions as having personal form. The universe is no longer a mere *It* to us, but a *Thou*, if we are religious; and any relation that may be possible from person to person might be possible here. For instance, although in one sense we are passive portions of the universe, in another we show a curious autonomy, as if we were

small active centres on our own account. We feel, too, as if the appeal of religion to us were made to our own active goodwill, as if evidence might be forever withheld from us unless we met the hypothesis halfway. To take a trivial illustration: just as a man who in a company of gentlemen made no advances, asked a warrant for every concession, and believed no one's word without proof, would cut himself off by such churlishness from all the social rewards that a more trusting spirit would earn—so here, one who should shut himself up in snarling logicality and try to make the gods extort his recognition willy-nilly, or not get it at all, might cut himself off forever from his only opportunity of making the gods' acquaintance. This feeling, forced on us we know not whence, that by obstinately believing that there are gods (although not to do so would be so easy both for our logic and our life) we are doing the universe the deepest service we can, seems part of the living essence of the religious hypothesis. If the hypothesis *were* true in all its parts, including this one, then pure intellectualism, with its veto on our making willing advances, would be an absurdity; and some participation of our sympathetic nature would be logically required. I, therefore, for one, cannot see my way to accepting the agnostic rules for truth-seeking, or wilfully agree to keep my willing nature out of the game. I cannot do so for this plain reason, that *a rule of thinking which would absolutely prevent me from acknowledging certain kinds of truth if those kinds of truth were really there, would be an irrational rule.* That for me is the long and short of the formal logic of the situation, no matter what the kinds of truth might materially be.

I confess I do not see how this logic can be escaped. But sad experience makes me fear that some of you may still shrink from radically saying with me, *in abstracto*, that we have the right to believe at our own risk any hypothesis that is live enough to tempt our will. I suspect, however, that if this is so, it is because you have got away from the abstract logical point of view altogether, and are thinking (perhaps without realizing it) of some particular religious hypothesis which for you is dead. The freedom to "believe what we will" you apply to the case of some patent superstition; and the faith you think of is the faith defined by the schoolboy when he said, "faith is when you believe something that you know ain't true." I can only repeat that this is misapprehension. *In concreto*, the freedom to believe can only cover living options which the intellect of the individual cannot by itself resolve; and living options never seem absurdities to him who has them to consider. When I look at the religious question as it really puts itself to concrete men, and when I think of all the possibilities which both practically and theoretically it involves, then this command that we shall put a stopper on our heart, instincts, and courage, and *wait*—acting of course meanwhile more or less as if religion were *not* true—till doomsday, or till such time as our intellect and senses working together may have raked in evidence enough—this command, I say, seems to me the queerest idol ever manufactured in the philosophic cave. Were we scholastic absolutists, there might be more excuse. If we had an infallible intellect with its objective certitudes, we might feel ourselves disloyal to such a perfect organ of knowledge in not trusting to it exclusively, in not waiting for its releasing word. But if we are empiricists, if we believe that no bell in us tolls to let us know for certain when truth is in our grasp, then it seems a piece of idle fantasticality to preach so solemnly our duty of waiting for the bell. Indeed we *may* wait if we will—I hope you do not think that I am denying that—but if we do so, we do so at our peril as much as if we believed. In either case we *act*, taking our life in our hands. No one of us ought to issue vetoes to the other, nor should we bandy words of abuse. We ought, on the contrary, delicately and profoundly to respect one another's mental freedom: then only shall we bring about the intellectual republic; then only shall we have that spirit of inner tolerance without which all our outer tolerance is soulless, and which is empiricism's glory; then only shall we live and let live, in speculative as well as in practical things.

I began by a reference to Fitz-James Stephen; let me end by a quotation from him. "What do you think of yourself? What do you think of the world? . . . These are questions with which all must deal as it seems good to them. They are riddles of the Sphinx, and in some way or other we must deal with them. . . . In all important transactions of life we have to take a leap in the dark. . . . If we decide to leave the riddles unanswered, that is a choice; if we waver in our answer, that, too, is a choice; but whatever choice we make, we make it at our peril. If a man chooses to turn his back altogether on God and the future, no one can prevent him; no one can show beyond reasonable doubt that he is mistaken. If a man thinks otherwise and acts as he thinks, I do not see that any one can prove that *he* is mistaken. Each must act as he thinks best; and if he is wrong, so much the worse for him. We stand on a mountain pass in the midst of whirling snow and blinding mist, through which we get glimpses now and then of paths which may be deceptive. If we stand still we shall be frozen to death. If we take the wrong road we shall be dashed to pieces. We do not certainly know whether there is any right one. What must we do? 'Be strong and of a good courage.' Act for the best, hope for the best, and take what comes. . . . If death ends all, we cannot meet death better."

STUDY QUESTIONS: JAMES, *THE WILL TO BELIEVE*

1. What is a *hypothesis?*
2. What does James mean by the difference between a *life* and *dead* hypothesis?
3. Are aliveness and deadness intrinsic properties of a hypothesis? Why? What does this mean?
4. Is a particular hypothesis alive or dead for all people everywhere equally? Or does it vary among people? Why? What is the significance of this?
5. What does James mean by *option?*
6. What is a *living* option?
7. What does James make of Pascal's wager?
8. Can you decide what to believe? Why?
9. What does James mean by the "fifth wheel of the coach" example?

10. Why do scientists tend not to look for evidence of, for instance, telepathy? What does this show?
11. What does it mean to leave a question open?
12. What is a *momentous* option?

PRAGMATISM

A New Name for Some Old Ways of Thinking

In this selection from his book, *Pragmatism: A New Name for Some Old Ways of Thinking*, James provides the philosophical background for his version of pragmatism, showing its solid roots in the best European philosophical traditions going back to Kant. The example of the squirrel at the beginning has become one of the most famous illustrations of how pragmatism resolves in a new way some of the oldest sorts of puzzles in philosophy, not by giving an answer one way or the other but by redirecting the conversation into a more fruitful sort of resolution without reliance on metaphysical answers. He gives his famous version of a pragmatic theory of truth that Bertrand Russell found so philosophically unpalatable. Pay close attention to how he quite overtly wants to free pragmatism from what he regards as an empty sort of intellectualism; this, in part, is what made his work so attractive to what many European philosophers at the time regarded as an anti-intellectual bent among American intellectuals. Notice, too, how he makes room both for religion and science, even while remaining staunchly critical and rigorously analytic, a sensibility that has become par for the course in American philosophy.

WHAT PRAGMATISM MEANS

Some years, ago, being with a camping party in the mountains, I returned from a solitary ramble to find every one engaged in a ferocious metaphysical dispute. The *corpus* of the dispute was a squirrel—a live squirrel supposed to be clinging to one side of a tree trunk; while over against the tree's opposite side a human being was imagined to stand. This human witness tries to get sight of the squirrel by moving rapidly round the tree, but no matter how fast he goes, the squirrel moves as fast in the opposite direction, and always keeps the tree between himself and the man, so that never a glimpse of him is caught. The resultant metaphysical problem now is this: *does the man go round the squirrel or not?* He goes round the tree, sure enough, and the squirrel is on the tree; but does he go round the squirrel? In the unlimited leisure of the wilderness, discussion had been worn threadbare. Every one had taken sides, and was obstinate; and the numbers on both sides were even. Each side, when I appeared, therefore appealed to me to make it a majority. Mindful of the Scholastic adage that whenever you meet a contradiction you must make a distinction, I immediately sought and found one, as follows: "Which party is right," I said, "depends on what you *practically mean* by 'going round' the squirrel. If you mean passing from the north of him to the east, then to the south, then to the west, and then to the north of him again, obviously the man does go round him, for he occupies these successive positions. But if on the contrary you mean being first in front of him, then on the right of him, then behind him, then on his left, and finally in front again, it is quite as obvious that the man fails to go round him, for by the compensating movements the squirrel makes, he keeps his belly turned towards the man all the time, and his back turned away. Make the distinction, and there is no occasion for any further dispute. You are both right and both wrong according as you conceive the verb 'to go round' in one practical fashion or the other."

James, from *Pragmatism: A New Name for Some Old Ways of Thinking*; 1907.

Although one or two of the hotter disputants called my speech a shuffling evasion, saying they wanted no quibbling or Scholastic hair-splitting, but meant just plain honest English "round," the majority seemed to think that the distinction had assuaged the dispute.

I tell this trivial anecdote because it is a peculiarly simple example of what I wish now to speak of as *the pragmatic method*. The pragmatic method is primarily a method of settling metaphysical disputes that otherwise might be interminable. Is the world one or many? Fated or free? Material or spiritual? Here are notions either of which may or may not hold good of the world; and disputes over such notions are unending. The pragmatic method in such cases is to try to interpret each notion by tracing its respective practical consequences. What difference would it practically make to any one if this notion rather than that notion were true? If no practical difference whatever can be traced, then the alternatives mean practically the same thing, and all dispute is idle. Whenever a dispute is serious, we ought to be able to show some practical difference that must follow from one side or the other's being right.

A glance at the history of the idea will show you still better what pragmatism means. The term is derived from the same Greek word πράγμα, meaning action, from which our words "practice" and "practical" come. It was first introduced into philosophy by Mr. Charles Peirce in 1878. In an article entitled "How to Make Our Ideas Clear," in the *Popular Science Monthly* for January of that year, Mr. Peirce, after pointing out that our beliefs are really rules for action, said that, to develop a thought's meaning, we need only determine what conduct it is fitted to produce: that conduct is for us its sole significance. And the tangible fact at the root of all our thought-distinctions, however subtle, is that there is no one of them so fine as to consist in anything but a possible difference of practice. To attain perfect clearness in our thoughts of an object, then, we need only consider what conceivable effects of a practical kind the object may involve—what sensations we are to expect from it, and what reactions we must prepare. Our conception of these effects, whether immediate or remote, is then for us the whole of our conception

of the object, so far as that conception has positive significance at all. . . .

PRAGMATISM'S CONCEPTION OF TRUTH

When Clerk-Maxwell was a child it is written that he had a mania for having everything explained to him, and that when people put him off with vague verbal accounts of any phenomenon he would interrupt them impatiently by saying, "Yes; but I want you to tell me the *particular go* of it!" Had his question been about truth, only a pragmatist could have told him the particular go of it. I believe that our contemporary pragmatists, especially Schiller and Dewey, have given the only tenable account of this subject. It is a very ticklish subject, sending subtle roots into all kinds of crannies, and hard to treat in the sketchy way that alone befits a public lecture. But the Schiller-Dewey view of truth has been so ferociously attacked by rationalistic philosophers, and so abominably misunderstood, that here, if anywhere, is the point where a clear and simple statement should be made.

I fully expect to see the pragmatist view of truth run through the classic stages of a theory's career. First, you know, a new theory is attacked as absurd; then it is admitted to be true, but obvious and insignificant; finally it is seen to be so important that its adversaries claim that they themselves discovered it. Our doctrine of truth is at present in the first of these three stages, with symptoms of the second stage having begun in certain quarters. I wish that this lecture might help it beyond the first stage in the eyes of many of you.

Truth, as any dictionary will tell you, is a property of certain of our ideas. It means their "agreement," as falsity means their disagreement, with "reality." Pragmatists and intellectualists both accept this definition as a matter of course. They begin to quarrel only after the question is raised as to what may precisely be meant by the term "agreement," and what by the term "reality," when reality is taken as something for our ideas to agree with.

In answering these questions the pragmatists are more analytic and painstaking, the intellectualists more offhand and irreflective. The popular notion is that a true idea must copy its reality. Like other popular views, this one follows the analogy of the most usual experience. Our true ideas of sensible things do indeed copy them. Shut your eyes and think of yonder clock on the wall, and you get just such a true picture or copy of its dial. But your idea of its "works" (unless you are a clockmaker) is much less of a copy, yet it passes muster, for it in no way clashes with the reality. Even though it should shrink to the mere word "works," that word still serves you truly; and when you speak of the "time-keeping function" of the clock, or of its spring's "elasticity," it is hard to see exactly what your ideas can copy.

You perceive that there is a problem here. Where our ideas cannot copy definitely their object, what does agreement with that object mean? Some idealists seem to say that they are true whenever they are what God means that we ought to think about that object. Others hold the copy-view all through, and speak as if our ideas possessed truth just in proportion as they approach to being copies of the absolute's eternal way of thinking.

These views, you see, invite pragmatistic discussion. But the great assumption of the intellectualists is that truth means essentially an inert static relation. When you've got your true idea of anything, there's an end of the matter. You're in possession; you *know*; you have fulfilled your thinking destiny. You are where you ought to be mentally; you have obeyed your categorical imperative; and nothing more need follow on that climax of your rational destiny. Epistemologically you are in stable equilibrium.

Pragmatism, on the other hand, asks its usual question. "Grant an idea or belief to be true," it says, "what concrete difference will its being true make in any one's actual life? How will the truth be realized? What experiences will be different from those which would obtain if the belief were false? What, in short, is the truth's cash value in experiential terms?"

The moment pragmatism asks this question, it see the answer: *true ideas are those that we can assimilate, validate, corroborate and verify. False ideas are those that we can not.* That is the practical difference it makes to us to have true ideas; that, therefore, is the meaning of truth, for it is all that truth is known as.

This thesis is what I have to defend. The truth of an idea is not a stagnant property inherent in it. Truth *happens* to an idea. It *becomes* true, is *made* true by events. Its verity *is* in fact an event, a process: the process namely of its verifying itself, its veri-*fication*. Its validity is the process of its valid-*ation*.

But what do the words verification and validation themselves pragmatically mean? They again signify certain practical consequences of the verified and validated idea. It is hard to find any one phrase that characterizes these consequences better than the ordinary agreement formula—just such consequences being what we have in mind whenever we say that our ideas "agree" with reality. They lead us, namely, through the acts and other ideas which they instigate, into or up to, or towards, other parts of experience with which we feel all the while—such feeling being among our potentialities—that the original ideas remain in agreement. The connections and transitions come to us from point to point as being progressive, harmonious, satisfactory. This function of agreeable leading is what we mean by an idea's verification. . . .

The possession of true thoughts means everywhere the possession of invaluable instruments of action; and that our duty to gain truth, so far from being a blank command from out of the blue, or a "stunt" self-imposed by our intellect, can account for itself by excellent practical reasons.

The importance to human life of having true beliefs about matters of fact is a thing too notorious. We live in a world of realities that can be infinitely useful or infinitely harmful. Ideas that tell us which of them to expect count as the true ideas in all this primary sphere of verification, and the pursuit of such ideas is a primary human duty. The possession of truth, so far from being here an end in itself, is only a preliminary means towards other vital satisfactions. If I am lost in the woods and starved, and find what looks like a cow path, it is of the utmost importance that I should think of a human habitation at the end of it, for if I do so and follow it, I save myself. The true thought is useful here because the house which is its object is useful. The practical value of true ideas is thus primarily derived from the practical importance of their objects to us. Their objects are, indeed, not important at all times. I may on another occasion have no use for the house; and then my idea of it, however verifiable, will be practically irrelevant, and had better remain latent. Yet since almost any object may some day become temporarily important, the advantage of having a general stock of *extra* truths, of ideas that shall be true of merely possible situations, is obvious. We store such extra truths away in our memories, and with the overflow we fill our books of reference. Whenever such an extra truth becomes practically relevant to one of our emergencies, it passes from cold storage to do work in the world and our belief in it grows active. You can say of it then either that "it is useful because it is true" or that "it is true because it is useful." Both these phrases mean exactly the same thing, namely that here is an idea that gets fulfilled and can be verified. True is the name for whatever idea starts the verification process, useful is the name for its completed function in experience. True ideas would never have been singled out as such, would never have acquired a class name, least of all a name suggesting value, unless they had been useful from the outset in this way.

From this simple cue pragmatism gets her general notion of truth as something essentially bound up with the way in which one moment in our experience may lead us towards other moments which it will be worth while to have been led to. Primarily, and on the commonsense level, the truth of a state of mind means this function of *a leading that is worthwhile*. When a moment in our experience, of any kind whatever, inspires us with a thought that is true, that means that sooner or later we dip by that thought's guidance into the particulars of experience again and make advantageous connection with them. This is a vague enough statement, but I beg you to retain it, for it is essential.

Our experience, meanwhile, is all shot through with regularities. One bit of it can warn us to get ready for another bit, can "intend" or be "significant of" that remoter object. The object's advent is the significance's verification. Truth, in these cases, meaning nothing but eventual verification, is manifestly incompatible with waywardness on our part. Woe to him whose beliefs play fast and loose with the order which realities follow in his experience; they will lead him nowhere or else make false connections.

By "realities" or "objects" here, we mean either things of common sense, sensibly present, or else commonsense relations, such as dates, places, distances, kinds, and activities. Following our mental image of a house along the cow path, we actually come to see the house; we get the image's full verifica-

tion. *Such simply and fully verified leadings are certainly the originals and prototypes of the truth-process.* Experience offers indeed other forms of truth-process, but they are all conceivable as being primary verifications arrested, multiplied or substituted one for another.

Take, for instance, yonder object on the wall. You and I consider it to be a "clock," although no one of us has seen the hidden works that make it one. We let our notion pass for true without attempting to verify. If truths mean verification process essentially, ought we then to call such unverified truths as this abortive? No, for they form the over whelmingly large number of the truths we live by. Indirect as well as direct verifications pass muster. Where circumstantial evidence is sufficient, we can go without eye-witnessing. Just as we here assume Japan to exist without ever having been there, because it *works* to do so, every thing we know conspiring with the belief, and nothing interfering so we assume that thing to be a clock. We *use* it as a clock, regulating the length of our lecture by it. The verification of the assumption here means its leading to no frustration or contradiction. Verif*ability* of wheels and weights and pendulum is as good as verification. For one truth process completed there are a million in our lives that function in this state of nascency. They turn us *towards* direct verification; lead us into the *surroundings* of the objects they envisage; and then, if everything runs on harmoniously, we are so sure that verification is possible that we omit it, and are usually justified by all that happens.

Truth lives, in fact, for the most part on a credit system. Our thoughts and beliefs "pass," so long as nothing challenges them, just as bank-notes pass so long as nobody refuses them. But this all points to direct face-to-face verifications somewhere, without which the fabric of truth collapses like a financial system with no cash basis whatever. You accept my verification of one thing. I yours of another. We trade on each other's truth. But beliefs verified concretely by *somebody* are the posts of the whole superstructure.

Another great reason—beside economy of time—for waiving complete verification in the usual business of life is that all things exist in kinds and not singly. Our world is found once for all to have that peculiarity. So that when we have once directly verified our ideas about one specimen of a kind, we consider ourselves free to apply them to other specimens without verification. A mind that habitually discerns the kind of thing before it, and acts by the law of the kind immediately, without pausing to verify, will be a "true" mind in ninety-nine out of a hundred emergencies, proved so by its conduct fitting everything it meets, and getting no refutation.

Indirectly or only potentially verifying processes may thus be true as well as full verification-processes. They work as true processes would work, give us the same advantages, and claim our recognition for the same reasons. All this on the common-sense level of matters of fact, which we are alone considering.

But matters of fact are not our only stock in trade. *Relations among purely mental ideas* form another sphere where true and false beliefs obtain, and here beliefs are absolute, or unconditional. When they are true they bear the name either of definitions or of principles. It is either a principle or a definition that 1 and 1 make 2, that 2 and 1 make 3, and so on; that white differs less from gray than it does from black; that when the cause begins to act the effect also commences. Such propositions hold of all possible "ones," of all conceivable "whites" and "grays" and "causes." The objects here are mental objects. Their relations are perceptually obvious at a glance, and no sense-verification is necessary. Moreover, once true, always true, of those same mental objects. Truth here has an "eternal" character. If you can find a concrete thing anywhere that is "one" or "white" or "gray" or an "effect," then your principles will everlastingly apply to it. It is but a case of ascertaining the kind, and then applying the law of its kind to the particular object. You are sure to get truth if you can but name the kind rightly, for your mental relations hold good of everything of that kind without exception. If you, then, nevertheless, failed to get truth concretely, you would say that you had classed your real objects wrongly.

In this realm of mental relations, truth again is an affair of leading. We relate one abstract idea with another, framing in the end great systems of logical and mathematical truth, under the respective terms of which the sensible facts of experience eventually arrange themselves, so that our eternal truths hold good of realities also. The marriage of fact and theory is endlessly fertile. What we say is here already true in advance of special verification, *if we have subsumed our objects rightly.* Our ready-made ideal framework for all sorts of possible objects follows from the very structure of our thinking. We can no more play fast and loose with these abstract relations than we can do with our sense experiences. They coerce us; we must treat them consistently, whether or not we like the results. The rules of addition apply to our debts as rigorously as to our assets. The hundredth decimal of π, the ratio of the circumference to its diameter, is predetermined ideally now, though no one may have computed it. If we should ever need the figure in our dealings with an actual circle we should need to have it given rightly, calculated by the usual rules; for it is the same kind of truth that those rules elsewhere calculate.

Between the coercions of the sensible order and those of the ideal order, our mind is thus wedged tightly. Our ideas must agree with realities, be such realities concrete or abstract; be they facts or be they principles, under penalty of endless inconsistency and frustration.

So far, intellectualists can raise no protest. They can only say that we have barely touched the skin of the matter.

Realities mean, then, either concrete facts, or abstract kinds of thing and relations perceived intuitively between them. They furthermore and thirdly mean, as things that new ideas of ours must no less take account of, the whole body of other truths already in our possession. But what now does "agreement" with such threefold realities mean?—to use again the definition that is current.

Here it is that pragmatism and intellectualism began to part company. Primarily, no doubt, to agree means to copy, but we saw that the mere word "clock" would do instead of a mental picture of its works, and that of many realities our ideas can only be symbols and not copies. "Past time," "power," "spontaneity"—how can our mind copy such realities?

To "agree" in the widest sense with a reality *can only mean to be guided either straight up to it or into its surroundings, or to be put into such working touch with it as to handle either it or something connected with it better than if we disagreed.* Better either intellectually or practically! And often agreement will only mean that nothing contradictory from the quarter of that reality comes to interfere with the way in which our ideas guide us elsewhere. To copy a reality is, indeed, one very important way of agreeing with it, but it is far from being essential. The essential thing is the process of being guided. Any idea that helps us to *deal*, whether practically or intellectually, with either the reality or its belongings, that doesn't entangle our progress in frustrations, that *fits*, in fact, and adapts our life to the reality's whole setting, will agree sufficiently to meet the requirement. It will hold true of that reality.

Thus, *names* are just as "true" or "false" as definite mental pictures are. They set up similar verification-processes, and lead to fully equivalent practical results.

All human thinking gets discursified; we exchange ideas; we lend and borrow verifications, get them from one another by means of social intercourse. All truth thus gets verbally built out, stored up, and made available for every one. Hence, we must *talk* consistently just as we must *think* consistently for both in talk and thought we deal with kinds. Names are arbitrary, but once understood they must be kept to. We mustn't now call Abel "Cain" or Cain "Abel." If we do, we ungear ourselves from the whole book of Genesis, and from all its connections with the universe of speech and fact down to the present time. We throw ourselves out of whatever truth that entire system of speech and fact may embody.

The overwhelming majority of our true ideas admit of no direct or face-to-face verification—those of past history, for example, as of Cain and Abel. The stream of time can be remounted only verbally, or verified indirectly by the present prolongations or effects of what the past harbored. Yet if they agree with these verbalities and effects, we can know that our *ideas of the past* are true. As *true as past time itself was*, so true was Julius Caesar, so true were antediluvian monsters, all in their proper dates and settings. That past time itself was, is guaranteed by its coherence with everything that's present. True as the present *is* the past *was* also.

Agreement, thus, turns out to be essentially an affair of leading—leading that is useful because it is into quarters that contain objects that are important. True ideas lead us into useful verbal and conceptual quarters as well as directly up to useful sensible termini. They lead to consistency, stability and flowing human intercourse. They lead away from eccentricity and isolation, from foiled and barren thinking. The untrammeled flowing of the leading-process, its general freedom from clash and contradiction, passes for

its indirect verification; but all roads lead to Rome, and in the end and eventually, all true processes must lead to the face of directly verifying sensible experiences *somewhere*, which somebody's ideas have copied.

Such is the large loose way in which the pragmatist interprets the word agreement. He treats it altogether practically. He lets it cover any process of conduction from a present idea to a future terminus, provided only it run prosperously. It is only thus that "scientific" ideas, flying as they do beyond common sense, can be said to agree with their realities. It is, as I have already said, *as if* reality were made of ether, atoms or electrons, but we mustn't think so literally. The term "energy" doesn't even pretend to stand for anything "objective." It is only a way of measuring the surface of phenomena so as to string their changes on a simple formula.

Yet in the choice of these man-made formulas we can not be capricious with impunity any more than we can be capricious on the common-sense practical level. We must find a theory that will *work*; and that means something extremely difficult; for our theory must mediate between all previous truths and certain new experiences. It must derange common sense and previous belief as little as possible, and it must lead to some sensible terminus or other that can be verified exactly. To "work" means both these things; and the squeeze is so tight that there is little loose play for any hypothesis. Our theories are wedged and controlled as nothing else is. Yet sometimes alternative theoretic formulas are equally compatible with all the truths we know, and then we choose between them for subjective reasons. We choose the kind of theory to which we are already partial; we follow "elegance" or "economy." Clerk-Maxwell somewhere says it would be "poor scientific taste" to choose the more complicated of two equally well-evidenced conceptions; and you will all agree with him. Truth in science is what gives us the maximum possible sum of satisfactions, taste included, but consistency both with previous truth and with novel fact is always the most imperious claimant.

I have led you through a very sandy desert. But now, if I may be allowed so vulgar an expression, we begin to taste the milk in the cocoanut. Our rationalist critics here discharge their batteries upon us, and to reply to them will take us out from all this dryness into full sight of a momentous philosophical alternative.

Our account of truth is an account of truths in the plural, of processes of leading, realized *in rebus* [in things], and having only this quality in common, that they *pay*. They pay by guiding us into or towards some part of a system that dips at numerous points into sense-percepts, which we may copy mentally or not, but with which at any rate we are now in the kind of commerce vaguely designated as verification. Truth for us is simply a collective name for verification-processes, just as health, wealth, strength, etc., are names for other processes connected with life, and also pursued because it pays to pursue them. Truth is *made*, just as health, wealth and strength are made, in the course of experience.

Here rationalism is instantaneously up in arms against us. I can imagine a rationalist to talk as follows:

"Truth is not made," he will say; "it absolutely obtains, being a unique relation that does not wait upon any process, but shoots straight over the head of experience, and hits its reality every time. Our belief that yon thing on the wall is a clock is true already, although no one in the whole history of the world should verify it. The bare quality of standing in that transcendent relation is what makes any thought true that possesses it, whether or not there be verification. You pragmatists put the cart before the horse in making truth's being reside in verification processes. These are merely signs of its being, merely our lame ways of ascertaining after the fact, which of our ideas already has possessed the wondrous quality. The quality itself is timeless, like all essences and natures. Thoughts partake of it directly, as they partake of falsity or of irrelevancy. It can't be analyzed away into pragmatic consequences."

The whole plausibility of this rationalist tirade is due to the fact to which we have already paid so much attention. In our world, namely, abounding as it does in things of similar kinds and similarly associated, one verification serves for others of its kind, and one great use of knowing things is to be led not so much to them as to their associates, especially to human talk about them. The quality of truth, obtaining *ante rem* [before the thing], pragmatically means, then, the fact that in such a world innumerable ideas work better by their indirect or possible than by their direct and actual verification. Truth *ante rem* means only verifiability, then; or else it is a case of the stock rationalist trick of treating the *name* of a concrete phenomenal reality as an independent prior entity, and placing it behind the reality as its explanation. Professor Mach quotes somewhere an epigram of Lessing's:

> Said crafty Hans to Cousin Fritz,
> "Why is it, Cousin Fritz,
> That those ranked richest in the world,
> The most wealth do possess?"

Hans here treats the principle "wealth" as something distinct from the facts denoted by the man's being rich. It antedates them; the facts become only a sort of secondary coincidence with the rich man's essential nature.

In the case of "wealth" we all see the fallacy. We know that wealth is but a name for concrete processes that certain men's lives play a part in and not a natural excellence found in Messrs. Rockefeller, and Carnegie, but not in the rest of us.

Like wealth, health also lives *in rebus*. It is a name for processes, as digestion, circulation, sleep, etc., that go on happily, though in this instance we are more inclined to think of it as a principle and to say the man digests and sleeps so well *because* he is so healthy.

With "strength" we are, I think, more rationalistic still, and decidedly inclined to treat it as an excellence pre-existing in the man and explanatory of the herculean performances of his muscles.

With "truth" most people go over the border entirely, and treat the rationalistic account as self-evident. But really all these words in *th* are exactly similar. Truth exists *ante rem* just as much and as little as the other things do.

The scholastics, following Aristotle, made much of the distinction between habit and act. Health *in actu* means, among other things, good sleeping and digesting. But a healthy man need not always be sleeping, or always digesting, any more than a wealthy man need be always handling money, or a strong man always lifting weights. All such qualities sink to the status of "habits" between their times of exercise; and similarly truth becomes a habit of certain of our ideas and beliefs in their intervals of rest from their verifying activities. But those activities are the root of the whole matter, and the condition of their being any habit to exist in the intervals.

"The true," to put it very briefly, is only the expedient in the way of our thinking, just as "the right" is only the expedient in the way of our behaving. Expedient in almost any fashion; and expedient in the long run and on the whole of course; for what meets expediently all the experience in sight won't necessarily meet all farther experiences equally satisfactorily. Experience, as we know, has ways of *boiling over*, and making us correct our present formulas.

The "absolutely" true, meaning what no farther experience will ever alter, is that ideal vanishing point towards which we imagine that all our temporary truths will some day converge. It runs on all fours with the perfectly wise man, and with the absolutely complete experience; and, if these ideals are ever realized, they will all be realized together. Meanwhile we have to live today by what truth we can get today, and be ready tomorrow to call it falsehood. Ptolemaic astronomy, euclidean space, aristotelian logic, scholastic metaphysics, were expedient for centuries, but human experience has boiled over those limits, and we now call these things only relatively true, or true within those borders of experience. "Absolutely" they are false; for we know that those limits were casual, and might have been transcended by past theorists just as they are by present thinkers.

When new experiences lead to retrospective judgments, using the past tense, what these judgments utter *was* true, even though no past thinker had been led there. We live forwards, a Danish thinker has said, but we understand backwards. The present sheds a backward light on the world's previous processes. They may have been truth processes for the actors in them. They are not so for one who knows the later revelations of the story.

This regulative notion of a potential better truth to be established later, possibly to be established some day absolutely, and having powers of retroactive legislation, turns its face, like all pragmatist notions, towards concreteness of fact, and towards the future. Like the halftruths, the absolute truth will have to be *made*, made as a relation incidental to the growth of a mass of verification experience to which the half-true ideas are all along contributing their quota.

I have already insisted on the fact that truth is made largely out of previous truths. Men's beliefs at any time are so much experience *funded*. But the beliefs are themselves parts of the sum total of the world's experience, and become matter, therefore, for the next day's funding operations. So far as reality means experienceable reality, both it and the truths men gain about it are everlastingly in process of mutation—mutation towards a definite goal, it may be—but still mutation.

Mathematicians can solve problems with two variables. On the Newtonian theory, for instance, acceleration varies with distance, but distance also varies with acceleration. In the realm of truth-processes facts come independently and determine our beliefs provisionally. But these beliefs make us act, and as fast as they do so, they bring into sight or into existence new facts which redetermine the beliefs accordingly. So the whole coil and ball of truth, as it rolls up, is the product of a double influence. Truths emerge from facts; but they dip forward into facts again and add to them; which facts again create or reveal new truth (the word is indifferent) and so on indefinitely. The "facts" themselves meanwhile are not *true*. They simply *are*. Truth is the function of the beliefs that start and terminate among them.

The case is like a snowball's growth, due as it is to the distribution of the snow on the one hand, and to the successive pushes of the boys on the other, with these factors codetermining each other incessantly.

The most fateful point of difference between being a rationalist and being a pragmatist is now fully in sight. Experience is in mutation, and our psychological ascertainments of truth are in mutation—so much rationalism will allow; but never that either reality itself or truth itself is mutable. Reality stands complete and ready-made from all eternity, rationalism insists, and the agreement of our ideas with it is that unique unanalyzable virtue in them of which she has already told us. As that intrinsic excellence, their truth has nothing to do with our experiences. It adds nothing to the content of experience. It makes no difference to reality itself; it is supervenient, inert, static, a reflection merely. It doesn't *exist*, it *holds* or *obtains*, it belongs to another dimension from that of either facts or fact-relations, belongs, in short, to the epistemological dimension—and with that big word rationalism closes the discussion.

Thus, just as pragmatism faces forward to the future, so does rationalism here again face backward to a past eternity. True to her inveterate habit, rationalism reverts to "principles," and thinks that when an abstraction once is named, we own an oracular solution.

The tremendous pregnancy in the way of consequences for life of this radical difference of outlook will only become apparent in my later lectures. I wish meanwhile to close this lecture by showing that rationalism's sublimity does not save it from inanity.

When, namely, you ask rationalists, instead of accusing pragmatism of desecrating the notion of truth, to define it themselves by saying exactly what *they* understand by it, the only positive attempts I can think of are these two:

1. "Truth is the system of propositions which have an unconditional claim to be recognized as valid."
2. Truth is a name for all those judgments which we find ourselves under obligation to make by a kind of imperative duty.

The first thing that strikes one in such definitions is their unutterable triviality. They are absolutely true, of course, but absolutely insignificant until you handle them pragmatically. What do you mean by "claim" here, and what do you mean by "duty"? As summary names for the concrete reasons why thinking in true ways is overwhelmingly expedient and good for mortal men, it is all right to talk of claims on reality's part to be agreed with and of obligations on our part to agree. We feel both the claims and the obligations, and we feel them for just those reasons.

But the rationalists who talk of claim and obligation *expressly say that they have nothing to do with our practical interests or personal reasons.* Our reasons for agreeing are psychological facts, they say, relative to each thinker, and to the accidents of his life. They are his evidence merely, they are no part of the life of truth itself. That life transacts itself in a purely logical or epistemological, as distinguished from a psychological, dimension, and its claims antedate and exceed all personal motivations whatsoever. Though neither man nor God should ever ascertain truth, the word would still have to be defined as that which *ought* to be ascertained and recognized.

There never was a more exquisite example of an idea abstracted from the concretes of experience and then used to oppose and negate what it was abstracted from.

Philosophy and common life abound in similar instances. The "sentimentalist fallacy" is to shed tears over abstract justice and generosity, beauty, etc., and never to know these qualities when you meet them in the street, because the circumstances make them vulgar. Thus I read in the privately printed biography of an eminently rationalistic mind: "It was strange that with such admiration for beauty in the abstract, my brother had no enthusiasm for fine architecture, for beautiful painting, or for flowers." And in almost the last philosophic work I have read, I find such passages as the following: "justice is ideal, solely ideal. Reason conceives that it ought to exist, but experience shows that it can not. . . . Truth, which ought to be, can not be. . . . Reason is deformed by experience. As soon as reason enters experience it becomes contrary to reason."

The rationalist's fallacy here is exactly like the sentimentalist's. Both extract a quality from the muddy particulars of experience, and find it so pure when extracted that they contrast it with each and all its muddy instances as an opposite and higher nature. All the while it is *their* nature. It is the nature of truths to be validated, verified. It pays for our ideas to be validated. Our obligation to seek truth is part of our general obligation to do what pays. The payments true ideas bring are the sole why of our duty to follow them. Identical whys exist in the case of wealth and health.

Truth makes no other kind of claim and imposes no other kind of ought than health and wealth do. All these claims are conditional; the concrete benefits we gain are what we mean by calling the pursuit a duty. In the case of truth, untrue beliefs work as perniciously in the long run as true beliefs work beneficially. Talking abstractly, the quality "true" may thus be said to grow absolutely precious and the quality "untrue" absolutely damnable: the one may be called good, the other bad, unconditionally. We ought to think the true, we ought to shun the false, imperatively.

But if we treat all this abstraction literally and oppose it to its mother soil in experience, see what a preposterous position we work ourselves into.

We can not then take a step forward in our actual thinking. When shall I acknowledge this truth and when that? Shall the acknowledgment be loud? or silent? If sometimes loud, sometimes silent, which *now?* When may a truth go into cold storage in the encyclopedia? And when shall it come out for battle? Must I constantly be repeating the truth "twice two are four" because of its eternal claim on recognition? or is it sometimes irrelevant? Must my thoughts dwell night and day on my personal sins and blemishes, because I truly have them? Or may I sink and ignore them in order to be a decent social unit, and not a mass of morbid melancholy and apology?

It is quite evident that our obligation to acknowledge truth, so far from being unconditional, is tremendously conditioned. Truth with a big T, and in the singular, claims abstractly to be recognized, of course; but concrete truths in the plural need be recognized only when their recognition is expedient. A truth must always be preferred to a falsehood when both relate to the situation; but when neither does, truth is as little of a duty as falsehood. If you ask me what o'clock it is and I tell you that I live at 95 Irving Street, my answer may indeed be true, but you don't see why it is my duty to give it. A false address would be as much to the purpose.

With this admission that there are conditions that limit the application of the abstract imperative, *the pragmatistic treatment of truth sweeps back upon us in its fullness:* Our duty to agree with reality is seen to be grounded in a perfect jungle of concrete expediencies.

When Berkeley had explained what people meant by matter, people thought that he denied matter's existence. When Schiller and Dewey now explain what people mean by truth, they are accused of denying *its* existence. These pragmatists destroy all objective standards, critics say, and put foolishness and wisdom on one level. A favorite formula for describing Mr. Schiller's doctrines and mine is that we are persons who think that by saying whatever you find it pleasant to say and calling it truth you fulfil every pragmatistic requirement.

I leave it to you to judge whether this be not an impudent slander. Pent in, as the pragmatist more than any one else sees himself to be, between the whole body of funded truths squeezed from the past and the coercions of the world of sense about him, who so well as he feels the immense pressure of objective control under which our minds perform their operations? If any one imagines that this law is lax, let him keep its commandment one day, says

Emerson. We have heard much of late of the uses of the imagination in science. It is high time to urge the use of a little imagination in philosophy. The unwillingness of some of our critics to read any but the silliest of possible meanings into our statements is as discreditable to their imaginations as anything I know in recent philosophic history. Schiller says the true is that which "works." Thereupon he is treated as one who limits verification to the lowest material utilities. Dewey says truth is what gives "satisfaction." He is treated as one who believes in calling everything true which, if it were true, would be pleasant.

Our critics certainly need more imagination of realities. I have honestly tried to stretch my own imagination and to read the best possible meaning into the rationalist conception, but I have to confess that it still completely baffles me. The notion of a reality calling on us to "agree" with it, and that for no reasons, but simply because its claim is "unconditional" or "transcendent," is one that I can make neither head nor tail of. I try to imagine myself as the sole reality in the world, and then to imagine what more I would "claim" if I were allowed to. If you suggest the possibility of my claiming that a mind should come into being from out of the void inane and stand and *copy* me, I can indeed imagine what the copying might mean, but I can conjure up no motive. What good it would do me to be copied, or what good it would do that mind to copy me, if further consequences are expressly and in principle ruled out as motives for the claim (as they are by our rationalist authorities) I can not fathom. When the Irishman's admirers ran him along to the place of banquet in a sedan chair with no bottom, he said, "faith, if it wasn't for the honor of the thing, I might as well have come on foot." So here: but for the honor of the thing, I might as well have remained uncopied. Copying is one genuine mode of knowing (which for some strange reason our contemporary transcendentalists seem to be tumbling over each other to repudiate); but when we get beyond copying, and fall back on unnamed forms of agreeing that are expressly denied to be either copyings or leadings or fittings, or any other processes pragmatically definable, the *what* of the "agreement" claimed becomes as unintelligible as the why of it. Neither content nor motive can be imagined for it. It is an absolutely meaningless abstraction.

Surely in this field of truth it is the pragmatists and not the rationalists who are the more genuine defenders of the universe's rationality. . . .

I am well aware how odd it must seem to some of you to hear me say that an idea is "true" so long as to believe it is profitable to our lives. That it is *good*, for as much as it profits, you will gladly admit. If what we do by its aid is good, you will allow the idea itself to be good in so far forth, for we are the better for possessing it. But is it not a strange misuse of the word "truth," you will say, to call ideas also "true" for this reason? . . .

. . . Let me now say only this, that truth is *one species of good*, and not, as is usually supposed, a category distinct from good, and coordinate with it. *The true is the name of whatever proves itself to be good in the way of belief, and good, too, for definite, assignable reasons.* Surely you must admit this, that if there were *no* good for life in true ideas, or if the knowledge of them were positively disadvantageous and false ideas the only useful ones, then the current notion that truth is divine and precious, and its pursuit a duty, could never have grown up or become a dogma. In a world like that, our duty would be to *shun* truth, rather. But in this world, just as certain foods are not only agreeable to our taste, but good for our teeth, our stomach, and our tissues; so certain ideas are not only agreeable to think about, or agreeable as supporting other ideas that we are fond of, but they are also helpful in life's practical struggles. If there be any life that it is really better we should lead, and if there be any idea which, if believed in, would help us to lead that life, then it would be really *better for us* to believe in that idea, *unless, indeed, belief in it incidentally clashed with other greater vital benefits.*

"What would be better for us to believe!" This sounds very like a definition of truth. It comes very near to saying "what we *ought* to believe"; and in *that* definition none of you would find any oddity. Ought we ever not to believe what it is *better for us* to believe? And can we then keep the notion of what is better for us, and what is true for us, permanently apart?

Pragmatism says no, and I fully agree with her. Probably you also agree, so far as the abstract statement goes, but with a suspicion that if we practically did believe everything that made for good in our own personal lives, we should be found indulging all kinds of fancies about this world's affairs, and all kinds of sentimental superstitions about a world hereafter. Your suspicion here is undoubtedly well founded, and it is evident that something happens when you pass from the abstract to the concrete that complicates the situation.

I said just now that what is better for us to believe is true *unless the belief incidentally clashes with some other vital benefit.* Now in real life what vital benefits is any particular belief of ours most liable to clash with? What indeed except the vital benefits yielded by *other beliefs* when these prove incompatible with the first ones? In other words, the greatest enemy of any one of our truths may be the rest of our truths. Truths have once for all this desperate instinct of self-preservation and of desire to extinguish whatever contradicts them.

STUDY QUESTIONS: JAMES, PRAGMATISM

1. What is the point of the squirrel example? What is it supposed to show?
2. How does James define *the pragmatic method*? What is its aim? How is this aim achieved?
3. What is the point of the Clerk-Maxwell childhood example?
4. What does James mean by saying that truth is something that *happens* to an idea?
5. What does James mean by saying that thoughts are instruments of action?
6. In what does the verification of an idea consist?
7. How are "realities," "objects," and "things of common sense," related?
8. What does James mean that truth lives, for the most part, on a "credit system?"
9. What is the point of the Cain/Abel example?
10. Do our true ideas admit of direct verification? Why? What does this show?
11. What does James mean by truth *ante rem?*
12. What is the "sentimentalist fallacy?"
13. What is the rationalist fallacy? How is it related to the sentimentalist?
14. What is the point of James' comparison of Berkeley, Schiller, and Dewey?

DOES CONSCIOUSNESS EXIST?

James' "Does 'Consciousness Exist?" presents a case study application of his version of a radical empiricist epistemology combined with the metaphysics of neutral monism. The subject matter is consciousness, of which he gives a detailed analysis. His conclusion, which any conscious reader should find startling, is that consciousness does not exist. What does exist, he calls "pure experience." This aspect of James' philosophy is presented as a natural, pragmatically inspired development of earlier philosophies of mind. It fore-shadows subsequent developments in twentieth-century physics and mathematics pio-neered by Einstein, Russell, and Bohr, wherein mind is regarded not as a passive observer but, along Kantian and Leibnizian lines, as an important and necessary aspect of the structuring of reality. In James' view, there is no Kantian "thing-in-itself" existing independently of the mind. Bertrand Russell had this to say about the article:

> Twenty-three years have elapsed since William James startled the world with his article entitled, "Does 'Consciousness' Exist?" In this article . . . he set out the view that "there is only one primal stuff or material in the world," and that the word "consciousness" stands for a function, not an entity. He holds that there are "thoughts," which perform the function of "knowing," but that thoughts are not made of any different "stuff" from that of which material objects are made. He thus laid the foundations for what is called "neutral monism," a view advocated by most American realists.

Many philosophers at the turn of the century became neutral monists, including Bertrand Russell, who regarded James' solution of the mind/body problem, according to which mind and matter are different aspects of what neither mental nor physical, as one of the most important philosophical innovations of the time. James' view of the "world of pure experience" is an attempt to go beyond the traditional philosophical categories of appearance versus reality. Notice, however, that in denying the existence of consciousness, which as he himself says is apt to strike you as absurd, he is not denying the existence of thoughts. Rather, he is claiming that the word consciousness does not denote (it does not refer to) any entity. Thus, consciousness is not a *thing* (i.e., not a substance) but a *function*, an act of knowing. The field of knowledge is thus active and yet impersonal: "Consciousness as such is entirely impersonal," is how he puts it in the article. He explains how the traditional separation between consciousness and content is bogus: the objects of perceptual experience are not *representations* of noumenal things in themselves but *presentations*. Consciousness as such is thus an external relation and therefore not subjective, as it had previously always been conceived.

"Thoughts" and "things" are names for two sorts of object, which common sense will always find contrasted and will always practically oppose to each other. Philosophy, reflecting on the contrast, has varied in the past in her explanations of it, and may be expected to vary in the future. At first, "spirit and matter," "soul and body," stood for a pair of equivalent substances quite on a par in weight and interest. But one day Kant undermined the soul and brought in the transcendental ego, and ever since then the bipolar relation has been very much off its balance. The transcendental ego seems nowadays in rationalist quarters to stand for everything, in empiricist quarters for almost nothing. . . .

James, from the *Journal of Philosophy, Psychology and Scientific Methods*, vol. I, no. 18, September, 1904.

[T]he spiritual principle attenuates itself to a thoroughly ghostly condition, being only a name for the fact that the "content" of experience *is known*. It loses personal form and activity—these passing over to the content—and becomes a bare *Bewusstheit* [consciousness] or *Bewusstsein überhaupt* [consciousness in general], of which in its own right absolutely nothing can be said.

I believe that "consciousness," when once it has evaporated to this estate of pure diaphaneity, is on the point of disappearing altogether. It is the name of a nonentity, and has no right to a place among first principles. Those who still cling to it are clinging to a mere echo, the faint rumor left behind by the disappearing "soul" upon the air of philosophy.... For twenty years past I have mistrusted "consciousness" as an entity; for seven or eight years past I have suggested its non-existence to my students, and tried to give them its pragmatic equivalent in realities of experience. It seems to me that the hour is ripe for it to be openly and universally discarded.

To deny plumply that "consciousness" exists seems so absurd on the face of it—for undeniably "thoughts" do exist—that I fear some readers will follow me no farther. Let me then immediately explain that I mean only to deny that the word stands for an entity, but to insist most emphatically that it does stand for a function. There is, I mean, no aboriginal stuff or quality of being, contrasted with that of which material objects are made, out of which our thoughts of them are made; but there is a function in experience which thoughts perform, and for the performance of which this quality of being is invoked. That function is *knowing*. "Consciousness" of supposed necessary to explain the fact that things not only are, but get reported, are known. Whoever blots out the notion of consciousness from his list of first principles must still provide in some way for that function's being carried on.

1.

My thesis is that if we start with the supposition that there is only one primal stuff or material in the world, a stuff of which everything is composed, and if we call that stuff "pure experience," then knowing can easily be explained as a particular sort of relation towards one another into which portions of pure experience may enter. The relation itself is a part of pure experience; one of its "terms" becomes the subject or bearer of the knowledge, the knower, the other becomes the object known. This will need much explanation before it can be understood. The best way to get it understood is to contrast it with the alternative view; and for that we may take the recentest alternative, that in which the evaporation of the definite soul-substance has proceeded as far as it can go without being yet complete. If neo-Kantism has expelled earlier forms of dualism, we shall have expelled all forms if we are able to expel neo-Kantism in its turn.

For the thinkers I call neo-Kantian, the word consciousness today does no more than signalize the fact that experience is indefeasibly dualistic in structure. It means that not subject, not object, but object-plus-subject is the minimum that can actually be. The subject-object distinction meanwhile is entirely different from that between mind and matter, from that between body and soul. Souls were detachable, had separate destinies; things could happen to them. To consciousness as such nothing can happen, for, timeless itself, it is only a witness of happenings in time, in which it plays no part. It is, in a word, but the logical correlative of "content" in an Experience of which the peculiarity is *that fact comes to light* in it, that *awareness of content* takes place. Consciousness as such is entirely impersonal—"self" and its activities belong to the content. To say that I am self-conscious, or conscious of putting forth volition, means only that certain contents, for which "self" and "effort of will" are the names are not without witness as they occur.

Thus, for these belated drinkers at the Kantian springs, we should have to admit consciousness as an, "epistemological" necessity, even if we had no direct evidence of its being there.

But in addition to this, we are supposed by almost every one to have an immediate consciousness of consciousness itself. When the world of outer facts ceases to be materially present, and we merely recall it in memory, or fancy it, the consciousness is believed to stand out and to be felt as a kind of impalpable inner flowing, which, once known in this sort of experience, may equally be detected in presentations of the outer world. . . .

This supposes that the consciousness is one element, moment, factor—call it what you like—of an experience of essentially dualistic inner constitution, from which, if you abstract the content, the consciousness will remain revealed to its own eye. Experience, at this rate, would be much like a paint of which the world pictures were made. Paint has a dual constitution, involving, as it does, a menstruum (oil, size or what not) and a mass of content in the form of pigment suspended therein. We can get the pure menstruum by letting the pigment settle, and the pure pigment by pouring off the size or oil. We operate here by physical subtraction; and the usual view is, that by mental subtraction we can separate the two factors of experience in an analogous way—not isolating them entirely, but distinguishing them enough to know that they are two.

2.

Now my contention is exactly the reverse of this. *Experience, I believe, has no such inner duplicity; and the separation of it into consciousness and content comes, not by way of subtraction, but by way of addition*—the addition, to a given concrete piece of it, of other sets of experiences, in connection with which severally its use or function may be of two different kinds.

The paint will also serve here as an illustration. In a pot in a paint shop, along with other paints, it serves in its entirety as so much saleable matter. Spread on a canvas, with other paints around it, it represents, on the contrary, a feature in a picture and performs a spiritual function. Just so, I maintain, does a given undivided portion of experience, taken in one context of associates, play the part of a knower, of a state of mind, of "consciousness"; while in a different context the same undivided bit of experience plays the part of a thing known, of an objective "content." In a word, in one group it figures as a thought, in another group as a thing. And, since it can figure in both groups simultaneously we have every right to speak of it as subjective and objective both at once. The dualism connoted by such double-barreled terms as "experience," "phenomenon," "datum," "*Vorfindung*"—terms which, in philosophy at any rate, tend more and more to replace the single-barreled terms of "thought" and "thing"—that dualism, I say, is still preserved in this account, but reinterpreted, so that, instead of being mysterious and elusive, it becomes verifiable and concrete. It is an affair of relations, it falls outside, not inside, the single experience considered, and can always be particularized and defined.

The entering wedge for this more concrete way of understanding the dualism was fashioned by Locke when he made the word "idea" stand indifferently for thing and thought, and by Berkeley when he said that what common sense means by realities is exactly what the philosopher means by ideas. Neither Locke nor Berkeley thought his truth out into perfect clearness, but it seems to me that the conception I am defending does little more than consistently carry out the "pragmatic" method which they were the first to use.

If the reader will take his own experiences, he will see what I mean. Let him begin with a perceptual experience, the "presentation," so called, of a physical object, his actual field of vision, the room he sits in, with the book he is reading as its centre; and let him for the present treat this complex object in the commonsense way as being "really" what it seems to be, namely, a collection of physical things cut out from an environing world of other physical things with which these physical things have actual or potential relations. Now at the same time it is just *those self-same things* which his mind, as we say, perceives; and the whole philosophy of perception from Democtitus's time downwards has been just one long wrangle over the paradox that what is evidently one reality should be in two places at once, both in outer space and in a person's mind! "Representative" theories of perception avoid the logical paradox, but on the other hand they violate the reader's sense of life, which knows no intervening mental image but seems to see the room and the book immediately just as they physically exist.

The puzzle of how the one identical room can be in two places is at bottom just the puzzle of how one identical point can be on two lines. It can, if it be situated at their intersection; and similarly, if the "pure experience" of the room were a place of intersection of two processes, which connected it with different groups of associates, respectively, it could be counted twice over, as belonging to either group, and spoken of loosely as existing in two places, although it would remain all the time a numerically single thing.

Well, the experience is a member of diverse processes that can be followed away from it along entirely different lines. The one self-identical thing has so many relations to the rest of experience that you can take it in disparate systems of association, and treat it as belonging with opposite contexts. In one of these contexts it is your "field of consciousness"; in another it is "the room in which you sit," and it enters both contexts in its wholeness, giving no pretext for being said to attach itself to consciousness by one of its parts or aspects, and to outer reality by another. What are the two processes, now, into which the room-experience simultaneously enters in this way?

One of them is the reader's personal biography, the other is the history of the house of which the room is part. The presentation, the experience, the *that* in short (for until we have decided *what* it is it must be a mere *that*) is the last term of a train of sensations, emotions, decisions, movements, classifications, expectations, etc., ending in the present, and the first term of a series of similar 'inner' operations extending into the future, on the reader's part. On the other hand, the very same *that* is the *terminus ad quem* of a lot of previous physical operations, carpentering, papering, furnishing, warming, etc., and the *terminus a quo* of a lot of future ones, in which it will be concerned when undergoing the destiny of a physical room. The physical and the mental operations form curiously incompatible groups. As a room, the experience has occupied that spot and had that environment for thirty years. As your field of consciousness it may never have existed until now. As a room, attention will go on to discover endless new details in it. As your mental state merely, few new ones will emerge under attention's eye. As a room, it will take an earthquake, or a gang of men, and in any case a certain amount of time, to destroy it. As your subjective state, the closing of your eyes, or any instantaneous play of your fancy will suffice. In the real world, fire will consume it. In your mind, you can let fire play over it without effect. As an outer object you must pay so much a month to inhabit it. As an inner content, you may occupy it for any length of time rent-free. If, in short, you follow it in the mental direction, taking it along with events of personal biography solely, all sorts of things are true of it which are false, and false of it which are true if you treat it as a real thing experienced, follow it in the physical direction, and relate it to associates in the outer world.

3.

So far, all seems plain sailing, but my thesis will probably grow less plausible to the reader when I pass from percepts to concepts, or from the case of things presented to that of things remote. I believe, nevertheless, that here also the same law holds good. If we take conceptual manifolds, or memories, or fancies, they also are in their first intention mere bits of pure experience, and, as such, are single *thats* which act in one context as objects, and in another context figure as mental states. By taking them in their first intention, I mean ignoring their relation to possible perceptual experiences with which they may be connected, which they may lead to and terminate in, and which then they may be supposed to "represent." Taking them in this way first, we confine the problem to a world merely "thought of" and not directly felt or seen. This world, just like the world of percepts, comes to us at first as a chaos of experiences, but lines of order soon get traced. We find that any bit of it which we may cut out as an example is connected with distinct groups of associates, just as our perceptual experiences are, that these associates link themselves with it by different relations, and that one forms the inner history of a person, while the other acts as an impersonal "objective" world, either spatial and temporal, or else merely logical or mathematical, or otherwise "ideal."

The first obstacle on the part of the reader to seeing that these non-perceptual experiences have objectivity as well as subjectivity will probably be due to the intrusion into his mind of *percepts*, that third group of associates with which the non-perceptual experiences have relations, and which, as a whole, they "represent," standing to them as thoughts to things. This important function of the non-perceptual experiences complicates the question and confuses it; for, so used are we to treat percepts as the sole genuine realities that, unless we keep them out of the discussion, we tend altogether to overlook the objectivity that lies in non-perceptual experiences by themselves. We treat them, "knowing" percepts as they do, as through and through subjective, and say that they are wholly constituted of the stuff called consciousness, using this term now for a kind of entity, after the fashion which I am seeking to refute.

Abstracting, then, from percepts altogether, what I maintain is, that any single non-perceptual experience tends to get counted twice over, just as a perceptual experience does, figuring in one context as an object or field of objects, in another as a state of mind: and all this without the least internal self-diremption on its own part into consciousness and content. It is all consciousness in one taking; and, in the other, all content. . . .

And yet, just as the seen room (to go back to our late example) is *also* a field of consciousness, so the conceived or recollected room is *also* a state of mind; and the doubling up of the experience has in both cases similar grounds.

The room thought-of, namely, has many thought-of couplings with many thought-of things. Some of couplings are inconstant, others are stable. In the reader's personal history the room occupies a single date—he saw it only once perhaps, a year ago. Of the house's history, on the other hand, it forms a permanent ingredient. Some couplings have the curious stubbornness, to borrow Royce's term of fact; others show the fluidity of fancy—we let them come and go as we please. Grouped with the rest of its house, with the name of its town, of its owner, builder, value, decorative plan, the room maintains a definite foothold, to which, if we try to loosen it, it tends to return, and to reassert itself with force. With these associates, in a word, it coheres, while to other houses, other towns, other owners, etc., it shows no tendency to cohere at all. The two collections, first of its cohesive, and, second, of its loose associates, inevitably come to be contrasted. We call the first collection the system of external realities, in the midst of which the room, as "real," exists; the other we call the stream of our internal thinking, in which, as a "mental image," it for a moment floats. The room thus again gets counted twice over. It plays two different roles, being thought-of-an-object, and the object-thought-of, both in one; and all this without paradox or mystery, just as the same material thing may be both low and high, or small and great, or bad and good, because of its relations to opposite parts of an environing world.

As "subjective" we say that the experience represents; as "objective" it is represented. What represents and what is represented is here numerically the same; but we must remember that no dualism of being represented and representing resides in the experience *per se*. In its pure state, or when isolated, there is no self-splitting of it into consciousness and what the consciousness is "of." Its subjectivity and objectivity are functional attributes solely, realized only when the experience is "taken," that is, talked of, twice, considered along with its two differing contexts respectively, by a new retrospective experience, of which that whole past complication now forms the fresh content.

The instant field of the present is at all times what I call the "pure" experience. It is only virtually or potentially either object or subject as yet. For the time being, it is plain, unqualified actuality, or existence, a simple *that*. In this *naïf* immediacy it is of course *valid*; it is *there*, we *act* upon it; and the doubling of it in retrospection into a state of mind and a reality intended thereby, is just one of the acts. The "state of mind," first treated explicitly as such in retrospection, will stand corrected or confirmed, and the retrospective experience in its turn will get a similar treatment; but the immediate experience in its passing is always "truth," practical truth, *something to act on*, at its own movement. If the world were then and there to go out like a candle, it would remain truth absolute and objective, for it would be "the last word," would have no critic, and no one would ever oppose the thought in it to the reality intended.

I think I may now claim to have made my thesis clear. Consciousness connotes a kind of external relation, and does not denote a special stuff or way of being. *The peculiarity of our experiences, that they not only are, but are known, which their 'conscious' quality is invoked to explain, is better explained by their relations—these relations themselves being experiences—to one another.*

4.

Were I now to go on to treat of the knowing of perceptual by conceptual experiences, it would again prove to be an affair of external relations. One experience would be the knower, the other the reality known; and I could perfectly well define, without the notion of 'consciousness,' what the knowing actually and practically amounts to—leading-towards, namely, and terminating in percepts, through a series of transitional experiences which the world supplies. But I will not treat of this, space being insufficient. I will rather consider a few objections that are sure to be urged against the entire theory as it stands.

5.

First of all, this will be asked: "If experience has not 'conscious' existence, if it be not partly made of 'consciousness,' of what then is it made? Matter we know, and thought we know, and conscious content we know, but neutral and simple 'pure experience' is something we know not at all. Say *what* it consists of—for it must consist of something—or be willing to give it up!"

To this challenge the reply is easy. Although for fluency's sake I myself spoke early in this article of a stuff of pure experience, I have now to say that there is no *general* stuff of which experience at large is made. There are as many stuffs as there are 'natures' in the things experienced. If you ask what any one bit of pure experience is made of, the answer is always the same: "It is made of *that*, of just what appears, of space, of intensity, of flatness, brownness, heaviness, or what not." Shadworth Hodgson's analysis here leaves nothing to be desired. Experience is only a collective name for all these sensible natures, and save for time and space (and, if you like, for 'being') there appears no universal element of which all things are made.

6.

The next objection is more formidable, in fact it sounds quite crushing when one hears it first.

"If it be the self-same piece of pure experience, taken twice over, that serves now as thought and now as thing," so the objection runs, "how comes it that its attributes should differ so fundamentally in the two takings. As thing, the experience is extended; as thought, it occupies no space or place. As thing, it is red, hard, heavy; but who ever heard of a red, hard, or heavy thought? Yet even now you said that an experience is made of just what appears, and what appears is just such adjectives. How can the one experience in its thing-function be made of them, consist of them, carry them as its own attributes, while in its thought-func-

tion it disowns them and attributes them elsewhere. There is a self-contradiction here from which the radical dualism of thought and thing is the only truth that can save us. Only if the thought is one kind of being can the adjectives exist in it 'intentionally' (to use the scholastic term); only if the thing is another kind, can they exist in it constitutively and energetically. No simple subject can take the same adjectives and at one time be qualified by it, and at another time be merely 'of' it, as of something only meant or known."

The solution insisted on by this objector, like many other commonsense solutions, grows the less satisfactory the more one turns it in one's mind. To begin with, *are* thought and thing as heterogeneous as is commonly said?

No one denies that they have some categories in common. Their relations to time are identical. Both, moreover, may have parts (for psychologists in general treat thoughts as having them); and both may be complex or simple. Both are of kinds, can be compared, added and subtracted and arranged in serial orders. All sorts of adjectives qualify our thoughts which appear in incompatible with consciousness, being as such a bare diaphaneity. For instance, they are natural and easy, or laborious. They are beautiful, happy, intense, interesting, wise idiotic, focal, marginal, insipid, confused, vague, precise, rational, casual, general, particular, and many things besides. Moreover, the chapters on 'Perception' in the psychology books are full of facts that make for the essential homogeneity of thought with thing. How, if 'subject' and 'object' were separated 'by the whole diameter of being,' and had no attributes in common, could it be so hard to tell, in a presented and recognized material object, what part comes in through the sense organs and what part comes 'out of one's own head'? Sensations and apperceptive ideas fuse here so intimately that you can no more tell where one begins and the other ends, than you can tell, in those cunning circular panoramas that have lately been exhibited, where the real foreground and the painted canvas join together.[1]

Descartes for the first time defined thought as the absolutely unextended, and later philosophers have

---

[1]Spencer's proof of his 'Transfigured Realism' (his doctrine that there is an absolutely non-mental reality) comes to mind as a splendid instance of the impossibility of establishing radical heterogeneity between thought and thing. All his painfully accumulated points of difference run gradually into their opposites, and are full of exceptions. [Cf. Spencer: *Principles of Psychology*, part VII, ch. XIX.]

accepted the description as correct. But what possible meaning has it to say that, when we think of a foot-rule or a square yard, extension is not attributable to our thought? Of every extended object the *adequate* mental picture must have all the extension of the object itself. The difference between objective and subjective extension is one of relation to a context solely. In the mind the various extents maintain no necessarily stubborn order relatively to each other, while in the physical world they bound each other stably, and, added together, make the great envelop-ing unit which we believe in and call real space. As 'outer,' they carry themselves adversely, so to speak, to one another, exclude one another and maintain their distances; while, as 'inner,' their order is loose, and they form a *durcheinander* in which unity is lost.[1] But to argue from this that inner experience is absolutely inextensive seems to me little short of absurd. The two worlds differ, not by the presence or absence of extension, but by the relations of the extensions which in both worlds exist.

Does not this case of extension now put us on the track of truth in the case of other qualities? It does; and I am surprised that the facts should not have been noticed long ago. Why, for example, do we call a fire hot, and water wet, and yet refuse to say that our mental state, when it is 'of' these objects, is either wet or hot? 'Intentionally,' at any rate, and when the mental state is a vivid image, hotness and wetness are in it just as much as they are in the physical experi-ence. The reason is this, that, as the general chaos of all our experiences gets sifted, we find that there are some fires that will always burn sticks and always warm our bodies, and that there are some waters that will always put out fires; while there are other fires and waters that will not act at all. The general group of experiences that *act*, that do not only possess their natures intrinsically, but wear them adjectively and energetically, turning them against one another, comes inevitably to be contrasted with the group whose members, having identically the same natures, fail to manifest them in the 'energetic' way. I make for myself now an experience of blazing fire; I place it near my body; but it does not warm me in the least. I lay a stick upon it, and the stick either burns or remains green, as I please. I call up water, and pour it on the fire, and absolutely no difference ensues. I account for all such facts by calling this whole train of experiences unreal, a mental train. Mental fire is what won't burn real sticks; mental water is what won't necessarily (though of course it may) put out even a mental fire. Mental knives may be sharp, but they won't cut real wood. Mental triangles are pointed, but their points won't wound. With 'real' objects, on the contrary, consequences always accrue; and thus the real experiences get sifted from the men-tal ones, the things from our thoughts of them, fanci-ful or true, and precipitated together as the stable part of the whole experience-chaos, under the name of the physical world. Of this our perceptual experiences are the nucleus, they being the originally *strong* experi-ences. We add a lot of conceptual experiences to them, making these strong also in imagination, and building out the remoter parts of the physical world by their means; and around this core of reality the world of laxly connected fancies and mere rhapsodi-cal objects floats like a bank of clouds. In the clouds, all sorts of rules are violated which in the core are kept. *Extensions there can be indefinitely located; motion there obeys no Newton's laws.*

7.

There is a peculiar class of experiences to which, whether we take them as subjective or as objective, we *assign* their several natures as attributes, because in both contexts they affect their associates actively, though in neither quite as 'strongly' or as sharply as things affect one another by their physical energies. I refer here to *appreciations*, which form an ambiguous sphere of being, belonging with emotion on the one hand, and having objective 'value' on the other, yet seeming not quite inner nor quite outer, as if a diremp-tion had begun but had not made itself complete.

Experiences of painful objects, for example, are usually also painful experiences; perceptions of loveli-ness, of ugliness, tend to pass muster as lovely or as ugly perceptions; intuitions of the morally lofty are lofty intuitions. Sometimes the adjective wanders as

---

[1] I speak here of the complete inner life in which the mind plays freely with its materials. Of course the mind's free play is restricted when it seeks to copy real things in real space.

if uncertain where to fix itself. Shall we speak of seductive visions or of visions of seductive things? Of wicked desires or of desires for wickedness? Of healthly thoughts or of thoughts of healthy objects? Of good impulses, or of impulses towards the good? Of feelings of anger, or of angry feelings? Both in the mind and in the thing, these natures modify their context, exclude certain associates and determine others, have their mates and incompatibles. Yet not as stubbornly as in the case of physical qualities, for beauty and ugliness, love and hatred, pleasant and painful can, in certain complex experiences, coexist.

If one were to make an evolutionary construction of how a lot of originally chaotic pure experiences became gradually differentiated into an orderly inner and outer world, the whole theory would turn upon one's success in explaining how or why the quality of an experience, once active, could become less so, and, from being an energetic attribute in some cases, elsewhere lapse into the status of an inert or merely internal 'nature.' This would be the 'evolution' of the psychical from the *bosom of the physical, in which the esthetic* moral and otherwise emotional experiences would represent a halfway stage.

8.

But a last cry of *non possumus* will probably go up from many readers. "All very pretty as a piece of ingenuity," they will say, "but our consciousness itself intuitively contradicts you. We, for our part, *know* that we are conscious. We *feel* our thought, flowing as a life within us, in absolute contrast with the objects which it so unremittingly escorts. We can not be faithless to this immediate intuition. The dualism is a fundamental *datum:* Let no man join what God has put asunder."

My reply to this is my last word, and I greatly grieve that to many it will sound materialistic. I can not help that, however, for I, too, have my intuitions and I must obey them. Let the case be what it may in others, I am as confident as I am of anything that, in myself, the stream of thinking (which I recognize emphatically as a phenomenon) is only a careless name for what, when scrutinized, reveals itself to consist chiefly of the stream of my breathing. The 'I think' which Kant said must be able to accompany all my objects, is the 'I breathe' which actually does accompany them. There are other internal facts besides breathing (intracephalic muscular adjustments, etc., of which I have said a word in my larger Psychology), and these increase the assets of 'consciousness,' so far as the latter is subject to immediate perception; but breath, which was ever the original of 'spirit,' breath moving outwards, between the glottis and the nostrils, is, I am persuaded, the essence out of which philosophers have constructed the entity known to them as consciousness. *That entity is fictitious, while thoughts in the concrete are fully real. But thoughts in the concrete are made of the same stuff as things are.*

I wish I might believe myself to have made that plausible in this article. In another article I shall try to make the general notion of a world composed of pure experiences still more clear.

STUDY QUESTIONS: JAMES, *DOES CONSCIOUSNESS EXIST?*

1. How are thoughts and things related?
2. Why is consciousness a *nonentity?* What does this mean?
3. What does James mean by *pure experience?* Is pure experience real? Is it the same as *consciousness?* Why?
4. What is neo-Kantianism? What view has it dispelled? Is James a neo-Kantian?
5. What is content? What is awareness of content?
6. What does it mean to be self-conscious?
7. Does James regard the separation of experience into consciousness and content as legitimate? Why?
8. What is the "wedge" put in place by Locke and Berkeley that James continues to apply to its logical conclusion?
9. What are percepts? How are percepts distinguished from concept? What is the nature of the relation between them?

10. What does James mean by *presentation*?
11. What does James mean when he says the room you're in gets "counted twice over?"
12. What is a pre-experience?
13. What does James think consciousness really is?
14. How does James' explanation in terms of an "external relation" make things any clearer?

A WORLD OF PURE EXPERIENCE

Here James puts forth his theory of *radical empiricism*, a "theory of everything" that is both phenomenalist and yet, at the same time, embraces naïve realism. The radical idea, as profound as it is subtle, is that ideas are the only *given* existent, but this does not logically entail that existence is *mental*. Thus James puts forth a theory in which certain fundamental presuppositions of absolute idealism hold without entailing the existence of an intrinsically subjective consciousness. This results in what might be thought of as a "pan-objectivism" of sorts, in which all relations in the universe are not internal, as Berkeley implicitly and Bradley explicitly claimed but, rather, *external relations*. This position, which has since come to be known as *neutral monism*, is a synthesis of earlier developments in the various idealisms and a precursor to the conceptual revolution in subsequent theories in physics developed by Einstein, Bohr, Heisenberg and Schrodinger, according to which the mind is not a passive observer but has an active role in structuring reality.

It is difficult not to notice a curious unrest in the philosophic atmosphere of the time, a loosening of old landmarks, a softening of oppositions, a mutual borrowing from one another on the part of systems anciently closed, and an interest in new suggestions, however vague, as if the one thing sure were the inadequacy of the extant school solutions. The dissatisfaction with these seems due for the most part to a feeling that they are too abstract and academic. Life is confused and super abundant, and what the younger generation appears to crave is more of the temperament of life in its philosophy, even though it were at some cost of logical rigor and of formal purity. Transcendental idealism is inclining to let the world wag incomprehensibly, in spite of its Absolute Subject and his unity of purpose. Berkeleyan idealism is abandoning the principle of parsimony and dabbling in panpsychic speculations. Empiricism flirts with teleology; and, strangest of all, natural realism, so long decently buried, raises its head above the turf, and finds glad hands outstretched from the most unlikely quarters to help it to its feet again. We are all biased by our personal feelings, I know, and I am personally discontented with extant solutions; so I seem to read the signs of a great unsettlement, as if the upheaval of more real conceptions and more fruitful methods were imminent, as if a true landscape might result, less clipped, straightedged and artificial.

If philosophy be really on the eve of any considerable rearrangement, the time should be propitious for any one who has suggestions of his own to bring forward. For many years past my mind has been growing into a certain type of *Weltanschauung*. Rightly or wrongly, I have got to the point where I can hardly see things in any other pattern. I propose, therefore, to describe the pattern as clearly as I can consistently with great brevity, and to throw my description into the bubbling vat of publicity where, jostled by rivals and torn by critics, it will eventually either disappear from notice, or else, if better luck befall it, quietly subside to the profundities, and serve as a possible ferment of new growths or a nucleus of new crystallization.

James, from *Journal of Philosophy, Psychology and Scientific Methods*, vol. I, no. 20 and no. 21 (1904).

1. Radical Empiricism

I give the name of 'radical empiricism' to my *Weltans-chauung*. Empiricism is known as the opposite of rationalism. Rationalism tends to emphasize universals and to make wholes prior to parts in the order of logic as well as in that of being. Empiricism, on the contrary, lays the explanatory stress upon the part, the element, the individual, and treats the whole as a collection and the universal as an abstraction. My description of things, accordingly, starts with the parts and makes of the whole a being of the second order. It is essentially a mosaic philosophy, a philosophy of plural facts, like that of Hume and his descendants, who refer these facts neither to Substances in which they inhere nor to an Absolute Mind that creates them as its objects. But it differs from the Humian type of empiricism in one particular which makes me add the epithet radical.

To be radical, an empiricism must neither admit into its constructions any element that is not directly experienced, nor exclude from them any element that is directly experienced. For such a philosophy, *the relations that connect experiences must themselves be experienced relations, and any kind of relation experienced must be accounted as 'real' as anything else in the system.* Elements may indeed be redistributed, the original placing of things getting corrected, but a real place must be found for every kind of thing experienced, whether term or relation, in the final philosophic arrangement.

Now, ordinary empiricism, in spite of the fact that conjunctive and disjunctive relations present themselves as being fully co-ordinate parts of experience, has always shown a tendency to do away with the connections of things, and to insist most on the disjunctions. Berkeley's nominalism, Hume's statement that whatever things we distinguish are as 'loose and separate' as if they had 'no manner of connection,' James Mill's denial that similars have anything 'really' in common, the resolution of the causal tie into habitual sequence, John Mill's account of both physical things and selves as composed of discontinuous possibilities, and the general pulverization of all experience by association and the mind-dust theory, are examples of what I mean.

The natural result of such a world picture has been the efforts of rationalism to correct its incoherencies by the addition of trans-experiential agents of unification, substances, intellectual categories and powers, or Selves; whereas, if empiricism had only been radical and taken everything that comes without disfavor, conjunction as well as separation, each at its face value, the results would have called for no such artificial correction. *Radical empiricism*, as I understand it, *does full justice to conjunctive relations*, without, however, treating them as rationalism always tends to treat them, as being true in some supernal way, as if the unity of things and their variety belonged to different orders of truth and vitality altogether.

2. Conjunctive Relations

Relations are of different degrees of intimacy. Merely to be 'with' one another in a universe of discourse is the most external relation that terms can have, and seems to involve nothing whatever so to farther consequences. Simultaneity and time-interval come next, and then space-adjacency and distance. After them, similarity and difference, carrying the possibility of many inferences. Then relations of activity, tying terms into series involving change, tendency, resistance, and the causal order generally. Finally, the relation experienced between terms that form states of mind, and are immediately conscious of continuing each other. The organization of the Self as a system of memories, purposes, strivings, fulfilments or disappointments, is incidental to this most intimate of all relations, the terms of which seem in many cases actually to compenetrate and suffuse each other's being.

Philosophy has always turned on grammatical particles. With, near, next, like, from, towards, against, because, for, through, my—these words designate types of conjunctive relation arranged in a roughly ascending order of intimacy and inclusiveness. A priori, we can imagine a universe of withness but no nextness; or one of nextness but no likeness, or of likeness with no activity, or of activity with no purpose, or of purpose with no ego. These would be universes, each with its own grade of unity. The universe of human experience is, by one or another of its parts, of each and all these grades. Whether or not it possibly enjoys some still more absolute grade of union does not appear upon the surface.

Taken as it does appear, our universe is to a large extent chaotic. No one single type of connection runs through all the experiences that compose it. If we take space-relations, they fail to connect minds into any regular system. Causes and purposes obtain only among special series of facts. The self-relation seems extremely limited and does not link two different selves together. *Prima facie*, if you should liken the universe of absolute idealism to an aquarium, a crystal globe in which goldfish are swimming, you would have to compare the empiricist universe to something more like one of those dried human heads with which the Dyaks of Borneo deck their lodges. The skull forms a solid nucleus; but innumerable feathers, leaves, strings, beads, and loose appendices of every description float and dangle from it, and, save that they terminate in it, seem to have nothing to do with one another. Even so my experiences and yours float and dangle, terminating, it is true, in a nucleus of common perception, but for the most part out of sight and irrelevant and unimaginable to one another. This imperfect intimacy, this bare relation of *withness* between some parts of the sum total of experience and other parts, is the fact that ordinary empiricism overemphasizes against rationalism, the latter always tending to ignore it unduly. Radical empiricism, on the contrary, is fair to both the unity and the disconnection. It finds no reason for treating either as illusory. It allots to each its definite sphere of description, and agrees that there appear to be actual forces at work which tend, as time goes on, to make the unity greater.

The conjunctive relation that has given most trouble to philosophy is *the co-conscious transition*, so to call it, by which one experience passes into another when both belong to the same self. About the facts there is no question. My experiences and your experiences are 'with' each other in various external ways, but mine pass into mine, and yours pass into yours in a way in which yours and mine never pass into one another. Within each of our personal histories, subject, object, interest and purpose *are continuous or may be continuous*. Personal histories are processes of change in time, and *the change itself is one of the things immediately experienced*. 'Change' in this case means continuous as opposed to discontinuous transition. But continuous transition is one sort of a conjunctive relation; and to be a radical empiricist means to hold fast to this conjunctive relation of all others, for this is the strategic point, the position through which, if a hole be made, all the corruptions of dialectics and all the metaphysical fictions pour into our philosophy. The holding fast to this relation means taking it at its face value, neither less nor more; and to take it at its face value means first of all to take it just as we feel it, and not to confuse ourselves with abstract talk *about* it, involving words that drive us to invent secondary conceptions in order to neutralize their suggestions and to make our actual experience again seem rationally possible.

What I do feel simply when a later moment of my experience succeeds an earlier one is that though they are two moments, the transition from the one to the other is *continuous*. Continuity here is a definite sort of experience; just as definite as is the *discontinuity-experience* which I find it impossible to avoid when I seek to make the transition from an experience of my own to one of yours. In this latter case I have to get on and off again, to pass from a thing lived to another thing only conceived, and the break is positively experienced and noted. Though the functions exerted by my experience and by yours may be the same (*e.g.*, the same objects known and the same purposes followed), yet the sameness has in this case to be ascertained expressly (and often with difficulty and uncertainty) after the break has been felt; whereas in passing from one of my own moments to another the sameness of object and interest is unbroken, and both the earlier and the later experience are of things directly lived.

There is no other *nature*, no other whatness than this absence of break and this sense of continuity in that most intimate of all conjunctive relations, the passing of one experience into another when they belong to the same self. And this whatness is real empirical 'content,' just as the whatness of separation and discontinuity is real content in the contrasted case. Practically to experience one's personal continuum in this living way is to know the originals of the ideas of continuity and of sameness, to know what the words stand for concretely, to own all that they can ever mean. But all experiences have their conditions; and over-subtle intellects, thinking about the facts here, and asking how they are possible, have ended by substituting a lot of static objects of conception for the direct perceptual experiences. "Sameness," they have said, "must be a stark numerical identity; it can't run on from next to next. Continuity can't mean mere absence of gap; for if you say two things are in immediate contact, *at* the contact how can they be two? If, on the other hand, you put a relation of transition between them, that itself is a third thing, and needs to be related or hitched to its terms. An infinite series is involved," and so on. The result is that from difficulty to difficulty, the plain conjunctive experience has been discredited by both schools, the empiricists leaving things permanently disjoined, and the rationalist remedying the looseness by their Absolutes or Substances, or whatever other fictitious agencies of union they may have employed. From all which artificiality we can be saved by a couple of simple reflections: first, that conjunctions and separations are, at all events, co-ordinate phenomena which, if we take experiences at their face value, must be accounted equally real; and second, that if we insist on treating things as really separate when they are given as continuously joined, invoking, when union is required, transcendental principles to overcome the separateness we have assumed, then we ought to stand ready to perform the converse act. We ought to invoke higher principles of *disunion*, also, to make our merely experienced *dis*junctions more truly real. Failing thus, we ought to let the originally given continuities stand on their own bottom. We have no right to be lopsided or to blow capriciously hot and cold.

3. The Cognitive Relation

The first great pitfall from which such a radical standing by experience will save us is an artificial conception of the *relations between knower and known*. Throughout the history of philosophy the subject and its object have been treated as absolutely discontinuous entities; and thereupon the presence of the latter to the former, or the 'apprehension' by the former of the latter, has assumed a paradoxical character which all sorts of theories had to be invented to overcome. Representative theories put a mental 'representation,' 'image,' or 'content' into the gap, as a sort of intermediary. Commonsense theories left the gap untouched, declaring our mind able to clear it by a self-transcending leap. Transcendentalist theories left it impossible to traverse by finite knowers, and brought an Absolute in to perform the salutatory act.

All the while, in the very bosom of the finite experience, every conjunction required to make the relation intelligible is given in full. Either the knower and the known are:

1. the self-same piece of experience taken twice over in different contexts; or they are
2. two pieces of *actual* experience belonging to the same subject, with definite tracts of conjunctive transitional experience between them; or
3. the known is a *possible* experience either of that subject or another, to which the said conjunctive transitions *would* lead, if sufficiently prolonged.

To discuss all the ways in which one experience may function as the knower of another, would be incompatible with the limits of this essay.[1] I have just treated of type 1, the kind of knowledge called perception. This is the type of case in which the mind enjoys direct 'acquaintance' with a present object. In the other types the mind has 'knowledge-about' an object not immediately there. Of type 2, the simplest sort of conceptual knowledge, I have given some account in two [earlier] articles. Type 3 can always formally and hypothetically be reduced to type 2, so that a brief description of that type will put the present reader sufficiently at my point of view, and make him see what the actual meanings of the mysterious cognitive relation may be.

Suppose me to be sitting here in my library at Cambridge, at ten minutes walk from 'Memorial Hall,' and to be thinking truly of the latter object. My mind may have before it only the name, or it may have a clear image, or it may have a very dim image of the hall, but such intrinsic differences in the image make no difference in its cognitive function. Certain *extrinsic* phenomena, special experiences of conjunction, are what impart to the image, be it what it may, its knowing office.

For instance, if you ask me what hall I mean by my image, and I can tell you nothing; or if I fail to point or lead you towards the Harvard Delta; or if, being led by you, I am uncertain whether the Hall I see be what I had in mind or not; you would rightly

---

[1]For brevity's sake I altogether omit mention of the type constituted by knowledge of the truth of general propositions. This type has been thoroughly and, so far as I can see, satisfactorily, elucidated in Dewey's *Studies in Logical Theory*. Such propositions are reducible to the *S-is-P* form; and the 'terminus' that verifies and fulfils is the *SP* in combination. Of course percepts may be involved in the mediating experiences, or in the 'satisfactoriness' of the *P* in its new position.

deny that I had 'meant' that particular hall at all, even though my mental image might to some degree have resembled it. The resemblance would count in that case as coincidental merely, for all sorts of things of a kind resemble one another in this world without being held for that reason to take cognizance of one another.

On the other hand, if I can lead you to the hall, and tell you of its history and present uses; if in its presence I feel my idea, however imperfect it may have been, to have led hither and to be now *terminated*; if the associates of the image and of the felt hall run parallel, so that each term of the one context corresponds serially, as I walk, with an answering term of the others; why then my soul was prophetic, and my idea must be, and by common consent would be, called cognizant of reality. That percept was what I *meant*, for into it my idea has passed by conjunctive experiences of sameness and fulfilled intention. Nowhere is there jar, but every later moment continues and corroborates an earlier one.

In this continuing and corroborating, taken in no transcendental sense, but denoting definitely felt transitions, *lies all that the knowing of a percept by an idea can possibly contain or signify*. Wherever such transitions are felt, the first experience *knows* the last one. Where they do not, or where even as possibles they can not, intervene, there can be no pretence of knowing. In this latter case the extremes will be connected, if connected at all, by inferior relations—bare likeness or succession, or by 'withness' alone. Knowledge of sensible realities thus comes to life inside the tissue of experience. It is *made*; and made by relations that unroll themselves in time. Whenever certain intermediaries are given, such that, as they develop towards their terminus, there is experience from point to point of one direction followed, and finally of one process fulfilled, the result is that *their starting point thereby becomes a knower and their terminus an object meant or known*. That is all that knowing (in the simple case considered) can be known as, that is the whole of its nature, put into experiential terms. Whenever such is the sequence of our experiences we may freely say that we had the terminal object 'in mind' from the outset, even although *at* the outset nothing was there in us but a flat piece of substantive experience like any other, with no self-transcendency about it, and no mystery save the mystery of coming into existence and of being gradually followed by

other pieces of substantive experience, with conjunctively transitional experiences between. That is what we *mean* here by the object's being 'in mind.' Of any deeper more real way of being in mind we have no positive conception, and we have no right to discredit our actual experience by talking of such a way at all.

I know that many a reader will rebel at this. "Mere intermediaries," he will say, "even though they be feelings of continuously growing fulfilment, only *separate* the knower from the known, whereas what we have in knowledge is a kind of immediate touch of the one by the other, an 'apprehension' in the etymological sense of the word, a leaping of the chasm as by lightning, an act by which two terms are smitten into one, over the head of their distinctness. All these dead intermediaries of yours are out of each other, and outside of their termini still."

But do not such dialectic difficulties remind us of the dog dropping his bone and snapping at its image in the water? If we knew any more real kind of union *aliunde*, we might be entitled to brand all our empirical unions as a sham. But unions by continuous transition are the only ones we know of, whether in this matter of a knowledge-about that terminates in an acquaintance, whether in personal identity, in logical predication through the copula 'is,' or elsewhere. If anywhere there were more absolute unions realized, they could only reveal themselves to us by just such conjunctive results. These are what the unions are *worth*, these are all that *we can ever practically mean* by union, by continuity. Is it not time to repeat what Lotze said of substances, that to *act like* one is to *be* one? Should we not say here that to be experienced as continuous is to be really continuous, in a world where experience and reality come to the same thing? In a picture gallery a painted hook will serve to hang a painted chain by, a painted cable will hold a painted ship. In a world where both the terms and their distinctions are affairs of experience, conjunctions that are experienced must be at least as real as anything else. They will be 'absolutely' real conjunctions, if we have no transphenomenal Absolute ready, to derealize the whole experienced world by, at a stroke. If, on the other hand, we had such an Absolute, not one of our opponents' theories of knowledge could remain standing any better than ours could; for the distinctions as well as the conjunctions of experience would impartially fall its prey. The whole question of how 'one' thing can know 'another' would cease to be a real one at all in a world where otherness itself was an illusion.[1]

So much for the essentials of the cognitive relation, where the knowledge is conceptual in type, or forms knowledge 'about' an object. It consists in intermediary experiences (possible, if not actual) of continuously developing progress, and, finally, of fulfilment, when the sensible percept, which is the object, is reached. The percept here not only *verifies* the concept, proves its function of knowing that percept to be true, but the percept's existence as the terminus of the chain of intermediaries *creates* the function. Whatever terminates that chain was, because it now proves itself to be, what the concept 'had in mind.'

The towering importance for human life of this kind of knowing lies in the fact that an experience that knows another can figure as its *representative*, not in any quasi-miraculous 'epistemological' sense, but in the definite practical sense of being its *substitute* in various operations, sometimes physical and sometimes mental, which lead us to its associates and results. By experimenting on our ideas of reality, we may save ourselves the trouble of experimenting on the real experiences which they severally mean. The ideas form related systems, corresponding point for point to the systems which the realities form; and by letting an ideal term call up its associates systematically, we may be led to a terminus which the corresponding real term would have led to in case we had operated on the real world. And this brings us to the general question of substitution.

4. Substitution

In Taine's brilliant book on 'Intelligence,' substitution was for the first time named as a cardinal logical function, though of course the facts had always been familiar enough. What, exactly, in a system of experiences, does the 'substitution' of one of them for another mean?

According to my view, experience as a whole is a process in time, whereby innumerable particular terms lapse and are superseded by others that follow upon them by transitions which, whether disjunctive or conjunctive in content, are themselves experiences, and must in general be accounted at least as real as the terms which they relate. What the nature of the event called 'superseding' signifies, depends altogether on the kind of transition that obtains. Some experiences simply abolish their predecessors without continuing them in any way. Others are felt to increase or to enlarge their meaning, to carry out their purpose, or to bring us nearer to their goal. They 'represent' them, and may fulfil their function better than they fulfilled it themselves. But to 'fulfil a function' in a world of pure experience can be conceived and defined in only one possible way. In such a world transitions and arrivals (or terminations) are the only events that happen, though they happen by so many sorts of path. The only function that one experience can perform is to lead into another experience; and the only fulfilment we can speak of is the reaching of a certain experienced end. When one experience leads to (or can lead to) the same end as another, they agree in function. But the whole system of experiences as they are immediately given presents itself as a quasi-chaos through which one can pass out of an initial term in many directions and yet end in the same terminus, moving from next to next by a great many possible paths.

Either one of these paths might be a functional substitute for another, and to follow one rather than another might on occasion be an advantageous thing to do. As a matter of fact, and in a general way, the paths that run through conceptual experiences, that is, through 'thoughts' or 'ideas' that 'know' the things in which they terminate, are highly advantageous paths to follow. Not only do they yield inconceivably rapid transitions; but, owing to the 'universal' character[2] which they frequently possess, and to their capacity for association with one another in great systems, they outstrip the tardy consecutions of the things

---

[1] Mr. Bradley, not professing to know his absolute *aliunde*, nevertheless derealizes Experience by alleging it to be everywhere infected with self-contradiction. His arguments seem almost purely verbal, but this is no place for arguing that point out. [Cf. F. H. Bradley; *Appearance and Reality* . . .]

[2] Of which all that need be said in this essay is that it also can be conceived as functional, and defined in terms of transitions, or of the possibility of such.

themselves, and sweep us on towards our ultimate termini in a far more labor-saving way than the following of trains of sensible perception ever could. Wonderful are the new cuts and the short circuits which the thought-paths make. Most thought-paths, it is true, are substitutes for nothing actual; they end outside the real world altogether, in wayward fancies, utopias, fictions or mistakes. But where they do re-enter reality and terminate therein, we substitute them always; and with these substitutes we pass the greater number of our hours.

This is why I called our experiences, taken all together, a quasi-chaos. There is vastly more discontinuity in the sum total of experiences than we commonly suppose. The objective nucleus of every man's experience, his own body, is, it is true, a continuous percept; and equally continuous as a percept (though we may be inattentive to it) is the material environment of that body, changing by gradual transition when the body moves. But the distant parts of the physical world are at all times absent from us, and form conceptual objects merely, into the perceptual reality of which our life inserts itself at points discrete and relatively rare. Round their several objective nuclei, partly shared and common and partly discrete, of the real physical world, innumerable thinkers, pursuing their several lines of physically true cogitation, trade paths that intersect one another only at discontinuous perceptual points, and the rest of the time are quite incongruent; and around all the nuclei of shared 'reality,' as around the Dyak's head of my late metaphor, floats the vast cloud of experiences that are wholly subjective, that are non-substitutional, that find not even an eventual ending for themselves in the perceptual world—the mere daydreams and joys and sufferings and wishes of the individual minds. These exist *with* one another, indeed, and with the objective nuclei, but out of them it is probable that to all eternity no interrelated system of any kind will ever be made.

This notion of the purely substitutional or conceptual physical world brings us to the most critical of all the steps in the development of a philosophy of pure experience. The paradox of self-transcendency in knowledge comes back upon us here, but I think

that our notions of pure experience and of substitution, and our radically empirical view of conjunctive transitions, are *Denkmittel*[1] that will carry us safely through the pass.

5. What Objective Reference Is

Whosoever feels his experience to be something substitutional even while he has it, may be said to have an experience that reaches beyond itself. From inside of its own entity it says 'more,' and postulates reality existing elsewhere. For the transcendentalist, who holds knowing to consist in a *salto mortale* across an 'epistemological chasm,' such an idea presents no difficulty; but it seems at first sight as if it might be inconsistent with an empiricism like our own. Have we not explained that conceptual knowledge is made such wholly by the existence of things that fall outside of the knowing experience itself—by intermediary experiences and by a terminus that fulfils? Can the knowledge be there before these elements that constitute its being have come? And, if knowledge be not there, how can objective reference occur?

The key to this difficulty lies in the distinction between knowing as verified and completed, and the same knowing as in transit and on its way. To recur to the Memorial Hall example lately used, it is only when our idea of the Hall has actually terminated in the percept that we know 'for certain' that from the beginning it was truly cognitive of *that*. Until established by the end of the process, its quality of knowing that, or indeed of knowing anything, could still be doubted; and yet the knowing really was there, as the result now shows. We were *virtual* knowers of the Hall long before we were certified to have been its actual knowers, by the percept's retroactive validating power. Just so we are 'mortal' all the time, by reason of the virtuality of the inevitable event which will make us so when it shall have come.

Now the immensely greater part of all our knowing never gets beyond this virtual stage. It never is completed or nailed down. I speak not merely of our ideas of imperceptibles like ether waves or dissociated 'ions,' or of 'ejects' like the contents of our neighbors' minds; I speak also of ideas which we might verify if we would take the trouble, but which we hold for true

---

[1][tools of thought (ed.)]

although unterminated perceptually, because nothing says 'no' to us, and there is no contradicting truth in sight. *To continue thinking unchallenged is, 99 times out of a 100, our practical substitute for knowing in the completed sense.* As each experience runs by cognitive transition into the next one, and we nowhere feel a collision with what we elsewhere count as truth or fact, we commit ourselves to the current as if the port were sure. We live, as it were, upon the front edge of an advancing wave crest, and our sense of a determinate direction in falling forward is all we cover of the future of our path. It is as if a differential quotient should be conscious and treat itself as an adequate substitute for a traced-out curve. Our experience, *inter alia,* is of variations of rate and of direction, and lives in these transitions more than in the journey's end. The experiences of tendency are sufficient to act upon— what more could we have *done* at those moments even if the later verification comes complete?

This is what, as a radical empiricist, I say to the charge that the objective reference which is so flagrant a character of our experiences involves a chasm and a mortal leap. A positively conjunctive transition involves neither chasm nor leap. Being the very original of what we mean by continuity, it makes a continuum wherever it appears. I know full well that such brief words as these will leave the hardened transcendentalist unshaken. Conjunctive experiences *separate* their terms, he will still say: they are third things interposed, that have themselves to be conjoined by new links, and to invoke them makes our trouble infinitely worse. To 'feel' our motion forward is impossible. Motion implies terminus; and how can terminus be felt before we have arrived? The barest start and sally forwards, the barest tendency to leave the instant, involves the chasm and the leap. Conjunctive transitions are the most superficial of appearances, illusions of our sensibility which philosophical reflection pulverizes at a touch. Conception is our only trustworthy instrument, conception and the Absolute working hand in hand. Conception disintegrates experience utterly, but its disjunctions are easily overcome again when the Absolute takes up the task.

Such transcendentalists I must leave, provisionally at least, in full possession of their creed. I have no space for polemics in this article, so I shall simply formulate the empiricist doctrine as my hypothesis, leaving it to work or not work as it may.

Objective reference, I say then, is an incident of the fact that so much of our experience comes as an insufficient and consists of process and transition. Our fields of experience have no more definite boundaries than have our fields of view. Both are fringed forever by a *more* that continuously develops, and that continuously supersedes them as life proceeds. The relations, generally speaking, are as real here as the terms are, and the only complaint of the transcendentalist's with which I could at all sympathize would be his charge that, by first making knowledge to consist in external relations as I have done, and by then confessing that nine-tenths of the time these are not actually but only virtually there, I have knocked the solid bottom out of the whole business, and palmed off a substitute of knowledge for the genuine thing. Only the admission, such a critic might say, that our ideas are self-transcendent and 'true' already, in advance of the experiences that are to terminate them, can bring solidity back to knowledge in a world like this, in which transitions and terminations are only by exception fulfilled.

This seems to me an excellent place for applying the pragmatic method. When a dispute arises, that method consists in auguring what practical consequences would be different if one side rather than the other were true. If no difference can be thought of, the dispute is a quarrel over words. What then would the self-transcendency affirmed to exist in advance of all experiential mediation or termination, be *known as?* What would it practically result in for *us,* were it true?

It could only result in our orientation, in the turning of our expectations and practical tendencies into the right path; and the right path here, so long as we and the object are not yet face to face (or can never get face to face, as in the case of ejects), would be the path that led us into the object's nearest neighborhood. Where direct acquaintance is lacking, 'knowledge about' is the next best thing, and an acquaintance with what actually lies about the object, and is most closely related to it, puts such knowledge within our grasp. Ether waves and your anger, for example, are things in which my thoughts will never *perceptually* terminate, but my concepts of them lead me to their very brink, to the chromatic fringes and to the hurtful words and deeds which are their really next effects.

Even if our ideas did in themselves carry the postulated self-transcendency, it would still remain true that their putting us into possession of such effects *would be the sole cash-value of the self-transcendency for us*. And this cash value, it is needless to say, is *verbatim et literatim* what our empiricist account pays in. On pragmatist principles therefore, a dispute over self-transcendency is a pure logomachy. Call our concepts of ejective things self-transcendent or the reverse, it makes no difference, so long as we don't differ about the nature of that exalted virtue's fruits—fruits for us, of course, humanistic fruits. If an Absolute were proved to exist for other reasons, it might well appear that *his* knowledge is terminated in innumerable cases where ours is still incomplete. That, however, would be a fact indifferent to our knowledge. The latter would grow neither worse nor better, whether we acknowledged such an Absolute or left him out.

So the notion of a knowledge still *in transitu* and on its way joins hands here with that notion of a 'pure experience' which I tried to explain in . . . 'Does Consciousness Exist?' The instant field of the present is always experience in its 'pure' state, plain unqualified actuality, a simple *that*, as yet undifferentiated into thing and thought, and only virtually classifiable as objective fact or as some one's opinion about fact. This is as true when the field is conceptual as when it is perceptual. 'Memorial Hall' is 'there' in my idea as much as when I stand before it. I proceed to act on its account in either case. Only in the later experience that supersedes the present one is this *naïf* immediacy retrospectively split into two parts, a 'consciousness' and its 'content,' and the content corrected or confirmed. While still pure, or present, any experience—mine, for example, of what I write about in these very lines—passes for 'truth.' The morrow may reduce it to 'opinion.' The transcendentalist in all his particular knowledges is as liable to this reduction as I am: his Absolute does not save him. Why, then, need he quarrel with an account of knowing that merely leaves it liable to this inevitable condition? Why insist that knowing is a static relation out of time when it practically seems so much a function of our active life? For a thing to be valid, says Lotze, is the same as to make itself

valid. When the whole universe seems only to be making itself valid and to be still incomplete (else why its ceaseless changing?) why, of all things, should knowing be exempt? Why should it not be making itself valid like everything else? That some parts of it may be already valid or verified beyond dispute, the empirical philosopher, of course, like any one else, may always hope.

6. How Can Two Minds Know the Same Thing?

With transition and prospect thus enthroned in pure experience, it is impossible to subscribe to the idealism of the English school. Radical empiricism has, in fact, more affinities with natural realism than with the views of Berkeley or of Mill, and this can be easily shown.

For the Berkeleyan school, ideas (the verbal equivalent of what I term experiences) are discontinuous. The content of each is wholly immanent, and there are no transitions with which they are consubstantial and through which their beings may unite. Your Memorial Hall and mine, even when both are percepts, are wholly out of connection with each other. Our lives are a congeries of solipsisms, out of which in strict logic only a God could compose a universe even of discourse. No dynamic currents run between my objects and your objects. Never can our minds meet in the *same*.

The incredibility of such a philosophy is flagrant. It is 'cold, strained, and unnatural' in a supreme degree; and it may be doubted whether even Berkeley himself, who took it so religiously, really believed, when walking through the streets of London, that his spirit and the spirits of his fellow wayfarers had absolutely different towns in view.

To me the decisive reason in favor of our minds meeting in *some* common objects at least is that, unless I make that supposition, I have no motive for assuming that your mind exists at all. Why do I postulate your mind? Because I see your body acting in a certain way. Its gestures, facial movements, words and conduct generally, are 'expressive,' so I deem it actuated as my own is, by an inner life like mine. This argument from analogy is my *reason*, whether an instinctive belief runs before it or not. But what is 'your body' here but a percept in *my* field? It is only as animating *that* object, *my* object, that I have any occasion to think of you at all. If the body that you actuate be not the very body that I see there, but some duplicate body of your own with which that has nothing to do, we belong to different universes, you and I, and for me to speak of you is folly. Myriads of such universes even now may coexist, irrelevant to one another; my concern is solely with the universe with which my own life is connected.

In that perceptual part of *my* universe which I call *your* body, your mind and my mind meet and may be called conterminous. Your mind actuates that body and mine sees it; my thoughts pass into it as into their harmonious cognitive fulfilment; your emotions and volitions pass into it as causes into their effects.

But that percept hangs together with all our other physical percepts. They are of one stuff with it; and if it be our common possession, they must be so likewise. For instance, your hand lays hold of one end of a rope and my hand lays hold of the other end. We pull against each other. Can our two hands be mutual objects in this experience, and the rope not be mutual also? What is true of the rope is true of any other percept. Your objects are over and over again the same as mine. If I ask you *where* some object of yours is, our old Memorial Hall, for example, you point to *my* Memorial Hall with *your* hand which *I* see. If you alter an object in your world, put out a candle, for example, when I am present, *my* candle *ipso facto* goes out. It is only as altering my objects that I guess you to exist. If your objects do not coalesce with my objects, if they be not identically where mine are, they must be proved to be positively somewhere else. But no other location can be assigned for them, so their place must be what it seems to be, the same.[1]

Practically, then, our minds meet in a world of objects which they share in common, which would still be there, if one or several of the minds were destroyed. I can see no formal objection to this supposition's being literally true. On the principles which I am defending, a 'mind' or 'personal consciousness' is the name for a series of experiences run together by certain definite transitions, and an objective reality is a series of similar experiences knit by different transitions. If one and the same experience can figure twice, once in a mental and once in a physical context (as I

have tried, in my article on 'Consciousness,' to show that it can), one does not see why it might not figure thrice, or four times, or any number of times, by running into as many different mental contexts, just as the same point, lying at their intersection, can be continued into many different lines. Abolishing any number of contexts would not destroy the experience itself or its other contexts, any more than abolishing some of the point's linear continuations would destroy the others, or destroy the point itself.

I well know the subtle dialectic which insists that a term taken in another relation must needs be an intrinsically different term. The crux is always the old Greek one, that the same man can't be tall in relation to one neighbor, and short in relation to another, for that would make him tall and short at once. In this essay I can not stop to refute this dialectic, so I pass on, leaving my flank for the time exposed. But if my reader will only allow that the same '*now*' both ends his past and begins his future; or that, when he buys an acre of land from his neighbor, it is the same acre that successively figures in the two estates; or that when I pay him a dollar, the same dollar goes into his pocket that came out of mine; he will also in consistency have to allow that the same object may conceivably play a part in, as being related to the rest of, any number of otherwise entirely different minds. This is enough for my present point: the common-sense notion of minds sharing the same object offers no special logical or epistemological difficulties of its own; it stands or falls with the general possibility of things being in conjunctive relation with other things at all.

In principle, then, let natural realism pass for possible. Your mind and mine *may* terminate in the same percept, not merely against it, as if it were a third external thing, but by inserting themselves into it and coalescing with it, for such is the sort of conjunctive union that appears to be experienced when a perceptual terminus 'fulfils.' Even so, two hawsers may embrace the same pile, and yet neither one of them touch any other part except that pile, of what the other hawser is attached to.

It is therefore not a formal question, but a question of empirical fact solely, whether, when you and I are said to know the 'same' Memorial Hall, our

---

[1]The notion that our objects are inside of our respective heads is not seriously defensible, so I pass it by.

minds do terminate at or in a numerically identical percept. Obviously, as a plain matter of fact, they do *not*. Apart from colorblindness and such possibilities, we see the Hall in different perspectives. You may be on one side of it and I on another. The percept of each of us, as he sees the surface of the Hall, is moreover only his provisional terminus. The next thing beyond my percept is not your mind, but more percepts of my own into which my first percept develops, the interior of the Hall, for instance, or the inner structure of its bricks and mortar. If our minds were in a literal sense *conterminous*, neither could get beyond the percept which they had in common, it would be an ultimate barrier between them— unless indeed they flowed over it and became 'coconscious' over a still larger part of their content, which (thought-transference apart) is not supposed to be the case. In point of fact the ultimate common barrier can always be pushed, by both minds, farther than any actual percept of either, until at last it resolves itself into the mere notion of imperceptibles like atoms or ether, so that, where we do terminate in percepts, our knowledge is only speciously completed, being, in theoretic strictness, only a virtual knowledge of those remoter objects which conception carries out.

Is natural realism, permissible in logic, refuted then by empirical fact? Do our minds have no object in common after all?

Yes, they certainly have *Space* in common. On pragmatic principles we are obliged to predicate sameness wherever we can predicate no assignable point of difference. If two named things have every quality and function indiscernible, and are at the same time in the same place, they must be written down as numerically one thing under two different names. But there is no test discoverable, so far as I know, by which it can be shown that the place occupied by your percept of Memorial Hall differs from the place occupied by mine. The percepts themselves may be shown to differ; but if each of us be asked to point out where his percept is, we point to an identical spot. All the relations, whether geometrical or causal, of the Hall originate or terminate in that spot wherein our hands meet, and where each of us begins to work if he wishes to make the Hall change before the other's eyes. Just so it is with our bodies. That body of yours which you actuate and feel from within must be in the same spot as the body of yours which I see or touch from without. 'There' for me means where I place my finger. If you do not feel my finger's contact to be 'there' in *my* sense, when I place it on your body, where then do you feel it? Your inner actuations of your body meet my finger *there*: it is *there* that you resist its push, or shrink back, or sweep the finger aside with your hand. Whatever farther knowledge either of us may acquire of the real constitution of the body which we thus feel, you from within and I from without, it is in that same place that the newly conceived or perceived constituents have to be located, and it is *through* that space that your and my mental intercourse with each other has always to be carried on, by the mediation of impressions which I convey thither, and of the reactions thence which those impressions may provoke from you.

In general terms, then, whatever differing contents our minds may eventually fill a place with, the place itself is a numerically identical content of the two minds, a piece of common property in which, through which, and over which they join. The receptacle of certain of our experiences being thus common, the experiences themselves might some day become common also. If that day ever did come, our thoughts would terminate in a complete empirical identity, there would be an end, so far as *those* experiences went, to our discussions about truth. No points of difference appearing, they would have to count as the same.

7. Conclusion

With this we have the outlines of a philosophy of pure experience before us. At the outset of my essay, I called it a mosaic philosophy. In actual mosaics the pieces are held together by their bedding, for which bedding the Substances, transcendental Egos, or Absolutes of other philosophies may be taken to stand. In radical empiricism there is no bedding; it is as if the pieces clung together by their edges, the transitions experienced between them forming their cement. Of course such a metaphor is misleading, for in actual experience the more substantive and the more transitive parts run into each other continuously, there is in general no separateness needing to be overcome by an external cement; and whatever separateness is actually experienced is not overcome, it stays and counts as separateness to the end. But the metaphor serves to symbolize the fact that Experience itself, taken at large, can grow by its edges. That one moment of it proliferates into the next by transitions which, whether conjunctive or disjunctive, continue the experiential tissue, can not, I contend, be denied. Life is in the transitions as much as in the terms connected; often, indeed, it seems to be there more emphatically, as if our spurts and sallies forward were the real firing line of the battle, were like the thin line of flame advancing across the dry autumnal field which the farmer proceeds to burn. In this line we live prospectively as well as retrospectively. It is 'of' the past, inasmuch as it comes expressly as the past's continuation; it is 'of' the future in so far as the future, when it comes, will have continued *it*.

These relations of continuous transition experienced are what make our experiences cognitive. In the simplest and completest cases the experiences are cognitive of one another. When one of them terminates a previous series of them with a sense of fulfilment, it, we say, is what those other experiences 'had in view.' The knowledge, in such a case, is verified; the truth is 'salted down.' Mainly, however, we live on speculative investments, or on our prospects only. But living on things *in posse* is as good as living in the actual, so long as our credit remains good. It is evident that for the most part it is good, and that the universe seldom protests our drafts.

In this sense we at every moment can continue to believe in an existing *beyond*. It is only in special cases that our confident rush forward gets rebuked. The beyond must, of course, always in our philosophy be itself of an experiential nature. If not a future experience of our own or a present one of our neighbor, it must be a thing in itself in Dr. Prince's and Professor Strong's sense of the term—that is, it must be an experience *for* itself whose relation to other things we translate into the action of molecules, ether waves, or whatever else the physical symbols may be.[1] This opens the chapter of the relations of radical empiricism to panpsychism, into which I can not enter now.

The beyond can in any case exist simultaneously—for it can be experienced *to have existed* simultaneously—with the experience that practically postulates it by looking in its direction, or by turning or changing in the direction of which it is the goal. Pending that actuality of union, in the virtuality of which the 'truth,' even now, of the postulation consists, the beyond and its knower are entities split off from each other. The world is in so far forth a pluralism of which the unity is not fully experienced as yet. But, as fast as verifications come, trains of experience, once separate, run into one another; and that is why I said, earlier in my article, that the unity of the world is on the whole undergoing increase. The universe continually grows in quantity by new experiences that graft themselves upon the older mass; but these very new experiences often help the mass to a more consolidated form.

These are the main features of a philosophy of pure experience. It has innumerable other aspects and arouses innumerable questions, but the points I have touched on seem enough to make an entering wedge. In my own mind such a philosophy harmonizes best with a radical pluralism, with novelty and indeterminism, moralism and theism, and with the 'humanism' lately sprung upon us by the Oxford and the Chicago schools. I can not, however, be sure that all these doctrines are its necessary and indispensable allies. It presents so many points of difference, both from the common sense and from the idealism that have made our philosophic language, that it is almost as difficult to state it as it is to think it out clearly, and if it is ever to grow into a respectable system, it will have to be built up by the contributions of many cooperating minds. It seems to me, as I said at the outset of this essay, that many minds are, in point of fact, now turning in a direction that points towards radical empiricism. If they are carried farther by my words, and if then they add their stronger voices to my feebler one, the publication of this essay will have been worth while.

---

[1] Our minds and these ejective realities would still have space (or pseudo-space, as I believe Professor Strong calls the medium of interaction between 'things-in-themselves') in common. These would exist *where*, and begin to act *where*, we locate the molecules, etc., and *where* we perceive the sensible phenomena explained thereby.

STUDY QUESTIONS: JAMES, A WORLD OF PURE EXPERIENCE

1. What does James mean by "radical empiricism?"
2. How are traditional empiricism and rationalism related?
3. What is a conjunctive relation?
4. How are sameness and continuity related?
5. What is the cognitive relation?
6. What is objective reference?
7. Do you and I perceive the same object when we are in the same room looking at, for example, a table? Why? What does this show?
8. Why does James call his theory of a world of pure experience a "mosaic philosophy?"

Philosophical Bridges: James' Influence

James was one of the most influential of American thinkers ever. His neutral monism, designed to transcend within language the subjective-objective distinction, was adapted and further elaborated by many thinkers of the time, including John Dewey. James' conception of the human being and the world as natural processes provided the foundation for twentieth-century naturalism and naturalized epistemology by breaking down the boundary between the knower and the known, yet remaining squarely within a positivistic outlook. His interactions not only with Peirce, Dewey, and Royce but with leading philosophers on both sides of the Atlantic—with F. H. Bradley, who was deeply critical but supportive, F. C. S. Schiller, a devoted disciple and supporter, Ernst Mach, Carl Stumpf, and Henri Bergson—created a network of philosophical exchange and understanding that ended America's philosophical provincialism and brought it to the forefront of philosophical activity in the world. Bergson, for instance, wrote that "I come to . . . William James, a philosopher my love and admiration for whom I can never adequately express." Not only in England and France, but in Italy as well, James had many enthusiastic followers, such as "The Pragmatic Club" in Rome consisting of influential Italian philosophers. In psychology, his *Principles of Psychology* is regarded as an essential work that everyone must study. Among philosophers today, James is held in as high regard as most of the great names throughout history. Many contemporary philosophers are directly inspired by James and hold him in the highest esteem, such as Daniel C. Dennett, whose theory of mind presented in his first book, *Content and Consciousness*, owed a lot to James, as did his widely influential work on free will, *Elbow Room*.

ROYCE (1855–1916)

Biographical History

Josiah Royce was born in Grass Valley, California, a mining town. After studying engineering at the University of California he went to Germany to study philosophy with various leading German idealists of the time, at Leipzig and Göttingen. The greatest influence on him, however, was Hegel, to whose philosophy he remained steadfastly loyal, developing it in a brilliant new direction, that of individualism. Upon returning to the United States he entered Johns Hopkins University and there he completed his Ph.D. He taught at several universities, including the University of California and Harvard University.

Philosophical Overview

Royce's individualist upgrade of Hegel's absolute idealism is a unique attempt among the American philosophers to create a complete system of thought that encompasses the whole of reality in the grand style of the great classical and modern philosophers. His philosophy of experience owes much to Peirce and James but is anything but pragmatic. Royce was the first and foremost American idealist philosopher and an inspirational source of virtually all subsequent idealist movements in American thought. Whereas British and German absolute idealists conceived of the Absolute as beyond the categories of thought and, therefore, inaccessible to the mind of an individual, Royce argues to the contrary, that full and complete knowledge of everything is possible by an "Absolute experience to which all facts are known and for which all facts are subject to universal law."

Royce's method begins with the fundamental proposition that the world itself and ourselves included is "such stuff as ideas are made of."

SPIRIT OF MODERN PHILOSOPHY

Royce

In this work Royce begins precisely where the sort of idealism propounded by Berkeley but also the German idealists ends; namely, he identifies each and every aspect of the world around us as being the immediate presence of the world soul. The world soul, the one mind who is all, is known and revealed not by faith but logic; it requires not religion but agnosticism.

The obvious question is, if reality is not material but mental, as Royce supposes, why then does reality appear to be so fixed and inevitable? Why can we not control the world around us? Here Royce offers a brilliant and original defense: The reason you cannot alter your experience and the objects within it as you would perhaps wish is because ideas can be more *stubborn* and *resilient* than the firmest conception of matter.

1.

I am very sorry that I cannot state my idealism in a simple and unproblematic form; but the nature of the doctrine forbids. I must first of all puzzle you with a paradox, by saying that my idealism has nothing in it which contradicts the principal propositions of what is nowadays called scientific Agnosticism, in so far, namely, as this agnosticism relates to that world of facts of experience which man sees and feels and which science studies. Of such agnosticism we learned something in our last lecture. But I must go on to say that the fault of our modern so-called scientific agnosticism is only that it has failed to see how the world in space and time, the world of causes and effects, the world of matter and of finite mind, whereof we know so little and long to know so much, is a very subordinate part of reality. It will be my effort to explain how we do know something very deep and vital about what reality is in its innermost essence. My explanation will indeed be very poor and fragmentary, but the outcome of it will be the very highly paradoxical assertion that while the whole finite world is full of dark problems for us, there is absolutely nothing, not even the immediate facts of our sense at this moment, so clear, so certain, as the existence and the unity of that infinite conscious Self of whom we have now heard so much. About the finite world, as I shall assert, we know in general only

Royce, from *The Spirit of Modern Philosophy*, 1892.

what experience teaches us and science records. There is nothing in the universe absolutely sure except the infinite. That will be the curious sort of agnosticism that I shall try in a measure to expound. Of the infinite we know that it is one and conscious. Of the finite things, that is, of the particular fashions of behavior in terms of which the infinite Consciousness gives himself form and plays the world-game, we know only what we experience. Yet doubtless it will at once seem to you that in *one* important respect my announced doctrine is in obvious conflict with a wise agnosticism. For is it not confessedly anthropomorphic in its character? And is not anthropomorphism precisely the defect that modern thinkers have especially taught us to avoid?

Anthropomorphism was the savage view, which led primitive man to interpret extraordinary natural events as expressions of the will of beings like himself. However he came by his fancy, whether by first believing in the survival of the ghosts of his ancestors, and then conceiving them as the agents who produced lightning, and who moved the sun, or by a simple and irreducible instinct of his childish soul, leading him to see himself in nature, and to regard it all as animate; in any case he made the bad induction, created the gods in his own image, and then constituted them as the causes of all natural events. His ignorant self-multiplication we must avoid. Shall our limited inner experience be the only test of what sorts of causation may exist in the world? What we know is that events happen to us, and happen in a certain fixed order. We do not know the ultimate causes of these events. If we lived on some other planet, doubtless causes of a very novel sort would become manifest to us, and our whole view of nature would change. It is self-contradictory, it is absurd, to make our knowledge the measure of all that is! The real world that causes our experience is a great *x*, wholly unknown to us except in a few select phenomena, which happen to fall within our ken. How wild to guess about the mysteries of the infinite!

But now *this* agnosticism, too, as I assure you, I ardently and frankly agree with, so far as it concerns itself with precisely *that* world in which it pretends to move, and to which it undertakes to apply itself. I have no desire to refute it. Touching all the world in space and time beyond experience, in the scientific

sense of the term experience, I repeat that I know nothing positive. I know, for instance, nothing about the stratification of Saturn, or the height of the mountains on the other side of the moon. For the same reason, also, I know nothing of any anthropomorphic demons or gods here or there in nature, acting as causes of noteworthy events. Of these I know nothing, because science has at present no need for such hypotheses. There may be such beings; there doubtless are in nature many curious phenomena; but what curiosities further experience might show us, we must wait for experience to point out ere we shall know. I repeat, in its own world, agnosticism is in all these respects in the right. For reasons that you will later see, I object indeed to the unhappy word *unknowable*. In the world of experience, as in the world of abstracter problems, there are infinitely numerous things unknown to us. But there is no rational question that could not somehow be answered by a sufficiently wise person. There are things relatively unknowable for us, not things absolutely so. There are numberless experiences that I shall never have, in my individual capacity; and there are numberless problems that I shall never solve. But the only absolute insoluble mysteries, as I shall hereafter point out to you, would be the questions that it is essentially absurd to ask. Still, not to quarrel over words, what many agnostics mean by unknowable is simply the stubbornly unknown, and, in that sense, I fully agree and indeed insist that human knowledge is an island in the vast ocean of mystery, and that numberless questions, which it deeply concerns humanity to answer, will never be answered so long as we are in our present limited state, bound to one planet, and left for our experience to our senses, our emotions, and our moral activities.

But, if I thus accept this agnostic view of the world of experience, what chance is left, you will say, for anything like an absolute system of philosophy? In what sense can I pretend to talk of idealism, as giving any final view of the whole nature of things? In what sense, above all, can I pretend to be a theist, and to speak of the absolute Self as the very essence and life of the whole world? For is this not mere anthropomorphism? Isn't it making our private human experience the measure of all reality? Isn't it making hypotheses in terms of our experience, about things beyond our experience? Isn't it making our petty notions of causation a basis for judging of the nature of the unknown first cause? Isn't it another case of what the savage did when he saw his gods in the thunderclouds, because he conceived that causes just like his own angry moods must be here at work? Surely, at best, this is sentiment, faith, mystical dreaming. It can't be philosophy.

I answer, just to change our whole view of the deeper reality of things, just to turn away our attention from any illusive search for first causes in the world of experience, just to get rid of fanciful faith about the gods in outer nature, and just to complete the spiritual task of agnosticism by sending us elsewhere than to phenomena for the true and inner nature of things, for just this end was the whole agony of modern philosophy endured by those who have wrestled with its problems. Is any one agnostic about the finite world? Then I am more. I know nothing of any first cause in the world of appearances yonder. I see no gods in the thunderclouds, no Keplerian angels carrying the planets in conic sections around the sun; I imagine no world-maker far back in the ages, beginning the course of evolution. Following Laplace, I need, once more, no such hypothesis. I await the verdict of science about all facts and events in physical nature. And yet that is just *why* I am an idealist. It is my agnosticism about the causes of my experience that makes me search elsewhere than amongst causes for the meaning of experience. The outer world which the agnostic sees and despairs of knowing is not the region where I look for light. The living God, whom idealism knows, is not the first cause in any physical sense, at all. No possible experience could find him as a thing amongst things or show any outer facts that would prove his existence. He isn't anywhere in space or in time. He makes from without no worlds. He is no hypothesis of empirical science. But he is all the more real for that, and his existence is all the surer. For causes are, after all, very petty and subordinate truths in the world, and facts, phenomena, as such, could never demonstrate any important spiritual truth. The absolute Self simply doesn't *cause* the world. The very idea of causation belongs to things of finite experience, and is only a mythological term when applied to the real truth of things. Not because I interpret the causes of my experience in terms of my

limited ideas of causation is the universe of God a live thing to me, but for a far deeper reason; for a reason which deprives this world of agnosticism of all substantiality and converts it once for all into mere show. I am ignorant of this world just because it is a show-world.

And this deeper reason of the idealist I may as well first suggest in a form which may perhaps seem just now even more mysterious than the problem which I solve by means of it. My reason for believing that there is one absolute World-Self, who embraces and is all reality, whose consciousness includes and infinitely transcends our own, in whose unity all the laws of nature and all the mysteries of experience must have their solution and their very being, is simply that the profoundest agnosticism which you can possibly state in any coherent fashion, the deepest doubt which you can any way formulate about the world or the things that are therein, already presupposes, implies, demands, asserts, the existence of such a World-Self. The agnostic, I say, already asserts this existence—unconsciously, of course, as a rule, but none the less inevitably. For, as we shall find, there is no escape from the infinite Self except by self-contradiction. Ignorant as I am about first causes, I am at least clear, therefore, about the Self. If you deny him, you already in denying affirm him. You reckon ill when you leave him out. "Him when you fly, he is the wings." He is the doubter and the doubt. You in vain flee from his presence. The wings of the morning will not aid you. Nor do I mean all this now as any longer a sort of mysticism. This truth is, I assure you, simply a product of dry logic. When I try to tell you about it in detail, I shall weary you by my wholly unmystical analysis of commonplaces. Here is, in fact, as we shall soon find, the very presupposition of presuppositions. You cannot stir, nay, you cannot even stand still in thought without it. Nor is it an unfamiliar idea. On the contrary, philosophy finds trouble in bringing it to your consciousness merely *because* it is so familiar. When they told us in childhood that we could not see God just *because* he was everywhere, just because his omnipresence gave us no chance to discern him and to fix our eyes upon him, they told us a deep truth in allegorical fashion. The infinite Self, as we shall learn, is actually asserted by you in every proposition you utter, is there at the heart, so to speak, of the very multiplication table. The Self is so little a thing merely guessed at as the unknowable source of experience, that already, *in* the very least of daily experiences you unconsciously know him as something present. This, as we shall find, is the deepest tragedy of our finitude, that continually he comes to his own, and his own receive him not, that he becomes flesh in every least incident of our lives; while we, gazing with wonder upon his world, search here and there for first causes, look for miracles, and beg him to show us the Father, since that alone will suffice us. No wonder that thus we have to remain agnostics. "Hast thou been so long time with me, and yet hast thou not *known* me?" Such is the eternal answer of the Logos to every doubting question. Seek him not as an outer hypothesis to explain experience. Seek him not anywhere yonder in the clouds. He is no "thing in itself." But for all that, experience contains him. He is the reality, the soul of it. "Did not our heart burn within us while he talked with us by the way?" And, as we shall see, he does not talk merely to our hearts. He reveals himself to our coolest scrutiny.

2.

But enough of speculative boasting. Coming to closer quarters with my topic, I must remind you that idealism has two aspects. It is, for the first, a kind of analysis of the world, an analysis which so far has no absolute character about it, but which undertakes, in a fashion that might be acceptable to any skeptic, to examine what you mean by all the things, whatever they are, that you believe in or experience. This idealistic analysis consists merely in a pointing out, by various devices, that the world of your knowledge, whatever it contains, is through and through such stuff as ideas are made of, that you never in your life believed in anything definable *but* ideas, that, as Berkeley put it, "this whole choir of heaven and furniture of earth," is nothing for any of us but a system of ideas which govern our belief and our conduct. Such idealism has numerous statements, interpretations, embodiments: forms part of the most various systems and experiences, is consistent with Berkeley's theism, with Fichte's ethical absolutism, with Professor Huxley's agnostic empiricism, with Clifford's mind-stuff theory, with countless other theories that have used such idealism as a part of their scheme. In this aspect idealism is already a little puzzling to our natural consciousness,

but it becomes quickly familiar, in fact almost commonplace, and seems after all to alter our practical faith or to solve our deeper problems very little.

The other aspect of idealism is the one which gives us our notion of the absolute Self. To it the first is only preparatory. This second aspect is the one which from Kant, until the present time, has formed the deeper problem of thought. Whenever the world has become more conscious of its significance, the work of human philosophy will be, not nearly ended (Heaven forbid an end), but for the first time fairly begun. For then, in critically estimating our passions, we shall have some truer sense of whose passions they are.

I begin with the first and the less significant aspect of idealism. Our world, I say, whatever it may contain, is such stuff as ideas are made of. This preparatory sort of idealism is the one that, as I just suggested, Berkeley made prominent, and after a fashion familiar. I must state it in my own way, although one in vain seeks to attain novelty in illustrating so frequently described a view.

Here, then, is our so real world of the senses, full of light and warmth and sound. If anything could be solid and external, surely, one at first will say, it is this world. Hard facts, not mere ideas, meet us on every hand. Ideas any one can mould as he wishes. Not so facts. In idea socialists can dream out Utopias, disappointed lovers can imagine themselves successful, beggars can ride horses, wanderers can enjoy the fireside at home. In the realm of facts, society organizes itself as it must, rejected lovers stand for the time defeated, beggars are alone with their wishes, oceans roll drearily between home and the wanderer. Yet this world of fact is, after all, not entirely stubborn, not merely hard. The strenuous will can mould facts. We can form our world, in part, according to our ideas. Statesmen influence the social order, lovers woo afresh, wanderers find the way home. But thus to alter the world we must work, and just because the laborer is worthy of his hire, it is well that the real world should thus have such fixity of things as enables us to anticipate what facts will prove lasting, and to see of the travail of our souls when it is once done. This, then, is the presupposition of life, that we work in a real world, where house walls do not melt away as in dreams, but stand firm against the winds of many winters, and can be felt as real. We do not wish to find facts wholly plastic; we want them to be stubborn, if only the stubbornness be not altogether unmerciful. Our will makes constantly a sort of agreement with the world, whereby, if the world will continually show some respect to the will, the will shall consent to be strenuous in its industry. Interfere with the reality of my world, and you therefore take the very life and heart out of my will.

The reality of the world, however, when thus defined in terms of its stubbornness, its firmness as against the will that has not conformed to its laws, its kindly rigidity in preserving for us the fruits of our labors—such reality, I say, is still something wholly unanalyzed. In what does this stubbornness consist? Surely, many different sorts of reality, as it would seem, may be stubborn. Matter is stubborn when it stands in hard walls against us, or rises in vast mountain ranges before the path-finding explorer. But minds can be stubborn also. The lonely wanderer, who watches by the seashore the waves that roll between him and his home, talks of cruel facts, material barriers that, just because they *are* material, and not ideal, shall be the irresistible foes of his longing heart. "In wish," he says, "I am with my dear ones, but alas, wishes cannot cross oceans! Oceans are material facts, in the cold outer world. Would that the world of the heart were all!" But alas! To the rejected lover the world of the heart *is* all, and that is just his woe. Were the barrier between him and his beloved only made of those stubborn material facts, only of walls or of oceans how lightly might his will before long transcend them all! Matter stubborn! Outer nature cruelly the foe of ideas! Nay, it is just an idea that now opposes him—just an idea, and that, too, in the mind of the maiden he loves. But in vain does he call this stubborn bit of disdain a merely ideal fact. No flint was ever more definite in preserving its identity and its edge than this disdain may be. Place me for a moment, then, in an external world that shall consist wholly of ideas—the ideas, namely, of other people about me, a world of maidens who shall scorn me, of old friends who shall have learned to hate me, of angels who shall condemn me, of God who shall judge me. In what piercing north winds, amidst what fields of ice, in the labyrinths of what tangled forests, in the depths of what thick-walled dungeons, on the edges of what tremendous precipices, should I be more genuinely in the presence of stubborn and unyielding facts than in that conceived world of ideas! So, as one sees, I by no means deprive my world of stubborn reality, if I merely call it a world of ideas. On the contrary, as every teacher knows, the ideas of the people are often the most difficult of facts to influence. We were wrong, then, when we said that while matter was stubborn, ideas could be molded at pleasure. Ideas are often the most implacable of facts. Even my own ideas, the facts of my own inner life, may cruelly decline to be plastic to my wish. The wicked will that refuses to be destroyed—what rock has often more consistency for our senses than this will has for our inner consciousness! . . .

No, here are barriers worse than any material chains. The world of ideas has its own horrible dungeons and chasms. Let those who have refuted Bishop Berkeley's idealism by the wonder why he did not walk over every precipice or into every fire if these things existed only in his idea, let such, I say, first try some of the fires and the precipices of the inner life, ere they decide that dangers cease to be dangers as soon as they are called ideal, or even subjectively ideal in me.

Many sorts of reality, then, may be existent at the heart of any world of facts. But this bright and beautiful sense world of ours—what, amongst these many possible sorts of reality, does that embody? Are the stars and the oceans, the walls and the pictures, real as the maiden's heart is real—embodying the ideas of somebody, but none the less stubbornly real for that? Or can we make something else of their reality? For, of course, that the stars and the oceans, the walls and the pictures have *some* sort of stubborn reality, just as the minds of our fellows have, our analysis so far does not for an instant think of denying. Our present question is, what sort of reality? Consider, then, in detail, certain aspects of the reality that seems to be exemplified in our sense world. The sublimity of the sky, the life and majesty of the ocean, the interest of a picture—to what sort of real facts do these belong? Evidently here we shall have no question. So far as the sense world is beautiful, is majestic, is sublime, this beauty and dignity exist only for the appreciative observer. If they exist beyond him, they exist only for some other mind, or as the thought and embodied purpose of some universal soul of nature. A man who sees the same world, but who has no eye for the fairness of it, will find all the visible facts, but will catch nothing of their value. At once, then, the sublimity and beauty of the world are thus truths that one who pretends to insight ought to see, and they are truths which have no meaning except for such a beholder's mind, or except as embodying the thought of the mind of the world. So here, at least, is so much of the outer world that is ideal, just as the coin or the jewel or the banknote or the bond has its value not alone in its physical presence, but in the idea that it symbolizes to a beholder's mind, or to the relatively universal thought of the commercial world. But let us look a little deeper. Surely, if the objects yonder are less than ideal and outer, odors and tastes and temperatures do not exist in these objects in just the way in which they exist in us. Part of the being of these properties, at least, if not all of it, is ideal and exists for us, or at best is once more the embodiment of the thought or purpose of some world-mind. About tastes you cannot dispute, because they are not only ideal but personal. For the benumbed tongue and palate of diseased bodily conditions, all things are tasteless. As for temperatures, a well-known experiment will show how the same water may seem cold to one hand and warm to the other. But even so, colors and sounds are at least in part ideal. Their causes may have some other sort of reality; but colors themselves are not in the things, since they change with the light that falls on the things, vanish in the dark (while the things remained unchanged), and differ for different eyes. And as for sounds, both the pitch and the quality of tones depend for us upon certain interesting peculiarities of our hearing organs, and exist in nature only as voiceless sound waves trembling through the air. All such sense qualities, then, are ideal. The world yonder may—yes, must—have attributes that give reasons why these qualities are thus felt by us; for so we assume. The world yonder may even be a mind that thus expresses its will to us. But these qualities need not, nay, cannot resemble the ideas that are produced in us, unless, indeed, that is because these qualities have place as ideas in some world mind. Sound waves in the air are not like our musical sensations; nor is the symphony as we hear it and feel it any physical property of the strings and the wind instruments; nor are the ether vibrations that the sun sends us like our ideas when we see the sun; nor yet is the flashing of moonlight on the water as we watch the waves a direct expression of the actual truths of fluid motion as the water embodies them.

Unless, then, the real physical world yonder is itself the embodiment of some world-spirit's ideas, which he conveys to us, unless it is real only as the maiden's heart is real, namely, as itself a conscious thought, then we have so far but one result: that real world (to repeat one of the commonplaces of modern popular science) is in itself, apart from somebody's eyes and tongue and ears and touch, neither colored nor tasteful, neither cool nor warm, neither light nor dark, neither musical nor silent. All these qualities belong to our ideas, being indeed none the less genuine facts for that, but being in so far ideal facts. We must see colors when we look, we must hear music when there is playing in our presence; but this *must* is a must that consists in a certain irresistible presence of an idea in us under certain conditions. *That* this idea must come is, indeed, a truth as unalterable, once more, as the king's settled remorse in Hamlet. But like this remorse, again, it exists as an ideal truth, objective, but through and through objective *for* somebody, and not *apart from* anybody. What this truth implies we have yet to see. So far it is only an ideal truth for the beholder, with just the bare possibility that behind it all there is the thought of a world-spirit. And, in fact, *so* far we must all go together if we reflect.

But now, at this point, the Berkeleyan idealist goes one step further. The real outside world that is still left unexplained and unanalyzed after its beauty, its warmth, its odors, its tastes, its colors, and its tones, have been relegated to the realm of ideal truths, what do you now *mean* by calling it real? No doubt it *is* known as somehow real, but *what* is this reality *known* as being? If you know that this world is still there and outer, as by hypothesis you know, you are bound to say *what* this outer character implies for your thought. And here you have trouble. Is the outer world, as it exists outside of your ideas, or of anybody's ideas, something having shape, filling space, possessing solidity, full of moving things? That would in the first place seem evident. The sound isn't outside of me, but the sound-waves, you say, are. The colors are ideal facts; but the ether-waves don't need a mind to know them. Warmth is ideal, but the physical fact called heat, this playing to and fro of molecules, is real, and is there apart from any mind. But once more, *is* this so evident? What do I *mean* by the shape of anything, or by the size of anything? Don't I mean just the idea of shape or of size that I am obliged to get under certain circumstances? What is the meaning of any property that I give to the real outer world? How can I express that property except in case I think it in terms of my ideas? As for the sound waves and the ether waves, what are they but things ideally conceived to explain the facts of nature? The conceptions have doubtless their truth, but it is an ideal truth. What I mean by saying that the things yonder have shape and size and trembling molecules, and that there is air with sound waves, and ether with lightwaves in it—what I *mean* by all this is that experience forces upon me, directly or indirectly, a vast system of ideas, which may indeed be founded in truth beyond me, which in fact *must* be founded in such truth if my experience has any sense, but which, like my ideas of color and of warmth, are simply expressions of how the world's order must appear to me, and to anybody constituted like me. Above all, is this plain about space. The real things, I say, outside of me, fill space, and move about in it. But what do I mean by space? Only a vast system of ideas which experience and my own mind force upon me. Doubtless these ideas have a validity. They have *this* validity, that I, at all events, when I look upon the world, am bound to see it in space, as much bound as the king in Hamlet was, when he looked within, to see himself as guilty and unrepentant. But just as his guilt was an idea—a crushing, an irresistible, an overwhelming idea—but still just an idea, so, too, the space in which I place my world is one great formal idea of mine. That is just why I can describe it to other people. "It has three dimensions," I say, "length, breadth, depth." I describe each. I form, I convey, I construct, an idea of it through them. I know space, as an idea, very well. I can compute all sorts of unseen truths about the relations of its parts. I am sure that you, too, share this idea. But, then, for all of us alike it is just an idea; and when we put our world into space, and call it real there, we simply think one idea into another idea, not voluntarily, to be sure, but inevitably, and yet without leaving the realm of ideas.

Thus, all the reality that *we* attribute to our world, in so far as *we* know and can tell what we mean thereby, becomes ideal. There is, in fact, a certain system of ideas, forced upon us by experience, which we have to use as the guide of our conduct. This system of ideas we can't change by our wish; it is

for us as overwhelming a fact as guilt, or as the bearing of our fellows towards us, but we know it only *as* such a system of ideas. And we call it the world of matter. John Stuart Mill very well expressed the puzzle of the whole thing, as we have now reached the statement of this puzzle, when he called matter a mass of "permanent possibilities of experience" for each of us. Mill's definition has its faults, but it is a very fair beginning. You know matter as something that either now gives you this idea or experience, or that would give you some other idea or experience under other circumstances. A fire, while it burns, is for you a permanent possibility of either getting the idea of an agreeable warmth, or of getting the idea of a bad burn, and you treat it accordingly. A precipice amongst mountains is a permanent possibility of your experiencing a fall, or of your getting a feeling of the exciting or of the sublime in mountain scenery. You have no experience just now of the tropics or of the poles, but both tropical and polar climates exist in your world as permanent possibilities of experience. When you call the sun 92,000,000 miles away, you mean that between you and the sun (that is, between your present experience and the possible experience of the sun's surface) there would inevitably lie the actually inaccessible, but still numerically conceivable series of experiences of distance expressed by the number of miles in question. In short, your whole attitude towards the real world may be summed up by saying: "I have experiences now which I seem bound to have, experiences of color, sound, and all the rest of my present ideas; and I am also bound by experience to believe that in case I did certain things (for instance, touched the wall, traveled to the tropics, visited Europe, studied physics), I then should get, in a determinate order, dependent wholly upon *what* I had done, certain other experiences (for instance, experiences of the wall's solidity, or of a tropical climate, or of the scenes of an European tour, or of the facts of physics)." And this acceptance of actual experience, this belief in possible experience, constitutes all that you mean by your faith in the outer world.

But, you say, is not, then, all this faith of ours after all well founded? Isn't there really something yonder that corresponds in fact to this series of experiences in us? Yes, indeed, there no doubt *is*. But what if this, which so shall correspond without us to the ideas within us, what if this hard and fast reality should itself be a system of ideas, outside of our minds but not outside of every mind? As the maiden's disdain is outside the rejected lover's mind, unchangeable so far for him, but not on that account the less ideal, not the less a fact in a mind, as, to take afresh a former fashion of illustration, the price of a security or the objective existence of this lecture is an ideal fact, but real and external for the individual person—even so why might not this world beyond us, this "permanent possibility of experience," be in essence itself a system of ideal experiences of some standard thought of which ours is only the copy? Nay, must it not be such a system in case it has any reality at all? For, after all, isn't this precisely what our analysis brings us to? Nothing whatever can I say about my world yonder that I do not express in terms of mind. *What* things are, extended, moving, colored, tuneful, majestic, beautiful, holy, *what* they are in any aspect of their nature, mathematical, logical, physical, sensuously pleasing, spiritually valuable, all this must mean for me only something that I have to express in the fashion of ideas. The more I am to know my world, the more of a mind I must have for the purpose. The closer I come to the truth about the things, the more ideas I get. Isn't it plain, then, that *if* my world yonder is anything knowable at all, it must be in and for itself essentially a mental world? Are my ideas to *resemble* in any way the world? Is the truth of my thought to consist in its *agreement* with reality? And am I thus capable, as common sense supposes, of *conforming* my ideas to things? Then reflect. What can, after all, so well agree with an idea as another idea? To what can things that go on in my mind conform unless it be to another mind? If the more my mind grows in mental clearness, the nearer it gets to the nature of reality, then surely the reality that my mind thus resembles must be in itself mental.

After all, then, would it deprive the world here about me of reality, nay, would it not rather save and assure the reality and the knowableness of my world of experience, if I said that this world, as it exists outside of my mind, and of any other human minds, exists in and for a standard, a universal mind, whose system of ideas simply constitutes the world? Even if I fail to prove that there is such a mind, do I not at least thus make plausible that, as I said, our world of common sense has no fact in it which we cannot interpret in terms of ideas, so that this world is throughout such stuff as ideas are made of? To say this, as you see, in no way deprives our world of its due share of reality. If the standard mind knows now that its ideal fire has the quality of burning those who touch it, and if I in my finitude are bound to conform in my experiences to the thoughts of this standard mind, then in case I touch that fire I shall surely get the idea of a burn. The standard mind will be at least as hard and fast and real in its ideal consistency as is the maiden in her disdain for the rejected lover; and I, in presence of the ideal stars and the oceans, will see the genuine realities of fate as certainly as the lover hears his fate in the voice that expresses her will.

I need not now proceed further with an analysis that will be more or less familiar to many of you, especially after our foregoing historical lectures. What I have desired thus far is merely to give each of you, as it were, the sensation of being an idealist in this first and purely analytical sense of the word idealism. The sum and substance of it all is, you see, this: you know your world in fact as a system of ideas about things, such that from moment to moment you find this system forced upon you by experience. Even matter you know just as a mass of coherent ideas that you cannot help having. Space and time, as you think them, are surely ideas of yours. Now, what more natural than to say that *if* this be so, the real world beyond you must in itself be a system of somebody's ideas? If it is, then you can comprehend what its existence means. If it isn't, then since all you can know of it is ideal, the real world must be utterly unknowable, a bare *x*. Minds I can understand, because I myself am a mind. An existence that has no mental attribute is wholly opaque to me. So far, however, from such a world of ideas, existent beyond me in another mind, seeming to coherent thought essentially *unreal*, ideas and minds and their ways, are, on the contrary, the hardest and stubbornest facts that we can name. *If* the external world is in itself mental, then, be this reality a standard and universal thought, or a mass of little atomic minds constituting the various particles of matter, in any case one can comprehend what it is, and will have at the same time to submit to its stubborn authority as the lover accepts the reality of the maiden's moods. If the world *isn't* such an ideal thing, then indeed all our science, which is through and through concerned with our mental interpretations of things, can neither have objective validity, nor make satisfactory progress towards truth. For as science is concerned with ideas, the world beyond all ideas is a bare x.

3.

But with this bare x, you will say, this analytical idealism after all leaves me, as with something that, spite of all my analyses and interpretations, may after all be there beyond me as the real world, which my ideas are vainly striving to reach, but which eternally flees before me. So far, you will say, what idealism teaches is that the real world can only be interpreted by treating it as if it were somebody's thought. So regarded, the idealism of Berkeley and of other such thinkers is very suggestive; yet it doesn't tell us what the true world is, but only that *so much* of the true world as we ever get into our comprehension has to be conceived in ideal terms. Perhaps, however, while neither beauty, nor majesty, nor odor, nor warmth, nor tone, nor color, nor form, nor motion, nor space, nor time (all these being but ideas of ours), can be said to belong to the extra-mental world—perhaps, after all, there does exist there yonder an extra-mental world, which has nothing to do, except by accident, with *any* mind, and which is through and through just extra-mental, something unknowable, inscrutable, the basis of experience, the source of ideas, but itself never experienced as it is in itself, never adequately represented by any idea in us. Perhaps it is there. Yes, you will say, *must* it not be there? Must not one accept our limitations once for all, and say, "What reality is, we can never hope to make clear to ourselves. That which has been made clear becomes an idea in us. But always there is the beyond, the mystery, the inscrutable, the real, the x. To be sure, perhaps we can't even know so much as that this x after all does exist. But then we feel bound to regard it as existent; or even if we doubt or deny it, may it not be there all the same?" In such doubt and darkness, then, this first form of idealism closes. If that were all there were to say, I should indeed have led you a long road in vain. Analyzing what the known world is for you, in case there is hardly any world known to you at all—this surely isn't proving that there is any real world, or that the real world can be known. Are we not just where we started?

No; there lies now just ahead of us the goal of a synthetic idealistic conception, which will not be content with this mere analysis of the colors and forms of things, and with the mere discovery that all these are for us nothing but ideas. In this second aspect, idealism grows bolder, and fears not the profoundest doubt that may have entered your mind as to whether there is any world at all, or as to whether it is in any fashion knowable. State in full the deepest problem, the hardest question about the world that your thought ever conceived. In this new form idealism offers you a suggestion that indeed will not wholly answer nor do away with every such problem, but that certainly will set the meaning of it in a new light. What this new light is, I must in conclusion seek to illustrate.

Note the point we have reached. *Either*, as you see, your real world yonder is through and through a world of ideas, an outer mind that you are more or less comprehending through your experience, *or else*, in so far as it is real and outer it is unknowable, an inscrutable x, an absolute mystery. The dilemma is perfect. There is no third alternative. Either a mind yonder, or else the unknowable; that is your choice. Philosophy loves such dilemmas, wherein all the mightiest interests of the spirit, all the deepest longings of human passion, are at stake, waiting as for the fall of a die. Philosophy loves such situations, I say, and loves, too, to keep its scrutiny as cool in the midst of them as if it were watching a game of chess, instead of the great world game. Well, try the darker choice that the dilemma gives you. The world yonder shall be an x, an unknowable something, outer, problematic, foreign, opaque. And you, you shall look upon it and believe in it. Yes, you shall for argument's sake first put on an air of resigned confidence, and say, "I do not only fancy it to be an extra-mental and unknowable something there, an impenetrable x, but I know it to be such. I can't help it. I didn't make it unknowable. I regret the fact. But there it is. I have to admit its existence. But I know that I shall never solve the problem of its nature." Ah, its nature is a *problem*, then. But what do you mean by this "*problem*"? Problems are, after a fashion, rather familiar things—that is, in the world of ideas. There are problems soluble and problems insoluble in that world of ideas. It is a soluble problem if one asks what whole number is the square root of 64. The answer is 8. It is an insoluble problem if one asks me to find what whole number is the square root of 65. There is, namely, no such whole number. If one asks me to name the length of a straight line that shall be equal to the circumference of a circle of a known radius, that again, in the world of ideas, is an insoluble problem, because, as can be proved, the circumference of a circle is a length that cannot possibly be exactly expressed in terms of any statable number when the radius is of a stated length. So in the world of ideas, problems are definite questions which can be asked in knowable terms. Fair questions of this sort either may be fairly answered in our present state of knowledge, or else they could be answered if we knew a little or a good deal more, or finally they could not possibly be answered. But in the latter case, if they could not possibly be answered, they always must resemble the problem how to square the circle. They then always turn out, namely, to be absurdly stated questions and it is their absurdity that makes these problems absolutely insoluble. Any fair question could be answered by one who knew enough. No fair question has an unknowable answer. But now, *if* your unknowable world out there is a thing of wholly, of absolutely problematic and inscrutable nature, is it so because you don't *yet* know enough about it, or because in its very nature and essence it is an absurd thing, an *x* that *would* answer a question, which actually it is nonsense to ask? Surely one must choose the former alternative. The real world may be unknown; it can't be essentially unknowable.

This subtlety is wearisome enough, I know, just here, but I shall not dwell long upon it. Plainly *if* the unknowable world out there is through and through in its nature a really inscrutable problem, this must mean that in nature it resembles such problems as, What is the whole number that is the square root of 65? Or, What two adjacent hills are there that have no valley between them? For in the world of thought such are the *only* insoluble problems. All others either may now be solved, or would be solved if we knew more than we now do. But, once more, *if* this unknowable is only just the real world as now unknown to us, but capable some time of becoming known, then remember that, as we have just seen, only a mind can ever become an object known to a mind. If I know you as external to me, it is only because you are minds. If I can come to know *any* truth, it is only in so

far as this truth is essentially mental, is an idea, is a thought, that I can ever come to know it. Hence, if that so-called unknowable, that unknown outer world there, ever could, by any device, come within our ken, then it is already an ideal world. For just that is what our whole idealistic analysis has been proving. Only ideas are knowable. And nothing absolutely unknowable can exist. For the absolutely unknowable, the *x* pure and simple, the Kantian thing in itself, simply cannot be admitted. The notion of it is nonsense. The assertion of it is a contradiction. Round squares, and sugar salt lumps, and Snarks, and Boojums, and Jabberwocks, and Abracadabras; such, I insist, are the only unknowables there are. The unknown, that which our human and finite selfhood hasn't grasped, exists spread out before us in a boundless world of truth; but the unknowable is essentially, confessedly, *ipso facto* a fiction.

The nerve of our whole argument in the foregoing is now pretty fairly exposed. We have seen that the outer truth must be, if anything, a "possibility of experience." But we may now see that a *bare* "possibility" as such, is, like the unknowable, something meaningless. That which, whenever I come to know it, turns out to be through and through an idea, an experience, must be in itself, before I know it, either somebody's idea, somebody's experience, or it must be nothing. What is a "possibility" of experience that is outside of me, and that is still nothing *for* any one else than myself? Isn't it a bare *x*, a nonsense phrase? Isn't it like an unseen color, an untasted taste, an unfelt feeling? In proving that the world is one of "possible" experience, we have proved that in so far as it is real it is one of actual experience.

Once more, then, to sum up here, *if*, however vast the world of the unknown, only the essentially knowable can exist, and *if* everything knowable is an idea, a mental somewhat, the content of some mind, then once for all we are the world of ideas. Your deepest doubt proves this. Only the nonsense of that inscrutable *x*, of that Abracadabra, of that Snark, the Unknowable of whose essence you make your real world, prevents you from seeing this.

To return, however, to our dilemma. *Either* idealism, we said, *or* the unknowable. What we have now said is that the absolutely unknowable is essentially an absurdity, a nonexistent. For any fair and stable problem admits of an answer. *If* the world exists yonder, its essence is then already capable of being known by some mind. If capable of being known by a mind, this essence is then already essentially ideal and mental. A mind that knew the real world would, for instance, find it a something possessing qualities. But qualities are ideal existences, just as much as are the particular qualities called odors or tones or colors. A mind knowing the real world would again find in it relations, such as equality and inequality, attraction and repulsion, likeness and unlikeness. But such relations have no meaning except as objects of a mind. In brief, then, the world as known would be found to be a world that had all the while been ideal and mental, even before it became known to the particular mind that we are to conceive as coming into connection with it. Thus, then, we are driven to the second alternative. The real world must be a mind, or else a group of minds.

4.

But with this result we come in presence of a final problem. All this, you say, depends upon my assurance that there is after all a real and therefore an essentially knowable and rational world yonder. Such a world would have to be in essence a mind, or a world of minds. But after all, how does one ever escape from the prison of the inner life? Am I not in all this merely wandering amidst the realm of my own ideas? My world, of course, isn't and can't be a mere *x*, an essentially unknowable thing, just because it *is* my world, and I have an idea of it. But then does not this mean that *my* world is, after all, forever just *my* world, so that I never get to any truth beyond myself? Isn't this result very disheartening? My world is thus a world of ideas, but alas! How do I then ever reach those ideas of the minds beyond me?

The answer is a simple, but in one sense a very problematic one. You, in one sense, namely, never *do* or can get beyond your own ideas, nor ought you to wish to do so, because in truth all those other minds that constitute your outer and real world are in essence one with your own self. This whole world of ideas is essentially *one* world, and so it is essentially the world of one self and *that art Thou.*

The truth and meaning of this deepest proposition of all idealism is now not at all remote from us. The considerations, however, upon which it depends are of the driest possible sort, as commonplace as they are deep.

Whatever objects you may think about, whether they are objects directly known to you, or objects infinitely far removed, objects in the distant stars, or objects remote in time, or objects near and present—such objects, then, as a number with 50 places of digits in it, or the mountains on the other side of the moon, or the day of your death, or the character of Cromwell, or the law of gravitation, or a name that you are just now trying to think of and have forgotten, or the meaning of some mood or feeling or idea now in your mind—all such objects, I insist, stand in a certain constant and curious relation to your mind whenever you are thinking about them—a relation that we often miss because it is so familiar. What is this relation? Such an object, while you think about it, needn't be, as popular thought often supposes it to be, the *cause* of your thoughts concerning it. Thus, when you think about Cromwell's character, Cromwell's character isn't just now *causing* any ideas in you—isn't, so to speak, doing anything to you. Cromwell is dead, and after life's fitful fever his character is a very inactive thing. Not as the *cause*, but as the *object* of your thought is Cromwell present to you. Even so, if you choose now to think of the moment of your death, that moment is somewhere off there in the future, and you can make it your object, but it isn't now an active cause of your ideas. The moment of your death has no present physical existence at all, and just now causes nothing. So, too, with the mountains on the other side of the moon. When you make them the object of your thought, they remain indifferent to you. They do not affect you. You never saw them. But all the same you can think about them.

Yet this thinking *about* things is, after all, a very curious relation in which to stand to things. In order to think *about* a thing, it is *not* enough that I should have an idea in me that merely resembles that thing. This last is a very important observation. I repeat, it is *not* enough that I should merely have an idea in me that resembles the thing whereof I think. I have, for instance, in me the idea of a pain. Another man has a pain just like mine. Say we both have toothache; or have both burned our fingertips in the same way. Now my idea of pain is just like the pain in him, but I am not on that account necessarily thinking about *his* pain, merely because what I am thinking about, namely my own pain, resembles his pain. No; to think about an object you must not merely have an idea that resembles the object, but you must *mean* to have your idea resemble that object. Stated in other form, to think of an object you must consciously aim at that object, you must pick out that object, you must already in some measure possess that object enough, namely, to identify it as what you mean. But how can you *mean*, how can you *aim at*, how can you *possess*, how can you *pick out*, how can you *identify* what is not already present in essence to your own hidden self? Here is surely a deep question. When you aim at yonder object, be it the mountains in the moon or the day of your death, you really say, "I, as my real self, as my larger self, as my complete consciousness, already in deepest truth possess that object, have it, own it, identify it. And that, and that alone, makes it possible for me in my transient, my individual, my momentary personality, to mean yonder object, to inquire about it, to be partly aware of it and partly ignorant of it." You can't mean what is utterly foreign to you. You mean an object, you assert about it, you talk about it, yes, you doubt or wonder about it, you admit your private and individual ignorance about it, only in so far as your larger self, your deeper personality, your total of normal consciousness already *has* that object. Your momentary and private wonder, ignorance, inquiry, or assertion, about the object, implies, asserts, presupposes, that your total self is in full and immediate possession of the object. This, in fact, is the very nature of that curious relation of a thought to an object which we are now considering. The self that is doubting or asserting, or that is even feeling its private ignorance about an object, and that still, even in consequence of all this, is *meaning,* is *aiming at* such object, is in essence identical with the self for which this object exists in its complete and consciously known truth.

So paradoxical seems this final assertion of idealism that I cannot hope in one moment to make it very plain to you. . . . But what I intend by thus saying that the self which thinks about an object, which really, even in the midst of the blindest ignorance and doubt concerning its object still means the object—that this self is identical with the deeper self which possesses and truly knows the object—what I intend hereby I can best illustrate by simple cases taken from your own experience. You are in doubt, say, about a name that you have forgotten, or about a thought that you just had, but that has now escaped you. As you hunt for the name or the lost idea, you are all the while sure that you mean just one particular name or idea and no other. But you don't yet know what name or idea this is. You try, and reject name after name. You query, "was this what I was thinking of, or this?" But after searching you before long find the name or the idea, and now at once you *recognize* it. "Oh, that," you say, "was what I meant all along, only, I didn't know what I meant." Did you know? Yes, in one sense you knew all the while—that is, your deeper self, your true consciousness knew. It was your momentary self that did not know. But when you found the long-sought name, recalled the lost idea, you recognized it at once, because it was all the while your own, because you, the true and larger self, who owned the name or the idea and were aware of what it was, now were seen to include the smaller and momentary self that sought the name or tried to recall the thought. Your deeper consciousness of the lost idea was all the while there. In fact, did you not presuppose this when you sought the lost idea? How can I mean a name, or an idea, unless I in truth am the self who knows the name, who possesses the idea? In hunting for the name or the lost idea, I am hunting for my own thought. Well, just so I know nothing about the far-off stars in detail, but in so far as I mean the far-off stars at all, as I speak of them, I am identical with that remote and deep thought of my own that already knows the stars. When I study the stars, I am trying to find out what I really mean by them. To be sure, only experience can tell me, but that is because only experience can bring me into relation with my larger self. The escape from the prison of the inner self is simply the fact that the inner self is through and through an appeal to a larger self. The self that inquires, either inquires without meaning, or if it has a meaning, this meaning exists in and for the larger self that knows.

Here is a suggestion of what I mean by Synthetic Idealism. No truth, I repeat, is more familiar. That I am always meaning to inquire into objects beyond me, what clearer fact could be mentioned? That only in case it is already I who, in deeper truth, in my real and hidden thought, *know* the lost object yonder, the object whose nature I seek to comprehend, that only in this case I can truly *mean* the thing yonder—this, as we must assert, is involved in the very idea of *meaning.* That is the logical analysis of it. You can mean what your deeper self knows; you cannot mean what your deeper self doesn't know. To be sure, the complete illustration of this most critical insight of idealism belongs elsewhere. Few see the familiar. Nothing is more common than for people to think that they mean objects that have nothing to do with themselves. Kant it was, who, despite his things in themselves, first showed us that nobody really means an object, really knows it, or doubts it, or aims at it, unless he does so by aiming at a truth that is present to his own larger self. Except for the unity of my true self, taught Kant, I have no objects. And so it makes no difference whether I know a thing or am in doubt about it. So long as I really *mean* it, that is enough. The self that *means* the object is identical with the larger self that possesses the object, just as when you seek the lost idea you are already in essence with the self that possesses the lost idea.

In this way I suggest to you the proof which a rigid analysis of the logic of our most commonplace thought would give for the doctrine that in the world there is but *one* Self, and that it is *his* world which we all alike are truly meaning, whether we talk of one another or of Cromwell's character or of the fixed stars or of the far-off eons of the future. The relation of my thought to its object has, I insist, this curious character, that *unless* the thought and its object are parts of one larger thought I can't even be *meaning* that object yonder, can't even be in error about it, can't even doubt its existence. You, for instance, are part of one larger self with me, or else I can't even be meaning to address you as outer beings. You are part of one larger self along with the most mysterious or most remote fact of nature, along with the moon, and all the hosts of heaven, along with all truth and all beauty. Else could you not even intend to speak of such objects beyond you. For whatever you speak of you will find that your world is meant by you as just your world. Talk of the unknowable, and it forthwith becomes your unknowable, your problem, whose solution, unless the problem be a mere nonsense question, your larger self must own and be aware of. The deepest problem of life is, "What is this deeper self?" And the only answer is, *It is the self that knows in unity all truth.* This, I insist, is no hypothesis. It is actually the presupposition of your deepest doubt. And that is why I say: Everything finite is more or less obscure, dark, doubtful. Only the Infinite Self, the problem solver, the complete thinker, the one who knows

what we mean even when we are most confused and ignorant, the one who includes us, who has the world present to himself in unity, before whom all past and future truth, all distant and dark truth is clear in one eternal moment, to whom far and forgot is near, who thinks the whole of nature, and in whom are all things, the Logos, the world-possessor—only his existence, I say, is perfectly sure.

5.

Yet I must not state the outcome thus confidently without a little more analysis and exemplification. Let me put the whole matter in a slightly different way. When a man believes that he knows any truth about a fact beyond his present and momentary thought, what is the position, with reference to that fact, which he gives himself? We must first answer, he believes that one who really knew his, the thinker's, thought, and compared it with the fact yonder, would perceive the agreement between the two. Is this *all*, however, that the believer holds to be true of his own thought? No, not so, for he holds not only that his thought, as it is, agrees with *some* fact outside his present self (as my thought, for instance, of my toothache may agree with the fact yonder called my neighbor's toothache), but also that his thought agrees with the fact with which it *meant* to agree. To *mean* to agree, however, with a specific fact beyond my present self, involves such a relation to that fact that if I could somehow come directly into the presence of the fact itself, could somehow absorb it into my present consciousness, I should become immediately aware of it as the fact that I all along had meant. Our previous examples have been intended to bring clearly before us this curious and in fact unique character of the relation called *meaning* an object of our thought. To return, then, to our supposed believer: he believes that he *knows* some fact beyond his present consciousness. This involves, as we have now seen, the assertion that he believes himself to stand in such an actual relation to the fact yonder that were it in, instead of out of his present consciousness, he would recognize it both as the object *meant* by his present thought, and also as in agreement therewith; and it is all this which, as he believes, an immediate observer of his own thought and of the object—that is, an observer who should include our believer's present self, and the fact yonder, and who should reflect on their relations—would find as the real relation. Observe, however, that only by *reflection* would this higher observer find out that real relation. Nothing but Reflective Self-consciousness could discover it. To believe that you know anything beyond your present and momentary self, is, therefore, to believe that you do stand in such a relation to truth as only a larger and reflectively observant self, that included you and your object, could render intelligible. Or once more, so to believe is essentially to appeal confidently to a possible larger self for approval. But now to say, I know a truth, and yet to say, This larger self to whom I appeal is appealed to only as to a possible self, that needn't be real—all this involves just the absurdity against which our whole idealistic analysis has been directed in case of all the sorts of fact and truth in the world. To believe, is to say, I stand in a *real* relation to truth, a relation which transcends wholly my present momentary self; and this real relation is of such a curious nature that only a larger inclusive self which consciously reflected upon my meaning and consciously possessed the object that I mean, could know or grasp the reality of the relation. If, however, this *relation* is a real one, it must, like the colors, the sounds, and all the other things of which we spoke before be real *for* somebody. Bare possibilities are nothing. Really possible things are already in some sense real. If, then, my relation to the truth, this complex relation of meaning an object and conforming to it, when the object, although at this moment meant by me, is not now present to my momentary thought—if this relation is genuine, and yet is such as only a possible larger self could render intelligible, then my possible larger self must be real in order that my momentary self should in fact possess the truth in question. Or, in briefest form, The relation of conforming one's thought to an outer object meant by this thought is a relation which only a Reflective Larger Self could grasp or find real. If the relation is real, the larger self is real, too.

So much, then, for the case when one *believes* that one has grasped a truth beyond the moment. But now for the case when one is actually in *error* about some object of his momentary and finite thought. Error is the actual failure to agree, not with any fact taken at random, but with just the fact that one had meant to agree with. Under what circumstances, then, is error possible? Only in case one's real thought, by virtue of

its meaning, does transcend his own momentary and in so far ignorant self. As the true believer, meaning the truth that he believes, must be in real relation thereto, even so the blunderer, really meaning, as he does, the fact yonder, in order that he should be able even to blunder about it, must be, in so far, in the same real relation to truth as the true believer. His error lies in missing that conformity with the meant object at which he aimed. Nonetheless, however, did he really mean and really aim; and, therefore, is he in error, because his real and larger self finds him to be so. True thinking and false thinking alike involve, then, the same fundamental conditions, in so far as both are carried on in moments; and in so far as, in both cases, the false moment and the true are such by virtue of being organic parts of a larger, critical, reflective, and so conscious self.

To sum up so far: of no object do I speak either falsely or truly, unless I mean that object. Never do I mean an object, unless I stand in such relation thereto that were the object in this conscious moment, and immediately present to me, I should myself recognize it as completing and fulfilling my present and momentary meaning. The relation of meaning an object is thus one that only conscious Reflection can define, or observe, or constitute. No merely *foreign* observer, no external test, could decide upon what is meant at any moment. Therefore, when what is meant is outside of the moment which means, only a Self inclusive of the moment and its object could complete, and so confirm or refute, the opinion that the moment contains. Really to mean an object, then, whether in case of true opinion or in case of false opinion, involves the real possibility of such a reflective test of one's meaning from the point of view of a larger self. But to say, My relation to the object is such that a reflective larger self, and *only* such a reflective and inclusive self, could see that I meant the object, is to assert a fact, a relation, an existent truth in the world, that either is a truth for nobody, or is a truth for an actual reflective self, inclusive of the moment, and critical of its meaning. Our whole idealistic analysis, however, from the beginning of this discussion, has been to the effect that facts must be facts for somebody, and can't be facts for nobody, and that *bare* possibilities are really impossible. Hence whoever believes, whether truly or falsely, about objects beyond the moment of his belief, is an organic part of a reflective and conscious larger self that has those objects immediately present to itself, and has them in organic relation with the erring or truthful momentary self that believes.

Belief, true and false, having been examined, the case of doubt follows at once. To doubt about objects beyond my momentary self is to admit the "possibility of error" as to such objects. Error would involve my inclusion in a larger self that has directly present to it the object meant by me as I doubt. Truth would involve the same inclusion. The inclusion itself, then, is, so far, no object of rational doubt. To doubt the inclusion would be merely to doubt whether I meant anything at all beyond the moment, and not to doubt as to my particular knowledge about the *nature* of some object beyond, when once the object had been supposed to be meant. Doubt presupposes then, whenever it is a definite doubt, the real possibility, and so, in the last analysis, the reality of the normal self-consciousness that possesses the object concerning which one doubts.

But if, passing to the extreme of skepticism, and stating one's most despairing and most uncompromising doubt, one so far confines himself to the prison of the inner life as to doubt whether one ever does mean any object beyond the moment at all, there comes the final consideration that in doubting one's power to transcend the moment, one has already transcended the moment, just as we found in following Hegel's analysis. To say, It is impossible to mean any object beyond this moment of my thought, and the moment is for itself "the measure of all things," is at all events to give a meaning to the words *this moment*. And *this moment* means something only in opposition to *other* moments. Yes, even in saying *this moment,* I have already left this moment, and am meaning and speaking of a past moment. Moreover, to deny that one can mean an object "beyond the moment" is already to give a meaning to the phrase *beyond the moment,* and then to deny that anything is meant to fall within the scope of this meaning. In every case, then, one must transcend by one's meaning the moment to which one is confined by one's finitude.

Flee where we will, then, the net of the larger Self ensnares us. We are lost and imprisoned in the thickets of its tangled labyrinth. The moments are not at all in themselves, for as moments they have no meaning; they exist only in relation to the beyond. The larger

Self alone is, and they are by reason of it, organic parts of it. They perish, but it remains; they have truth or error only in its overshadowing presence.

And now, as to the unity of this Self. Can there be many such organic selves, mutually separate unities of moments and of the objects that these moments mean? Nay, were there *many* such, would not their manifoldness be a truth? Their relations, would not these be real? Their distinct places in the world order, would not these things be objects of possible true or false thoughts? If so, must not there be once more the inclusive real Self for whom these truths were true, these separate selves interrelated, and their variety absorbed in the organism of its rational meaning?

There is, then, at last, but one Self, organically, reflectively, consciously inclusive of all the selves, and so of all truth. I have called this self, Logos, problem solver, all-knower. Consider, then, last of all, his relation to problems. In the previous lecture we doubted many things; we questioned the whole seeming world of the outer order; we wondered as to space and time, as to nature and evolution, as to the beginning and the end of things. Now he who wonders is like him who doubts. Has his wonder any rationality about it? Does he *mean* anything by his doubt? Then the truth that he means, and about which he wonders, has its real constitution. As wonderer, he in the moment possesses not this solving truth; he appeals to the self who can solve. That self must possess the solution just as surely as the problem has a meaning. The real nature of space and time, the real beginning of things, where matter was at any point of time in the past, what is to become of the world's energy: these are matters of truth, and truth is necessarily present to the Self as in one all-comprehending self-completed moment, beyond which is naught, within which is the world.

The world, then, is such stuff as ideas are made of. Thought possesses all things. But the world isn't unreal. It extends infinitely beyond our private consciousness, because it is the world of a universal mind. What facts it is to contain only experience can inform us. There is no magic that can anticipate the work of science. Absolutely the *only* thing sure from the first about this world, however, is that it is intelligent, rational, orderly, essentially comprehensible, so that all its problems are somewhere solved, all its darkest mysteries are known to the supreme Self. This Self infinitely and reflectively transcends our consciousness, and therefore, since it includes us, it is at the very least a person, and more definitely conscious than we are; for what it possesses is self-reflecting knowledge, and what is knowledge aware of itself, but consciousness? Beyond the seeming wreck and chaos of our finite problems, its eternal insight dwells, therefore, in absolute and supreme majesty. Yet it is not far from every one of us. There is no least or most transient thought that flits through a child's mind, or that troubles with the faintest line of care a maiden's face, and that still does not contain and embody something of this divine Logos.

STUDY QUESTIONS: ROYCE, *SPIRIT OF MODERN PHILOSOPHY*

1. Why can't Royce state his version of idealism in simple and unproblematic form?
2. What is anthropomorhpism? Why does Royce call it a "savage" view?
3. Why does Royce reject the idea that the world is ultimately unknowable?
4. Does Royce believe in God?
5. What is the World-Self?
6. What reason does Royce give for believing in the World-Self?
7. Are you and I the same Self? Why?
8. Why is the world "stubborn?" What does this mean? Why is it important?
9. Is all reality ideal? Why?
10. What does he mean by *analytical idealism?*
11. Is the real world a mind? Why?
12. What is my "larger self?" How is this revealed in experience?
13. What is the Logos?

THE WORLD AND THE INDIVIDUAL
Royce

In this, one of his major works, Royce constructs his elaborate philosophy without ever moving beyond the realm of ideas known immediately and directly in our experience. To him, idealism is not just the correct assessment of the true nature of reality but a historical evolution of thought along the liens envisaged by Hegel. Here he distinguishes four stages of philosophical development. They are realism, mysticism, critical rationalism, and teleological idealism. The first can be summed up in the proposition that *to be is to be independent*, the second in the proposition that *to be is to be immediate* and the third in the proposition that *to be is to be valid.* Although each stage ultimately involves self-contradiction, the best elements of each are incorporated in the fourth conception, summarized with the ancient mystic proposition, "That art thou."

There is an ancient doctrine that whatever is, is ultimately something Individual. Realism early came to that view; and only Critical Rationalism has ever explicitly maintained that the ultimate realities are universals, namely, valid possibilities of experience, or mere truths as such. Now at the close of the last lecture, after analyzing the whole basis of Critical Rationalism, the entire conception of the Real as merely valid, we reinstated the Individual as the only ultimate form of Being. In so far we returned to a view that, in the history of thought, Realism already asserted. But we gave a new reason of our own for this

---

Royce, from *The World and the Individual* (New York: Macmillan, 1899).

view. Our reason was that the very defect of our finite ideas which sends us seeking for Being lies in the fact that whether we long for practical satisfaction, or think of purely theoretical problems, we, as we now are, are always seeking another object than what is yet present to our ideas. Now any ultimate reality, for us while as finite thinkers we seek it, is always such another fact. Yet this other object is always an object for our thought only in so far as our thought already means it, defines it, and wills it to be our object. But what is for us this other? In its essence it is already defined even before we undertake to know it. For this other is precisely the fulfilment of our purpose, the satisfaction of the will now imperfectly embodied in our ideas, the completion of what we already partially possess in our finite insight. This completion is for us another, solely because our ideas, in their present momentary forms, come to us as general ideas—ideas of what is now merely a kind of relative fulfilment and not an entire fulfilment. Other fulfilment of the same general kind is needed before we can face the whole Being that we seek. This kind of fulfilment we want to bring, however, to some integral expression, to its own finality, to its completeness as a whole fact. And this want of ours, so I asserted, not only sets us looking for Being, but gives us our only ground and means for defining Being.

Being itself we should directly face in our own experience only in case we experienced finality, that is, full expression of what our finite ideas both mean and seek. Such expression, however, would be given to us in the form of a life that neither sought nor permitted another to take its own place as the expression of its own purpose. Where no other was yet to be sought, there alone would our ideas define no other, no Being, of the type in question, lying yet beyond themselves, in the direction of their own type of fulfilment. The other would be found, and so would be present. And there alone should we consequently stand in the presence of what is real. Conversely, whoever grasps only the nature of a general concept, whoever merely thinks of light or colors, or gravitation, or of man, whoever lacks, longs, or in any way seeks another, has not in his experience the full expression of his own meaning. Hence it is that he has to seek his object elsewhere. And so he has not yet faced any ultimate Being. He has upon his hands mere fragments, mere aspects of Being. Thus an entire instance of Being must be precisely that which permits your ideas to seek no other than what is present. Such a being is an Individual. Only, for our present conception of Being, an individual being is not a fact independent of any experience, nor yet a merely valid truth, nor yet a merely immediate datum that quenches ideas. For all these alternatives we have already faced and rejected. On the contrary an individual being is a Life of Experience fulfilling Ideas, in an absolutely final form. And this we said is the essential nature of Being. The essence of the Real is to be Individual, or to permit no other of its own kind, and this character it possesses only as the unique fulfilment of purpose.

Or, once more, as Mysticism asserted, so we too assert of your world, *that art thou*. Only the Self which is your world is your completely integrated Self, the totality of the life that at this instant you fragmentarily grasp. Your present defect is a matter of the mere form of your consciousness at this instant. Were your eyes at this instant. Were your eyes at this instant open to your own meaning, your life as a whole would be spread before you as a single and unique life, for which no other could be substituted without a less determinate expression of just your individual will. Now this complete life of yours, is. Only such completion can be. Being can possess no other nature than this. And this, in outline, is our Fourth Conception of Being. . . .

But with this result we come in presence of a final problem. All this, you say, depends upon my assurance that there is after all a real and therefore an essentially knowable and rational world yonder. Such a world would have to be in essence a mind, or a world of minds. But after all, how does one ever escape from the prison of the inner life? Am I not in all this merely wandering amidst the realm of my own ideas? My world, of course, isn't and can't be a mere *x*, an essentially unknowable thing, just because it *is* my world, and I have an idea of it. But then does not this mean that *my* world is, after all, forever just *my* world, so that I never get to any truth beyond myself? Isn't this result very disheartening? My world is thus a world of ideas, but alas! How do I then ever reach those ideas of the minds beyond me?

The answer is a simple, but in one sense a very problematic one. You, in one sense, namely, never *do* or can get beyond your own ideas, nor ought you to wish to do so, because in truth all these other minds that constitute your outer and real world are in essence one with your own self. This whole world of ideas is essentially *one* world, and so it is essentially the world of one self and *that art Thou.*

The truth and meaning of this deepest proposition of all idealism is now not at all remote from us. The considerations, however, upon which it depends are of the dryest possible sort, as commonplace as they are deep.

Whatever objects you may think about, whether they are objects directly known to you, or objects infinitely far removed, objects in the distant stars, or objects remote in time, or objects near and present—such objects, then, as a number with fifty places of digits in it, or the mountains on the other side of the moon, or the day of your death, or the character of Cromwell, or the law of gravitation, or a name that you are just now trying to think of and have forgotten, or the meaning of some mood or feeling or idea now in your mind—all such objects, I insist, stand in a certain constant and curious relation to your mind whenever you are thinking about them—a relation that we often miss because it is so familiar. What is this relation? Such an object, while you think about it, needn't be, as popular thought often supposes it to be, the *cause* of your thoughts concerning it. Thus, when you think about Cromwell's character, Cromwell's character isn't just now *causing* any ideas in you—isn't, so to speak, doing anything to you. Cromwell is dead, and after life's fitful fever his character is a very inactive thing. Not as the *cause*, but as the *object* of your thought is Cromwell present to you. Even so, if you choose now to think of the moment of your death, that moment is somewhere off there in the future, and you can make it your object, but it isn't now an active cause of your ideas. The moment of your death has no present physical existence at all, and just now causes nothing. So, too, with the mountains on the other side of the moon. When you make them the object of your thought, they remain indifferent to you. They do not affect you. You never saw them. But all the same you can think about them.

Yet this thinking *about* things is, after all, a very curious relation in which to stand to things. In order to think *about* a thing, it is *not* enough that I should have an idea in me that merely resembles that thing. This last is a very important observation. I repeat, it is

not enough that I should merely have an idea in me that resembles the thing whereof I think. I have, for instance, in me the idea of a pain. Another man has a pain just like mine. Say we both have toothache; or have both burned our finger-tips in the same way. Now my idea of pain is just like the pain in him, but I am not on that account necessarily thinking about *his* pain, merely because what I am thinking about, namely my own pain, resembles his pain. No; to think about an object you must not merely have an idea that resembles the object, but you must *mean* to have your idea resemble that object. Stated in other form, to think of an object you must consciously aim at that object, you must pick out that object, you must already in some measure possess that object enough, namely, to identify it as what you mean. But how can you *mean*, how can you *aim at*, how can you *possess*, how can you *pick out*, how can you *identify* what is not already present in essence to your own hidden self? Here is surely a deep question. When you aim at yonder object, be it the mountains in the moon or the day of your death, you really say, "I, as my real self, as my larger self, as my complete consciousness, already in deepest truth possess that object, have it, own it, identify it. And that, and that alone, makes it possible for me in my transient, my individual, my momentary personality, to mean yonder object, to inquire about it, to be partly aware of it and partly ignorant of it." You can't mean what is utterly foreign to you. You mean an object, you assert about it, you talk about it, yes, you doubt or wonder about it, you admit your private and individual ignorance about it, only in so far as your larger self, your deeper personality, your total of normal consciousness already *has* that object. Your momentary and private wonder, ignorance, inquiry, or assertion, about the object, implies, asserts, presupposes, that your total self is in full and immediate possession of the object. This, in fact, is the very nature of that curious relation of a thought to an object which we are now considering. The self that is doubting or asserting, or that is even feeling, its private ignorance about an object, and that still, even in consequence of all this, is *meaning*, is *aiming at* such object, is in essence identical with the self for which this object exists in its complete and consciously known truth.

So paradoxical seems this final assertion of idealism that I cannot hope in one moment to make it very plain to you. . . . But what I intend by thus say-ing that the self which thinks about an object, which really, even in the midst of the blindest ignorance and doubt concerning its object still means the object—that this self is identical with the deeper self which possesses and truly knows the object—what I intend hereby I can best illustrate by simple cases taken from your own experience. You are in doubt, say, about a name that you have forgotten, or about a thought that you just had, but that has now escaped you. As you hunt for the name or the lost idea, you are all the while sure that you mean just one particu-lar name or idea and no other. But you don't yet know what name or idea this is. You try, and reject name after name. You query, "was this what I was thinking of, or this?" But after searching you erelong find the name or the idea, and now at once you *recognize* it. "Oh, that," you say, "was what I meant all along, only, I didn't know what I meant." Did you know? Yes, in one sense you knew all the while, that is, your deeper self, your true consciousness knew. It was your momentary self that did not know. But when you found the long-sought name, recalled the lost idea, you recognized it at once, because it was all the while your own, because you, the true and larger self, who owned the name or the idea and were aware of what it was, now were seen to include the smaller and momentary self that sought the name or tried to recall the thought. Your deeper consciousness of the lost idea was all the while there. In fact, did you not presuppose this when you sought the lost idea? How can I mean a name, or an idea, unless I in truth am the self who knows the name, who possesses the idea? In hunting for the name or the lost idea, I am hunt-ing for my own thought. Well, just so I know nothing about the far-off stars in detail, but in so far as I mean the far-off stars at all, as I speak of them, I am identi-cal with that remote and deep thought of my own that already knows the stars. When I study the stars, I am trying to find out what I really mean by them. To be sure, only experience can tell me, but that is because only experience can bring me into relation with my larger self. The escape from the prison of the inner self is simply the fact that the inner self is through and through an appeal to a larger self. The self that inquires, either inquires without meaning, or if it has a meaning, this meaning exists in and for the larger self that knows.

Here is a suggestion of what I mean by Synthetic Idealism. No truth, I repeat, is more familiar. That I am always meaning to inquire into objects beyond me, what clearer fact could be mentioned? That only in case it is already I who, in deeper truth, in my real and hidden thought, *know* the lost object yonder, the object whose nature I seek to comprehend, that only in this case I can truly *mean* the thing yonder—this, as we must assert, is involved in the very idea of *meaning*. That is the logical analysis of it. You can mean what your deeper self knows; you cannot mean what your deeper self doesn't know. To be sure, the complete illustration of this most critical insight of idealism belongs elsewhere. Few see the familiar. Nothing is more common than for people to think that they mean objects that have nothing to do with themselves. Kant it was, who, despite his things in themselves, first showed us that nobody really means an object, really knows it, or doubts it, or aims at it, unless he does so by aiming at a truth that is present to his own larger self. Except for the unity of my true self, taught Kant, I have no objects. And so it makes no difference whether I know a thing or am in doubt about it. So long as I really *mean* it, that is enough. The self that *means* the object is identical with the larger self that possesses the object, just as when you seek the lost idea you are already in essence with the self that possesses the lost idea.

In this way I suggest to you the proof which a rigid analysis of the logic of our most commonplace thought would give for the doctrine that in the world there is but *one* Self, and that it is *his* world which we all alike are truly meaning, whether we talk of one another or of Cromwell's character or of the fixed stars or of the far-off eons of the future. The relation of my thought to its object has, I insist, this curious charac-ter, that *unless* the thought and its object are parts of one larger thought I can't even be *meaning* that object yonder, can't even be in error about it, can't even doubt its existence. You, for instance, are part of one larger self with me, or else I can't even be meaning to address you as outer beings. You are part of one larger self along with the most mysterious or most remote fact of nature, along with the moon, and all the hosts of heaven, along with all truth and beauty. Else could you not even intend to speak of such objects beyond you. For whatever you speak of you will find that your world is meant by you as just your world. Talk of the unknowable, and it forthwith becomes your unknowable, your problem, whose solution, unless the problem be a mere nonsense question, your larger self must own and be aware of. The deepest problem of life is, "what is this deeper self?" And the only answer is, *it is the self that knows in unity all truth.* This, I insist, is no hypothesis. It is actually the presupposition of your deepest doubt. And that is why I say: everything finite is more or less obscure, dark, doubtful. Only the Infinite Self, the problem-solver, the complete thinker, the one who knows what we mean even when we are most confused and ignorant, the one who includes us, who has the world present to himself in unity, before whom all past and future truth, all distant and dark truth is clear in one eternal moment, to whom far and forgot is near, who thinks the whole of nature, and in whom are all things, the Logos, the world possessor— only his existence, I say, is perfectly sure.

STUDY QUESTIONS: ROYCE, *THE WORLD AND THE INDIVIDUAL*

1. What is *critical rationalism?*
2. What is Royce's view of mysticism?
3. What is the significance of the proposition, "that art thou?"
4. What is *synthetic idealism?* How is it related to *analytic* idealism?
5. What is Royce's view of Kant?
6. What is the Infinite Self?

Philosophical Bridges: Royce's Influence

The profound, expansive individualistic idealism constructed by Royce became a philosophical bridge, literally, between the great nineteenth century European philosophers who had inherited and further developed the great Greek wisdom and the advent of philosophical idealism in the United States. His vision of a labyrinthine world in which each individual, as a corridor, opens up into every other as the one self who is all, the world soul, everywhere all at once, always everyone, is a startling revival at the dawn of the twentieth century of some of the most ancient philosophies. Spanning through the great medieval mystics, both in the Christian and Islamic traditions, from Averroes and Bruno to Spinoza, all the way back to the ancient Greek mystics, Royce gave a new voice to an old idea that inspired American thinkers and writers for generations to come. You can see elements of his philosophy in works such as Mark Twain's *Mysterious Stranger,* and in poems that have become the staple of the American literary scene, such as Walt Whitman's *Song of Myself.*

Royce's view that both the will and the intellect seek the Absolute in the individual, results in a deeply secular inspirational view of moral life that has inspired many American moral theorists to follow Royce's identification of the ultimate human moral virtue in terms of the concept of *loyalty.* Because we must seek the meaning of our individual lives by identifying ourselves with meaning that is always larger than and beyond ourselves, loyalty becomes the means for individual self-fulfillment and the foundation for a society of diverse individuals living in pluralistic harmony with each other and with nature.

Philosophical Bridges: The Influence of the American Pragmatists and Idealists

From its inception, the United States of America has been a haven for European and other immigrants seeking refuge from religious and economic oppression. The majority of immigrants were poor and religious. Their simple outlook on life was tempered by necessity and tolerance, in so far as they found themselves among a vast array of other peoples struggling to survive. Even the cultural centers, mainly in New England, were settled predominantly by English Protestants, many of them Puritans and Calvinists. They too tended to be deeply religious followers of the Bible and passionately conservative. They rarely permitted themselves to question the traditional beliefs of their ancestors, which, typically, were extremely primitive from a philosophical point of view. Their philosophical roots, in so far as they had any, were strictly in the past, backward looking. Moreover, the ties between fundamental religions and government were close, and the clergy and politicians were intimately entwined by a steadfast Christian faith. Likewise, on the frontier, where people were drawn in a great expansion ever westward, the mind had neither inclination nor time for philosophical speculation. Experience was ground in immediate reality, defined by day-to-day needs that had no place for abstract thinking.

Few educated Europeans of the time could have imagined that philosophy would ever arise—not to mention flourish—in the new world. Yet the handful of American philosophers presented in this section inspired virtually overnight students of the new world to aspire to the heights of wisdom, to welcome one more, unlikely immigrant to its shores: namely, philosophy herself. That philosophy found its new home and began suddenly to thrive, apparently from out of nowhere, virtually overnight, in the United States, way beyond what Peirce, James and Royce ever envisioned, is in and of itself a remarkably wonderful testament to their great legacy.

BIBLIOGRAPHY

GENERAL

Ayer, A. J., *Origins of Pragmatism: Studies in the Philosophy of Charles Sanders Peirce and William James*, Macmillan, 1968

De Wall, C., *On Pragmatism*, Wadsworth, 2004

James, W., *Peragmatism*, Longmans, Green & Co., 1907

Kuklick, B., *The Rise of American Philosophy*, Yale University Press, 1977

Murphy, J., *Pragmatism: From Perice to Davidson*, Westview Press, 1990

Reck, A., *Recent American Philosophy*, Pantheon, 1962

Scheffler, I., *Four Pragmatists*, Humanities Press, 1974

Smith, J., *The Spirit of American Philosophy*, Oxford University Press, 1963

Winn, R. B., ed., *American Philosophy*, 1955

PEIRCE: Primary

Selected Writings, ed. J. B., Harcourt, Brace & Concept, 1939

The Essential Peirce, Peirce Edition Project, Indiana University Press, 1992–98

Writings of Charles S. Peirce: A Chronological Edition, Peirce Edition Project, Indiana University Press, 1982

Collected papers of Charles Sanders Peirce, C. Hartshorne, P. Weiss, and A. Burks, eds., Harvard University Press, 1931–58

New Elements of Mathematics, ed. C. Eisele, Mouton, 1976

Historical Perspectives on Peirce's Logic of Science, ed. C. Eisele, Mouton, 1985

Secondary

Brent, J., *Charles Sanders Peirce: A Life*, Indiana University Press, 1993

De Wall, C., *On Peirce*, Wadsworth, 2001

Hausman, C., *Charles S. Peirce's Evolutionary Philosophy*, Cambridge University Press, 1993

Hookway, C., *Peirce*, Routledge, 1985

His Glassy Essence: An Autobiography of Charles Sanders Peirce, ed. K. Ketner, Vanderbilt University Press, 1998

Murphy, M., *The Development of Peirce's Philosophy*, Harvard University Press, 1961

JAMES: Primary

The Varieties of Religious Experience: A Study in Human Nature, Longmans, Green and Co., 1902

Essays in Pragmatism, ed. A. Castell, Macmillan, 1948

Memories and Studies, Longmans, Green and Co., 1917

The Principles of Psychology, Holt, 1890

Some Problems of Philosophy: A Beginning of an Introduction to Philosophy, Longmans, Green & Co., 1911

Essays in Radical Empiricism, R. B. Perry, ed., Longmans, Green & Co., 1912

A Pluralistic Universe, Longmans, Green & Co., 1909

Will to Believe and Other Essays in Popular Philosophy, Longmans, Green & Co., 1897

Talks to Teachers on Psychology and to Students on Some of Life's Ideals, Longmans, Green & Co., 1897

Pragmatism: A New Name for Some Old Ways of Thinking, Longmans, Green & Co., 1909

The Meaning of Truth: A Sequel to "Pragmatism," Longmans, Green, and Co., 1909

Secondary

Allen, G. W., *William James*, Viking, 1967

De Wall, C., *On Peirce*, Wadsworth, 2001

The Writings of William James, ed. J. McDermott, Random House, 1967

Myers, G. E., *William James: His Life and Thought*, University Press, 1986

Peirce, C. S., *Essays in the Philosophy of Science*, Liberal Arts Library, 1957

Perry, R. B., *The Thought and Character of William James*, 2 vols, Harper, 1935

Rowe, S., *The Vision of James*, Element, 1996

Skrupskelis, I. and Berkeley, E.M., *The Correspondence of William James*, 12 vols., University Press of Virginia, 1992–2004

Wild, J., *The Radical Empiricism of William James*, Greenwood Press, 1980

ROYCE: Primary

The Basic Writings of Josiah Royce, vol. 1, ed. J. McDermott, University of Chicago Press, 1969

The Basic Writings of Josiah Royce, vol. 2, ed. John McDermott, University of Chicago Press, 1969

Royce's Logical Essays, ed. D. S. Robinson, Wm. C. Brown Company, 1951

Secondary

Clendenning, *The Life and Thought of Josiah Royce*, Vanderbilt University Press, 1999

Kuklick, B., *Josiah Royce: An Intellectual Biography*, Hackett, 1985

Oppenheim, F., *Royce's Mature Philosophy of Religion*, University of Notre Dame Press, 1987

Trotter, G., *On Royce*, Wadsworth, 2001

The Philosophy of Josiah Royce, ed. J. K. Roth, Hackett Publishing Company, 1982

SOURCES

SECTION I: THE LEGACY OF KANT: AVATER OF NINETEENTH CENTURY PHILOSOPHY

Schopenhauer, A Critique of the Kantian Philosophy translated, edited, and annotated by Richard E. Aquila, © Richard E. Aquila. Translation based on the third edition (1859) of Volume One of *Die Welt als Wille und Vorstellung* (first edition, (1819), according to the version of the text edited by Julius Frauenstädt, revised by Arthur Hübscher, and published as reviewed by Angelika Hübscher, as Volume Two of Schopenhauer's *Sämtliche Werke* (F. A. Brockhaus, 1988 [4th ed.]).

SECTION II: THE GERMAN IDEALISTS

1. Fichte, Johann, *The Science of Knowledge,* from *Erste Einleitung in die Wissenschaftslehre,* translated by Benjamin Rand, Sammtlichte Werke, 1845, ch. 1

2. Schelling, Friedrich, *System of Transcendental Idealism,* translated by Benjamin Rand, Sammtlichte Werke, 1908, chs. 1–3.

3. Hegel, George Friedrich,
   a. *Philosophy of Mind: Part III of the Encyclopaedia of the Philosophical Sciencies,* translated by William Wallace, Oxford, 1892
   b. *The Logic,* translated by William Wallace, Clarendon Press, 1842, Introduction, Chs. 2–5, 7, 8: Parts A, B, C, 9: Parts A, B, C
   c. *Phenomenology of Mind,* translated by Josiah Royce in *Modern Classical Philosophers,* Houghton Mifflin, 1908.
   d. *Philosophy of History,* translated by J. Sibree, Citadel Press, 1900, Introduction, I 1–4; II 1–4; III 1–12

4. Schopenhauer, Arthur, *The World as Will and Idea,* trans. R.B. Haldane and J. Kemp, London: Trubner, 1883

SECTION III: THE EXISTENTIALISTS

5. Kierkegaard, Soren,
   a. *Either/Or,* translated by D.F. Swenson and L.M. Swenson, Princeton University Press, 1941, "An Ecstatic Lecture."
   b. *Concluding Unscientific Postscript,* translated by D. F. Swenson, Princeton University Press, 1941, compounded selections.

6. Nietzsche, Friedrich
   a. *Beyond Good and Evil,* translated by Helen Zimmern, Foulis, 1914. ch. 1, §§ 1–7, 11, 16, 19; ch. 2, §§ 24–30, 32, 36, 44.
   b. *The Will to Power* translated by A. M. Ludovici, Allen & Unwin, 1924: Preface, Book One: chs. 1–3.

SECTION IV: THE SOCIAL PHILOSOPHERS

7. Comte, Auguste, *The Positive Philosophy,* London 1853, vol 1, ch. 1

8. Feuerbach, Ludwig, *The Essence of Christianity,* translated by George Eliot, 1854

9. Bentham, Jeremy, *Principles of Morals and Legislation,* Oxford, 1823, chs. I–V

10. Mill, John Stuart
    a. *Utilitarianism,* 1863, chs. 1–5, abridged
    b. *On Liberty,* 1859, chs. 1–3, abridged

11. Marx, Karl
    a. and Engels, Friedrich, *Communist Manifesto,* translated by Samuel Moore, 1888
    b. "Alienation," from *Economic and Philosophic Manuscripts of 1844,* translated by Martin Milligan
    c. "The Power of Money," from *Economic and Philosophic Manuscripts of 1844,* translated by Martin Milligan

SECTION V: THE AMERICAN PRAGMATISTS AND IDEALISTS

12. Peirce, Charles,
    a. "The Fixation of Belief," *Popular Science Monthly,* 1877
    b. Pierce, Charles, "How to Make Our Ideas Clear" *Popular Science Monthly,* 1878

13. James, William,
    a. "The *Will to Believe,*" address to the Philosophical Clubs of Yale and Brown, New World, June 1896
    b. "Does Consciousness Exist?" from *Journal of Philosophy, Psychology, and Scientific Methods,* vol I, no. 18, 1904
    c. "A World of Pure Experience," from *Journal of Philosophy, Psychology, and Scientific Methods,* vol I, no. 20 and no. 21, 1904

14. Royce, Josiah
    a. *The Spirit of Modern Philosophy: Reality and Idealism: The Inner World and Its Meaning,* Houghton, Mifflin and Co., 1892
    b. *The World and the Individual,* Macmillan, 1899